Preaching

and

The Victory of the Gospel

By John M Otis

Scripture quotations are from the New American Standard Bible.

Triumphant Publications Ministries

www.triumphantpublications.com

Email: cjotis2@yahoo.com

ISBN: 978-0-9772800-7-0

Dedication

This book is dedicated to all of Gods' faithful preachers down through the ages. Jesus refers to them as His "little ones." These men have been the voice of the King of kings and Lord of lords. They have been and will continue to be the stewards of the mysteries of God to the end of the world. As Christ's ambassadors, they have and will continue to boldly and fearlessly proclaim the excellencies of their Master. They often have been destitute, afflicted, and ill treated. More than a few have been stoned, sawn in two, put to death with the sword, hanged, and burned at the stake. They are men of whom the world is not worthy, and though often tempted to grow weary in well doing, they will reap a glorious crown of righteousness on that great Day. They will hear the loving words of their Redeemer – "Well done, thou good and faithful servant."

Acknowledgments

My writing ministry would be significantly curtailed if it were not for the loving and skillful efforts of my dear wife, Christine. She is my technical expert and typesetter. In many ways, she is the backbone to Triumphant Publications.

I am greatly indebted to my proof reader Kaity Moore who labored through my manuscript, being sure that I conformed to proper grammar rules.

Table of Contents

Introduction

As we enter the second decade of the 21st Century, we must take a sober look at the spiritual condition of Christ's visible church. Whatever problems exist is not Christ's fault, and they are surely no surprise to the living God. One of the great theological tensions is the relationship of divine sovereignty to human responsibility. In other words, how does a God who has planned human history from start to finish, who has determined the end from the beginning, and who possesses absolute power govern the peoples of this earth while holding men simultaneously accountable for their actions? In some ways it is mysterious to us, only because we are not God. The problem with many people is that they do not have a high enough view of God. Just because we cannot understand perplexing issues doesn't mean that they are problems with God. Men need a healthy dose of humility on a regular basis. Isaiah 55:8-11 says:

> ^{8}'For My thoughts are not your thoughts, nor are your ways My ways,' declares the Lord. ^{9}'For as the heavens are higher than the earth, so are My ways higher than your ways and My thoughts than your thoughts. ^{10}For as the rain and the snow come down from heaven and do not return there without watering the earth and making it bear and sprout, and furnishing seed to the sower and bread to the eater; ^{11}so will My word be which goes forth from My mouth; It will not return to Me empty without accomplishing what I desire, and without succeeding in the matter for which I sent it.'

The reason we don't understand certain things is because we are not God! The creature cannot even begin to fathom God in His perfections. Simply because I don't understand how divine sovereignty and human responsibility function simultaneously doesn't mean it is a problem with God. God is God, and the creature is the creature!

God has predestined all that will come to pass. Nothing is arbitrary to a sovereign God. Everything will most certainly occur exactly as He has planned. Nothing catches Him by surprise. Nevertheless, men are not puppets in the hands of such a sovereign God; their moral actions stem from a heart and will that is under no divine compulsion. Men freely choose certain actions, and those actions carry personal consequences, either to their well being or to their harm. The truth is: men will always choose in accordance with the condition of their hearts. If their heart is in bondage to sin, they will choose sin. If their heart has been regenerated, then they have the capacity to choose that which is good, though they don't always due to the remaining effects of sin. While God does not constrain men against their wills, this does not mean that men are autonomous beings, that is, beings outside of God's control. One of the things that is awe inspiring about God is that He can allow men to freely act, but those "free" actions always correspond to God's eternal decrees.

One thing is most certain in Scripture. God will do always what He chooses to do, and man is impotent to stop it. We read in Isaiah 14:24, 27:

> [24]*The Lord of hosts has sworn saying, "Surely, just as I have intended so it has happened, and just as I have planned so it will stand ...* [27]*For the Lord of hosts has planned, and who can frustrate it? And as for His stretched-out hand, who can turn it back?*

What does all of this have to do with preaching and the victory of the gospel? The gospel is God's message to man. God is sovereign and will accomplish all His holy will. The question is: is the gospel going to prevail in human history or not? I suppose we could phrase it another way. Is it possible for God not to be victorious? Someone could respond, "Well, God can do all things, but He may have decreed for His gospel not to prevail in human history." My follow up question to this person would be – why would an omnipotent God choose to fail? Moreover, the all important question is: what does the Scripture clearly reveal? Does the Bible teach failure or victory for the gospel? It all comes down to careful exegesis. Yes, we must be willing to engage in exegetical hand to hand combat with those who deny the victory of the gospel in human history prior to Christ's Second Coming.

I will be so bold to assert that the Bible overwhelmingly teaches victory, not defeat for the church and the gospel. The idea of God's purposes and His gospel not prevailing in history is inconceivable. Such a notion strikes at the heart of God's prophetic message. It is totally inconsistent with the One who sits presently at the right hand of God in heaven. Before Jesus' ascension into heaven, He came to His disciples after His resurrection and gave His Great Commission as recorded in Matthew 28:18-20:

¹⁸And Jesus came up and spoke to them, saying, "All authority has been given to Me in heaven and on earth. ¹⁹Go therefore and make disciples of all the nations, baptizing them in the name of the Father and the Son and the Holy Spirit, ²⁰teaching them to observe all that I commanded you; and lo, I am with you always, even to the end of the age.

The very nature of the Great Commission exudes with victory, not defeat! Jesus has all the authority. How much? All authority! If one has all authority, it presumes all power. So, what are the chances of the Great Commission being fulfilled? 100%! Who can resist Him? The fact that Jesus says that He will be with His church to the end of the world guarantees the church's success in carrying out the task. Jesus' abiding presence, who has all authority and power, guarantees the victory.

My explicit goal in this book is to exegetically prove from the Word of God that the gospel will prevail in human history. Revelation 11:15 will come to pass prior to Jesus' Second Coming:

> *The kingdom of the world has become the kingdom of our Lord and of His Christ, and He will reign forever and ever.*

Is this book about eschatology? Is it purporting a certain millennial view? Of course it is. Is it the typical book on postmillennialism? I don't think so. My goal is to focus on one all consuming truth. The gospel is and will be victorious, and preaching is the primary means by which the gospel succeeds, and this preaching is undergirded by earnest prayer of the saints.

I did use the word, "postmillennial." What do I mean by this eschatological position? The distinctive feature of postmillennial eschatology is the victory of the gospel during the millennial age. Of course, this raises another important question – when does the millennium occur with reference to Christ's Second Coming? One of the distinctives of postmillennialism, but not solely restricted to this position, is that we are presently in the millennium, that Jesus is presently reigning victoriously from God's right hand. Such a notion would be viewed as nearly heretical in the minds of many American Christians today, only because the millennial view of premillennialism has gained preeminence in the modern Christian church. This preeminence is not because of the theological superiority of the position, but because it is fraught with much imagination. Exegetically, it cannot withstand careful scrutiny. One of my goals is to conclusively demonstrate exegetically that Jesus is presently reigning.

The problem with today's church is the pessimism that has infected it. Until the present visible church recovers its God given mandate, we will continually see a cultural irrelevancy of the church's ministry. This irrelevancy is not because the church is irrelevant; it is because the church has been unfaithful to its mandated mission. This is where my earlier comments about human responsibility enter in. Our God has revealed His Scripture; He has set forth His promises of victory scattered all through the Old and New Testaments. We, as moral agents, must choose to believe these promises or not. Our worldview does impact our future view! Premillennialism is self-consciously defeatist in its outlook on the future in terms of the gospel permeating the nations.

As the 1950s radio preacher J. Vernon McGee put it, "You don't polish brass on a sinking ship." I know that some well meaning Bible teachers still insist that though God may have prophesied defeat for the church in history, meaning that things will get worse and worse culminating in Jesus coming back to rescue His church out of the mess, one can still have a positive outlook. The only positive outlook is the belief that my soul is saved, and maybe God will save a few more souls along the way. You cannot convince me that such a pessimistic worldview is motivates the soul to be vigorous in the Lord's business. Now, I do realize that a person can be faithful despite tremendous opposition. The usual comeback is that we must be zealous because God wants us to be zealous, despite a prophetic view of defeat. While it is true that we must be faithful no matter what, a pessimistic worldview has tremendous implications on a day by day basis of how I live as a Christian in this world.

As a pastor, I can assure you that one of my greatest struggles is to remain focused and not get discouraged at the apparent lethargy in the church in many places and the ongoing slide of our nation into increasing ungodliness. I have to continually remind myself that my work is not in vain in the Lord, that what I am doing for the kingdom somehow is making a difference in the long haul. Pessimism is not the fertile ground that promotes evangelistic zeal. On the other hand, a reaffirmation of the biblical promises of gospel victory is that fertile soil from which the fruit of faith grows; these promises prod us on to fight the good fight. Optimism in God's blessed promises is inspiring!

One of the chapters of this book demonstrates that the postmillennial hope was indeed the theological impetus for missions particularly during the 18th Century. World missions are the natural offshoot of an eschatology of victory.

As mentioned, men are morally accountable to God for their actions; they must give an account to the Lord Jesus one day. One of the most amazing biblical truths is: God has ordained preaching to be the primary method of the discipling of the nations. This is the divinely sanctioned method of evangelization; this is the primary means of teaching Christians all that Jesus commanded. Isaiah 11:9 asserts:

> ... *For the earth will be full of the knowledge of the Lord as the waters cover the sea.*

It will not come with cleverly devised human innovations. The present Christian church, in my opinion, is in a state of crisis, only because we have forsaken God's ordained methods, thinking that our methods are better than the divinely revealed ones. Plays, skits, Power Point presentations, and music designed specifically for the purpose of identifying with certain "worldly" practices are no substitute for preaching!

Several years ago, a Christian minster and I attended a supposed Christian music festival. Our purpose in attending was to hand out Christian tracts, CDs, and other Christian material designed to give some in depth Christian teaching. I have rarely been so dismayed and righteously angry over what I witnessed. It was an all day event with one "Christian" music group performing after another. While it was not designed to be a worship service, it was designed as a "Christian" event where the promoters of the event were soliciting churches to participate in help sponsoring it. My criticism of the event was not due to my different taste in music, but the physical appearance of the "Christian" group and the failure of all the groups to clearly enunciate a Christian message. Essentially, it was no different in many respects from a typical rock concert being performed by worldly entertainers. During the whole event, there was absolutely no preaching at all, not even a two minute homilee on who Jesus is. Group after group bombarded the audience with music so loud and so confusing that despite my attempts to get close to hear the supposed "Christian lyrics" I could not make out what they were singing. The groups danced on the stage in a manner that was no different from a pop rock band (not that I have ever been to one but I have seen video clips). They looked no different. Many had their spiked hair! This was supposedly a Christian event? Who was attending? I saw my fair share of young people with shaved heads, and colored spiked Mohawk haircuts. It was simply disheartening. I personally handed out CDs to band members who had finished their performance to see their reaction. They accepted my handout but didn't show any enthusiasm of receiving free hours of theological discussions on important biblical issues.

This is the crisis that we are facing today in the visible Christian church, especially in America. We have become "worldly" in order to attract the world. But God is not honored. Many go to churches that offer the latest series on how to be a better parent, have a better marriage, etc. and to be entertained with certain types of music. Is there anything wrong with messages on parenting and marriage? Of course not. But, if this is the typical emphasis, which it often is, then we have a serious issue. So much "church" today has been exclusively man centered and not God centered. If one examines the revivals of the past several centuries, the emphasis was upon preaching the gospel. It was not unusual for these preachers to speak hour long messages to people who were willing to hear.

The great sin of today's modern visible church in America is its abandonment of God's ordained methods for humanly devised methods designed to amuse the audience. When I ministered in Corpus Christi, Texas several years ago, I was appalled at a post card mailed out from a local so called "church."[1] For several years, I and thousands of other households in the community had received postcard mailings from this "church." I had always thought the postcards to be ridiculous, but this particular mailing finally angered me. These mailings were always designed to take some topic and cleverly phrase it with contemporary appeal. This mailing was an 8"x 4" postcard titled, *"Victorious Secrets"* with the subtitle as *"Victorious Secrets… The Intimacy Collection; A Collection of secret truths that will change your relationships."* The card was a stripped pink card with a silver bow insignia. The series of four messages being advertised to take place over four consecutive Sundays were: "Undressing Your Relational problems," "His secrets," "Her secrets," and "The Secret Sin of Omission: It's not what you're doing; it's what you're not doing." This was a cleverly devised appeal based on the

---

[1] This mailing came from a church called Bay Area Fellowship. They had just built a huge facility that held thousands of people. In April 2010, the "church" made national news for its Easter promotions. The controversy was over their 'Ultimate Easter Giveaway.' Bay Area Fellowship was giving away over $2 million in prizes including items such as cars, televisions, furniture, bikes, entertainment tickets, and much more. Among the criticism was the 'materialism' and 'consumerism' associated with these giveaways and many questions as to what that had to do with Easter. Both in his blog and on various interviews, which was seen on the Bay Area Fellowship site, Pastor Bill Cornelius reassured the public that the intent of this event was not to focus on the materialism of the things around us in our daily lives, but rather to focus on the 'Ultimate Free Giveaway,' that is the love of Jesus Christ and his gift to mankind, giving his life for us. In that context, the giveaway was to call those who have strayed from the church or those who have never been in church, to find their way back or to experience Jesus' saving grace for themselves.

Victoria Secret women's lingerie company. Anyone who has seen a television commercial of Victoria Secret is exposed to what I call an essentially pornographic commercial. I was so incensed by the postcard that I wrote a letter to the pastor of this "church" appealing to him as a fellow pastor to end this type of activity, that I was personally offended by the contents of the mail out, and that it was a disgrace to the Christian community. I went to his newly built facility to hand deliver the letter with the hopes of a face to face meeting. The "pastor" was not in, so I left my letter with his receptionist. I urged this "pastor" to contact me in keeping with Matthew 5:24 in terms of an offended brother, because I was that offended brother. Of course, I heard nothing from him. I deliberately have put in quotes the terms "church" and "pastor" because I have serious doubts as to whether we can legitimately refer to this body as a true church of the Lord Jesus Christ.

Until we repent of our unfaithfulness as the visible church, we will not be blessed. What we must do is get on our knees and beg God to be merciful to us and to send us a true revival whereby people are preached to with His glorious gospel message, calling men to repent and believe in Jesus alone for salvation. The postmillennial confidence is that God will eventually do this, but let's exercise our moral responsibility in asking our Lord to do it sooner than later. We must never be guilty of an unbiblical pragmatism – that the end justifies the means. Those promoting humanly devised methods should not think that the Lord will bless their endeavors. Why should the God of heaven and earth bless methods derived from the world? I John 2:15-17 states:

> *Do not love the world nor the things in the world. If anyone loves the world, the love of the Father is not in him. For all that is in the world, the lust of the flesh and the lust of the eyes and the boastful pride of life, is not from the Father, but is from the world. The world is passing away, and also its lusts; but the one who does the will of God lives forever.*

The Scripture exhorts us to utilize divinely ordained weapons for spiritual warfare by which we destroy speculations and every lofty thing raised up against the knowledge of Christ and bring every thought captive to Christ's obedience (II Corinthians 10:3-5). The text does not directly reveal what these weapons are, but I believe that a study of Scripture reveals that the foremost weapons are: preaching and prayer. In this book, we will take a close look as to why these are divinely sanctioned weapons.

The thesis of this book is that preaching is the foremost instrument that Jesus uses to carry out God's eternal decrees in human history. Christ's church is His invincible instrument in subduing all His and our enemies.

God's Word is inerrant; it is comprehensively authoritative in both the Old and New Testaments; it prophesies victory to Christ's church. Though Christ's bride has suffered numerous persecutions throughout history with Tertullian aptly saying, "The blood of the martyrs is the seed of the church," the church will ultimately prevail in history. Persecution of Christ's bride in no way negates the ultimate victory. Any war entails casualties. What victorious army did not normally suffer casualties in the securing of its victory? We need to keep in mind what Revelation 20:4 says:

> *Then I saw thrones, and they sat on them, and judgment was given to them, and I saw the souls of those who had been beheaded because of their testimony of Jesus and because of the word of God, and those who had not worshiped the beast or his image, and had not received the mark on their forehead and on their hand; and they came to life and reigned with Christ for a thousand years.*

Let me clarify what I mean by a casualty. I mean those who are killed for their testimony for Christ as set forth in this passage. As Paul said so aptly in Philippians 1:21:

> *For to me, to live is Christ, and to die is gain.*

Death is not the end all for the Christian! It is only the portal opening into eternal life. Jesus did say in John 11:25-26:

> *.. I am the resurrection and the life; he who believes in Me will live even if he dies, and everyone who lives and believes in Me will never die...*

This 19th Century hymn is most fitting. Here are the stanzas of the well known hymn, *Onward Christian Soldiers*[2]:

1   Onward, Christian soldiers, Marching as to war,
    With the Cross of Jesus Going on before.
    Christ the Royal Master Leads against the foe,

---

[2]   Taken from http://www.hymnary.org/text/onward_christian_soldiers_marching_as.

Forward into battle, See, His banners go.
Onward, Christian soldiers, Marching as to war,
With the Cross of Jesus Going on before.

2   At the sign of triumph Satan's host doth flee;
On, then, Christian soldiers, On to victory.
Hell's foundations quiver At the shout of praise;
Brothers, lift your voices, Loud your anthems raise.
Onward, Christian soldiers, Marching as to war,
With the Cross of Jesus Going on before.

3   Like a mighty army Moves the Church of God;
Brothers, we are treading Where the saints have trod;
We are not divided, All one body we,
One in hope, and doctrine, One in charity.
Onward, Christian soldiers, Marching as to war,
With the Cross of Jesus Going on before.

4   Crowns and thrones may perish, Kingdoms rise and wane,
But the Church of Jesus Constant will remain;
Gates of hell can never 'Gainst that Church prevail;
We have Christ's own promise, And that cannot fail.
Onward, Christian soldiers, Marching as to war,
With the Cross of Jesus Going on before.

5   Onward, then, ye people, Join our happy throng,
Blend with ours your voices In the triumph-song;
Glory, laud, and honour, Unto Christ the King,
This through countless ages Men and Angels sing.
Onward, Christian soldiers, Marching as to war,
With the Cross of Jesus Going on before.

Why will Christ's church prevail in history? It's because the Scripture promises it! Numbers 23:19 states:

> *God is not a man that he should lie, nor a son of man, that He should repent; Has He said: and will He not do it? Or has He spoken, and will He not make it good?*

Jesus is presently reigning from God the Father's right hand, subduing all His enemies under His feet, and who can defy the Lord Jesus, who has all authority and power?

I know that there are well meaning Christians who think otherwise, who think Israel and the church are separate entities in history, who think the church is destined to have no lasting impact in history. I know there are some who think that there will be a literal 1000 year kingdom of Christ on earth after Christ's Second Coming. My response to them is: you are sincerely wrong.

Yes, I am more than willing to do theological hand-to-hand exegetical combat. I will let the reader decide if the exegesis set forth in this book is accurate or not.

I would concur with what early 20th Century theologian, Benjamin B. Warfield, said and what 19th Century Southern Presbyterian preacher and theologian, James Henley Thornwell, said about the preaching of the gospel and the necessity of earnestness in our optimism in God's Word. In his commentary on Revelation 19, Warfield wrote:

> The section opens with a vision of the victory of the Word of God, the King of Kings and Lord of Lords over all His enemies. We see him come forth form heaven girt for war, followed by the armies of heaven... The thing symbolized is obviously the complete victory of the Son of God over all the hosts of wickedness... The conquest is wrought by the spoken word – in short, by the preaching of the gospel... What we have here, in effect, is a picture of the whole period between the first and second advents, seen from the point of view of heaven. It is the period of advancing victory of the Son of God over the world... As emphatically as Paul, John teaches that the earthly history of the Church is not a history merely of conflict with evil, but of conquest over evil: and even more richly than Paul, John teaches that this conquest will be decisive and complete. The whole meaning of the vision of Revelation 19:11-21 is that Christ Jesus comes forth not to war merely but to victory, and every detail of the picture is laid in with a view precisely to emphasizing the thoroughness of this victory. The Gospel of Christ is, John being witness, completely to conquer the world... A progressively advancing conquest of the earth by Christ's gospel implies a coming age deserving at least the relative name of "golden."[3]

Concerning the urgency of maintaining a spirit of biblical optimism, James Henley Thornwell said:

---

[3] Greg Bahnsen, *Victory in Jesus: The Bright Hope of Postmillennialism*, (Texarkana, Arkansas: Covenant Media Press, 1999), pp. 112-113, who quotes B.B. Warfield, *The Millennium and the Apocalypse, Biblical Doctrines*, (New York: Oxford University Press, 1929), pp. 647-648, 662.

... if the Church could be aroused to a deeper sense of the glory that awaits her, she would enter with a warmer spirit into the struggles that are before her. Hope would inspire ardour... It is our unfaithfulness, our negligence and unbelief, our low and carnal aims that retard the chariot of the Redeemer. The Bridegroom cannot come until the Bride has made herself ready. Let the Church be in earnest after greater holiness in her own members, and in faith and love undertake the conquest of the world, and she will soon settle the question whether her resources are competent to change the face of the earth.[4]

We have an omnipotent King and Savior who reigns, who has endowed His church with invincible spiritual weapons. The only question is: are we willing to use them.

---

[4]   Bahnsen, p. 113.

Chapter 1

The Necessity of Understanding
God's Covenant of Salvation

If we are going to assert that the gospel will be victorious in human history and that King Jesus uses preaching as the primary means in bringing this to pass, then it is incumbent upon us to understand the biblical teaching of God's covenant of salvation.

The Covenant of Works

In order to understand the kingdom of God, we must also understand God's covenant with man. A covenant essentially can be defined as "a bond in blood sovereignly administered."[1] God comes to man in covenant and sets forth the stipulations of that covenant. God issues forth the terms of the covenant to which man must comply. Though two parties participate, God and man, man has no choice. He is but the creature, and God owns man. Romans 9:20-21 emphatically states:

> [20]*On the contrary, who are you, O man, who answers back to God? The thing molded will not say to the molder, 'Why did you make me like this,' will it?* [21]*Or does not the potter have a right over the clay, to make from the same lump one vessel for honorable use and another for common use?*

The parties of the covenant are not equals; there is no bargaining. The terms of the covenant are quite severe. Whichever party violates the terms of the covenant must die. This is why a covenant is said to be "in blood." Of course, a sovereign God, who is eternal spirit, cannot die. The true and living God is perfect in every respect. God cannot sin. The only party that can break the terms of the covenant is man. Though Adam and Eve were created perfect in body and soul, they did have the capacity to change. In other words, man could choose to disobey and incur the penalty of breaking the covenant.

---

[1]   This is how O. Palmer Robertson has defined a covenant.

The first covenant made with man is termed as the "covenant of works." In this covenant, God promises eternal life to Adam and Eve as long as they continue to obey the terms of this covenant – do not eat of the tree of the knowledge of good and evil. If they ever ate of this tree, then they would become covenant breakers, thereby becoming subject to the penalties of the covenant. Disobedience would lead to immediate spiritual death and eventually physical death. This covenant of works demanded perfect, personal, and perpetual obedience of Adam and Eve.

One of the realities of this covenant of works is that Adam stood as the representative head of the human race. Theologically, this is referred to as the "federal headship of Adam." This great theological truth is set forth with great clarity in Romans 5:12-21. All mankind was present in the Garden of Eden through its representative head, Adam. When Adam sinned by partaking of the forbidden fruit by his one act of disobedience, all mankind became guilty of Adam's sin (Romans 5:12). In Adam's sin we all stand guilty representatively in Adam, but we also stand polluted by sin due to the passing on of this sinful nature by ordinary generation. This is called Original Sin. Consequently, the entire human race stands condemned before a holy God whose perfect justice demands our condemnation in hell forever; hence, all mankind stands in need of a Savior. Since God demands personal, perfect, and perpetual obedience to His law, there is no hope of deliverance in ourselves. As James 2:10 states:

> For whoever keeps the whole law and yet stumbles in one point,
> he has become guilty of all.

All it takes is one sin in thought, word, or deed to condemn a person to hell forever. This is why Romans 3:19-20 states:

> [19]Now we know that whatever the Law says, it speaks to those who are under the Law, so that every mouth may be closed and all the world may become accountable to God; [20]because by the works of the Law no flesh will be justified in His sight; for through the Law comes the knowledge of sin.

The Covenant of Grace

It is God's love for fallen mankind that led to the instituting of the covenant of grace. In this covenant, God would choose according to the counsel of His own good pleasure to redeem a certain and fixed number for salvation (Ephesians 1:5-11). The motive for this grace and mercy shown to God's elect is nothing in the creature itself. It is all in God's eternal decree. Grace is an act of God's love whereby He gives the elect that which they do not deserve – salvation. Mercy is an act of God's love whereby God pities the fallen race of sinners and does not give them what they personally deserve. Why does God choose some for salvation while passing over others? It is purely in God's eternal decree, but there is nothing unjust in this whatsoever. We read in Romans 9:15-24:

15For He says to Moses, 'I will have mercy on whom I have mercy, and I will have compassion on whom I have compassion.' 16So then it does not depend on the man who wills or the man who runs, but on God who has mercy. 17For the Scripture says to Pharaoh, 'For this very purpose I raised you up, to demonstrate My power in you, and that My name might be proclaimed throughout the whole earth.' 18So then He has mercy on whom He desires, and He hardens whom He desires. 19You will say to me then, 'Why does He still find fault? For who resists His will?' 20On the contrary, who are you, O man, who answers back to God? The thing molded will not say to the molder, 'Why did you make me like this,' will it? 21Or does not the potter have a right over the clay, to make from the same lump one vessel for honorable use and another for common use? 22What if God, although willing to demonstrate His wrath and to make His power known, endured with much patience vessels of wrath prepared for destruction? 23And He did so to make known the riches of His glory upon vessels of mercy, which He prepared beforehand for glory, 24even us, whom He also called, not from among Jews only, but also from among Gentiles.

As we can see, God owns us and can do with us as He pleases. He is the potter, and we are the clay. God would have been just to leave all mankind in the state of sin and misery, doomed to everlasting destruction. Moreover, we all sin voluntarily; no one compels us to sin against God's holy law. We are not innocent. The fact that God saves some is amazing! The fact that God chooses to pass over some is for the purpose of magnifying the riches of His glory in showing mercy to those whom He has chosen. Those redeemed out of sin, who are easily prone to point a finger at God, complaining, "It is not fair that God saves some and not others," don't complain that God showed them grace and mercy in the Lord Jesus Christ. Men may complain about the consequences of Adam's representative headship, but they do not complain about the effects of Jesus Christ's representative headship on their behalf.

This covenant of grace is made with Jesus Christ and God's elect. Romans 5:15-21 beautifully sets forth that Jesus Christ's one act of obedience in justifying His people has undone all the damage by Adam. Adam's sin condemned the human race whereas Jesus' perfect law keeping and atoning sacrifice has secured salvation for all in union with Him. This is why the Bible refers to Jesus as the "second" or "last Adam." Salvation is by representation. Jesus is the substitute for His people.

The glory and uniqueness of the Christian faith is that salvation from start to finish originates with God, not us. All other religions of the world are totally man centered, meaning that it is a vain attempt at self righteousness. Non- Christian religions are futile attempts to do something to merit God's favor or attempts to perfect ourselves through good works. The reality is: As the Scripture says (Romans 3:10, 23) there are none who are good, and all have fallen short of God's glory. We cannot save ourselves; we are in need of a Savior, one who can pay the penalty for our transgressions in our place, and one who can present to God the Father a perfect life in our place so that we can be in the presence of a holy God. I John 4:10 says:

> In this is love, not that we loved God, but that He loved us and sent His Son to be the propitiation for our sins.

 This passage definitively informs us that salvation originates from God. God's love is manifested in the Father sending His only begotten Son into this world to be the propitiation for our sins. Propitiation is a word that means – the satisfaction of divine justice by means of a bloody sacrifice. Meanings of biblical words are determined by how they are used in Scripture. When one looks at "propitiation" we see this definition set forth clearly in Romans 3:21-25:

> [21]But now apart from the Law the righteousness of God has been manifested, being witnessed by the Law and the Prophets, [22]even the righteousness of God through faith in Jesus Christ for all those who believe; for there is no distinction; [23]for all have sinned and fall short of the glory of God, [24]being justified as a gift by His grace through the redemption which is in Christ Jesus; [25]whom God displayed publicly as a propitiation in His blood through faith This was to demonstrate His righteousness, because in the forbearance of God He passed over the sins previously committed.

The text affirms our failure before God because of our sins. If we are going to be righteous, it is through having faith in Jesus Christ. The basis for our righteousness is not our faith, but Jesus Christ alone as our righteousness. Redemption conveys the ransoming of someone – a price paid to secure their release. Jesus' blood is the ransom price. The blood of Jesus is the propitiatory sacrifice. Notice that Romans 3:25 emphasizes "His" righteousness, that is Jesus' righteousness, not our own. Faith is only the means or instrument by which we possess Christ's righteousness.

I have mentioned all of this for one important purpose: This is the gospel!! The gospel is God's message to a fallen race. The gospel is the glorious message of God stooping to us in love demonstrating His grace and mercy. It is not man reaching up to God in obedience; it is God descending to us through His eternally begotten Son, who became a man in order to save us. The Westminster Larger Catechism in two questions (numbers 38 and 39) asks: Why was it requisite that the Mediator should be God, and why was it requisite that the Mediator should be man? The mediator needed to be God because only God is perfect, only God can keep the perfect demands of His law, and only God can render a life and sacrifice sufficient to bring His elect to everlasting salvation. The Mediator had to become a real man because Adam was a real man. Since a real man failed as the representative head of the human race, a real man needed to be the redeemer. The redeemer had to keep the Law perfectly in the flesh, and the redeemer must be a real man to shed real blood to atone for the sins of His elect people. Hebrews 10:5-14 demonstrates the absolute necessity for the incarnation of the Son of God to possess a human body:

> *[5]Therefore, when He comes into the world, He says, "Sacrifice and offering You have not desired, but a body You have prepared for Me." [6]In whole burnt offerings and sacrifices for sin You have taken no pleasure. [7]Then I said, "Behold, I have come in the scroll of the book it is written of Me to do your will, O God." [8]After saying above, "Sacrifices and offerings and whole burnt offerings and sacrifices for sin You have not desired, nor have You taken pleasure in them" (which are offered according to the Law), [9]then He said, "Behold, I have come to do Your will." He takes away the first in order to establish the second. [10]By this will we have been sanctified through the offering of the body of Jesus Christ once for all. [11]Every priest stands daily ministering and offering time after time the same sacrifices, which can never take away sins; [12]but He, having offered one sacrifice for sins for all time, sat down at the right hand of God, [13]waiting from that time onward until His enemies be made a footstool for His feet. [14]For by one offering He has perfected for all time those who are sanctified.*

The gospel is a message of God becoming a man in order to save His elect people. It is God coming to us! In affirming the uniqueness of Christianity over against the other religions of the world, that are vain efforts in trying to save ourselves, I must stress that there are perversions within the pale of Christianity. Those perversions essentially affirm the same thing as pagan religions – attempts to earn our salvation by good works. These perversions would be seen in the doctrinal teaching of Roman Catholicism and in a hybrid form of Romanism known as Federal Vision theology. Both of these theologies deny the blessed doctrine of justification by Christ alone and by faith alone.

The covenant of grace is administered in two Testaments, the Old and New. *The Westminster Confession of Faith* speaks of the Old Testament as an administration of the covenant of grace "in the time of the Law" and in the New Testament as "under the gospel." This does not mean that men were saved by the law under the Old Testament. The essential element of the covenant of grace is faith in the Messiah in order to be saved. Under the Old Testament, the covenant of grace was administered by promises, prophecies, sacrifices, circumcision, the paschal lamb, and other types but **all foresignifying Christ to come**.

The salient point is that the Old Testament was very Christological, pointing to Christ. Chapter Seven of *The Westminster Confession of Faith* sets forth the following truths. The elect possessed salvation by faith in the promised Messiah. Key to the Old Testament administration is the phrase, "they had full remission of sins and eternal salvation."

We could simply say that God's elect were saved by faith in the Old Testament in the Messiah **to come**, while the elect in the New Testament were saved by faith in the Messiah **who has come**. But all were saved by faith in Christ!

The term "gospel" as applied to the New Testament age by *The Westminster Confession of Faith* is not to be understood in a rigid sense as if there was no gospel in the Old Testament, for we know from Scripture that the gospel was preached in the Old Testament to Abraham (Galatians 3:8). More on this when I discuss the Abrahamic covenant.

There are not therefore two covenants of grace differing in substance, but one and the same under various eras. There are not separate gospels. There is only one gospel. There is only one Messiah, only one savior who saved men in both Testaments in the same way – by faith.

Old Testament saints were saved by trusting in Christ to come. Though the sacrificial system of the Old Testament, with its animal sacrifices, could not atone for sins in themselves; nonetheless, when an elect Israelite, whose heart was circumcised, brought a sacrifice to the priests, he was identifying himself with the death of that animal believing that his sins deserved death. But the animal sacrifice was a type; the real substance was the "lamb of God" that takes away the sins of the world as John the Baptist declared. This explains why Hebrews 10:4 states:

> *For it is impossible for the blood of bulls and goats to take away sins.*

This is why Hebrews 10:5-15 sets forth the necessity of the Messiah to have a body in order to shed His blood to take away sins. The animal sacrificial blood typified Jesus' shed blood.

Let's now look at various features of the covenants that comprise the covenant of grace.

Adamic Covenant

When we think of the victory of the gospel in history, we find the first promise of it immediately after Adam and Eve's fall into sin. This is when the covenant of grace was first inaugurated as recorded in Genesis 3:14-15:

> [14]*The Lord God said to the serpent, 'Because you have done this, cursed are you more than all cattle, and more than every beast of the field; on your belly you will go, and dust you will eat all the days of your life,* [15]*and I will put enmity between you and the woman, and between your seed and her seed; He shall bruise you on the head, and you shall bruise him on the heel.'*

This is sometimes theologically referred to as the "protoevangelium." There will be war between the seed of the woman (Christ, the Messiah, and His elect people) and the seed of the serpent (the Devil and his deceived). The holy war reaches an apex in the person and work of Jesus Christ in the new covenant, although it is not the end of the spiritual warfare. The significant thing to note is that the **victor** is already determined. The seed of the woman defeats the seed of the serpent in history and on earth. The serpent bruises the woman's seed on the heel, but He crushes the head of the serpent. More will be said about this definitive defeat of Satan when I discuss the binding of Satan during the millennium.

Noahic Covenant

In this covenant, we see that there was a synthesis between the two seed lines. The seed line of the Serpent (those descending from Cain), united with the seed of the woman, (those descending from Seth), and the result was devastating.

God showed His attitude on the two seed lines. He totally wiped out the seed of the serpent, and showed free unmerited grace on the seed of the woman, particularized in only one family – (Noah's).

This Noahic covenant has been known as the covenant of preservation (Genesis 8:20-22). This covenant has tremendous eschatological implications. God binds Himself to a covenant never again to destroy the earth's inhabitants, but will preserve the earth until the end of time (Genesis 9:9-16). In other words, no catastrophe in human history will prevent the fulfillment of God's redemptive plan of the victory of the gospel.

Abrahamic Covenant

This covenant has tremendous eschatological implications. As noted previously, the gospel is not restricted to the New Testament era. Though it may be fully realized in the New Testament, it was preached in the Old Testament to Abraham. Galatians 3:8 states:

> The Scripture, foreseeing that God would justify the Gentiles by faith, preached the gospel beforehand to Abraham, saying, 'All the nations will be blessed in you.'

Another vital passage is John 8:56-58:

> [56]Your father Abraham rejoiced to see My day, and he saw it and was glad. [57]So the Jews said to Him, 'You are not yet fifty years old, and have You seen Abraham?' [58]Jesus said to them, 'Truly, truly, I say to you, before Abraham was born, I am.'

How was the gospel preached to Abraham? How was it that Abraham saw Jesus' day and was glad? These passages have been a "thorn in the side" of dispensational premillennialists who contend that there are two distinct peoples of God, Israel and the church, who are never joined into one body. According to this popular but novel view of Scripture, the gospel is peculiar to the church age, not existing among God's ancient people, the Jews.

Let's begin with understanding Jesus' comments in John 8:56-58. Jesus said that Abraham rejoiced to see "My day" and saw it. Perhaps another biblical passage is essential for us to examine that will cast light on Jesus' comments. It is Hebrews 11:13-19:

> *¹³All these died in faith, without receiving the promises, but having seen them and having welcomed them from a distance, and having confessed that they were strangers and exiles on the earth. ¹⁴For those who say such things make it clear that they are seeking a country of their own. ¹⁵And indeed if they had been thinking of that country from which they went out, they would have had opportunity to return. ¹⁶But as it is, they desire a better country, that is, a heavenly one therefore God is not ashamed to be called their God; for He has prepared a city for them. ¹⁷By faith Abraham, when he was tested, offered up Isaac, and he who had received the promises was offering up his only begotten son; ¹⁸it was he to whom it was said, 'In Isaac your descendants shall be called' ¹⁹He considered that God is able to raise people even from the dead, from which he also received him back as a type.*

Abraham saw Jesus' day by faith when he believed the promises of God that through his seed all the families of the earth would be blessed. That blessing would be realized in the coming of the Lord Jesus Christ. It is evident that Abraham believed that through Isaac's seed line this world wide blessing would come. We must not sell short what our Old Testament saints understood. Since Scripture is the best interpreter of Scripture, we must accept that Abraham saw Jesus' day. Abraham was yearning for a city whose foundation was laid by God. Though he never received the fulfillment of the promise in the sense that New Testament saints have received it; nevertheless, he "welcomed it from a distance." He saw it with the eyes of faith!

How was the gospel preached to Abraham as Galatians 3:8 indicates? The book of Galatians is a polemic against the Judaizers who were insisting that "works" were necessary in addition to faith in order to be justified. Inspired Paul refutes this notion by affirming that the Gentiles are being saved by faith just as it was prophesied in the Abrahamic covenant. The heart of the Abrahamic covenant was the foretold promise that through Abraham's seed all the families of the earth would be blessed. This is the gospel! The gospel is that in Jesus Christ all the families of the nations would be brought into God's fold. This doesn't mean every single person without exception will believe, but it does imply a substantial number will believe. This substantial number is reflected in God's promise to Abraham. God first gave this promise to Abraham as reflected in Genesis 12:2-3:

> *²And I will make you a great nation, and I will bless you, And make your name great; And so you shall be a blessing; ³and I will bless those who bless you, And the one who curses you I will curse, and in you all the families of the earth will be blessed.*

Then we come to Genesis 15. Abraham is concerned about how this promise can be possible seeing that he has no heir. God tells Abraham to go outside and look at the stars and try to count them. God promises that from a seed coming from his own body, his descendants will be as numerous as the heavenly host. To get a full appreciation of this visual object lesson, it is helpful to have seen the stars in a desert setting, especially when there are no city lights. Of course in biblical times, there would have been no lights to hinder the splendor of such a sight. On two occasions in my life, I have been awe struck by viewing a vast canopy of stars in such a setting. Imagine Abraham looking at this innumerable host and believing that one day in human history, his seed would be as innumerable. It really took faith, but the Bible says in Romans 4:20 about Abraham:

> *Yet, with respect to the promise of God, he did not waver in unbelief, but grew strong in faith, giving glory to God.*

This New Testament passage reflects what Genesis 15:5-6 says:

> *⁵And He took him outside and said, 'Now look toward the heavens, and count the stars, if you are able to count them and He said to him, ⁶'so shall your descendants be.' Then he believed in the Lord; and He reckoned it to him as righteousness.*

This passage in Genesis 15 is so crucial to biblical theology. Paul uses this Old Testament passage in Romans 4 as the basis to prove that men are justified by faith and not by works (Romans 4:1-13).

In the Abrahamic covenant, God would reaffirm this covenantal promise to Abraham on two other occasions – in Genesis 17 and 22. In Genesis 17:4-11, we see that Abram's name was changed to Abraham to reflect that the promise encompasses a multitude of nations. The name "Abraham" means "a father of a multitude." Genesis 17:7 indicates that

God's covenantal promise is an everlasting promise to his seed throughout their generations. It is most noteworthy that Romans 4:13 is based upon Genesis 17:7. As I quote Romans 4:13, be careful to observe the words that inspired Paul used in reference to Abraham's promise. Romans 4:13 reads:

> *The promise to Abraham or to his descendants that he would be heir of the world was not through the Law, but through the righteousness of faith.*

The text says "world." Did Paul misquote Genesis? Of course not. The New Testament always interprets accurately the Old Testament. The land promise of the Abrahamic covenant was **never restricted to the Jewish nation!** It actually foretold of the incorporation of the Gentile nations. This is why Paul states that the gospel was preached beforehand to Abraham. The land promise of the Abrahamic covenant during the time of its historical administration was the geographical territory of Canaan, but this was only a down payment of God's wider promise that Paul alludes to. The Abrahamic covenant promise always pertained to the world! This is why God told Abraham that his seed would be as numerous as the stars of the sky.

The other reaffirmation of the covenant promise to Abraham is seen in Genesis 22:17-18:

> *[17] Indeed I will greatly bless you, and I will greatly multiply your seed as the stars of the heavens and as the sand which is on the seashore; and your seed shall possess the gate of their enemies. [18] 'in your seed all the nations of the earth shall be blessed, because you have obeyed My voice.'*

This event transpired some twenty years or more after God's initial promise to Abraham. God reaffirms His promise to Abraham due to his faithfulness in willing to sacrifice Isaac. Another image is introduced to convey the notion of "innumerable." It is the phrase, "and I will greatly multiply your seed... as the sand which is on the seashore." How many grains of sand on a seashore? A vast number!

One of the most important aspects of the Abrahamic covenant is its emphasis upon quantity. This is why postmillennialism believes in a vast number of people being saved in history before Christ's Second Coming. The blessing to all the nations cannot be restricted to only a few in history. It is a blessing that encompasses the world, the families of the earth that are as numerous as the stars of the sky and the sand of the seashore. Revelation 5:9 conveys the magnificent doxology of the redeemed church in all the ages represented by the twenty-four elders. They proclaim:

> *And they sang a new song, saying, 'Worthy are You to take the book and to break its seals; for You were slain, and purchased for God with Your blood men from every tribe and tongue and people and nation. You have made them to be a kingdom and priests to our God; and they will reign upon the earth.'*

This enumerable number of the redeemed of God is gathered from every tribe, tongue, people, and nation. This is fulfillment of Abraham's covenant promise.

There is another very important theological point raised in Genesis 22:17. This innumerable seed of Abraham is said to **"possess the gate of their enemies."** Hence, the Abrahamic covenant at its very heart pictures gospel victory! More will be said later about the concept of "possessing the gate of their enemies." But for the time being, we can clearly see that the gospel was preached in promise form in the Old Testament during the Abrahamic covenant. Abraham did see Jesus' day in promise form by faith in God's promise to him that his seed would be a blessing to all families of the earth. As Galatians 3:8 affirms, Scripture foreseeing that God would justify the Gentiles by faith preached the gospel beforehand to Abraham. This means that the salvation of the Gentile nations was a crucial part of the Abrahamic covenant. It is not restricted to some future promise held out for an exclusively Jewish element in a thousand year kingdom after Christ's Second Coming. Dispensationalism, in its insistence that the millennial kingdom is after Christ's Second Coming where the Jews will be prominent in the earth, is simply a myth according to the Word of God. This theological outlook is a system of beliefs arbitrarily imposed upon the Scripture. We must never allow our system of beliefs to dictate the exegesis of Scripture; we must allow Scripture to dictate our exegesis.

Since we have seen that gospel victory is central to the Abrahamic covenant, we need to carefully understand who this "seed" is that is promised in this covenant. Understanding this vital point is paramount to our understanding of Christ's millennial kingdom, and the victorious nature of this kingdom **before** Christ's Second Coming.

Dispensational Premillennial Errors Pertaining to the Abrahamic Covenant

Critical to the debate in eschatology among the varying millennial views is the ascertaining of who Israel really is. For the dispensational premillennialist, one of the fundamental tenets of his system is: Israel is Israel, and the church is the church - two distinct peoples of God with two different purposes in history. One is not a dispensationalist without believing this.[2]

A determination of who really constitutes "the seed of Abraham" or "the true Israel" is crucial in our understanding of Scripture. It is a key in properly understanding prophecy. It is vital in understanding the nature of the millennium and how Jesus reigns during this millennium. It is no minor point! Dispensationalists make a radical distinction between Israel and the church, believing that the church Age is the time frame for the preaching of the gospel but not the preaching of the kingdom. The preaching of the kingdom supposedly is restricted to the millennial kingdom after Jesus' Second Coming.

While this book is not exclusively a polemic against dispensational premillennial teaching, I cannot be remiss in bringing out what I believe to be serious theological errors in this system. One's present worldview (theological perspective) does impact one's mission to the world. Believing that the church has been or will be a failure is no minor thing. Believing that Jesus will not reign as King of kings and Lord of lords until after His Second Coming is no minor deviation from biblical theology. Believing that there will be a salvation according to the Law in the millennial kingdom is a theological error of tremendous import – heresy!

The following quotes are from various dispensational proponents over the past century. Several Dispensational teachers make a distinction between the church and the kingdom, and a distinction between the kingdom of

---

[2]   Charles C. Ryrie has long been recognized as a leading Dispensational teacher. In his book *Dispensationalism Today* (Chicago: Moody Press, 1965), he defines one of the salient features of this interpretation of Scripture. He says, "What, then, is the sine qua non of dispensationalism? A dispensationalist keeps Israel and the Church**Error! Bookmark not defined.** distinct" (p.44). Ryrie quotes fellow dispensationalist, Lewis Sperry Chafer, as saying, "The dispensationalist believes that throughout the ages God is pursuing two distinct purposes: one related to the earth with earthly people and earthly objectives involved which is Judaism; while the other is related to heaven with heavenly people and heavenly objectives involved, which is Christianity" (p.45). Ryrie goes on to say, "A man who fails to distinguish Israel and the Church will inevitably not hold to dispensational distinctions, and one who does, will" (p.45). Ryrie emphatically states, "The essence of dispensationalism, then, is the distinction between Israel and the Church" (p. 47).

heaven and the kingdom of God. Dispensationalist, Clarence Larkin taught:

> The "church" and the "kingdom" are not identical. They are never confounded in the Scriptures… Christ is the "Head" of the Church, but He is never spoken of as its "king."…The church is here, the kingdom is **to come**… the church is an invisible and heavenly spiritual organism, entered by the "new birth", and to be "caught out" while the kingdom is an outward, visible, and earthly "political organization" that is to be "set up" on the EARTH, of which the Jewish Nation will be the "Head" (Deuteronomy 28:11-13), and will have a King, a Throne, and a capital city – Jerusalem.
>
> The kingdom is characterized by a "throne" the church by a "table." Thus we see that the Church and the kingdom have "spheres" of work and different "time periods" in which to do that work. Therefore what God has separated let no man join together.
>
> There is much confusion as to the difference between the "kingdom of God," "the kingdom of heaven," and the church. No amount of sophistical argument can make them synonymous… The "kingdom of heaven" is a New Testament term…It is the earthly sphere of the "kingdom of God" and is outward and visible… In it is a mixture of "good" and "evil" and "wheat and tares."[3]

Dispensationalism still remains one of the most popular views today. Now while there are some variations in this system, the points under discussion are rather consistent throughout all dispensational thought. C.I. Scofield has said in his reference Bible:

> Therefore, in approaching the study of the Gospels, the mind should be freed, so far as possible, from such presuppositions as that the Church is to be equated with the true Israel, and that the O.T. promises to Israel and the foreview of the kingdom relate only to the Church.[4]

Scofield has also said:

---

[3]   Clarence Larkin**Error! Bookmark not defined.**, *The Second Coming of Christ*, (Philadelphia: Rev. Clarence Larkin Estate, 1918-1922), p.47.
[4]   C.I. Scofield, *The New Scofield Reference Bible*, (New York: Oxford Press, 1967), p. 987.

The kingdom thus made way for the church, which was a distinct and separate entity which can never be merged with the kingdom, neither in time nor in eternity. And the message is no longer "the gospel of the kingdom," but the "gospel of the grace of God..." The church corporately is not in the vision of the Old Testament prophets.[5]

S.D. Gordon (1859-1936) was a popular writer and speaker in the late nineteenth and early twentieth centuries. As a Dispensationalist, his views on God's plan as it pertains to the Church are disconcerting. It is a lengthy quote, but it is necessary to show Dispensational thinking. Here are excerpts from his talk on world winning – past failures:

God fails, sometimes. That is to say, the plan He has made and set His heart upon fails.

Eden was God's plan for man... and in the midst of all God Himself walking and working in closest touch with man in all his enterprises--that was God's Eden plan for man. But it failed.

The Israel plan was a failure, too. The main purpose of Israel being made God's peculiar people has failed up to the present hour... They were to be wholly unlike the other nations, utterly unambitious politically, neither exciting war upon themselves by others nor ever making war upon others. Their great mission was to be a teacher-nation to all the earth, teaching the great spiritual truths; and, better yet, embodying these truths in their personal and national life. But the plan failed.

Then God worked with them where they would work with Him. He planned a great kingdom to overspread the earth in its rule and blessed influence, but not by the aggression of war and oppression... Yet when the King came they rejected Him and then killed Him. They failed at the very point that was to have been their great achievement. God's plan failed. The Hebrew people from the point of view of the direct object of their creation as a nation have been a failure up to the present hour.

Jesus' plan for Judas failed. The sharpest contrasts of possible good and actual bad came together in his career in the most

---

[5]   Old Scofield Bible, p.711.

startling way. He failed at the very point where he should have been strongest--his personal loyalty to his Chief.

There can be no doubt that Jesus picked him out for one of His inner circle because of his strong attractive traits. He had in him the making of a John, the intimate, the writer of the great fourth Gospel. He might have been a Peter, rugged in his bold leadership of the early Church... Jesus planned Judas the apostle. He became Judas the apostate, the traitor. He was to be a leader and teacher of the Gospel. He became a miserable reproach and by-word of execration to all men. Jesus' plan failed.

Will you please mark very keenly that the failure always comes because of man's unwillingness to work with God? It always takes two for God's plan--Himself and a man. All His working is through human partnership. In all His working among men He needs to work with men.

Some good earnest people don't like, and won't like, that blunt statement that God fails sometimes. It seems to them to cast a reproach upon God... There is reproach. Every failure that could have been prevented by honest work and earnest faithfulness spells reproach. And there is reproach here. But it isn't upon God; it is upon man. God's plan depends upon man. It is always man's failure to do his simple part faithfully that causes God's plan to fail.

But the practical thing to burn in deep just now is this, that we can hinder God's plan. His plans have been hindered, and delayed, and made to fail, because we wouldn't work with Him.

And God lets His plan fail. It is a bit of His greatness. He will let a plan fail before He will be untrue to man's utter freedom of action. He will let a man wreck his career, that so through the wreckage the man may see his own failure, and gladly turn to God. Many a hill is climbed only through a swamp road.

God cares more for a man than for a plan. The plan is only for the sake of the man. You say, of course. But, you know, many men think more of carrying through the plan on which they have set themselves, regardless of how it may hurt or crush some man in the way. God's plan is for man, and so it is allowed to fail, for the man's sake.

Now, God had and has a plan for His Church. That plan is simply this: The Church was to be His messenger to the nations of the earth. There are other matters of vast importance committed to the Church, without doubt: the service of worship and the training and developing of the life of its members. But these, be it said very thoughtfully, are distinctly secondary to the service of taking the Gospel to all men.

These two, the chief and the secondary, are interwoven, each contributing to and dependent upon the other. But there is always a main purpose. And that here, without question, is the carrying of the message of Jesus fully to all the earth. In each generation the chief plan, to which all else was meant to be contributory, was that all men should hear fully and winsomely the great thrilling story of Jesus.

Shall I say that that plan has failed? It hurts too much even to repeat such words. I will not say the Church has failed. But I will ask you to note God's plan for the Church, and then in your inner heart to make your own honest answer.

And in making it, remember the practical point is this--the Church is you. I am the Church. Its mission is mine. If I say it has failed I am talking about myself. I can keep it from failing, so far as part of it is concerned, the part that I am. My concern is not to be asking abstractly, theoretically, about the Church, but about so much of it as I am.

But the Church was not meant by the Master to be a rich institution in money and property; though it has grown immensely so. The Master's thought was that its power and faithfulness should be revealed entirely in the extent to which all men of all nations know about Himself and have been won to Him.

If we think only a little bit into the past history of the Church, and then into present world conditions, we know the answer to that hurting question about the Church being a failure.

We shudder to attempt to think into what these centuries would have been without the influence of the Church.

But at present we are talking about something else. Let me ask you, softly, if God's plan for the Church was that it was to be His messenger to all men, as you think back through nineteen centuries and then think out into the moral world conditions to-day, would you say the plan had succeeded? Or has?

It looks very much as though the Master's coming has been delayed, and His plans delayed, because we have not done the preparatory part assigned us.

The restless millions wait the light, Whose coming maketh all things new. Christ also waits; but men are slow and late. Have we done what we could? Have I? Have you? [6]

Here are some of the immense problems with the above perspective of S.D. Gordon, who does articulate the general thrust of dispensational teaching. To assert that God's plan has failed because man has somehow been unfaithful is a direct assault upon the glory of God. While Gordon refers to God's sovereignty, he does so in such a way that actually distorts a biblical understanding of God's sovereignty. God cannot be sovereign if God's plan can be nullified! Let's think about this carefully. If man, in any shape or form, can alter or set aside God's original intent, then who really is the architect of history? God or Man? Dispensational theology is not consistent with the following Scripture.

Isaiah 46:9-10 affirms:

> [9]*Remember the former things long past, for I am God, and there is no other; I am God, and there is no one like Me,* [10]*declaring the end from the beginning and from ancient times things which have not been done, saying, 'My purpose will be established, and I will accomplish all My good pleasure.'*

Isaiah 14:24, 27 states:

> [24]*The Lord of hosts has sworn saying, "Surely, just as I have intended so it has happened and just as I have planned so it will stand ...* [27]*For the Lord of hosts has planned, and who can frustrate it? And as for His stretched-out hand, who can turn it back?*

---

[6]   S.D. Gordon, *Quiet Talks With World Winners, Chapter 6: World-Winning – The Past Failure* found on http://www.raptureready.com/resource/gordon/gordon39.html.

Gordon appears to be sensitive to the fact that there is something odd about asserting that God's plan can be frustrated, that the church can fail. This is because there is something terribly wrong with this assertion. God's sovereignty does not make God a reactor but sovereign planner. Probably the most serious flaw in dispensational thinking is that history is not determined until man has acted, but then, that makes man sovereign, not God. The Arminian concept about God's foreseeing is totally inadequate. The typical explanation advanced about "predestination" is that God somehow foresees what man will do and having somehow seen it, God then rewinds the tape of human history, declaring, "This is My plan." Sorry, but this makes no sense, and is very dishonoring to God. What did Isaiah 14:27 emphatically state? God says, "For the Lord of hosts has planned, and who can frustrate it?" There is no failure in God's plan! There is no planning based first on what man will do! No, God's plan remains an eternal decree that will be accomplished exactly as God planned it. Does this plan incorporate the actions of men, allowing them to freely act according to their hearts' desires? Of course it does. God who has ordained the end has simultaneously ordained the means to that end, but incorporating men's acts in a plan does not make men the orchestrators of history; man's unfaithfulness does not alter God's plan.

Gordon blatantly asserts that the church has failed, that God's plan has failed. This is no theology that bows to God's absolute authority, and it is no theology that truly prompts us to press on during this so called "church age" as dispensationalism calls this present time period.

This deficient theology is further set forth in dispensational radio preacher, M.R. DeHann:

> ... the kingdom of heaven is the reign of heaven's king on earth. This Jesus offered to the nation of Israel when he came the first time, but they rejected it and he went to the cross.[7]

Such statements make Jesus' death on the cross as a change in God's plan due to Israel's rejection of the kingdom. This is an incredible admission! Jesus' atoning sacrifice an alternate plan? How can this be? Consider DeHann's statement in light of the following biblical texts:

> *Men of Israel, listen to these words: Jesus the Nazarene, a man attested to you by God with miracles and wonders and signs which God performed through Him in your midst, just as you*

---

[7] M.R. DeHann, *The Second Coming of Jesus*, (Grand Rapids: Kregel Publications, 1996), p. 98.

yourselves know-- this Man, delivered over by the predetermined plan and foreknowledge of God, you nailed to a cross by the hands of godless men and put Him to death. (Acts 2:22-23)

For truly in this city there were gathered together against Your holy servant Jesus, whom You anointed, both Herod and Pontius Pilate, along with the Gentiles and the peoples of Israel, to do whatever Your hand and Your purpose predestined to occur. (Acts 4:27-28)

Dispensational theology consistent with Arminian theology, doesn't really believe in "predestination." They believe in what I call, "postdestination." Predestination means exactly what it implies. The prefix, "pre" means "before." The word "destination" infers a "destiny or plan." Predestination, therefore, means to plan beforehand. Jesus' death was predestined, that is, planned beforehand, which would occur exactly as God the Father planned!

A Different Mode of Salvation in the Kingdom?

The idea that Jesus would have set up the kingdom of God if the Jews had accepted the offer, and that its rejection led to His death on the cross is a view that makes the atoning sacrifice of Christ as an alternate plan B is fundamentally heretical, meaning that it is false doctrine at its worse.

The Old Testament sacrificial system was a type prefiguring the atoning sacrifice of Christ. Jesus was always a kingly priest. The book of Hebrews shows that the New Testament was a better covenant than the old, but it was always in the plan of God.

Revelation 13:8 refers to the Lamb having been slain from the foundation of the world. The plan of redemption reaches back into eternity past. Ephesians 1:3-9 clearly indicates that God the Father chose us in Christ before the foundation of the world, as verse 5 states, *"He predestined us to adoption as sons through Jesus Christ to Himself."*

The notion that there is a gospel of the kingdom that is distinct from the gospel of grace, meaning that the church was never in the vision of the Old Testament is equally an aberrant view, for it purports that there was a different plan of salvation in the Old Testament and that this Old Testament saving plan will be implemented in the millennial kingdom.

Historic dispensationalism then purports that salvation in the Old Testament was not of grace. If it is not of grace, then what is it? Of works? The following quotes from some dispensationalists are not encouraging at all.

Concerning the difference between the Mosaic dispensation and the New Testament dispensation, C.I. Scofield said this in his reference Bible:

> The point of testing is no longer legal obedience as the condition of salvation, but acceptance or rejection of Christ...[8]

Lewis Sperry Chafer was the founder and first president of Dallas Theological Seminary and he made the following quotes:

> The essential elements of a grace administration- faith as the sole basis of acceptance with God, unmerited acceptance through a perfect standing in Christ, the present possession of eternal life, and absolute security from all condemnation, and the enabling power of the indwelling Spirit – are not found in the kingdom administration. On the other hand, it is declared to be the fulfilling of "the law and the prophets, and is to be an extension of the Mosaic law into the realm of meritorious obligation...[9]

> A distinction must be observed here between just men of the Old Testament and those justified according to the New Testament. According to the Old Testament men were just because they were true and faithful in keeping the Mosaic law... Men were therefore just because of their own works for God, whereas New Testament justification is God's work for man in answer to faith.[10]

> ... The kingdom teachings, like the Law of Moses, are based on a covenant of works. The teachings of grace, on the other hand, are based on a covenant of faith. In the one case, righteousness is demanded; in the other it is provided, both imputed and imparted, or inwrought. One is of a blessing to be bestowed because of a

---

[8] Scofield Reference Bible, (New York: Oxford University Press, 1945), p.1115.
[9] Lewis Sperry Chafer, *Dispensationalism*, p. 416. Quoted in Curtis I. Crenshaw and Grover E. Gunn, III, *Dispensationalism Today, Yesterday, and Tomorrow*, (Memphis, TN: Footstool Publications, 1985).
[10] Chafer, *Systematic Theology*, 7:219.

perfect life, the other of a life to be lived because of a perfect blessing already received.[11]

Under grace, the fruit of the Spirit is, which indicates the present possession of the blessing through pure grace; while under the kingdom, the blessing shall be to such as merit it by their own works.[12]

In this age, God is dealing with men on the ground of His grace as it is in Christ. His dealings with men in the coming age are based on a very different relationship. At that time, the King will rule with a rod of iron. There is no word of the cross, or of grace, in the kingdom teachings.[13]

While it is amazing that L.S. Chafer would teach a two fold plan of salvation and that the millennial kingdom would be a return to the Old Testament plan of salvation, he made this comment about the Mosaic dispensation:

Israel made a foolish and rash mistake at Mount Sinai by accepting the meritorious Mosaic covenant. [14]

Now think about the immense problem in this theological system. The Jews made a rash mistake by accepting the Mosaic covenant, but this "foolish and rash mistake" is the mode of salvation in the millennial reign of the Lord Jesus Christ? This erroneous system of interpretation then means that the Lord Jesus Christ along with us glorified "church saints" will supervise a world where salvation is not by grace but by works.

We continue with some other very problematic quotes from Lewis Sperry Chafer:

As the Christian may be forgiven and cleansed on the ground of confession of his sin to God (I John 1:9), so Israelites both individually and nationally were restored by sacrifices.[15]

The kingdom saint's righteousness under Messiah's reign will exceed the righteousness of the scribes and Pharisees. Indeed,

---

[11]   Chafer, *Systematic Theology*, 4:215-216.
[12]   Chafer, 4:219.
[13]   Chafer, 4:222.
[14]   Chafer, 4:162-163.
[15]   Chafer, 4:159.

such personal quality and merit are demanded for entrance into that kingdom at all.[16]

Another dispensationalist, William Evans, has said:

> This sometimes called the age of the church, or the church period. The characteristic of this age is that salvation is no longer by legal obedience, but by the personal acceptance of the finished work of Jesus Christ, who by his meritorious ministry has procured for us a righteousness of God.[17]

Concerning the Tribulation period of seven years between the Rapture and Second Coming dispensationalism teaches that the Jews are in dominance and large numbers of people are converted. Regarding this period, dispensationalist John Walvoord has said:

> The tribulation period, also, seems to revert back to Old Testament conditions in several ways; and in the Old Testament period, saints were never permanently indwelt except in isolated instances, though a number of instances of the filling of the Spirit and of empowering for service are found. Taking all the factors into consideration, there is no evidence for the indwelling of the Holy Spirit in believers in the tribulation.[18]

These are very serious theological errors. To purport that there was a time and will be a future time where men can be saved outside of the grace of God, independent of the atoning work of Christ, is not just wrong; it is heresy.

Where in all of God's Word do we have any hint of people being saved apart from the application of saving grace by the Holy Spirit? Nowhere! Titus 3:5-7 is vital:

> *He saved us, not on the basis of deeds which we have done in righteousness, but according to His mercy, **by the washing of regeneration and renewing by the Holy Spirit**, whom He poured out upon us richly through Jesus Christ our Savior, so that being justified by His grace we would be made heirs according to the hope of eternal life.* (Emphasis mine)

---

[16]   Chafer, 5:106.
[17]   William Evans, *Outline Study of the Bible*, p. 34.
[18]   John F. Walvoord, *The Holy Spirit*, p.230.

Charles Ryrie, has made these criticisms of those who hold to covenant theology:

> The covenant theologian in his zeal to make Christ all in all is guilty of superimposing Him arbitrarily on the Old Testament. He does the same with the doctrine of the Church and with the concept of salvation through faith in Christ.[19]

> The hermeutical straitjacket which covenant theology forces on the Scriptures results in reading the New Testament back into the Old Testament and in an artificial typological interpretation.[20]

My personal interaction to this criticism of Covenant Theology is that I enthusiastically stand guilty of making Christ the "yes" to all the covenant promises, and accepting what Jesus said in Luke 24: 44:

> *These are My words which I spoke to you while I was still with you, that all things which are written about Me in the Law of Moses, and the Prophets and the Psalms must be fulfilled.*

And yes, I will enthusiastically let the New Testament inspired writers tell me what the Old Testament prophecies really mean. As Romans 3:4 states:

> *Let God be found true, though every man be found a liar...*

I will say this about Charles Ryrie, who studied under Lewis Sperry Chafer. Ryrie has been very sensitive about what appears to be a works salvation in the dispensational system and has offered his own somewhat modification. For Ryrie states:

> The basis for salvation in every age is the death of Christ; the requirement for salvation in every age is faith; the object of faith in every age is God; the content of faith changes in the various dispensations.[21]

Then we have Dallas Theological Seminary's doctrinal statement:

> ... we believe that it was historically impossible that (Old Testament saints) should have had as the conscious object of their

---

[19]   Ryrie, p. 187.
[20]   Ryrie, p. 190.
[21]   Ryrie, p. 123.

faith the incarnate, crucified Son, the Lamb of God (John 1:29), and that it is evident that they did not comprehend as we do that the sacrifices depicted the person and work of Christ.[22]

There is a very serious problem with saying that the Old Testament did not comprehend, as we do, that the sacrifices depicted the person and work of Christ. Jesus explicitly said, as recorded in John 8:56, that Abraham rejoiced to see His day and saw it. While it is true that New Testament saints have faith in the substance of the Old Testament promise of a Messiah, we must affirm that in essence it is no different than Old Testament saints trusting in the promise of the Messiah yet to come. *The Westminster Confession of Faith*, in speaking about the covenant of grace, says it beautifully when it states:

> This covenant was differently administered in the time of the law, and in the time of the gospel, under the law it was administered by promises, prophecies, sacrifices, circumcision, the paschal lamb, and other types and ordinances delivered to the people of the Jews, all foresignifying Christ to come, **which were for that time sufficient and efficacious, through the operation of the Spirit, to instruct and build up the elect in faith in the promised Messiah, by whom they had full remission of sins, and eternal salvation,** and is called the Old Testament" (WCF 7:5 Emphasis mine).

Whether it is salvation in a Messiah to come or has come, it is still salvation by grace through faith in Christ alone.

The Old Testament saints were trusting in Christ for the New Testament explicitly says they were. I Corinthians 10:1-4 states:

> *[1]For I do not want you to be unaware, brethren, that our fathers were all under the cloud and all passed through the sea; [2]and all were baptized into Moses in the cloud and in the sea; [3]and all ate the same spiritual food;[4] and all drank the same spiritual drink, for they were drinking from a spiritual rock which followed them; **and the rock was Christ**.* (Emphasis mine)

Dispensationalism advocates what is known as the postponement theory and the parenthesis of the church age. This view believes that the Kingdom was rejected by the Jews and God postponed the kingdom, and in its place

---

[22]   Dallas Theological Seminary doctrinal statement, p. 11.

was the church age, that period of time between the rejection and the rapture of the church.

In fact, Clarence Larkin states this about the OT prophets:

> ...the Old Testament prophets failed to distinguish between the "First" and "Second" Comings. From the prophet's view point he saw the birth of Jesus, the Crucifixion, the Outpouring of the Holy Spirit, the Antichrist, the Sun of righteousness, the Millennial Kingdom, Ezekiel's Temple and the New Heavens and the New Earth, as "mountain peaks" of one great mountain, but we standing off to the side see these peaks as belonging to two different mountains with the "valley of the church" in between.[23]

Who Is the True Israel?

Properly understanding the Abrahamic covenant is essential in understanding the glorious continuity in God's Word. I cannot stress too strongly the theological truth that the church of the New Testament is de facto the seed of Abraham, possessing all the promises pictured in that covenant. Dispensationalists emphatically deny this truth, but they are clearly wrong.

Romans 2:28-29 and Romans 9:3-8

A very important theological point is that there is an **external** and **internal** aspect of God's covenant. Romans 2:28-29 refers to a circumcision that is outward in the flesh and to a circumcision that is inward according to the Holy Spirit. The text reads:

> [28]*For he is not a Jew who is one outwardly, nor is circumcision that which is outward in the flesh.* [29]*But he is a Jew who is one inwardly; and circumcision is that which is of the heart, by the Spirit, not by the letter; and whose praise is not from men, but from God.*

Romans 9:3-8 says that not all those who are descended from Israel are Israel, and the true children of Abraham are not those descended from the flesh but are the children of the promise. This text reads:

---

[23] Larkin, pp. 6-7.

> *³For I could wish that I myself were accursed, separated from Christ for the sake of my brethren, my kinsmen according to the flesh, ⁴who are Israelites, to whom belongs the adoption as sons, and the glory and the covenants and the giving of the Law and the temple service and the promises, ⁵whose are the fathers, and from whom is the Christ according to the flesh, who is over all, God blessed forever. Amen. ⁶But it is not as though the word of God has failed. For they are not all Israel who are descended from Israel; ⁷nor are they all children because they are Abraham's descendants, but: "through Isaac your descendants will be named." ⁸That is, it is not the children of the flesh who are children of God, but the children of the promise are regarded as descendants.*

Hence, there is a distinction between children of the flesh and children of the promise. The two persons serving as the object lesson of this great truth are Esau and Jacob who are set forth in Romans 9:9-13. Obviously, Jacob, whom God loves, is a child of the promise while Esau, whom God hates, is a child of the flesh. While Esau was circumcised just like Jacob, and while both were members in the visible covenant community, God's saving grace was applied only to Jacob. Hebrews 12:14-17 brings out the spiritual bankruptcy of Esau. The text states:

> *¹⁴Pursue peace with all men, and the sanctification without which no one will see the Lord. ¹⁵See to it that no one comes short of the grace of God; that no root of bitterness springing up causes trouble, and by it many be defiled; ¹⁶that there be no immoral or godless person like Esau, who sold his own birthright for a single meal. ¹⁷For you know that even afterwards, when he desired to inherit the blessing, he was rejected, for he found no place for repentance, though he sought for it with tears.*

Let's examine more closely the great truths set forth in Romans 2:28-29. The emphasis of the text is the value of the **internal** work of the Holy Spirit as opposed to trusting in the external rite. The Jews believed that mere possession of the external rite was valuable in itself. The tendency was to neglect the weightier matters of the Law, as Jesus told the self-righteous and blind Pharisees. The emphasis is on the internal work. This is why Paul says that the Gentiles who do not have circumcision but who keep the Law are actually circumcised (Romans 2:26). How could they be circumcised, but not be circumcised? The answer is in verses 27-29. The real Jew is the one who is circumcised in his heart! In fact, Paul says that a

real Jew is not even one who is circumcised in the flesh (v. 28). Paul even says that circumcision is not even that which is outward in the flesh (v. 28). What? Circumcision is "not even that which is outward in the flesh." Paul says in verse 29 that the real Jew is the one who is **circumcised in the heart, which is by the Spirt, not by the letter.**

> This "circumcision of the heart" was always emphasized, even in the old covenant. The following texts illustrate this truth. Deuteronomy 10:16 states – *"So circumcise your heart, and stiffen your neck no longer."* Jeremiah 4:4 states – *"Circumcise yourselves to the Lord and remove the foreskins of your heart, men of Judah and inhabitants of Jerusalem, lest My wrath go forth like fire and burn with none to quench it, because of the evil of your deeds."* Jeremiah 9:25-26 also states – *"Behold, the days are coming, declares the Lord, that I will punish all who are circumcised and yet uncircumcised- Egypt and Judah, and Edom and the sons of Ammon, and Moab and all those inhabiting the desert who clip the hair on their temples; for all the nations are uncircumcised, and all the house of Israel are uncircumcised of heart."*

Now, this does not disparage the outward rite of circumcision at all. It was still necessary in the old covenant. It simply meant that the outward rite was a sign and seal of that which was **internally done by the Spirit of God.**

John Calvin understood Romans 2:25-29 as stressing the internal work of the Spirit. Calvin stated the following about Romans 2:28-29:

> The meaning is, that a real Jew is not to be ascertained, either by natural descent, or by profession, or by an external symbol; that the circumcision which constitutes a Jew, does not consist in an outward sign only, but that both are inward. And what he subjoins with regard to true circumcision, is taken from various passages of Scripture, and even from its general teaching; for the people are everywhere commanded to circumcise their hearts, and it is what the Lord promises to do. The fore-skin was cut off, not indeed as the small corruption of one part, but as that of the whole nature. Circumcision then signified the mortification of the whole flesh.

> What he then adds, in the spirit, not in the letter, understand thus: He calls the outward rite, without piety, the letter, and the spiritual design of this rite, the spirit; for the whole importance of signs and

rites depends on what is designed; when the end in view is not regarded, the letter alone remains, which in itself is useless. And the reason for this mode of speaking is this, - where the voice of God sounds, all that he commands, except it be received by men in sincerity of heart, will remain in the letter, that is, in the dead writing; but when it penetrates into the heart, it is in a manner transformed into spirit. And there is an allusion to the difference between the old and the new covenant, which Jeremiah points out in Jeremiah 31:33; where the Lord declares that his covenant would be firm and permanent when engraven on the inward parts. Paul had also the same thing in view in another place, (2 Corinthians 3:6) where he compares the law with the gospel, and calls the former "the letter," which is not only dead but killeth; and the latter he signalizes with the title of "spirit." But extremely gross has been the folly of those who have deduced a double meaning from the "letter," and allegories from the "spirit." [24]

John Murray saw the emphasis in Romans 2:28, 29:

The apostle now proceeds to show that which truly constitutes a person a Jew and that in which circumcision truly consists; he shows who is a **true** Jew and what is **true** circumcision ... The contrast instituted is that between what is outward and what is inward. The outward in the case of the Jew is, ostensibly, natural descent from Abraham and the possession of the privileges which that relation entailed ... the inward as it pertains to the Jew is not explained any further than as that which is "in the secret," that is to say, in that which is hidden from external observation (cf. 2:16; I Corinthians 4:5; 14:25; II Corinthians 4:2; I Peter 3:4), the hidden man of the heart, and is to be understood of that which a man is in the recesses of the heart in distinction from external profession. The inward as it pertains to circumcision is defined as "that of the heart, in the spirit not in the letter." "That of the heart" is perspicuous enough and, in terms of the Old Testament, means the renewal and purification of the heart (Deuteronomy 10:16; 30:6; Jeremiah 4:4; 9:25-26)... The contrast is that between the Holy Spirit and the law as externally administered a contrast between the life-giving power which the Holy Spirit imparts and the impotence which belongs to law as mere law. We shall have to adopt this contrast here. Hence what the apostle says is that the

---

[24]   John Calvin, *The Epistles of Paul the Apostle to the Romans,* (Grand Rapids: Eerdmans Publishing Company, 1973), pp. 56-57.

circumcision which is of the heart is by the Holy Spirit and not by the law.[25]

Philippians 3:1-2

The apostle Paul sets forth a distinction between "the false circumcision" and "the true circumcision" in Philippians 3:1-2:

> *Finally, my brethren, rejoice in the Lord. To write the same things again is no trouble to me, and it is a safeguard for you. Beware of the dogs, beware of the evil workers, beware of the false circumcision, for we are the true circumcision, who worship in the Spirit of God and glory in Christ Jesus and put no confidence in the flesh,*

In verse 2, Paul refers to certain men as dogs, who are evil workers, and who are "the false circumcision." On the other hand, "the true circumcision" in verse 3 is those who worship in the Spirit, glorifying Christ and not the flesh, meaning that they are not trusting in the fact that they are physically circumcised. Who is Paul referring to as the true circumcision, who worships in the Spirit? **It is obviously the church!**

Thus far, Paul has been clearly stating that Gentile converts to Christ in Rome are true Jews over against those Jews actually descending from Abraham. Gentile believers are more Jewish than physical Jews! And the Philippian Gentile believers in Jesus are the true circumcision as opposed to the false circumcision, being those physical Jews who are advocating a works salvation paradigm, insisting that one cannot be saved without submitting to the Law of Moses.

Colossians 2:11-12

One of the most significant New Testament passages bringing together the promises of the Abrahamic Covenant with those in the New Covenant is Colossians 2:11-12 which states:

> *and in Him you were also circumcised with a circumcision made without hands, in the removal of the body of the flesh by the circumcision of Christ; having been buried with Him in baptism,*

---

[25]   John Murray, *Epistle to the Romans,* (Grand Rapids: Eerdmans Publishing Company, 1959), p. 88.

in which you were also raised up with Him through faith in the working of God, who raised Him from the dead.

Colossians 2:11-12 is direct grammatical and theological proof that baptism has replaced circumcision as the sign and seal of the new covenant in the covenant of grace. The Colossian believers are said to be circumcised with a circumcision made without hands in the removal of the body of the flesh by the circumcision of Christ. The phrase, "body of flesh," refers to the bondage to the sin nature. The allusion to a circumcision without hands obviously alludes to a "spiritual circumcision." Who is responsible for this spiritual circumcision? Jesus is!

We already have seen from the book of Romans how this spiritual circumcision is accomplished, that is, who is doing it. According to Romans 2:29, the Holy Spirit is the one performing the inward circumcision of the heart that makes one a true Jew. Hence, Christ circumcises Christians internally by the power of the Holy Spirit. Biblically speaking, Christ dwells in all believers by the Holy Spirit, who is said in Scripture to be "the Spirit of Christ."

Moving on to Colossians 2:12, we see that the phrase "having been buried with Him in baptism" continues the thought of verse 11. Now here is the direct, incontrovertible, exegetical, and explicit proof that baptism has replaced circumcision as the sign and seal of the covenant of grace.

The Greek grammar is most instructive. The phrase "having been buried with Him in baptism" is known as a participle. What are participles? Dana and Mantey's *A Manual Grammar of the Greek New Testament* helps us. It states:

> ... The participle has a pronounced adjective function, following the adjective rule of agreement with the noun, and declined in both numbers and in all the genders and cases... In keeping with its essential character, the participle may be used directly to limit or qualify a noun... The participle may denote an affirmation that distinguishes the noun which it qualifies as in some way specially defined, or marked out in its particular identity. [26]

Participles are known as "verbal adjectives." What does an adjective do? It describes something. So, when I say the "beautiful landscape," "beautiful"

---

[26] Dana and Mantey, *A Manual Grammar of the Greek New Testament,* (Toronto: The Macmillian Company, 1927), pp. 222-224.

is the adjective telling me something about the landscape. It is beautiful as opposed to an ugly landscape. So, a participle tells me something about what it modifies (the association). In other words, it further defines it in some capacity. Therefore, the participial phrase "having been buried with Him in baptism" is describing something further about what it modifies. Grammatically speaking, we must ask then what does the participial phrase modify? It either modifies "circumcision" in verse 11 as the noun, or it modifies the verb of the sentence, which is "you were circumcised" in verse 11.

Either way, it directly links baptism with circumcision. In other words, "having been buried with Him in baptism" describes what Christ is doing by the Holy Spirit in the life of the believer. Spiritual baptism is equated with spiritual circumcision performed by Christ via the Holy Spirit. And, physical baptism is a sign and seal of what is going on internally by the Spirit, just as physical circumcision was a sign and seal of what the Holy Spirit was doing in the hearts of those spiritually circumcised.

Whether it was spiritual circumcision in the Old Testament or spiritual baptism in the New Testament, they both represented **union with God** in the deepest spiritual sense.

Romans 4:11 and Romans 6:4-9

The sign and seal that Paul refers to in Romans 4:11 is physical circumcision! The physical circumcision was applied to Abraham as confirmatory of his faith in Christ. Physical baptism does exactly the same thing; it is confirmatory of faith in Christ. We must remember that the external rites, be they circumcision or baptism, are designed to reflect what God, the Holy Spirit, has done or will do in the hearts of his elect. The external rites are of no ultimate value unless something occurs internally. The external rites are valuable in that they bring people into the "visible community of believers" which carries certain privileges; however, unless the Holy Spirit circumcises or baptizes the hearts of those receiving the external rite, they remain in bondage to sin.

This union with Christ is what Romans 6:4-9 entails. The text reads:

> [4]*Therefore we have been buried with Him through baptism into death, so that as Christ was raised from the dead through the glory of the Father, so we too might walk in newness of life. [5]For if we have become united with Him in the likeness of His death, certainly we shall also be in the likeness of His resurrection,*

⁶knowing this, that our old self was crucified with Him, in order that our body of sin might be done away with, so that we would no longer be slaves to sin; ⁷for he who has died is freed from sin. ⁸Now if we have died with Christ, we believe that we shall also live with Him, ⁹knowing that Christ, having been raised from the dead, is never to die again; death no longer is master over Him.

The fundamental concept of baptism is set forth – that of union with Christ. We died with Him, and we were raised with Him. Our bondage to sin, represented by the "old self" was crucified and buried, meaning that it no longer has dominion over us. When Jesus was raised from the dead, we were raised with Him to newness of life. But these wonderful spiritual truths apply only to God's elect, who God intends to save from their sins. Those in the Old Testament who believed in the promise of the Messiah to come, whose hearts were truly circumcised were saved by faith. Likewise, those in the New Testament who believe in the Messiah who has come, whose hearts have been baptized by the Holy Spirit, are saved by faith.

I Corinthians 10:1-4

There is another New Testament passage that links circumcision with baptism, demonstrating that baptism has replaced circumcision as the sign and seal of God's covenant of grace. It is I Corinthians 10:1-4:

¹For I do not want you to be unaware, brethren, that our fathers were all under the cloud and all passed through the sea; ²and all were baptized into Moses in the cloud and in the sea; ³and all ate the same spiritual food; ⁴and all drank the same spiritual drink, for they were drinking from a spiritual rock which followed them; and the rock was Christ.

We have already quoted this passage earlier, but we now look at it from a different angle. Notice that it says the Old Testament covenant people, national Israel, were said to be **baptized!** I thought that baptism was not implemented until the New Testament. Well, it was, but in a very real spiritual sense, it is said they were baptized. The sign and seal of those Israelites was circumcision, but Paul refers to them as being baptized. Again, who are we going to believe? Dispensationalists who are mere men or the inspired apostle Paul?

The importance of this passage is that which baptism fundamentally means is what is being applied to national Israel. Again, that fundamental meaning being - **union with God.**

Israel was in covenantal union with Jehovah. In I Corinthians 10, the covenantal union is an external union, not necessarily a spiritual union because I Corinthians 10:5-6 says that most of those baptized in the Red Sea were spiritual unbelievers, failing to enter God's rest. Hebrews 3:7-4:1-2 reflects the sad story of most of physical Israel failing to enter Canaan due to their hardness of heart, failing to believe in their heart the promises of God. Hebrews 4:2-3 states:

> *²For indeed we have had good news preached to us, just as they also; but the word they heard did not profit them, because it was not united by faith in those who heard. ³For we who have believed enter that rest, just as He has said, 'As I swore in My wrath, they shall not enter My rest.'*

What is the purpose for all of this exegesis of various passages? **It is to prove that Christians in the New Testament, even the Gentiles, are said to be the true Israel of God.**

Galatians 3:16, 26-29

If it isn't clear enough, Galatians 3:16, 26-29 should be the definitive proof as to who constitutes the seed of Abraham. This passage reads:

> *Now the promises were spoken to Abraham and to his seed. He does not say, "And to seeds," as referring to many, but rather to one, "And to your seed," that is, Christ (v. 16).*

> *For you are all sons of God through faith in Christ Jesus. For all of you who were baptized into Christ have clothed yourselves with Christ. There is neither Jew nor Greek, there is neither slave nor free man, there is neither male nor female; for you are all one in Christ Jesus. And if you belong to Christ, **then you are Abraham's descendants**, heirs according to promise (verses 26-29, Emphasis mine).*

The Gentiles are explicitly said to be the seed of Abraham who have exercised faith in Jesus Christ. This means that the church of the New Testament is the rightful heir to all of the promises of the Abrahamic covenant.

These truths are a devastating blow to dispensational theology. The Abrahamic promises are **not** restricted to Jews in a millennium after the Second Coming; they belong to the church **before the Second Coming.**

Before we move on to another of the covenants of promise in the Old Covenant, there are several other passages we need to address.

Galatians 5:1-6

> *¹It was for freedom that Christ set us free; therefore keep standing firm and do not be subject again to a yoke of slavery. ²Behold I, Paul, say to you that if you receive circumcision, Christ will be of no benefit to you. ³And I testify again to every man who receives circumcision, that he is under obligation to keep the whole Law. ⁴You have been severed from Christ, you who are seeking to be justified by law; you have fallen from grace. ⁵For we through the Spirit, by faith, are waiting for the hope of righteousness. For in Christ Jesus neither circumcision nor uncircumcision means anything, but faith working through love.*

In Galatians chapter 5, Paul is emphasizing the true freedom of those who walk in the Spirit, having trusted Christ as opposed to those who have put confidence in the flesh, having been physically circumcised. Those who think they are saved by outward rites are gravely mistaken and have fallen from grace - fallen from grace in that salvation is now by works. Those who want to be saved by works are bound to keep all the law or be cursed. However, true Christians are those who wait for their hope of righteousness by faith in Christ, through the Spirit.

The bottom line is in verse 6: Faith in Christ and the love that stems from that faith as fruit. Circumcision or uncircumcision means nothing apart from Christ. Hearing the gospel does not save anyone. Men must believe what was preached. They must have faith. This is why Jesus would say, "He who has ears to hear, let him hear."

Consider this powerful statement of Jesus in John 8:47:

He who is of God hears the words of God; for this reason you do not hear them, because you are not of God."

The bottom line is this: if one is **of** the covenant, circumcised (Old Testament) or baptized (New Testament), then one must hear the good news and appropriately respond in faith to what he has heard.

There has never been in any era of human history where men have been saved by the works of the law. Dispensationalists who think that those in the Old Testament and those in the coming millennium are going to be saved by the works of the law **are not preaching the true gospel.**

Matthew 21:33-46

Let us consider Matthew 21:33-46:

> [33]*Listen to another parable. "There was a landowner who planted a vineyard and put a wall around it and dug a wine press in it, and built a tower, and rented it out to vine-growers and went on a journey.* [34]*When the harvest time approached, he sent his slaves to the vine-growers to receive his produce.* [35]*The vine-growers took his slaves and beat one, and killed another, and stoned a third.* [36]*Again he sent another group of slaves larger than the first; and they did the same thing to them.* [37]*But afterward he sent his son to them, saying, 'They will respect my son.'* [38]*But when the vine-growers saw the son, they said among themselves, 'This is the heir; come, let us kill him and seize his inheritance.'* [39]*They took him, and threw him out of the vineyard and killed him.* [40]*Therefore when the owner of the vineyard comes, what will he do to those vine-growers?"* [41]*They said to Him, "He will bring those wretches to a wretched end, and will rent out the vineyard to other vine-growers who will pay him the proceeds at the proper seasons."* [42]*Jesus said to them, "Did you never read in the Scriptures, the stone which the builders rejected, this became the chief corner stone; this came about from the Lord, and it is marvelous in our eyes?* [43]*Therefore I say to you, the kingdom of God will be taken away from you and given to a people, producing the fruit of it.* [44]*And he who falls on this stone will be broken to pieces; but on whomever it falls, it will scatter him like dust."* [45]*When the chief priests and the Pharisees heard His parables, they understood that He was speaking about them.* [46]*When they sought to seize Him, they feared the people, because they considered Him to be a prophet.*

In this parable, Jesus says that the kingdom of God will be taken away from the original vine growers, which were the unbelieving Jews. This is one parable where men were granted an ability to understand. The chief priests and Pharisees understood that Jesus was speaking it against them. Dispensationalists do acknowledge that the kingdom of God was rejected by unfaithful Jews; however, they mistakenly think that the kingdom of God is a millennium after Jesus' Second Coming where God will show mercy to His ancient people and make all the kingdom promises of the Old Testament come to pass in this period, a period that glorifies Judaism.

Romans 9:27-33

Nothing could be further from the truth. The rejection of the kingdom by unfaithful Jews and given to a people deserving of it applies to not only believing Jews but to **believing Gentiles!** This truth is brought out in Romans 9:27-33:

> [27]*And Isaiah cries out concerning Israel, 'Though the number of the sons of Israel be as the sand of the sea, it is the remnant that will be saved;* [28]*for the Lord will execute His word upon the earth, thoroughly and quickly,'* [29]*and just as Isaiah foretold, 'Except the Lord of Sabaoth had left to us a posterity, we would have become as Sodom, and would have resembled Gomorrah.'* [30]*What shall we say then? That Gentiles, who did not pursue righteousness, attained righteousness, even the righteousness which is by faith,* [31]*but Israel, pursuing a law of righteousness, did not arrive at that law.* [32]*Why? Because they did not pursue it by faith, but as though it were by works. They stumbled over the stumbling stone,* [33]*just as it is written, 'Behold, I lay in Zion a stone of stumbling; and a rock of offense, and He who believes in Him will not be disappointed.'*

Paul is saying that Israel, seeking to pursue righteousness by law keeping did not make it, but the Gentiles seeking righteousness by faith found it. So much for the notion purported by dispensationalists that salvation in the Old Testament was by the works of the law. Inspired Scripture clearly affirms that any kind of pursuing righteousness by the works of the law is a stumbling over the chief cornerstone, which is Christ. No one has ever or ever will be saved by keeping the law!

Ephesians 2:11-22

One of the most important texts in all of Scripture is Ephesians 2:11-22:

> [11]*Therefore remember that formerly you, the Gentiles in the flesh, who are called "Uncircumcision" by the so-called "Circumcision," which is performed in the flesh by human hands--* [12]*remember that you were at that time separate from Christ, excluded from the commonwealth of Israel, and strangers to the covenants of promise, having no hope and without God in*

the world. [13]But now in Christ Jesus you who formerly were far off have been brought near by the blood of Christ. [14]For He Himself is our peace, who made both groups into one and broke down the barrier of the dividing wall, [15]by abolishing in His flesh the enmity, which is the Law of commandments contained in ordinances, so that in Himself He might make the two into one new man, thus establishing peace, [16]and might reconcile them both in one body to God through the cross, by it having put to death the enmity. [17]And He came and preached peace to you who were far away, and peace to those who were near. [18]For through Him we both have our access in one Spirit to the Father. [19]So then you are no longer strangers and aliens, but you are fellow citizens with the saints, and are of God's household, [20]having been built on the foundation of the apostles and prophets, Christ Jesus Himself being the corner stone, [21]in whom the whole building, being fitted together, is growing into a holy temple in the Lord, [22]in whom you also are being built together into a dwelling of God in the Spirit.

This thrilling passage doesn't teach that there are two peoples of God in history that are forever distinct. Dispensationalism denies a fundamental tenet of the Word of God – a tenant that sets forth that believing Jews and Gentiles are united into ONE body through mutual faith in Jesus Christ. Both groups are now of the **same household.** Jesus is the chief cornerstone of this new house, called the **church.** They who were formerly excluded from the commonwealth of Israel and strangers to the covenants of promise are now brought near by the blood of Jesus. In Christ there is only one people of God, comprised of believing Jews and Gentiles. The dividing wall between Jew and Gentile has been broken down by Christ. To maintain that there are two separate peoples of God with two distinct purposes in history is to blatantly attack the glorious gospel of Christ that has made the two, one.

Hebrews 2:9-17

Let's continue in our exegetical documentation that the seed of Abraham is equated with the church of the Lord Jesus Christ. Hebrews 2:9-17:

[9]But we do see Him who was made for a little while lower than the angels, namely, Jesus, because of the suffering of death crowned with glory and honor, so that by the grace of God He might taste death for everyone. [10]For it was fitting for Him, for whom are all things, and through whom are all things, in

*bringing **many sons** to glory, to perfect the author of their salvation through sufferings. [11]For both He who sanctifies and those who are sanctified are all **from one Father**; for which reason He is not ashamed to call them **brethren,** [12]saying, 'I will proclaim Your name to My brethren, in the midst of **the congregation** I will sing Your praise. I will put My trust in Him.' [13]And again, 'Behold, I and the children whom God has given Me.' [14]Therefore, since the children share in flesh and blood, He Himself likewise also partook of the same, that through death He might render powerless him who had the power of death, that is, the devil, [15]and might free those who through fear of death were subject to slavery all their lives. [16]For assuredly He does not give help to angels, but He gives help to the **descendant of Abraham**. [17]Therefore, He had to be made like His brethren in all things, so that He might become a merciful and faithful high priest in things pertaining to God, to make propitiation for the sins of **the people**.* (Emphasis mine)

The importance of the passage is multi-faceted. For my purpose presently, I want to emphasize several of the phrases being used. We have "many sons," "from one Father," "brethren," "the congregation," "the children," "descendant of Abraham," and "the people." One of the great truths set forth is that the church for whom Jesus died is identified with the elect of the Old Testament. Jesus died for true Israel, that is a given. He died for the "seed of Abraham" whether they are in the old or new covenant. Verse 9 states that Jesus tasted death for all. Words mean what they mean in any given context, and the fact that it says that Jesus tasted death to "all" should not be interpreted to mean He died for everyone in the whole wide world regardless of who they are. This is not biblical teaching; there are none in hell for whom Jesus died. Jesus' atoning death is effectual, that is, not one drop of His blood was shed in vain. Jesus' death actually is the ransom that does secure the release of those in bondage to sin. There is no maybe or possibility about it. Jesus' death accomplishes forgiveness of sins for which He died.

Our context in Hebrews 2 abundantly sets forth the meaning of "all" for us in the verses following verse 9. The "everyone" of verse 9 is defined in verse 10 as "bringing many sons to glory." These many sons are brought to glory; there is no uncertainty about it. Obviously, anyone in hell has not been brought to glory; hence, Jesus did not die for the reprobate of mankind. Verse 11 indicates that Jesus is not ashamed to call as "brethren" all who are sanctified and who are from one Father. Verse 12 quotes Psalm 22:22. The writer to Hebrews did not quote Psalm 22:23 but he could have. Here is what Psalm 22:23 states, *"You who fear the Lord, praise Him; All you descendants of Jacob, glorify Him, and stand in awe of Him all you descendants of Israel."* The "brethren" of Psalm 22:22 are the same as those in the "assembly." And they are the same as the "descendants of Israel" in verse 23. The Septuagint (LXX) is the Greek translation of the Old Testament. The term "assembly" or "congregation," depending on one's translation, is the Greek word, *"ekklesia."* Need I inform those familiar with the New Testament that this is the Greek word for "church?" In some English translations there is often a note in the reference column saying "congregation" is "church."

Hebrews 2:11 carries over these "all" and "many sons" as those who are "sanctified." These "sanctified" ones are called "brethren." This passage clearly states **that the church was in the OT in its visible and invisible aspect. The brethren who are sanctified are in the MIDST of the congregation or church. In other words, the circumcised of heart who are physically circumcised.** Keep in mind that these sanctified children in the midst of the church are sanctified by the death of Christ.

In Hebrews 2:14, we see that the emphasis is upon Jesus Christ sharing the same "flesh and blood" in order to carry out His atoning death on behalf of "the children." Jesus' death rendered powerless the devil who had the power of death. More will be said on this later, but, for the time being, Jesus' death does deliver "the children" from the fear of death. This is true regardless of whether the children are in the Old or New Testaments.

Hebrews 2:16 explicitly affirms that Jesus gives help to **"the descendants of Abraham."** This explicitly states that Jesus died for "the seed of Abraham." Obviously, Jesus died for those in the church, and we have seen that the church is in both the Old and New Testaments. In other words, the true seed of Abraham is any person who is redeemed by Christ. The death of Jesus obviously reaches back into the Old Testament. We already have proven that the saints of the Old Testament really and truly believed in Jesus Christ through promise form, in a Messiah yet to come. They had full remission of sins.

Hebrews 2:17 emphasizes the necessity of the Son of God to be incarnated as a real human being – to be "made like His brethren" in all things so that He might become a merciful and faithful high priest in order to make propitiation for the sins "of the people." It is quite apparent that "the people" are the "seed of Abraham" regardless of which covenant they are in. "Propitiation" is the biblical term denoting "the satisfaction of divine justice by means of a bloody sacrifice." Romans 3:24-25 portrays how the shed blood of Jesus brings about propitiation to those who have faith in Jesus.

The Hebrew word for "people" is the word "עַם" pronounced "am." The Septuagint would be "*laos*." This particular word is used numerous times in the Old Testament to refer to "national Israel." It refers to "the Israel of God." The unmistakable testimony of Scripture is that the church was indeed in the Old Testament; it was "the congregation." Jesus died for the elect of "the people."

Acts 7:37-38

Who else said that the "church" was in the Old Testament? Stephen did. In Acts 7:37-38 we read:

> *[37]This is the Moses who said to the sons of Israel, 'God will raise up for you a prophet like me from Your brethren.' [38]This is the one who was in the congregation in the wilderness together with the angel who was speaking to him on Mount Sinai, and who was with our fathers; and he received living oracles to pass on to you.*

The Greek word for "congregation" as we saw earlier is the word, "*ekklesia*" or "church."

Galatians 4:21-26

Galatians 4:21-26 is an allegory put forth by inspired Paul. What is a biblical allegory? Milton S. Terry, in his book, *Biblical Hermeneutics: A Treatise on the Interpretation of the Old and New Testaments* makes these comments about biblical allegory:

> An allegory is usually defined as an extended metaphor... An allegory contains its interpretation within itself, and the thing signified is identified with the image... The allegory is a figurative use and application of some supposable fact or history... It is a discourse in which the main subject is represented by some other subject to which it has a resemblance.[27]

---

[27]   Milton S. Terry, *Biblical Hermeneutics: A Treatise on the Interpretation of the Old and New Testaments*, (Grand Rapids: Zondervan Publishing, 1974), p. 302.

Paul is writing to the Galatians of whom many were Gentiles of course. The Book of Galatians is fundamentally a polemic against the Judaizers who were insisting that one had to submit to the ceremonial laws of Moses, namely circumcision, in order to be saved. The Judaizers essentially taught salvation by keeping the law.

Paul actually uses the term "allegory" as he sets forth who really are the people of God, who really is Israel, and who are the inheritors of the promises of the Father. Paul sets forth the spiritual meaning by means of a familiar story – that of two women who dwelt in Abraham's tent, namely Hagar (his personal slave) and Sarah (his wife). Hagar bore Ishmael while Sarah bore Isaac. Sarah and her son are described as representing all those free people who live by faith. Hagar and her son represent those spiritually enslaved, who live by the law.

Paul's ultimate concern is to discredit the heretical teaching of the Judaizers who were teaching that one must keep the Law of Moses in order to be saved in addition to faith in Christ. The Judaizers prided themselves as being "the seed of Abraham." After all, they were Jews, descending physically from Abraham. The Judaizers looked in disdain upon the Gentiles who thought that only faith in Jesus was sufficient for salvation. The Judaizers' boast was in their physical descent from Abraham. But Paul wants to remind them that Abraham had two sons. Those who want to boast in their physical genealogy are no better off than the Ishmaelites, descending from Hagar.

Paul's emphasis is that there is a huge difference between the son of Hagar, the slave woman, and the son of Sarah, the free woman. The difference is not in terms of physical descent but one of spiritual reality. The contrast that Paul is making in the allegory is between those who live by law and those who live by faith. The issue is: Who is the rightful heir? Is it Ishmael, or is it Isaac? In Galatians 4:23, Paul says that the son of the slave woman was flesh born (Ishmael), while the the son of the free woman (Isaac) was born through promise.

Paul mentions that there are two covenants. One precedes from Mt. Sinai which is said to be slaves, and who is said to be represented by Hagar, the bond woman. The other covenant is said to be the "heavenly Jerusalem." Isaac, born to the free woman, Sarah, is said to be "the child of promise."

Paul is making it very clear that those who labor slavishly to attain righteousness through their own efforts are doomed to failure. On the other hand, those who live by faith do attain the promises of Abraham. Isaac, being the child of promise, is the one born of the Spirit. This imagery is used for the Holy Spirit who is the One who brings about the promise. Unless the Spirit first works, there will be no faith.

Paul ends in verse 31 with the declaration that we are not the children of the bondwoman but of the free woman. It is of incredible import that those of the free woman are said to be the true heirs of the promise, who are said to be the "**heavenly Jerusalem**." This is amazing that Gentiles who believe in Jesus are said to be the heavenly Jerusalem. This is a very "Jewish" terminology to be applied to Gentiles, but it is thoroughly biblical because as was revealed in Galatians 3:29 any person who believes in Jesus is the seed of Abraham. **The church of the New Testament is the heavenly Jerusalem**, plain and simple, which includes Jews who believe in Jesus along with Gentiles who also believe.

Galatians 6:15-16

> *[15]For neither is circumcision anything, nor uncircumcision, but a new creation. [16]And those who will walk by this rule, peace and mercy be upon them, and upon the Israel of God.*

This text does require some careful exegesis. The dispensationalist would simply say that it is apparent that two groups are being emphasized – those who walk as new creatures and those who are called "the Israel of God," meaning the Jews separately, who receive peace and mercy. They would interpret the Greek conjunction (*kai*) as being something additional in a sequence, which would make the meaning of "the Israel of God" as a separate group. This interpretation is fraught with many problems, and the only reason one would attempt to interpret it this way is that it would fit into one's theological system.

Here are the exegetical reasons why we must reject the dispensationalist contention. First, words or phrases mean what they mean in their context. The context entails the immediate verse, surrounding verses in the chapter, the entire New Testament book, and the whole Bible. We can never interpret any passage so as to contradict other portions of Scripture. The immediate context of the verse itself is not presenting separate groups. In the Scripture, the Jews were known as the "circumcised" while the Gentiles were known as the "uncircumcised." Why would Paul, in verse 15, say that circumcision and uncircumcision mean nothing but being a new creature, if he wanted to give separate blessings to separate groups? II Corinthians 5:17 says that any man who is in Christ is a new creature. The new man in Christ has God's blessings on him. We have understood from

Romans 9:6-8 that Paul has referred to those who are the true children of God as the children of promise, who are said to be Israel, not after the flesh. True Israel constitutes all those who have faith in Jesus Christ, be they circumcised or uncircumcised. Galatians 3:15-16 is simply echoing what Romans 9 has said. Already in Paul's allegory as seen in Galatians 4:28, the children of promise are seen as those who exercise faith as opposed to those seeking justification by the works of the law.

To interpret this passage as a blessing upon two distinct groups that share differing promises is flatly wrong.

The fact is: the preposition "*kai*" has three generally accepted classifications and meanings. "*Kai*" can be seen as transitional or continuative, meaning "and," as adjunctive, meaning "also," and as ascensive, meaning "even."[28] Hence, to restrict the interpretation of "*kai*" in this passage to the first use, making it to mean a completely separate group is not grammatically responsible. When we consider the conjunction in the context of the verse itself, the book of Galatians, and the rest of Scripture, the interpretation that is exegetically correct is the one that sees the new man in Christ as the "Israel of God." The "Israel of God" belong to both circumcised and uncircumcised who have had faith in Jesus alone for their justification.

Hebrews 12:18-24

> [18]*For you have not come to a mountain that can be touched and to a blazing fire, and to darkness and gloom and whirlwind,* [19]*and to the blast of a trumpet and the sound of words which sound was such that those who heard begged that no further word be spoken to them.* [20]*For they could not bear the command, 'if even a beast touches the mountain, it will be stoned.'* [21]*And so terrible was the sight, that Moses said, 'I am full of fear and trembling.'* [22]*But you have come to Mount Zion and to the city of the living God, the heavenly Jerusalem, and to myriads of angels,* [23]*to the general assembly and church of the firstborn who are enrolled in heaven, and to God, the Judge of all, and to the spirits of the righteous made perfect,* [24]*and to Jesus, the mediator of a new covenant, and to the sprinkled blood, which speaks better than the blood of Abel.*

This passage pictures Old Testament and New Testament saints as being included in the "Heavenly Jerusalem." We have already seen in several

---

[28] Dana and Mantey, p. 250.

other passages that the "heavenly Jerusalem" pictures all who have faith in Jesus; that is the church! This passage vividly portrays the "church" as having Old Testament designations.

In this passage, the writer stresses the difference between the old and new covenant. New Testament believers are different from Old Testament believers in that they have come to different mountains. Old Testament believers (v.18) came to Mt. Sinai where they received the Ten Commandments. The Israelites saw the spectacle of fire, smoke, and storm. They saw God in veiled form. God spoke to them in His Decalogue. But as the Scripture says elsewhere, this law was written on tablets of stone, and not upon their hearts with power. Israel was filled with awe and fear of the majestic God.

In v.22, the writer says BUT you have come to a different mountain than Old Testament believers. You have come to Mt. Zion and to the city of the living God, the heavenly Jerusalem. So, the contrast is between Mt. Sinai and Mt. Zion.

Mt. Zion is God's city, the heavenly Jerusalem. **Note that Mt. Zion is said to be God's city and declared to be the heavenly Jerusalem.** It should be obvious that Mt. Zion is not an earthly city because it says explicitly that it is a **heavenly Jerusalem.** The heavenly Jerusalem then is the permanent place where Jesus, the mediator of a new covenant dwells.

Zion is where God dwells with all His saints.

The writer of Hebrews says that "you" in contrast to Old Testament saints have come to eight things and all eight things:

1) to Mt. Zion
2) to the city of the living God, the heavenly Jerusalem
3) to myriads of angels
4) to the general assembly and church, the first born enrolled in heaven
5) to God, the Judge of all
6) to the spirits of righteous men made perfect
7) to Jesus, the mediator of a new covenant
8) to sprinkled blood, which is better than the blood of Abel

The "you" refers to New Testament believers in Hebrews 12:1-2 who are running the race, fixing their eyes on Jesus, who interestingly is said to be the author, and **perfecter** of faith. Note that in 11:40 the saints of the Old Testament are not made perfect without us.

The perfecter of our faith has sat down at the right hand of the throne of God. This is but another place where the Scripture identifies God's throne with David's throne, but that fact will be looked at in greater detail in an upcoming chapter in this book.

As set forth in Hebrews 9:24-25, Jesus enters a holy place different than the Aaronic priests. This holy place is not a mere copy of the true one like the tabernacle of the Old Testament, but it is the **true** one, which is not on earth, but in heaven itself.

Jesus enters into the presence of God, which is what the throne of God is. In our text in Hebrews 12:22ff, the New Testament saints are said to come Mt. Zion and to the city of the living God, the heavenly Jerusalem. Key is the fact that New Testament saints are linked in with Old Testament terminology. They have come to myriads of angels like Daniel 7 refers to the throne of God. The angels constitute a joyful assembly.

The New Testament saints have come to the general assembly, the church *"ekklesia"* of the first born enrolled in heaven. This is an allusion to the Book of Life where all the elect are written. The New Testament saints have come to God as the judge of all men where we will have to give an account.

We have come to spirits of righteous men made perfect. This alludes to Hebrews 11:39-40. This teaches us that in heaven, all the saints are perfect. When we temporarily shed our bodies, our souls are made perfect. We have come to Jesus, the mediator of a new covenant and to sprinkled blood. In the first covenant, the high priest sprinkled blood on the altar signifying the forgiveness of sins. In the New Covenant, Jesus' blood is the blood that atones for sin once and for all. The blood of Jesus is better than the blood of Abel. Abel's blood demanded vengeance. Christ's blood removed the curse placed upon fallen man and affected reconciliation and peace between God and man.

Similar thoughts to this passage in Hebrews are also seen in the book of Revelation as we shall see.

Revelation 21:2-3, 9-14

> [2]*And I saw the holy city, new Jerusalem, coming down out of heaven from God, made ready as a bride adorned for her husband.* [3]*And I heard a loud voice from the throne, saying, 'Behold, the tabernacle of God is among men, and He will dwell*

among them, and they shall be His people, and God Himself will be among them.'

[9]Then one of the seven angels who had the seven bowls full of the seven last plagues came and spoke with me, saying, 'Come here, I will show you the bride, the wife of the Lamb.' [10]And he carried me away in the Spirit to a great and high mountain, and showed me the holy city, Jerusalem, coming down out of heaven from God, [11]having the glory of God. Her brilliance was like a very costly stone, as a stone of crystal-clear jasper.[12] It had a great and high wall, with twelve gates, and at the gates twelve angels; and names were written on them, which are the names of the twelve tribes of the sons of Israel. [13]There were three gates on the east and three gates on the north and three gates on the south and three gates on the west. [14]And the wall of the city had twelve foundation stones, and on them were the twelve names of the twelve apostles of the Lamb.

The holy city, Jerusalem, is said to be a bride, made ready for her husband. This imagery of a bride made ready for her husband is found in Ephesians 5:25-27.

In Revelation 21:3, a voice cries out that "the tabernacle of God" shall dwell among them, and God Himself shall be among them. This reminds us of what John said in his gospel account in John 1:1-3, 14 where it says that the eternal "logos" became flesh and dwelt among us, and we beheld His glory as the only begotten of the Father, full of grace and truth. This is said to be none other than the Lord Jesus Christ (John 1:17).

In Revelation 21:9-10, we see explicit reference in verse 9 that one of the angels spoke to John, saying, "Come here, I shall show you the bride, the wife of the Lamb." Then in verse 10, the angel carries John away to a mountain where he sees this bride. The bride is a holy city called Jerusalem. The holy city, Jerusalem, is said to have a high wall with twelve gates. The names written on the twelve gates are said to be the twelve tribes of the sons of Israel. And the wall of the city had twelve foundations stones, which were the twelve apostles of the Lamb.

The holy city is said to be Jerusalem, and it is comprised of believers from the Old Testament and New Testament. Those citizens in the Old Testament are represented by the twelve tribes of Israel. Those citizens in the New Testament are represented by the apostles of the Lamb. The bride of the Lamb is said to be constituted as the holy city, Jerusalem. The tribes of Israel and the apostles are integral parts of this one city. **What is pictured is the complete church of Christ as pictured in the Old and New Testaments.**

It is noteworthy that the Old Testament name "Jerusalem" is equated with the New Testament bride of Christ. There is only ONE city, not two. Old Testament saints are in the same city as New Testament saints. Together they constitute the one church of Christ.

Hence, the Scripture, when carefully examined, does not teach that there are two distinct peoples with differing purposes. The idea that the kingdom is being reserved for "the seed of Abraham" after Christ's Second Coming and that the "church age" is a time for the Gentiles to prosper before the Second Coming is simply a theological fabrication.

Concluding Thoughts on the Abrahamic Covenant

There is a very good reason why I have labored extensively on the Abrahamic Covenant. It greatly develops the promise for the victory of God's people in history. It carries forward the great promise. The gospel was preached to Abraham; Abraham saw Jesus' day and rejoiced. He saw it with the eyes of faith in God's promise to him to make him a blessing to all the nations of the earth. The true seed of Abraham constitutes all those united to Christ by faith, be they Jew or Gentile and be they in the Old or New Testaments.

The church has been in existence since the dawn of man's creation. If the church is truly the seed of Abraham, possessing all the spiritual promises of Abraham, then this means that the church of the New Testament is no parenthesis in human history. It was always in the plan of God; it was always pictured as being the true Israel of God, inheritor of all of Abraham's promises. The kingdom of God is **not** some period of time after Christ's Second Coming. The Kingdom of God, the millennial age, is **before the Second Coming. Jesus is presently reigning from David's throne which is in heaven at the right hand of God.** We shall now exegetically prove these truths in the next two chapters.

I will reserve comments on the Davidic Covenant until an upcoming chapter where it will be shown that Jesus is presently sitting on David's throne, subduing all His enemies right now!

Chapter 2

The Nature of the Kingdom of God

In seeking to establish the main thesis of this book, the victory of the gospel through preaching, I must simultaneously deal with incorrect views of the kingdom of God because our understanding of the kingdom is essential to understanding how God works out His sovereign decree in human history.

One of the crucial issues in Eschatology revolves around the "kingdom of God" or "the millennium" What was exactly prophesied? When will it come? How long is it? What is its nature?

Other questions are pertinent as well: Does the Christian church fulfill, or does it interrupt the fulfillment of Old Testament prophecies? Was the church age unknown to the prophets, or did they predict it?

Regarding these issues, Reformed Theology and dispensationalism stand in stark contrast. For the dispensationalist, there are several things that mark their understanding of the kingdom of God: 1) The Messiah's kingdom will be future, earthly, and political, 2) It necessitates the physical presence of Christ on earth, ruling from a physical Jerusalem and sitting on a physical throne of David, in a rebuilt temple, and 3) This kingdom will be fundamentally Jewish in its scope

Expressions of Christian Zionism

There are varying degrees of Christian Zionism, some of which are very radical. Fundamentally, Christian Zionism is the belief that physical Jews today have a biblical right to possess the land of Palestine because of supposed prophetic promises. Much stress is put on the promises to Abraham. The dispensationalist is regimented in the belief that this promise must always pertain to a geographical territory prior to Christ's return. The dispensationalist sees the land promise of the Abrahamic covenant as Jewish, unconditional, and unfulfilled, which can only be truly fulfilled in a future millennium on earth.

Dispensationalist, Lewis Sperry Chafer, said:

> ... there is an eschatology of Judaism and an eschatology of
> Christianity and each, though wholly different in details, reaches
> on into eternity. One of the great burdens of predictive prophecy is
> the anticipation of the glories of Israel in a transformed earth
> under the reign of David's Son, the Lord Jesus Christ, the Son of
> God.[1]

> The dispensationalist believes that through the ages God is
> pursuing two distinct purposes: one related to the earth with
> earthly people and earthly objectives involved, which is Judaism;
> while the other is related to heaven with heavenly people and
> heavenly objectives involved, which is Christianity.[2]

J. Dwight Pentecost wrote:

> The promises in the Abrahamic covenant concerning the land and
> the seed are fulfilled in the millennial age... [3]

Dispensationalists Wayne House and Tommy Ice make this assertion in
their book *Dominion Theology: Blessing or Curse:*

> That Christ will soon rapture his Bride, the church, and that we
> will return with him in victory to rule and exercise dominion with
> him for a thousand years upon the earth.[4]

> This is the point: once Israel is restored to the place of blessing
> and the tabernacle of David is rebuilt, then will follow the third
> phase in the plan of God. That period will be the time of the
> millennium, when the nations will indeed be converted and ruled
> over by Christ.[5]

Consistent with dispensational theology, House and Ice state that a proper
distinction between Israel and the church demands "a consistent distinction
between the Bible's use of Israel and the church." It is evident that
dispensationalists don't speak of victory until after Christ's Second

---

[1]   Chafer, 4:27, p. 310.
[2]   Chafer, 4:401, p. 312.
[3]   J. Dwight Pentecost, *Things to Come*, p. 476 as quoted in Crenshaw and Gunn, p. 313.
[4]   Wayne House and Tommy Ice, *Dominion Theology: Blessing or Curse: An Analysis of Christian
       Reconstruction*, (Portland, Oregon: Multnomah Press, 1988), p. 10.
[5]   House, p. 169.

Coming in a millennium on earth. Only then do dispensationalists speak of a conversion of the world, and also note that dispensationalists only speak of the reign of Christ as a reality after His Second Coming, not before. Though this point will be developed later, the idea that Jesus has ascended into heaven and presently sits at God's right hand but is supposedly not reigning is an oddity at best. Obviously, the Great Commission given to the church before His ascension will be a great failure according to dispensational thought.

Dispensationalists assert that "Christ offered to Israel a literal, earthly kingdom, but that the Jews rejected it, thus causing its postponement."[6] The dispensationalist insists that the millennium or the kingdom prophesied in the Old Testament is strictly a Jewish time of glory. The church age, the time between the first advent of Christ and the rapture, is a parenthesis in human history, meaning that the prophets did not really prophesy the church age.

Clarence Larken, a dispensationalist of the early 20th Century wrote in his book, *The Second Coming of Christ*, the following about the prophets not seeing the church age in their prophecies. In one of his famous charts (depicted after quote) he demonstrates this. Larken writes:

> On Chart 2 we see how it was that the Old Testament Prophets failed to distinguish between the "First" and "Second" Comings. From the prophet's view- point he saw the birth of Jesus, the Crucifixion, the Outpouring of the Holy Spirit, the Antichrist, the Sun of Righteousness, the Millennial Kingdom, Ezekiel's Temple and the New Heavens and the New Earth, as "Mountain Peaks" of one great mountain, but we standing off to the side see these peaks as belonging to two different mountains with the "Valley of the church" in between. And more we see that there are two more valleys, one, the "Millennial Valley," separates the "Second Coming" from the "Renovation of the Earth by Fire" (II Peter 3:7-13), and the other is the Valley of the "Perfect Age."

---

[6]   J. Dwight Pentecost, *Things To Come: A Case Study in Biblical Eschatology,* (Grand Rapids: Zondervan, 1958), p. 456.

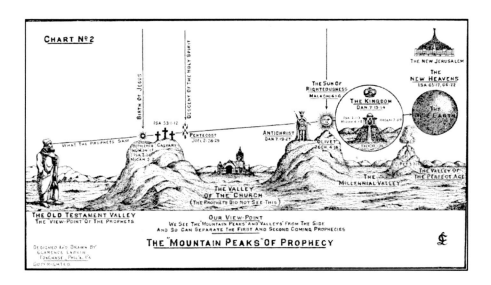

Larken is a very good example of imposing a theological system upon the
Scripture rather than allowing the Scripture to dictate for him his
theological system. Larken's view is a very dishonoring view of the
prophets but ultimately an insult to God. Who inspired the prophets? How
can an inspired prophet fail to distinguish something, if prophecy is the
revelation of biblical truth to man? How can this prophet accurately see
major events in the future and then have "a weak moment" and fail to see
something as momentous as the Church? Larken's diagram implies that the
prophet can't see over the mountain tops. The prophet somehow misses the
church because it is in a valley. But, somehow, the prophet manages to see
the other valley, the "Millennial Valley." See how arbitrary such thinking
is! Oh, the prophet can see one valley but is unable to see another valley.

The problem is not with the inspired prophets of God but with men who
arbitrarily impose their own interpretations upon the Bible in such a way
as to deny huge portions of God's Word. No, the prophets clearly saw the
Church and prophesied concerning it. Again, the New Testament is the
best interpreter of the Old Testament unless of course one wants to say that
an inspired New Testament writer is mistaken, having vision problems too.

If the previous quotes are not radical enough, Daniel Fuller gave a
dissertation at Northern Baptist Theological Seminary in 1957. He said:

> If the dispensational interpretation of the millennial situation is
> correct, then the party of the circumcision who wanted Gentiles

admitted into the church as they had been admitted into the synagogue (i.e. circumcised proselytes) could have made better use of this passage (Acts 15) than did James. They could have argued that the prophesied inferior status of spiritually blessed millennial Gentiles is evidence for a similarly inferior status for church age Gentiles.

I find this comment incredible and heretical. For one, those he is referring to are the Judaizers who Paul argued with vehemently which led to the great Jerusalem Council in Acts 15. The Judaizers were preaching another gospel according to Paul in Galatians. How can the Judaizers make better use of the passage than inspired James? Incredible!

There is a view of Christian Zionism that pushes not only churches but our government to be sure to treat modern day Israel as a special status group. In his book, the *Fundamentalist Phenomenon*, published in 1981, Jerry Falwell spelled out what he called the evangelical attitude toward Israel. He said: "To stand against Israel is to stand against God. We believe that history and scripture prove that God deals with nations in relation to how they deal with Israel."[7] He is referring to the present Israeli state formed by the United Nations in 1948.

One of the greatest dangers of this form of Christian Zionism is that it emphasizes physical Jewish lineage in a very unbiblical way. One of the most ardent Christian Zionists today is Pastor John Hagee of Cornerstone Church in San Antonio, Texas. He has considerable clout in various circles, and here are his quotes as recorded in the *Houston Chronicle* in April 1988:

'I'm not trying to convert the Jewish people to the Christian faith,' he said.

'In fact, trying to convert Jews is a "waste of time,"' he said. 'The Jewish person who has his roots in Judaism is not going to convert to Christianity. There is no form of Christian evangelism that has failed so miserably as evangelizing the Jewish people. They (already) have a faith structure.'

---

[7]   Jerry Falwell, *Fundamentalist Phenomenon*, (Garden City, N.Y.: Doubleday, 1981) as quoted in http://www.rense.com/general41/aagi.htm.

'Everyone else, whether Buddhist or Baha'i, needs to believe in Jesus, he says. But not Jews. Jews already have a covenant with God that has never been replaced by Christianity,' he says.

'The Jewish people have a relationship to God through the law of God as given through Moses,' Hagee said. 'I believe that every Gentile person can only come to God through the cross of Christ. I believe that every Jewish person who lives in the light of the Torah, which is the word of God, has a relationship with God and will come to redemption.'

'The law of Moses is sufficient enough to bring a person into the knowledge of God until God gives him a greater revelation. And God has not,' said Hagee, giving his interpretation of Romans 11:25. 'Paul abandoned the idea (of Jews knowing Christ). In the book of Romans, he said, `I am now going to go to the Gentiles from this time forward.' Judaism doesn't need Christianity to explain its existence. But Christianity has to have Judaism to explain its existence.'[8]

The above quote by a supposed evangelical pastor is unconscionable. I would consider this comment heretical, not just erroneous. Notice what Hagee contends. He has clearly put forth two ways of salvation, one for the Gentile and another for the Jew. He openly advocates "works righteousness" for the Jew. There is no need to try to convert a Jew? Somehow Buddhists and Muslims need Jesus but not Jews?

In his article about John Hagee proclaiming another gospel, G. Richard Fisher writes:

Hagee's view, with a slight twist, was promoted during the 1980s by Wim Malgo, editor of the magazine *The Midnight Call*. In a letter to *The Jerusalem Post*, Malgo assured the newspaper's readers:

"...we strongly reject any missionary work in Israel itself, since it is our belief that Israel is God's chosen people, and therefore in the hands of God. Our rejection of missionary work in Israel stems

---

[8]   Comment made by Pastor John Hagee as found in Julia Dunn, "San Antonio Fundamentalist Battles Anti-Semitism," Sat. 4/30/1988 Houston Chronicle, Section religion found at http://www.chron.com/CDA/archives/archive.mpl?id=1988_540301

also from our belief that Israel is a nation which has had to endure so much, and should be shown love and understanding."[40]

It seems that Malgo's brand of the "Two Covenant" idea saw Jews in Israel as automatically saved.

This was confirmed in a Sept. 20, 1983, letter to this writer by *Midnight Call* spokesman Arno Froese, which suggested that missionary activity to Jews ended with Paul and that the Great Commission was only for Gentiles. Froese then emphatically added: "To summarize, we, as Gentile Christians, have no Biblical basis to go to Israel and preach the Gospel there."[9]

The theological problems are immense for dispensational premillennialism. Just what does the Bible really say about the kingdom of God (the millennium)? Let's let Scripture interpret Scripture.

Jesus' View of the Kingdom of God

One would think that the Son of God, the Lord of glory, the promised Messiah, and the King of kings and Lord of lords ought to know the nature of God's kingdom. It is His kingdom after all.

Matthew's Gospel account begins in 1:1 stating that this is a genealogy of Jesus Christ, **the son of David, the son of Abraham.** This clearly states that the promises given to Abraham and David are fulfilled in Jesus Christ. Jesus is the long awaited One who will fulfill the covenant promises. Through Him all the families of the earth will be blessed (as THE seed of Abraham). And, He will establish the kingdom of David forever.

The last great prophet of the Old Testament era was John the Baptist. As the promised forerunner of the Messiah, John confidently preached:

> [1]*Now in those days John the Baptist came, preaching in the wilderness of Judea, saying,* [2]*'Repent, for the kingdom of heaven is at hand.' For this is the one referred to by Isaiah the prophet when he said, 'The voice of one crying in the wilderness, 'Make ready the way of the Lord, make His paths straight!'*(Matthew 3:1-3)

---

[9]   G. Richard Fisher, *"The Other Gospel of John Hagee: Zionism and Ethnic Salvation"*, http://www.pfo.org/jonhagee.htm.

Note, John the Baptist said that the kingdom of heaven is at hand! Therefore repent.

In Mark 1:9-15, we see what Jesus preached:

> [9]*In those days Jesus came from Nazareth in Galilee and was baptized by John in the Jordan.* [10]*Immediately coming up out of the water, He saw the heavens opening, and the Spirit like a dove descending upon Him;* [11]*and a voice came out of the heavens: 'You are My beloved Son, in You I am well-pleased.'* [12]*Immediately the Spirit impelled Him to go out into the wilderness.* [13]*And He was in the wilderness forty days being tempted by Satan; and He was with the wild beasts, and the angels were ministering to Him.* [14]*Now after John had been taken into custody, Jesus came into Galilee, preaching the gospel of God, and saying, 'The time is fulfilled, and the kingdom of God is at hand; repent and believe in the gospel.'*

The forerunner of the Messiah said the "kingdom of God" was at hand, and now, the Messiah, Himself, preaches that the "kingdom of God" is at hand. Does this sound like the kingdom or millennium is far off into the future after Jesus' Second Coming? Jesus has officially started His ministry declaring that the kingdom had arrived.

One might wonder, "Why was Jesus baptized? Did He need to confess sin? Was he a personal sinner?" Of course not.

The fundamental meaning of baptism conveys "union with God," which is the same as what circumcision conveyed in the Old Testament. It was at Jesus' baptism that He was anointed with the Holy Spirit and declared to be the Father's beloved Son with whom God was well pleased.

This is the official beginning of Jesus' ministry. He is the new Israel of God. He is the promised Messiah, God in the flesh.

Jesus has come as the second Adam to undo what the first Adam did. The first Adam, as the covenantal head of the human race, failed and brought sin and misery into the world. The second Adam, as the covenantal head of His people, will faithfully discharge His duties. This is brought out in Galatians 4:4-5:

> [4]*But when the fullness of the time came, God sent forth His Son, born of a woman, born under the Law,* [5]*so that He might redeem*

those who were under the Law, that we might receive the adoption as sons.

Jesus must keep the law perfectly, and must pay the penalty for the transgressions of His people. II Corinthians 5:21 states:

He made Him who knew no sin to be sin on our behalf, so that we might become the righteousness of God in Him.

After His baptism, Jesus went into the wilderness, led by the Holy Spirit! For forty days, He was tempted by the serpent, who is the Devil. Jesus' victory in the wilderness in resisting the temptations of the Devil was the beginning of His crushing the head of the serpent (Genesis 3). Whereas Old Testament Israel failed in the wilderness, Jesus, as the New Israel, was victorious in the wilderness. And then after John the Baptist's arrest, thereby ending the ministry of the forerunner, Jesus came preaching the **Gospel of God.** Jesus proclaimed emphatically that "**the time is fulfilled.**" What time? The time prophesied of David's greater Son, that one day, the Messiah would establish His kingdom. This is why Jesus says, "**the kingdom of God** is at hand."

Jesus was sent by the Father "in the fullness of time" (Galatians 4:4) to inaugurate "the favorable year of the Lord." There is close affinity of Mark with Luke 4:16-21. The text reads:

[16]And He came to Nazareth, where He had been brought up; and as was His custom, He entered the synagogue on the Sabbath, and stood up to read. [17]And the book of the prophet Isaiah was handed to Him. And He opened the book and found the place where it was written, [18]'The Spirit of the Lord is upon Me, because He anointed Me to preach the gospel to the poor. He has sent Me to proclaim release to the captives, and recovery of sight to the blind, to set free those who are downtrodden,[19] to proclaim the favorable year of the Lord.' [20]And He closed the book, gave it back to the attendant and sat down; and the eyes of all in the synagogue were fixed on Him. [21]And He began to say to them, "Today this Scripture has been fulfilled in your hearing."

As verse 21 says, "Today this Scripture has been fulfilled in your hearing."

Isaiah 61 prophesied that the "acceptable year of the Lord" has come. The verb "has come" is in the perfect tense, meaning that at a given point the acceptable year has come and the effect of that event will continue.

In Mark 1, Jesus states, **"the kingdom of God is at hand.**" Jesus clearly meant that the Kingdom of God had arrived. Jesus condemned Jerusalem as recorded in Matthew 23:37 and Luke 19:44 because it did recognize "the time of your visitation."

Dispensationalism,[10] on one hand, states that the kingdom of God was offered to the Jews, and because they rejected the offer, somehow the kingdom was postponed. But then the Dispensationalists turn around and say that the prophets never saw the church age. Of course, a true Dispensationalist would assert that the church age was God's plan B, which explains why they think it was a "parenthesis" in history.

---

[10] I am fully aware that there is, if I may use this term, an "evolving" of dispensational thought. What I have been stating as the tenets of dispensational thought is historic, mainline dispensationalism. There is a new view known as "progressive dispensationalism." It had its moorings in the mid 1980s. It came about because there were some who were very uncomfortable with mainline Dispensational teaching, which led to a dialogue between Dispensationalists and non-dispensationalists. The following information is taken from: http://www.middletownbiblechurch.org/dispen/progresi.htm.

Keith Mathison, author of the postmillennial book, *Postmillennialism: An Eschatology of Hope* has made these observations about this new form of dispensationalism. He states: "Progressive dispensationalists have moved closer to Reformed theology on a number of doctrines. They now acknowledge that the kingdom has been inaugurated and that there is a present as well as a future aspect of the kingdom. They have also recognized the two-peoples-of-God theory to be unbiblical, which, ironically, brings us to the negative side of progressive dispensationalism. If the defining doctrine of dispensationalism is the two-peoples-of-God theory, then to reject that theory is to reject dispensationalism itself. "Progressive dispensationalism" is therefore both an encouraging trend and a misleading or confusing title."). Darrell Bock who has co-authored a 1993 book titled *Progressive Dispensationalism* has made these comments about this hybrid form of dispensationalism. He states: "Virtually every piece I have written has affirmed my commitment to a future for national Israel in a millennium (this includes a belief in sacrifices, a future temple, and pre-tribulationism). While there may be an appearance of a move towards Covenant Theology, it is clearly not Covenant Theology. While it is not Covenant Theology there are some similar teachings in certain areas."

Progressive Dispensationalists teach that Christ is already reigning on the throne of David in heaven, and that He assumed this throne at the time of the ascension. Progressive dispensationalists are distancing themselves from the notion that the Church is a parenthesis in God's plan. It is rejecting the notion that the kingdom was postponed. With Progressive dispensationalism's movement towards Covenant Theology, it is not surprising to learn that mainline dispensationalists are bemoaning the defection of some. Wayne House, a former professor of Systematic Theology at Dallas Theological Seminary has said: "One of my best students, and a research assistant to me at DTS, had told me in the mid-1990's that he had accepted progressive dispensationalism. My next meeting with him at the Dallas Seminary bookstore just two years ago I discovered that he had embraced amillennialism and covenant theology. When I asked him about this he commented to me that it was an easy move to make from progressive dispensationalism to amillennialism" (H. Wayne House, "Dangers of Progressive Dispensationalism to Pre-Millennial Theology," Pre-Trib. CD 2003, page 3).

I find it absolutely amazing that something of this grandeur, as the onset of the kingdom of God, would be relegated to a "parenthesis" in human history.

One of the strange teachings of dispensationalism is that it wants to distinguish between the kingdom of heaven and the kingdom of God. Is John the Baptist's "kingdom of heaven" any different from Jesus' "kingdom of God?" Of course not.

One of the clearest documentation that the Kingdom of heaven was a present reality in Jesus' ministry is Matthew 12:22-29 which states:

> *[22]Then a demon-possessed man who was blind and mute was brought to Jesus, and He healed him, so that the mute man spoke and saw. [23]All the crowds were amazed, and were saying, 'This man cannot be the Son of David, can he?' [24]But when the Pharisees heard this, they said, 'This man casts out demons only by Beelzebul the ruler of the demons.' [25]And knowing their thoughts Jesus said to them, 'Any kingdom divided against itself is laid waste; and any city or house divided against itself will not stand. [26]'If Satan casts out Satan, he is divided against himself; how then will his kingdom stand? [27]If I by Beelzebul cast out demons, by whom do your sons cast them out? For this reason they will be your judges. [28]But if I cast out demons by the Spirit of God, then the kingdom of God has come upon you. [29]Or how can anyone enter the strong man's house and carry off his property, unless he first binds the strong man? And then he will plunder his house.'* (Emphasis mine)

The kingdom of God has come upon them by virtue of the fact that Jesus cast out demons, thereby plundering Satan's house. The fact that Satan's kingdom had been invaded and plundered is the proof that the kingdom has come.

Another vital text is Luke 17:20-21 which states:

> *[20]Now having been questioned by the Pharisees as to when the kingdom of God was coming, He answered them and said, "The kingdom of God is not coming with signs to be observed; [21]nor will they say, 'Look, here it is!' or, 'There it is!' For behold, the kingdom of God is in your midst."* (Emphasis mine)

The Pharisees wanted to know when the kingdom of God was coming. The kingdom is "not coming with signs to be observed," Jesus said, but the **"kingdom of God is in your midst" or "within you."** Hence, Jesus was speaking of the kingdom of God as a **present reality**.

Interestingly, during His trial Jesus said some most illuminating things about the kingdom of God. Let's consider John 18:33-37:

> *[33]Therefore Pilate entered again into the Praetorium, and summoned Jesus and said to Him, "Are You the King of the Jews?" [34]Jesus answered, "Are you saying this on your own initiative, or did others tell you about Me?" [35]Pilate answered, "I am not a Jew, am I? Your own nation and the chief priests delivered You to me; what have You done?" [36]Jesus answered, "My kingdom is not of this world. If My kingdom were of this world, then My servants would be fighting so that I would not be handed over to the Jews; but as it is, My kingdom is not of this realm." [37]Therefore Pilate said to Him, "So You are a king?" Jesus answered, "You say correctly that I am a king For this I have been born, and for this I have come into the world, to testify to the truth Everyone who is of the truth hears My voice."*

Pilate asks Him point blank, "Are you the King of the Jews?" In Luke's account of the same incident (Luke 23:3) Jesus affirms, "It is as you say." Jesus affirms that He is the king of the Jews. Of course, Jesus did not tell the inhabitants that they were wrong when he came riding into Jerusalem on a donkey and they were proclaiming in Matthew 21:9:

> *The crowds going ahead of Him, and those who followed, were shouting,"Hosanna to the Son of David; blessed is He who comes in the name of the; Hosanna in the highest!"*

Matthew of course affirmed that Jesus was indeed the promised king of the Jews when he said in Matthew 21:4-5:

> *[4]This took place to fulfill what was spoken through the prophet: [5]'Say to the daughter of Zion, Behold your king is coming to you, gentle, and mounted on a donkey, even on a colt, the foal of a beast of burden.'*

This was a fulfillment of Zechariah's prophecy in Zechariah 9:9 which stated:

> *Rejoice greatly, O daughter of Zion! Shout in triumph, O daughter of Jerusalem! Behold, your king is coming to you; He is just and endowed with salvation, humble, and mounted on a donkey, even on a colt, the foal of a donkey.*

Returning to the passage in John 18, Jesus says in 18:36, "**My kingdom is not of this world!**" It is not fundamentally a political realm; hence, in this sense, it is no threat to Rome in terms of a physical army fighting the Romans.

Jesus' kingdom is not of this realm. In verse 37, Jesus says that He is a king; He was born a king; and for this reason He has come into the world to bear witness that He is the promised king of the Jews, and the promised One to establish David's throne.

Hence, Jesus is saying that the kingdom of God is a **spiritual kingdom.** When He says that His kingdom is spiritual and not of this world, He means that its origin is not of this world; it is not an earthly political realm. It doesn't derive its authority or power from this world. Now, this doesn't mean that the spiritual kingdom has no relevancy for political institutions, for after all, Psalm 2 does say that the installed king of the Father would be given the nations as His inheritance, that He would rule them with a rod of iron, and that failure to do homage to Him would be that nation's demise. In reality, Jesus' spiritual kingdom was a great threat to Rome.

Daniel 2 prophesies just how this kingdom was a threat to Rome.

Daniel 2:31-45

The text states Daniel's interpretation of Babylonian King Nebuchadnezzar's dream:

> [31]*You, O king, were looking and behold, there was a single great statue; that statue, which was large and of extraordinary splendor, was standing in front of you, and its appearance was awesome.* [32]*The head of that statue was made of fine gold, its breast and its arms of silver, its belly and its thighs of bronze,* [33]*its legs of iron, its feet partly of iron and partly of clay.* [34]*You continued looking until a stone was cut out without hands, and it struck the statue on its feet of iron and clay and crushed them.* [35]*Then the iron, the clay, the bronze, the silver and the gold were*

crushed all at the same time and became like chaff from the summer threshing floors; and the wind carried them away so that not a trace of them was found **But the stone that struck the statue became a great mountain and filled the whole earth.** [36]*This was the dream; now we will tell its interpretation before the king.* [37]*You, O king, are the king of kings, to whom the God of heaven has given the kingdom, the power, the strength and the glory ;*[38]*and wherever the sons of men dwell, or the beasts of the field, or the birds of the sky, He has given them into your hand and has caused you to rule over them all. You are the head of gold.* [39]*After you there will arise another kingdom inferior to you, then another third kingdom of bronze, which will rule over all the earth.* [40]*Then there will be a fourth kingdom as strong as iron; inasmuch as iron crushes and shatters all things, so, like iron that breaks in pieces, it will crush and break all these in pieces.* [41]*In that you saw the feet and toes, partly of potter's clay and partly of iron, it will be a divided kingdom; but it will have in it the toughness of iron, inasmuch as you saw the iron mixed with common clay.* [42]*As the toes of the feet were partly of iron and partly of pottery, so some of the kingdom will be strong and part of it will be brittle.* [43]*And in that you saw the iron mixed with common clay, they will combine with one another in the seed of men; but they will not adhere to one another, even as iron does not combine with pottery.* [44]***In the days of those kings the God of heaven will set up a kingdom which will never be destroyed***, *and that kingdom will not be left for another people;* ***it will crush and put an end to all these kingd****oms, but it will itself endure forever.* [45]*Inasmuch as you saw that a stone was cut out of the mountain without hands and that it crushed the iron, the bronze, the clay, the silver and the gold, the great God has made known to the king what will take place in the future; so the dream is true and its interpretation is trustworthy.* (Emphasis mine)

In Daniel's interpretation the statue represents four kingdoms. Historically, they are as follows:

1) The head of gold – Babylonian Empire
2) The breast and arms of silver – Medo-Persian Empire
3) The belly and thighs of bronze – The Greek Empire
4) The legs of iron and feet of iron and clay – the Roman Empire

Daniel says, in verses 34-35, that a stone was cut out without hands, meaning it was not of human origin. This stone that struck the statue became a great mountain that filled the whole earth. **Does this sound like a victory for the kingdom of God in history? It surely is!**

Then in v.44 we are told that in the days of those kings, the God of heaven will set up a kingdom which will never be destroyed, and it will crush or put an end to all these kingdoms. In verse 45 a stone is cut out of a mountain without hands, and it crushes all kingdoms.

Historically, Jesus was born during the reign of Caesar Augustus. Caesar decreed that a tax should be taken of the Roman world which required all to go to the city of their origin. Both Joseph and Mary were of the house of David. Bethlehem was the city of David where Jesus was born. In the providence of God, God orchestrated all of these events in order to have Mary, great with child, end up in Bethlehem where, according to Micah 5:1-5, the ruler of Israel would come.

Micah 5:1-5

> [1]*Now muster yourselves in troops, daughter of troops; They have laid siege against us; with a rod they will smite the judge of Israel on the cheek.* [2]*But as for you, Bethlehem Ephrathah, too little to be among the clans of Judah, from you One will go forth for Me to be ruler in Israel His goings forth are from long ago, From the days of eternity.* [3]*Therefore He will give them up until the time when she who is in labor has borne a child then the remainder of His brethren will return to the sons of Israel.* [4]*And He will arise and shepherd His flock in the strength of the Lord, in the majesty of the name of the Lord His God and they will remain, because at that time He will be great to the ends of the earth.* [5]*This One will be our peace when the Assyrian invades our land, when he tramples on our citadels, then we will raise against him seven shepherds and eight leaders of men.*

We can readily see that our majestic God is sovereign over the affairs of men; His decrees cannot be thwarted in the least. Whatever He plans, He accomplishes. The notion presented by many dispensationalists that God's original plan can be thwarted is nonsense and God dishonoring. God's providence orchestrates the details of human history in the minutiae of life so that people are where they need to be at the precise time they need to be there. Does this negate human responsibility? Not in the least. Men make moral decisions that carry either blessing or curse, but those decisions always, without exception, fulfill God's predestined plan. One of the greatest passages demonstrating this correlation of divine sovereignty with human responsibility is Mark 14:21 which states:

> *For the Son of Man is to go just as it is written of Him; but woe to that man by whom the Son of Man is betrayed! It would have been good for that man if he had not been born.*

There you have it. Jesus said that as the Son of Man, He is to go (to the cross) as it had been prophesied, but woe to the man (referring to Judas Iscariot) who betrayed Him. It would have been better if he had never been born. God's prophecy cannot be diverted! Men have no power to thwart God's plan! And prophets of God don't overlook anything, such as the Church age!

The Expansion of the Kingdom

We know that Jesus came preaching the gospel of the kingdom of heaven (the Kingdom of God), telling men to repent and believe. Jesus sent out His disciples to preach, declaring that the Kingdom of heaven (the Kingdom of God) was at hand.

Besides being spiritual and internal, what else did Jesus teach about the Kingdom of God? We have already alluded to this passage in chapter one.

We read in Matthew 21:33-46:

> *[33]Listen to another parable. There was a landowner who planted a vineyard and put a wall around it and dug a wine press in it, and built a tower, and rented it out to vine-growers and went on a journey. [34]When the harvest time approached, he sent his slaves to the vine-growers to receive his produce. [35]The vine-growers took his slaves and beat one, and killed another, and stoned a third. [36]Again he sent another group of slaves larger than the first; and they did the same thing to them. [37]But afterward he sent his son to them, saying, 'They will respect my son.' [38]But when the vine-growers saw the son, they said among themselves, 'This is the heir; come, let us kill him and seize his inheritance.' [39]They took him, and threw him out of the vineyard and killed him. [40]Therefore when the owner of the vineyard comes, what will he do to those vine-growers?" [41]They said to Him, 'He will bring those wretches to a wretched end, and will rent out the vineyard to other vine-growers who will pay him the proceeds at the proper seasons.' [42]Jesus said to them, 'Did you*

never read in the Scriptures, the stone which the builders rejected, this became the chief corner stone; this came about from the Lord, and it is marvelous in our eyes? [43]Therefore I say to you, the kingdom of God will be taken away from you and given to a people, producing the fruit of it. [44]And he who falls on this stone will be broken to pieces; but on whomever it falls, it will scatter him like dust.' [45]When the chief priests and the Pharisees heard His parables, they understood that He was speaking about them. [46]When they sought to seize Him, they feared the people, because they considered Him to be a prophet.

The kingdom of God belongs to those producing godly fruit, not to those who have been given outward privileges but then who do not believe in the promise. Those to whom the promise really belongs are those who repent and believe, like the tax gatherers and harlots in Matthew 21:32:

For John came to you in the way of righteousness and you did not believe him; but the tax collectors and prostitutes did believe him; and you, seeing this, did not even feel remorse afterward so as to believe him.

Of course, this promise belongs to all Gentiles who repent and believe in Jesus. These believers did not stumble over the choice cornerstone, but the Pharisees did stumble over it. The main point of the parable is that external privilege is no guarantee of God's blessing. Moreover, the spiritual promise is not restricted to Jews but available to any who believe. The clear implication is that the kingdom of God was never meant to be exclusive to national Israel. So much for the dispensational belief that the kingdom of God is for national Israel to shine.

Jesus' Kingdom Parables Concerning Expansion

Parable of the Sower and the Seed

Matthew 13 contains the kingdom parables of Jesus. In Matthew 13:19-23, we have the parable of the sower and the seed. It reads:

[19]When anyone hears the word of the kingdom and does not understand it, the evil one comes and snatches away what has been sown in his heart. This is the one on whom seed was sown beside the road. [20]The one on whom seed was sown on the rocky places, this is the man who hears the word and immediately receives it with joy; [21]yet he has no firm root in himself, but is

only temporary, and when affliction or persecution arises because of the word, immediately he falls away. [22]And the one on whom seed was sown among the thorns, this is the man who hears the word, and the worry of the world and the deceitfulness of wealth choke the word, and it becomes unfruitful. [23]And the one on whom seed was sown on the good soil, this is the man who hears the word and understands it; who indeed bears fruit and brings forth, some a hundredfold, some sixty, and some thirty.

Here we have Jesus identifying who the real subjects of His kingdom are: it is only those who hear the Word and then manifest fruit due to their hearing. In John 15:8, Jesus said that those who bear fruit prove to be His disciples; these are those branches who abide in Him as the true vine.

Parable of the Tares and Wheat

In Matthew 13:24-30, we have the parable of the tares and wheat. It reads:

[24]Jesus presented another parable to them, saying, 'The kingdom of heaven may be compared to a man who sowed good seed in his field. [25]But while his men were sleeping, his enemy came and sowed tares among the wheat, and went away. [26]But when the wheat sprouted and bore grain, then the tares became evident also.' [27]The slaves of the landowner came and said to him, 'Sir, did you not sow good seed in your field? How then does it have tares?' [28]And he said to them, 'An enemy has done this!' The slaves said to him, 'Do you want us, then, to go and gather them up?' [29]But he said, 'No; for while you are gathering up the tares, you may uproot the wheat with them. [30]Allow both to grow together until the harvest; and in the time of the harvest I will say to the reapers, First gather up the tares and bind them in bundles to burn them up; but gather the wheat into my barn.'

Jesus said the kingdom of heaven is compared to a man who sowed good seed in his field but an enemy also sowed tares. The tares are left to grow in the field until the harvest, when the tares will be destroyed. In this world there is a mixture of righteous and unrighteous. But keep in mind, it is a wheat field and not a tare field.

Parable of the Mustard Seed

In Matthew 13:31-32 we find the parable of the mustard seed. It states:

[31] He presented another parable to them, saying, 'The kingdom of heaven is like a mustard seed, which a man took and sowed in his field; [32] and this is smaller than all other seeds, but when it is full grown, it is larger than the garden plants and becomes a tree, so that the birds of the air come and nest in its branches'.

The kingdom of heaven is like a mustard seed that is the smallest of all other seeds, but when it is full grown it is the largest of the plants, so big that birds can nest in it. The point should be obvious. The kingdom of heaven gradually grows from small beginnings to a large tree. It is clear that the governing principle of the parable is upon size – from small to large.

This is very similar to an Old Testament imagery taken from Ezekiel 17:22-24:

[22] Thus says the Lord God, 'I will also take a sprig from the lofty top of the cedar and set it out; I will pluck from the topmost of its young twigs a tender one and I will plant it on a high and lofty mountain.' [23] On the high mountain of Israel I will plant it, that it may bring forth boughs and bear fruit and become a stately cedar. And birds of every kind will nest under it; they will nest in the shade of its branches. [24] All the trees of the field will know that I am the Lord; I bring down the high tree, exalt the low tree, dry up the green tree and make the dry tree flourish. I am the Lord; I have spoken, and I will perform it.'

With the royal family of Judah brought to desolation, the question would be – what about the promise of God to David to seat one his on his throne forever. Comfort is seen here. God takes a small sprig of a cedar and plants it on the high mountain of Israel so that it is conspicuous. It will grow and bear fruit and become a **stately cedar** where birds will come and nest in its branches.

The point is that while God takes down great trees, He then takes a sprig and exalts it as a great tree. **The idea is that of a universal greatness and exaltation of the kingdom of heaven.** So, the mustard seed parable shows how extensive the kingdom of heaven will become. It will be great!

The old line dispensational interpretation of the parable of the fig tree is totally skewed, and shows how dispensationalists will desperately attempt to foster their own ideas upon Scripture. Clarence Larken is one such teacher, for he says about the parable of the fig tree the following:

In the Parable of the "Mustard Seed" we see how the visible church is sought as a "roosting place" by the "birds of the air," the emissaries of Satan (Matthew 13:4, 19), who lodge in its branches, not so much for shelter as to befoul the tree. These are the "False Teachers" of II Peter 2:1-2, which are so evident in our day.[11]

Another common dispensational understanding of this parable is to view the mustard seed growing into a large tree as a monstrosity. Here is this interpretation:

Now there are few passages of Scripture which have suffered more at the hands of commentators than the third and fourth parables of Matthew 13. They have been turned completely upside down; that is to say, they have been made to mean the very opposite of what the Lord Jesus taught. The main cause of this erroneous interpretation may be traced back to a wrong understanding of the expression "kingdom of heaven." Those who have failed in their definition of this term are, necessarily, all at sea, when they come to the details of these parables.

The popular and current explanation of these parables is that they were meant to announce the glorious success of the Gospel. Thus, that of the mustard-seed is regarded as portraying the rapid extension of Christianity and the expansion of the church of Christ. Beginning insignificantly and obscurely, its proportions have increased immensely, until ultimately it shall cover the earth. Let us first show how untenable and impossible this interpretation is.

First, it must be steadily borne in mind that these seven parables form part of one connected and complete discourse whose teaching must necessarily be consistent and harmonious throughout. Therefore, it is obvious that this third one cannot conflict with the teaching of the first two. In the first parable, instead of drawing a picture of a field in which the good Seed took root and flourished in every part of it, our Lord pointed out that most of its soil was unfavorable, and that only a fractional proportion bore an increase. Moreover, instead of promising that the good-ground section of the field would yield greater and greater returns, He announced that there would be a decreasing harvest— 'some an hundredfold, some sixty, some thirty.' In the

---

[11]   Larken, p. 59.

second parable, our Lord revealed the field as over-sown with "tares," and declared that these should continue until the harvest-time, which He defined as "the end of the age." This fixes beyond all doubt the evil consequences of the Enemy's work, and positively forbids the expectation of a world won to Christ during this present dispensation, Christ plainly warned us that the evil effects of the Devil's labors at the beginning of the age would never be repaired. The crop as a whole is spoiled! Thus this third parable *cannot* teach that the failure of things in the hands of men will be removed and reversed.

Second, the *figure* here selected by Christ should at once expose the fallacy of the popular interpretation. Surely our Lord would never have taken a mustard-seed which afterwards became a "tree," ever rooting itself deeper and deeper in the earth, to portray that people whose calling, hope, citizenship, and destiny *is heavenly*. Again and again He affirmed that His people were "*not* of the world." Again, a great tree with its towering branches speaks of prominence and loftiness, but lowliness and suffering, not prominence and exaltation, are the present portion of the New Testament saints. The more any church of Christ climbs the ladder of worldly fame the more it sinks spiritually. That which is represented by this "tree" is *not* a people who are "strangers and pilgrims" down here, but a system whose roots lie deeply in the earth and which aims at greatness and expansion in the world.

Third, that which Christ here describes is a *monstrosity*. We are aware that this is denied by some, but our Lord's own words are final. He tells us that when this mustard-seed is grown it is the "greatest among *herbs*, and *becomes* a tree" (v. 32). "Herbs" are an entirely different specie from trees. That which distinguished them is that their stems never develop woody tissue, but live only long enough for the development of flowers and seeds. But this "herb" became a "tree;" that is to say, it developed into something entirely *foreign* to its very nature and constitution. How strange that sober men should have deemed this unnatural growth, this abnormal production, a fitting symbol of the *saints* of God in their corporate form!

Thus we may discern in the first three parables of Matthew 13 a striking and sad forecast of the *development of evil*. In the first, the Devil caught away part of the good Seed. In the second, he is seen engaged in the work of imitation. Here, in the third, we are shown a corrupted Christianity affording him shelter.[12]

It is not at all encouraging that sincere Christians can have such varied and contradictory interpretations of the Word of God. So, who is right? Of course, I contend that this dispensational interpretation is very wrong and not consistent with Scripture's tenor, and that it is an interpretation presuppositionally imposed upon the text in order to preserve dispensational assumptions.

To contend that Jesus is referring to an aberration in the size of the mustard tree from a small seed is totally erroneous. Why should a tree growing from a small seed be seen as monstrous? In one sense, all trees come from seeds. Jesus simply said that one of the smallest seeds in the garden grows into a tree and is larger than the other plants in the garden. There is nothing monstrous about a full grown mustard tree. These trees fully grown can reach a height of twenty feet and be almost as large in width as height. This is common!

Parables were designed to take commonly understood images to teach spiritual truths. Milton S. Terry states in his book on hermeneutics how to approach interpreting parables:

> First, we should determine the historical occasion and aim of the parable; secondly, we should make an accurate analysis of the subject matter, and observe the nature and properties of the things employed as imagery in the similitude; and thirdly we should interpret the several parts with strict reference to the general scope and design of the whole, so as to preserve a harmony of proportions, maintain the unity of all the parts, and make prominent the great central truth. [13]

The dispensational interpretation is bizarre, and it violates biblical principles of interpretation. Dispensationalists have no right to impose foreign ideas upon the parable. Jesus is simply stating a common horticultural fact – mustard seeds are smaller than other seeds and often grow large enough where birds can nest. This is the natural interpretation. The nesting of birds in the mustard tree's branches is simply saying that the tree is big enough to allow this. Hence, the natural interpretation is: the kingdom of heaven starts small but eventually grows into a large tree.

---

[12]   Taken from http://www.pbministries.org/books/pink/Parables/parables_03.htm.
[13]   Terry, pp. 281-282.

However, the dispensational interpretation rejects such simplicity, arguing for subtle complexity. Why should birds be seen as "Satan's emissaries?" Every parable must be seen in its own context. Yes, in the parable of the sower and the seed, the clear teaching by Jesus is that the birds represent Satan coming and snatching up the seed before it has a chance (Luke 18:12). The birds are equated with Satan in this parable because **Jesus said so**. Does Jesus say explicitly in the parable of the mustard seed that the birds represent the devil? No! In this parable, the birds are used only to demonstrate the largeness of the tree so that they can build nests in it. For the dispensationalist to insist that birds always mean "evil emissaries" is hermeneutically irresponsible. We know that words can shift their meaning depending upon the context. For example, one Greek word for "world" is "cosmos," and it doesn't always mean the same. It can mean "the created realm" (Matthew 24:21), or "material possessions" (Mark 8:36), or " the human race in various nations" (Luke 12:30) or "representatives of the human race" (John 1:10), or "those for whom Jesus died" (John 1:29), or "the human race" (John 3:17), or "a limited or certain restricted group" (John 12:19), or "certain nations of the world" (Matthew 26:13)," or "a system of thinking contrary to God," (I John 2:15; I Corinthians 2:12), "unbelievers who are condemned in judgment" (I Corinthians 11:32), or "the elect or redeemed only" (John 17:9)," or "certain unbelievers" (John 17:14, 25), or "people in general" (John 18:25), or "the entire human race as sinners" (Romans 3:19), or "believers by faith only as heirs of Abraham's promise" (Romans 4:13), or "those in rebellion against God" (I John 5:19).

I know it may have been somewhat "overkill" to list so many differing uses of the word "world" (cosmos), but it was to serve as an illustration that it is exegetically irresponsible to simply take the use of a word in one place and infer it is obviously the meaning in that context. To insinuate that "birds" are emissaries of Satan in the parable of the mustard seed is unjustified.

The natural interpretation of this parable is that the kingdom of heaven starts small but grows large. Dispensationalists cannot accept this interpretation because it contradicts their theological system of failure, of a presuppositional commitment to a distinction between Israel and the church. For them, this parable cannot teach victory for the kingdom of heaven because their theology doesn't permit it. The church, to them, is a failure in the present age. For them, the kingdom promises cannot belong to the church, for the church is distinct from Israel. Hence, they must impose all kinds of interpretations that are not contextually justified.

Dispensationalists want to accuse others, especially covenant theologians, of imposing presuppositions on the text and supposedly non-literal interpretations, but it is they who are guilty of not taking the texts in their normal way. They bring all kinds of complexity to a text that corresponds to their theology.

And notice that Jesus says that "the **kingdom of heaven** is like...." Dispensationalists want to view then "the kingdom of heaven" in a very negative light, not only in this parable but also in the next parable for our consideration – the parable of the leaven.

Parable of the Leaven

We have the parable of the leaven in Matthew 13:33:

> *He spoke another parable to them, "The kingdom of heaven is like leaven, which a woman took, and hid in three pecks of meal, until it was all leavened."*

C.I. Scofield gives the typical dispensational premillennial interpretation of this parable when he says:

> Leaven, as a fermenting process, is uniformly regarded in Scripture as typifying the presence of impurity or evil (Ex. 12:15, 19; 13:7; Lev. 2:11; Dt. 16:4; Mt. 16:6, 12; Mark 8:15; Luke 12:1; I Corinthians 5:6-9; Gal. 5:9)... The use of leaven in the three measures of meal seems intended likewise to represent evil within the kingdom of heaven. The teaching that leaven in this parable represents the beneficient influence of the Gospel pervading the world has no Scriptural justification. Nowhere in Scripture does leaven represent good; the idea of a converted world at the end of the age is contradicted by the presence of tares among the wheat and bad fish among the good in the kingdom itself... The parable is, therefore, a warning that true doctrine, represented by the meal, would be corrupted by false doctrine (cp. 1 Timothy 4:1-3; 2 Timothy 2:17-18; 4:3-4; 2 Peter 2:1-3).[14]

Again, here is the hermeneutical problem. One cannot use other places to assert that the meaning of a word is always the same! In looking at Scofield's proof texts, for him to assert that "leaven" is uniformly or

---

[14]   New Scofield Reference Bible notes, p. 1015 on the meaning of the parable of the leaven in Matthew 13:33.

always used to refer to evil is clearly wrong. In the Old Testament passages concerning the command to not eat anything but unleavened bread, Scofield mentions Deuteronomy 16:4 that forbids Israel to eat unleavened bread for seven days. Why didn't he mention verse 3? Deuteronomy 16:3 reads:

> *You shall not eat leavened bread with it; seven days you shall eat with it unleavened bread, the bread of affliction (for you came out of the land of Egypt in haste), in order that you may remember all the days of your life the day when you came out of the land of Egypt.*

First, this command is with respect to the Old Testament observance of Passover, commemorating Israel's deliverance from Egypt. It is evident that "leaven" is not seen as evil but is representative of the fact that they left in "haste" (Exodus 12:30-34). It takes time for leaven to permeate a loaf. Israel did not have much time, for they were urged by the Egyptians, by Pharaoh, to leave in "haste" because of the final plague of the death of Egypt's first born. Pharoah wanted the cursed Israelites out of his land as soon as possible! The issue is one of "haste" not leaven being evil. In fact, we are told in Exodus 12:34 that Israel was used to eating "leavened" bread. The text reads, *"So the people took their dough before it was leavened, with their kneading bowls bound up in the clothes on their shoulders."* Moreover, God never commanded Israel that they could never eat leavened bread; God simply said that for seven days they could not eat it during the Passover observance in commemoration of having to leave in haste. Scofield is clearly wrong! He has completely misinterpreted the text.

In one of Scofield's other proof texts to prove that "leaven" is always bad, he quotes Matthew 16:6 where Jesus warns people to avoid the "leaven" **of the Pharisees and Sadducees.** Is any leaven condemned? No. It is the leaven of the Pharisees and Sadducees, of which Luke 12:1 calls the leaven as "hypocrisy." "Leaven" as a whole is not condemned, but a certain kind of leaven is – the leaven of hypocrisy of the Pharisees and Sadducees.

Context, context, context and, I repeat, context determines the meanings of words. Hence, Scofield has no warrant of imposing on Matthew 13:33 a meaning of "leaven" as evil. Moreover, let's keep in mind that Jesus says explicitly that the **kingdom of heaven is like leaven.** Dispensationalism's false hermeneutic leads them to commit another serious theological error – to called the kingdom of heaven evil! Dispensationalism states that the "kingdom of heaven" or the church age is permeated or corrupted by a pervasive evil. In other words, evil abounds greatly and is supposedly the main characteristic of the church age. Scofield openly states in his notes on this parable that the postmillennial notion of victory cannot be true because of the nature of leaven. He has no proper understanding of postmillennialism, for he asserts that the presence of tares at the coming of Jesus is proof that it cannot be true. For one, postmillennialism never asserts that the victory of the gospel or the fulfillment of the Great Commision demands every single person without exception be converted, but it does imply massive conversions for sure.

This brings us to another serious error of dispensationalism – a view that there is a distinction between "the kingdom of heaven" and "the kingdom of God." Clarence Larkin promotes this belief:

> There is much confusion as to the difference between the "Kingdom of God," the "kingdom of heaven," and the "church." No amount of sophistical argument can make them synonymous. The "kingdom of God" is the all inclusive Kingdom, or rule of the Triune God (Father, Son, and Holy Spirit) over the whole Universe, especially over all moral intelligences, angelic or human, and includes "Time" and "Eternity," "Heaven" and "Hell." It is SPIRITUAL, and "cometh not with observation" (outward show). Luke 17:20-21. It is entered by the "New Birth" (John 3:5), and is not "meat" and "drink," but "Righteousness" and "Peace," and "Joy" in the HOLY GHOST. Romans 14:17, (See Chart page 48), The "Kingdom of Heaven" is a New Testament term, and is found in Matthews' Gospel only, where it is mentioned 27 times. It is the early sphere of the "Kingdom of God," and is outward and visible. Its character is described in the 12 "Kingdom of heaven Parables" given in Matthew 13:1-50; 18:23-35; 20:1-16; 22:1-14; 25:1-30. From these Parables we see that the "Kingdom of Heaven" is limited as to its "Time" and "Sphere." Its "Time" is from the first to the Second Coming of Christ, and its "Sphere" is over that part of the world that we call Christendom. In it there is a mixture of "Good" and "Evil," of "Wheat" and "Tares," of "Wise Virgins" and "Foolish Virgins," of "Good Fish" and "Bad Fish."[15]

The following are the famous charts from his book, *The Second Coming of Christ.*

---

[15]   Larken, p. 47.

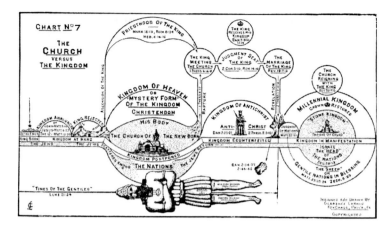

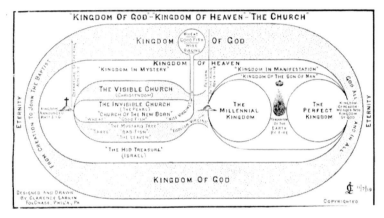

One of the amazing errors of dispensationalism is its uncanny ability to complicate something very simple. The parable of the leaven simply states that the kingdom of heaven is LIKE leaven. Leaven is yeast and once introduced, it spreads to the entire loaf. This deals with the intensive progress of the kingdom of heaven in this world. Jesus said that the kingdom of heaven or the kingdom of God is like leaven; the idea is that the kingdom of God keeps growing and growing and growing until it encompasses the world.

Is there a biblical distinction between the kingdom of God and the kingdom of heaven? Not really.

In Matthew 3:2, John the Baptist comes proclaiming *"Repent, for the kingdom of heaven is at hand."* In Matthew 4:17, Jesus comes proclaiming *"Repent, for the kingdom of heaven is at hand."* So, Matthew records both John the Baptist and Jesus using the phrase "kingdom of heaven."

But, let's see how Mark's Gospel account records these same instances. Mark 1:15 has Jesus proclaiming *"The time is fulfilled, and the kingdom of God is at hand; repent and believe in the gospel."* Now, if there is an absolute distinction between the phrases "kingdom of heaven" and "kingdom of God," then we have a real problem. Which did Jesus preach after the wilderness temptation? Was it the kingdom of heaven or the kingdom of God? We obviously don't have a contradiction between Matthew and Mark for both are inspired. Both gospel accounts are speaking of exactly the same event.

Matthew 11:12-13 reads, "From the days of John the Baptist until now the **kingdom of heaven** suffers violence, and violent men take it by force. For all the prophets and the Law prophesied until John" (Emphasis mine). In Luke 16:16 we read, "The Law and the Prophets were proclaimed until John; since that time the gospel of the **kingdom of God** has been preached, and everyone is forcing his way into it" (Emphasis mine). In speaking about the same thing, Matthew uses the phrase "kingdom of heaven" while Luke uses the phrase "kingdom of God." It is obvious that the terms are synonymous.

In Matthew 10:7, Jesus sent out the Twelve to preach saying, "**the kingdom of heaven** is at hand." Luke 9:1-2 reads, *"And He called the twelve together, and gave them power and authority over all the demons and to heal diseases. And He sent them out to proclaim the **kingdom of God** and to perform healing"* (Emphasis mine). Both Matthew and Luke are referencing the same event; however, one uses the phrase "kingdom of heaven" while the other uses "kingdom of God." Therefore, the terms must be synonymous.

Matthew 19:23-24 is very instructive for us, for it uses in the same verses the two terms interchangeably. The text reads:

> *And Jesus said to His disciples, 'Truly I say to you, it is hard for a rich man to enter **the kingdom of heaven**. Again I say to you, it is easier for a camel to go through the eye of a needle, than for a rich man to enter **the kingdom of God**.'* (Emphasis mine)

How can it be clearer? When Jesus reiterates what He has just said, He changes to the phrase, "kingdom of God." The kingdom of God and the kingdom of heaven are **not** separate concepts, but the same.

We are told in Daniel 2:44 that the "kingdom of heaven" will be set up a kingdom that will never be destroyed. Why the difference in phraseology?

Probably the phrase "kingdom of heaven" stresses the origin or source of the kingdom – it is from heaven; it is not earthly originating with man, but it is God's kingdom.

Old Testament Prophecies about the Kingdom of God

We saw in the Abrahamic covenant that there is the promise of his seed being as numerous as the stars and the sand of the seashore, and Romans 4:13 affirmed that this promise was obviously meant to encompass the world, not some limited geographical territory in the Middle East.

In Psalm 22:27-31, we have a psalm of David which reads:

> *[22]All the ends of the earth will remember and turn to the Lord, and all the families of the nations will worship before You. [28]For the kingdom is the Lord's, and He rules over the nations. [29]All the prosperous of the earth will eat and worship, all those who go down to the dust will bow before Him, even he who cannot keep his soul alive. [30]Posterity will serve Him; it will be told of the Lord to the coming generation. [31]They will come and will declare His righteousness to a people who will be born, that He has performed it.*

Psalm 22:1-21 is that classic section portraying the Messiah's suffering. Keep in mind that this Psalm was quoted by Christ when He was on the cross in Matthew 27:46. Additionally, we see clear attestation to both the Abrahamic and Davidic covenants. All the families of the earth are coming and worshipping. The Lord is pictured as ruling over the nations with their coming to bow down before Him. **The most important aspect of this is that we don't have to wait until after the Second Coming of Jesus to earth for the setting up of this kingdom. The kingdom of God is upon us, and the Old Testament prophesied it for this present age.**

Psalm 47 is a very significant passage, for it speaks of the Lord reigning on His throne, subduing peoples and nations under "our feet." And, it associates the "princes of the people" as the people of the God of Abraham.

Psalm 47

> *O clap your hands, all people; shout to God with voice of joy. For the Lord Most High is to be feared, a great king over all the earth. He subdues peoples **under us**, and nations **under our feet**.*

He chooses our inheritance for us, the glory of Jacob whom He loves. Selah. God has ascended with a shout, the Lord, with the sound of a trumpet. Sing praises to god, sing praises; sing praises to our King, sing praises. For God is the King of all the earth; sing praises with a skillful psalm. God reigns over the nations, God sits on His holy throne. The princes of the people have assembled themselves as the people of the God of Abraham; for the shields of the earth belong to God; He is highly exalted. (Emphasis mine)

The first thing that we must see in this passage is that the King is none other than the promised Messiah, the Lord Jesus Christ. This is not disputed by dispensationalists, but they think that this is a promise restricted to national Israel, and it won't come to pass until after Jesus' Second Coming. They think Jesus then sets up His millennial kingdom, where He sits on a literal throne of David, from a literal rebuilt temple in Jerusalem, and where the Jews (the glory of Jacob) will exercise dominion over the nations. This is the typical dispensational premillennial interpretation. But, we will prove throughout this book that this interpretation, particularly of Psalm 47, is flatly wrong.

We must not miss the powerful statement that *"The princes of the people have assembled themselves as the people of the God of Abraham."* This is not a prophecy of a glorious restoration of Judaism; it is a prophecy of the glory of Christ's church, which incorporates both Jew and Gentile **as the people of the God of Abraham**. I could have quoted this passage in the previous chapter where I demonstrate from Scripture that the church constitutes the new Israel of God.

We need to understand that Psalm 47 refers to God having **ascended** with a shout to His holy throne where He is reigning from that throne, and the effect of that reign is that the princes of the people have assembled as the people of the God of Abraham. Dispensationalists totally miss the import of Psalm 47. There is a definitive difference between "ascending" and "descending." The inspired word of God says that God **ascends to His throne.** The Second Coming of Jesus is a "descending" to earth, not an ascending. As we shall see in the next chapter, the ascension of the Messiah is clearly set forth not only in this passage of Psalm 47, but it is set forth in Daniel 7:13-14 and then in Acts 2:29-36. What does Psalm 47 say that the King is doing from His holy throne to which He has ascended? Verse 3 states explicitly that *"He subdues peoples **under us**, and nations **under our feet**."* We will see that this is consistent teaching with Psalm 110 and with Acts 2 where Psalm 110 is directly quoted by Peter. The whole thrust of Psalm 47 points to victory! The Messiah (the King) is victorious over all the nations, and the King exercises that victory "under us" or "under our feet." This victory is specifically seen in the princes of the people being assembled as the people of the God of Abraham. This is obviously a picturing of the conversion of the nations as the true people of God. It is a direct reference to the conversion of the Gentiles who then become constituted as "the people of the God of Abraham."

Galatians 3 is as definitive as it gets in setting forth that the Gentile nations are the recipients of the promises to Abraham. We have already mentioned that Galatians 3:8 states that the gospel was preached to Abraham in promise form – "all the nations shall be blessed in you." Galatians 3:9 affirms, "*So then those who are of faith are blessed with Abraham, the believer.*" This blessed truth about the Gentiles being constituted as the new Israel of God by faith is seen in Galatians 3:14 – "*In order that in Christ Jesus the blessing of Abraham might come to the Gentiles, so that we might receive the promise of the Spirit through faith.*"

The Gentiles believing in Jesus are the true inheritors of Abraham's promises and are his seed. As Psalm 47 teaches, the ascended Messiah **from** His throne is subduing enemies under whose feet? **Our feet!** The feet belong to Jesus' people, who are the church! This theological truth I will further establish in the next chapter.

It is most illuminating what the great commentator, Matthew Henry, said about Psalm 47. He stated:

> … It was the honour of Israel that they were *the people of the God of Abraham,* as they were Abraham's seed and taken into his covenant; and, thanks be to God, this blessing of Abraham has come upon the isles of the Gentiles, Gal. iii. 14… It was well with Israel when the princes of their people were gathered together to consult for the public welfare. The unanimous agreement of the great ones of a nation in the things that belong to its peace is a very happy omen, which promises abundance of blessings. 2. It may be applied to the calling of the Gentiles into the church of Christ, and taken as a prophecy that in the days of the Messiah the kings of the earth and their people should join themselves to the church, and bring their glory and power into the New Jerusalem, that they should all become *the people of the God of Abraham,* to whom it was promised that he should be the *father of many nations.* The volunteers of the people (so it may be read); it is the same word that is used in Ps. cx. 3, *Thy people shall be willing;* for

those that are gathered to Christ are not forced, but made freely willing, to be his. *When the shields of the earth*, the ensigns of royal dignity (1 Kings xiv. 27, 28), are surrendered to the Lord Jesus, as the keys of a city are presented to the conqueror or sovereign, when princes use their power for the advancement of the interests of religion, then Christ is greatly exalted.[16]

God's promise to bring blessing to all the families of the earth through the seed of Abraham will be fulfilled by bringing together all the families of the earth under Christ's rule on David's throne.

Union with Christ is by faith, and faith is through the gospel; hence, belief in gospel preaching is the fulfilling of the Abrahamic promise. Jesus, from His throne in heaven, is subduing His enemies foremost **by converting them through the preaching of His church.**

Dispensational premillennialism cannot see this clear biblical truth because of its proclivity to its unbiblical distinctions. Actually, all forms of premillennial thinking cannot see this, and amillennialists, while understanding that Jesus is presently reigning in His kingdom, cannot see this blessed truth either.

Further Dispensational Errors Regarding the Kingdom of God

The purpose of this book is not foremost a polemic against dispensationalism; it is to exegetically demonstrate that Jesus' kingdom is victorious, and that this kingdom is before and not after the Second Coming. I am constrained nonetheless to demonstrate the serious errors of dispensational thinking for the purpose of showing that their interpretation of Scripture is not accurate. As elders of the church, we are obligated to confront theological error, particularly when it is dishonoring to our Lord and detrimental to the church of the Lord Jesus. Titus 1:9 exhorts elders to do the following:

> *Holding fast the faithful word which is in accordance with the teaching, that he may be able both to exhort in sound doctrine and to refute those who contradict.*

Dispensationalism has had a virtual "stranglehold" upon the evangelical community throughout much of the Twentieth Century. In other words, for

---

[16]   Matthew Henry's Commentary on Psalm 47.

someone to question dispensational thinking is tantamount to being anti-Christian in some circles. But, as I noted in the introduction, because something is popular, doesn't mean that it is biblical. The Christian church has not historically held to dispensational thinking throughout its history. Dispensational theology is essentially "the new kid on the block." It definitely was not the theology of the Protestant Reformation.

Many times we must point out error in order to instruct in truth. The goal, then, in pointing out these dispensational errors regarding the kingdom of God is to show that these errors are contrary to the truth about the nature of God's kingdom. It is to show that dispensational theology cannot hold up against careful exegetical study. The Word of God is not contradictory, and it is unthinkable to purport that there is a return to the "shadows" once the "substance" has come. The theology of a millennial kingdom after the Second Coming simply cannot be biblically supported. Therefore, all forms of premillennialism cannot be sustained, but especially dispensational premillennialism. I am fully aware that many passages are put forth by all proponents of premillennial thought. I am contending that their hermeneutic is biblically flawed. More will be said about hermeneutics later.

I have already alluded to some serious theological errors in chapter one and in the earlier part of this chapter, but there are some other errors that need to be addressed. I have already pointed out that the belief that a sovereign God's plan can be thwarted is biblically untenable and dishonoring to the Lord of glory. The notion that the prophets failed to distinguish between the comings of Jesus is equally untenable and dishonoring to God. God doesn't make mistakes with His inspired prophets!

A Millennium Dominated By Jews?

It is evident that dispensationalists cannot see that the kingdom of God is now because they cannot divorce themselves from this Israel/church distinction. Dispensationalists J. Dwight Pentecost, Charles L. Feinberg, and John F. Walvoord have made the following statements:

> "Israel in the millennium will be exalted above the Gentiles," "the Gentiles will be Israel's servants," and "the distinction of Israel from the Gentiles will again be resumed."[17]

> "The nations in the kingdom will recognize the favored condition of Israel..." and "... Israel will also rule over the nations under the direct command of the king."[18]

> In contrast to the present church age in which Jew and Gentile are on an equal plane of privilege, the millennium is clearly a period of time in which Israel is in prominence and blessing.[19]

One of the other dispensational errors pertains to their insistence that the millennial kingdom is an earthly, political organization, where the Jews rule the world with Jesus with an iron hand.

Due to the Roman occupation of Palestine during Jesus' time, there were Jewish zealots who were determined to resist this occupation by force. It would eventually lead to the Jew's total annihilation as a nation by Rome in the Jewish Wars, culminating in Jerusalem's destruction in 70 AD.

John 6:14-15 states:

> *Therefore when the people saw the sign which He had performed, they said, "This is truly the Prophet who is to come into the world." So Jesus, perceiving that they were intending to come and take Him by force to make Him king, withdrew again to the mountain by Himself alone.*

Jesus responds to Pontius Pilate's question as to whether He is the king of the Jews. In John 18:36 Jesus states:

---

[17]   Pentecost, pp. 507-08, 519-20 in Crenshaw and Gunn, p. 183.
[18]   Feinberg, p. 186 in Crenshaw and Gunn, p. 183.
[19]   Walvoord, pp. 302-03 in Crenshaw and Gunn, p. 183.

Jesus answered, 'My kingdom is not of this world. If My kingdom were of this world, then My servants would be fighting so that I would not be handed over to the Jews; but as it is, My kingdom is not of this realm.'

Jesus' kingdom is not of political or earthly origin that must be defended by a sword. Why did Jesus resist being made a political king? It is because it is not the fundamental nature of His kingdom. If you notice in John 6 the people perceived Jesus to be the great prophet prophesied in Deuteronomy18:15-18.

The idea of a Messianic king that has a political realm that forcibly keeps subjects in line is thinking very near to what the Pharisees perceived the Messiah to be. Their problem was that they did not perceive Messiah to be a suffering servant, that humiliation preceded exaltation. The notion that Jesus offered the Jews a political and exalted kingdom that they rejected, thereby forcing God to have a plan B, which resulted in a "gospel of grace" and the preaching of the cross, is not that far off from a Pharisaical understanding.

There appears to some varying understandings of the millennial age by dispensationalists.

Dispensationalist writer Hal Lindsey has said the following about the millennial kingdom in his book *There's a New World Coming:*

> The oldest interpretation is called pre-millennialism. This view holds that Christ will literally and bodily return to earth *before* the thousand year Kingdom begins. He will set up this Kingdom and reign from the throne of David out of a rebuilt city of Jerusalem … regardless of Israel's past history of spiritual failures, God will *literally fulfill* all His promises during this thousand-year Kingdom period. [20]

> Even with Satan not active, there will still be a certain amount of sin during the Millennium. The Tribulation believers still in their physical bodies will have sinful natures, they and their children can choose to rebel against God, and some will.[21]

---

[20]   Hal Lindsey, *There's A New World Coming*, (Santa Ana, CA: Vision House Publishers, 1973), p.267.

[21]   Lindsey, p. 272.

> Man will enjoy a peace filled thousand years on this old earth. But at the end of this time, after the mortals have had perfect government by the perfect God-man in the most perfect surroundings imaginable, some will end up rebelling and blowing it again at their first opportunity.[22]

The picture that some dispensationalists portray of this one thousand year reign of Christ on earth with glorified church saints is not what some may think. Dispensational writer of the 19th Century, J.H. Brooks, said:

> That which is born of the flesh is flesh and though restrained during the Millennium it will manifest its inherent pravity at the first favorable opportunity, like a tiger long caged and curbed that will bound back to its native jungle with unquenchable thirst for blood when the iron bars are removed.[23]

Dispensationalists have always contended that the prophecies of Isaiah chapters 2 and 11 apply to the millennial reign of Christ, which doesn't occur until after Christ's Second Coming. In Isaiah's prophecies it pictures the nations beating their swords into plowshares and learning war no more; it pictures the supposed changes in ferocious meat eating animals into passive, vegetating animals. In their plea to be "literalists," Dispensationalists have a peculiar understanding of world peace. So, it is more than strange to see some dispensationalists believing that the Messianic kingdom is essentially a seething undercurrent of rebellious spirits having to be kept in physical check by Jesus Himself and His glorified saints (church having been raptured prior to the Second Coming). This doesn't sound like the nations have beat the swords into plowshares and learned war no more.

For dispensationalists, the realm of Messiah will be kept in line only by a rod of iron rule on David's throne. The picture is that of Jesus on David's throne having to put down this undercurrent of rebellion when it shows itself. The nations will have physical force exerted against them to keep them in line. After all, it says that the Messiah will rule with "a rod of iron."

If according to the dispensational system, the physical animals have been constitutionally altered where actual lions will no longer desire to eat

---

[22]   Lindsey, pp. 284-285.
[23]   Oswald T. Allis, *Prophecy and the Church*, (Philadelphia: Presbyterian and Reformed Publishing, 1977), p.240 who quotes J.H. Brookes, *Maranatha*, p.490.

lambs and where cobra snakes are no longer poisonous, isn't it rather strange that men's hearts have not been changed to internally desire peace, but are kept in check by a rod of iron?

Yes, the Scripture does say that the Messiah will rule the nations with a rod of iron, but we need to appreciate the frequent poetic language used in Scripture. Yes, Psalm 2:9 refers to the Messianic king's reign as being one where *"Thou shalt break them with a rod of iron, Thou shall shatter them like earthenware."* The imagery is one of subduing one's enemies. As we shall see, Psalm 110:1-3 states:

> *[1]The Lord says to my Lord: 'Sit at My right hand until I make Your enemies a footstool for Your feet.' [2]The Lord will stretch forth Your strong scepter from Zion, saying, 'Rule in the midst of Your enemies. [3]Your people will volunteer freely in the day of Your power; in holy array, from the womb of the dawn, Your youth are to You as the dew.*

Rather than forcefully seeking to keep in check a rebellious spirit, it is a more Scriptural understanding to see that Christ subdues His enemies fundamentally by **converting them!** It says that His people will "volunteer freely" in the day of His power. The biblical emphasis is hardly picturing the nations as "caged tigers being forcibly detained."

According to dispensationalists, the Psalms have their central theme as Christ and the Jewish remnant in the millennial age. Isaiah has its emphasis on Jesus Christ and His sufferings to be followed by the glory in the Davidic kingdom. The theme of Ezekiel is seen as Israel in the land during the millennial age. During the millennial age, the Jews will be preeminent among the nations. The millennium will be a Jewish age.

Jesus on a Physical Throne, in a Rebuilt Temple, with Sacrifices Being Performed?

One of the other serious errors of dispensational theology is its belief that Jesus will sit on a "literal" throne of David in a "literal" temple, and in a "literal" rebuilt Jerusalem. Jesus is supposedly physically reigning over the world from one place. There are immense theological problems with this interpretation of Scripture.

Since the millennial kingdom is for the glory of the Jews that was suspended when the Jews did not accept the offer of the kingdom by Jesus, the temple and the Levitical sacrifices will be reinstituted.

Dispensationalists believe that the prophecies in Ezekiel of the glorified temple are exclusively intended for the kingdom age where Jesus will be sitting on a literal rebuilt throne of David. The priests who are Levites of Zadok are to officiate. This means that the Levitical priesthood and the Mosaic rituals are resumed.

Anyone who knows the New Testament, particularly the book of Hebrews, should ask, "What about Hebrews 10:4?" This verse states - *"For it is impossible for the blood of bulls and goats to take away sins."* The whole purpose of Hebrews is a warning to the readers against the temptation of returning to an obsolete inferior covenant. Hebrews 8 specifically addresses this point of the obsolete nature of the old covenant.

Dispensationalists are also sensitive of the charges leveled against this theological perspective that this would be negating the atoning work of Christ.

C.I. Scofield has stated:

> Doubtless these offerings will be memorial, looking back to the cross, as the offerings under the old covenant were anticipatory, looking forward to the cross.[24]

Other dispensationalists have followed suit in seeing the resumed sacrifices as only memorials but not propitiatory, but they have a serious internal flaw. Dispensationalists proudly wear the badge, "we are literalists." They have insisted that the kingdom prophecies do enter the kingdom age "absolutely unchanged."

The real problem with dispensational theology on the sacrifices of the kingdom being "memorials" and not "propitious" is that this is not how Ezekiel pictured them. Regarding the nature of the sacrifices we see in Ezekiel 45:13-20:

> [13]*This is the offering that you shall offer: a sixth of an ephah from a homer of wheat; a sixth of an ephah from a homer of barley;* [14]*and the prescribed portion of oil (namely, the bath of oil), a tenth of a bath from each kor (which is ten baths or a homer, for ten baths are a homer);* [15]*and one sheep from each flock of two hundred from the watering places of Israel--for a grain offering, for a burnt offering and for peace offerings, to*

---

[24]   Scofield Reference Bible, p. 890.

__make atonement for them__, declares the Lord God. [16]All the people of the land shall give to this offering for the prince in Israel. [17]It shall be the prince's part to provide the burnt offerings, the grain offerings and the drink offerings, at the feasts, on the new moons and on the sabbaths, at all the appointed feasts of the house of Israel; he shall provide __the sin offering__, the grain offering, the burnt offering and the peace offerings, to make atonement for the house of Israel. [18]Thus says the Lord GOD, 'In the first month, on the first of the month, you shall take a young bull without blemish and cleanse the sanctuary. [19]The priest shall take some of the blood from the __sin offering__ and put it on the door posts of the house, on the four corners of the ledge of the altar and on the posts of the gate of the inner court. [20]And thus you shall do on the seventh day of the month for everyone who goes astray or is naive; so you shall __make atonement for the house__.' (Emphasis mine)

As one can readily see, the sacrifices of Ezekiel were propitious; they did forgive sin as they typified Jesus' coming one time sacrifice of Himself. They were not simply memorials. The idea of the re-institution of "animal" sacrifices is unfathomable. In fact, it is openly insulting to the Lord of glory; it fundamentally assaults the one time propitiatory sacrifice of Jesus. All of biblical revelation in the old covenant was anticipatory, picturing the coming of the "lamb of God" that would take away the sins of the world. The entire sacrificial system of the Mosaic covenant is said to be "a shadow" of good things to come (Hebrews 10:1). In a correct understanding of biblical theology, there is no such thing as a return to "shadows." There is no such thing as the re-institution of animal sacrifices. But, this is the immense problem that dispensationalism faces with its faulty understanding of the kingdom.

Hal Lindsey is still convinced that there will be a physical Jerusalem with Jesus on a physical throne.

> To us the biggest issue is over the question, "Does God keep His promises?" For God unconditionally promised Abraham's descendants a literal world-wide kingdom over which they would rule through their Messiah who would reign upon King David's throne. The Jews who believe in the Messiah will also possess the land...[25]

---

[25]   Lindsey, *The Late Great Planet Earth*, p. 165.

> It is promised that Jerusalem will be the spiritual center of the entire world and that all people of the earth will come annually to worship Jesus who will rule there (Zechariah14:16-21; Isaiah 2:3; Micah 4:1-3). The Jewish believing remnant will be the spiritual leaders of the world and teach all nations the ways of the Lord (Zechariah 8:20-23; Isaiah 66:23).[26]

God does keep His promises, but not the way Lindsey thinks. He has made wonderful promises to the seed of Abraham, and praise God that into one body, whether it is male or female, Jew or Gentile, those who trust in Jesus are the seed of Abraham and heirs of the promise as Galatians 3:28-29 so beautifully states. It is not restricted to some "church age"distinct from the millennial age.

Praise God that there is no need of some physical temple that God couldn't be contained in anyway. Praise God that He is joining both Jew and Gentile into one holy temple of the Lord, and is building that temple **in the Spirit** as Ephesians chapter two tells us.

Further, Lindsey has completely misunderstood the Scripture, and in his attempt to be a so called "literalist," he has brought the majesty of the Most High God down to some mundane absurd condition. Since when do we view the prophecies of Isaiah and Micah depicting the nations of the world streaming supposedly to one physical city to worship? In order to learn of the law of God are we to think that this infers an annual and physical pilgrimage to Jerusalem in the millennial age, like Muslims make to Mecca today?

Are we to think that Jesus sitting on a physical throne, from a physical temple, is more glorious than His ascension to the right hand of God the Father as both Lord and Christ as inspired Peter said on the Day of Pentecost? The apostle Peter said that Jesus' resurrection and ascension is the fulfillment of the promise of God to seat one of his descendants forever upon His throne.

Just like many of the Jews of Jesus' ministry failed to see the Day of their visitation, so dispensationalists have failed to see the glorious fulfillment of all these prophesies in the New Testament. While they have not had the spirit of unbelief like those Jews, they have, nonetheless, missed the whole import of Jesus' comments.

---

[26]   Lindsey, p. 165.

God has not forgotten His promises to Israel. Many have come to pass in this age. Romans 2:29 says that he is a Jew who is one inwardly, who may even be uncircumcised physically.

Which is more honoring to Christ? To see prophesy the way dispensationalism does or seeing it as having been fulfilled in Christ's first advent and His continual ministry among His people, the church? As I set forth in chapter one, the New Testament explicitly views the church as the true Israel of God.

Is it really honoring to see Jesus restricted to a literal throne, a literal temple, and a literal Jerusalem where animal sacrifices are being practiced, and where salvation is the resumption of personal works? Nay, I say it is not Covenant theology that has imposed a system of theology on biblical texts, but it is dispensationalism with its faulty hermeneutic that has led it to incredible admissions that are actually heretical in many respects. The glory of the Gospel can never be replaced by a system of works.

There is no question that Scripture teaches that the Messiah would come and sit on David's throne, but how are we to understand this? Ezekiel, indeed, prophesies the Messiah as sitting on David's throne. Ezekiel 37:24-28 states:

> *[24]My servant David will be king over them, and they will all have one shepherd; and they will walk in My ordinances and keep My statutes and observe them. [25]They will live on the land that I gave to Jacob My servant, in which your fathers lived; and they will live on it, they, and their sons and their sons' sons, forever; and David My servant will be their prince forever. [26]I will make a covenant of peace with them; it will be an everlasting covenant with them and I will place them and multiply them, and will set My sanctuary in their midst forever. [27]My dwelling place also will be with them; and I will be their God, and they will be My people. [28]And the nations will know that I am the LORD who sanctifies Israel, when My sanctuary is in their midst forever.*

Dispensationalism is forced to relegate this prophecy to a millennium that is after Christ's Second Coming. It is forced to think of Jesus occupying this Davidic throne after His Second Coming, and it understands the promises as being fulfilled in a time frame after the Second Coming. The truth is: the promises pictured by Ezekiel were and are being fulfilled presently with the reigning of Jesus right now from David's throne! This truth will be proved exegetically in the next chapter.

With respect to Jesus having to sit on a literal throne, in a literal temple, and from a literal city, we could take a lesson from Stephen's great sermon in Acts 7:44-49:

> [44]*Our fathers had the tabernacle of testimony in the wilderness, just as He who spoke to Moses directed him to make it according to the pattern which he had seen.* [45]*And having received it in their turn, our fathers brought it in with Joshua upon dispossessing the nations whom God drove out before our fathers, until the time of David.* [46]*And David found favor in God's sight, and asked that he might find a dwelling place for the God of Jacob.* [47]*But it was Solomon who built a house for Him.* [48]*However, the Most High does not dwell in houses made by human hands; and the prophet said,* [49]*'Heaven is My throne, and earth is the footstool of My feet; what kind of house will you build for Me? says the Lord; Or what place is there for My repose? Was it not My hand which made all these things?'*

This is a momentous passage because Stephen is inspired by the Holy Spirit to say these things. Acts 6:8-10 affirms that Stephen was full of grace, wisdom, and the Spirit, and he was performing great wonders and signs among the people. For this, Stephen found himself at great odds with the ruling Jewish Sandhedrin. The accusation against Stephen was that he had been supposedly preaching that Jesus would destroy the temple and do away with the Mosaic customs (Acts 6:14). Hence, the Sanhedrin, via the high priest, asks him if this was the case. All of Acts 7 is Stephen's defense and is a masterful synopsis of biblical history up to that point. Of course, Stephen's whole defense was to magnify the Lord Jesus Christ, to point out that Jesus was the promised Messiah, and that Jesus was already sitting on David's throne from heaven and that all men must repent and believe in Him.

In the passage quoted above, Stephen affirms the Davidic covenant, but he makes a most illuminating point: the Davidic covenant never promised some "literal" throne. How could it according to Stephen? He actually quotes Isaiah 66:1 to prove his point. God doesn't dwell in human temples! Heaven is God's throne! Stephen was pointing out that the Davdic covenant was essentially teaching a great spiritual truth – that the emphasis was never upon a "physical" throne in a "physical" place. While it is true that in the old covenant God manifested His presence in the temple during the Davidic covenant, it was not the ultimate picture of God's reign. The ultimate picture would be the coming Messiah, who would dwell among His people, and who would sit on that throne establishing God's kingdom forever. Just as the Mosaic sacrificial system pictured in shadow form the one time sacrifice of Christ, the Davidic covenant in shadow form pictured the reigning of the Messiah, the Lord Jesus, from the throne of God which is at God's right hand in heaven.

Stephen ends his historical recounting by rebuking the Jews for being stiff necked and uncircumcised in heart. This did not go over well with these unbelieving Jews who drove him out of Jerusalem and stoned him to death. Interestingly before his death, Stephen was enabled to see into heaven the Lord Jesus standing at God's right hand (Acts 7:55-56). What throne do you think Jesus was standing by? David's throne in heaven! In the next chapter, we will look in more depth at what Acts 2:29-36 reveals, but for the moment, we understand that Peter preached during the Day of Pentecost a magnificent sermon explicitly stating that Jesus has ascended to heaven to sit on David's throne because he quotes Psalm 110.

The dispensational view that Jesus will sit on a literal throne of David, in a millennial kingdom yet in the future is simply unbiblical. Stephen and Peter refuted this notion, and I will always go with inspired writers of the New Testament over the opinions of men. The idea of the necessity of a physical throne, temple, and city is not consistent with the progress of biblical revelation.

We must never forget what Jesus said to the Samaritan woman at Jacob's well as recorded in John 4:20-24:

> *Our fathers worshiped in this mountain, and you people say that in Jerusalem is the place where men ought to worship. Jesus said to her, 'Woman, believe Me, an hour is coming when neither in this mountain nor in Jerusalem will you worship the Father. You worship what you do not know; we worship what we know, for salvation is from the Jews. But an hour is coming, and now is, when the true worshipers will worship the Father in spirit and truth; for such people the Father seeks to be His worshipers. God is spirit, and those who worship Him must worship in spirit and truth.'*

I fully understand how Dispensationalists approach this passage. They would totally agree that it is true, but only true of "the church age," but not true of the coming millennial kingdom. But, again, this only demonstrates how dishonoring this is to the Lord Jesus Christ's work. Jesus doesn't differentiate between worshipping God during some so called "church age" and "a millennial kingdom" where worship in a literal Jerusalem will be resumed.

What is so sad is that dispensationalism, while affirming these passages as true, relegates them to an age supposedly never seen by the prophets, the church age - this glorious age where Jesus fulfills all these prophecies. Dispensationalism wants us to believe that this glorious age of grace will give way to an age of shadows and meritorious works, where Jesus is confined to a place on earth for a thousand years.

The insistence on some kind of hermeneutic that fails to see metaphors and symbolism of the Old Testament that speak of a more glorious age, an age where Jews and Gentiles are in one glorious spiritual temple, which is being built by the reigning Jesus from David's throne, is a hermeneutic that has failed.

Glorified Christians Living with Mortal Men?

There is one other anomaly of the dispensational premillennial understanding of the kingdom of God. Actually, it is a problem that all premillennialists face. All premillennialists believe that the "rapture" (the catching up of the saints) will occur either before or at the time of the Second Coming, and all premillennialists believe in a thousand year reign on earth after the Second Coming.

According to the dispensational system, the secret Rapture of the church occurs before the Second Coming of Christ. At the supposed second phase of the Second Coming, the raptured church returns with their glorified bodies along with the saints of the Old Testament who also have glorified bodies. Hence, the glorified saints (perfect in body and soul) come to rule with Jesus for a thousand years on earth. They enter the thousand year Judaistic kingdom age as immortal perfected beings. As such, the resurrected Christian has no sin, and cannot even sin, for they are perfected forever, and obviously cannot die.

Supposedly, Jesus and all of us who are with Him, are forcibly ruling the nations with a rod of iron, meaning that we are keeping in check a world that is still affected by sin where death is still going on. Is this the glorious hope that the Scripture speaks? Will I have to put up with sinful human beings for one thousand years as a glorified saint? Will I have to somehow physically keep sinners in check?

Where in all of God's Word to have any hint whatsoever that the glorified saint will be in any place other than with Jesus in the new heavens and new earth? Where does God's Word say that as a glorified saint I have to put up with sin and force people to submit to Jesus? The Scripture is silent of course because such a notion is unthinkable. Dispensationalism's only attempted defense is to assert that such a situation is true because the system demands it. Does this sound like biblical exegesis? No, it is *eisegesis* (reading into the text a foreign concept).

While it is true that historic premillennialists don't buy into the dispensational understanding of a Judaistic millennial kingdom, they still cannot escape from this notion that glorified beings are living with moral beings.

Hal Lindsey has attempted to try to deal with this fact that immortals and mortals are living together. Since he believes that the New Jerusalem is a physical city and not a metaphorical depiction of the church, this is what he says:

> It may be that the Holy City will be suspended above the earth during the thousand-year Kingdom, and that the immoral believers will principally live there. This would help to explain the question of how mortal and immortal beings can live together in the Millennium since the mortals (those believers who live through the Tribulation) will continue to marry, have children, and live ordinary lives. This, of course, won't be true of the immortal believers, since these saints will already have received their resurrection bodies.[27]

We can save ourselves much speculation that is unbiblical if we just accept the fact that the millennial age is **not** separate from the church age. There is no such thing as a distinction between the kingdom of heaven and the kingdom of God. There is no such distinction between Israel and the church. There is no need to complicate that which is plainly and simply stated in God's Word. There is no need of trying to speculate how mortal and immortal beings can live together. There is no need of believing that there are two separate bodily resurrections, separated by a thousand year millennial kingdom. When we force theological systems on the Bible, we get into all sorts of trouble.

---

[27]   Lindsey, *There's A New World Coming*. p. 289.

In this next chapter, I will demonstrate exegetically that we are presently in the millennial kingdom, that Jesus is presently reigning from David's throne in heaven, subduing all His enemies.

Chapter 3

The Millennium

This book's title is – *Preaching and the Victory of the Gospel*. I am fully aware that I have spent considerable time in the previous two chapters seeking to delve into the nature of the covenants of promise contained in the covenant of grace and the nature of what the kingdom is and is not. To advocate that preaching is the primary means for the victory of the gospel requires that we lay a solid foundation – a foundation rooted in sound exegesis of various texts. There must be sufficient biblical warrant to assert that the Great Commission will be fulfilled in history **prior to Christ's Second Coming**, and that we are presently in the Lord Jesus' millennial kingdom. I agree that all issues of eschatology are hermeneutical in scope. It does come down to the exegesis (interpretation) of biblical texts. Who has done a better job at exegesis – dispensationalists, other premillennialists, amillennialists, or postmillennialists? Of course, I am convinced that the postmillennial perspective is the most faithful and accurate exegesis of the Scripture. I wasn't always convinced. Even while I was at Reformed Theological Seminary in the 1970s, I was still not convinced of where I stood. The reason was because I had never studied carefully the issue of eschatology. I knew that being a panmil was totally unacceptable. This is no real view of eschatology, but it has humorously conveyed the attitude of some – it will all pan out in the end. I can assure you that eschatology is no minor point in theology. As set forth in the introduction of this book, our future view is rooted in our eschatological views.

To understand the nature of the "millennium" we need to look at more than just the passage in the book of Revelation that discusses it. All millennial views understand that this period of time encompasses the idea of "the reign of Christ." Therefore, we need to examine those passages that deal with Christ's reign. We need to look at any passage that deals with the Messiah sitting on David's throne. We have to look at any concept associated with Christ's reign. We have to look at the whole picture.

Let's start with the one passage that mentions the thousand year reign of Christ – Revelation 20:1-6:

> *[1]Then I saw an angel coming down from heaven, holding the key of the abyss and a great chain in his hand. [2]And he laid hold of the dragon, the serpent of old, who is the devil and Satan, and bound him for a thousand years; [3]and he threw him into the abyss, and shut it and sealed it over him, so that he would not deceive the nations any longer, until the thousand years were completed; after these things he must be released for a short time. [4]Then I saw thrones, and they sat on them, and judgment was given to them. And I saw the souls of those who had been beheaded because of their testimony of Jesus and because of the word of God, and those who had not worshiped the beast or his image, and had not received the mark on their forehead and on their hand; and they came to life and reigned with Christ for a thousand years. [5]The rest of the dead did not come to life until the thousand years were completed. This is the first resurrection. [6]Blessed and holy is the one who has a part in the first resurrection; over these the second death has no power, but they will be priests of God and of Christ and will reign with Him for a thousand years.*

We could say that Revelation is the focus point for our understanding of the millennium since it is the only chapter in the Bible where we find an explicit mention of "the thousand years." Of course, a millennium is a period of one thousand years. This is the only place in the Bible that associates "a thousand years" with the reign of Christ. We must not forget that the mentioning of the thousand year reign is in the most figurative book in the Bible.

All forms of premillennialism believe this period of time occurs after the Second Coming of Christ. As noted in another chapter, dispensational premillennialists believe this to be a literal "one thousand years" where Christ will reign on earth from a rebuilt Jerusalem, on a literal throne of David, and in a literal rebuilt temple.

Historic premillennialists while agreeing with Dispensationalists that the millennium is an earthly reign of Christ on earth after the Second Coming**Error! Bookmark not defined.**, do not necessarily restrict the millennium to one thousand years. These historic premillennialists do not believe that Jesus is reigning from a literal throne of David or from a rebuilt Jerusalem. For them there is not a return to Judaism as in dispensationalism. It will be a time of worldwide peace, prosperity, and cultural renewal.

Amillennialism and postmillennialism both deny that the millennium is an earthly reign of Christ after the Second Coming. Both place the millennium **before** the Second Coming, and both views understand the thousand years as a figurative term denoting a long period of time between the First and Second Advent of Christ.

The key is: whose exegesis of the relevant texts is the most faithful in understanding the biblical concepts associated with the millennium? Which exegesis lets Scripture interpret Scripture?

Let's now begin breaking down the text in Revelation 20. Obviously, paramount to understanding the nature of the millennium is an understanding of **"the reign of Christ."** What is the nature of the reign? What is the time frame of the reign? Both of these questions are absolutely crucial. Revelation 20 is not the only place in the Bible that refers explicitly to Christ's reigning or infers the reign of Christ. It may be the only place where one thousand years is mentioned, but it is not the only place that Christ's reign is mentioned.

Since the book of Revelation is a very figurative book, the question arises – is it possible for the one thousand years to be taken figuratively without corrupting its meaning? The answer is a definite yes!

The figure represents a perfect cube of ten (10x10x10). The one thousand years is not more literal than what is said in Psalm 50:10 where it says that God owns the cattle on a thousand hills. Does this mean that God doesn't own the cattle on the thousand and first hill? Or when God promises to Israel in Deuteronomy 1:10-11 that he would increase them a thousand fold and bless them, is it really intended to be restricted to a finite number? The text reads:

> *The Lord your God has multiplied you, and behold, you are this day like the stars of heaven in number. May the Lord, the God of your fathers, increase you a thousand-fold more than you are and bless you, just as He has promised you!*

It is obvious that "a thousand-fold" is figurative language for the purpose of conveying God's ongoing blessing to those faithful to Him. This blessing is so huge that it is like "the stars of heaven in number."

Then we have Deuteronomy 7:9 saying:

Know therefore that the Lord your God, He is God, the faithful God, who keeps His covenant and His lovingkindness to a thousandth generation with those who love Him and keep His commandments.

Does His love stop at the one thousand and first generation, or are there only one thousand generations?

A generation in the Bible is commonly seen as around forty years, so if we want to get as literal as Dispensationalists often want, then there are at least 40,000 years in human history, and we are only in the 6000 year range presently.

We also have the imagery of one thousand years being as one day in God's sight. II Peter 3:8 states:

... with the Lord one day is as a thousand years, and a thousand years as one day.

Consequently, there is nothing unusual about figuratively understanding the notion of one thousand years, particularly in the most figurative book in the Bible.

A "Literal" vs. a "Figurative" Interpretation

It is necessary to discuss the nature of figurative language as it pertains to the discipline of hermeneutics (principles of interpretation). In the ongoing theological debate between Covenant theologians and Dispensationalists, this is a hot issue. Dispensationalists claim they are "literalists" and that their approach to Scripture is the only faithful and legitimate way to address biblical texts. They accuse Covenant theology of spiritualizing away God's word.

Dispensationalists like to say that the controversy is between a "literal" versus a "figurative" interpretation, and that they are the champions of a literal view. Charles Ryrie has stated:

The dispensationalist claims to use the normal principle of interpretation consistently in all of his study of the Bible.[1]

If one does not use the plain, normal, or literal method of interpretation, all objectivity is lost. What check would there be on the variety of interpretations which man's imagination could produce if there were not an objective standard which the literal principle provides?[2]

Ryrie has stated that a "literal" approach to Scripture does not rule out the use of figurative language. He states:

Dispensationalists claim that their principle of hermeneutics is that of literal interpretation. This means interpretation which gives to every word the same meaning it would have in normal usage, whether employed in writing, speaking or thinking. This is sometimes called the principle of grammatical-historical interpretation since the meaning of each word is determined by grammatical and historical considerations. The principle might also be called normal interpretation since the literal meaning of words is the normal approach to their understanding in all languages. It might also be designated plain interpretation so that no one receives the mistaken notion that the literal principle rules out figure of speech. Symbols, figures of speech and types are all interpreted plainly in this method and they are in no way contrary to literal interpretation... The *literalist* (so called) is not the one who denies that *figurative* language, that *symbols*, are used in prophecy, nor does he deny that great *spiritual* truths are set forth therein; his position is, simply, that the prophecies are to be *normally* interpreted (i.e., according to the received laws of language) as any other utterances are interpreted – that which is manifestly figurative being so regarded.[3]

Actually, I would not argue with Ryrie on the above quote for the most part. Therefore, there should be no problem in interpreting the one thousand years of Revelation 20 as not being limited to a fixed number of years. We could say that there are certain portions of Scripture where a "literal" interpretation demands an adoption of a figurative meaning;

---

[1]   Ryrie, p. 86.
[2]   Ryrie, p. 88.
[3]   Ryrie, pp. 86-87.

hence, it really isn't accurate to make a dichotomy between a "literal" and "figurative" hermeneutic.

I have always found it perplexing the frequent criticism that dispensationalists level against Covenant theology in its use of figurative language. In their quest for supposed "literalness" Dispensationalists are indeed very inconsistent. They demand literalism in prophetic passages, but then, in some historical passages, they become quite fanciful.

For dispensationalists, Israel must mean Israel, and it can never refer to the church. Canaan must mean Canaan, never heaven. But incredibly, they at times refer to Eve, Rebekah, Ruth, the Shulamite, and Vashi as "types." If Ruth is seen "as a fore view of the church" and the Song of Solomon as the church (not that I agree with this), then why can't Isaiah's prophecies refer to the church?

How is it that Gog and Magog according to Hal Lindsey are modern day Russians? How is it that the kings of the East are the modern day Red Chinese and not what most in history have said - the Assyrians? Why is it that those of the North are not viewed as Babylon but some future Russian army? And why is it that the 250 million of Revelation 9:16 must be literal, and why must it be referring to some future modern day Chinese army, possessing these many foot soldiers?

Why must the 70th week of Daniel's prophecy then not literally follow the 69th week? And why is the entire gap between the 69th and 70th week already four times longer than the entire prophecy of Daniel? I thought prophecy was to be literal? And why must the fourth empire of Daniel's vision be the ten nation Common Market of today? Was this literally stated?

Lindsey dogmatically states in his book, *The Late Great Planet Earth*:

> The time is ripe and getting riper for the Great Dictator, the one we call the "Future Fuehrer." This is the one who is predicted in the Scriptures **very clearly** and called the "Antichrist."[4] (Emphasis mine)

Is that so? Very clearly predicted? And where is that Mr. Lindsey? The word "antichrist" is **never** used to refer to a singular man. Antichrist is not used in Daniel where he is supposedly prophesied by the Dispensationalist.

---

[4]   Lindsey, *The Late Great Planet Earth*, p. 92.

I thought prophecy was to be very literal? So, why is the word "Antichrist" not used there?

Lindsey states:

> This person, the Antichrist, is called the beast because from God's viewpoint that is exactly what he is. The passage is **obviously** talking about a person because the personal pronoun "he" is used.[5] (Emphasis mine)

So, is it obvious? Nowhere in Revelation does it literally say Antichrist is the beast. And why is it obviously "future" events when Revelation says that the events are "soon" to take place. It literally says "soon take place," but dispensationalism, the supposed defender of literalism, ignores the literal historical context of the book of Revelation.

The term "antichrist" is only used four times in the Bible, and they are all found in John's epistles (I John 2:18; I John 2:22; I John 4:2-3; II John 1:7). In I John 2:18, the apostle refers to "many antichrists" that have arisen. In I John 2:22, the apostle specifies exactly who the antichrist is – it is one who denies that Jesus is the Christ. The antichrist is anyone who denies the deity of Christ and who fails to accept Him as the Messiah (Christ). I John 4:2-3 refers to "the spirit of antichrist." This spirit is said to not confess Jesus as coming in the flesh, which is denying His full humanity. And finally, II John 1:7, states that **the** deceiver and **the** antichrist is anyone who does not acknowledge Jesus' full humanity. Theologically, the apostle John is dealing with the Gnostic heresy of the first century that denied the deity and humanity of Jesus. Therefore, Hal Lindsey and all other Dispensationalists who want to refer to the beast as the Antichrist and assign this to some person yet in the future are terribly misinterpreting the texts and guilty of not allowing Scripture to interpret Scripture.

Hal Lindsey sees the 144,000 of Revelation as the following:

> After the Christians are gone, God is going to reveal Himself in a special way to 144,000 physical, literal Jews who are going to believe with a vengeance that Jesus is the Messiah. They are going to be 144,000 Jewish Billy Grahams turned loose on this earth- the earth will never know a period of evangelism like this period…They are going to have the greatest number of converts in

---

[5]   Lindsey, p. 92.

all history. Revelation 7:9-14 says they bring so many to Christ that they can't be numbered.[6]

Really? And how does this incredible evangelism take place without the Holy Spirit who was raptured with the saints before the Tribulation? A bunch of literal Jews are going to accomplish something that the church of Jesus could not accomplish with the Holy Spirit for 2000 years? Now, where is the absolute proof of that again?

Let's consider the liberty that Hal Lindsey took in his interpretation of other portions of Revelation. In his *Apocalypse Code* (1997), essentially an unattributed revision of *There's a New World Coming* (1973), Lindsey thinks that the images that the apostle John saw could easily refer to the following[7]:

*   Supersonic jet aircraft with missiles...
*   Advanced attack helicopters
*   Modern main battle tanks
*   Intercontinental ballistic missiles with Multiple Independently Targeted Reentry vehicles tipped with thermonuclear warheads (ICBM's that are MIRVed).
*   Battlefield artillery and missiles with neutron-nuclear warheads
*   Biological and chemical weapons
*   Aircraft carriers, missile cruisers, nuclear submarines
*   Laser weapons
*   Space stations and satellites
*   the new super secret HAARP weapon system (High-frequency Active Auroral Research Program)

So, in Lindsey's inspired bible code, John's "locusts" become helicopters, "horses prepared for battle" are heavily armed attack helicopters, "crowns of gold" are the helmets worn by pilots, and the "sound of their wings" are the "thunderous sound of many attack helicopters flying overhead." Just as imaginatively, the "bow" wielded by the Antichrist in Revelation 6:1-2, is apparently, "...a code for long range weapons like ICBM's." The reference to the "color of fire and of hyacinth and of brimstone" in Revelation 9:17 become the "Chinese national flag"..."emblazoned on the military vehicles." Lindsey applies the same hermeneutical technique to Zechariah 14:12.

---

6   Lindsey, pp. 99-100.
7   Lindsey, *The Apocalypse Code*, (Palos Verdes, California, Western Front, 1997), p. 36.

Says Lindsey:

> This is exactly the way a neutron bomb works. A soldier is hit by a burst of radiation that leaves only a skeleton within a nanosecond. How could Zechariah have known such a thing 2500 years ago? Once again, the Apocalypse code unlocks the meaning of something not understood for centuries, because the technology for such things did not exist until now.[8]

Now, we can let the Bible's imagery speak for itself, or we can allow dispensationalist Hal Lindsey, who is the supposed "literalist," tell us what is meant in Matthew 24:29 by the strange stellar imagery.

In his book *The 1980's: Countdown to Armageddon,* Lindsey says this about stellar phenomenon:

> Authorities now admit that there have been confirmed sightings of unidentified flying objects. There are even some baffling cases where people under hypnosis say they were taken aboard UFOs by beings from space.

> It's my opinion that UFO's are real and that there will be a proven "close encounter of the third kind" soon. And I believe that the source of the phenomenon is some type of alien being of great intelligence and power.

> According to the Bible, a demon is a spiritual personality in a state of war with God. Prophecy tells us that demons will be allowed to use their powers of deception in a grand way during the last days of history (2 Thess. 2:8-12). I believe these demons will stage a spacecraft landing on Earth. They will claim to be from an advanced culture in another galaxy.[9]

In all seriousness, Hal Lindsey and other dispensationalists do not have any right to accuse those adherents of Covenant theology as violating

---

[8] Quoted from http://www.preteristarchive.com/.

[9] Hal Lindsey, *The 1980's: Countdown to Armageddon,* pp. 34-35. And if reading this isn't convincing enough that Lindsey said it, one can watch him say it on his television show that airs presently as of 2011. One can listen to him discuss demons and UFOs at www.youtube.com/watch?v=olG2R_-2k7c. Such beliefs are very distressing. Nothing Lindsey said in the 1970s that would happen in the 1980s has come to pass. But, as long as he can sell his books, be invited to "prophecy conferences," and have a weekly television program to tout the latest proof for his views, the world will have to put up with his fanciful and unbiblical teaching.

; of "literalness." In the insistence upon a "literal" interpretation, Charles Ryrie has said:

> What check would there be on the variety of interpretations which man's imagination could produce if there were not an objective standard which the literal principle provides?[10]

Does this admonition apply to Hal Lindsey's fanciful imagination? How should we generally approach the subject of hermeneutics? Biblical doctrine should be determined by careful exegesis of texts, comparing Scripture to Scripture.

The Westminster Confession of Faith in 1:9 states:

> The infallible rule of interpretation of Scripture is the Scripture itself; and therefore, when there is a question about the true and full sense of any Scripture, (which is not manifold, but one,) it must be searched and known by other places that speak more clearly.

To conclude this section on hermeneutics, here are some general guidelines that are always important to keep in focus:

1) Scripture is the best interpreter of Scripture
2) Contexts determine the meaning of words
3) The Bible does employ figurative language in many places
4) The New Testament is the best explainer of Old Testament texts
5) Inspired New Testament writers are reliable interpreters of Old Testament texts

Key Elements in the Millennium of Revelation 20

Having taken an excursus to deal with hermeneutical principles, I return to an exegesis of Revelation 20:1-6. What are some of the key elements of Revelation 20:1-6? These questions need to be asked: Who is the angel coming down from heaven with the key to the abyss? What does it mean for this angel to bind the devil for one thousand years? Who are the individuals sitting on thrones with the power to judge? Who is this beast that required some to have his mark on their forehead? Who came to life

---

[10] Ryrie, p. 88.

and reigned a thousand years? What is the first resurrection? And, who are these priests of God that will reign with Jesus for one thousand years?

I am going to give succinct answers to the aforementioned questions, but I will then delve into the exegetical proofs for the answers. Who is the angel coming down from heaven with the key to the abyss who binds the devil for one thousand years? It is none other than the Lord Jesus Christ. Revelation 1:17-18 is contextual proof within the book of Revelation that Jesus Christ is the great angel. The text reads:

> *[17]When I saw Him, I fell at His feet like a dead man, and He placed His right hand on me, saying, 'Do not be afraid; I am the first and the last, [18]and the living One; and I was dead, and behold, I am alive forevermore, and I have the keys of death and of Hades.'*

What does it mean for Jesus Christ to bind the devil for one thousand years? It doesn't mean total cessation of activity for the devil, but it does mean, as the text explicitly states, that the devil no longer has the ability to deceive the nations as he did before Christ's first advent. The abyss is not the final abode for the devil. That is the lake of fire (Matthew 25:41; Jude 6 and 7).

Who are the individuals sitting on thrones with the power to judge? We are given certain clues in the text itself. They are sitting on multiple thrones and judging. The time frame of their sitting on the thrones is the same as when they did not worship the beast nor receive his mark. While the devil is bound, these people participate in the reign of Christ. These persons include both the martyred saints in heaven (the souls of those who had been beheaded for their witness) and those saints who persevered on earth (those who had not worshipped the beast). These persons lived and reigned with Christ a thousand years; hence, these persons are throughout the entirety of Christ's reign. Seeing that these persons are found in the entirety of the millennial reign, they are obviously judging throughout the entirety of the millennium; therefore, it has nothing to do with occupying a throne in the final Day of Judgment. These persons are the saints - Christians! They constitute the church of the Lord Jesus Christ!

Who is this beast that required some to have his mark on their forehead? Without delving into this in great detail, let me just say that Revelation chapters 13 and 17 reveal who this beast of the sea is. The number of his name is 666, and the beast of the sea is said to have seven heads which are seven mountains and seven kings. The beast of the sea is generically imperial Rome with 666 referring specifically to Nero Caesar.[11] While much of Revelation deals with figures of the First Century, it is evident that the Roman Empire represents any establishment raised up in rebellion to Christ and His rule. Psalm 2:6-12 speaks of the installed King upon Mount Zion who is the Son of God and to whom the Father has given the nations as His inheritance. The Son rules the nations with a rod of iron and all those earthly potentates who don't worship the Son will be crushed. The saints who are reigning with Christ during the millennium are exercising regal authority, that is, they are judging. In a forthcoming chapter, we shall see that the church is the agent of the ascended Christ by which Jesus subdues the nations, by which His dominion manifests itself. The saints judging upon thrones are an image of great power backed up by the authority of Christ Himself.

Who came to life and reigned a thousand years? And, what is the first resurrection? The saints who are reigning with Christ, judging on thrones are those who came to life. They have participated in the first resurrection over which the second death has no power; moreover, this same group is said to be priests of God and of Christ who are reigning with Him. The Bible does speak of a spiritual resurrection and a bodily resurrection.

Who are these priests of God and of Christ? They are the saints. The church is clearly said to be a kingdom of priests (Revelation 1:5-6; 5:9-10).

The previous points are a brief summary of the salient features of Revelation 20:1-6. I will now delve into the exegetical proofs of these points. I shall prove from Scripture, by allowing Scripture to interpret Scripture, that Jesus is presently reigning in His millennial kingdom. I shall prove that the church is clearly set forth as the agent of Christ's dominion. I shall prove that Jesus is sitting presently on David's throne. And, I shall prove that the millennial kingdom must be before Christ's Second Coming and that there is only one bodily resurrection and only one judgment that occur on the last day, which is Christ's Second Coming.

All forms of premillennialism cannot be true. Amillennialism, while holding to virtually all of the points I shall make, is deficient in one major area, which is no minor deficiency. It does not believe in the victory of the gospel during the millennial age, and this is amillennialism's Achilles heel. It doesn't fully grasp the magnitude of Jesus' power at the right hand of

---

[11]   For a detailed study of the Beast of Revelation, I encourage readers to see Kenneth L. Gentry, *The Beast of Revelation*, (Tyler, Texas: Institute for Christian Economics, 1989).

God the Father. Only historic and biblical postmillennialism provides us with a hermeneutic that ties all the Scripture together in a glorious presentation of the victorious King of kings and Lord of lords who goes forth conquering to conquer.

Understanding the Devil and His Defeat

Let's now take a look at the biblical texts that substantiate several of the key elements of Revelation 20:1-6. One major key to understanding when the millennium occurs is to understand when Satan, the devil, is bound. The Son of God, as the great angel, comes down from heaven with a great chain to bind the devil for a thousand years. In the immediate context of Revelation 20, Satan is thrown into the abyss for the distinct purpose of not **deceiving the nations any longer** until he is released for a short time at the end of the millennium only to be utterly defeated and thrown into the lake of fire to be tormented forever.

The major feature of Satan's binding is his restriction to deceive the nations. If we can exegetically establish when this binding specifically takes place, we have established the timing of the millennium. This can be ascertained by applying the hermeneutical principle of allowing Scripture to interpret Scripture. This principle, I believe, conclusively demonstrates that the binding of Satan started with the first advent of Jesus, and it is continuing throughout this present age, which is the millennial age. The binding of Satan is not a future event any more than the kingdom of God is a future event.

Jesus Christ has principally defeated Satan by His very advent into this world. His incarnation marked the defeat of Satan; His earthly ministry demonstrated his defeat, and His death on the cross sealed his defeat in fulfillment of biblical prophecy. In I John 3:8 we read:

> *The one who practices sin is of the devil; for the devil has sinned from the beginning. The Son of God appeared for this purpose,* ***to destroy the works of the devil.*** (Emphasis mine)

Jesus' very appearance upon the stage of human history marked the definitive defeat of the devil. To understand how Jesus' incarnation and ministry marked the devil's defeat, we must go back to the dawn of human history – the Garden of Eden. God gave the explicit command to Adam and Eve not to eat of the forbidden fruit of the tree of the knowledge of good and evil. With their subsequent transgression of this command, which is sin, they fell from their original righteousness and communion with God and became dead in sin, and thoroughly polluted or defiled in all areas of soul and body. Nothing escaped sin's pollution; their mind, heart, and will were all impacted. In their physical bodies they bore the consequences of their sin. They would eventually be subject to a physical death.

Adam, being the head of the human race (Genesis 1:26-27; Romans 5:12-14; I Timothy 2:12-15; I Corinthians 11:3, 8, 12) passed on the guilt of sin to all mankind. Romans 5:12-14 specifically states that Adam's one transgression brought death to "all" because "all" sinned. Adam was the representative head of the human race; therefore, his sin became "all" mankind's sin. We could say that the entire human race was in the Garden of Eden with Adam as its representative head. Not only has the guilt of Adam's sin been imputed (transferred) to all mankind, but the corrupt nature has been passed on to all subsequent generations by means of ordinary generation. This explains why David said in Psalm 51:5 that he was conceived in sin and why he says in Psalm 58:3 that we all go astray from birth. This guilt of Adam's sin and this inheritance of a corrupt nature from Adam is known theologically as "Original Sin." *The Westminster Confession of Faith* states the condition of mankind rather succinctly. In chapter 6:4 it says – "From this original corruption, whereby we are utterly indisposed, disabled, and made opposite to all good, and wholly inclined to all evil, do proceed all actual transgressions." Romans chapter three is one of the most specific chapters dealing with all mankind's corruption.

With man's fall into sin, we see in Genesis 3:14-15 the following:

> *The LORD God said to the serpent, "Because you have done this, Cursed are you more than all cattle, and more than every beast of the field; on your belly you will go, and dust you will eat all the days of your life; and I will put enmity Between you and the woman, and between your seed and her seed; He shall bruise you on the head, and you shall bruise him on the heel."*

In dealing with the curse upon the serpent, we do understand from Scripture that the devil inhabited the serpent in order to entice Eve to sin (Genesis 3:1-5; II Corinthans 11:3; I Timothy 2:14; John 8:44). Revelation 12:9 refers to the old serpent.

Revelation 12:9:

> *And the great dragon was thrown down, the serpent of old who is called the devil and Satan, who deceives the whole world; he*

*was thrown down to the earth, and his angels were thrown down
with him.*

More will be said about Revelation 12 in a moment, but Genesis 3:14-15
sets forth a conflict that will mark human history up to the end of the
world. There are two seed lines mentioned: the seed of the woman and the
seed of the serpent. Genesis 3:15 is theologically known as the
"protevangelium." This is the first promise of a Savior to the fallen race.
The seed of the woman is the coming Lord Jesus Christ, together with all
His seed, that is, the church of Christ. The seed of the serpent is the devil
and all who belong to him, that is, the reprobate of mankind. God's
prophesy concerning the devil is that the historic conflict climaxes in the
phraseology "He shall bruise you on the head, and you shall bruise him on
the heel." Satan's defeat in history is promised at the outset of human
history. The prophesy concerning the devil will definitively transpire at the
cross of Calvary. Here, Satan bruises Jesus on the heel, by instigating the
death of Jesus, but it is only a heel bruise because Jesus cannot remain
under the power of death but will rise again. But even the death of Jesus
simultaneously spelled the crushing of the head of the serpent.

The Diabolical Nature of Satan, the Devil

Before I discuss the impact of Jesus' death upon the defeat of Satan, it
would be helpful to consider how diabolical that Satan, the devil, really is.
Names in the Bible reveal the character of a person. God reveals His holy
character via His names; likewise, the devil's diabolical character is
demonstrated via the various names given to him throughout Scripture.
The Hebrew name for the "angel of the abyss" is "Abaddon" and
"Apollyon" in Greek. These words mean "**destroyer**." Hence, Satan is, by
his very nature, a destroyer; he is intent on destroying men's souls, and if
he could destroy Christians, which he cannot, he would.

In John 8:44, Jesus called Satan, the "**father of lies**," and a "**murderer
from the beginning**."

I Peter 5:8 speaks of the devil as our "**adversary**," and as a "**roaring lion**
seeking someone to devour."

In Revelation 12:10, the devil is said to be the "**accuser of the brethren**."
This is one of Satan's favorite tactics, which every Christian needs to be
aware of. Some people think that their sins are so great that they can never
be forgiven.

In II Corinthians 11:12-15, Satan is said to be **"an angel of light**." This of course emphasizes his cunning ability to deceive people into thinking he is light! False apostles are said to be Satan's servants "who disguise themselves as servants of righteousness," when in reality, they are wolves in sheep's clothing. The apostle Paul was speaking here of the Judaizers, who taught that one must submit to the law of Moses in order to be saved. In Galatians 1:6-9, Paul says that the Judaizers were perverting or distorting the gospel, which is why they deserve to be accursed of God.

In Revelation 12:9, Satan is said to be **"the deceiver**," and of course in Revelation 20:3, he is the **"deceiver of the nations**."

In Matthew 13:39 (cf Luke 8:12), John 17:15, and I John 5:19, Satan is called **"the evil one**." In Jesus' parable of the sower and the seed, "the evil one" comes and snatches up the seed that was fallen by the road side. The seed represents the Word of God. In Luke 8:12, Jesus says:

> *And those beside the road are those who have heard; then the devil comes and takes away the word from their heart, so that they may not believe and be saved.*

Corresponding with the devil snatching up the word from men's hearts preventing them from believing and being saved, II Corinthians 4:3-4 states:

> *[3]And even if our gospel is veiled, it is veiled to those who are perishing, [4]in whose case **the god of this world** has blinded the minds of the unbelieving so that they might not see the light of the gospel of the glory of Christ, who is the image of God.* (Emphasis mine)

Some explanation is needed here that is often misunderstood by some Christians. When it says that Satan is the "god of this world," it does not mean that Satan is the owner of this world, nor does it mean that the devil is any kind of rival force to God in the sense that the outcome is questionable as to who will win. Satan is the "god of this world" as the master mind behind the system of belief in rebellion against God, which of course encompasses all those in bondage to him. As the "god of this world," Satan deceives men by blinding their minds, disabling them from seeing the truth of the Gospel and coming to saving faith. Men may think that they have free use of their minds, that their minds are completely autonomous (self-governed). Nothing could be further from the truth. II Timothy 2:24-26 states:

> *[24]The Lord's bond-servant must not be quarrelsome, but be kind to all, able to teach, patient when wronged, [25]with gentleness correcting those who are in opposition, if perhaps God may grant them repentance leading to the knowledge of the truth, [26]and they may come to their senses and escape from the snare of the devil, having been held captive by him to do his will.*

This passage definitively informs us that the devil ensnares men, making them his slaves to do his will. Non-Christians may think they are free, but they aren't. They may think their minds are functioning very well, but they aren't. In a spiritual sense, unbelievers are brain damaged who need to "come to their senses." They may think they know truth, but they don't because genuine truth can only be ascertained via repentance.

In Ephesians 2:1-2, Satan is said to be "**the prince of the powers of the air**." He is a spirit that works in the "sons of disobedience." Satan is the energizing force behind all rebellion to God; he is behind all wars. As Ephesians 2:3 brings out, as sons of disobedience, men live in accord with the lusts of their flesh, indulging in fleshly desires, and are, by nature, children of wrath. Satan is the head of a demonic realm that fell with him.

In John 12:32, Jesus said that Satan is the "**ruler of this world**." This is fundamentally the same as being called the "god of this world." Again, the word "world" can have multiple meanings, but in this context as others, it is a world in rebellion against God. This can be seen in I John 2:15-17 which reads:

> *[15]Do not love the world nor the things in the world. If anyone loves the world, the love of the Father is not in him. [16]For all that is in the world, the lust of the flesh and the lust of the eyes and the boastful pride of life, is not from the Father, but is from*

the world. [17]The world is passing away, and also its lusts; but the one who does the will of God lives forever.

Lust, pride, and covetousness are all characteristics that the "ruler of this world" seeks to foster. It constituted one of the temptations of the devil to Jesus – worship me and I will give you all the glories of the kingdoms of the world. James 4:4 states that "friendship with the world" is hostility toward God.

In Matthew 4:3, the devil is called the "**tempter.**"

In Ephesians 6:16, Satan is **"the evil one"** who shoots fiery arrows at the Christian.

In II Corinthians 6:15, Satan is diametrically opposed to everything that Christ stands for. There is no harmony between Christ and Satan at any point. The devil is devoted to hindering or destroying the kingdom of God. Of course, he cannot prevail in the latter.

Revelation 12

The whole chapter is very instructive in our understanding of Satan and his influence. It demonstrates that there is war between Satan, the great dragon, and the woman with child, who represents the people of God in the Old Testament. Revelation 12:1-2 reads:

A great sign appeared in heaven: a woman clothed with the sun, and the moon under her feet, and on her head a crown of twelve stars; and she was with child; and she cried out, being in labor and in pain to give birth.

The imagery is drawn from that of the Old Testament. The imagery of a pregnant woman travailing to give birth was often used (Isaiah 26:17; 66:7-9; Micah 4:10; 5:3). The imagery of the sun, moon, and twelve stars is definitely drawn from aspects of Joseph's dream (Genesis 37:9). The twelve stars on the woman's crown allude to the twelve tribes of Israel. The child that the woman is about to give birth is no less than Jesus Christ. This is evident from Revelation 12:5:

And she gave birth to a son, a male child, who is to rule all the nations with a rod of iron; and her child was caught up to God and to His throne.

We learn from Psalm 2:6-9 that the king that God installs on Zion is His only begotten Son who is given the nations as His inheritance, and who rules them with a rod of iron. In Isaiah 9:6-7, a son will be born whose government of peace will know no end. This is appropriate imagery because in terms of physical lineage, Israel did give birth to the Messiah. Two of the greatest names in the Old Testament are those of Abraham and David. Matthew's gospel account begins by declaring the genealogy of Jesus Christ as being the son of Abraham and David (Matthew 1:1). Romans 9:5 states that the Christ has come from the fathers according to the flesh; hence, the notion of the people of God of the old covenant (the woman) gives birth to a child, who is the Messiah, is only fitting.

The adversarial relationship of the great dragon with the woman is seen in Revelation 12:3-4:

> *Then another sign appeared in heaven: and behold, a great red dragon having seven heads and ten horns, and on his heads were seven diadems. And his tail swept away a third of the stars of heaven and threw them to the earth. And the dragon stood before the woman who was about to give birth, so that when she gave birth he might devour her child.*

Satan is portrayed as a great red dragon, a monster. This imagery too is drawn from the Old Testament where the enemies of God's people are referred to as dragons (Isaiah 27:1; 51:9). Here in Revelation, the dragon is pictured with having ten horns and seven heads. This imagery of the dragon having a tail that swept away a third of the stars of heaven and throwing them to the earth seeks to portray Satan's rebellion against God. Satan is Beelzebul, the ruler of the demons (Matthew 12:24), and he did lead a third of the angels of heaven in rebellion against God. As Jude 6 indicates, they abandoned their proper abode and are being kept in eternal bonds of darkness for the great Day of Judgment. Revelation 9:1 alludes to Satan as a star from heaven that fell to earth, who has the key of the bottomless pit to unleash a host of demonic spirits.

When Christ was born, Satan was there seeking to devour Him. Historically, King Herod sought to destroy the child that the magi declared to be the Messiah, the King of the Jews (Matthew 2). An angel of the Lord had warned Joseph to flee to Egypt with the child and His mother, which they did. Revelation 12:6 corresponds with what Matthew 2 describes. It reads:

> *Then the woman fled into the wilderness where she had a place prepared by God, so that there she would be nourished for one thousand two hundred and sixty days.*

The church, in her infancy stage, was nourished for the allotted time, the time frame until King Herod died. Upon Herod's death, an angel of the Lord appears to Joseph informing him of Herod's death and that it was safe to return Israel (Matthew 2:19). The going in and out of Egypt with the Christ child was a fulfillment of prophecy (Matthew 2:15; cf Hosea 11:1). It is most interesting how the prophecy of Hosea 11:1 is stated:

> *When Israel was a youth I loved him, and out of Egypt I called My son.*

This demonstrates that in the Lord Jesus Christ, we have Him representing the people of God because the prophecy refers to the infant child as "Israel." The imagery, then, in Revelation 12 corresponds very well with the notion that Satan is out to destroy the church by seeking to destroy its head, but he will obviously fail.

Revelation 12:7-9 conveys the spiritual warfare that is cosmic in scope. This is consistent with what was set forth in Genesis 3:15 where there was prophesied warfare between the seed of the serpent and the seed of the woman. Revelation 12:7-9 states:

> [7]*And there was war in heaven, Michael and his angels waging war with the dragon. The dragon and his angels waged war,* [8]*and they were not strong enough, and there was no longer a place found for them in heaven.* [9]*And the great dragon was thrown down, the serpent of old who is called the devil and Satan, who deceives the whole world; he was thrown down to the earth, and his angels were thrown down with him.*

This warfare entails the Archangel Michael leading God's angels against Satan. This conflict is intense especially in the establishment of God's kingdom in the birth and ministry of the Lord Jesus Christ. The kingdom of God was prophesied by Daniel to be established during the time of the fourth kingdom, which history demonstrated to be the Roman Empire. Jesus was born during the reign of Caesar Augustus. More will be said later about this great prophecy in Daniel 2, but it does emphatically state that the kingdom of God did dawn upon human history in the birth of the Messiah to whom all the nations of the earth belong as his inheritance. This is why the kingdom of God will crush the greatest of human empires and continue to grow in an unprecedented way.

In this spiritual warfare between good and fallen angels pictured in Revelation 12, we see the archangel Michael being successful in driving Satan and his demonic realm "from heaven" and "down to the earth." It is important to understand the imagery's import. It is not so much emphasizing where Satan has fallen to, as much as it conveys Satan losing his influence. The context of Revelation 12 in conjunction with Jesus' ministry conveys this truth. We must keep in mind what I John 3:8 teaches – the Son of God appeared in order to destroy the works of the devil. Satan is being systematically defeated on all fronts. Satan failed to destroy the Christ child; Satan failed to succeed in his temptation of Jesus in the wilderness. Putting this into theological perspective, the temptation of Jesus was an attempt of the devil to destroy the church by having the head of the church sin. Jesus is referred to as the "last Adam" (I Corinthians 15:45; Romans 5:14). Jesus is the representative head of His church, the new Israel. Jesus' baptism by John the Baptist obviously isn't because He is a sinner needing to repent of anything. Jesus' baptism marked his official beginning of His mediatorial ministry as the "last Adam." Jesus must succeed; otherwise, man's redemption fails. Everything was at stake with Jesus' victory over the devil during His forty days of temptation by the devil. We must always understand who sent Jesus into the wilderness after His baptism. It was the Holy Spirit! Mark1:12 states, *"And immediately the Spirit impelled Him to go out into the wilderness."* As it were, the devil threw everything at Him, but he would not succeed. This was a monumental defeat for Satan, which is part of the imagery conveyed in Revelation 12 of Satan being thrown down from heaven to earth. Man's salvation was at stake as to whether Jesus, as the representative head of His people, would succeed. Romans 5:15-21 speaks of the "one act of obedience" of Jesus Christ in securing justification for all in union with Him. This "one act of obedience" actually spans the entirety of Jesus' life leading up to Calvary's cross, which is the climatic death blow to Satan's influence.

Revelation 12:10-11 sets forth the methodical defeat of Satan:

> [10]*Then I heard a loud voice in heaven, saying, 'Now the salvation, and the power, and the kingdom of our God and the authority of His Christ have come, for the accuser of our brethren has been thrown down, he who accuses them before our God day and night.'* [11]*And they overcame him because of the blood of the Lamb and because of the word of their testimony, and they did not love their life even when faced with death.*

This is a magnificent display of the complete victory of Jesus and His church over Satan. One thing to note is that verse 10 explicitly says that *"the kingdom of our God and the authority of His Christ have come."* The kingdom is now. What is the impact of the kingdom having come? Salvation and power has come. The fruit of this salvation with power is that "the accuser of the brethren" has been thrown down. This shows that the phraseology of "been thrown down" means that Satan's influence is being destroyed. The "accuser of the brethren" has lost the power over death that he once had.

The climatic victory of Jesus over the devil in fulfillment of Genesis 3:15 is seen in Hebrews 2:14-17:

> *[14]Therefore, since the children share in flesh and blood, He Himself likewise also partook of the same, **that through death He might render powerless him who had the power of death**, that is, the devil, [15]and might free those who through fear of death were subject to slavery all their lives. [16]For assuredly He does not give help to angels, but He gives help to the descendant of Abraham. [17]Therefore, He had to be made like His brethren in all things, so that He might become a merciful and faithful high priest in things pertaining to God, to make propitiation for the sins of the people.* (Emphasis mine)

This passage explains in more full detail what Romans 5:15-21 conveys about the last Adam, the Lord Jesus Christ whose one act of obedience brings justification of life for all in union with Him. Let's understand how Jesus rendered powerless the devil and just how the devil once had the power of death. The text states that Jesus shares in our humanity. In order to save us from our sins, Jesus had to become a human. Why? Adam as our representative head was a human who brought sin and misery to the human race; hence, the last Adam had to have a real body in order to shed real blood to atone for the sins of His people. This necessity for a body is brought out in Hebrews 2:5-10:

> *Therefore, when He comes into the world, He says, 'Sacrifice and offering You have not desired, but a body You have prepared for Me. In whole burnt offerings and sacrifices for sin You have taken no pleasure'. Then I said, 'Behold, I have come in the scroll of the book it is written of Me to do your will, O God.' After saying above, 'Sacrifices and offerings and whole burnt offerings and sacrifices for sin You have not desired, nor have You taken pleasure in them' (which are offered according to the Law), then He said, 'Behold, I have come to do Your will.' He takes away the first in order to establish the second. By this will we have been sanctified through the offering of the body of Jesus Christ once for all.*

In our being sanctified through Jesus' one sacrifice, we are told in the Hebrews 2 passage that Jesus' death was a propitiation for the sins of His people (v.17). Propitiation is the satisfaction of divine justice by means of a bloody sacrifice. Romans 3:25 demonstrates that Jesus' shed blood is the propitiation for His people's sins. Romans 5:9-10 demonstrates that Jesus' shed blood saves us from God's wrath and reconciles us to a holy God. The Scripture abundantly shows that our sins have separated us from God and have condemned us (Isaiah 59:1-2; Romans 3:10, 19-20; Romans 6:23).

How did Satan have the power of death before the cross? It is as follows: The Bible does show that we are all sinners, having transgressed God's holy law. As I John 3:4 states, sin is defined as transgression of the law. Romans 3:19-20 informs us that we are under the law; therefore, every mouth is stopped. No one can boast that he is innocent before God. To be "under the law" is to be under the constant demand of having to keep it perfectly or else. To be "under the law" is to be under the "dominion of sin." And what does the Bible say that our sins bring as lawbreakers? Death! In fact, there is the fear of death and the instinctive knowledge that we deserve judgment.

The devil had the power of death in the sense that he is the "tempter" of men. When the devil tempts us, he knows that our sinful natures will take over and carry through to the thought and performance of that sin. At least this is the case in the unbeliever who is enslaved to sin and Satan. Because of our sins, we know we deserve judgment, which brings a definite element of fear into our lives. As slaves of Satan in our natural or unbelieving state, we are constantly being dominated by fear, which is exactly what the devil wants. One of the blessed realities when we by faith trust in Christ is that we are delivered from the devil's bondage, from his oppressive accusations against us. In Christ, the Christian no longer has to live in fear of judgment because Jesus has paid for his sins once and for all. I John 4:16-18 states:

> *We have come to know and have believed the love which God has for us. God is love, and the one who abides in love abides in God, and God abides in him. By this, love is perfected with us, so that we may have confidence in the day of judgment; because as He is, so also are we in this world. There is no fear in love; but perfect love casts out fear, because fear involves punishment, and the one who fears is not perfected in love.*

Even though Jesus' atoning death has provided the actual basis for our reconciliation to a holy God and removed any just reason for us being condemned, the devil still wants to come to "Jesus' brethren" and accuse them day and night. What we must always do is this: whenever Satan wants to accuse us because of the still remaining presence of sin in us, we must simply tell him to get lost! We must boldly say to the devil, "I know I still have sin, but praise God, my redeemer Jesus paid the price for my transgressions, and I stand forgiven in Him. So devil, you haven't reminded me of something I don't already know. I know I am unworthy to receive anything, but thankfully, my salvation is not based on my actions but upon the actions of my atoning substitute, so get lost!"

Jesus has rendered the devil powerless through His death and subsequent resurrection from the dead. Because Jesus was victorious over death, all those in union with Him will also be victorious (Romans 6:6-10; I Corinthians 15:50-58). I Corinthians 15:55-57 is magnificent:

> *O death where is your victory? O death, where is your sting? The sting of death is sin, and the power of sin is the law; but thanks be to God, who gives us the victory through our Lord Jesus Christ.*

Note the phrase, "the power of sin is the law." As the apostle Paul mentioned in Romans 7:7-13, the problem with all of us is not the law of God, for it is holy, righteous, and good. The culprit is sin, for it takes the law and "throws it into our face." The law shows us our sin. Death's sting is due to sin, and sin derives its power to condemn from God's law. Satan, in tempting us to sin which we did, had the power of death in this sense. But, with the atoning sacrifice of Jesus for the sins of His people, the "accuser of the brethren" has indeed been cast down! The devil has lost his stranglehold upon us. This is why Revelation 12:11 can say that "they" (the church) overcame him because of the blood of the Lamb and because of the word of their testimony. By faith we enter into that vital union with Christ. Every time that a sinner is saved by grace through faith, Satan experiences more and more defeat.

Colossians 2:13-15 expresses most beautifully Jesus' triumph over Satan and the demonic realm at His death:

> *When you were dead in your transgressions and the uncircumcision of your flesh, He made you alive together with Him, having forgiven us all our transgressions, having canceled out the certificate of debt consisting of decrees against us, which was hostile to us; and He has taken it out of the way, having nailed it to the cross. When He had disarmed the rulers and*

authorities, He made a public display of them, having triumphed over them through Him.

This beautifully shows that the massive "certificate of debt of decrees" against us was cancelled out. That certificate debt of decrees was the law of God demanding perfect obedience. Since we all miserably fail what a blessing when all our transgressions are erased as if they never existed! Hence, Jesus' death was indeed a disarming of rulers and authorities demonstrating that they had been defeated.

The Binding of Satan

Revelation 20 clearly mentions that Jesus would bind the devil for a thousand years. This binding manifests itself in his **inability to deceive the nations** as he once did. Revelation 12:9 clearly refers to Satan's casting down to the earth as, essentially, his inability to deceive the nations.

As I noted previously, one of the most important eschatological questions is: **when is the millennium?** So much depends upon when this occurs. Is the millennium before or after the Second Coming? This is equally paramount. One of the keys to understanding when the millennium occurs pertains to when Satan is said to be bound. If we can exegetically prove that Satan's binding occurs before Jesus' Second Coming, then every expression of premillennialism suffers a fatal blow.

We are told that Satan was bound during Jesus' earthly ministry, prior to his death and therefore prior to His Second Coming.

Matthew 12:22-29

[22]Then a demon-possessed man who was blind and mute was brought to Jesus, and He healed him, so that the mute man spoke and saw. [23]All the crowds were amazed, and were saying, 'This man cannot be the Son of David, can he?' [24]But when the Pharisees heard this, they said, 'This man casts out demons only by Beelzebul the ruler of the demons.' [25]And knowing their thoughts Jesus said to them, 'Any kingdom divided against itself is laid waste; and any city or house divided against itself will not stand. [26]If Satan casts out Satan, he is divided against himself; how then will his kingdom stand? [27]If I by Beelzebul cast out demons, by whom do your sons cast them out? Consequently they shall be your judges. [28]But if I cast out demons by the Spirit

of God, then the kingdom of God has come upon you." [29]Or how can anyone enter the strong man's house and carry off his property, unless he first binds the strong man? And then he will plunder his house.'

This passage definitively states that **Jesus bound Satan**. Satan is the strong man in Jesus' comments. The whole text deals with Jesus casting out demons. The Pharisees accused Jesus of casting out demons by the ruler of the demons, Beelzebul. This is ridiculous according to Jesus because a kingdom cannot stand if it is divided. In other words, Satan would never cast out his own demons. We must not miss the momentous comment of Jesus: "but if I cast out demons by the Spirit of God, then **the kingdom of God has come upon you.**" Jesus just told us when the kingdom of God has come. It **has** come! It is already here! **This means that the millennium is now!** One of the salient features of Satan's binding is that demons are subject to Jesus' authority And, as we shall see, demons are not only subject to Jesus' direct authority but also to those who have been given a derivative authority from Jesus – His apostles. Jesus gave this derivative power to His disciples (Matthew 10:1; Mark 6:7; 9:38; Luke 10:17; Acts 5:16; 8:7; 16:16-18; 19:12).

Luke 10:8-11; 17-19

One of the passages that deserves special attention describing the derivative authority given to Jesus' disciples is Luke 10:8-11; 17-19 which states:

*[8]Whatever city you enter and they receive you, eat what is set before you; [9]and heal those in it who are sick, and say to them, 'The **kingdom of God has come near to you.**' [10]But whatever city you enter and they do not receive you, go out into its streets and say, [11]'Even the dust of your city which clings to our feet we wipe off in protest against you; yet be sure of this, that **the kingdom of God has come near.**' [17]The seventy returned with joy, saying, 'Lord, even the demons are subject to us in Your name.' [18]And He said to them, '**I was watching Satan fall from heaven like lightning.**' [19]Behold, I have given you authority to tread on serpents and scorpions, and **over all the power of the enemy**, and nothing will injure you. (Emphasis mine)*

I noted in Revelation 9:1 and 12:9 that Satan was said to have fallen from heaven to earth as a star, and that he who deceived the world had been thrown down to the earth. With the demons subject to the disciples of Jesus, Jesus said that Satan had fallen from heaven like lightning. This is figurative language denoting that the kingdom of Satan is being deposed by the onset of the kingdom of God.

When Jesus sent the seventy out to preach, He empowered them to preach the gospel of the kingdom. Matthew 4:23 and 9:35 both mention that Jesus was going throughout the villages and cities preaching the gospel of the kingdom. **The kingdom of God had already arrived!** In the kingdom's arrival, Satan is seen as falling from heaven like lightning.

The main aspect of Satan's kingdom and power was his ability to deceive the nations. In the Old Testament, the devil was always deceiving nations; he was always the source behind all idolatry. Jesus referred to Satan as Beelzebub. Baal worship was a pervasive form of idolatry in the pagan world that even had greatly infected national Israel. The world was deceived; it was in darkness and spiritual death. As the "god of or ruler of this (age)," the world was in the vice grip of Satan's kingdom for the most part. So, when the devil offered the kingdoms of the world to Jesus, it was the nations under his slavery to do his will. As noted earlier in the various names of Satan, Satan has blinded the minds of the unbelieving so that they could not see the gospel (II Corinthians 4:3-4); those in unbelief are held captive by him to do his will (II Timothy 2:26); those dead in their sins are walking according to the course of this world indulging in all kinds of evil behavior, walking according to the prince of the power of the air, of the spirit that is now working in the sons of disobedience (Ephesians 2:1-3). While this is still true of unbelievers today, it is not the same because of the gospel.

Luke 4:14-21

The world prior to Jesus' first advent lay in deception, darkness, and spiritual death. Satan had a free hand in deceiving the nations, but this all changed with Christ's coming. Isaiah 61:1-2 had prophesied the following:

> *[1]The Spirit of the Lord God is upon me, Because the Lord has anointed me to bring good news to the afflicted; He has sent me to bind up the brokenhearted, to proclaim liberty to captives and freedom to prisoners; [2]to proclaim the favorable year of the Lord and the day of vengeance of our God; to comfort all who mourn,*

This prophecy was principally fulfilled in Luke 4:14-21:

> *[14]And Jesus returned to Galilee in the power of the Spirit, and news about Him spread through all the surrounding district. [15]And He began teaching in their synagogues and was praised by*

all. [16]And He came to Nazareth, where He had been brought up; and as was His custom, He entered the synagogue on the Sabbath, and stood up to read. [17]And the book of the prophet Isaiah was handed to Him. And He opened the book and found the place where it was written, [18]'The Spirit of the Lord is upon Me, because He anointed Me **to preach the gospel to the poor***. He has sent Me to proclaim release to the captives, and recovery of sight to the blind, to set free those who are oppressed, [19]to proclaim the favorable year of the Lord.' [20]And He closed the book, gave it back to the attendant and sat down; and the eyes of all in the synagogue were fixed on Him. [21]And He began to say to them, 'Today this Scripture has been fulfilled in your hearing.'*
(Emphasis mine)

The first advent of Jesus changed everything. It affected a radical change in Satan's kingdom. His stranglehold of power over men was broken. The favorable year of the Lord had come! Captives were being set free, spiritually blind men were now seeing, and those being oppressed by the devil were being set free. We are reminded of what Jesus said in John 8:36 – *"If therefore the Son shall make you free, you shall be free indeed."* What was the mechanism for this blessed activity? **The preaching of the gospel!** We will develop this point more fully in another chapter, but one should see why I titled this book, *Preaching and the Victory of the Gospel.*

The exorcisms performed by Jesus and His disciples marked the great conflict between the kingdom of Satan and the kingdom of God. And who is winning? Peter, in Acts 10:38, described the ministry of Jesus as one anointed of God with the Holy Spirit and with power to heal all who were oppressed by the devil. Not only did Jesus' casting out demons testify to His divinity (Mark 3:11), but it testified to their eventual torment (Matthew 8:29). Jesus' exorcisms and those done by His disciples in His name marked the plundering of Satan's house and that God's kingdom had arrived with great power.

John 12:27-33

God the Father had confirmed from heaven that Jesus had come to do His will. We read in John 12:27-33:

Now My soul has become troubled; and what shall I say, 'Father, save Me from this hour'? But for this purpose I came to this hour. 'Father, glorify Your name' Then a voice came out of heaven: 'I have both glorified it, and will glorify it again.' So the crowd of people who stood by and heard it were saying that it *had thundered; others were saying, 'An angel has spoken to Him.'Jesus answered and said, 'This voice has not come for My sake, but for your sakes. **Now judgment is upon this world; now the ruler of this world will be cast out.** And I, if I am lifted up from the earth, will draw all men to Myself.' But He was saying this to indicate the kind of death by which He was to die.* (Emphasis mine)

We must learn, in our quest to do sound biblical exegesis, that we must let Scripture interpret Scripture. If only there would be more serious attention to this, then we would be spared so much divergence of opinion in the Christian community. We can never interpret one portion of Scripture so as to contradict another. Hence, when Jesus said that judgment is upon this world and that the ruler of this world will be cast out, we must accept this as true and not try to explain it away with our theological biases. Satan is now being cast out! How so? We know that Satan's activity isn't completely stopped, for the apostles after Jesus' death had to contend with demons. We know that Peter says that Satan walks about like a roaring lion seeking someone to devour. We know Paul said that those in the church at Ephesus should not give an opportunity to the devil (Ephesians 4:27), and we know that Paul told the Thessalonians that he had been hindered by Satan from coming to them as planned (I Thessalonians 2:18).

Proper exegesis must always consider words in their context; it must take into account figurative language; and it must allow Scripture to interpret Scripture. The phrase "now the ruler of this world will be cast out" is essentially the same as "plundering the strong man's house," as "seeing Satan fall from heaven like lightning," and as "being cast down from heaven to earth." They are all various designations of the same concept- Satan's domain is being destroyed! Notice in the John 12 passage that Jesus' comment about the ruler of this world being judged and cast out is juxtaposed with his comment that He, if lifted up, will draw all men to Himself. This is consistent with all that we have said. When Jesus read from Isaiah's scroll (Isaiah 61) in the synagogue at Nazareth, He said, "*Today this Scripture has been fulfilled in your hearing*" (Luke 4:21). The gospel is a proclamation that through Jesus' death, salvation has come to men once held in captivity to the devil. Jesus alludes to His being lifted up (His death on the cross) as the basis of exercising faith in Him (John 3:14-16). Every time a person cries out in repentance of sins and turns in faith to Jesus, Satan's kingdom has been assaulted and decimated.

The binding of Satan is specifically said to have occurred during Jesus' ministry. This is exactly in conformity with Revelation 20:1-3. **This**

means that we are in the millennium right now! It means that Jesus is presently reigning! Not only does this one truth confirm the present reality of Jesus' millennial kingdom, but there are other aspects of Revelation 20 that confirm it.

Saints Reigning With Jesus

Revelation 20:4-6

> *⁴Then I saw thrones, and they sat on them, and judgment was given to them. And I saw the souls of those who had been beheaded because of their testimony of Jesus and because of the word of God, and those who had not worshiped the beast or his image, and had not received the mark on their forehead and on their hand; and they came to life and reigned with Christ for a thousand years. ⁵The rest of the dead did not come to life until the thousand years were completed. This is the first resurrection. ⁶Blessed and holy is the one who has a part in the first resurrection; over these the second death has no power, but they will be priests of God and of Christ and will reign with Him for a thousand years.*

There is another avenue to take to prove that we are presently in the millennial kingdom and that it is before Christ's Second Coming. It is the proof of the saints reigning with Jesus. If we can ascertain from Scripture **when the saints reign**, then we have determined the time frame of the millennium. What do we see from this passage? We see saints sitting on thrones. Surely, these are not physical thrones. Note it is plural (thrones). There are not millions of physical thrones all over the earth where Christians are sitting on them exercising authority over subjects. This should serve as a hermeneutical lesson to all Dispensationalists who insist that Jesus' throne in the millennial kingdom must be in a literal city and upon a literal throne. Well, if this is the hermeneutic they constrain themselves to, then there are also millions and millions of little, literal thrones somehow scattered around the earth with Christians literally sitting on them. I trust that one can see how this is not good exegesis. A "throne" is a figure of speech denoting the reign of the saint, that is, his regal authority derived from Christ.

There are several New Testament passages referring to Christians as presently judging.

I Corinthians 6:1-4

> *[1]Does any one of you, when he has a case against his neighbor, dare to go to law before the unrighteous and not before the saints? [2]Or do you not know that **the saints will judge the world**? If the world is judged by you, are you not competent to constitute the smallest law courts? [3]Do you not know that **we will judge angels**? How much more matters of this life? [4]So if you have law courts dealing with matters of this life, do you appoint them as judges who are of no account in the church?* (Emphasis mine)

The pertinent questions are: when and how do the saints, reigning with Jesus, judge? The first thing we must observe is that the judging of the world and of angels pertains to the millennial age. It does not pertain to the Great Day of Judgment. The two passages reflecting this Great Day of Judgment are Revelation 20:11-15 and Matthew 25:31-46. On this Day of Judgment all men will be judged by the Lord Jesus and those whose sins were covered by Jesus, who had experienced the first resurrection (spiritual), will be exonerated. Nothing is ever said of saints judging on that day but being judged. In the judgment of angels, it must be referring to "fallen angels" when the saints exercise authority over them in casting them out. God's holy angels have nothing to be judged about – they are perfectly holy.

How is it that the saints will judge the world? John Calvin's comments are helpful:

> Here we have an argument from the less to the greater; for Paul, being desirous to show that injury is done to the church of God when judgments on matters of dispute connected with earthly things are carried before unbelievers, as if there were no one in the society of the godly that was qualified to judge, reasons in this strain:"Since God has reckoned the saints worthy of such honor, as to have appointed them to be judges of the whole world, it is unreasonable that they should be shut out from judging as to small matters, as persons not qualified for it." Hence it follows, that the Corinthians inflict injury upon themselves, in resigning into the hands of unbelievers the honor that has been conferred upon them by God.

> What is said here as to *judging the world* ought to be viewed as referring to that declaration of Christ: When the Son of Man shall come, ye shall sit, etc. (Matthew 19:28). For all power of

judgment has been committed to the Son, (John 5:22), in such a manner that he will receive his *saints* into a participation with him in this honor, as assessors. Apart from this, they *will judge the world*, as indeed they begin already to do, because their piety, faith, fear of the Lord, good conscience, and integrity of life, will make unbelievers altogether inexcusable, as it is said of Noah, that *by his faith he condemned* all the men of his age (Hebrews 11:7).

...What he finds fault with in the Corinthians is simply this, that they carry their disputes before unbelieving judges, as if they had none in the church that were qualified to pass judgment, and farther, he shows how much superior is the judgment that God has assigned to his believing people.

...The words rendered *in you* mean here, in my opinion, *among you*. For whenever believers meet in one place, under the auspices of Christ, there is already in their assembly a sort of image of the future judgment, which will be perfectly brought to light on the last day. Accordingly Paul says, that the world is judged in the Church, because *there* Christ's tribunal is erected, from which he exercises his authority.[12]

Matthew 19:28 and Luke 22:29-30

And Jesus said to them, "Truly I say to you, that you who have followed Me, in the regeneration when the Son of Man will sit on His glorious throne, you also shall sit upon twelve thrones, judging the twelve tribes of Israel. (Matthew 19:28)

[29]And just as My Father has granted Me a kingdom, I grant you [30]that you may eat and drink at My table in My kingdom, and you will sit on thrones judging the twelve tribes of Israel. (Luke 22:29-30)

---

[12]   Calvin's New Testament Commentaries on I Corinthians 6:1-3, pp. 118-119.

The two passages are essentially referring to the same teaching of Jesus but from two different gospel writers. Matthew uses the word "regeneration" while Luke uses the word "kingdom." This should help us understand what Matthew means by "regeneration." It refers to the kingdom of God, and it refers to the period beginning with Jesus' ministry. John Calvin makes these comments on the meaning of "regeneration:"

> *In the regeneration.* Some connect this term with the following clause. In this sense, *regeneration* would be nothing else than the renovation which shall follow our restoration, when life shall swallow up what is mortal, and when our mean body shall be transformed into the heavenly glory of Christ. But I rather explain *regeneration* as referring to the first coming of Christ; for then the world began to be renewed, and arose out of the darkness of death into the light of life. And this way of speaking occurs frequently in the Prophets, and is exceedingly adapted to the connection of this passage. For the renovation of the Church, which had been so frequently promised, had raised an expectation of wonderful happiness, as soon as the Messiah should appear; and therefore, in order to guard against that error, Christ distinguishes between the beginning and the completion of his reign.[13]

Regarding the meaning of those sitting on thrones and judging the twelve tribes of Israel, Calvin makes this observation:

> *Verily I say to you.* That the disciples may not think that they have lost their pains, and repent of having begun the course, Christ warns them that the glory of his kingdom, which at that time was still hidden, was about to be revealed. As if he had said, "There is no reason why that mean condition should discourage you; for I, who am scarcely equal to the lowest, will at length ascend to my throne of majesty. Endure then for a little, till the time arrive for revealing nay glory." And what does he then promise to them? They shall be partakers of the same glory. *You also shall sit on twelve thrones.* By assigning to them *thrones,* from which they may *judge the twelve tribes of Israel,* he compares them to assessors, or first councilors and judges, who occupy the highest seats in the royal council. We know that the number of those who were chosen to be apostles was *twelve,* in order to testify that, by the agency of Christ, God purposed to collect the remnant of his people which was scattered. This was a very high rank, but hitherto was concealed; and therefore Christ holds their wishes in

---

[13] Calvin's New Testament Commentaries, Matthew, Mark, and Luke, Vol.2, p. 262.

suspense till the latest revelation of his kingdom, when they will fully receive the fruit of their election. And though the kingdom of Christ is, in some respects, manifested by the preaching of the Gospel, there is no doubt that Christ here speaks of the last day.[14]

Later, I shall develop more fully the magnificent passage in Acts 2 where Peter confirms that Jesus ascended to David's throne, which is in heaven, in fulfillment of II Samuel 7, Daniel 7, and Psalm 110. We see Jesus testifying that when He sits on His throne, His apostles (His preachers) shall also sit on twelve thrones judging the twelve tribes of Israel. Jesus' preachers demonstrate their judgment upon the twelve tribes by their gospel preaching. This is seen throughout the book of Acts, particularly Paul's preaching. Who was Paul's greatest adversary in his ministry? Apostate Judaism! Paul makes this scathing remark about the apostate Jews in I Thessalonians 2:14 -16:

> [14]*For you, brethren, became imitators of the churches of God in Christ Jesus that are in Judea, for you also endured the same sufferings at the hands of your own countrymen, even as they did from the Jews,* [15]*who both killed the Lord Jesus and the prophets, and drove us out. They are not pleasing to God, but hostile to all men,* [16]*hindering us from speaking to the Gentiles so that they may be saved; with the result that they always fill up the measure of their sins but wrath has come upon them to the utmost.*

We also see this most telling judgment upon apostate Judaism in Acts 13:44-47:

> [44]*The next Sabbath nearly the whole city assembled to hear the word of the Lord.* [45]*But when the Jews saw the crowds, they were filled with jealousy and began contradicting the things spoken by Paul, and were blaspheming.* [46]*Paul and Barnabas spoke out boldly and said, 'It was necessary that the word of God be spoken to you first; since you repudiate it and judge yourselves unworthy of eternal life, behold, we are turning to the Gentiles.'* [47]*For so the Lord has commanded us, 'I have placed you as a light for the Gentiles, that you may bring salvation to the end of the earth.'*

In Paul and Barnabas' preaching, the unbelieving Jews **judged themselves** unworthy. We must understand that once Jesus ascended to God's throne, which is David's throne, He began to subdue all His enemies, and some of

---

[14]   Calvin, Vol.2, pp. 261-262.

the first were apostate Jews. Whenever anyone rejects the preaching of His anointed preachers, they reject Jesus, thereby condemning themselves. It is wholly true that when Jesus sat on His glorious throne, then the saints sat on thrones rendering judgment.

Yes, it does say in Matthew 25:31-46 that when Jesus comes in His glory with all the angels that He will sit on His throne and gather all the nations before Him and pass the final judgment. This does not mean that this is when He assumed His throne because Scripture already stated that Jesus was on His throne (Daniel 7:13-14; Acts 2:29-36). This simply means that Jesus will sit on His throne and judge the nations. Anytime a king sits on his throne, he renders judgment. Matthew 25 isn't the first time Jesus will sit on His throne.

Two Types of Resurrection

In Revelation 20, there are two types of resurrection being referred to. One is experienced by the saints who are sitting on the thrones, and who are also called priests of God. They experience what is called, "the first resurrection." The text says that the rest of the dead did not come to life until after the thousand years. Those who experience the first resurrection are those over which the second death has no power. Moreover, those experiencing the first resurrection are said to be "priests of God and of Christ" who are reigning with Christ for a thousand years.

First Resurrection- A Spiritual One

Those saints who are sitting on thrones and judging are reigning with Jesus during the millennium. They are also those who have experienced the blessed first resurrection, which is a spiritual one. This resurrection, which is just as powerful as a physical one, raises those who are dead in their sins to newness of life.

John 5:24-29

The words of Jesus should be quite sufficient to prove there are two resurrections, but one is spiritual and the other is bodily. John 5:24-29 states the words of Jesus:

> *24Truly, truly, I say to you, he who hears My word, and believes Him who sent Me, has eternal life, and does not come into*

judgment, but has passed out of death into life. ^{25}Truly, truly, I say to you, an hour is coming and now is, when the dead will hear the voice of the Son of God, and those who hear will live. ^{26}For just as the Father has life in Himself, even so He gave to the Son also to have life in Himself; ^{27}and He gave Him authority to execute judgment, because He is the Son of Man. ^{28}Do not marvel at this; for an hour is coming, in which all who are in the tombs will hear His voice, ^{29}and will come forth; those who did the good deeds to a resurrection of life, those who committed the evil deeds to a resurrection of judgment.

Let's follow the words of Jesus very carefully and see how they substantiate what Revelation 20 teaches. First, Jesus affirms that every one who hears "My word" and believes Him who sent me has eternal life. Jesus is clearly talking about the resurrection of a soul. This person who believes in His word does not come into judgment, but has passed out of death into life. The one who hears the Word and believes in Christ "**has passed**" out of death into life. The verb tense "*metabebayken*" is the perfect tense, meaning that which has occurred at a given point but then whose result continues. In other words, upon belief in Jesus, the Christian possesses eternal life, and this eternal life continues on into the future. Is this not what Revelation 20:6 states? The one experiencing the first resurrection has nothing to fear of the second death, which is a casting into the lake of fire (Revelation 20:14). Jesus said that an hour is coming and **now is** when the dead will hear the voice of the Son of God, and those who hear will live. This confirms that this is a spiritual resurrection because Jesus said the hour "now is." There are other places in the New Testament that speak of a spiritual resurrection.

Then Jesus says that "an hour is coming" in which all in their **tombs** will hear Jesus' voice and will come forth, that is, physically resurrected. In this bodily resurrection, there are two aspects to it but still only one resurrection. This bodily and general resurrection entails the good who are raised to life, and those who did evil and are raised to judgment. It is noteworthy that the first resurrection referred to in verse 24 pertains to "an hour that is" as opposed to a resurrection in verse 28 pertaining "to an hour that is coming." Two things key us in that the latter resurrection is a bodily resurrection. The text refers to "tombs." Nothing is said in verse 24 about tombs. Also, those who hear Jesus in this resurrection is yet in the future. We can safely conclude that verse 24 pertains to a spiritual resurrection (first resurrection) while verse 28 pertains to a physical resurrection (second resurrection).

John 10:27-28

> ^{27}*My sheep hear My voice, and I know them, and they follow Me;* ^{28}*and I give eternal life to them, and they will never perish; and no one will snatch them out of My hand.*

In this first or spiritual resurrection, those who were dead must hear the voice of Jesus in order to live. Those who hear Jesus' voice become His disciples and are eternally secure in Christ.

John 8:47

> *He who is of God hears the words of God; for this reason you do not hear them, because you are not of God.*

What a magnificent passage that simply but profoundly sets forth the wonderful doctrine of God's election. Only those of God hear the words of God; the reprobate of mankind doesn't hear them and respond.

Romans 10:13-14

> ^{13}*For whoever will call on the name of the Lord will be saved.* ^{14}*How then will they call on Him in whom they have not believed? How will they believe in Him whom they have not heard? And how will they hear without a preacher?*

To be saved, a person must call on Jesus, but how can they call on Jesus unless they hear Jesus speak unto their hearts? A man must hear the voice of the Son in order to be raised to newness of life. And, as we shall see in a later chapter, the role of a human preacher is absolutely essential in the overall plan of God, not that He is restricted to human agents.

Romans 6:5-11

Baptism pictures union with Christ as its dominating idea. The passage states:

> ^{5}*For if we have become united with Him in the likeness of His death, certainly we shall also be **in the likeness of His resurrection**, ^{6}knowing this, that our old self was crucified with Him, in order that our body of sin might be done away with, so that we would no longer be slaves to sin; ^{7}for he who has died is freed from sin. ^{8}Now if we have died with Christ, we believe that **we shall also live with Him**, ^{9}knowing that Christ, having been raised from the dead, is never to die again; death no long is*

*master over him. [10]For the death that He died, He died to sin, once for all; but the life that He lives, He lives to God. [11]Even so consider yourselves to be dead to sin, but **alive to God in Christ Jesus**.* (Emphasis mine)

In this union with Christ, we are united with Him in the likeness of His death, and we shall also be with Him in the likeness of His resurrection. Baptism pictures the death of our old nature in Christ. When He was buried, our sins were buried with Him. The bondage to the sinful nature is forever gone. We are freed from sin's enslaving power. If we have died in Jesus, we shall also live with Him. In Jesus, we are alive. Just as Jesus was raised from dead with death no longer master over Him, we too are spiritually raised from the dead to no longer have sin as our master.

Romans 5:17

For if by the transgression of the one, death reigned through the one, much more those who receive the abundance of grace and of the gift of righteousness will reign in life through the One, Jesus Christ.

This is a very fitting passage corresponding closely with Revelation 20 where those experiencing the first resurrection will reign with Christ for a thousand years and where the second death has no power over them. In our passage in Romans 5, the contrast is being drawn between Adam and Christ. Adam brought death for all in union with him, but Jesus brought life for all in union with Him.

Colossians 2:12-13

*[12]Having been buried with Him in baptism, in which you were also **raised up with Him through faith** in the working of God, who **raised Him from the dead**. [13]When you were dead in your transgressions and the uncircumcision of your flesh, He **made you alive together with Him**, having forgiven us all our transgressions.* (Emphasis mine)

This passage speaks of a spiritual resurrection very closely aligned with Romans 6. Note that faith is the operative instrument that brings about the reality of "raised up with Him." We are made alive via this spiritual resurrection.

Ephesians 2:4-6

> *⁴But God, being rich in mercy, because of His great love with which He loved us, ⁵even when we were dead in our transgressions, **made us alive together with Christ** (by grace you have been saved), ⁶and **raised us up with Him, and seated us with Him in the heavenly places in Christ Jesus,** (Emphasis mine)

This clearly speaks of a spiritual resurrection – we were dead in our transgressions but then made alive and raised up with Him. It even says we are seated with Him in the heavenly places. How can this be true seeing that Christ has ascended into heaven where He is seated at God the Father's right hand? We are not physically raised up, and we are not physically seated with Him in heaven either. This can only be understood as a spiritual resurrection. Remember, Revelation 20:4 says that during the millennium the saints are sitting on thrones and judging. This sure sounds like the saints are presently reigning with Jesus on thrones right now, meaning that the saints are exercising spiritual authority. The disciples of Jesus were definitely exercising spiritual authority when they also cast out demons in Jesus' name. Also, spiritual authority was exercised in their preaching because those rejecting it were condemned and judged worse than the sexual deviants of Sodom and Gomorrah (Matthew 10:12-15).

Colossians 3:1-3

> *¹Therefore if you have been raised up with Christ, keep seeking the things above, where Christ is, seated at the right hand of God. ²Set your mind on the things above, not on the things that are on earth. ³For you have died and your life is hidden with Christ in God.*

We need to see this passage in conjunction with Ephesians 2:4-6. Figuratively, we have been raised up and seated with Christ in the heavenly places; consequently, we should behave in light of what is spiritually true of us. We need to live with our minds focused on heavenly things even though physically we are still on earth.

In determining the timing of the millennium of Revelation 20, we can exegetically demonstrate from the reign of the saints that we are presently in the millennial age. Thus far, I have documented that the binding of Satan and the reign of the saints places the millennium **before** the Second Coming of Christ, but there is additional proof that we are in the millennium. It pertains to what Revelation 20:6 states about those who have experienced the first resurrection. They will be "priests of God and of Christ."

The Reign of the Martyrs- Revelation 20:4

During the millennial age, the reigning saints, who are sitting on thrones and judging, will often experience persecution. A persecuted church is **not** a defeated church; it is still a victorious church. As the Christian leader Tertullian said in the Third Century, "The blood of the martyrs is the seed of the church." A victorious church in history does not negate the reality of a persecuted church for a portion of its existence.

We must remember that the millennial age is an age of spiritual warfare – the reigning Jesus is subduing all His enemies under His feet. As we shall see in an upcoming chapter, Jesus uses His church as the primary means in subduing the nations. Jesus' church is on the offensive; it is engaged in holy spiritual warfare. It is assaulting the "gates of hell." While Satan is bound in terms of being a deceiver of the nations as he once was, he is still a "roaring lion" seeking whom he may devour. Much of the book of Revelation portrays this warfare between the devil and his seed and Christ and His seed.

Suffering and martyrdom are no strangers to the saints in the history of the church over the past two millennia. Jesus told His disciples to expect it. We read in John 15:18-20:

> *[18]If the world hates you, you know that it has hated Me before it hated you. [19]If you were of the world, the world would love its own; but because you are not of the world, but I chose you out of the world, because of this the world hates you. [20]Remember the word that I said to you, 'A slave is not greater than his master.' If they persecuted Me, they will also persecute you; if they kept My word, they will keep yours also.*

The apostle Paul was one well acquainted with suffering and like many of the other apostles was martyred for the Faith. In his conversion and simultaneous calling to be "the apostle to the Gentiles," Jesus informed Ananias that He had chosen Saul of Tarsus (Paul) to be a chosen instrument of His to bear His name before the Gentiles and sons of Israel, and Jesus said, "*For I will show him how much he must suffer for My name's sake*" (Acts 9:15-16). Paul said we should expect persecution – *"And indeed, all who desire to live godly in Christ Jesus will be persecuted"* (II Timothy 3:12). Paul clearly understood the magnitude of the spiritual warfare he was engaged in. In II Corinthians 11:24-28, he sets forth the extent of this suffering:

²⁴Five times I received from the Jews thirty-nine lashes. ²⁵Three times I was beaten with rods, once I was stoned, three times I was shipwrecked, a night and a day I have spent in the deep. ²⁶I have been on frequent journeys, in dangers from rivers, dangers from robbers, dangers from my countrymen, dangers from the Gentiles, dangers in the city, dangers in the wilderness, dangers on the sea, dangers among false brethren; ²⁷I have been in labor and hardship, through many sleepless nights, in hunger and thirst, often without food, in cold and exposure. ²⁸Apart from such external things, there is the daily pressure on me of concern for all the churches.

The apostle Peter fully recognized the spiritual intense conflict as well. We read in I Peter 2:19-23:

¹⁹For this finds favor, if for the sake of conscience toward God a person bears up under sorrows when suffering unjustly. ²⁰For what credit is there if, when you sin and are harshly treated, you endure it with patience? But if when you do what is right and suffer for it you patiently endure it, this finds favor with God. ²¹For you have been called for this purpose, since Christ also suffered for you, leaving you an example for you to follow in His steps, ²²who committed no sin, nor was any deceit found in His mouth, ²³and while being reviled, He did not revile in return; while suffering, He uttered no threats,

The intensity of the persecutions of the church is vividly expressed by Peter in I Peter 4:12-14:

¹²Beloved, do not be surprised at the fiery ordeal among you, which comes upon you for your testing, as though some strange thing were happening to you; ¹³but to the degree that you share the sufferings of Christ, keep on rejoicing, so that also at the revelation of His glory you may rejoice with exultation. ¹⁴If you are reviled for the name of Christ, you are blessed, because the Spirit of glory and of God rests on you.

It is an historical fact that Nero was the first Roman Emperor that greatly persecuted Christians, even using them as torches in his courtyard. The Roman historian Tacitus states:

> But all human efforts, all the lavish gifts of the emperor, and the propitiations of the gods, did not banish the sinister belief that the conflagration was the result of an order. Consequently, to get rid of the report, Nero fastened the guilt and inflicted the most exquisite tortures on a class hated for their abominations, called 'Chrestians' by the populace.[15]

> Yet no human effort, no princely largess nor offerings to the gods could make that infamous rumor disappear that Nero had somehow ordered the fire. Therefore, in order to abolish that rumor, Nero falsely accused and executed with the most exquisite punishments those people called Christians, who were infamous for their abominations. The originator of the name, Christ, was executed as a criminal by the procurator Pontius Pilate during the reign of Tiberius; and though repressed, this destructive superstition erupted again, not only through Judea, which was the origin of this evil, but also through the city of Rome, to which all that is horrible and shameful floods together and is celebrated. Therefore, first those were seized who admitted their faith, and then, using the information they provided, a vast multitude were convicted, not so much for the crime of burning the city, but for hatred of the human race. And perishing they were additionally made into sports: they were killed by dogs by having the hides of beasts attached to them, or they were nailed to crosses or set aflame, and, when the daylight passed away, they were used as nighttime lamps. Nero gave his own gardens for this spectacle and performed a Circus game, in the habit of a charioteer mixing with the plebs or driving about the race-course. Even though they were clearly guilty and merited being made the most recent example of the consequences of crime, people began to pity these sufferers, because they were consumed not for the public good but on account of the fierceness of one man.[16]

---

[15]   From *Annals*, 15.44 as found in http://www.livius.org/cg-cm/christianity/tacitus.html.
[16]   *Annuals.* as found in http://warandgame.com/2009/04/10/tacitus-on-nero%E2%80%99s-persecution-of-the-christians/.

The persecutions under Nero were the beginning of centuries of persecutions under the beast[17] and its image, which is the Roman Empire and all worldly institutions throughout history in rebellion to God. In our text in Revelation 20:4, we must understand that it had a first century application since John was writing to Christian churches in Asia Minor (Revelation 1:3, 9), but it is not restricted only to the first century; it spans the entirety of the millennial age regarding those who have been martyred for the Faith. The point is: suffering and persecution does mark aspects of the millennial age, but this is not inconsistent for the millennial age to be marked as an age of ongoing victory for Christ and His reigning saints. We have no idea exactly how long the millennial age is. As stated previously, it is a figurative term denoting a long period of time, and long enough for people to think that Jesus is never coming back (II Peter 3:1-3).

Amillennialists want to interpret Revelation 20:4 as referring to the "souls" of the martyred saints as disembodied spirits, thereby placing these souls in heaven and not on earth. There are real problems with this interpretation. There is no compelling exegetical reason that mandates that the Greek word, *psuche,* must be seen as a disembodied spirit. It can be translated as "life" (Matthew 2:20: Luke 12:22; Acts 20:10; John 10:11, 15, 17; 12:25; 13:37, 38; 15:13; I John 3:16; Revelations 8:9; Revelations 12:11). In other words, the verse is referring to "persons."

Revelation 20:4 pictures the millennium as the gospel age where the saints are reigning victoriously with Jesus regardless of suffering or martyrdom.

Priests of God and of Christ

Revelation 20:6

> *Blessed and holy is the one who has a part in the first resurrection; over these the second death has no power, but they will be **priests of God and of Christ** and will reign with Him for a thousand years.* (Emphasis mine)

If we can determine when those experiencing the first resurrection become priests of God and of Christ, then we have exegetically proved when the millennium occurs because it says that they will be priests **and reign** with Christ for a thousand years. Even those of the Dispensational persuasion

---

[17] For a biblical understanding of the "beast of Revelation" see Kenneth Gentry, *The Beast of Revelation,* (Tyler, Texas: Institute for Christian Economics, 1989).

acknowledge that the saints being priests occur during the millennial reign. The problem is that dispensationalism totally misunderstands the timing of the millennium, and they make the great mistake of believing that there is the re-institution of the Levitical sacrificial system; hence, somehow the saints of the millennial kingdom will be a priesthood of this Old Testament order.

In contrast to this false belief, we need to assert that the "priesthood of believers" applies to the church, that it was always intended to apply to the church of the new covenant. If we can demonstrate that the phrase "they will be priests of God and Christ" applies to the church now, then we have demonstrated from another angle that we are presently in the millennium.

Revelation 1:4-6

> *[4]John to the seven churches that are in Asia: Grace to you and peace, from Him who is and who was and who is to come, and from the seven Spirits who are before His throne, [5]and from Jesus Christ, the faithful witness, the firstborn of the dead, and the ruler of the kings of the earth. To Him who loves us and released us from our sins by His blood, [6]and He has made us to be a kingdom, priests to His God and Father - to Him be the glory and the dominion forever and ever. Amen.*

The text clearly states that John's message is to the **churches** in Asia. He is not referring to some millennial kingdom after Christ's coming that is distinct from the church age. Such interpretations directly contradict the basic hermeneutical principle of allowing Scripture to interpret Scripture. Jesus secured the redemption of "us" by His own blood. Simultaneous with this redemption is the truth that these redeemed are made a kingdom and priests to God. The church is presently a kingdom of priests to God! This truth is confirmed by other Scriptures.

Revelation 5:1-10

> *[1]I saw in the right hand of Him who sat on the throne a book written inside and on the back, sealed up with seven seals. [2]And I saw a strong angel proclaiming with a loud voice, 'Who is worthy to open the book and to break its seals?' [3]And no one in heaven or on the earth or under the earth was able to open the book or to look into it. [4]Then I began to weep greatly because no one was found worthy to open the book or to look into it; [5]and one of the elders said to me, 'Stop weeping; behold, the Lion that*

*is from the tribe of Judah, the Root of David, has overcome so as to open the book and its seven seals.' ⁶And I saw between the throne (with the four living creatures) and the elders a Lamb standing, as if slain, having seven horns and seven eyes, which are the seven Spirits of God, sent out into all the earth. ⁷And He came and took the book out of the right hand of Him who sat on the throne. ⁸When He had taken the book, the four living creatures and the twenty-four elders fell down before the Lamb, each one holding a harp and golden bowls full of incense, which are the prayers of the saints. ⁹And they sang a new song, saying, 'Worthy are You to take the book and to break its seals; for You were slain, and purchased for God with Your blood men from every tribe and tongue and people and nation. ¹⁰You have made them to be a kingdom and **priests** to our God; and they will reign upon the earth.'* (Emphasis mine)

This portion of Scripture continues the heavenly vision that powerfully depicts Jesus Christ as a victorious judge. It depicts what Jesus has done for His church. The vision begins with God the Father holding a book in His right hand that is sealed up. An angel is crying out, "Who is worthy to open the book and break its seals?" What is the book? The commentator Matthew Henry argues for this understanding:

> The designs and methods of divine Providence towards the church and the world are stated and fixed; they are resolved upon and agreed to, as that which is written in a book. The great design is laid, every part adjusted, all determined, and every thing passed into decree and made a matter of record. The original and first draught of this book is the book of God's decrees, laid up in his own cabinet, in his eternal mind: but there is a transcript of so much as was necessary to be known in the book of the scriptures in general, in the prophetical part of the scripture especially, and in this prophecy in particular. 2. God holds this book in his right hand, to declare the authority of the book, and his readiness and resolution to execute all the contents thereof, all the counsels and purposes therein recorded.[18]

Who is able to delve into the mind of God? Who really can reveal the eternal counsel of God? No creature can do so. No creature is worthy to open the book, that is, to reveal the decrees of God. This failure for any creature to open the book makes John weep, but then an elder speaks to

---

[18]   Matthew Henry's Commentary on Revelation 5:1.

John, "*Stop weeping; behold, the Lion that is from the tribe of Judah, the Root of David, has overcome so as to open the book and its seven seals.*" There is no question that the Lord Jesus Christ is the one portrayed. He is the Lion from the tribe of Judah; He is the root of David (Revelation 22:16). As the mediator between God and man, the Lord Jesus Christ is worthy to execute the eternal decrees of God the Father. He is said to be standing in the midst or middle of the throne separating the four living creatures and the elders as a slain lamb. This conveys the ministry of mediation – one who is able to reconcile God with man. Was not Jesus declared by John the Baptist as "the lamb of God that takes away the sin of the world" (John 1:29)? Revelation 13:8 refers to the lamb slain from the foundation of the world. The plan of redemption was an eternal plan, that is, from the foundation of the world. Yes, the actual death of Jesus was in space and time, but since it was the eternal plan of God for men's salvation, it can be said that Jesus was slain from the foundation of the world. It is a sure thing that no man can stop. This is why Acts 2:23 and 4:27-28 refer to the death of Jesus as being a predetermined plan.

Jesus Christ comes and takes the book out of the right hand of Him who sat on the throne. With this act, there begins a doxology, praises to God among the heavenly host (four living creatures) and the twenty-four elders. The twenty-four elders are representative of the church of the Lord Jesus Christ as comprised in the old and new covenant. As noted in an earlier chapter, the church of Christ is pictured as a litany of images - as the heavenly Jerusalem, the city of the living God, Mount Zion, the general assembly, and church. In other words, the church is all these things metaphorically pictured. Revelation 21:10-14 pictures the New Jerusalem as having a great wall with twelve gates with names written on them. The names are specifically said to be the twelve tribes of Israel. Moreover, the great city's wall had twelve foundation stones with the names of the twelve apostles of the lamb. The imagery of course is picturing the completed people of God, the church, as constituted in the new covenant. As Ephesians 2:19-20 states, the church, as God's household, is built upon the foundation of the apostles and prophets.

The imagery of the golden bowls full of incense is specifically said to be **"the prayers of the saints."** And what was the nature of the new song of praise? Revelation 5:9 says that the song was one of praise to God suited to the new state of the church, the gospel state accomplished by the Son of God's mediation. Jesus Christ is praised as worthy of taking the book and breaking its seal. Why? Because He was slain and did purchase for God with His blood men from every tribe and tongue and people and nation. Revelation 5:10 specifically continues the effects of Christ's mediatorial work – "A*nd thou has made them to be a kingdom and priests to our God; and they will reign upon the earth."* As kings, members of the redeemed church govern their own spirits and conquer Satan. They possess the power to prevail with God in prayer and to judge the world. Jesus' accomplished mediatorial work has made His church priests to God. As priests what do they do? They offer spiritual and acceptable sacrifices. Hebrews 13:15 states:

> *Through Him then, let us continually offer up a sacrifice of praise to God, that is, the fruit of lips that give thanks to His name.*

As Revelation 5:8 reveals, the golden bowls of incense are the prayers of the saints. The Lord Jesus Christ is victorious as His church engages in the ministry of prayer! In fact, we have free access to the Father because of Jesus; we can be bold in our prayers, and we can be assured that these prayers are brought into the very presence of God the Father. We no longer need an earthly priest to intercede for us; we can intercede directly for ourselves through our mediator Jesus. We now as the church constitute a kingdom of priests. Hebrews 4:14-16 beautifully states:

> *[14]Therefore, since we have a great high priest who has passed through the heavens, Jesus the Son of God, let us hold fast our confession. [15]For we do not have a high priest who cannot sympathize with our weaknesses, but One who has been tempted in all things as we are, yet without sin. [16]Therefore let us draw near with confidence to the throne of grace, so that we may receive mercy and find grace to help in time of need.*

We can boldly approach God the Father in prayer because of the mediatorial work of Jesus. We read in Hebrews 9:24-28:

> *[24]For Christ did not enter a holy place made with hands, a mere copy of the true one, but into heaven itself, now to appear in the presence of God for us; [25]nor was it that He would offer Himself often, as the high priest enters the holy place year by year with blood that is not his own. [26]Otherwise, He would have needed to suffer often since the foundation of the world; but now once at the consummation of the ages He has been manifested to put away sin by the sacrifice of Himself. [27]And inasmuch as it is appointed for men to die once and after this comes judgment, [28]so Christ also, having been offered once to bear the sins of many, will appear a second time for salvation without reference to sin, to those who eagerly await Him.*

Revelation 5:10 is a powerful passage that continues the effect of Jesus' sacrificial work as explained in 5:9. Therefore, the all important question is: when did the church become constituted as a kingdom of priests who reign on earth? **The answer: at the time the church was redeemed!** This truth is substantiated as well in I Peter 2:4-10.

I Peter 2:4-10

> *[4]And coming to Him as to a living stone which has been rejected by men, but is choice and precious in the sight of God, [5]you also, as living stones, are being built up **as a spiritual house for a holy priesthood, to offer up spiritual sacrifices** acceptable to God through Jesus Christ. [6]For this is contained in Scripture: 'Behold, I lay in Zion a choice stone, a precious corner stone and he who believes in Him will not be disappointed.' [7]This precious value, then, is for you who believe; but for those who disbelieve, The stone **which the builders rejected, this became the very corner stone.** [8]and, a stone of stumbling and a rock of offens; for they stumble because they are disobedient to the word, and to this doom they were also appointed. [9]But you are a chosen race, **a royal priesthood**, a holy nation, a people for God's own possession. so that you may proclaim the excellencies of Him who has called you out of darkness into His marvelous light; [10]for you once were not a people, but now you are the people of God; you had not received mercy, but now you have received mercy.* (Emphasis mine)

This passage in I Peter is about as clear proof as possible to demonstrate that the present church is a holy and royal priesthood. We don't become royal priests after the Second Coming. God's Word says we are royal priests now, and that the sacrifices we offer are **spiritual** sacrifices, not literal animal sacrifices of a Levitical priesthood re-instituted in a millennium after the Second Coming.

One of the purposes of God creating this royal priesthood is for the distinct purpose for the redeemed people to *"proclaim the excellencies of Him who has called you out of darkness into His marvelous light."* The Apostle Paul's ministry to the Gentile world is described by himself in Acts 26:18:

> *To open their eyes so that they may turn from darkness to light and from the dominion of Satan to God, that they may receive forgiveness of sins and an inheritance among those who have been sanctified by faith in Me.*

We also see this beautiful description of Christ's saving work among the Gentiles in Colossians 1:13-14:

> *[13]For He rescued us from the domain of darkness, and transferred us to the kingdom of His beloved Son, [14]in whom we have redemption, the forgiveness of sins.*

Dispensational premillennialists would acknowledge Paul's ministry as being one performed during the so called "church age." The immense problem that this theological system faces is that Paul's ministry and all preachers who have followed him have functioned as a kingdom of priests (royal priests), reigning with Jesus, preaching the glorious gospel and seeing people delivered out of darkness to light. This means that the millennium is now, not later after the Second Coming.

Isaiah 61:6

> *But you will be called the **priests of the Lord**; You will be spoken of as ministers of our God. You will eat the wealth of nations, and in their riches you will boast.* (Emphasis mine)

We know this prophecy was meant for the present age because Jesus quotes from Isaiah 61 to prove to those in the synagogue at Nazareth that He was the promised Messiah. Jesus said that Isaiah 61 **was fulfilled at His reading.** The favorable year of the Lord had arrived.

The Release of Satan

Revelation 20:7-9

> *[7]When the thousand years are completed, Satan will be released from his prison, [8]and will come out to deceive the nations which are in the four corners of the earth, Gog and Magog, to gather them together for the war; the number of them is like the sand of the seashore. [9]And they came up on the broad plain of the earth and surrounded the camp of the saints and the beloved city, and fire came down from heaven and devoured them.*

At the beginning of the millennium, the Lord Jesus bound Satan in the sense that he is no longer deceiving the nations as he once was. He is still the "god of this age;" he is still prowling like a roaring lion seeking to devour men spiritually, but he is a defeated foe, whose kingdom has been plundered by Jesus and His church. Because he has been bound, the nations have been progressively discipled which has brought an unprecedented blessing to the world. The nations have beaten their swords into plowshares and learned war no more (Isaiah 11:4). It is not a perfect world yet, but the gospel has triumphed over the citadel of hell.

At the completion of the thousand year kingdom, Satan will be released from his prison to deceive the nations again, but this rebellion will be of short duration as Revelation 20:3 stated, "... *after these things he must be released for a short time.*" During this short period, Satan will organize a sizable force of rebels from the various nations, symbolized as Gog and Magog. They are enemies of the people of God. This final conflict has its roots pictured in Ezekiel 38. In this passage, Gog is said to be the ruler of Magog and the prince of Meshech and Tubal. Trying to identify them specifically is not necessary. They are representative of the enemies of God's people, the godless among the nations of the world.

Commentator Matthew Henry understands Ezekiel 38 as having future implications for the church. He states:

> Now it is said, This shall be *in the latter days,* namely, in the latter days of the Old-Testament church; so the mischief that Antiochus did to Israel was; but in the latter days of the New-Testament church another like enemy should arise, that should in like manner be defeated. Note, Effectual securities are treasured up in the word of God against the troubles and dangers the church may be brought into a great while hence, even in the latter days.[19]

These unbelievers will seek to overthrow the prevailing Christian influence. Revelation 20:9 says that the huge rebel force comes and *"surrounds the camp of the saints, and the beloved city."* We have seen that the church in the New Testament is called "the city of the living God, the heavenly Jerusalem" (Hebrews 12:22). Since Ezekiel 38 pictures this rebellion, we need to see the parallels of the Old Testament imagery with that of Revelation 20.

Ezekiel 38:8 is most illuminating:

> *After many days you will be summoned; in the latter years you will come into the land that is restored from the sword, whose inhabitants have been gathered from many nations to the mountains of Israel which had been a continual waste; but its*

---

[19]   Matthew Henry's Commentary on Ezekiel 38.

*people were brought out from the nations, and they are living
securely, all of them.*

Those who are being summoned are the nations in rebellion to God
(Ezekiel 38:1-7). Verse 8 corresponds with what is said in Revelation
20:7-9. In Ezekiel 38:8, the godless nations are summoned in the latter
years to come into the land that has been restored from the sword. What
does being restored from the sword mean except that there has been world
peace for a considerable time. Remember, Isaiah 2:4 said that during the
millennial kingdom, the nations have beaten their swords into plowshares
and learned war no more. Verse 8 also states that "the land" that has been
restored is comprised of *"whose inhabitants have been gathered from
many nations to the mountains of Israel; but its people were brought out
from the nations, and they are living securely, all of them."* Just from this
text alone, we immediately see that the land is **not** restricted to the
geographical piece of real estate in the Middle East known as "Israel." Our
text distinctly says the inhabitants of the land were **brought out of the
nations**. Moreover, all of these inhabitants are living securely, meaning
that peace has marked those in the land.

Dispensational premillennialists, being the Zionists that they are, insist that
Ezekiel 38 refers to the actual land of Israel consisting of Jews and a
physical Jerusalem. But, as noted in a previous chapter in this book,
dispensationalists are greatly in error, failing to understand that the
Abrahamic covenant land promise was never intended to be restricted to
the physical land of Canaan. As Romans 4:13 states, it encompassed the
world. Moreover, it was established as well that the church of the New
Testament clearly constitutes the "new Israel." Christians are emphatically
said to be "the seed of Abraham" (Galatians 3:29). The apostle James
explicitly said in Acts 15 that the conversion of the Gentiles by the
ministries of Peter and Paul is a fulfillment of Amos 9 in the rebuilding of
David's tabernacle. And, did not Isaiah 2:2 say that in the *"last days the
mountain of the house of the Lord will be established as the chief of the
mountains, and will be raised above the hills?"* The people of God, the
church, are the highest mountain. And where will the nations be gathered
to? Isaiah 2:3 answers it – *"And many peoples will come and say, 'Come,
let us go up to the mountain of the Lord, the house of the God of Jacob,
that He may teach us concerning His ways, and that we may walk in His
paths. For the law will go forth from Zion, and the word of the Lord from
Jerusalem."* We have seen that this is a clear reference to the millennial
age where the nations will come to the church and be discipled just as the
Great Commission of Matthew 28 states. Ezekiel 38:8 specifically refers to
the nations coming "to the mountains of Israel."

Dispensational premillennialists insist that Ezekiel 38 speaks of the great battle of Armageddon, and that this occurs before Christ's Second Coming. Hal Lindsey was the first to give his most imaginative and non-literal description of Ezekiel 38 in his book *The Late Great Planet Earth*. According to the dispensationalist Lindsey, all of the events of Ezekiel 38 take place after the church has been secretly raptured. Lindsey says that the Antichrist's take over of Jerusalem has precipitated growing world tension. Chapter 5 of Lindsey's *Late Great Planet Earth* is titled, "Russia is Gog." Supposedly the great army of the north that invades physical Israel is Russian (Ezekiel 38:14-16). Lindsey then seeks to weave into Ezekiel 38 certain chapters of Revelation that he insists refer to the same time frame. Lindsey maintains that Revelation 9:14, 15 and 16:12 refer to the "kings of the east" having an army of 200 million soldiers can only be the Red Chinese. Only Red China has this many people to field an army of this size. With the Russian invasion of Israel, it prompts a revived Roman Empire to attack the Russian army with tactical nuclear weapons, which Lindsey says is the meaning of "a torrential rain of hailstones, fire, and brimstone" that Ezekiel 38:22 refers to. Then, this supposed Red Chinese army of 200 million men reaches the Euphrates River and plans to attack the Antichrist who is in Israel. This is what Revelation 16:12 refers to according to Lindsey. Then there will be a massive shootout between forces of the Western civilization headed by a Roman dictator against the Red Chinese army. Things will escalate and thermonuclear war will erupt destroying one third of mankind.

With the deliverance of Israel from the Russian army, this will supposedly convict one-third of the Jewish people to get converted to Christ, which is rather odd because it is a common belief among dispensational premillennialists that the Holy Spirit has been removed from the earth with the rapture of the church. Dispensationalist writer Tommy Ice explains:

> Second Thessalonians 2:1-12 discusses a man of lawlessness being held back until a later time. Interpreting the restrainer of evil (2:6) as the indwelling ministry of the Holy Spirit at work through the body of Christ during the current age, supports the pretribulational interpretation. Since "the lawless one" (the beast or Antichrist) cannot be revealed until the Restrainer (the Holy Spirit) is taken away (2:7-8), the tribulation cannot occur until the church is removed. Of all the rapture positions, only the pre-trib position can be harmonized when we understand that the Restrainer is referring to the Holy Spirit.

> Therefore, it is not surprising that since the tribulation cannot start until after the church is completed and taken to heaven in the

rapture that the man of lawlessness is restrained through the presence of the Holy Spirit on earth indwelling church age Believers. This current work of the Holy Spirit is unique to the church. Dr. John Walvoord explains, "We search the prophetic Scriptures in vain for any reference to baptism of the Spirit except in regard to the church, the body of Christ (1 Corinthians 12:13). While, therefore, the Spirit continues a ministry in the world in the tribulation, there is no longer a corporate body of believers knit into one living organism. There is rather a return to national distinctions and fulfillment of national promises in preparation for the millennium."

Those who do not hold to pretribulationism often mischaracterize our view of the Holy Spirit in the tribulation. They often say that we do not believe that the Holy Spirit will be present during the tribulation. This is not what we are saying. We do believe that the Holy Spirit will be present and active during the tribulation. We do believe the Holy Spirit will not be carrying out His present unique ministry related to the church since all members of that body will be in heaven. Further, we are saying that the Holy Spirit will be present in His transdispensational ministry of bringing the elect of the tribulation to faith in Christ, even though they will not be part of the body of Christ-the church. The Holy Spirit will also aid tribulation Believers as they live holy lives unto the Lord. The Holy Spirit will also function to seal and protect the 144,000 Jewish witnesses for their great evangelistic ministry as noted in Revelation 7 and 14 and the two witnesses of Revelation 11.[20]

The above comments just prove the amazing lengths that men will go to in order to preserve a theological position. A transdispensational ministry of the Holy Spirit? A group of believers in Jesus who are not part of the church? Where is that in the Bible? Nowhere! If one is a believer in Jesus, the Bible de facto says that he is in the church with Christ as the head. There is no such thing as a believer in Jesus (a Christian) who is not part of His church.

According to dispensational premillennial thought, as the battle of Armageddon reaches its climax, Jesus returns with His church in the supposed "second phase of the Second Coming" to rescue mankind from

---

[20] Thomas Ice, "The Holy Spirit and the Pretribulational Rapture" found at http://www.according2prophecy.org/hsrap.html.

self destruction. Then Jesus sets up His millennial kingdom on earth for a thousand years.

Hal Lindsey, typical of mainstream dispensationalism, says this about Satan's release at the end of the millennium.

> The first thing Satan does when he is released from the abyss after the Millennium is to organize a war. War is one his favorite enterprises. He gets together some of the descendants of the enemies of Israel (Gog and Magog) who were born during the millennium, and surrounds Jerusalem. But the rebellion doesn't even get off the ground. God zaps them all with fire and brimstone from heaven and they are annihilated.[21]

This dispensational understanding of events surrounding the rapture, the Second Coming and events at the end of the millennium is fraught with immense problems. The most prominent problem with the dispensationalist's understanding of Satan's release at the end of the millennium is this: how can any human being pose any threat whatsoever against Jesus and immortal beings (resurrected church saints)? Did it ever occur to these people this immense theological problem: what kind of threat could Satan pose to the Lord of lords and King of kings who has all authority in heaven and earth? What kind of weapon could exist that would harm any of us glorified immortal beings with Jesus in Jerusalem? Where is one verse in the Bible that explicitly states or even remotely infers that immortal glorified saints live on earth with sinful men?

The only reason that dispensationalism believes in this incredible scenario is because its unbiblical distinction of Israel and the church demands it! This is the epitome of the imposition of human speculation upon the Word of God, stemming from a faulty hermeneutic.

Postmillennialism, which we have been advocating throughout this book, does believe that at the end of the millennial reign, Satan will be loosed to deceive the nations again. The binding of Satan began in Jesus' ministry and has continued throughout the present age (millennial age). The reason for the success of the gospel worldwide has been and will be due to Satan's binding.

Upon release from his prison, Satan will gather a rebellion among the nations symbolized as Gog and Magog. They are enemies of the people of

---

[21]   Lindsey, *There's A New World Coming,* pp.277-278.

God. This final conflict is pictured in Ezekiel 38. Gog is said to be the ruler of Magog and the prince of Meshech and Tubal. Trying to identify them specifically is not necessary. They are representative of the enemies of God's people, the godless nations of the world. If we understand Revelation 20 to be what we have been noting, then we are presently in the millennial age with the gospel being advanced. This uprising is simply part of the subduing of all His enemies under his feet. In the biblical scheme, the destruction of Satan's rebellion appears to be the near conclusion of His subjugation of all His enemies. As we shall see from I Corinthians 15:26, the last enemy to be destroyed will be death itself. This occurs at the conclusion of the millennial age with Christ's Second Coming and the resurrection of the dead.

Revelation 20:11-15

We are told in Revelation 20:11-15 when the second death occurs. The text reads:

> [11]*Then I saw a great white throne and Him who sat upon it, from whose presence earth and heaven fled away, and no place was found for them.* [12]*And I saw the dead, the great and the small, standing before the throne, and books were opened; and another book was opened, which is the book of life; and the dead were judged from the things which were written in the books, according to their deeds.* [13]*And the sea gave up the dead which were in it,* [14]*and death and Hades gave up the dead which were in them; and they were judged, every one of them according to their deeds. Then death and Hades were thrown into the lake of fire. This is the second death, the lake of fire.* [15]*And if anyone's name was not found written in the book of life, he was thrown into the lake of fire.*

In this passage, there are the dead who are standing before a great white throne and books are opened out of which these dead are judged. All those whose names are not in the book of life are condemned and thrown into the lake of fire, which is called the second death. The great white throne judgment pictured here is also pictured in Matthew 25:31-46 where Jesus is sitting on a throne where all the nations are gathered before Him. Those whose deeds demonstrated their genuine faith in Jesus are commended and beckoned to inherit the kingdom prepared for them from the foundation of the world (Matthew 25:34). Those whose deeds demonstrated no genuine faith are condemned and sent away to eternal fire prepared for the devil and his angels (Matthew 25:41). In Revelation 20, those who have experienced the first resurrection have nothing to fear in the great Day of

Judgment. This is but one clue that the first resurrection is a **spiritual resurrection, not a bodily resurrection.** Dispensationalists and even some historic premillennialists insist that Revelation is speaking about two bodily resurrections. Again, the only reason why one would want to hold to two bodily resurrections is because his theological system necessitates it. Somehow, the premillennialist must account for a bodily resurrection at the rapture of the saints either before or at the same time as Christ's Second Coming and subscribe to another bodily resurrection after the millennial kingdom on earth, where he asserts that death is still present. Hence, their theology demands two bodily resurrections separated by at least a thousand years. Why should we have two bodily resurrections when the issue is readily solved by maintaining a spiritual resurrection, called the first resurrection, and a second resurrection, which is the bodily resurrection at the end of the millennium when Christ comes?

Summary Statement on Revelation 20

To summarize what we have seen thus far from Revelation 20, the key elements of the millennial reign entail the binding of Satan for the thousand years. Jesus began binding him during His earthly ministry, and the preaching of the gospel ever since has shown that the deceiver of the nations has lost his stranglehold on the nations. Those reigning with Christ have experienced the first resurrection. They have been born again from above; they are the redeemed of the Lord over which the second death has no power. And, those reigning with Christ are a kingdom of priests to the Lord, rendering sacrifices of praise and thanksgiving for Christ's redemption of their souls. This royal priesthood is proclaiming the glorious gospel and watching the power of the Gospel transfer men from darkness to light.

The Davidic Covenant and the Reign of Christ

I have deliberately waited until now to discuss the magnificent theology of the Davidic covenant which sets forth the great truths of Christ's Messianic reign. Understanding the Davidic Covenant promises is absolutely essential in understanding the true nature of the kingdom of God.

As we look at this covenant in detail, we will find the answers to the following questions: What was exactly prophesied? When will it come?

How long is it? What is its nature? The Davidic covenant and its New Testament fulfillment in the New Covenant provide us with the answers.

At the outset, we need to make an important observation. **God identifies David's throne with the throne of God.** We read in I Chronicles 29:23:

> *And they made Solomon the son of David king a second time, and they anointed him as ruler for the Lord and Zadok as priest. Then Solomon **sat on the throne of the Lord** as king instead of David his father; and he prospered, and all Israel obeyed him.* (Emphasis mine)

This is an absolutely vital truth to keep in mind when we enter the New Testament and discover when Jesus Christ sat on David's throne. One of the things about the throne of David as God's throne is that the king has the authority to bind the people of God to the covenant law (i.e. Mosaic theocratic law). Let's consider II Kings 23:1-3:

> *[1]Then the king sent, and they gathered to him all the elders of Judah and of Jerusalem. [2]The king went up to the house of the Lord and all the men of Judah and all the inhabitants of Jerusalem with him, and the priests and the prophets and all the people, both small and great; and he read in their hearing all the words of the book of the covenant which was found in the house of the Lord. [3]The king stood by the pillar and made a covenant before the Lord, to walk after the Lord, and to keep His commandments and His testimonies and His statutes with all his heart and all his soul, to carry out the words of this covenant that were written in this book. And all the people entered into the covenant.*

In the progress of biblical revelation and in seeing the continuity and unity of the various covenants of the covenant of grace, we must remind ourselves that the seed of David is the seed of Abraham and part of the Mosaic congregation of Jehovah that is circumcised of heart.

Let's now look at the inauguration of the Davidic covenant.

Great Promises of the Davidic Covenant in II Samuel 7:8-17

> *[8]Now therefore, thus you shall say to My servant David, 'Thus says the LORD of hosts, I took you from the pasture, from following the sheep, to be ruler over My people Israel. [9]I have been with you wherever you have gone and have cut off all your*

enemies from before you; and I will make you a great name, like the names of the great men who are on the earth. [10]*I will also appoint a place for My people Israel and will plant them, that they may live in their own place and not be disturbed again, nor will the wicked afflict them any more as formerly,* [11]*even from the day that I commanded judges to be over My people Israel; and I will give you rest from all your enemies The LORD also declares to you that the LORD will make a house for you.* [12]*When your days are complete and you lie down with your fathers, I will raise up your descendant after you, who will come forth from you, and I will establish his kingdom.* [13]*He shall build a house for My name, and I will establish the throne of his kingdom forever.* [14]*I will be a father to him and he will be a son to Me; when he commits iniquity, I will correct him with the rod of men and the strokes of the sons of men,* [15]*but My lovingkindness shall not depart from him, as I took it away from Saul, whom I removed from before you.* [16]*Your house and your kingdom shall endure before Me forever; your throne shall be established forever.'* [17]*In accordance with all these words and all this vision, so Nathan spoke to David.*

There are tremendous promises set forth in the Davidic covenant. In verses 8-9, Jehovah promises to make his name great. Does this sound familiar to God's promise to Abram in Genesis 12 of making him a blessing to the nations? It should.

The Davidic Promise of an Everlasting Possession

In verse 10, God promises a "place" for his generations to live and prosper. Sound familiar to the promise to Abraham in Genesis 17:8 where God will give his seed a "land" as **an everlasting possession?** The "land" promised to Abraham was but a down payment to God's covenant people down through their generations. Romans 4:13 demonstrates that the promise really entailed the entire world! Jesus said the meek shall inherit the "earth."

The Davidic Promise of a Dwelling Place among His people

In verse 11, God promises David rest from his enemies, and that the Lord will make a "house," a dwelling place for His glory among His people.

The Davidic Promise of a Seed Who Will Establish His Kingdom

In verse 12, God promises to raise up "a seed" after he is gone, who will be from him and who will establish his kingdom. We must be observant as to **when** the kingdom will be established.

The Davidic Promise That David's Throne and Kingdom Will Be Established Forever

In verses 13 and 16, David's throne and kingdom will be established forever.

In verses 14-15, God promises that the seed of David who builds His house shall be shown mercy when he sins, and that God's lovingkindness will not be removed from him as with Saul. We need to understand that there is a temporal and a future fulfillment to this covenant promise. We know that Solomon, David's son, will be the one who builds the temple, the house of God. And when that temple was built, the Ark of the Covenant, representing God's presence on earth with His people was moved from the tabernacle, the movable tent, to the permanent temple in Jerusalem.

The phrase, "when he commits sin," refers to Solomon's great unfaithfulness seen in I Kings 11 where his foreign wives led him to bring into Israel the pagan worship of Egypt, the Baals, etc.

But God's lovingkindness would not depart from him. When he was born, it said God loved him (II Samuel 12:24). Yes, God will discipline him greatly, but Solomon will be restored, and Ecclesiastes is an example of this restoration. The temporal fulfillment of the promise pertains to Solomon, a human who could and did sin.

In verse 16 we see the wonderful promise that David's house and kingdom shall endure before God forever. David's throne will be established forever, and how is this accomplished? It is accomplished through the primary promise of the Davidic covenant – the promise of the coming Messiah (Jesus Christ).

Since David, Solomon, and all the kings on David's throne physically died, how can it be that the kingdom and the throne will be established forever? It can only be true if the passage has Messianic overtones. The promise obviously finds fulfillment in the Lord Jesus Christ, and the New Testament explicitly states this, particularly in Acts 2:30-36. More will be stated later on this vital passage.

The Davidic covenant promises the following regarding the Messiah (Jesus Christ):

1) David's seed is Messiah, the God/man.
2) Messiah conquers His enemies from David's throne
3) Messiah is promised the nations as His inheritance.

John 1:14 states, "And the Word became flesh, and dwelt among us, and we saw His glory, glory as of the only begotten from the Father, full of grace and truth." Jesus Christ is the logos, the eternal Word, made flesh. He is the dwelling place of Jehovah, and one of the great principles and themes of the Old Testament is the Immanuel principle.

Isaiah 7:13-14

[13]*Then he said, 'Listen now, O house of David! Is it too slight a thing for you to try the patience of men, that you will try the patience of my God as well?* [14]*Therefore the Lord Himself will give you a sign: Behold, a virgin will be with child and bear a son, and she will call His name Immanuel.'*

We see that this Old Testament promise is definitively fulfilled in the birth of Jesus as recorded in Matthew 1:18-23:

[18]*Now the birth of Jesus Christ was as follows: when His mother Mary had been betrothed to Joseph, before they came together she was found to be with child by the Holy Spirit.* [19]*And Joseph her husband, being a righteous man and not wanting to disgrace her, planned to send her away secretly.* [20]*But when he had considered this, behold, an angel of the Lord appeared to him in a dream, saying, 'Joseph, son of David, do not be afraid to take Mary as your wife; for the Child who has been conceived in her is of the Holy Spirit.* [21]*She will bear a Son; and you shall call His name Jesus, for He will save His people from their sins.'* Now all this took place to fulfill what was spoken by the Lord through the prophet: 'Behold, the virgin shall be with child and shall bear a son, and they shall call His name Immanuel,' which translated means, 'God with us.'*

As this passage states, Jesus Christ is "Immanuel," and the term means, "God with us." Indeed, as John 1:14 brings out, Jesus did tabernacle with us in His incarnation. It is no coincidence that Mathew 1:1 in its genealogy of Jesus emphasizes both the Abrahamic and Davidic covenants. Galatians 3:16 affirms that Jesus Christ is the promised seed of Abraham through whom all the families of the earth will be blessed. And, Jesus Christ is the Son of David.

Isaiah 9:6-7

In continuing with this great Immanuel principle, we turn our attention to Isaiah 9:6-7:

> *For a child will be born to us, a son will be given to us; And the government will rest on His shoulders; And His name will be called Wonderful Counselor, Mighty God, Eternal Father, Prince of Peace. There will be no end to the increase of His government or of peace, on the throne of David and over his kingdom, to establish it and to uphold it with justice and righteousness from then on and forevermore. The zeal of the LORD of hosts will accomplish this.*

It is evident that all government rests on His shoulder, meaning He is the sovereign Lord of all. He is the mighty God; there will be no end to the increase of His government of peace since He is the Prince of Peace. Note the explicit reference to the establishment of David's throne with justice and righteousness. Since there will be no end to the government of Immanuel, this is what is meant in II Samuel 7:16 that David's throne will be established forever.

Luke 1:26-35

This Immanuel principle is beautifully set forth in Luke 1:26-35:

> [26]*Now in the sixth month the angel Gabriel was sent from God to a city in Galilee called Nazareth,* [27]*to a virgin engaged to a man whose name was Joseph, of the descendants of David; and the virgin's name was Mary.* [28]*And coming in, he said to her, 'Greetings, favored one! The Lord is with you.'* [29]*But she was very perplexed at this statement, and kept pondering what kind of salutation this was.* [30]*The angel said to her, 'Do not be afraid, Mary; for you have found favor with God.* [31]*And behold, you will conceive in your womb and bear a son, and you shall name Him Jesus.* [32]*He will be great and will be called the Son of the Most High; and the Lord God will give Him the throne of His father David;* [33]*and He will reign over the house of Jacob forever, and His kingdom will have no end.'* [34]*Mary said to the angel, 'How can this be, since I am a virgin?'* [35]*The angel answered and said to her, 'The Holy Spirit will come upon you, and the power of the*

Most High will overshadow you; and for that reason the holy Child shall be called the Son of God'.

The angel Gabriel was sent to Joseph and Mary, and in this passage, the angel informs Mary that she is blessed of all women for she will be the bearer of the Savior of the world. There is no coincidence that Mary's son will be great, for it conveys the truth of II Samuel 7:9 where God promised to make David a great name. As Matthew 1:1 states, Jesus Christ is the son of David. David's name is great in the earth because the Messiah (Jesus) is David's son, the greatest of all. Concerning Jesus' greatness, He will be called the Son of the Most High, the Son of God. Is this not what is promised in Isaiah's prophecy concerning Immanuel? Immanuel is said to be the mighty God.

It is most telling what Matthew 26:63 conveys – *"But Jesus kept silent. And the high priest said to Him, I adjure You by the living God, that You tell us whether You are the Christ, the Son of God."* The reprobate Jews knew in one sense the Old Testament prophecies. They understood that Messiah (Christ) was the son of God; they just couldn't believe that Jesus was that Messiah. It is this spiritual blindness which explains Jesus' comment that many of the Jews did not recognize the day of their visitation.

In Luke 1:32, the angel Gabriel also told Mary that her son will be given the throne of his father David. This is an explicit tying in of Jesus as that promised seed referred to in II Samuel 7. The angel also announced that Jesus would reign over the house of Jacob forever and that the kingdom would have no end. One can see that what the angel Gabriel announced is exactly the same thing revealed in II Samuel 7:13, 16 and in Isaiah 9:7.

The Davidic Promise That the Messiah Would Conquer His Enemies from David's Throne

Mary's response to the news that she will bear the Son of God causes her to praise God. One of the things that she praises God for is that the Messiah will scatter those who are proud in heart, and will bring down rulers from their thrones (Luke 1:50-51).

Genesis 49:8-10

There is a powerful prophetic passage in Genesis 49:8-10 that pertains to the coming Messiah. The passage states:

> *[8]Judah, your brothers shall praise you; Your hand shall be on the neck of your enemies; Your father's sons shall bow down to you. [9]Judah is a lion's whelp; from the prey, my son, you have gone up. He couches, he lies down as a lion, and as a lion, who dares rouse him up? [10]The scepter shall not depart from Judah, nor the ruler's staff from between his feet, until Shiloh comes, and to him shall be the obedience of the peoples.*

The promise is a familiar one – that of victory over one's enemies. Notice the phraseology, "Your hand shall be on the neck of your enemies." Judah is a lion's welp, a lion of Judah. Verse 10 affirms that the scepter shall not depart from Judah. A scepter is a king's ruling symbol of his power. It is no coincidence either of the location of the king's scepter. It is **between his feet.** This will have tremendous import once we take a look at Psalm 110, but for the moment, we recognize that the scepter belongs to "Shiloh," which means "to whom it belongs."

We read in Revelation 5:5 and 22:16 respectively:

> *And one of the elders said to me, 'Stop weeping; behold, the Lion that is from the tribe of Judah, the Root of David, has overcome so as to open the book and its seven seals.'*

> *I, Jesus, have sent My angel to testify to you these things for the churches. I am the root and the offspring of David, the bright morning star.*

The one who is worthy to open the book in Revelation is called the lion from the tribe of Judah, the root of David. This is undoubtedly the Lord Jesus Christ. He is the lion from the tribe of Judah. Jesus is Shiloh; the scepter belongs to Jesus. Since the scepter is said to be between His feet, this is amazingly similar to how the Messiah is portrayed in Psalm 110.[22]

---

[22] The 110th Psalm is the most frequently quoted Messianic prophecy in the entire New Testament. It is quoted or alluded to in Matthew 22:43-45, Mark 12:36-37, Luke 20:42-44, Acts 2:34-36 1 Corinthians 15:25, and especially in the Book of Hebrews 1:3, 13; 5:6, 10: 6:20; 7:3, 11-28; 8:1; 10:12-13; and 12:2.

Psalm 110

> [1]*The LORD says to my Lord: 'Sit at My right hand Until I make Your enemies a footstool for Your feet.' The LORD will stretch forth Your strong scepter from Zion, saying, "Rule in the midst of Your enemies." [3]Your people will volunteer freely in the day of Your power; In holy array, from the womb of the dawn, Your youth are to You as the dew. [4]The LORD has sworn and will not change His mind, 'You are a priest forever according to the order of Melchizedek.' [5]The Lord is at Your right hand; He will shatter kings in the day of His wrath. [6]He will judge among the nations, He will fill them with corpses, He will shatter the chief men over a broad country. He will drink from the brook by the wayside; therefore He will lift up His head.*

This Messianic Psalm pictures David's Lord sitting at the right hand of God. What is David's Lord doing at the right hand? He is sitting until His enemies are made a **footstool for his feet.** The parallel with Genesis 49:8-10 is unmistakable. In Genesis, the scepter belonging to Shiloh is between His feet. Here in Psalm 110:2, the Lord stretches forth His strong scepter from Zion, saying, "rule in the midst of Thine enemies." In Genesis 49:8, Judah's hand shall be upon the neck of his enemies indicating the subjugation of enemies to one's power. The effect of the scepter between Shiloh's feet in Genesis 49:10 is that it leads to "the obedience of the peoples." Here in Psalm 110:3, the effect of ruling in the midst of His enemies is that "Thy people will volunteer freely in the day of Thy power." Whether the image is that of a scepter between the feet of the Messiah or the Messiah's enemies made as a footstool for His feet, the Messiah's rule brings about the conversion of previous enemies.

We must not miss the momentous truth that the Messiah destroys His enemies **while he is seated at the Father's right hand.** He does not destroy His enemies in His Second Coming, for they have already been destroyed. Victory is secured while Jesus is seated and reigning. As we shall soon see, Jesus doesn't come back to earth until the victory is complete.

We know from New Testament evidence that Jesus Christ is the one pictured as David's Lord sitting at the right hand of the Lord (the Father). It is quite illuminating what Jesus says in Matthew 22:41-45:

> [41]*Now while the Pharisees were gathered together, Jesus asked them a question: [42]'what do you think about the Christ, whose son is He?' They said to Him, 'The son of David.' [43]He said to*

them, *'Then how does David in the Spirit call Him 'Lord,'* *saying,* [44]*'The Lord said to My Lord, "Sit at My right hand, until I put your enemies beneath your feet?" If David then calls Him 'Lord,' how is He his son?'*

Jesus informed the Pharisees that He was the Messiah (Christ), the Son of David, who is David's Lord at the same time. Of course, the Pharisees could not understand. How can David's son be David's Lord? There is no problem theologically once we understand that Jesus is a man and God at the same time – the God/Man. Messiah is God/Man. In one sense, the Pharisees knew that Messiah was the Son of God, but what they could not grasp is how Messiah was fully God while being fully human. In His humanity, Jesus was David's son, and in His deity, Jesus was David's Lord. This idea of God being a man was beyond the comprehension of the Pharisees; they refused to accept such a notion despite what Psalm 110:1 said.

According to Psalm 110:4, this Lord sitting at the right hand of the Lord, is said to be a priest, but not of the priesthood of Aaron, but He is of the priesthood of Melchizedek. In other words, Messiah would be a priestly/king.

Hebrews 6: 19; 7:1-3 states:

[19]*This hope we have as an anchor of the soul, a hope both sure and steadfast and one which enters within the veil, where Jesus has entered as a forerunner for us, having become a high priest forever according to the order of Melchizedek.* [1]*For this Melchizedek, king of Salem, priest of the Most High God, who met Abraham as he was returning from the slaughter of the kings and blessed him,* [2]*to whom also Abraham apportioned a tenth part of all the spoils, was first of all, by the translation of his name, king of righteousness, and then also king of Salem, which is king of peace.* [3]*Without father, without mother, without genealogy, having neither beginning of days nor end of life, but made like the Son of God, he remains a priest perpetually.*

As Psalm 110:5 says, the Messiah, who is at the Father's right hand will shatter kings in the day of His wrath.

Psalm 2

[1]*Why are the nations in an uproar and the peoples devising a vain thing?* [2]*The kings of the earth take their stand And the*

rulers take counsel together against the LORD and against His Anointed, saying, ³'Let us tear their fetters apart and cast away their cords from us!' ⁴He who sits in the heavens laughs, The Lord scoffs at them. Then He will speak to them in His anger and terrify them in His fury, saying, ⁶'But as for Me, I have installed My King Upon Zion, My holy mountain. ⁷I will surely tell of the decree of the LORD:' He said to Me, 'You are My Son, Today I have begotten You. ⁸Ask of Me, and I will surely give the nations as Your inheritance, And the very ends of the earth as Your possession. ⁹You shall break them with a rod of iron, You shall shatter them like earthenware.' ¹⁰Now therefore, O kings, show discernment; Take warning, O judges of the earth. ¹¹Worship the LORD with reverence and rejoice with trembling. ¹²Do homage to the Son, that He not become angry, and you perish in the way, for His wrath may soon be kindled. How blessed are all who take refuge in Him!

The Psalm presents the nations in rebellion to God with the imagery of raising their puny fists in God's face with the delusion that they can have nothing to do with God and His anointed. This is expressed by the phrase, "Let us tear their fetters apart, and cast away their cords from us!" How foolish of reprobate men to think that they are autonomous (self rule) and not accountable to and governed by a sovereign God. Does God worry that men don't honor Him? Does the rebellion of men somehow thwart the plan of God? Hardly! Psalm 2:4-5 states that God laughs and scoffs at rebellious nations. God's sovereignty is absolute, and the joint plan of nations means nothing before such a majestic God. Isaiah 40:21-25 sets forth God's sovereignty over the nations:

²¹Do you not know? Have you not heard? Has it not been declared to you from the beginning? Have you not understood from the foundations of the earth? ²²It is He who sits above the circle of the earth, and its inhabitants are like grasshoppers, who stretches out the heavens like a curtain and spreads them out like a tent to dwell in. ²³He it is who reduces rulers to nothing, who makes the judges of the earth meaningless. ²⁴Scarcely have they been planted, scarcely have they been sown, scarcely has their stock taken root in the earth, but He merely blows on them, and they wither, and the storm carries them away like stubble. ²⁵'To whom then will you liken Me that I would be his equal?' says the Holy One.

Psalm 2 pictures God as laughing and scoffing at the nations in defiance of Him and His anointed. He will speak to them in His anger and will terrify them. The question is: how does God terrify the nations in rebellion to Him? First, the New Testament ties together the crucifixion of Jesus in Acts 4:25-28 with Psalm 2:1-2. Acts 4:25-27 reads:

> [25]*Who by the Holy Spirit, through the mouth of our father David Your servant, said, 'Why did the Gentiles rage, and the peoples devise futile things?* [26]*The kings of the earth took their stand, and the rulers were gathered together against the Lord and against His Christ.'* [27]*For truly in this city there were gathered together against Your holy servant Jesus, whom You anointed, both Herod and Pontius Pilate, along with the Gentiles and the peoples of Israel to do whatever Thy hand and Thy purpose predestined to occur.*

The passage in Acts does not convey everything that Psalm 2 conveys but only a part of it. The Messiah must first be crucified and then raised from the dead. The rest of Psalm 2 speaks of the Messianic role of subduing the nations in keeping with them being His inheritance. It would encompass the activity of the installed king during His Messianic reign. For example, the apostle Paul makes reference to Psalm 2:7 in his successful preaching among the Gentiles as recorded in Acts 13:32-39. More will be said shortly with reference to this passage.

Psalm 2:6 states, *"but as for Me, I have installed My king upon Zion, My holy mountain."* Who is this king? First, we know "His anointed" in Psalm 2:2 is a reference to the Messiah. The term "Anointed One" is the Hebrew word, "Messiah." Hence, the Messiah is the One who is installed as king upon Mt. Zion. Psalm 2:7 expands on the nature of this installation. The Messiah speaks, *"I will surely tell of the decree of the Lord: He said to Me, 'Thou art My Son, today I have begotten Thee.'"*

The term "Zion" originally applied to the physical site that included Mount Moriah where Solomon built the temple (Isaiah 8:18; Joel 3:17; Micah 4:7). But, the reference to Mt. Zion came to mean far more than a reference to a physical site; it primarily came to refer to Jerusalem itself (2 Kings 19:21; Psalm 48:2, 11-13, 69:35; Isaiah 1:8), the whole Jewish nation (Isaiah 40:9; Zechariah 9:13), and most importantly to the church of God.[23]

---

[23]   See discussion on the church being referred to as Zion in Chapter 1, page 45-46.

If there is any doubt that Psalm 2 and II Samuel 7:14 are referring to the Lord Jesus Christ, we only have to cite Hebrews 1:5; 5:5-6:

> *"For to which of the angels did He ever say, 'Thou are My Son, today I have begotten Thee?' And again, 'I will be a Father to Him and He shall be a Son to Me?' 'So also Christ did not glorify Himself so as to become a high priest, but who said to Him, 'Thou art My Son, today I have begotten Thee.' Just as He says also in another passage, 'Thou art a priest forever according to the order of Melchizedek.'"*

The writer of the book of Hebrews, in speaking about the majesty of the Lord Jesus Christ, states in Hebrews 1:8 – *"but of the Son He says, 'Thy throne, O God, is forever and ever, and the righteous scepter is the scepter of His kingdom.'"* This is a direct reference to Psalm 45:6 which is basically what II Samuel 7:16 states when it says, "Y*our kingdom shall endure before Me forever; your throne shall be established forever.*" And then of course, Hebrews 1:13 references Psalm 110:1 when it says, "*But to which of the angels has He ever said, 'Sit at My right hand, until I make Thine enemies a footstool for Thy feet?'"*

There is no question that the Lord Jesus Christ is the king being installed on Mt. Zion in Psalm 2, and the Davidic covenant promises world wide blessing through David's seed.

The Davidic Covenant Promises Messiah (Christ) the Nations as His Inheritance

Psalm 2:7-9 refers to the reigning Messiah king having inherited the nations as His inheritance and that the king breaks the nations with a rod of iron and shatters them like earthenware. While Psalm 2 goes on to warn the judges of the earth to do homage to the Son or perish, we should not view the breaking of the nations and the shattering of them to exclusively be a reference to their physical destruction. Throughout Scripture this imagery is used to refer to spiritual destruction and even to spiritual conversion. The most definitive demonstration of this is Psalm 110:1-4 which has been alluded to already. The stretching forth of the Son's scepter to rule in the midst of His enemies is specifically said to be expressed in His people volunteering freely in the day of His power. Moreover, the scepter between Shiloh's feet as set forth in Genesis 49:10 shall lead to the "obedience of the peoples." In another chapter, I will demonstrate that the preaching of the Gospel is how Jesus rules the nations with a rod of iron, and with the "breath of His lips" He slays the wicked.

Psalm 22:27-28

Psalm 22:27-28 is a glorious Messianic Psalm depicting the victory of Christ's kingdom. The text states:

> [27]*All the ends of the earth will remember and turn to the Lord, and all the families of the nations will worship before Thee.* [28]*For the kingdom is the Lord's and He rules over the nations.*

The Lord will save the nations because they are His inheritance per Psalm 2:8.

Psalm 72

This Messianic Psalm is a magnificent depiction of not only the extensive reign of the Messiah (from sea to sea) (v.8), it also conveys the success of His reign in defeating His enemies, causing them to "lick the dust." (v.9) The Messianic kingdom is perpetual throughout the generations (vv. 15-17). It will bring tremendous social reformation – justice to the poor and needy and economic prosperity to the nations (vv. 2-4, 12-14). The spiritual benefits of His reign are immense in that the nations will call Him blessed (v. 17). The whole earth will be filled with His glory (v.19).

The chapter reads:

> [1]*Give the king Your judgments, O God, and Your righteousness to the king's son.* [2]*May he judge Your people with righteousness and Your afflicted with justice.* [3]*Let the mountains bring peace to the people, and the hills, in righteousness.* [4]*May he vindicate the afflicted of the people, save the children of the needy and crush the oppressor.* [5]*Let them fear You while the sun endures, and as long as the moon, throughout all generations.* [6]*May he come down like rain upon the mown grass, like showers that water the earth.* [7]*In his days may the righteous flourish, and abundance of peace till the moon is no more.* [8]*May he also rule from sea to sea and from the River to the ends of the earth.* 9*Let the nomads of the desert bow before him, and his enemies lick the dust.* [10]*Let the kings of Tarshish and of the islands bring presents; the kings of Sheba and Seba offer gifts.* [11]*And let all kings bow down before him, all nations serve him.* [12]*For he will deliver the needy when he cries for help, the afflicted also, and him who has no helper.* [13]*He will have compassion on the poor and needy, and the lives of the needy he will save.* [14]*He will rescue their life from oppression and violence, and their blood will be precious in his sight;* [15]*So may he live, and may the gold of Sheba be given to*

him; and let them pray for him continually; Let them bless him all day long. [16]May there be abundance of grain in the earth on top of the mountains; its fruit will wave like the cedars of Lebanon; and may those from the city flourish like vegetation of the earth. [17]May his name endure forever; may his name increase as long as the sun shines; and let men bless themselves by him; let all nations call him blessed. [18]Blessed be the LORD God, the God of Israel, Who alone works wonders. [19]And blessed be His glorious name forever; and may the whole earth be filled with His glory. Amen, and Amen. [20]The prayers of David the son of Jesse are ended.

John Calvin has some noteworthy comments on Psalm 72 in his Old Testament commentary:[24]

> David, therefore, teaches us that as God defends the earth from the heat of the sun by watering it, so he in like manner provides for the welfare of his Church, and defends it under the government of the king. But this prediction has received its highest fulfillment in Christ, who, by distilling upon the Church His secret grace, renders her fruitful...

> Moreover, when David represents the life of the king as prolonged to the end of the world, this shows more clearly that he not only comprehends his successors who occupied an earthly throne, but that he ascends even to Christ, who, by rising from the dead, obtained for himself celestial life and glory, that he might govern his Church for ever...

> The Prophet immediately adds, that *the enemies of the king shall lick the dust* in token of their reverence. This, as is well known, was in ancient times a customary ceremony among the nations of the East; and Alexander the Great, after he had conquered the East, wished to compel his subjects to practice it, from which arose great dissatisfaction and contentions, the Macedonians disdainfully refusing to yield such a slavish and degrading mark of subjection. The meaning then is, that the king chosen by God in Judea will obtain so complete a victory over all his enemies, far and wide, that they shall come humbly to pay him homage...

---

[24]　Calvin's Old Testament commentary on Psalm 72.

V. 11 And all kings shall prostrate themselves before him. This verse contains a more distinct statement of the truth, that the whole world will be brought in subjection to the authority of Christ... From this we also learn, that in the Church and flock of Christ there is a place for kings; whom David does not here disarm of their sword nor despoil of their crown, in order to admit them into the Church, but rather declares that they will come with all the dignity of their station to prostrate themselves at the feet of Christ...

V. 16 A handful of corn shall be in the earth upon the top of the mountains... By this figure is portrayed the large abundance of all good things which, through the blessing of God, would be enjoyed under the reign of Christ. To this is added the increase of children. Not only would the earth produce an abundance of all kinds of fruits, but the cities and towns also would be fruitful in the production of men.

Acts 2:25-36

This passage is probably the most definitive New Testament proof that Jesus' Messianic reign has already begun; it establishes undeniably that the Messianic reign officially began with Jesus' resurrection and ascension to the Father's right hand in fulfillment of Psalm 110.

Acts 2:25-36:

[25]*For David says of Him, 'I saw the Lord always in my presence; for He is at my right hand, so that I will not be shaken.* [26]*Therefore my heart was glad and my tongue exulted; moreover my flesh also will live in hope;* [27]*because you will not abandon My soul to Hades, nor allow Your Holy One to undergo decay.* [28]*You have made known to me the ways of life; you will make me full of gladness with your presence.'* [29]*Brethren, I may confidently say to you regarding the patriarch David that he both died and was buried, and his tomb is with us to this day.* [30]*And so, because he was a prophet and knew that God had sworn to him with an oath to seat one of his descendants on his throne,* [31]*he looked ahead and spoke of the resurrection of the Christ, that He was neither abandoned to Hades, nor did His flesh suffer.* [32]*This Jesus God raised up again, to which we are all witnesses.* [33]*Therefore having been exalted to the right hand of God, and having received from the Father the promise of the Holy Spirit, He has poured forth this which you both see and*

hear. For it was not David who ascended into heaven, but he himself says: 'The Lord said to my Lord, sit at My right hand, until I make your enemies a footstool for Your feet.' Therefore let all the house of Israel know for certain that God has made Him both Lord and Christ--this Jesus whom you crucified.'

In verses 25-28, Peter alludes to David as a prophet and quotes Psalm 16:8-11. In verse 29, Peter clarifies that Psalm 16 promised that God would not abandon the Messiah's body to the grave. David died and saw corruption but not the Holy One. In verse 31, Peter emphatically states that David prophesied of the resurrection of the Christ. Neither David nor Peter can err when they prophesy. Peter confirms that he and others are witnesses of Jesus' resurrection. We must remember that part of the promise of the Davidic covenant was that one will come forth from David and sit on his throne, establishing it forever. Notice carefully how inspired Peter links the promise of the Davidic covenant and the establishment of David's throne as beginning with Jesus' resurrection. We have already established from Scripture earlier that David's throne is also God's throne, and it is Messiah's throne! Peter wants his Jewish audience to understand without doubt that Jesus Christ is the promised seed of David and is the promised One to sit on David's throne; hence, He is the Messiah.

In verse 33, Peter links **the ascension of Christ to God's right hand** to the Messianic prophecy in Psalm 110:1 by directly referring to it. Luke 1:32-33 has the angel Gabriel affirming that Jesus indeed is the promised seed to sit on David's throne and would reign forever.

When did Jesus sit on David's throne? It occurred when Jesus was resurrected and ascended to God the Father's right hand! Here is definitive, inspired proof when it happened. Notice that it does not say that Jesus sat on some physical throne, nor does it say it happened after the Second Coming in some future period of time. This is biblical proof that all forms of Premillennialism are incorrect.

Peter confirms that Jesus is sitting presently on David's throne **in heaven** and subduing all His enemies from this position. What is Peter's proof? It is the outpouring of the Holy Spirit on the Day of Pentecost that led to Spirit empowered preaching that brought about the conversion of 3000 souls. When the Messiah sat at God's right hand in Psalm 110, did this not promise that He would stretch out His scepter from Zion and rule in the midst of His people? Did it not promise that "Thy people would volunteer freely in the day of Thy power?" This explains how 3000 people volunteered freely by repenting and getting saved. Did not the Scripture promise in the Abrahamic covenant that the lion of the tribe of Judah is also Shiloh and that the scepter of Shiloh was between His feet bringing about the obedience of the people? Did not Peter quote Psalm 110 that emphasizes that Messiah would sit at the right hand of God **until** God the Father makes His enemies a footstool for His feet?

This glorious ascension and session of Christ was magnificently prophesied in the Old Testament. Daniel 7:13-14 and Zechariah 6:9-15 are prime examples.

Daniel 7:13-14

One of the most important Old Testament prophecies of Christ's enthronement as King of kings and Lord of lords is Daniel 7:13-14:

> *[13] I kept looking in the night visions, and behold, with the clouds of heaven One like a Son of Man was coming, and He came up to the Ancient of Days and was presented before Him. [14] And to Him was given dominion, Glory and a kingdom that all the peoples, nations and men of every language might serve Him. His dominion is an everlasting dominion which will not pass away; and His kingdom is one which will not be destroyed.*

Virtually all Dispensationalists believe that this passage speaks of Christ's Second Coming, but this interpretation is incorrect and fails to follow the wording of the text. In Jesus' Second Coming, He will descend to earth. Nothing is said here of a descent. The text says that One like a Son of Man "came up to" the Ancient of Days. The only synonym that fits the text is "ascend." The term "Son of Man" refers to Jesus Christ, who used this term for Himself more than the phrase "Son of God." The whole passage pictures One coming to royalty, "the Ancient of Days," to receive a kingdom. Daniel 7:13-14, II Samuel 7:8-17, Psalm 2:6-8, and Acts 2:25-36 all are speaking of Christ's enthronement as King of the universe.

Daniel's prophecy reveals that Jesus Christ, upon His coming up to the Ancient of Days, is given dominion, glory, and a kingdom. As Psalm 2:6-8 indicates, the Father promised the Son all the nations as His inheritance, and the Son received them in principle at His ascension to God the Father's right hand in heaven. From Father's right hand, the Son, the Lord Jesus Christ is exercising His full authority, having all the power. He is subduing all His enemies upon David's throne in heaven. Any theological view that brings Jesus down to earth to sit on some physical throne, in a rebuilt temple, and in one city on earth simply does not understand or appreciate the greatness of Christ's present spiritual reign.

On the Day of Pentecost, Daniel's prophecy was wonderfully fulfilled, and nothing has been the same sense. From that day, the risen Lord Jesus has been exercising dominion over His inheritance. Pentecost is the beginning of what Jesus told His disciples just prior to His ascension recorded in Acts 1:8 – *"But you will receive power when the Holy Spirit has come upon you; and you shall be My witnesses both in Jerusalem, and in all Judea and Samaria, and even the remotest part of the earth."*

Zechariah 6:9-15

This is another marvelous Old Testament prophecy regarding the coming priestly king. The text states:

> *⁹The word of the LORD also came to me, saying, ¹⁰'Take an offering from the exiles, from Heldai, Tobijah and Jedaiah; and you go the same day and enter the house of Josiah the son of Zephaniah, where they have arrived from Babylon. ¹¹Take silver and gold, make an ornate crown and set it on the head of Joshua the son of Jehozadak, the high priest.' ¹²Then say to him, 'Thus says the LORD of hosts, Behold, a man whose name is Branch, for He will branch out from where He is; and He will build the temple of the LORD. ¹³Yes, it is He who will build the temple of the LORD, and He who will bear the honor and sit and rule on His throne. Thus, He will be a priest on His throne, and the counsel of peace will be between the two offices.' ¹⁴Now the crown will become a reminder in the temple of the LORD to Helem, Tobijah, Jedaiah and Hen the son of Zephaniah. ¹⁵Those who are far off will come and build the temple of the LORD. Then you will know that the LORD of hosts has sent me to you. And it will take place if you completely obey the LORD your God.*

The commentators Kiel and Delitsch and Matthew Henry make astute observations of this great Messianic prophecy:

> The series of visions... sets before the eye the figure of the mediator of salvation, who, as crowned high priest, or as priestly king, is to build the kingdom of God, and raise it into a victorious power over all the kingdoms of this world, for the purpose of comforting and strengthening the congregation.[25]

---

[25] Kiel-Delitzsch, *Commentary on the Old Testament* Vol. 10, (Grand Rapids, MI: William B. Erdmans Publishing Co., 1977), p. 296.

It is observable that there should be two eminent types of Christ in the Old Testament that were both named *Joshua* (the same name with *Jesus,* and by the LXX., and in the New Testament, rendered *Jesus,* Acts vii. 45) -- Joshua the chief captain, a type of Christ the captain of our salvation, and Joshua the chief priest, a type of Christ the high priest of our profession, and both in their day saviours and leaders into Canaan. And this is peculiar to Joshua the high priest, that here was something done to him by the divine appointment on purpose that he might be a type of Christ, a priest after the order of Melchizedek, who was both a king and a priest.[26]

John Calvin understands this as a glorious promise of the coming Christ who will build His temple, the church:

And further, the possession of the land was not of itself desirable, except with reference to the hope given them; that is, because God had promised by his Prophets that the kingdom of David would again be made glorious, and also that the grandeur and glory of the temple would be greater than ever before... when the kingly office and the priesthood flourished: for these were the chief ornaments, or the two eyes, as it were, of the body — the priest, a mediator between God and men — and the king, sustaining the person of God in governing the people. We hence see that by the two crowns is set forth the restoration of the Church: but we must also observe that the two crowns are placed on the head of Joshua, which was new and unusual...

Here then we find a union of royalty and priesthood in the same person, which had never before been the case; for God had in his law made a distinction between the two offices. We hence see that something unknown before is set forth by this prophecy, even this, that the same person would be both a king and a priest...

The Prophet is bid to *set the two crowns on the head of the high priest.* This, as I have said, was intended as a symbol to denote the union of the two dignities in the person of Christ... It is then no wonder that God brought forth the high priest Joshua, who was a type and representative of Christ; and he brought him forth with a double crown, because he who was to come would unite, according to what follows, the priesthood with the kingly office...

---

[26]   Matthew Henry, *Matthew Henry's Commentary of the Whole Bible* Vol. 2, (Wilmington, DE: Sovereign Grace Publishers, 1972), p. 1475.

Hence he says, that there would be a *man*, whose name was to be *Branch*... He then says, *And he shall build the temple of Jehovah*. This is a remarkable passage: it hence appears that the temple which the Jews had then begun to build, and which was afterwards built by Herod, was not the true temple of which Haggai had prophesied, when he said, "The glory of the second house shall be greater than that of the first." ...Christ indeed himself was a temple as to his body, for the fullness of the Godhead dwelt in him, Colossians 2:6;) but he built a temple to God the Father, when he raised up everywhere pure worship, having demolished superstitions, and when he consecrated us to be a royal priesthood... *He, he shall build the temple of Jehovah*; by which he means, "Let not your eyes remain fixed on this temple, for to look at it weakens your faith and almost disheartens you; but hope for another temple which ye see not now, for a priest and a king shall at length come to build a better and a more excellent temple."
...

Bear shall he the glory, and shall sit and rule on his throne. He fully confirms what we have already referred to — that this man, who was to grow by God's hidden power, would be made both a king and a priest, but by no earthly instrumentality... The Prophet also states, that men would come from remote lands to contribute labor or wealth towards the building of the temple; for the word building may refer to either of these two things. *Come* then *shall those from far...* We then see that this prophecy cannot be otherwise referred than to the building of the spiritual temple, when Gentiles, formerly remote from God's people, joined them as friends, and brought their labor to the work of building the temple, not with stones or wood, or with other corruptible materials, but with the doctrine and the gifts of the Holy Spirit.[27]

We know from the Scriptures that the Lord Jesus Christ is Branch, and indeed as Zechariah prophesies, He will branch out and build His temple. Christ is the kingly priest. As Zechariah 6:13 indicates, Branch will be a priest as He sits on His throne, and the **counsel of peace** will be between the two offices of priest and king. How do we understand the "counsel of peace" between these offices? For one, we know according to Isaiah 9:6-7 that the virgin born son's name shall be called, "Prince of Peace." Christ, as Branch, shall manifest peace in His dual capacity. As king, peace will

---

[27]   John Calvin, *Calvin's Commentaries*, Vol. 15, (Grand Rapids, MI: Baker Book House, 1981), pp. 152-163.

be the hallmark of His kingdom. In other words, His reign shall be one of peace. Is this not how Isaiah 2:1-4 and 11:6-10 portray the millennial kingdom? It shall be characterized by universal peace. Messiah's reign will be marked by peace among the nations, but before men can live at peace with one another, they must first be at peace with God. As the Scripture affirms, men, in their unconverted state, are estranged from God. Our sins have separated us from God (Isaiah 59:1-2); a state of hostility exists between sinful men and a holy God. We must be reconciled to our God.

Messiah is also a priest on His throne. As our great High Priest, the Lord Jesus reconciles us to God the Father through His atoning death. Romans 5:1 beautifully states:

> *Therefore having been justified by faith, we have peace with God through our Lord Jesus Christ.*

And Romans 5:10-11 states:

> *[10]For if while we were enemies we were reconciled to God through the death of His Son, much more, having been reconciled, we shall be saved by His life. [11]And not only this, but we also exult in God through our Lord Jesus Christ, through whom we have now received the reconciliation.*

The most explicit New Testament verification that Jesus is the priestly king ministering to His people is Hebrews 8:1-2:

> *[1]Now the main point in what has been said is this: we have such a high priest, who has taken His seat at the right hand of the throne of the Majesty in the heavens, [2]a minister in the sanctuary and in the true tabernacle, which the Lord pitched, not man.*

Jesus is the High Priest who ministers in the sanctuary, in the true tabernacle. From the right hand of God, our great High Priest takes the benefits of His sacrificial death and ministers to His people.

One vital way He does this is to bring reconciliation to His elect by converting them. Every time one of God's elect is regenerated and brought to saving faith, peace has been established between the kingly office and the priestly office of the Branch. As Zechariah 6:12 says, Branch will **build the temple of the Lord, the Lord's house.** According to the New Testament, who is the temple of the Lord? Outside of Jesus being referred to as the temple of the Lord, it refers to the church of the Lord Jesus (Ephesians 2:18-22; I Peter 2:1-10).

We can summarize the main points of Zechariah 6:9-15 as:

1) Joshua, the high priest, is coronated
2) A diadem is placed on his head,
3) Joshua is a type of Christ,
4) The type is called BRANCH,
5) Branch will build God's temple,
6) Branch is a kingly priest where peace exists in His offices,
7) Branch will build God's temple by use of the Gentiles

In keeping with the ongoing fulfillment of Zechariah's prophecy, the ministry of the apostle Paul is proof of the Gentiles (those far off) being used to build the temple of the Lord, the church of the Lord Jesus Christ. In keeping with the Scripture that the gospel should first go to the Jews, being the covenant people of God, Paul's missionary team boldly proclaims to the Jews that God is preaching the good news of the promise made to the fathers. However, the Jews in Asia Minor will demonstrate themselves to have hardened hearts, but the Gentiles will gladly receive the gospel.

Acts 13:32-41, 44-49

[32]And we preach to you the good news of the promise made to the fathers, [33]that God has fulfilled this promise to our children in that He raised up Jesus, as it is also written in the second Psalm, 'You are My Son; Today I have begotten You'. [34]As for the fact that He raised Him up from the dead, no longer to return to decay, He has spoken in this way: 'I will give You the holy and sure blessings of David' [35]Therefore He also says in another Psalm, 'You will not allow Your Holy One to undergo decay.' [36]For David, after he had served the purpose of God in his own generation, fell asleep, and was laid among his fathers and underwent decay; [37]but He whom God raised did not undergo decay. [38]Therefore let it be known to you, brethren, that through Him forgiveness of sins is proclaimed to you, [39]and through Him everyone who believes is freed from all things, from which you could not be freed through the Law of Moses. [40]Therefore take heed, so that the thing spoken of in the Prophets may not come upon you: [41]'Behold, you scoffers, and marvel, and perish; for I am accomplishing a work in your days, a work which you will never believe, though someone should describe it to you.'

[44]The next Sabbath nearly the whole city assembled to hear the word of the Lord. [45]But when the Jews saw the crowds, they were

filled with jealousy and began contradicting the things spoken by Paul, and were blaspheming. ⁴⁶Paul and Barnabas spoke out boldly and said, 'It was necessary that the word of God be spoken to you first; since you repudiate it and judge yourselves unworthy of eternal life, behold, we are turning to the Gentiles. ⁴⁷For so the Lord has commanded us, 'I have place you as a light for the Genitles, that you may bring salvation to the end of the earth.' ⁴⁸When the Gentiles heard this, they began rejoicing and glorifying the word of the Lord; and as many as had been appointed to eternal life believed. ⁴⁹And the word of the Lord was being spread through the whole region.

Several noteworthy things must be observed. First, this passage proves that the blessings of David do not wait until after the Second Coming of Christ, but belong to the present age, demonstrating that Jesus is presently reigning. And, the passage demonstrates that the apostolic preaching is in fulfillment of Psalm 2:7-8, Hence, as gospel preaching goes forth, the Messiah is converting the nations in keeping with the promise of the Father that all nations were given to the Son for His inheritance.

The apostle Paul says exactly the same thing as Peter concerning the promises of the Davidic covenant being fulfilled with the resurrection of Jesus. Paul's preaching of the gospel to the Gentiles is the fulfillment of the sure blessings of David. Paul's preaching is the effect of Jesus sitting on David's throne in heaven. As men believe in Jesus through preaching, they are freed from the bondage of sin, experiencing forgiveness of sins. Peter's preaching on the Day of Pentecost demonstrated the blessings of David, as well as Paul's preaching.

Second, this was Paul's first missionary journey, and, in keeping with going to the Jews first with the Gospel, sadly, the Jews will reject the Gospel due to their hardened hearts precipitating Paul turning to the Gentiles, who will gladly embrace the Gospel. Paul quotes Isaiah 42 and 49 as being fulfilled in his ministry to the Gentiles. Indeed, those far off (Gentiles) will build the temple of the Lord as Zechariah prophesied.

Acts 15:12-18

¹²All the people kept silent, and they were listening to Barnabas and Paul as they were relating what signs and wonders God had done through them among the Gentiles. ¹³After they had stopped speaking, James answered, saying, 'Brethren, listen to me. ¹⁴Simeon has related how God first concerned Himself about *taking from among the Gentiles a people for His name.' [15]With this the words of the Prophets agree, just as it is written, [16]'After these things I will return, and I will **rebuild the tabernacle of David** which has fallen, and I will rebuild its ruins, and I will restore it, [17]so that the rest of mankind may seek the Lord, and all the Gentiles who are called by My name, [18]says the Lord, who makes these things known from long ago.'* (Emphasis mine)

This passage demonstrates as well that the preaching to the Gentiles whether it was by Peter or Paul, was an ongoing fulfillment of the Davidic covenant. The apostle James quotes from Amos 9:11-15 in order to show that what God was doing among the Gentiles was indeed a fulfillment of Amos' passage, that David's tabernacle was being rebuilt. The historic reality was that David's tabernacle was ruined and fallen down. There had not been for ages a king of the house of David; the scepter had departed from Judah. The royal family had been buried in obscurity. We noted earlier from Luke 1:32-33 that the angel Gabriel affirmed to Mary that her child would be given the throne of David and that He would reign over it forever.

We know from Peter's sermon on Pentecost (Acts 2:25-36) that Jesus' resurrection and ascension was the definitive proof that Christ had assumed David's throne. From Acts 2:25-36 and Acts 13:32-39, we see that the preaching of the Gospel particularly to the Gentiles is the rebuilding of David's tabernacle. Jesus is the promised seed who would sit on David's throne, establishing His kingdom forever. Inspired James says that the incorporating of the Jews and Gentiles into the church is the rebuilding of David's tabernacle.

In opposition to inspired James, we have the view of dispensationalist C.I. Scofield on Acts 15:

> After God has taken out a people for His name from among the Gentiles to form the church (which Simeon related would occur first before the second advent), the second advent of Christ will occur and Christ will reestablish the Davidic rule over Israel in order that Israelites may seek after the Lord and also in order that all the millennial Gentiles may do the same.[28]

Dispensationalists interpret "after these things I will return" as the Second Coming of Christ. This dispensational understanding of Acts 15 is

---

[28]   Scofield Bible notes on Acts 15

indicative of the exegetical gymnastics that must be exercised to fit the Bible into a certain theological model rather than allowing the Scripture to naturally reveal the meaning of the text. Is there anything in Acts 15 that explicitly or even remotely refers to some millennial period after the Second Coming of Christ?

"After these things" must be interpreted in its historical context in Amos where Amos' prophecy was directed against the northern kingdom of Israel. The context of Amos refers to the scattering of the northern kingdom of Israel that was carried out by the Assyrians in 722 B.C. "After this" refers to the time of the establishment of the NT church. It should be clear that James is using Amos to prove that the Messianic age is a time of Gentile spiritual blessings, not an age of Jewish blessing. The context of Acts 15 pertains to how the Jewish Christians are to view the great conversions among the Gentiles that occurred under Peter and Paul's ministries, particularly Paul's missionary journeys. But the dispensational position is that the Messianic age spoken of in Amos is not the church age, but a yet future Jewish millennium and that James quoted Amos in order to prove that the time of special Jewish blessing would come after a time of Gentile blessing. This only demonstrates that the dispensational presupposition that God has two distinct peoples with distinct purposes is a faulty view that the Scripture explicitly refutes.

The nature of Christ's Messianic reign is for the building of a holy temple, which we know emphatically from the New Testament to be **His church**. The reign of Christ from David's throne in heaven is for the subduing of His enemies, for the building up of His church, the temple of the Lord. This church incorporates both Jew and Greek into one body. Hence, the millennial kingdom is not an exclusively Jewish rule.

Where is God's throne? It is in heaven, not on some physical piece of furniture or in some physical city that cannot even begin to convey the regal authority of Christ.

When did the millennium begin? It officially began with the coronation of Jesus' kingship when He sat down at God's right hand!

Jesus was prophesied to be a king; He was born a king, but His official enthronement was not until His state of humiliation was complete (from his conception to His burial). His state of exaltation began with His resurrection which extended to His ascension and seating at God's right hand and continues with His Second Coming at the end of the world.

Summary Points of David's Covenant Pertaining to Christ's Millennial Reign

1) Christ is David's seed
2) David's seed is also Abraham's seed
3) Christ will establish David's kingdom
4) David's kingdom (Christ's kingdom) will endure forever
5) Jesus Christ is on God's throne in heaven
6) God's throne is David's throne
7) Christ's kingdom grants rest to God's people by subduing their enemies
8) Jesus' resurrection and ascension is when He sat on David's throne
9) Jesus Christ is a kingly priest on David's throne
10) Christ is promised the nations as His inheritance
11) Christ's reign is marked by earthly peace
12) Jesus Christ is building God's temple, His church, from David's throne
13) God's temple is comprised of both Jews and Gentiles as one body, one house
14) Christ's kingdom cannot be exclusively a Jewish time for glory
15) Christ's reign is fundamentally a spiritual reign
16) the Great Commission is the exercise of Christ's Messianic reign
17) Christ, from David's throne, makes His people willing in the day of His power

A Victorious Reign and Then the End of the World

Differences among the varying millennial views fundamentally revolve around two issues: **1) the nature and character of the millennium, and 2) the timing of the Second Coming.** The names given to various millennial views are determined mostly by what one believes about the timing of the Second Coming. When timing is discussed, there are essentially two millennial views – premillennialism and postmillennialism. The differences are determined by **when** the Second Coming occurs with reference to the millennium. If one believes that the Second Coming is **before** a millennium, then one is (pre) millennial. If one believes the Second Coming is **after** the millennium, then one is (post) millennial.

For most of this chapter, emphasis has been upon the nature of the millennium and proving that we are presently in the millennial age. Now, emphasis will be upon the timing of the Second Coming, and when the end of the world will come without setting dates.

Jesus' disciples were curious as to the timing of the end of the age and Jesus' Second Coming, just like many Christians throughout history. Matthew 24 is a pivotal biblical passage, but one that is greatly misunderstood.

Matthew 24

One of the most often used passages used in determining eschatological events is that of Matthew 24. It is especially a favorite of dispensational premillennialists. It is an important passage to understand, and there is a considerable difference of opinion as to its meaning. Amillennialists and postmillennialists would take great exception to dispensationalism's understanding.

In order to understand Matthew 24, one must understand the backdrop of the chapter, and that backdrop is Matthew 23:23-39. Israel had come to the point where it was going to fill up the measure of the guilt of their fathers. This will be the guilt of their crucifixion of Jesus, their Messiah. They will crucify the Son of God, the Son of David. What greater crime could they commit?

To understand the magnitude of national Israel's guilt, we need to jump ahead for a moment to show the incredible tragedy that was to befall Israel during this generation as expressed in Matthew 27:24-25. When Jesus was sent to the Roman governor, Pontius Pilate, by the Jewish Sanhedrin, Pilate can find no guilt in Jesus to merit His death, and Pilate will try to find a way out of the situation by offering the release of either Jesus or a known criminal, Barabbas. What transpired is a terrifying reality for this generation of Jews.

Matthew 27:15-26:

> [15]*Now at the feast the governor was accustomed to release for the people any one prisoner whom they wanted.* [16]*At that time they were holding a notorious prisoner, called Barabbas.* [17]*So when the people gathered together, Pilate said to them, 'Whom do you want me to release for you? Barabbas, or Jesus who is called Christ?'* [18]*For he knew that because of envy they had handed Him over.* [19]*While he was sitting on the judgment seat, his wife sent him a message, saying, 'Have nothing to do with that righteous Man; for last night I suffered greatly in a dream*

*because of Him.' * ^20^*But the chief priests and the elders persuaded the crowds to ask for Barabbas and to put Jesus to death. * ^21^*But the governor said to them, 'Which of the two do you want me to release for you?' And they said, 'Barabbas.' * ^22^*Pilate said to them, 'Then what shall I do with Jesus who is called Christ?' They all said, 'Crucify Him!' * ^23^*And he said, 'Why, what evil has He done?' But they kept shouting all the more, saying, 'Crucify Him!' * ^24^*When Pilate saw that he was accomplishing nothing, but rather that a riot was starting, he took water and washed his hands in front of the crowd, saying, 'I am innocent of this Man's blood; see to that yourselves.' * ^25^***And all the people said, 'His blood shall be on us and on our children!' *** ^26^*Then he released Barabbas for them; but after having Jesus scourged, he handed Him over to be crucified* (Emphasis mine).

This self proclaimed curse will indeed transpire in 70 A.D. with the destruction of Jerusalem by the Roman legions under Titus. This event is the great Tribulation that Jesus spoke of in the first portion of Matthew 24.

There are two major sections in Matthew 24:

Section 1 - events to befall contemporary generation of Jesus, the destruction of Jerusalem and the temple (Matthew 24:1-35)

Verse 34 – dividing point

Section 2 - events occurring at the Second Coming of Christ at the end of the world (Matthew 24:36-51)

We can say that the events found in verses 1-35 were fulfilled in the generation specified by Christ. Verses 36-51 deal with events at the Second Coming at the end of the world. This interpretation could be generally classified as a **"partial or moderate preterism"** approach to Matthew 24 and also which would govern an interpretation of the book of Revelation.[29]

---

[29] This is not a novel interpretation of Matthew 24. For other books coming from this "partial preterest" understanding of Matthew 24, I refer the reader to other works, and even among these books there is not total agreement concerning the entirety of Matthew 24. For a defense of the position similar to the one in this book, I refer readers to the following books: *An Eschatology of Victory* by Marcellus Kik, John Calvin's *New Testament Commentaries, An Exposition of the New Testament* by John Gil, and an unpublished syllabus on Matthew 24 by Joe Morecraft III. While Kenneth Gentry does not discuss Matthew 24:36-51 in his book *He Shall Have Dominion*, he does express essentially the same view as this book when he answered questions in an

What do we mean by preterism? Preterism is based on the Latin word, "preter," meaning past. Hence, certain eschatological passages have already come to pass. Partial preterism would hold that many of the prophecies of Revelation and the first portion of the Olivet Discourse of Matthew 24 were fulfilled in the events surrounding Jerusalem's fall in 70 A.D.

Partial preterism is to be distinguished from "full preterism" or "hyper preterism" which **erroneously** teaches that all of Matthew 24 events have been fulfilled, that the Second Coming and resurrection occurred at the fall of Jerusalem.

Since we are saying that Matthew 24:34 is the pivotal passage in the Olivet Discourse, let's take a look at it- *"Truly I say to you, this generation will not pass away until all these things take place."* How should we understand "generation"? The meanings of words are found in their immediate and broad context. So, does Jesus mean the generation to whom he is talking to? Or, is He meaning some distant generation that sees the events He is referring to. The most literal approach would be to think that Jesus is referring to His contemporary generation. How does Matthew typically use "generation?" That is very important. Matthew 11:16 gives some insight:

> *But to what shall I compare this generation? It is like children sitting in the market places, who call out to other children.*

In Matthew 12:38-45, the scribes and Pharisees were insisting upon signs from Jesus. Jesus condemns "this evil generation" for craving signs. In this passage, Jesus is clearly referring to the present generation of Jews.

---

interview conducted for *The Word, Volume 12, Issue 6 (July 2001)* found on: http://preteristsite.com/docs/gentrypretpost.html. Gentry also wrote a 2008 article titled *On the transitional verses of Matthew 24* where he lays out the exegetical case for dividing Matthew 24 into two major sections with the first major section (Matthew 24:1-34) pertaining to the fall of Jerusalem, and the second major section (Matthew 24:36-51) pertaining to the Second Coming. This article can be read at: http://www.forerunner.com/beast/X0003_Gentry_on_Matthew_24.html.

For other books that would agree that the Great Tribulation was fulfilled in 70 A.D. I refer readers to: *Postmillennialism: An Eschatology of Hope* by Keith A. Matthison; *He Shall Have Dominion* by Kenneth L. Gentry Jr.; *Last Days Madness* by Gary DeMar; *Victory in Jesus: The Bright Hope of Postmillennialism* by Greg L. Bahnsen.

The most significant usage of "this generation" is seen in Matthew 23:36. Jesus states:

Truly, I say to you, all these things shall come upon this generation.

In verses 32-35, Jesus had just rebuked the present generation of Jews who were filling up the measure of the guilt of their fathers who had murdered the prophets. The cup of guilt would be full when the present generation would crucify Him, their Messiah. This passage is virtually identical to Matthew 24:34. Moreover, the fact that the demonstrative pronoun "this" precedes the word, "generation," is further exegetical proof that it is a contemporary generation Jesus is referring to, not some future generation thousands of years later. This "generation" is Jesus' contemporary generation.

As I have noted already, Jesus had given a railing rebuke to the religious leaders of Israel for their hypocrisy and that upon them, "this generation" (Matthew 23:36) shall fall the guilt of all the righteous blood on earth.

And when those who preferred Barabbas to Jesus and were willing to have Jesus' crucified blood on their and their children's hands, they were pronouncing their own judgment upon themselves just like Pharaoh in the last plague on Egypt.

In Luke 23:26-30 we read:

[26]When they led Him away, they seized a man, Simon of Cyrene, coming in from the country, and placed on him the cross to carry behind Jesus. [27]And following Him was a large crowd of the people, and of women who were mourning and lamenting Him. [28]But Jesus turning to them said, 'Daughters of Jerusalem, stop weeping for Me, but weep for yourselves and for your children. [29]For behold, the days are coming when they will say, 'Blessed are the barren, and the wombs that never bore, and the breasts that never nursed.' [30]Then they will begin to say to the mountains, 'fall on us,' and to the hills, cover us.'

As Jesus was being led away to be crucified, a great number of women were following Him and weeping, and Jesus said the above words. What was to befall them in the fall of Jerusalem was more horrifying than they could ever imagine. God was abandoning national Israel for her sins. To think that Jesus was referring to some event thousands of years into the future makes no sense whatsoever, and violates the most natural and clear meaning of His words. The women constituted the very generation that would go through the great tribulation of 70 A.D.

We must stress the importance of Matthew 23:37-39:

> *[37]Jerusalem, Jerusalem, who kills the prophets and stones those who are sent to her! How often I wanted to gather your children together, the way a hen gathers her chicks under her wings, and you were unwilling. [38]Behold, your house is being left to you desolate! [39]For I say to you, from now on you will not see Me until you say, 'Blessed is He who comes in the name of the Lord!'*

Jesus wept over the great city of Jerusalem, the city where God chose to put His name, the city where the temple resided, the holiest place on earth in the Old Covenant, where God's presence was symbolized. Yet, as we have seen in other sections, God's promises do not fall automatically to a physical seed or to a physical city. God destroyed Israel in the past for its unfaithfulness. He destroyed Solomon's temple and sent the visible covenant people off to captivity. Just as Jeremiah lamented the fall of Jerusalem, Jesus wept over her that was once great over the nations. Now, it will be no different than what Jeremiah says of Jerusalem in his time. Lamentations 1:8 states:

> *Jerusalem sinned greatly; therefore she has become an unclean thing. All who honored her despise her because they have seen her nakedness; even she herself groans and turns away.*

It is noteworthy what Jesus said as He came out of the temple as recorded in Matthew 24:1-3:

> *[1]Jesus came out from the temple and was going away when His disciples came up to point out the temple buildings to Him. [2]And He said to them, 'Do you not see all these things? Truly I say to you, not one stone here will be left upon another, which will not be torn down.' [3]As He was sitting on the Mount of Olives, the disciples came to Him privately, saying, 'Tell us, when will these things happen, and what will be the sign of Your coming, and of the end of the age?'*

Because of her hard heartedness, Jerusalem is doomed. Look what Jesus says in v.38 – "B*ehold your house is being left to you desolate.*" Earlier, the temple was His house, a house of prayer that they were corrupting. Well, it is no longer His house but their house. God has left the temple. The glory of God has departed. What a grievous reality! Their doom is sealed. Consequently, Jesus said that not one stone of the Temple would be left upon another that will not be torn down. For the Jew, the temple was the glory and beauty of the earth; it was unthinkable that God would abandon the temple during the Messianic age.

1)   Jesus' prophetic words prompted the disciples to ask two key questions: When would these things come about?

2)   What will be the sign that these things were about to be accomplished and the end of the age?

 The disciples wanted to know for one when the destruction of this temple would take place. And, they wanted to know what **sign** would precede this destruction. Interestingly, neither Mark nor Luke in their accounts of this event express this event the same as Matthew. Only Matthew says "sign of **Your coming and end of the age.**" Mark and Luke mention that the disciples wanted to know about the sign pertaining to the temple. According to Matthew, the disciples associated the "coming" of Christ with the end of the age. It is apparent that the disciples thought that the end of the temple was the end of the age. The disciples had been taught by Jesus in the parables of the tares (Matthew 13:39-40) and the drag net (Matthew 13:47-50) that the Judgment would come at the end of the age. Hence, the disciples wanted to know what the sign was for the end of the Messianic age. Whatever the disciples may have thought, Jesus, in his answer, will separate the destruction of Jerusalem and its temple from the end of the Messianic age.

Hence, section one of the Olivet discourse pertains to when this destruction of the temple will come and its sign. This is in Matthew 24:1-35. Section two pertains to when and what sign there is for end of the Messianic age (Matthew 24:36-51).

Section 1

Events to Befall Jesus' Contemporary Generation - the Destruction of Jerusalem and the Temple (Matthew 24:1-35)

Many present day Christians make the flawed assumption that a "coming" of Jesus must mean the Second Coming. Let's emphatically state that there will be a physical Second Coming of Christ at the end of the world, but it is an exegetical mistake to assume any New Testament reference to "coming" has to refer to Christ's Second Coming. We will see that there is significant biblical proof demonstrating that Jesus' coming in the first section of Matthew 24 does not pertain to the Second Coming at the end of the world but to His coming in judgment to apostate Israel. The various signs that Jesus alludes to in Matthew 24:4-34 pertain to His coming in judgment to national Israel. We must not overlook the context for these signs. Jesus declared that the temple would be physically destroyed, which prompted the disciples' question as to when this would occur. Hence, the signs that Jesus gives in the following verses is a specific answer to their question.

Sign of False Christs (Matthew 24:4-5)

In answering the disciples' questions, Jesus tells them in Matthew 24:4-5 not to be misled by those proclaiming to be the Messiah or the Christ. An early Christian church father, Jerome, referred to the bold Messianic claims of Simon Magus, the magician mentioned in Acts 8.

Jerome says that Simon Magus said, "I am the Word of God, I am the Comforter, I am Almighty, I am all there is of God." And the church father Irenaus said that Simon Magus claimed to be the Son of God and creator of angels.[30]

Josephus, who will witness the fall of Jerusalem mentions "the deceivers and imposters, under pretense of divine inspiration fostering revolutionary changes" (Josephus, *Wars of the Jews* 2:13:4).

Josephus also tells of a certain imposter named Theudas who persuaded a great number to follow him to the river Jordan which he said would divide for their crossing.

Sign of Wars and Rumors of Wars (Matthew 24:6-7a)

The church father, Origen, and other historians referred to the "Pax Romana," as the age of peace that was said to last about 200 years.[31] This began with Caesar Augustus in 17 B.C. to 180 A.D.

This peace would remain for the most part intact until the time of Nero. The greatest crisis was the Year of Four Emperors in A.D. 69, followed by

---

[30]   Quoted in J. Marcellus Kik, *An Eschatology of Victory*, p.92 who cited Mansel, *The Gnostic Heresies*, p. 82.
[31]   Gentry, *p. 344.*

three others (including Claudius, Domitian, and Marcus Aurelius). It was definitely ruptured with the onset of the Jewish Wars (68-69 A.D.). According to the Roman historian Tacitus, these wars nearly brought down the end of the Roman Empire.[32]

So, "wars and rumors of wars" would definitely be a sign during a time of relative peace.

Sign of Famines and Earthquakes (Matthew 24:7b)

Jesus then mentions the sign of famines and earthquakes (Matthew 24:7). Beginning with the book of Acts, famines were common in the time frame leading up to 70 A.D. The famine was so bad in Jerusalem that the church of Corinth helped in the relief. Historians such as Tacitus, Suetonius, and Josephus all mention other famines during this time frame. Tacitus records in 51 A.D. of a famine in Rome which also included earthquakes.[33]

Historians mention earthquakes occurring all over the Mediterranean from Crete, Smyrna, Miletus, Chios, Samos, Laodicea, Hierapolis, Colossae, Rome, and Judea.

Josephus describes an earthquake in Judea of such magnitude "and then it was also that there was an earthquake in Judea, such a one as had not happened at any other time, and which earthquake brought a great destruction upon the cattle in that country. About ten thousand men also perished by the fall of houses…"[34] Josephus continues to write that this earthquake was no common calamity, dictating that God Himself had brought it about for a special purpose.

---

[32]   Gentry.
[33]   Gentry, p. 344 who quotes Tacitus, *Annals*, 16:13 and Suetonius, *Nero*, p. 39.
[34]   Josephus, *Antiquities of the Jews*, Book 15, chapter 5:2.

Sign of Terrors and Great Signs from Heaven (Luke 21:11)[35]

According to Luke's version (21:11) of Jesus' comments paralleling Matthew 24, there would be the sign of terrors and great signs from heaven. Matthew's account does not have this, but Luke's account does. A comet appeared around 60 A.D. during the reign of Nero. The public viewed such signs as changes in the political landscape. The Roman historian Tacitus mentions:

> As if Nero were already dethroned, men began to ask who might be his successor. Nero took the comet's threat seriously. This is the man who murdered his mother, his two wives, and most of his family, burned Rome, and used Christians as flaming torches.[36]

In 66 A.D. Haley's comet appeared. The comet was viewed as an omen of the fall of Jerusalem four years before the Roman siege. In addition to Haley's comet, Josephus recounted that a series of omens foretold the disaster that was about to befall the Temple:

> Thus it was that the wretched people were deluded at that time by charlatans and pretended messengers of the deity; while they neither heeded nor believed in the manifest portents that foretold the coming desolation, but, as if thunderstruck and bereft of eyes and mind, disregarded the plain warnings of God. So it was when a star, resembling a sword, stood over the city, and a comet which continued for a year.[37]

As Matthew 24:8 says, Jesus said that these are only the beginning of the birth pains.

---

[35] Because of the popularity of the Dispensational view of Scripture, present day Christians might view what I have been stating as a strange interpretation of the signs of Matthew 24. First, the interpretations that I am giving are not novel, but several respected Bible scholars have held similar views in church history. And, which is a more natural understanding of Scripture? The interpretation above or the fanciful views of modern day Christian Bible teachers who think these signs from heaven are 50 lb. chunks of ice falling from the sky (Chuck Smith, *The Second Coming Any Day Now, Charisma and Christian Life*, (February 1989), p. 46 as quoted in Gary DeMar, *Last Days Madness*, p. 131. Or, Hal Lindsey's view that the Jupiter Effect in 1982 (a special alignment of planets with reference to the sun) would bring about cataclysmic effects on earth (Hal Lindsey, *The 1980's: Countdown To Armageddon*, p. 31). But this is not the most fanciful and ridiculous view of Hal Lindsey. As pointed out in an earlier chapter of this book, Lindsey still believes that these "terrors and great signs from heaven" could likely refer to a staged alien landing with the pilots of these spacecrafts as demons (Lindsey, *The 1980's*, pp. 34-35). Seriously, whose interpretations of Scripture are more faithful to the Word of God?

[36] Quoted from Gary DeMar, *Last Days Madness*, (Atlanta, GA: American Vision, 1999), pp. 81-82 who quotes Nigel Calder, *The Comet Is Coming!*

[37] Josephus, *Wars of the Jews*, Book 6:5:3

Sign of Persecution, Apostasy, False Prophets, and Lawless Living (Matthew 24:9-12)

In Matthew 24:9-12, Jesus mentions the sign of persecution, apostasy, false prophets, and lawless living. One only has to read the book of Acts and the journeys of Paul and Peter's epistles to know that the church was persecuted by Jews and by the Romans. Stephen will be martyred, James, the brother of John will be killed by Herod; and Paul and Peter will die before 70 A.D. as martyrs.

In his epistles, Paul wrote of those forsaking him and going back to the world. During the persecution by Nero, it was not uncommon for professing Christians to betray their fellow Christians. Roman historian, Tacitus discusses the persecution of Christians:

> In the meantime, the number of the Christians being now very large, it happened that Rome was destroyed by fire while Nero was stationed at Antium. But the opinion of all cast the odium of causing the fire upon the emperor, and the emperor was believed in this way to have sought for the glory of building a new city. And in fact, Nero could not by any means that he tried escape from the charge that the fire had been caused by his orders. He therefore turned the accusation against the Christians, and the most cruel tortures were accordingly inflicted upon the innocent. Nay, even new kinds of death were invented, so that, being covered in the skins of wild beasts, they perished by being devoured by dogs, while many were crucified or slain by fire, and not a few were set apart for this purpose, that, when the day came to a close, they should be consumed to serve for light during the night. It was in this way that cruelty first began to be manifested against the Christians. Afterward, too, their religion was prohibited by laws which were given, and by edicts openly set forth it was proclaimed unlawful to be a Christian. At that time Paul and Peter were condemned to capital punishment, of whom the one was beheaded with a sword, while Peter suffered crucifixion.[38]

Regarding false prophets, Peter warned that there would be false teachers among you who would bring damnable heresies. Paul warned the Ephesian elders that wolves in sheep's clothing would arise among themselves seeking to gather disciples after themselves. Paul contended with the

---

[38]   Tacitus, *Annals.*

Judaizers, who taught salvation by works of the Law. The apostle John warned of many false prophets, antichrists, gone out into the world, some of whom were once part of the fold (I John 2:18-24).

The epistles contain sufficient testimony of immoral living, even in the church, such as at Corinth. Not only was lawlessness in the church, but the names of Caligula and Nero were prominent examples of "lawlessness."

In Matthew 24:13, Jesus says that he who endures to the end shall be saved. This is indicative of apostolic warnings and those of Christ to the seven churches in Revelation. In Hebrews 3:6, 14 we read:

> *[6]But Christ was faithful as a Son over His house whose house we are, if we hold fast our confidence and the boast of our hope firm until the end... [14]For if we have become partakers of Christ, if we hold fast the beginning of our assurance firm until the end.*

Then of course we have the words of Jesus in Revelation 3:21:

> *He who overcomes, I will grant to him to sit down with Me on My throne, as I also overcame and sat down with My father on His throne.*

Sign of the Gospel Preached to the World as a Witness (Matthew 24:14)

Matthew 24:14 says that the gospel shall be preached to the whole world for a witness and then the end shall come. We need to carefully exegete this passage. First, it does not say the nations will be discipled as Jesus said in the Great Commission. Discipling and witnessing are different. How could all the nations have the gospel of the kingdom preached to them? We are told on the Day of Pentecost (Acts 2:5) that devout men from **every nation under heaven** were in Jerusalem and heard the gospel.

Colossians 1:5-6, 23:

> *[5]Because of the hope laid up for you in heaven, of which you previously heard in the word of truth, the gospel, [6]which has come to you just **as in all the world**... [23]If indeed you continue in the faith firmly established an steadfast, and not moved away from the hope of the gospel that you have heard, which was proclaimed **in all creation under heaven**, and of which, I, Paul, was made a minister.* (Emphasis mine).

Romans 1:8:

> *First, I thank my God through Jesus Christ for you all, because your faith is being proclaimed **throughout the whole world**.* (Emphasis mine)

Romans 16:25-27:

> *My gospel and the preaching of Jesus Christ ... has been made known **to all the nations**, leading to the obedience of faith.* (Emphasis mine)

The key to understanding this biblical phraseology is that the Roman Empire was viewed as the "whole world." For example, in Luke 2:1 we read that a decree from Caesar Augustus was to be taken of "all the inhabited earth." Hence, we can say according to biblical examples that the gospel was preached to all the nations prior to 70 A.D.

Sign of the Abomination of Desolation

(Matthew 24:15-20)

The definitive sign that the end is near is the **Abomination of Desolation** (Matthew 24:15). As much as wars, famines, pestilences, earthquakes, persecutions, false prophets, spiritual coldness were signs of the coming judgment upon Jerusalem, the most notable sign is what Jesus calls the Abomination of Desolation spoken of by the prophet Daniel.

As a quick aside, the fact that Jesus quotes Daniel's prophecy in Daniel 9 as a sign of the coming destruction of Jerusalem is a most powerful point that dispensational premillennialism is totally wrong. The Abomination of Desolation is **not** some future period, not some delayed 70th week where the Antichrist defiles a rebuilt Jewish temple.

When you see the Abomination of Desolation of Daniel, Jesus said in Matthew 24:15-20:

> *[15]Therefore when you see the ABOMINATION OF DESOLATION which was spoken of through Daniel the prophet, standing in the holy place (let the reader understand), [16]then those who are in Judea must flee to the mountains. [17]Whoever is on the housetop must not go down to get the things out that are in his house. [18]Whoever is in the field must not turn back to get his cloak. [19]But woe to those who are pregnant and to those who are*

nursing babies in those days! ^{20}*But pray that your flight will not be in the winter, or on a Sabbath.*

What is the Abomination of Desolation? The parallel passage in Luke tells us specifically. The Abomination of Desolation is: the surrounding of Jerusalem by Roman armies who will desecrate the temple and destroy Jerusalem. Luke 21:20-24 states:

> ^{20}*But when you see Jerusalem surrounded by armies, then recognize that her desolation is near.* ^{21}*Then those who are in Judea must flee to the mountains, and those who are in the midst of the city must leave, and those who are in the country must not enter the city;* ^{22}*because these are days of vengeance, so that all things which are written will be fulfilled.* ^{23}*Woe to those who are pregnant and to those who are nursing babies in those days; for there will be great distress upon the land and wrath to this people;* ^{24}*and they will fall by the edge of the sword, and will be led captive into all the nations; and Jerusalem will be trampled under foot by the Gentiles until the times of the Gentiles are fulfilled.*

Why was the Roman army viewed as "the abomination of desolation?" The Roman army carried ensigns consisting of eagles and images of the emperor to whom divine honors were given by the army. The Caesars saw themselves as gods. Emperor worship was common in the empire. Josephus recounts in his *Antiquities of the Jews* that Pontius Pilate was the first who brought such images to Palestine and set them up in the city. There was an incident in which the Jews complained greatly to Pilate about these images in Jerusalem. Incensed about their audacious complaint, Pilate had his army surround them ready to kill any who did not leave. Josephus records that these Jews willingly laid bare their heads to be removed before they would see their laws transgressed. Pilate moved by their resolve ordered the images removed from Jerusalem to Caesarea.[39] To the Jews, such images were an abomination.

Josephus comments upon what the Romans did in the Jerusalem temple once they had burnt the house:

> And now the Romans, upon the flight of the seditious into the city, and upon the burning of the holy house itself, and of all the buildings lying round about it brought their ensigns to the temple, and set them over against its eastern gate; and there did they offer

[39]   Josephus, *Antiquities of the Jews*, Book 18: 3:1.

sacrifices to them, and there did they make Titus imperator with the greatest acclamations of joy.[40]

In Matthew 24:16-20, Jesus gives this instruction to His disciples:

> *[16]Then those who are in Judea must flee to the mountains.*
> *[17]Whoever is on the housetop must not go down to get the things*
> *out that are in his house. [18]Whoever is in the field must not turn*
> *back to get his cloak. [19]But woe to those who are pregnant and to*
> *those who are nursing babies in those days! [20]But pray that your*
> *flight will not be in the winter, or on a Sabbath.*

The church historian Eusebius, (270-340 A.D.) who wrote the only surviving account of the church during its first 300 years, writes:

> The whole body, however, of the church at Jerusalem, having
> been commanded by a divine revelation, given to men of approved
> piety there before the war, removed from the city, and dwelt at a
> certain town beyond the Jordan, called Pella. Here those that
> believed in Christ, having removed from Jerusalem, as if holy men
> had entirely abandoned the royal city itself, and the whole land of
> Judea; the divine justice, for their crimes against Christ and his
> apostles finally overtook them, totally destroying the whole
> generation of these evildoers from the earth.[41]

When did the Christians have the opportunity to flee on the housetops once they saw the city surrounded with armies? There were several Roman campaigns against Jerusalem before the infamous and successful siege by the Roman general Titus. In 66 A.D. one Roman campaign was led by Cestius Gallus. Josephus has this interesting comment on Cestius' temporary cessation of attacks upon Jerusalem:

> But when Cestius was come into the city, he set the part called
> Bezetha, which is also called Cenopolis, (or the new city) on fire;
> as he did also to the timber Market; after which he came into the
> upper city... It then happened that Cestius was not conscious
> either how the besieged despaired of success, nor how courageous
> the people were for him; and he recalled his soldiers from the
> place, and by despairing of any expectation of taking it, without

---

40   Josephus, *Wars of the Jews,* Book 6:6:1.
41   Eusebius, *History of the Church,* 3:5.

having received any disgrace, he retired from the city without any reason in the world.[42]

The translator of Josephus' *Wars of the Jews* gives this illuminating comment:

> There may another very important, and very providential, reason be here assigned for this strange and foolish retreat of Cestius; which, if Josephus had been now a Christian, he might probably have taken notice of also; and that is, the affording the Jewish Christians in the city an opportunity of calling to mind the prediction and caution given them by Christ about thirty-three years and a half before, that 'when they should see the abomination of desolation' [the idolatrous Roman armies, with the images of their idols in their ensigns, ready to lay Jerusalem desolate] 'stand where it ought not;' or, 'in the holy place;' or, 'when they should see Jerusalem any one instance of a more impolitic, but more providential, compassed with armies;' they should then 'flee to the mountains.' By complying with which those Jewish Christians fled to the mountains of Perea and escaped this destruction... Nor was there, perhaps, any one instance of a more upolitic, but more providential conduct than this retreat of Cestius, visible during this whole siege of Jerusalem, which yet was providentially such a Great Tribulation, as had not been from the beginning of the world to that time; no, nor ever should be.[43]

The next Roman campaign against Jerusalem was in 68 A.D. under Vespasian. The emperor Nero had appointed him as the replacement to Cestius in order to bring the Jews back under control. In the Spring of 68 A.D., Vespasian laid siege to Jerusalem. During this time, certain generals plotted the overthrow of Nero in Rome. In June of 68 A.D. Nero will commit suicide. During a very turbulent time in Rome with a rapid succession of emperors, Vespasian will be made emperor, and will decide to terminate the Jewish wars. It will be in the spring of 70 A.D. that Vespasian will appoint his son, Titus, as general over the Roman armies, and the siege of Jerusalem will resume. By September 70 A.D., the destruction of Jerusalem will be complete.

There is no record of any Jewish Christian dying in the siege of Jerusalem. They remembered what Jesus said and fled. Actually, construction of

---

[42]   Josephus, *War of the Jews*, Book 2:19:4, 7.
[43]   William Whiston, noted in Josephus, *War of the Jews*, Book 2:19:6.

houses in Jerusalem made it possible to actually flee from housetop to housetop.

The Great Tribulation

(Matthew 24:21-22)

Jesus warned that there was coming a "great tribulation" that was and will be unique in the world. Matthew 24:21-22 states Jesus as saying:

> *[21]For then there will be a great tribulation such as has not occurred since the beginning of the world until now, nor ever shall. [22]And unless those days had been cut short, no life would have been saved; but for the sake of the elect those days shall be cut short.*

It is quite clear that believers were to flee in order to avoid this great tribulation. The reason for the haste is due to this impending catastrophe of immense proportions. Josephus detailed the accounts of the magnitude of suffering in his *War of the Jews*. The suffering in Jerusalem was mind boggling. Civil war, an instance of cannibalism, and starvation took place. The temple was burned and the Roman soldiers sacrificed to their ensigns in the temple. The number of deaths was placed at 1.1 million in one city! The war captives were 97,000.[44] Jesus said in Luke 21:23-24:

> *[23]Woe to those who are pregnant and to those who are nursing babies in those days; for there will be great distress upon the land and wrath to this people; [24]and they will fall by the edge of the sword, and will be led captive into all the nations; and Jerusalem will be trampled under foot by the Gentiles until the times of the Gentiles are fulfilled.*

One thing to keep in mind is that Jesus is referring to a single event experienced by the Jewish nation. Matthew 24:22 states that the tribulation period would be cut short for the sake of the elect. Luke saw the tribulation period as associated with **the land** and **this people**. The land of Israel and "this people" refers to the Jews living in Israel at the time when Jerusalem was surrounded by armies.

---

[44]   Josephus, *War of the Jews*, Book 6:9:3.

The Meaning of "*Parousia*"

(Matthew 24:27-31)

We have looked at the importance of hermeneutics already. It is very important that we understand that words mean what they do in context, and we saw that the same Greek word can have differing meanings in different contexts. This is true regarding the word "coming." The Greek word is "*parousia*." Most think that "parousia" always refers to Christ's physical Second Coming. This is a mistake. Whereas the great majority of the uses of "parousia" in the New Testament do refer to what we believe to be the personal and physical return of Jesus, known as the Second Coming, it is not exclusively used this way.

There is another Greek word that is translated as "coming." It is "*erchomai*." Depending on the context, it can refer to either the fall of Jerusalem or the Second Coming. "*Erchomai*" is used in Matthew 24:30 and 26:64. Some want to rush and say that "*erchomai*" always refers to Jesus' invisible but real coming to Jerusalem in 70 A.D., and that "*parousia*" refers to the physical Second Coming. The problem is that exegetically it cannot be maintained that this is **always** the case. For example, in Matthew 24:27, the use of "coming" is the word "*parousia*," but then in Matthew 24:30, the word for coming is "*erchomai*;" **however, the context is clear that it is referring to the same event of the impending fall of Jerusalem.**

Also, with reference to Christ's physical Second Coming, there is a use of both words to refer to the same event. Mark 13:35-36 uses "*erchomai*," while Matthew 24:35-51, uses both "*erchomai*" and "*parousia*" to refer to Christ's Second Coming. We just need to recognize that sometimes there is a "coming" of Christ that does **not** refer to Christ's Second Coming. There are instances in Scripture where the idea of "coming" refers to a "coming" in judgment. One such instance is found in Matthew 24:27-30:

> [27]*For just as the lightning comes from the east, and flashes even to the west, so shall the coming of the Son of Man be.* [28]*Wherever the corpse is, there the vultures gather.* [29]*But immediately after the tribulation of those days the sun will be darkened, and the moon will not give its light, and the stars will fall from the sky, and the powers of the heavens will be shaken,* [30]*and then the sign of the Son of man will appear in the sky, and then all the tribes of the earth will mourn, and they will see the Son of Man coming on the clouds of the sky with power and great glory.*

In this passage, Jesus is coming, but He is not physically coming to earth. His coming has terrible consequences for national Israel. He is coming upon the clouds in power and glory. He is coming in judgment to destroy Jerusalem.

Jesus said that His coming would be "just as the lightning comes from the east." This is figurative language denoting that which is quick and without warning. Lightning can signify the **presence of the Lord in a fearful way.** With reference to Israel coming to Mount Sinai, Exodus 19:16 states:

> *So it came about on the third day, when it was morning, that there were thunder and lightning flashes and a thick cloud upon the mountain and a very loud trumpet sound, so that all the people who were in the camp trembled.*

In Job 36:30, lightning is used to portray simply the presence of the Lord – "*Behold, He spreads His lightning about Him…*"

Deuteronomy 33:2 refers to the spiritual presence and coming of the Lord:

> *So it came about on the third day, when it was morning, that there were thunder and lightning flashes and a thick cloud upon the mountain and a very loud trumpet sound, so that all the people who were in the camp trembled.*

Ezekiel 21:14-15 refers to a "coming" in judgment:

> *[14]You therefore, son of man, prophesy and clap hands together; and let the sword be doubled the third time, the sword for the slain. It is the sword for the great one slain, which surrounds them, [15]that hearts may melt, and many fall at all their gates. **I have given the glittering sword. Ah! It is made like lightning, it is wrapped up for slaughter.*** (Emphasis mine)

In Zechariah 9:14-16, we see lightning being associated with judgment of Judah's enemies:

> *[14]Then the Lord will appear over them, and **His arrow will go forth like lightning**; and the Lord God will blow the trumpet, and will march in the storm winds of the south. [15]The Lord of hosts will defend them. And they will devour and trample on the sling stones; and they will drink and be boisterous as with wine; and they will be filled like a sacrificial basin, drenched like the corners of the altar. [16]And the Lord their God will save them in*

that day as the flock of His people; for they are as the stones of a crown, sparkling in His land. (Emphasis mine)

In 586 B.C. the Babylonian king, Nebuchadnezzar destroys Jerusalem and carries off a remnant to Babylon, but the Scripture emphatically states that God is the One who ordained Jerusalem's destruction. We read in Isaiah 42:24-25:

²⁴Who gave Jacob up for spoil and Israel to plunderers? Was it not the LORD, against whom we have sinned, and in whose ways they were not willing to walk, and whose law they did not obey? ²⁵So He poured out on him the heat of His anger and the fierceness of battle; and it set him aflame all around, yet he did not recognize it; and it burned him, but he paid no attention.

For our purposes here, Jesus came like lightning to set Jerusalem aflame. The wrath of the Lamb was brought against Jerusalem. One of the most important passages tying together the notion of "coming" with judgment is Jesus' own words before the Sanhedrin as recorded in Matthew 26:59-65:

⁵⁹Now the chief priests and the whole Council kept trying to obtain false testimony against Jesus, so that they might put Him to death. ⁶⁰They did not find any, even though many false witnesses came forward. But later on two came forward, ⁶¹and said, 'This man stated, 'I am able to destroy the temple of God and to rebuild it in three days.' ⁶²The high priest stood up and said to Him, 'Do You not answer? What is it that these men are testifying against You?' ⁶³Jesus kept silent. And the high priest said to Him, 'I adjure You by the living God, that You tell us whether You are the Christ, the Son of God.' ⁶⁴Jesus said to him, 'You have said it yourself; nevertheless I tell you, hereafter you will see the Son of Man sitting at the right hand of power, and coming on the clouds of Heaven' ⁶⁵Then the high priest tore his robes and said, 'He has blasphemed! What further need do we have of witnesses? Behold, you have now heard the blasphemy.'

Contextually, we must understand that Jesus was speaking about something that would come to those with whom He was speaking. The "you" probably should be viewed as that being inclusive of the entire Sanhedrin, not just to Caiaphas, the high priest. Moreover, the Sanhedrin was the Jewish ruling body, representing the nation of the Jews. The Sanhedrin, as the ruling body, condemned Jesus, handing Him over to Pontius Pilate with the distinct purpose of having Him put to death.

Jesus' words are to be taken figuratively in the sense that the Sanhedrin could not physically see Him sitting at the right hand of power, but they would surely see the devastating effects of Jesus' session at the Father's right hand. The Sanhedrin would see Jesus coming in great power to decimate Jerusalem. God's power ordains whatsoever comes to pass to orchestrate history and its empires to accomplish His divine plan.

The reference to "sitting at the right hand of Power" is a reference to His enthronement that occurred at His ascension. From God's right hand, which is a position of authority and power, Jesus comes to men in various ways. Jesus, who has all authority and power in heaven and earth, came to men with great power on the Day of Pentecost, saving them from their sins and continuing to do so during His Messianic reign.

Also, Jesus comes to men in judgment. In this case, Jesus says that the coming destruction of Jerusalem is My coming on the clouds. You will see My power. And, in keeping with His statements in Matthew 23:36; 24:34, these events will come upon "**this generation.**" We must not forget what the Jews swore in their insistence on having Barabbas freed and not Jesus when Pilate offered them a choice. In Matthew 27:25:

> *And all the people answered and said, 'His blood be on us and on our children!'*

While Jesus was in His state of humiliation leading up to and including the cross, He voluntarily set aside access to divine power. For example, when He was being arrested, Peter defended Jesus with his sword, but Jesus told Peter to put his sword back because His kingdom would not be advanced by the sword. Jesus said that He could call more than twelve legions of angels to rescue Him, but He wouldn't because He must go to the cross.

When Jesus was resurrected, He was exalted to the utmost and uses His regal power to convert or destroy. "Coming in the clouds" is a figurative phrase denoting a coming in judgment. The Bible does use this phraseology of "coming in the clouds" historically as a figurative expression for God coming in judgment to wreak vengeance upon wicked nations.

Isaiah 19:1:

> *The oracle concerning Egypt. Behold, the LORD is riding on a swift cloud and is about to come to Egypt; The idols of Egypt will tremble at His presence, and the heart of the Egyptians will melt within them.*

This "coming" of Jehovah to Egypt occurred in 671 B.C. when the Assyrian King, Esarhaddon, conquered Egypt.

On his way to the cross, Jesus told women crying not to cry for Him but "for yourselves." Luke 23:28-30 states:

> ^{28}*But Jesus turning to them said, "Daughters of Jerusalem, stop weeping for Me, but weep for yourselves and for your children. ^{29}For behold, the days are coming when they will say, 'Blessed are the barren, and the wombs that never bore, and the breasts that never nursed.' ^{30}Then they will begin to say to the mountains, 'fall on us,' and to the hills, 'cover us.'"*

Jesus quotes from Hosea 10:8-10 which is significant because this text clearly indicates God's punishment of Israel for its unfaithfulness, and Jesus is quoting it as directly applying to the weeping women and their children's generation as He was being led away to His death. The text reads:

> ^{8}*Also the high places of Aven, the sin of Israel, will be destroyed; thorn and thistle will grow on their altars; Then they will say to the mountains, "Cover us!" and to the hills, "Fall on us!" ^{9}From the days of Gibeah you have sinned, O Israel; There they stand! Will not the battle against the sons of iniquity overtake them in Gibeah? ^{10}When it is My desire, I will chastise them; the peoples will be gathered against them when they are bound for their double guilt.*

Many of the visions in the book of Revelation apply directly to Christ's coming in judgment upon faithless Israel. Without getting into a full fledged discussion of how we should interpret most of Revelation, I have already noted that the book of Revelation is dealing with events for the most part leading up to 70 A.D. while the temple is still standing. Revelation deals with the two enemies of God's elect people (His invisible church). Those two enemies are apostate Jews and the Roman state, both referred to as a Beast.

Revelation 6:16-17:[45]

> *[16]And they said to the mountains and to the rocks, 'Fall on us and hide us from the presence of Him who sits on the throne, and from the wrath of the Lamb; [17]for the great day of their wrath has come, and who is able to stand?'*

Revelation 6 deals with the opening of the sixth seal which brings about terrible destruction. It is the Lamb of God that brings judgment upon the Jewish nation and Jerusalem for its sins. We must remember that Jesus said that "this generation"is filling up the measure of the guilt of their forefathers. No wonder Jesus wept over Jerusalem because He knew that His wrath was soon to be poured out on a rebellious nation, for it was about to crucify its Messiah.

Following Jesus' comment that the coming of the Son of Man will be like lightning, He prophesies the gathering of eagles over a corpse. Matthew 24:28 reads:

> *Wherever the corpse is there the vultures will gather.[46]*

Wherever the corpse is the "vultures" or "eagles" will gather. We are reminded again that the ensign of the Roman armies was the eagle, and when the Romans put the eagles in the temple and offered sacrifices to them, they desecrated the temple. The ultimate insult had come upon faithless Israel.

Imagery of the Sun, Moon, and Stars

Matthew 24:29 deals with a most interesting imagery that comes immediately after the tribulation of those days. The imagery is that of heavenly bodies not shining and stars falling from the sky, and the power of the heavens shaken. The text reads:

> *But immediately after the tribulation of those days the sun will be darkened, and the moon will not give its light, and the stars will fall from the sky, and the powers of the heavens will be shaken.*

---

[45]   Several authors would agree that this passage in Revelation 6 refers to the fall of Jerusalem in 70 A.D. These are: Matthew Henry's commentary on Revelation 6:16-17; Greg Bahnsen, *Victory in Jesus: The Bright Hope of Postmillennialism*, p. 13; Gary Demar, *Last Days Madness*, p. 121.

[46]   The King James Version translates the Greek word, *"aetos"* as eagles.

Dispensationalists such as Hal Lindsey and Chuck Smith have given some rather fanciful interpretations of this passage in an attempt to remain "literal."[47] I want to reiterate that "literalness" does not have to reflect some rigid understanding of the expressions. For example, stars falling from heaven? Really? What would be the impact of a literal star falling to earth? Our own solar system's sun is about 109 times bigger than the earth. Such a rigid "literal" interpretation would lead to the earth's utter annihilation. Figurative expressions do express actual historical events, but the Bible defines its own use of its "figurative expressions." We could say that the Bible needs to be "literally" understood "figuratively." Expressions of the sun and moon being darkened and stars falling are biblical expressions of great national judgments and great events of theological import. The Scripture is **always** its best interpreter!

Consider God's judgment against Babylon as seen in Isaiah 13:1, 10-13:

> [1]*The oracle concerning Babylon which Isaiah the son of Amoz saw…* [10]*For the stars of heaven and their constellations will not flash forth their light; the sun will be dark when it rises and the moon will not shed its light.* [11]*Thus I will punish the world for its evil and the wicked for their iniquity; I will also put an end to the arrogance of the proud and abase the haughtiness of the ruthless.* [12]*I will make mortal man scarcer than pure gold and mankind than the gold of Ophir.* [13]*Therefore I will make the heavens tremble and the earth will be shaken from its place at the fury of the LORD of hosts in the day of His burning anger.*
> (Emphasis mine)

Consider God's judgment of all rebellious nations as seen in Isaiah 34:1-5:

> [1]*Draw near, O nations, to hear; and listen, O peoples! Let the earth and all it contains hear, and the world and all that springs from it.* [2]*For the LORD'S indignation is against all the nations, and His wrath against all their armies; He has utterly destroyed them, He has given them over to slaughter.* [3]*So their slain will be thrown out, and their corpses will give off their stench, and the mountains will be drenched with their blood.* [4]**And all the host of heaven will wear away, and the sky will be rolled up like a scroll; all their hosts will also wither away as a leaf withers from the vine,** *or as one withers from the fig tree.* [5]*For My sword is satiated in heaven,* **Behold it shall descend for judgment**

---

[47]   See footnote number 94 in this chapter for these interpretations.

upon Edom and upon the people whom I have devoted to destruction. (Emphasis mine)

Consider God's judgment of Egypt as seen in Ezekiel 32:2, 7-8, 11-12:

> [2]*Son of man, take up a lamentation over Pharaoh king of Egypt and say to him,...* [7]*'And when I extinguish you, I will cover the heavens and darken their stars; I will cover the sun with a cloud and the moon will not give its light.* [8]*All the shining lights in the heavens I will darken over you and will set darkness on your land,' declares the Lord GOD...* [11]*For thus says the Lord GOD, 'The sword of the king of Babylon will come upon you.* [12]*By the swords of the mighty ones I will cause your hordes to fall; all of them are tyrants of the nations, and they will devastate the pride of Egypt, and all its hordes will be destroyed.'* (Emphasis mine)

Consider God's judgment upon His covenant people in the following three texts. Jeremiah 4:22-24 states:

> [22]*For My people are foolish, they know Me not; they are stupid children and have no understanding. They are shrewd to do evil, but to do good they do not know.* [23]***I looked on the earth, and behold, it was formless and void; and to the heavens, and they had no light.*** [24]*I looked on the mountains, and behold, they were quaking, and all the hills moved to and fro.* (Emphasis mine)

Amos 5:18:

> *Alas, you who are longing for the day of the LORD, For what purpose will the day of the LORD be to you?* ***It will be darkness and not light.*** (Emphasis mine)

Amos 8:9:

> *'It will come about in that day,' declares the Lord GOD, 'That* ***I will make the sun go down at noon And make the earth dark in broad daylight.*** (Emphasis mine)

In these contexts, the phrase "day of the Lord" will be darkness and not light for Israel. It denotes God's coming to His covenant people in judgment (in darkness). But the "day of the Lord" can be light as is expressed in the following passages regarding the Day of Pentecost.

Concerning the great theological significance of the Day of Pentecost, Peter says that the events of the Day of Pentecost are the fulfillment of Joel 2:10, 28-32. Joel's prophecy reads:

> [10]***Before them the earth quakes, the heavens tremble, the sun and the moon grow dark and the stars lose their brightness*** *...* [28]*It will come about after this that I will pour out My Spirit on all mankind; and your sons and daughters will prophesy, your old men will dream dreams, your young men will see visions.* [29]*Even on the male and female servants I will pour out My Spirit in those days.* [30]***I will display wonders in the sky and on the earth, blood, fire and columns of smoke.*** [31]***The sun will be turned into darkness and the moon into blood before the great and awesome day of the LORD comes***. [32]*And it will come about that whoever calls on the name of the LORD will be delivered; for on Mount Zion and in Jerusalem there will be those who escape, as the LORD has said, even among the survivors whom the LORD calls*. (Emphasis mine)

Inspired Peter proclaims to the inhabitants of Jerusalem the following as recorded in Acts 2:14-21:

> [14]*But Peter, taking his stand with the eleven, raised his voice and declared to them: 'Men of Judea and all you who live in Jerusalem, let this be known to you and give heed to my words.* [15]*For these men are not drunk, as you suppose, for it is only the third hour of the day;* [16]*but this is what was spoken of through the prophet Joel.* [17]*And it shall be in the last days God says, that I will pour forth of My Spirit upon all mankind; and your sons and your daughters shall prophesy, and your young men shall see visions,* [18]*even upon My bondslaves, both men and women, I will in those days pour forth of My Spirit and they shall prophesy.* [19]*And I will grant wonders in the sky above, and signs on the earth beneath, blood, and fire, and vapor of smoke,* [20]*the sun shall be turned into darkness, and the moon into blood, before the great and glorious Day of the Lord shall come.* [21]*And it shall be, that everyone who calls on the name of the Lord shall be saved.'*

Stellar cataclysmic language is used to refer to the profound theological significance of Pentecost. Pentecost is the official inauguration of the enthronement of Jesus Christ as King of kings and Lord of lords. It is the beginning of Jesus' defeat of all His enemies as prophesied in Psalm 110. We saw that Psalm 110:3 stated that *"Thy people will volunteer freely in the day of Thy power.*" Peter boldly proclaims that the glorious Day of the Lord pertains to whoever calls on the Lord shall be saved, and 3000 called on the Lord at Pentecost! In this context, the phrase "Day of the Lord" references the great conversion of God's elect. In typical Old Testament imagery, this fantastic conversion is expressed as the sun being darkened and the moon turning into blood.

When we allow the Scripture to interpret Scripture, allowing inspired New Testament apostles to apply Old Testament passages, and then we clearly see that the language of the heavenly host being darkened is a figurative expression of God's judgment and of great events marking the onset of the Messianic age.

Stars were used scripturally to represent people and nations. They were used as symbols of earthly rulers and families. We see this in the following passages.

Genesis 37:9-11 pertains to Joseph's dream:

> *⁹Now he had still another dream, and related it to his brothers, and said, 'Lo, I have had still another dream; **and behold, the sun and the moon and eleven stars were bowing down to me.**' ¹⁰He related it to his father and to his brothers; and his father rebuked him and said to him, "What is this dream that you had? Shall I and your mother and your brothers actually come to bow ourselves down before you to the ground?" ¹¹His brothers were jealous of him, but his father kept the saying in mind.* (Emphasis mine)

Judges 5:19-20 uses stars as representative of kings:

> *¹⁹The kings came and fought; then fought the kings of Canaan at Taanach near the waters of Megiddo; they took no plunder in silver. ²⁰**The stars fought from heaven,** from their courses they fought against Sisera.* (Emphasis mine)

By combining the imagery of the sun, moon, and stars in Matthew 24:29, Jesus is using Old Testament terminology to represent Israel. Matthew 24:29 is essentially the Lord's declaration that lights are out for national Israel. It is under the judging hand of the Son of Man.

Jesus' comments in Matthew 24:30 reflect what He will soon say to Caiaphas and the Sanhedrin at His mock trial. The text reads:

And then the sign of the Son of Man will appear in the sky, and then all the tribes of the earth will mourn, and they will see the Son of Man coming on the clouds of the sky with power and great glory.

This is an instance where the NASB's translation is misleading and not the best rendering of the original Greek. The KJV translation is virtually identical to the Greek text. It reads:

And then shall appear the sign of the Son of man in heaven: and then shall all the tribes of the earth mourn, and they shall see the Son of man coming in the clouds of heaven with power and great glory.

We should note that "a sign" was not going to appear in the sky. No, a sign would be given of the Son of Man in heaven. The Son, not the sign, is in heaven. The sign is that Jesus, the Son of Man, is enthroned in heaven with power, coming on the clouds of judgment upon national Israel for her sins. The tribes of the land will mourn, for the Jewish nation is finished. The sign is that the Son of Man is enthroned in heaven with power. The "tribes of the earth (land) will mourn. The tribes of the land are representative of the tribes of Israel. They will mourn, for national Israel will be no more. It is the end of an age. What national Israel will see is the enthroned Jesus, who is in heaven, visiting Jerusalem with horrible judgment for her sins. The apostate Jews will see Jesus coming in the clouds of judgment, just like Jehovah did in earlier Jewish history. The phraseology of "the tribes of the land" denotes the Jewish nation. We see this in Revelation 1:7 which reads:

Behold, He is coming with the clouds, and every eye will see Him, even those who pierced Him; and all the tribes of the earth will mourn over Him. So it is to be. Amen.

It is important to see Matthew 24:30 in conjunction with Matthew 26:64 and Revelation 1:7. The common phrase among all these verses is the Son of Man "coming on or with the clouds." Jesus fulfilled the self proclaimed curse that the Jews pledged upon themselves in having Jesus crucified – *"And all the people answered and said, 'His blood be on us and on our children,"* (Matthew 27:25). Josephus' horrifying description of the suffering and destruction of Jerusalem in 70 A.D. is most fitting with "the tribes of the earth" mourning over Him. It was that generation of apostate

Jews that crucified Jesus. In Matthew 23:36, Jesus said that "this generation" would fill up the measure of the guilt of their fathers.

After declaring His judgment upon apostate Israel, Jesus states in Matthew 24:31:

> And He will send forth His angels with great trumpet and they will gather together His elect from the four winds, from one end of the sky to the other.

Again, we must keep in mind that this passage still falls into the first major section of Jesus' Olivet discourse pertaining to signs surrounding "this generation." Grant it, the terminology of "angels" gathering God's elect is similar to Jesus' parable of the wheat and tares in Matthew 13:36-43. But, there is a significant difference between the two, and one of the most important hermeneutical principles is that words or phrases can shift in their meaning according to their context.

The "coming of the Son of Man" can refer to Jesus' coming in judgment upon faithless Israel, and then it can mean His coming at the end of the age or world, referring to His Second Coming. Moreover, the use of "a great trumpet" in association with His coming is not exclusively used to refer to His Second Coming.

The question then before us is whether Matthew 24:31 can be exegetically linked with the events leading up to and subsequent to the destruction of Jerusalem in 70 A.D. The answer is a definite yes. In Matthew 13:36-43, Jesus speaks of the world having the seed sown in it. The wheat and tares are the sons of the kingdom and the evil one, respectively. The harvest occurs at "the end of the age." The reapers sent forth at the end of the age are angels who gather the tares (sons of the devil) to be cast into the furnace of fire. This whole scene is consistently seen in the New Testament as occurring at the "last day," which is the great Day of Judgment where the righteous and wicked are separated (Matthew 13:47-50; 22:13; 24:51; 25: 30-46; Luke 12:47-48; Revelation 20:11-15).

In our passage in Matthew 24:31, we simply see "angels" going forth at a great trumpet to gather His elect from the four winds. Nothing is explicitly said or alluded to of the wicked being judged.

With the destruction of national Israel, one of the greatest threats and obstacles to the proclamation of the gospel was removed. One must recall that the reprobate, unbelieving Jews, always caused problems for Paul wherever he went.

Trumpets in the OT were associated with victory, celebration, and deliverance. Trumpets announced the year of Jubilee. The Jubilee was a celebration of liberty from slavery. Who are the angels going forth with a trumpet, gathering His elect from the four winds, from one end of the sky to another?

"Angellos" in the New Testament has a multiple usage depending upon the context. It can refer to a holy angel, an unfallen angel (demon), or a human messenger who proclaims the gospel message. This is but another instance of biblical words changing their meaning depending upon the context.

Jesus referred to John the Baptist as an *"angellos"* in Matthew 11:9-11:

> *⁹But why did you go out? To see a prophet? Yes, I say to you, and one who is more than a prophet. ¹⁰This is the one about whom it is written, "Behold, I send My messenger before your face, who will prepare your way before you. ¹¹Truly, I say to you, among those born of women there has not arisen anyone greater than John the Baptist; yet he who is least in the kingdom of heaven is greater than he.*

The previous text is an example how the word *"angellos"* is translated sometimes as "messenger." You do have heavenly "messengers," the holy angels, but the Bible does speak of other *"angelloi"* or "messengers." **They are God's preachers!**

The same Greek word is used to refer to either heavenly beings or preachers. The context will determine which one. In Luke 7:24, the disciples of John the Baptist who were sent to inquire of Jesus were called *"angelloi"* or messengers. In Luke 9:52, the messengers that Jesus sent ahead to a village of the Samaritans were called *"angelloi."*

Christ's first advent was the joyous proclamation of the **"Jubilee of Salvation."** Jesus brought this out when He read from Isaiah's scroll in the synagogue in Luke 4, quoting that Isaiah 61:1-3 was fulfilled in their hearing. Gospel preaching by *"angelloi"* (messengers) is the blowing of a trumpet of Jubilee that salvation has come to God's elect, who are set free from their bondage to sin.

With the destruction of Jerusalem, the end of the temple and their sacrifices, national Israel was in utter shambles, but this paved the way for gospel preaching that has spread to the ends of the earth. The four winds and "from one end to another" simply indicates the universality of gospel success. Isaiah 27:13 connects a trumpet with great deliverance leading to the worship of the Lord:

> *It will come about also in that day that a great trumpet will be blown, and those who were perishing in the land of Assyria and who were scattered in the land of Egypt will come and worship the LORD in the holy mountain at Jerusalem.*

What is the essential meaning of Matthew 24:31? Gospel preachers are sent forth to all nations proclaiming a great deliverance from sin through the Lord Jesus Christ. Paul references the impact of the cutting off of apostate Judaism in Romans 11:12:

> *Now if their transgression be riches for the world and their failure be riches for the Gentiles, how much more will their fulfillment be?*

The natural branches (national Israel) were cut off, allowing the wild olive branches (Gentiles) to be grafted on to the tree.

Jesus' parable of the fig tree in Matthew 24:32-33 is the last sign associated with the passing of the Old Testament era and the inauguration of the New Testament age. This text reads:

> *Now learn the parable from the fig tree: when its branch has already become tender and puts forth its leaves, you know that summer is near; so, you too, when you see all these things, recognize that He is near, right at the door.*

Jesus' parable of the fig tree teaches that summer is approaching, that there will be fruit. With the events leading to the horrible fall of Jerusalem, a great harvest would result with the conversion of the Gentile nations. Jesus wanted His disciples to learn the meaning of the parable of the fig tree. And what lesson did Jesus want them to grasp? It is this – the events surrounding the destruction of Jerusalem in 70 A.D. were signs that summer was near, not winter. When the branch becomes tender and the leaves show up, then know that summer is near. With the coming of summer for a fig tree means that there will be productivity, growth, and fruit. The parable teaches that the fall of Jerusalem marked the beginning of a great future for the church. It was the beginning of a world wide harvest of souls.

As noted earlier, Matthew 24:34 is the pivotal passage of the chapter. Jesus said that **this generation** (the one to whom He was speaking) would not pass away until all these things take place. What things? All the events represented by the signs leading up to and including the cataclysmic fall of Jerusalem.

In Matthew 24:35, Jesus boldly proclaims what will surely come to pass. Jesus said:

> *Heaven and earth will pass away but My words shall not pass away.*

All the signs that Jesus referred to in verses 4-33 were things Jesus spoke, and they all came to pass in a generation. They were ordained by the sovereign God, and in fulfillment of Daniel's 70 weeks prophecy.

Section 2

Events Occurring at Christ's Second Coming at the End of the World (Matthew 24:36-51)

Beginning in Matthew 24:36, we see the second section of the Olivet Discourse. In verses 36-51, Jesus deals with events that pertain to His physical return at the end of the world – His Second Coming. There are exegetical reasons justifying the division of Matthew 24 into two major sections. I will briefly set forth some of these reasons.[48]

The opening Greek phrase in verse 36 suggests a definite change in topic. The phrase "but concerning" is referring to a day and hour that no one knows, not even Jesus. Jesus said that this day and hour references "the coming of the Son" (v.37). As I mentioned earlier, the context governs the meaning of words and phrases, and this is a prime example of a change in meaning within one chapter. Verse 34 gives all appearance of being a summary statement of preceding events. As Jesus said, the various signs expressed in verses 4-33 occur to "this generation." Note the contrast of "this generation" (v.34) with "that day" (v.36). "This generation" encompasses many distressing days that Jesus called "the beginning of birth pains" and culminating in a series of days known as the Great Tribulation. The siege of Jerusalem in 70 A.D. spanned several months. "That day" in verse 36 references a Second Coming that occurs in a

---

[48] Several of these points are derived from Ken Gentry's 2008 article titled *On the Transitional Verses of Matthew 24* which can be read at: http://www.forerunner.com/beast/X0003_Gentry_on_ Matthew_24.html.

moment, in the twinkling of an eye. One of the most conspicuous absences in Matthew 24:36-51 is no mention of signs. In contrast, "this generation" (v. 34) is told to look for signs, signs that point to the nearness of Christ's judgment upon Jerusalem. It is no minor point that Jesus pleads ignorance of when His Second Coming will occur.[49] Concerning the signs in verses 4-33, Jesus knows the timing of these events, which is why He warns people to flee Jerusalem when they see armies surrounding the city. Jesus says in Matthew 24:25, "*Behold, I have told you in advance.*" In contrast to this is His Second Coming which is like the days of Noah. How were the days of Noah different than the signs leading to Jerusalem's destruction? Destruction came upon the wicked suddenly, totally unexpected. It is here that some people theologically go astray because of the imposition of their theological systems upon the Scripture. Dispensationalist Hal Lindsey comments upon Matthew 24:40-44 in support of his so called "secret rapture." Lindsey states:

> Jesus described the sudden parting of believers from unbelievers when He comes secretly for His own. He said two men will be working in a field, and one will be taken and the other left. Two women will be employed side-by-side, and one will suddenly disappear and the other one will be left (Matthew 24:40-44) (Lindsey, *There's A New World Coming*, p.82)

So, dispensationalism views those taken away as those who were secretly raptured. But, let's look closely at Matthew 24:38-39:

> [38]*For as in those days before the flood they were eating and drinking, marrying and giving in marriage, until the day that Noah entered the ark,* [39]*and they did not understand until the flood came and **took them all away**; so will the coming of the Son of Man be.* (Emphasis mine)

Who is taken away? It is not Noah's family; it is **the wicked!** Taken away how? **In Judgment!** The righteous were **left** and lived by entering the Ark.[50] Jesus said his unexpected Second Coming would be like the days of Noah where people were living normal lives, where everything seemed

---

[49] This ignorance of Jesus should be explained as a choice by the God/Man not to know the time of His Second Coming. Being God, Jesus does know all things or is capable of knowing them, but Jesus is also a true man. There is a certain mystery regarding how the two natures in one person operate. However explainable, Jesus says that He does not know the date of His return. He has deliberately chosen not to access this knowledge, even though He is God.

[50] Tim Lahaye and Jerry B. Jenkins have authored a 16 volume series titled *Left Behind*. Since 1997, this series has sold a staggering 65 million copies worldwide. The series presents the Dispensational Premillennial view of a secret rapture. This is a prime example of how popularity doesn't necessarily equate with biblical truth.

okay, and where life was going on as usual – eating, drinking, and marrying. What did the wicked not understand? They had no idea that judgment was coming upon them.

The difference between the signs that Jesus' generation was to see and act upon and Jesus' Second Coming are seen in Matthew 24:40-51. In verses 40-44 we read:

> *40Then shall two be in the field; the one shall be taken, and the other left. 41Two women shall be grinding at the mill; the one shall be taken, and the other left. 42Watch therefore: for ye know not what hour your Lord doth come. 43But know this, that if the good man of the house had known in what watch the thief would come, he would have watched, and would not have suffered his house to be broken up. 44Therefore be ye also ready: for in such an hour as ye think not the Son of man cometh.*

Concerning the "coming of the Son of Man" as it pertains to Christ's Second Coming, the above text indicates suddenness and uncertainty. There is no looking for signs as warnings; we are to be prepared for His coming at any time. The readiness for the Lord's coming does not teach the imminent return of Christ as dispensationalists teach. It simply teaches the principle of preparedness by living a faithful life. The Scripture emphatically teaches that Jesus will not return until all His enemies are defeated (I Corinthians 15:20-28; Hebrews 10:12-13). Presently, all His enemies are not defeated.

While it is true that there will be a generation living when Jesus physically returns to earth, most generations of Christians will die without seeing that glorious day. Seeing that two thousand years have elapsed since this Scripture was given, how should we understand these passages that appear to teach Christ's imminent return? The stress in these passages (Matthew 24:42-51; 25:1-30) is for us to be found doing the Master's will. Those not prepared by not believing in Jesus as their Lord and Savior will be cut in pieces and assigned to the outer darkness where there is weeping and gnashing of teeth.

Though these passages are dealing with that glorious and terrible day of the Lord at the end of the world, there is a sense that Jesus comes for every man at his death. In Jesus' parable of the rich fool recorded in Luke 12:15-21, Jesus says to the rich fool:

> *You fool! This very night your soul is required of you, and now who will own what you have prepared?*

None of us know the time of our death; therefore, we must be prepared to meet the Lord Jesus on Judgment Day. Hebrews 9:27 affirms:

> *And inasmuch as it is appointed for men to die once and after this comes judgment.*

The Second Coming Is the End of the World

The Second Coming is the end of the world, not the beginning of a thousand year reign of Christ on earth. Where one places the millennium with respect to Christ's Second Coming determines whether one is premillennial or postmillennial. All premillennialists believe that Christ's Second Coming ushers in the millennial age while all postmillennialists believe that it brings to a close this phase of human existence, ushering in the eternal state. The differences are profound, and both cannot be correct. The Bible knows nothing of a so called "eschatological liberty" where one can choose to believe whatever they want about the end times. No, the Bible teaches a particular truth, and we must diligently strive to discern what that truth is.

When we allow Scripture to interpret Scripture, then we will discern that the postmillennial scheme is the most faithful interpretation of Scripture. For most of this chapter, discussion has focused upon the nature of the millennium. Now, our focus is upon the **timing** of the millennium.

Concerning events at the end of human history, several events are seen as conterminous, meaning that they occur essentially at the same time or shortly after one another. There is no gap of a thousand years between them.

These coterminous biblical events are:

1) The Second Coming
2) A general resurrection of both the righteous and unrighteous
3) A general judgment of both the righteous and unrighteous
4) The Second Coming is at the last day or the end of the world

We do affirm that there will be a physical Second Coming of the Lord Jesus Christ. While the phrase "His coming on the clouds" can be a reference to His coming in judgment upon faithless Israel in 70 A.D., this does not negate the bodily return of Christ at the end of the world.

A Physical Return

We do affirm that Jesus Christ returns physically, personally, visibly, and publicly in the clouds of glory on the very last day of human history. Since context determines the meaning of words, there is every reason to believe that these are physical clouds in the sky because this is how Jesus ascended into heaven. In His ascension, Jesus physically was lifted up into the sky, and He disappeared in a cloud.

Acts 1:11:

> *And after He had said these things, He was lifted up while they were looking on, and a cloud received Him out of their sight. And as they were gazing intently into the sky while He was going, behold, two men in white clothing stood beside them. They also said, "Men of Galilee, why do you stand looking into the sky? This Jesus, who has been taken up from you into heaven, will come in just the same way as you have watched Him go into heaven."*

I Thessalonians 4:13-17:

> *[13]But we do not want you to be uninformed, brethren, about those who are asleep, so that you will not grieve as do the rest who have no hope. [14]For if we believe that Jesus died and rose again, even so God will bring with Him those who have fallen asleep in Jesus. [15]For this we say to you by the word of the Lord, that we who are alive and remain until the coming of the Lord, will not precede those who have fallen asleep. [16]For the Lord Himself will descend from heaven with a shout, with the voice of the archangel and with the trumpet of God, and the dead in Christ will rise first. [17]Then we who are alive and remain will be caught up together with them in the clouds to meet the Lord in the air, and so we shall always be with the Lord.*

A Biblical View of the Rapture

In I Thessalonians 4:14, Paul states that those who have died in Jesus will be brought back with Jesus when He returns, that is, the souls of those who have died in Jesus will come with Him.

In verse 15 Paul affirms that those living at the time of Christ's Coming will not precede those who have died in Christ.

What is the mode of the Second Coming? Jesus descends from heaven, with a shout and a trumpet of God, and the dead in Christ will rise first. This means that the resurrection of believers occurs at the Second Coming. Now, the Dispensationalist will say, "See, it does not say the wicked are raised at the same time; hence, there must be two bodily resurrections." The focus of this passage is on giving comfort to Christians who have lost loved ones to death. The doctrine of the resurrection of the righteous at the Second Coming of Christ is a blessed doctrine. Jesus reminded grieving Martha about her deceased brother Lazarus. Though Jesus will immediately raise Lazarus, his resurrection was but a foretaste of that great event at the end of the world. In John 11:25-26, Jesus told Martha:

> *I am the resurrection and the life; he who believes in Me will live even if he dies, and everyone who lives and believes in Me will never die. Do you believe this?*

Earlier, I established from Scripture that there is a general physical resurrection of the dead, not two, separated by a thousand years. It is beyond the scope of what Paul wants to convey to discuss the resurrection of the wicked at Jesus' Second Coming in I Thessalonians 4. Jesus alluded to this general resurrection of both the righteous and the wicked in John 5:28-29.

The dead in Christ have their souls and bodies united at Christ's coming. The first to have this glorious reunion are those who have died. Those who are alive at His coming are "caught up" together with Christ when the others are raised, and we will all be together with the Lord.

Dispensationalists refer to this catching up as the "secret Rapture." Enough books and films (*Left Behind* series) have been written and made about this supposed "secret rapture" of Christians before a great Tribulation. Unfortunately, though sincere in their belief, the idea of a "secret" rapture is totally the fabrication of dispensationalists whose faulty interpretations of biblical events demand this "secret" rapture.

The word "rapture" is not found in the Bible, but the concept is taught, though there are varying views of what it is. Those who correctly discredit the idea of a "secret rapture" before a Great Tribulation must be careful not to convey a wrong notion that there is no rapture at all, because there is a biblical view of the rapture.

In I Thessalonians 4:14, the phrase, "caught up," is translated in Greek as "*harpazo*." But, in Latin, it is translated as "*rapturo*;" hence, "rapture" is the English rendering of this Latin word. The "catching up" of all believers in Christ at Christ's Second Coming is a biblical event at the end of the world. The "rapture" is the immediate changing of the living from mortal to immortal beings, from corruptible to incorruptible. It is the final redemption of the Christian (perfect soul united with perfect body). The "rapture" then is that biblical event at Christ's Second Coming where those alive on earth will be instantly translated from mortal to immortal and given their glorified bodies in the twinkling of an eye (I Corinthians 15:50-56). I Corinthians 15:52 affirms that this changing will be "at the last trumpet." This trumpet sounding corresponds with the trumpet of I Thessalonians 4.

The rapture is **not** a first phase of the Second Coming as Dispensationalists contend; their system demands an anti-biblical position. We must allow Scripture to interpret Scripture. The rapture is at the Second Coming. The biblical proof for this is determined by understanding that the Second Coming, the general resurrection of both the righteous and the unrighteous, and the Judgment Day all occur essentially at the same time. The following biblical texts should conclusively prove this point.

One of the most important passages that teaches about the nature of the millennium and specifies the timing of the Second Coming with reference to the reign of Christ (the millennium) is I Corinthians 15:20-28:

> *[20]But now Christ has been raised from the dead, the first fruits of those who are asleep. [21]For since by a man came death, by a man also came the resurrection of the dead. [22]For as in Adam all die, so also in Christ all will be made alive. [23]But each in his own order: Christ the first fruits, after that those who are Christ's at His coming, [24]then comes the end, when He hands over the kingdom to the God and Father, when He has abolished all rule and all authority and power. [25]For He must reign until He has put all His enemies under His feet. [26]The last enemy that will be abolished is death. [27]For He has put all things in subjection under His feet. But when He says, "All things are put in subjection," it is evident that He is excepted who put all things in subjection to Him. [28]When all things are subjected to Him, then the Son Himself also will be subjected to the One who subjected all things to Him, so that God may be all in all.*

This is one of the clearest texts supporting the postmillennial perspective in all of Scripture. This text clearly determines the timing issue in Eschatology. **When is the millennium with respect to the Second Coming? The millennium is before the Second Coming;** therefore, any view that places the millennium after the Second Coming is in direct opposition to this text. This rules out both forms of premillennialism, both of which place the millennium after the Second Coming.

I Corinthians 15 begins with an emphasis that Jesus Christ is the first fruits of those who rise from the dead. Jesus rose first and guarantees by His victory that all in union with Him will likewise be victorious over death. There is an order in the resurrection – Christ is first and then all His believers. This passage also teaches that **there will be only one bodily resurrection which is at His Second Coming.** This passage confirms that there is nothing after the Second Coming of Christ because it says at His coming **"then comes the end."** At the Second Coming, Christ hands over the kingdom to God the Father, **when He has abolished all rule and authority and power.** Notice the completed action. Jesus "has abolished" all His enemies. It says He must reign **until** all His enemies are under His feet. This is an obvious allusion to Psalm 110 which we know came to fruition at Jesus' ascension/enthronement. This passage clearly places the "reign of Christ" before the Second Coming.

The last enemy that is abolished is death. This obviously takes place at the resurrection which we know is at the Second Coming. We are told in I Corinthians 15:54-55 that at the resurrection of the redeemed, death is swallowed up in victory, for death has lost its sting.

The imagery of I Corinthians 15:20-28 is that of a victorious king, who having won complete victory over all enemies, hands over this victorious kingdom to the ultimate sovereign. This alludes back to Psalm 2 where God the Father installs God the Son on His holy mountain, giving Him all the nations as His inheritance.

I Corinthians 15:27-28 states that God the Father has put all things in subjection to the Son. This is consistent with Psalm 2:7-8 where God the Father gives God the Son all the nations as His inheritance, and the very ends of the earth as His possession. It is consistent with Daniel 7:13-14 where the Son of Man comes up to the "Ancient of Days" who gives Him dominion, glory, and a kingdom so that all peoples might serve Him. The Son's dominion is everlasting, and His kingdom cannot be destroyed.

I Corinthians 15:27-28 pictures the final act of the Son delivering over to His Father a conquered kingdom, as it were, the spoils of holy and spiritual warfare. God the Son accomplished the task given to Him in subduing all His enemies, and now gives to His Father the spoils of war – all the nations have been won! The Great Commission has been fulfilled! The earth is full of the glory of the Lord as the waters cover the sea. Now the truth of Revelation 11:15 can be seen in its ultimate sense:

The kingdom of the world has become the kingdom of our Lord, and of His Christ, and He will reign forever.

Hebrews 10:12-13 is very instructive at this point, for it says:

[12]But He, having offered one sacrifice for sins for all time, sat down at the right hand of God, [13]waiting from that time onward until His enemies be made a footstool for His feet.

This passage teaches exactly what is said in I Corinthians 15. Jesus is not coming back from heaven until victory has been secured over all His enemies. This means that the millennium is before the Second Coming. This means that Jesus is presently reigning from heaven; it means that His reign is foremost a spiritual kingdom. It is a spiritual war that is being waged by the Lord Jesus, but what is amazing is that His church is the instrument by which He carries out this spiritual warfare.

I Corinthians 15:50-58 is a good corollary passage to both I Thessalonians 4:13-17 and I Corinthians 15:20-28. I Corinthians 15:50-58 reads:

[50]Now I say this, brethren, that flesh and blood cannot inherit the kingdom of God; nor does the perishable inherit the imperishable. [51]Behold, I tell you a mystery; we will not all sleep, but we will all be changed, [52]in a moment, in the twinkling of an eye, at the last trumpet; for the trumpet will sound, and the dead will be raised imperishable, and we will be changed. [53]For this perishable must put on the imperishable, and this mortal must put on immortality. [54]But when this perishable will have put on the imperishable, and this mortal will have put on immortality, then will come about the saying that is written, 'Death is swallowed up in victory.' [55]O death, where is your victory? O death, where is your sting? [56]The sting of death is sin, and the power of sin is the law; [57]but thanks be to God, who gives us the victory through our Lord Jesus Christ. [58]Therefore, my beloved brethren, be steadfast, immovable, always abounding in the work of the Lord, knowing that your toil is not in vain in the Lord.

This passage is clearly referencing the resurrection of believers. This resurrection occurs at the "last trump." It teaches that there are some who will not "sleep" (that is die), but we all will be instantaneously transformed from mortal to immortal. This wonderful transformation is the definitive destruction of death's power over us. Nothing directly in the passage references Christ's Second Coming, but we can infer that it must be referencing the Second Coming. From I Corinthians 15:26, we learn that the last enemy that is destroyed at Christ's coming is death. Moreover, we can infer that the changing in the twinkling of an eye from mortal to immortal is what is meant by the rapture in I Thessalonians 4:17 where those alive at His coming will be "caught up" in the air to meet the Lord.

From these passages, we can establish the indisputable fact that the resurrection of believers from the dead occurs at the Second Coming of Christ. There are not multiple resurrections, and there is nothing in the Bible at all that says that there are two different bodily resurrections separated by a thousand years. I have already demonstrated that the first and second resurrections mentioned in Revelation 20 must be referencing a spiritual resurrection and a physical resurrection. Our texts in I Corinthians and I Thessalonians both refer to a bodily resurrection occurring at the Second Coming.

A General Resurrection of the Dead at the Last Day

One of the distinctives of all forms of premillennial thought is that there are two bodily resurrections. The first bodily resurrection occurs either at the rapture or at the Second Coming depending upon whether one is a dispensationalist or a historic premillennialist. The second bodily resurrection supposedly occurs at the end of the millennial kingdom on earth. This view of two bodily resurrections is based upon a false understanding of Revelation 20. Moreover, this false view is necessitated by the belief in a millennial kingdom on earth after Christ's Second Coming. If life is still continuing on earth after His coming, then people are still dying, and those who believe in Christ during this millennial kingdom must be raised from the dead.

The problem with a view of two bodily resurrections separated by a millennial kingdom is biblically untenable. It simply cannot be exegetically demonstrated; it is the imposition of a system of belief upon Scripture rather than letting Scripture interpret Scripture. The following verses demonstrate a general resurrection (one bodily resurrection) of both the righteous and the unrighteous at the "last day."

A general resurrection is seen in Daniel 12:2:

> *And many of those who sleep in the dust of the ground will awake, these to everlasting life, but the others to disgrace and everlasting contempt.*

It is also seen in John 5:28-29 which states:

> [28]*Do not marvel at this; for an hour is coming, in which all who are in the tombs will hear His voice,* [29]*and will come forth; those who did the good deeds to a resurrection of life, those who committed the evil deeds to a resurrection of judgment.*

Who are the "all" in this text? It encompasses those who did good and bad deeds, which means every single human being that has ever lived. There is a resurrection unto life and one unto judgment, but it all occurs simultaneously. Nothing in the text alludes to a separation of a thousand years. The literal and natural way to interpret the text is to understand that the resurrection of the dead has a dual aspect – some are raised to glory and others to condemnation.

In the Apostle Paul's defense before Felix, he alludes to a general resurrection in Acts 24:14-15:

> *But this I admit to you, that according to the Way which they call a sect I do serve the God of our fathers, believing everything that is in accordance with the Law and that is written in the Prophets; having a hope in God, which these men cherish themselves, that there shall certainly be a resurrection of both the righteous and the wicked.*

If we look again at Revelation 20:1-15 there is not a time gap of a thousand years between the two resurrections once we understand that the "first" resurrection is the spiritual resurrection and the one that Jesus referred to in John 5:24-25 and the one that Paul speaks of in being raised up with Christ when we are made alive in Christ. We should never interpret a multitude of verses by one verse, especially if the one verse can easily be understood in light of the multitude. That is, don't interpret Daniel, John, and Acts by Revelation 20 when this chapter can be understood in light of the others.

A very important question is: When does the resurrection occur with reference to the Second Coming? Answer: at the same time and at the end of the world! We have already documented from our study of I Corinthians 15:20-24 that the resurrection occurs at His coming and then comes the end. We noted in I Corinthians 15:24-27 that the end doesn't come until all of Christ's enemies are subdued, and the last one is death. Death is subdued at a resurrection and the resurrection of all the dead is at the **Last Day!**

I must emphasize the obvious. How many days are after the "last day?" None of course! If there are no days after the "last day," how can there be a thousand more days after the "last day?" Since death is the last enemy destroyed, and since death is defeated by the resurrection, and since the resurrection of the dead is at Christ's Second Coming (I Corinthians 15:23-27), how can there be a thousand more days on earth where death occurs and where another bodily resurrection occurs?

Jesus said that the resurrection of all the dead occurs on the "last day." We read in John 6:44, 54 states:

> [44]*No one can come to Me unless the Father who sent Me draws him; and **I will raise him up on the last day**... [54]He who eats My flesh and drinks My blood has eternal life, and **I will raise him up on the last day.*** (Emphasis mine)

Even Martha, the sister of Lazarus, understood this theological truth, for she says in John 11:24:

> *Martha said to Him, 'I know that he will rise again in the resurrection on the last day.'*

Judgment Day is at Christ's Second Coming

If the resurrection is at the "last day," what about the judgment of the dead? Judgment Day is also at the "last day." John 12:48 states:

> *He who rejects Me and does not receive My sayings, has one who judges him; the word I spoke is what **will judge him at the last day.*** (Emphasis mine)

A dispensationalist would have a tremendous problem associating the resurrection of all the dead (both righteous and unrighteous) at the "last day." A dispensationalist understands Revelation 20:11-15 as the Great White Throne Judgment pertaining **only** to the wicked dead. Again, the dispensationalist's theological system is imposed upon Scripture. This can be seen in dispensationalist Clarence Larkin's comment:

> The Scriptures speak of "two resurrections." One of the "just" (the Justified, or Righteous), the other of the "unjust" (the Unjustified,

or Wicked). Acts 24:15. The character of these Resurrections is different, for one is unto "Life" (Eternal Life), the other is unto "Damnation" (Eternal Punishment), John 5:28-29. The "Time Space" between these Resurrections is 1000 years, and they are designated as the "First" and "Second" Resurrections. Revelations 20:4-6. As a "day" with the Lord is as a "1000 years" (II Peter 3:8), and the Millennium is a 1000 years long, then the "First" Resurrection (that of the Righteous) will take place on the Morning of the "Millennial Day," and the "Second" Resurrection (that of the Wicked) as the Evening Shadows Fall.[51]

The unwarranted assumptions that dispensationalists make are: 1) that "the reign of Christ" must be after the Second Coming; 2) that the two resurrections in Revelation must be physical; and 3) that only the wicked are at the Great White Throne Judgment in Revelation 20. The belief that only the wicked are judged at the Great White Throne Judgment cannot be exegetically supported. In fact, an exegesis of the text directly refutes this view. The text states that "the book of life" is opened (v.12), and anyone not found in this book is cast into the lake of fire (v.15). The "book of life" is mentioned in Revelation 3:5; 13:8; 17:8 which contain the names of the redeemed, and any not found in this book are destroyed. The clear inference of Revelation 20:12, 15 is that all humanity is at the Great White Throne Judgment.

A biblical view of the Judgment Day is that it has a dual aspect: 1) Acquit the righteous, whose deeds reflect their justification in Christ, and 2) Condemn the wicked to eternal hell for ungodly deeds.

Since John 12:48 affirms that the Day of Judgment is at the "last day," which is also when all the dead are raised, this means that the resurrection of the dead and the judgment of all the dead are coterminous events. And since we know that the resurrection of the dead is at the Christ's Second Coming, then the judgment of all the dead is likewise at the Second Coming.

II Thessalonians 1:5-10 explicitly states that the wicked and the saints are present before the Lord Jesus at the **same time.** The text reads:

> [5]*This is a plain indication of God's righteous judgment so that you will be considered worthy of the kingdom of God, for which indeed you are suffering.* [6]*For after all it is only just for God to*

---

[51]   Larkin, p. 39.

*repay with affliction those who afflict you, [7]and to give relief to
you who are afflicted and to us as well when **the Lord Jesus will
be revealed from heaven with His mighty angels in flaming
fire, [8]dealing out retribution to those who do not know God and
to those who do not obey the gospel of our Lord Jesus.** [9]These
will pay the penalty of eternal destruction, away from the
presence of the Lord and from the glory of His power, [10]when
He comes to be glorified in His saints on that day, and to be
marveled at among all who have believed, for our testimony to
you was believed.* (Emphasis mine)

Paul is dealing with the question about what happens to those who
persecute the church. In v.6 God will repay with affliction those who
afflict His people. This repayment with affliction is expressed in v.7ff
when it says that the Lord Jesus will be revealed from heaven with His
mighty angels in flaming fire to deal out retribution to all who don't know
God, and who don't obey the gospel. It is apparent that Paul is referring to
the day when fire consumes those who refused to accept the Gospel. Verse
9 says that these who reject the Gospel will bear the penalty of eternal
destruction away from His presence. Verse 10 is continuing the thought of
v.7 about Jesus' revelation from heaven. Not only does He judge the
wicked when He comes, but v.10 says that the saints will be glorified on
that day. What is "that day"? That day is the coming of the Lord; it is the
Day of Judgment. Moreover, both the righteous and the wicked are present
at the same time.

The fact that the righteous and the wicked are present at the same time is
the overwhelming testimony of Scripture. A corollary passage to II
Thessalonians 1:5-10 is Matthew 25:31-46.

Matthew 25:31-46:

*[31]But when the Son of Man comes in His glory, and all the angels
with Him, then He will sit on His glorious throne. [32]All the
nations will be gathered before Him; and He will separate them
from one another, as the shepherd separates the sheep from the
goats; [33]and He will put the sheep on His right, and the goats on
the left. [34]Then the King will say to those on His right, 'Come,
you who are blessed of My Father, inherit the kingdom prepared
for you from the foundation of the world. [35]For I was hungry,
and you gave Me something to eat; I was thirsty, and you gave
Me something to drink; I was a stranger, and you invited Me in;
[36]naked, and you clothed Me; I was sick, and you visited Me; I
was in prison, and you came to Me.' Then the righteous will*

answer Him, 'Lord, when did we see You hungry, and feed You, or thirsty, and give You something to drink? And when did we see You a stranger, and invite You in, or naked, and clothe You? When did we see You sick, or in prison, and come to You?' The King will answer and say to them, 'Truly I say to you, to the extent that you did it to one of these brothers of Mine, even the least of them, you did it to Me.' Then He will also say to those on His left, 'Depart from Me, accursed ones, into the eternal fire which has been prepared for the devil and his angels; for I was hungry, and you gave Me nothing to eat; I was thirsty, and you gave Me nothing to drink; I was a stranger, and you did not invite Me in; naked, and you did not clothe Me; sick, and in prison, and you did not visit Me.' Then they themselves also will answer, 'Lord, when did we see You hungry, or thirsty, or a stranger, or naked, or sick, or in prison, and did not take care of You?' Then He will answer them, 'Truly I say to you, to the extent that you did not do it to one of the least of these, you did not do it to Me.' These will go away into eternal punishment, but the righteous into eternal life.

Verse 31 speaks of the Son of Man coming in His glory with His angels. Does this sound familiar with II Thessalonians 1:7? It ought to. Both refer to His coming in glory and with angels. Note that v.31 says, "then He will sit on His glorified throne." Dispensationalism says that this event in Matthew 25 occurs during the second phase of the Second Coming regarding the judgment of the nations just prior to the beginning of the thousand year millennial reign. The wording "then He will sit on His glorified throne" sounds like Jesus has not already been seated on His throne, David's throne. But, we must interpret Scripture in light of Scripture. We know from Acts 2:30ff that Jesus at His resurrection and ascension sat on David's throne and began His kingdom reign. Matthew 25 doesn't mean that this is when Jesus began to rule on David's throne. That view would contradict Scripture. So what does it mean here? It simply means that in sitting on His throne, He is exercising the kingly role of eternal judge. It is a throne of judgment. When a king sits on his throne, he is using a facet of his regal authority.

Matthew 25 fits in perfectly with II Thessalonians 1:5-10 and with Revelation 20:11-15. In Matthew 25:51, the wicked are condemned to eternal punishment, but the righteous will go away into eternal life. This is a judgment that happens at **the same event**, because it says that Jesus has gathered before Him sheep and goats. The sheep are His believing saints, and the goats are unbelievers. This passage definitely proves that the judgment of the righteous and the unrighteous is together. And we observe from Revelation 20:15 that whoever was not found in the book of life was thrown into the lake of fire.

All of these passages also fit perfectly with Matthew 13:30, 36-43 concerning the parable of the wheat and tares. The passage states:

> [30]*Allow both to grow together until the harvest; and in the time of the harvest I will say to the reapers, 'First gather up the tares and bind them in bundles to burn them up; but gather the wheat into my barn.'...* [36]*Then He left the crowds and went into the house. And His disciples came to Him and said, 'Explain to us the parable of the tares of the field.'* [37]*And He said, 'The one who sows the good seed is the Son of Man,* [38]*and the field is the world; and as for the good seed, these are the sons of the kingdom; and the tares are the sons of the evil one;* [39]*and the enemy who sowed them is the devil, and the harvest is the end of the age; and the reapers are angels.* [40]*So just as the tares are gathered up and burned with fire, so shall it be at the end of the age.* [41]*The Son of Man will send forth His angels, and they will gather out of His kingdom all stumbling blocks, and those who commit lawlessness,* [42]*and will throw them into the furnace of fire; in that place there will be weeping and gnashing of teeth.* [43]*Then the righteous will shine forth as the sun in the kingdom of their Father. He who has ears, let him hear.'*

II Peter 3:3-15

This passage demonstrates the following events as simultaneous: the Coming of Christ; the day of Judgment; the day of the Lord; and the day of God. It is devastating to all forms of premillennialism since at Christ's coming, the human race is judged, and the cosmos is destroyed (rejuvenated). How can there be an earthly millennium of a thousand days **after** Christ's coming, if the end of the world comes with Christ's Second Coming?

II Peter 3:3-15:

> [3]*Know this first of all, that in the last days will come with their mocking, following after their own lusts,* [4]*and saying, 'Where is the promise of His coming? For ever since the fathers fell asleep, all continues just as it was from the beginning of creation.'* [5]*For when they maintain this, it escapes their notice that by the word of God the heavens existed long ago and the earth was formed*

*out of water and by water, ⁶through which the world at that time
was destroyed, being flooded with water. ⁷But by His word the
present heavens and earth are being reserved for fire, kept for
the day of judgment and destruction of ungodly men. ⁸But do not
let this one fact escape your notice, beloved, that with the Lord
one day is like a thousand years, and a thousand years like one
day. ⁹ The Lord is not slow about His promise, as some count
slowness, but is patient toward you, not wishing for any to perish
but for all to come to repentance. ¹⁰But the day of the Lord will
come like a thief, in which the heavens will pass away with a
roar and the elements will be destroyed with intense heat, and
the earth and its works will be burned up. ¹¹Since all these things
are to be destroyed in this way, what sort of people ought you to
be in holy conduct and godliness, ¹²looking for and hastening the
coming of the day of God, because of which the heavens will be
destroyed by burning, and the elements will melt with intense
heat! ¹³But according to His promise we are looking for new
heavens and a new earth, in which righteousness dwells.
¹⁴Therefore, beloved, since you look for these things, be diligent
to be found by Him in peace, spotless and blameless, ¹⁵and
regard the patience of our Lord as salvation; just as also our
beloved brother Paul, according to the wisdom given him, wrote
to you,*

Verses 3-4 indicate that in the "last days" (more on this in a separate section), mockers will come saying, and "Where is the promise of His coming?" In other words, He is not coming because He hasn't come yet. The inference here in "His coming" in the whole context is that Christ is coming in judgment to destroy the unbelievers, and the mockers are hardly concerned. There is no fear of God; they think there is no day of reckoning. We are not accountable for our sins, so they think. It is no different from what Paul encountered in Athens with the Epicurean and Stoic philosophers who saw no life after death and no Day of Judgment. Of course, this does not impede Paul from declaring to them in Acts 17:30-31 that God is now declaring to men everywhere that they should repent because God has fixed a day in which He will judge the world in righteousness through a man who has been raised from the dead.

Just like the pagan philosophers of Athens, the mockers here in II Peter have their own argument that Jesus is not coming because the creation remains steadfast, constant since the beginning of creation.

In verses 5-6, Peter mentions that these mockers have made a fatal flaw in their reasoning. They failed to know that God destroyed the earth once during Noah's flood. In verse 7, while the Bible has made the promise that God will not destroy the world again by a flood, the present heavens and earth are being reserved for fire, kept for the Day of Judgment and destruction of ungodly men. In other words, a great Day of Judgment is coming upon the world where fire is involved. When this day comes, the ungodly will be destroyed just like in the days of Noah, except this time by a different mode.

In verse 8, Peter refutes the argument of the mockers found in verses 5-6. Peter warns - don't allow yourself to think that delay means no return and no judgment. With God, who is eternal, one day is as a thousand years, and a thousand years as one day. What to man appears as a "never event" due to the length of days is nothing to God.

Verse 9 is an often misunderstood passage. The Arminian believes that this text teaches that God wants "all men without exception" to repent as if any man can repent in his own ability. First of all, in the context, Peter is dealing with the certainty of an awful Day of Judgment for the ungodly. What is this promise referred to in verse 9? We must understand that one of the promises of the Noahic covenant is that the end of the world will not come until God achieves all of His covenantal promises in this world such as the subjugation of all His enemies. What is God patient towards? Us! The world will not come to an end until the very last elect person has repented and come to saving faith. When the last elect person is saved, then the end will come.

In verse 10, Peter says BUT (transition carrying the thought over) **the day of the Lord** will come as a thief where the heavens and earth will be consumed with intense heat. Notice what we have seen thus far: His coming (Jesus' Second Coming) in verse 3 is simultaneous with the "Day of Judgment" in verse 7. Moreover, this Day of Judgment of ungodly men is called "the day of the Lord" in verse 10.

Verse 11 warns us to be vigilant, to seek after godliness, seeing that a terrible day of reckoning is coming for sinners.

Verse 12 encourages us to look forward to and hasten **"the day of God"**where the heavens and earth will be destroyed by fire. Hence, it is obvious that the "day of the Lord" and "the day of God" are the same.

In verses 13-15, we see that God promises a new heaven and a new earth that comes about as the result of the destruction of the present cosmos. In this new cosmos, righteousness will dwell.

The Christian is to look forward to these events. The Christian has no fear of judgment day; he is secure in Christ.

As v.15 states, the patience of God in not bringing about the end of the world is that the elect will be saved.

In summary of this passage in II Peter 3, what do we see? All forms of premillennialism are proved wrong, especially dispensational premillennialism. Remember that in their view, at the Second Coming, there is no resurrection of the wicked and no judgment of the wicked, but this is not what II Peter 3 informs us. Dispensationalism has the resurrection and judgment of the wicked AFTER the millennium. But the world has been destroyed by intense heat at the coming of the Lord. Therefore, there can be no earthly millennium after Christ's Second Coming.

A General Statement of the Day of Judgment

1) It follows immediately after the resurrection
2) It occurs concurrent with Christ's Second Coming
3) It will be accompanied by the purging of the universe with fire

When Are the Last Days?

Somehow each generation has a tendency to think that they are the final generation before Christ's Second Coming. Present day dispensational premillennial advocates are notorious for believing this. They often insist that we are in the "last days." By "last days," they mean that we are in the terminal generation; the last one just before Christ's Second Coming. The assumption is that the "last days" refers to this terminal generation. Popular dispensationalist, Hal Lindsey, wrote a book in 1976 called, *The Terminal Generation.*[52] Lindsey insists that this present generation is that terminal generation. Dispensationalist and Christian Zionist, John Hagee, in his book *Beginning of the End, The Assassination of Yitzhak Rabin and*

---

[52] This book sold 100,000 copies in its first three months.

the Coming Antichrist teaches that there are ten signs indicating that we are in this terminal generation. Dispensationalist, Charles Ryrie, has taught that our present generation is the only generation where the events of Ezekiel 37 are beginning to be fulfilled. In his 1978 book *Future Survival,* Chuck Smith said:

> We're the generation that saw the fig bud forth, as Israel became a nation again in 1948. As a rule, a generation in the Bible lasts 40 years... Forty years after 1948 would bring us to 1988.
>
> From my understanding of bible prophecies, I'm convinced that the Lord is coming for His church before the end of 1981. I could be wrong, but it is a deep conviction in my heart, and all my plans are predicated upon that belief.
>
> The Lord said that towards the end of the Tribulation period the sun would scorch men who dwell upon the face of the earth (Revelation 16). The year 1986 would fit just about right.[53]

The list of date setters could go on and on. We are in desperate need of allowing the Scripture to be its best interpret of itself, rather than the fanciful imaginations of men. The biblical truth is: we have been in the "last days" since the time of Christ! Hebrews 1:1-2 states:

> [1]*God, after He spoke long ago to the fathers in the prophets in many portions and in many ways,* [2]***in these last days*** *has spoken to us in His Son, whom He appointed heir of all things, through whom also He made the world.* (Emphasis mine)

With Jesus' first advent, He inaugurated a new covenant thereby setting aside an old one. The old covenant consisted of dreams, visions, prophecies, types, promises, and sacrifices all forsignifying Christ and His redemptive and kingly work. I Peter 1:20 states:

> *For He was foreknown before the foundation of the world, but has appeared **in these last times** for the sake of you.* (Emphasis mine)

And Hebrews 9:26 states:

> *Otherwise, He would have needed to suffer often since the foundation of the world; but now once **at the consummation of***

---

[53]   Chuck Smith, *Future Survival,* (Santa Ana, Ca: Word For Today, 1978) pp. 17, 20, 21.

the ages He has been manifested to put away sin by the sacrifice of Himself. (Emphasis mine)

The biblical evidence is that the "last days" spans the entirety of the millennial age, which we have proven to be the period between Christ's first and Second Advent, officially beginning at His resurrection, ascension and session. The apostle Peter states that the Day of Pentecost is the fulfillment of Joel's prophecy (Joel 2:28-32). Acts 2:17-21 states:

> [17]*And it shall be in the **last days**, God says, that I will pour forth of My Spirit upon all mankind; and your sons and your daughters shall prophesy, and your young men shall see visions, and your old men shall dream dreams;* [18]*even upon My blondslaves, both men and women, I will in those days pour forth of My Spirit and they shall prophesy.* [19]*And I will grant wonders in the sky above, and signs on the earth beneath, blood, and fire, and vapor of smoke.* [20]*The sun shall be turned into darkness, and the moon into blood, before the great and glorious Day of the Lord shall come.* [21]*And it shall be, that everyone who calls on the name of the Lord shall be saved.* (Emphasis mine)

Contrary to the popular dispensational belief that this imagery is some rigidly literal cosmic upheaval associated with Christ's Second Coming, the inspired[54] apostle states that the marvelous outpouring of the Holy Spirit at Pentecost leading to the conversion of 3000 souls is part of the "last days!" The "last days" mark the triumphant reign of Jesus as King of kings and Lord of lords. Isaiah 2:1-4 pictures the glorious Messianic reign of Christ:

> [1]*The word which Isaiah the son of Amoz saw concerning Judah and Jerusalem.* [2]*Now it will come about that **in the last days** the mountain of the house of the LORD will be established as the chief of the mountains, and will be raised above the hills; and all the nations will stream to it.* [3]*And many peoples will come and say, 'Come, let us go up to the mountain of the LORD, to the house of the God of Jacob; that He may teach us concerning His ways and that we may walk in His paths.' For the law will go forth from Zion and the word of the LORD from Jerusalem.* [4]*And*

---

[54] I do want to stress that the apostles are "inspired" conveyers of Scripture who are never wrong because God is incapable of error. However, a seemingly endless number of modern day teachers continue to confidently assert that their interpretations are true, indicating that we are in the "last days" leading up to Christ's Second Coming. These so called modern prophets should pay closer attention to God's condemnation of false prophets in Deut. 18:20-23 and cease this embarrassment to the Lord Jesus and His church.

He will judge between the nations, and will render decisions for many peoples; and they will hammer their swords into plowshares and their spears into pruning hooks. Nation will not lift up sword against nation, and never again will they learn war. (Emphasis mine)

In the "last days" the mountain of the house of the Lord will be established as the chief of the mountains with all the nations streaming to it and learning the ways of the Lord. First, we must understand this Old Testament imagery as it pertains to the coming millennial kingdom of Jesus. Second, we must understand what the Scripture says is **when** "the last days" occur. Actually, the immediate context does specify when the "last days" occur; it occurs during the millennial age. More on this in a moment, but first, we must understand the imagery. The nations will come to the "mountain of the Lord," and to "the house of Jacob." As the nations come, they come to "Zion," and "Jerusalem." Our text states that the law will go forth from Zion, and the word of the Lord from "Jerusalem."

The term "mountain of the Lord" is a general reference to God's people, to God's kingdom. We have seen in Daniel 2 that God's kingdom is referred to as a stone that grows into a great mountain filling the earth. In the Old Testament, Mount Zion was in Jerusalem where the temple stood. This was the dwelling place and sanctuary of Jehovah where the King of Israel resided. Hebrews 12:22-23 is most illuminating:

[22]But you have come to Mount Zion and to the city of the living God, the heavenly Jerusalem, and to myriads of angels, [23]to the general assembly and church of the firstborn who are enrolled in heaven, and to God, the Judge of all, and to the spirits of the righteous made perfect.

The terms "Mount Zion," "Jerusalem," "The House of Jacob," and "the mountain of the Lord" all correspond to the church of the New Testament in the Hebrews passage. In Hebrews 12:22, the city of God is said to be the "heavenly Jerusalem." The "House of Jacob" is the "household and temple of God" in Ephesians 2:19-22.

In Isaiah 2:3 the world's nations will come up to the house of God so that they can be taught God's law, for it says, "For the law will go forth from Zion, and the word of the Lord from Jerusalem." Is this not what the Great Commission pictures? The result of learning of the ways of the Lord is world peace.

All of this occurs during the "last days;" therefore, if we can discern when the "last days" are, then we have discerned the millennium, and since we know the millennium is before the Second Coming, the "last days" are before Christ's return. Even premillennialists acknowledge that Isaiah 2:1-4 refers to Christ's millennial kingdom, but they have an immense problem because all premillennialists believe the millennial kingdom is after Christ's Second Coming. How can this be, seeing that the "last days," even in their scheme, always pertain to events prior to Jesus' return? Inadvertently, premillennialists, in holding to the "last days" being associated with the "church age," which is before Jesus' return, have actually demonstrated their system to be wrong.

Isaiah's prophecy anticipated the establishment of Mount Zion/Jerusalem as the chief of the mountains where the nations will be taught the ways of the Lord. The New Testament affirms this prophecy as coming to pass with the church's preaching. As the gospel proliferates, souls will be brought out of darkness into light, and nations will be transformed as they are discipled.

Thus, the "last days" mark the victorious millennial reign of Christ before the Second Coming. It does not pertain to a terminal generation just prior to Christ's Second Coming. The Son of God came into this world to save sinners, and He is continually saving them throughout the "last days."

Present day Christians should quit going to these so called prophecy conferences and buying up millions of copies of books that deny biblical truth. We need to quit looking for signs of the end and be about the Lord's business of saving souls and building a godly civilization!

Chapter 4

The Church as Jesus' Conquering Instrument

The one thing separating biblical postmillennialism from all other eschatological views is its clear affirmation of the victory of the gospel during the millennial age. While many would acknowledge that God has all power, they would still maintain that He has ordained the defeat of the church in terms of carrying out the Great Commission. But, how can a sovereign God be defeated? Why would He ordain defeat? While all eschatological views believe that the Great Commission was given to the church prior to Christ's Second Coming, only the postmillennial perspective believes that there will be a conspicuous and pervasive accomplishment of the Great Commission.

In his book, *A Case for Amillennialism: Understanding the End Times*, Kim Riddlebarger, while acknowledging many similarities with postmillennialism, insists that the New Testament pictures Christ's return to a wicked and unbelieving world like during the days of Noah, and that the New Testament pictures the millennial age as a suffering church.[1] I pointed out in the previous chapter that the postmillennial perspective does not demand a 100% conversion of every human being, and it does acknowledge an apostasy at the very end of the millennial age due to Satan's release, which would account for unbelievers in existence at Christ's return. The emphasis in Matthew 24:37-38 is the fact that judgment comes upon those not ready to meet God. It is not intended to speak to some quantitative nature of the ratio between believers and unbelievers. If this were the case, then only a handful of people will be Christians at Christ's return since there were only eight persons saved during Noah's Flood. Riddlebarger also argues that the New Testament pictures the church as a suffering church, not as much as a victorious church. There is no question that Christians have and will continue to suffer during the millennial age, but this is hardly a refutation of the

---

[1] Kim Riddlebarger, *A Case for Amillennialism: Understanding the End Times*, (Grand Rapids: Baker Books, 2003), pp. 237-238.

success of the gospel. The ultimate question is: what is the preponderance of the evidence? The evidence is overwhelmingly in favor of seeing Christianity's successful influence during the millennial age.

Will It Be Faith or Fear?

If Jesus has all authority and power in heaven and earth (Matthew 28:18), and has promised to be with His church to the end of the world (Matthew 28:20), how can the church fail to disciple the nations? Isaiah prophesies of a time where the earth will be filled with the knowledge of the Lord as the waters cover the sea (Isaiah 11:9). The promises of the Davidic Covenant are being fulfilled. Jesus is sitting on David's throne in heaven and is conquering all His enemies in fulfillment of Psalm 110. Satan's stranglehold on the nations has been broken, and his domain is being systematically plundered. Just because these promises have yet to be fulfilled in their totality does not mean they will not eventually be accomplished. This is the error that amillennialist Kim Riddlebarger makes when he states – "Indeed, the nagging question remains, 'If postmillennarians are correct about their millennial expectations, what does this say of the progress of the kingdom thus far.'"[2]

Our problem is fundamentally a lack of faith in God's promises, and we must resist the temptations of looking at the present circumstances. One of the invaluable lessons that we learn from Israel's initial failure of entering the land of Canaan is precisely this point. The sad story is recounted in Numbers 13 and 14. Moses was given divine assurance that Israel would be victorious in their conquest of the land. Numbers 13:1-2 states:

> *¹Then the Lord spoke to Moses saying, ²'Send out for yourself men so that they may spy out the land of Canaan, **which I am going to give to the sons of Israel**; you shall send a man from each of their fathers' tribes every one a leader among them'.* (Emphasis mine)

The divine command to send out spies before the attack was not to determine whether or not Israel should attack; it was essentially a military reconnaissance mission. We see the nature of the reconnaissance mission in Numbers 13:18-20:

> *¹⁸And see what the land is like, and whether the people who live in it are strong or weak, whether they are few or many. ¹⁹And*

---

2   Riddlebarger, p.238.

how is the land in which they live, is it good or bad? And how are the cities in which they live, are they like open camps or with fortifications? ²⁰*And how is the land, is it fat or lean? Are there trees in it or not? Make an effort then to get some of the fruit of the land.*

Why bring back some of the fruit of the land? I think it was to prove to Israel that God's word is true – the land does flow with milk and honey. God is not lying. I also think that the report was to encompass what kind of people inhabited the land and their living arrangements for the express purpose of seeing whether Israel would believe God's promises over against seemingly unconquerable circumstances. Would Israel have faith or not?

The spying of the land took forty days, and the report given by ten of the spies was recorded in Numbers 13:27-28:

> ²⁷*Thus they told him, and said, 'We went into the land where you sent us, and it certainly does flow with milk and honey, and this is its fruit. Nevertheless, the people who live in the land are strong, and the cities are fortified and very large; and moreover, we saw the descendants of Anak there.* ²⁸*Amalek is living in the land of the Negev and the Hittites and Jebussites and the Amorites are living the hill country, and the Canaanites are living by the sea and by the side of the Jordan.'*

God said that ten of the spies gave what God called, a bad report. The only exceptions were Caleb and Joshua. Putting it bluntly, the distinguishing feature between the viewpoint of the ten spies over against two others was a lack of faith on the part of the ten. This distinction is recorded in Numbers 13:30-33:

> ³⁰*Then Caleb quieted the people before Moses, and said, 'We should by all means go up and take possession of it, for we shall surely overcome it.'* ³¹*But the men who had gone up with him said, 'We are not able to go up against the people, for they are too strong for us.'* ³²*So they gave out to the sons of Israel a bad report of the land which they had spied out, saying, 'The land through which we have gone, in spying it out, is a land that devours its inhabitants; and all the people whom we saw in it are men of great size.* ³³*There also we saw the Nephilim (the sons of Anak are part of the Nephilim); and we became like grasshoppers in our own sight, and so we were in their sight.'*

Why does God call the report of the ten spies a bad report? Was there something not factual about it? No. Did Caleb and Joshua see something different from the other spies? No. They all saw that the land was a very productive land like God promised. They all saw giants (the Nephilim). They all saw some of the inhabitants living in great fortified cities. So, what was the distinguishing mark? Caleb and Joshua exercised faith! The other spies looked at the circumstances and shrank in fear, a fear that became very infectious. This fear spread to the entire camp of Israel so much so that the people wept and began to grumble against anointed leadership, wanting new leaders to take them back to the slavery in Egypt of all places.

Joshua and Caleb sought to persuade the people to live by faith, but the people wouldn't listen. In Numbers 14: 8-9 they said:

> *⁸If the Lord is pleased with us, then He will bring us into this land, and give it to us – a land which flows with milk and honey. ⁹Only do not rebel against the Lord; and do not fear the people of the land, for they shall be our prey. Their protection has been removed from them, and the Lord is with us; do not fear.*

Choosing to not live by faith in the promises of God is rebellion against God. When we ignore the clear promises of God and concentrate on the external circumstances, we choose to live by fear and not by faith. Fear is paralyzing, but faith is liberating. Faith always clings to a divine promise thereby dispelling fear. **Where there is faith, there is no fear!**

Because of its unbelief in God's promises, a whole generation of adults wandered in the wilderness for forty years until they all died with the exception of Joshua and Caleb. The spies who gave the bad report died of a plague (Numbers 14:37).

According to Hebrews 3, this unbelieving generation never knew the Lord despite being in God's external covenant. Hebrews 4:1-2 states it bluntly:

> *¹Therefore, let us fear lest, while a promise remains of entering His rest, any one of you should seem to have come short of it. ²For indeed we have had good news preached to us, just as they also; but the word they heard did not profit them, because it was not united by faith in those who heard.*

There is a lack of faith in God's promises that is destructive of one's soul like the example above, and then there is a lack of faith in a Christian that deserves God's rebuke as we see in Jesus' rebuke of His disciples for their lack of faith. The incident is recorded in Mark 4:35-41:

> *35On that day, when evening came, He said to them, 'Let us go over to the other side.' 36Leaving the crowd, they took Him along with them in the boat, just as He was; and other boats were with Him. 37And there arose a fierce gale of wind, and the waves were breaking over the boat so much that the boat was already filling up. 38Jesus Himself was in the stern, asleep on the cushion; and they woke Him and said to Him, 'Teacher, do You not care that we are perishing?' 39And He got up and rebuked the wind and said to the sea, 'Hush, be still.' And the wind died down and it became perfectly calm. 40And He said to them, 'Why are you afraid? Do you still have no faith?' 41They became very much afraid and said to one another, 'Who then is this, that even the wind and the sea obey Him?'*

The circumstances seemed perilous for the disciples, and some might even think for good reason since water was already filling the boat; however, Jesus sternly reprimands His disciples for their fear and lack of faith. Why? What was there to fear with the Lord of creation in the same boat?

There is the attitude of those mockers in II Peter 3 who think that a delay in Jesus' return is indicative of no return at all. God forbid that Christians should adopt anything remotely like such skepticism.

The bottom line is this: If God has given us divine promises of the victory of the gospel in the present age, then it is an act of unbelief not to believe those promises despite what the current trends may be.

I have spent a large portion of this book demonstrating from Scripture the biblical evidence for the victory of the gospel. It is incumbent upon all who profess Jesus as their Lord and Savior to believe these promises and not recoil in doubt.

How is Jesus accomplishing His victorious reign? It is through His beloved church! I noted earlier that Revelation 20 indicates that the saints, who have experienced the first resurrection and who are priests to God, will sit on thrones and reign with Christ for a thousand years. Exactly how do the saints do this? Since Jesus is presently reigning and presently defeating all His enemies, He has ordained His church to be the ordained agent for the spiritual conquest of the world. Contrary to dispensational premillennial views, the church is not destined for defeat. No, the church has yet seen its most glorious days. This is not wishful thinking; it is based upon a divine promise of a Messiah who is sitting victoriously at the right hand of the Father in heaven.

We must learn to be enthralled with the greatness of our union with Christ. He is the head of His church, and the victory that He possesses we likewise possess. This is the glorious testimony of Scripture as we shall see. The victory that belongs to Christ is imparted to His church. This is how Jesus subdues His enemies under His feet – through His divinely ordained agent, His spiritual body, the church. This truth is magnificently set forth in Ephesians 1:18-23:

Ephesians 1:18-23

> [18]*I pray that the eyes of your heart may be enlightened, so that you will know what is the hope of His calling, what are the riches of the glory of His inheritance in the saints, [19]and what is the surpassing greatness of His power toward us who believe. These are in accordance with the working of the strength of His might [20]which He brought about in Christ, when He raised Him from the dead and seated Him at His right hand in the heavenly places, [21]far above all rule and authority and power and dominion, and every name that is named, not only in this age but also in the one to come. [22]And He put all things in subjection under His feet,* **and gave Him as head over all things to the church,** [23]**which is His body, the fullness of Him who fills all in all.** (Emphasis mine)

The apostle Paul is addressing the church of Ephesus and is speaking to those who have experienced the surpassing greatness of God's power to the true church (those elect who have come to saving faith). God's power is manifested in three special ways to His people. First, they have experienced the new birth; they have been transformed by the power of the living God and have been transferred from spiritual darkness to light (I Thessalonians 1:2-5, 9; Colossians 1:13). It takes the power of God to raise the dead, seeing that we are all dead in our sins (Ephesians 2:1-6). Second, it is the power of God that works in us to continually sanctify us (Ephesians 3:16, 20; Colossians 1:11; II Peter 1:3). And, third, His church receives power to preach and bear witness of the gospel (Acts 1:8; Romans 15:18-19). The greatest emphasis of God's power in this text is upon this third aspect – power granted to the church by the risen/enthroned Christ. The power of God was exercised in raising Jesus from the dead and seating Him at God's right hand in heaven. The Father bestowed power to the Son that is far above all other authority and power in the universe. The Father put all things under Jesus' feet. This is consistent with Psalm 110 and Daniel 7:13-14. What follows is absolutely amazing. The text explains how God the Father put all things under the Son's feet. He did so by making Jesus head over all things **to the church.** Moreover, the church is viewed as the "spiritual" body of Jesus, which is the fullness of Him who fills all in all. **The church is the fullness of Christ who fills all.** How is this possible? This passage demonstrates the greatness of Christ in His capacity as mediator. The great commentator Matthew Henry said:

> And yet the church is said to be his fullness, because Christ as Mediator would not be complete if he had not a church. How could he be a king if he had not a kingdom? This therefore comes in to the honour of Christ, *as Mediator, that the church is his fulness.*[3]

Calvin says this about Ephesians 1:23 and the meaning of "the fullness of Him:"

> This is the highest honor of the Church, that, until He is united to us, the Son of God reckons himself in some measure imperfect. What consolation is it for us to learn, that, not until we are along with him, does he possess all his parts, or wish to be regarded as complete! Hence, in the First Epistle to the Corinthians, when the apostle discusses largely the metaphor of a human body, he includes under the single name of Christ the whole Church. *That filleth all in all.* This is added to guard against the supposition that any real defect would exist in Christ, if he were separated from us. His wish to be filled, and, in some respects, made perfect in us, arises from no want or necessity; for all that is good in ourselves, or in any of the creatures, is the gift of His hand; and His goodness appears the more remarkably in raising us out of nothing, that He, in like manner, may dwell and live in us. There is no impropriety in limiting the word *all* to its application to this passage; for, though all things are regulated by the will and power of Christ, yet the subject of which Paul particularly speaks is the spiritual government of the Church. There is nothing, indeed, to hinder us from viewing it as referring to the universal government of the world; but to limit it to the case in hand is the more probable interpretation.[4]

---

[3]   Matthew Henry's Commentary on Ephesians 1:23.
[4]   Calvin's New Testament Commentary on Ephesians 1:23.

The beauty of this passage is: Christ is the Lord who reigns, defeating all His enemies through the agency of His church! This needs to sink in. We are the ordained tool of Christ in His spiritual conquest of the earth.

This truth is also pictured in Hebrews 1 and 2. In these two chapters, we see a wonderful presentation of the majesty and supremacy of the reigning Christ and how He uses His church to accomplish His purposes.

In Hebrews 1:5, the writer quotes portions of Psalm 2 and 110 to confirm that Jesus Christ is the Lord who is sitting on His throne at God's right hand. Having established Jesus' deity and present rule, the writer of Hebrews, in chapter 2, sets forth the primacy of apostolic preaching that was confirmed by God's witness through both signs and wonders, various miracles, and other gifts of the Holy Spirit (2:1-4). Those neglecting that preached word that brings so great a salvation shall be doomed.

Hebrews 2:5-9

> *5For He did not subject to angels the world to come, concerning which we are speaking. 6But one has testified somewhere, saying, 'What is man, that you remember him? Or the son of man, that you are concerned about Him? 7You have made Him for a little while lower than the angels; You have crowned Him with glory and honor, and have appointed Him over the works of Your hands; 8You have put all things in subjection under His feet.' 9For in subjecting all things to him, He left nothing that is not subject to him. But now we do not yet see all things subjected to him. But we do see Him who was made for a little while lower than the angels, namely, Jesus, because of the suffering of death crowned with glory and honor, so that by the grace of God He might taste death for everyone.*

In this passage, it is most illuminating how the writer utilizes a reference from Psalm 8 about mankind's dominion as the image bearer of God with the New Testament's clear reference to Psalm 8 as prefiguring the Lord Jesus Christ. Which is it? Is this referring to man or Christ? It is both! First, verse 5 begins with a transitional word, "for." This means that he is continuing the previous thoughts pertaining to the preached word performed by the apostles, testified to by signs, wonders, and miracles. Verse 5 emphasizes that the world was not made subject to angels but to man, even the Son of Man. While Psalm 8 beautifully brings out the dominion mandate of Genesis 1:28, the writer to Hebrews goes beyond this. He uses Psalm 8 to reveal the majesty of the Lord Jesus Christ, the one who is called the Son of Man, and who we know was the Messiah of Psalm 2 and 110. We know all things were put under the feet of the Messiah, so then how does this fit in with the use of Psalm 8? The key is the last part of verse 8 – "*For in subjecting all things to him, He left nothing that is not subject, but now we do not yet see all things subject to him.*" We need to appreciate the thrust of Psalm 8 as originally given in Scripture. The Psalm magnifies man as the image bearer of God, created as God's vice-regent (co-ruler) under Him, giving man dominion over the creation. The latter part of verse 8 stresses the fact that we don't see all things subjected to "him" (man). Verse 9 begins with "*But we do see Jesus who has been made for a little while lower the angels...*" A contrast is being made between verses 8 and 9 as to "him" and "HIM;" however, there is simultaneously a vital union. This interplay between man and Christ makes total sense once we understand that the "man" of verse 8 is **redeemed man in Christ.** All things are not **yet** subjected to him, but we do see Jesus. Since we know that all things have been put under Christ's feet (Psalm 110; Ephesians 1:22), it is just a matter of time before all things are subjected to redeemed man as the agent of Christ in world dominion. As Ephesians 1:23 says, Jesus is the head of the church, a church which is the fullness of Him that fills all in all. Jesus is the kingly priest as Hebrews 7 beautifully stresses, and His saints are "redeemed man" who we know to be a kingdom of priests (Revelation 1:6; 5:10; I Peter 2:9).

F.F. Bruce, in his commentary on Hebrews makes these pertinent observations on this passage:

> There is a minor *crux interpretation* here: when our author says that "now we see not yet all things subjected to him,"does "to him" (Greek αὐτῷ) mean "to man" or "to Christ"? The *crux* is only a minor one, because in any case Christ is in view as the representative Man. But in the first instance the reference is probably to man (so Westcott, Moffatt; cf. NEB: "But in fact we do not yet see all things in subjection to man"). We do not see man exercising his God-given right as lord of creation, but we do see God's Man invested with universal sovereignty. The writer confesses that is not easy to recognize in man the being who the psalmist describes as "crowned with glory and honor" and enjoying dominion over all the works of the Creator's hands. "Man's unfulfilled promise, however, he sees fulfilled in Christ and for mankind fulfilled through Christ" (A.E. Garvie, "Shadow and Substance," EX Txxviii [1916-1917], p. 461). For the view that αὐτῷ means "to Christ" cf. Spicq, *ad loc.:* "Jesus is still far

from having been accepted and acclaimed as king by all the universe: 'unbelieving sinners and demons are not yet subject to him' (St. Thomas). The author must here be expressing the anguish, if not the discouragement of the despised and persecuted Christians, vainly awaiting God's kingdom on earth (II Peter 3:4). The truth is that Christ's militant kingdom is progressive; he must put down his enemies (ch.1:13) before its plenary and triumphant realization." Our author recognizes that, even in exaltation and enthronement, Christ is waiting "till his enemies be made the footstool of his feet" (Ch.10:13); this implies that while He is the rightful ruler of all, all do not yet acknowledge His sovereignty. So, while man is primarily indicated by αὐτῷ, the Son of Man cannot be totally excluded from its scope.[5]

The amazing truth is that Christ, from His throne at God's right hand, has been given universal dominion; the nations have been given to Him as His inheritance. Jesus is using His church, "redeemed man," restored in the image of God to subdue the nations. The truths of Genesis 1:26 (the dominion mandate) and Psalm 8 (on the dignity and task of man made in God's image) merge into a glorious realization of what redeemed man can accomplish in the power of the Head of the church – the Lord Jesus Christ. The church by its use of divinely powerful weapons is the divinely ordained instrument in subduing all of Christ's enemies. We must understand that this portion in Hebrews was given in the context of the importance of apostolic preaching.

Wherever a church is established, Christ is there pouring His gifts out upon His people in order to advance the kingdom of God. The church really is the fullness of Christ in His mediatorial capacity.

William Symington's *Messiah the Prince or, The Mediatorial Dominion of Jesus Christ.*

William Symington was one of Scotland's most accomplished preachers of the 19th Century. His book, *Messiah the Prince or, The Mediatorial Dominion of Jesus Christ,* is a masterful treatise of the relationship between Christ and His church. The basic tenets of a postmillennial eschatology and of a theonomic ethic abound in this work. Some excerpts

---

[5]   F.F. Bruce, *The Epistle to the Hebrews,* (Grand Rapids, MI: Wm. B. Eerdmans Publishing Co., 1964), footnote on p.37.

from his tremendous work shows how he understood the relationship between Christ and His church.

> The outward ordinances of visible Christianity shall be universally spread abroad; efficacy shall be given to the means of grace, by the outpouring of the Spirit; and every obstruction to the triumphant progress of the chariot of salvation shall be effectually removed. Ignorance shall be dispelled before the spreading beams of gospel light... Every usurper of the right sand prerogatives of Zion's King shall be pushed from his seat. Every rival kingdom shall be over thrown. The civil and ecclesiastical constitutions of the earth shall be regulated by the infallible standard of God's word; their office-bearers, of every kind, shall acknowledge the authority of Messiah the Prince; and the greatest kings on earth shall cast their crowns at his feet. All enemies shall be put under his feet.[6]

> By spiritual conversion or judicial destruction, he shall effect the entire subjugation of the globe. And, at the last, there shall not be a spot on the face of the habitable earth where the true church of Christ shall not have effected a footing, nor a single tribe of the vast family of man which shall not have felt the meliorating and blissful influence of Christian laws and institutions... The church, thus universally diffused, shall be effectually perpetuated. The government of Messiah shall not only increase, but it shall have "no end."[7]

> Without such extent of power, he could never open up a way for the diffusion of his gospel among the nations of the earth; could never, either subordinate their administration, or overrule their rebellion, so as to bring about the period when the kingdoms of this world shall become the kingdoms of our Lord and of his Christ.[8]

---

[6]   William Symington, *Messiah the Prince, or The Mediatorial Dominion of Jesus Christ*, pdf online book by Still Waters Revival Books, p. 185.

[7]   Symington, p. 186.

[8]   Symington, pp. 193-94.

Symington understood that Christ's mediatorial dominion was not restricted to the ministry of the visible church, but that it extended to ministry of the civil rulers to advance the cause of the church:

> A prominent feature of these times shall be the subserviency of civil rulers to the church, which surely supposes their subjection to Christ her Head. *Kings shall he thy nursing-fathers* is a similitude which imports the most tender care, the most endearing solicitude; not mere protection, but active and unwearied nourishment and support.[9]

> It does not follow that kings are referred to only in their private capacity... On the contrary, the prediction before us leads us to conclude, that, in the times of the gospel, persons of the most exalted public stations shall exert their influence on behalf of the church of Christ; and this certainly supposes the subjection of such to Christ himself.[10]

Symington's understanding of Christ's dominion prompted a biblical understanding of missions. In fact, one of Symington's city missionaries to Glasgow, Scotland was none other than John G. Paton, who later became the famous missionary to the cannibal islands of the New Hebrides. Symington states:

> Without the supremacy of Christ over the nations, however, the missionaries of the Cross could have no right thus to penetrate into all lands;—the apostolic commission could not, indeed, be lawfully executed.[11]

Symington's exuding confidence in the transformation of all facets of human society by the reign of Christ is undeniably seen in these comments:

> When "kings shall be nursing fathers and their queens nursing mothers to the Church;" when "the Zion of the Holy One of Israel shall suck the breasts of kings;" when "the kingdoms of this world shall become the kingdoms of our Lord and of his Christ;" the nations of this earth will assume an aspect very different from the present. The basis of their organization will then be the Word of God, and the aim of their administration, the glory of Christ: their

---

[9]   Symington, p. 199.
[10]   Symington, p. 201.
[11]   Symington, p. 226.

officers shall be peace and their exactor's righteousness; and the spirit which shall pervade all their actions, shall be the pure spirit of the Gospel. But by whom is this change to be effected? How is this marvelous revolution to be brought about? By the overruling providence and gracious energy of Him who is Governor among the nations. He will shake all nations with the thunder of his power, till everything connected with them that is opposed to his cause is overthrown, and they are led to hail himself 'as the Desire of all nations.' He will purge out the leaven of infidelity and antichristianism with searching scrutiny, and liberally infuse the opposite principles till they leaven the whole lump. He will overturn, overturn, overturn, till he come whose right it is; and he will give it him. The secular tyrannies of the Latin Earth shall be broken to pieces, shall become like the chaff of the summer thrashing floor, and be carried away by the wind till no place be found for them; and the kingdoms that shall succeed will be actuated with the spirit of that kingdom which is represented by the stone cut out without hands, which is to become a great mountain and fill the whole earth. Thus to purify, sanctify, revolutionise, nay Christianise, the nations of the world, is what none but he could perform; and where it not that he is Head of the nations, as well as Head of the Church, we should have to despair of these glorious anticipations being ever realised.[12]

Symington was acutely aware that there was only one law that must be the law of all nations – the law of God. In this sense, he was a thorough going theonomist:

It is the duty of nations, as the subjects of Christ, to take his law as their rule. They are apt to think it enough that they take, as their standard of legislation and administration, human reason, natural conscience, public opinion, or political expediency. None of these, however, nor indeed all of them together, can supply a sufficient guide in affairs of state.[13]

We contend, then, that the Bible is to be our rule, not only in matters of a purely religious nature, in matters connected with conscience and the worship of God, but in matters of a civil or political nature. Indeed, if nations are moral subjects, they are bound to regulate their conduct by whatever laws their moral

---

[12]   Symington, pp. 229-30.
[13]   Symington, p. 234.

Governor has been pleased to give them; and as they are the subjects of the Mediator, they must be under the law of the Mediator as contained in the scriptures.[14]

When, therefore, we find civil rulers, king and judges, commanded to **be wise** and to **be instructed,** must we not understand them as required to go to the Bible for the instruction they need, and to extract from this sacred repository their lessons of political wisdom?[15]

Nations, as such, are under the obligation of the moral law; they are bound to regulate their affairs by the principles and precepts of the Decalogue. Every precept of that law they are bound to obey.[16]

This leads us to a vital understanding of the relationship that Jesus sustains to His preachers.

Jesus and His Preachers

Romans 10:13-17

> [13]*For Whoever will call on the name of the Lord will be saved.* [14]*How then will they call on Him in whom they have not believed? How will they believe in Him whom they have not heard? And how will they hear without a preacher?* [15]*And how will they preach unless they are sent? Just as it is written, 'How beautiful are the feet of those who bring glad tidings of good things!'* [16]*However, they did not all heed the good news; for Isaiah says, 'Lord, who has believed our report?'* [17]*So faith comes from hearing, and hearing by the word of Christ.*

The free offer of the gospel is seen in v.13 - "Whoever calls on Jesus will be saved." But verse 14 asks a very important question – "How then shall they call upon Him (meaning Jesus) in whom they have not believed? And how shall they believe in Him (Jesus) whom they have not heard?"

---

[14]   Symington, p. 235.
[15]   Symington, p. 238.
[16]   Symington, p. 239.

In order to believe **one must hear Jesus.** Without hearing Jesus no one can believe. This is consistent with what Jesus said in John 10:26-27:

> *[26]But you do not believe, because you are not of My sheep. [27]My sheep hear My voice, and I know them, and they follow Me.*

Unless one is Jesus' sheep, he cannot hear Jesus, but all who are His sheep (the elect) do hear His voice and follow Him. In John 8:47, Jesus said:

> *He who is of God hears the words of God; for this reason you do not hear them, because you are not of God.*

So, a man must hear Jesus. Romans 10:14, 15 affirms, *"How shall they hear without a preacher?"* and *"How shall they preach unless they are sent?"* Paul then quotes Isaiah 52:7 as applicable to preachers of the gospel. Men are not invested with power from on High unless they are sent by the sovereign. They are called "ambassadors." Ambassadors are official representatives of a sovereign king who sends them. Paul uses this term several times. He said that he and his apostolic team were "ambassadors for Christ" (II Corinthians 5:20). In this context, their responsibility was that of entreating men to come to Christ in order to be reconciled. Paul uses the term in Ephesians 6:20 where he says he was "an ambassador in chains" who must speak boldly. Ambassadors can and must speak boldly, for they are announcing the word of the King! Malachi 2:7 demonstrates the role of an ambassador, though the word is not directly used. The text states:

> *For the lips of a priest should preserve knowledge, and men should seek instruction from his mouth; for he is the messenger of the LORD of hosts.*

As Jesus commissions His preachers, they proceed with His divine authority, speaking His words. In the Romans 10 passage, Paul quotes Isaiah 52:7 to demonstrate what Jesus is doing. Isaiah 52:6 is glorious when it says:

> *Therefore, My people shall know My name; therefore in that day I am the one who is speaking, here I am.*

Then Isaiah continues in 52:7:

> *How lovely on the mountains are the feet of him who brings good news, who announces peace and brings good news of happiness, who announces salvation, and says to Zion, "Your God reigns!"*

How clearer can it be? God says that in the preaching of His preachers, He is speaking! God says, *"I am the one who is speaking, 'Here I am.'"* In human preachers, God comes speaking and revealing salvation through them. In speaking salvation through them, the preachers are saying to Zion – **Your God reigns!** Since inspired writers of the New Testament can never err, then Paul, in using Isaiah 52, is saying that Jesus is presently reigning through the message of His preachers. This corresponds perfectly with Psalm 110, Ephesians 1:18-23, and Hebrews 1 and 2.

Not only is the term "ambassador" used with reference to preachers, but the term "herald" is used most often. A *keruyx* is the Greek word for a "preacher." A *keruyx* is a herald who proclaims the word of the king. The *keruyx*, the preacher, brings the good news. The *keruyx* can be considered an "ambassador" as II Corinthians 5:20 pictures in bringing the word of reconciliation.

Romans 10:17 simply reiterates the importance of verse 14 that faith comes from hearing **the word of Christ.** Jesus speaks through His preachers. Rejecting the message of one of Jesus' preachers brings serious ramifications. Luke 10:16 states:

> *The one who listens to you listens to Me, and the one who rejects you rejects Me; and he who rejects Me rejects the One who sent Me.*

Jesus had sent out His disciples to preach the gospel of the kingdom of God to the cities and villages of Israel. Since the church is said to be "the fullness of Him who fills all in all," wherever the preachers go, even to the remotest parts of the earth, their feet are said to be beautiful, for they are bringing the good news of God – "I am here to save!"

John Murray makes these comments pertaining to Romans 10:13-17:

> The main point is that the saving relation to Christ involved in calling upon his name is not something that can occur in a vacuum; it occurs only in a context created by the proclamation of the gospel on the part of those commissioned to proclaim it. The sequence is therefore; authorized messengers, proclamation, hearing, faith, calling on the Lord's name. This is summed up in verse 17; "faith is of hearing, and hearing through the word of Christ."

> A striking feature of this clause is that Christ is represented as being heard in the gospel when proclaimed by the sent

messengers. The implication is that Christ speaks in the gospel proclamation... the dignity of the messengers, reflected on later, is derived from the fact that they are the Lord's spokesmen...the apostle is thinking of the institution which is the ordinary and most effectual means of propagating the gospel, namely, the official preaching of the Word by those appointed to this task.[17]

John Calvin makes these observations on Romans 10:17:

This is a noteworthy passage on the efficacy of preaching, for Paul declared that faith is produced by preaching. He has just stated that by itself preaching is profitless, but when the Lord is pleased to work, it is the instrument of His power. Certainly the human voice cannot by its own power penetrate into the soul. Too much honour would be paid to a mere mortal if it were said that he had power to regenerate us. The light of faith also is too exalted to be able to be conferred by man. But all these things do not prevent God from acting effectually by the voice of man, so as to create faith in us by his ministry.[18]

I noted in the previous chapter that this wonderful truth of Jesus preaching through His preachers was seen in the marvelous conversion of 3000 souls on the Day of Pentecost (Acts 2:25-41). Peter's sermon was performed in the power of the Spirit from the risen Christ who Peter says was sitting at the right hand of the Father in fulfillment of Psalm 110.

Romans 16:25-26

The incredible thing is that **Jesus preaches through His preachers**! Hence, the primacy of preaching is set forth. This same truth is set forth in Romans 16:25-26:

*[25]Now to Him who is able to establish you according to my gospel and **the preaching of Jesus Christ**, according to the revelation of the mystery which has been kept secret for long ages past, [26]but now is manifested, and by the Scriptures of the prophets, according to the commandment of the eternal God, has been made known to all the nations, leading to obedience of faith.* (Emphasis mine)

---

[17]   Murray, p. 58.
[18]   John Calvin, *The Epistles of Paul the Apostle to the Romans and to the Thessalonians*, (Grand Rapids, MI: Wm. B. Eerdman's Publishing Co., 1973), p. 233.

The church is the fullness of Christ who fills all in all. Wherever preachers go into the remotest parts of the earth, Jesus is going with them and empowering them. **Understanding these precious truths should be the compelling motive for world missions!** In speaking about world missions, the foremost passage in the New Testament is the Great Commission expressed in Matthew 28:18-20.

Matthew 28:18-20

> *[18]And Jesus came up and spoke to them, saying, 'All authority has been given to Me in heaven and on earth. [19]Go therefore and make disciples of all the nations, baptizing them in the name of the Father and the Son and the Holy Spirit, [20]teaching them to observe all that I commanded you; and lo, I am with you always, even to the end of the age.'*

This passage is most commonly known as the Great Commission. Jesus specifically commands His apostles to disciple the nations. The command entails much more than the commonly understood notion of evangelism. Of course, it involves evangelism – God saving men out of darkness and bringing them to light. But discipling goes beyond evangelism. The discipling of the nations involves individual, family, and cultural transformation. A disciple is a person who is committed to the Lordship of Christ in all areas of his life. He walks consciously in holiness of life through the power of the Spirit. The family is the fundamental building block of any civilization, and for a culture to prosper, a godly family is a necessity. The command to baptize and to teach in the Commission points to God's emphasis upon the family. The church must help families to educate their children in the nurture and admonition of the Lord. Christian education is no option, be it in a Christian school or in Christian homeschooling. The cultural implications of the Great Commission are that the word of God permeates all facets of civilization. All national institutions must be transformed by the Christian worldview. The institutions of economics, education, industry, and law must all fly the banner of Christ.

Really and truly, the Great Commission is the New Testament expression of the Dominion Mandate of Genesis 1:28. Redeemed man is to have dominion over **all** of life.

The Great Commission is founded upon one central and absolutely essential truth – Jesus has all authority in heaven and earth. Verse 18 serves as the foundation for the success of the Commission. The risen

Christ comes to His disciples just prior to His ascension with this glorious fact – I have all authority and power in the universe! The Greek word for authority is *exousia*, meaning the right of privilege and power to rule. Jesus said that He had it all! Who can defy the living God? This all embracing authority and power undergirds the Great Commission, guaranteeing its success. Jesus guarantees victory for the church's mission by His promise – "*I am with you always, even to the end of the age.*" In these glorious words of Jesus' abiding presence with His church, He is showing forth the magnificent words of Deuteronomy 20: 1, 3, 4:

> *[1]When you go out to battle against your enemies and see horses and chariots and people more numerous than you, do not be afraid of them; for the LORD your God, who brought you up from the land of Egypt, is with you... [3]He shall say to them, 'Hear, O Israel, you are approaching the battle against your enemies today. Do not be fainthearted. Do not be afraid, or panic, or tremble before them ... [4]for the LORD your God is the one who goes with you, to fight for you against your enemies, to save you.*"

Jesus Christ is Jehovah Sabaoth, "the Warrior of Israel." Jesus is the "Captain of the hosts of the Lord" who leads the heavenly hosts in war against His enemies. The fact that Jesus is with His church in this capacity and "with them until the end of the age" assures the success of His Great Commission. Who can defeat God? This means His church is invincible in its capacity to be His agent in the spiritual conquest of the world.

We must remember that Psalm 110 tells us that Christ, in the stretching forth of His scepter from Zion, is ruling in the midst of His enemies. Christ's scepter that rules in the midst of His enemies is from Zion, His church. The church is the divine instrument of Christ's scepter in subjugating the nations.

The victory of Christ in the millennial age utilizing the church is seen in several other passages.

Revelation 19:11-19

> *[11]And I saw heaven opened, and behold, a white horse, and He who sat on it is called Faithful and True, and in righteousness He judges and wages war. [12]His eyes are a flame of fire, and on His head are many diadems; and He has a name written on Him which no one knows except Himself. [13]He is clothed with a robe dipped in blood, and His name is called The Word of God. [14]And*

the armies which are in heaven, clothed in fine linen, white and clean, were following Him on white horses. [15]From His mouth comes a sharp sword, so that with it He may strike down the nations, and He will rule them with a rod of iron; and He treads the wine press of the fierce wrath of God, the Almighty. [16]And on His robe and on His thigh He has a name written, 'KING OF KINGS, AND LORD OF LORDS.' [17]Then I saw an angel standing in the sun, and he cried out with a loud voice, saying to all the birds which fly in mid heaven, 'Come, assemble for the great supper of God, [18]so that you may eat the flesh of kings and the flesh of commanders and the flesh of mighty men and the flesh of horses and of those who sit on them and the flesh of all men, both free men and slaves, and small and great.' [19]And I saw the beast and the kings of the earth and their armies assembled to make war against Him who sat on the horse and against His army.

The main points of this highly figurative picture are:

1) It is a vision of victory, where One is riding on a white horse. The one sitting on the horse is called "Faithful and True."
2) In righteousness He comes judging and waging war.
3) His robe is dipped in blood, demonstrating He is engaged in destroying His enemies.
4) The name written upon Him is the Word of God.
5) Following Him are the armies of heaven who are clothed in white linen, also riding on white horses.
6) From His mouth comes a sharp sword that smites the nations; He rules them with a rod of iron; His wrath is poured out upon all His enemies.
7) On His robe and thigh, a name is written: King of kings, and Lord of lords.
8) An angel beckons birds to come and assemble for the great supper of God where the flesh of kings, commanders, mighty men, of both free men and slaves, small and great are devoured.
9) The armies of the beast and kings of the earth are assembled to war against Christ and His army.

A common misunderstanding of this passage is often seen in dispensational premillennial teaching. They describe this as the Second Coming, but this is totally wrong. They have missed the advents of Christ. This imagery does not pertain to the Second Coming but Christ's First Coming. The Second Coming according to Acts 1:11 has Jesus ascending into heaven in the clouds, which is in line with similar imagery found in I

Thessalonians 4:17. In Acts 1:11, the angels are declaring, *"This Jesus, who has been taken up from you into heaven, will come in just the same way as you have watched Him go into heaven."*

The Second Coming is not a time of making war on earth. As I Corinthians 15 teaches, when Jesus returns, "then comes the end." His enemies have already been defeated. The Second Coming is the final day of history; it is the "last day," referring to the day of resurrection and judgment.

However, the imagery of Revelation 19 conveys imagery of intense warfare. Some insist that this present age cannot be the millennium, for there is too much turmoil; it is supposed to be a time of great peace. The biblical answer to this is: the millennial age according to Psalm 110 is when Jesus sits on David's throne, stretching forth His scepter from Zion saying, *"Rule in the midst of Thine enemies."* It is an age of spiritual warfare, for He must reign until He has put all His enemies under His feet. The millennial age is a time where His kingdom plunders Satan's house. The millennial age is distinctly a time of great warfare where Jesus and those with Him are destroying their enemies. But the millennial age is indeed a time of great worldwide peace. When men are converted to Christ, they are at peace with God and with men. Jesus' destruction of His enemies brings peace in those who are defeated!

Jesus comes riding on a white horse, which was a common ancient symbol of a hero coming in triumph over his enemies. The One sitting on the white horse is called "Faithful and True." He comes judging and waging war in righteousness. His robe is dipped in blood, an imagery of intense warfare whereby His robe is stained with the blood of His defeated enemies. His name is interestingly called, "The Word of God." Those following him are an army riding on white horses clothed in white linen, a symbol of purity. This is not an imagery of angels with Jesus, but that of His purified church who are waging war with Him. We must remember that the saints are reigning with Jesus and judging, and as I have just noted previously, the church is the agent of discipling the nations.

It is noteworthy that a sharp sword is coming out of His mouth by which He smites the nations, ruling them with a rod of iron. Remember, His name is "The Word of God." This sword coming out of his "mouth" slays His enemies. What could possibly be the meaning of this sharp sword protruding from His mouth? **It is the preaching of God's Word**. We remember that Jesus preaches through His preachers! This army in white linen is the church engaged as the agent of defeating Jesus' enemies with Him. It is no coincidence that Ephesians 6:17 says that the divinely ordained part of the Christian's armor that is an offensive weapon is his sword, which is the sword of the Spirit, which is called the Word of God. Does not Hebrews 4:12 refer to the Word of God that is sharper than any ordinary two edged sword? It penetrates into the depths of men's souls accomplishing God's perfect will.

Hebrews 4:12

> *For the word of God is living and active and sharper than any two-edged sword, and piercing as far as the division of soul and spirit, of both joints and marrow, and able to judge the thoughts and intentions of the heart.*

It was noted from Psalm 110 that the enemies of Christ are defeated by being converted. As Christ stretches forth His royal scepter, ruling in the midst of His enemies, His people volunteer freely in the day of His power. It was noted earlier that men must hear Jesus preaching to them in order to be converted, and it is the Holy Spirit taking God's word that is the very means of their conversion. Jesus does slay His enemies with the sword coming out of His mouth! He slays them through His church that preaches His word in the power of the Spirit.

Isaiah 11:4-5

The imagery of a sword out of His mouth and smiting the nations is an Old Testament image of the role of the Messiah. Isaiah 11 is most illuminating. The Messiah is from the "branch of Jesse." Jesus is that branch according to His own testimony (Revelation 22:16). Isaiah 11:4-5 states:

> *⁴But with righteousness He will judge the poor... and He will strike the earth with the rod of His mouth, and with the breath of His lips He will slay the wicked. ⁵Also righteousness will be the belt about His loins, and faithfulness the belt about His waist.*

There is no coincidence either between this description of the coming Messiah and that of Jesus in Revelation 19. Isaiah says He judges the poor with righteousness. Revelation 19 says that in righteousness He comes judging and waging war. Isaiah says that Messiah strikes the earth with the "rod of His mouth," and by the "breath of His lips" He slays the wicked. Revelation 19 says that He smites the nations with "the sharp sword coming out of His mouth" and rules them with a rod of iron. Isaiah says that Messiah has the belt of "faithfulness." Revelation 19 says that the One riding on the white horse is called, "Faithful and True."

Isaiah 11 pictures the coming Messiah whose reign will bring about peace. All millennial views believe that Isaiah 11 pictures the reign of Christ. Premillennialists believe that the kingdom of Christ is a time of unprecedented peace on earth and so do postmillennialists. Their differences are in the timing of the millennial age and in the nature of that millennium. The fact that one can link the imagery of Isaiah 11 (the millennial age) with that of Revelation 19 demonstrates that Revelation 19 pertains to the first coming of Christ not His Second Coming; it pictures the subduing of the nations to Christ through the agency of His church, who preaches the gospel. Preaching is indeed "the sword out of His mouth" that smites the nations. Revelation 19 says that Jesus rules the nations with a rod of iron. Did not Psalm 2:8-9 inform us that the nations have been given to the Son as His inheritance and that He shall break them with a rod of iron?

There is a wonderful parallel between the imagery of the Old Testament prophecies concerning Christ with that imagery of the New Testament, although it is not exactly the same wording, but the meaning is the same. A "rod of His mouth" that strikes the earth means the same as "a sharp sword coming out of His mouth" that smites the nations.

Revelation 6:1-2

Revelation 6:1-2 conveys a very similar thought as Revelation 19. It says:

> *¹And I saw when the Lamb broke one of the seven seals, and I heard one of the four living creatures saying as with a voice of thunder, "Come!" ²And I looked and behold, a white horse, and he who sat on it had a bow; and a crown was given to him; and he went out conquering and to conquer.*

Jesus is reigning; He is going out conquering and to conquer. He is subduing the nations; He is smiting them with the rod of His mouth. His preaching is destroying His enemies; His gospel is the very power of God that transforms enemies of God into His friends. Jesus does all of this through His church! His church is the fullness of Him that fills all in all in terms of His role as mediator. This agency of the church being used in holy warfare is seen in even other texts.

Matthew 16:16-18

> *¹⁶Simon Peter answered, 'You are the Christ, the Son of the living God.' ¹⁷And Jesus said to him, 'Blessed are you, Simon Barjona, because flesh and blood did not reveal this to you, but*

My Father who is in heaven. [18]I also say to you that you are Peter, and upon this rock I will build My church; and the gates of Hell will not overpower it.'

Jesus had asked His disciples, "Who do men say that the Son of Man is?" While some of His disciples were saying that others thought him to be Elijah or John the Baptist or Jeremiah returned from the dead, it was Peter who said, "You are the Christ, the Son of the living God." Jesus had elicited a response from Peter as to His true identity. With Peter's accurate confession, Jesus stated that any such illumination is an act of God's revealing grace because flesh and blood cannot understand it. It is upon such a confession that Jesus builds His church. No one is a genuine Christian who does not receive Him as Lord, who does not confess Him as the God/Man (I John 2:20-23). This is the glorious truth set forth in the gospel that the church preaches.

Notice as well, that Jesus said that the gates of Hell will not overpower the church. This is often misunderstood. Many view this passage as stating that the church is a blessed stronghold that not even the devil and his entire demonic realm can defeat. This view pictures the devil on the attack while the church is on the defensive, but prevailing. This is not what Jesus meant, and it is not an accurate view of the church and its relationship to the devil and his forces. Yes, it is true that Ephesians 6 pictures the Christian with his full armor who is standing firm against the devil and his schemes (Ephesians 6:12), whose shield of faith does quench all the fiery darts of the evil one (Ephesians 6:16). We must always understand passages in their context, and how the Scripture uses various concepts. The individual Christian is engaged in a holy war with the devil and his seed, but this doesn't mean the church is on the defense. No, this simply reflects how the Christian is protected. The church is not on the defense, but **it is on the offense!** Our text in Matthew 16:18 says it is **not** "the gates of the church," but it is "the gates of hell" that will not prevail. Gates are not offensive structures; they are defensive. The citadel of the devil is under attack by the church! And, the "gates," which is the entrance to the fortress cannot overpower the church, that is, it cannot withstand the church's assault.

Genesis 22:17-18

It is no coincidence that Jesus uses this imagery of His church in Matthew. It has Old Testament roots. Genesis 22:17-18 states:

[17]Indeed I will greatly bless you, and I will greatly multiply your seed as the stars of the heavens and as the sand which is on the

seashore; [18]*and your seed shall possess the gate of their enemies. In your seed all the nations of the earth shall be blessed, because you have obeyed My voice.* (Emphasis mine).

We know this to be a very important aspect and promise of the Abrahamic covenant. We have established already that the church of Jesus is the seed of Abraham (Galatians 3:29). The promise is that Abraham's seed will possess the "gate" of their enemies, signifying the defeat of the enemies of God by the seed of Abraham. It is more than reasonable that Jesus, who is THE seed of Abraham (Galatians 3:16) was referring to this when He spoke to His church. Possessing the gates of one's enemies means the same as the gates of hell not prevailing against the church.

How does the church of Christ attack the gates of hell?

Divinely Ordained Weapons: Preaching and Prayer

II Corinthians 10:3-5

[3]*For though we walk in the flesh, we do not war according to the flesh,* [4]*for the weapons of our warfare are not of the flesh, but divinely powerful for the destruction of fortresses.* [5]*We are destroying speculations and every lofty thing raised up against the knowledge of God, and we are taking every thought captive to the obedience of Christ.*

The possessing of the gates of our enemies is not a physical warfare, but a spiritual one. We are engaged in warfare, but our weapons are spiritual and divinely powerful for the destruction of fortresses. In speaking about the church, Paul says that we are attacking fortresses. Sounds a lot like Genesis 22:17 and Matthew 16:18 doesn't it?

The nature of the warfare is spiritual, for it says that with divinely powerful weapons we are destroying speculations raised up against the knowledge of God and taking captive every thought to the obedience of Christ. Is this not the scope of the Great Commission? Is this not the discipling of the nations whereby we teach them to observe ALL things that Jesus commanded? And what was the promise of Jesus? As the "warrior of Israel," as "the Captain of the Lord's host" is He not with His church always, assuring them of victory? Jesus said He had all authority (power) in the universe; therefore, what is the likelihood of the divinely ordained weapons He has given to His church prevailing against the fortress of hell? Hell's citadel stands no chance!

Oh yes, you bet our weapons are divinely powerful, so powerful that Hell's gates, Hell's citadel stands no chance! How do we as the church bring all thoughts captive to Christ's obedience? It is by the faithful preaching and teaching of the Word of God and diligent prayer. These are the divinely powerful weapons!

The Power of Preaching

It took power for Jesus to raise men physically from death to life; it took power for Jesus to be raised Himself from physical death, and, in one sense, it takes as much divine power to raise a deadened soul to spiritual life.

As Jesus said, He has all the power in the universe. Who can resist the omnipotent King of kings and Lord of lords? If Jesus is empowering His preachers, preaching through them, how is it possible for the gospel not to be victorious in history?

Romans 1:1-6

> *[1]Paul, a bond-servant of Christ Jesus, called as an apostle, set apart for the gospel of God, [2]which He promised beforehand through His prophets in the holy Scriptures, [3]concerning His Son, who was born of a descendant of David according to the flesh, [4]who was declared the Son of God with power by the resurrection from the dead, according to the Spirit of holiness, Jesus Christ our Lord, [5]through whom we have received grace and apostleship to bring about the obedience of faith among all the Gentiles for His name's sake, [6]among whom you also are the called of Jesus Christ.*

Verse 4 says that Jesus was declared to be the Son of God with power by the resurrection. It does not say that Jesus became God at the resurrection, only that He was declared to be the Son of God. The resurrection was the crowning testimony to His divinity. The key idea here is the phrase, "with power." Jesus is the Son of God with power! The resurrection of Christ was the beginning of His exaltation. His ascension and session at the Father's right hand marked His possession of the nations as His inheritance as promised in Psalm 2 and Daniel 7.

Verse 5 stresses the fact that through Christ Jesus grace and apostleship has been given. For the apostle Paul, God's grace to him and his call to apostleship came together for one great purpose – **to bring about the obedience of faith** among the Gentiles. This phrase, "the obedience of faith" is an important one to understand. While it is true that there is a union of obedience to faith, it is one where obedience is the fruit of faith. In this context, the "obedience of faith" is the call to exercise faith. Faith is seen as an act of obedience to the demands of the gospel. So, when the gospel is preached, what does God expect? Obey the call to believe! I John 3:23 states, "*And this is His commandment, that we believe in the name of His Son Jesus Christ...*"

We see the same meaning expressed in Romans 1:5 set forth in Romans 16:25-26.

Romans 16:25-26

The incredible thing is that **Jesus preaches through His preachers**! Hence, the primacy of preaching is set forth. This same truth is set forth in Romans 16:25-26:

> *[25]Now to Him who is able to establish you according to my gospel and **the preaching of Jesus Christ**, according to the revelation of the mystery which has been kept secret for long ages past, [26]but now is manifested, and by the Scriptures of the prophets, according to the commandment of the eternal God, has been made known to all the nations, **leading to obedience of faith**.* (Emphasis mine)

The church is the fullness of Christ who fills all in all. Wherever preachers go into the remotest parts of the earth, Jesus is going with them and empowering them. When Jesus goes to save His elect, there is nothing in the universe that can prevent it. When Jesus preaches through His earthly preachers, men are led to faith most assuredly.

The power of the invincible Christ was manifested to Saul of Tarsus (who became Paul the apostle). This is vividly seen in Paul's testimony to the Galatians in Galatians 1:11-16.

Galatians 1:11-16

> *[11]For I would have you know, brethren, that the gospel which was preached by me is not according to man. [12]For I neither received it from man, nor was I taught it, but I received it*

through a revelation of Jesus Christ. [13]For you have heard of my former manner of life in Judaism, how I used to persecute the church of God beyond measure and tried to destroy it; [14]and I was advancing in Judaism beyond many of my contemporaries among my countrymen, being more extremely zealous for my ancestral traditions. [15]But when God, who had set me apart even from my mother's womb and called me through His grace, was pleased [16]to reveal His Son in me so that I might preach Him among the Gentiles, I did not immediately consult with flesh and blood,

The conversion of Saul of Tarsus is undoubtedly one of the surest biblical examples of the power of Christ to sovereignly save sinners. Saul of Tarsus was zealous to defend Judaism against Christians. He was feared by believers for his persistent persecution of the Faith. In fact, Saul was on his way to Damascus to arrest more Christians when Jesus encounters him (Acts 9:1-19). Saul was definitely not seeking the Lord when Jesus came to him, but when Jesus goes to save, nothing in the universe can stop it. In the Galatians text, we see one of the greatest examples of predestination unto eternal life. Paul states that God had set him apart from his mother's womb to be a recipient of God's saving grace and predestined to be the apostle to the Gentiles. Jesus revealed Himself to Saul of Tarsus and saved him. We see this predestination of Saul to be the great apostle to the Gentiles by Jesus' words to Ananias as recorded in Acts 9:15 – *"But the Lord said to him, 'Go, for he is a chosen instrument of Mine to bear My name before the Gentiles and kings and the sons of Israel, for I will show him how much he must suffer for My name's sake."*

Saul, the great persecutor of the church, was saved by the omnipotent power of God from spiritual death to spiritual life. This same power that saved him was also the same power that empowered him to preach the gospel. We read in Acts 26:15-18:

[15]And I said, 'Who are You, Lord?' And the Lord said, 'I am Jesus whom you are persecuting. [16]But get up and stand on your feet; for this purpose I have appeared to you, to appoint you a minister and a witness not only to the things which you have seen, but also to the things in which I will appear to you; [17]rescuing you from the Jewish people and from the Gentiles, to whom I am sending you, [18]to open their eyes so that they may turn from darkness to light and from the dominion of Satan to God, that they may receive forgiveness of sins and an inheritance among those who have been sanctified by faith in Me.'

This is a highly significant passage that teaches us several vital truths. First, it affirms again God's predestination in choosing His preachers. Jesus said that He "appointed" Saul of Tarsus to be a minister. Second, Jesus is the One who sends His preachers to deliver men from their spiritual darkness – "*To open their eyes so that they may turn from darkness to light and from the dominion of Satan to God.*" This demonstrates the purpose of gospel preaching. The gospel invades the domain of darkness, Satan's domain, to set men free! This reminds us of what was stated in an earlier chapter that even during Jesus' earthly ministry, His disciples were empowered by Him to preach the gospel of the kingdom. Consequently, Jesus said that He saw Satan fall from heaven like lightning (Luke 10:18), meaning that Satan's domain was being assaulted and overcome by the **power of preaching!**

God's Power to Regenerate

Actually, every person who believes in Jesus must have Jesus revealed to him/her. Jesus made this truth evident when He responded to Peter in Matthew 16:16-17:

> [16]*And Simon Peter answered and said, 'Thou are the Christ, the Son of the living God. *[17]*And Jesus answered and said to him, 'Blessed are you, Simon Barjona, because flesh and blood did not reveal this to you, but My Father who is in heaven.'*

We must have the Holy Spirit reveal biblical truth to us about the gospel because we are dead in our sins, not simply sick. Theologically, this is called the doctrine of total depravity, meaning that sin has affected every aspect of a man's being - his heart, mind, and will.

Ephesians 2:1-6

> [1]*And you were dead in your trespasses and sins,*[2] *in which you formerly walked according to the course of this world, according to the prince of the power of the air, of the spirit that is now working in the sons of disobedience. *[3]*Among them we too all formerly lived in the lusts of our flesh, indulging the desires of the flesh and of the mind, and were by nature children of wrath, even as the rest. *[4]*But God, being rich in mercy, because of His great love with which He loved us, *[5]*even when we were dead in our transgressions, made us alive together with Christ(by grace you have been saved), *[6]*and raised us up with Him, and seated us with Him in the heavenly places in Christ Jesus.*

The text affirms that we are dead in our sins. Dead men cannot do anything but remain dead. It is obvious that dead men have no power in themselves whatsoever to change their spiritual condition. The text also affirms that the "prince of the power of the air" (a reference to Satan) works in all who are dead in their sins. By nature we are children of wrath, meaning that unless God does something amazing to intervene, we will all perish in our sins. But, this text also reveals the glorious fact that God is rich in mercy toward those whom He loves and determines to save, despite the fact they are spiritually dead. God in Christ makes us alive by showing His grace to us. These two wonderful acts of God are given to His elect – His mercy and grace. Mercy is not receiving what we deserve; we all deserve Hell because of our transgressions. Grace is receiving that which we did not deserve.

While it is true that men must believe in the gospel that is offered to them, it is not true that men have the power in themselves to believe. Dead men cannot reach out to a Savior in their own strength. This biblical truth is clearly stated in Isaiah.

Isaiah 64:6-7

> [6]*For all of us have become like one who is unclean, and all our righteous deeds are like a filthy garment; and all of us wither like a leaf, and our iniquities, like the wind, take us away.* [7]*There is no one who calls on Your name, Who arouses himself to take hold of You; For You have hidden Your face from us and have delivered us into the power of our iniquities.*

The text affirms that all of us without exception have nothing good in us. Our iniquities (sins) have taken us away, and God has given us over to the power of our iniquities. This explains why unbelievers cannot help but sin. It explains what Ephesians 2:1-2 stated – that we live in our lusts, indulging in the desires of the flesh. The Isaiah text openly states that **no one arouses himself to take hold of God.** How clearer can it be? A sinner enslaved to sin has no ability to reach out to God! Those in bondage to sin are at the complete mercy and grace of God.

Moreover, the Bible affirms that men dead in their sins have no desire to seek God's face; they hate Jesus as Jesus stated and recorded in John's gospel account.

John 3:19-20

> [19]*This is the judgment, that the Light has come into the world, and men loved the darkness rather than the Light, for their deeds were evil.* [20]*For everyone who does evil hates the Light, and does not come to the Light for fear that his deeds will be exposed.*

Men don't come to Jesus because they don't want to. They hate the light and love the darkness, and unless something supernaturally acts upon them, nothing spiritually will change. In addition to being in bondage to our sins, the Bible asserts that we are slaves of Satan to do his will.

II Timothy 2:24-26

> [24]*The Lord's bond-servant must not be quarrelsome, but be kind to all, able to teach, patient when wronged,* [25]*with gentleness correcting those who are in opposition, if perhaps God may grant them repentance leading to the knowledge of the truth,* [26]*and they may come to their senses and escape from the snare of the devil, having been held captive by him to do his will.*

In a very real spiritual sense, unbelievers are "out of their mind." Their thinking is completely skewed due to the bondage to their sin nature. The hideous spiritual truth is that all unbelievers are pawns of the devil, in bondage to him, to do his evil bidding. The unbeliever has no spiritual capacity to embrace Christ as offered in the gospel.

II Corinthians 4:3-6

> [3]*And even if our gospel is veiled, it is veiled to those who are perishing,* [4]*in whose case the god of this world has blinded the minds of the unbelieving so that they might not see the light of the gospel of the glory of Christ, who is the image of God.* [5]*For we do not preach ourselves but Christ Jesus as Lord, and ourselves as your bond-servants for Jesus' sake.* [6]*For God, who said, 'Light shall shine out of darkness,' is the One who has shone in our hearts to give the Light of the knowledge of the glory of God in the face of Christ.*

The spiritual deadness of a sinner is clearly set forth. The idea that spiritually dead men can, of their own free will, choose Christ as offered in the gospel is totally false, thoroughly unbiblical. This text states that the gospel is veiled to unbelievers. Satan, the god of this world, has blinded the minds of the unbelieving so that they might not see the light of the gospel. As Jesus said, men don't come to Him because they hate the light and love the darkness. Dead men cannot do anything! But note that if there is deliverance, it must be initiated by God Himself. God must shine in our hearts, enlightening us with the knowledge of the glory of God in Christ. How does this come? Verse 5 states that **"we do not preach ourselves but Christ Jesus as Lord."** This glorious act of God shedding light in our dead souls normally comes through the agency of preaching! Jesus did say that only He can deliver men from such bondage.

John 8:34-36

> [34]*Jesus answered them, 'Truly, truly, I say to you, everyone who commits sin is the slave of sin.* [35]*The slave does not remain in the house forever; the son does remain forever.* [36]*So if the Son makes you free, you will be free indeed'.*

The only one who can free us from our sin and misery is the Lord Jesus Christ. If Christ frees us, then we are really and truly free from our slavery to sin and the devil. How does Jesus do this? He does this through the power of the Holy Spirit, who is commonly designated as the Spirit of Christ because the Holy Spirit does the bidding of the Son. The Holy Spirit accomplishes this through the marvelous work of regeneration – the transformation of a dead sinner into one who is spiritually alive. It is a supernatural transformation of a man's heart. This is exactly how the Scripture pictures it. Jesus told Nicodemus that he must be "born again."

John 3:1-8

> [1]*Now there was a man of the Pharisees, named Nicodemus, a ruler of the Jews;* [2]*this man came to Jesus by night and said to Him, 'Rabbi, we know that You have come from God as a teacher; for no one can do these signs that You do unless God is with him.'* [3]*Jesus answered and said to him, 'Truly, truly, I say to you, unless one is born again he cannot see the kingdom of God.'* [4]*Nicodemus said to Him, 'How can a man be born when he is old? He cannot enter a second time into his mother's womb and be born, can he?'* [5]*Jesus answered, 'Truly, truly, I say to you, unless one is born of water and the Spirit he cannot enter into the kingdom of God.* [6]*That which is born of the flesh is flesh, and that which is born of the Spirit is spirit.* [7]*Do not be amazed that I said to you, 'You must be born again.'* [8]*The wind blows where it wishes and you hear the sound of it, but do not know where it*

comes from and where it is going; so is everyone who is born of the Spirit.'

Jesus said that men must be born again in order to see the kingdom of God, and that it is a spiritual rebirth. A man must be born again with water and the Spirit. Water is often a symbol of cleansing. Every sinner needs a spiritual cleansing, which only the Holy Spirit can accomplish. Men cannot make themselves born again, just like no man is the cause of his own birth. The Arminian claims that the exercise of faith causes one to be born again. This is totally incorrect. As the Scripture states, dead men can do nothing to arouse themselves to take hold of God. The spiritual rebirth, as Jesus told Nicodemus, is like the wind. One does not know from where it comes or goes, but we do see the power of it. When the Holy Spirit regenerates a soul, then the person's heart has been totally transformed, and his will has been set free to choose Christ as offered freely in the gospel. We must understand the proper sequence: **faith does not lead to one being born again, but being born again leads one to faith.** This spiritual truth is also taught in John 1:12-13.

John 1:12-13

[12]But as many as received Him, to them He gave the right to become children of God, even to those who believe in His name, [13]who were born, not of blood nor of the will of the flesh nor of the will of man, but of God.

The biblical sequence for salvation is: born of God, then faith, and then adoption into God's family. Verse 13 is the foundation. Please note there are people "who were born" not of the will of man, but by God. Regeneration (born again) leads to faith, and then once we exercise faith, we are adopted into God's family.

The biblical message is thoroughly consistent. Salvation is of God's mercy and grace, not of man's doing. However, we must not misunderstand Scripture in its call of sinners to repent and have faith in Christ. Men must choose to follow Jesus. Men must choose to follow Christ, but they must have their hearts transformed and their "wills" set free to see Christ and want Him.

This biblical doctrine of regeneration is seen in the Old Testament most gloriously taught in Ezekiel, as well as other places. Israel had been severely judged for its spiritual apostasy; all their hope had been vanquished. Was there any hope at all for them?

Ezekiel 36:24-27

> [24]*For I will take you from the nations, gather you from all the lands and bring you into your own land.* [25]*Then I will sprinkle clean water on you, and you will be clean; I will cleanse you from all your filthiness and from all your idols.* [26]*Moreover, I will give you a new heart and put a new spirit within you; and I will remove the heart of stone from your flesh and give you a heart of flesh.* [27]*I will put My Spirit within you and cause you to walk in My statutes, and you will be careful to observe My ordinances.*

This is a wonderful exposition of God's initiative in saving sinners, who deserve nothing but His wrath. First, God is pictured as the "initiator." Note how many times "I" is used to describe what God is doing. God must sprinkle clean water on us to be clean. Is this not what Jesus told Nicodemus in John 3? We must be born of the Spirit and of water. God must cleanse us from our spiritual filthiness. Moreover, God gives a new heart and puts a new spirit in us. Obviously it doesn't exist until God does it. God removes the heart of stone, giving us a heart of flesh. Essentially this is what was taught in II Corinthians 4:3-6. The hardened heart must be changed into a soft one. And finally, God puts His Spirit in us, who then motivates us to walk in God's statutes, that is, obeying all that God commands us. This truth is beautifully pictured in the New Testament in Romans 8:6-9.

Romans 8:6-9

> [6]*For the mind set on the flesh is death, but the mind set on the Spirit is life and peace,* [7]*because the mind set on the flesh is hostile toward God; for it does not subject itself to the law of God, for it is not even able to do so,* [8]*and those who are in the flesh cannot please God.* [9]*However, you are not in the flesh but in the Spirit, if indeed the Spirit of God dwells in you. But if anyone does not have the Spirit of Christ, he does not belong to Him.*

Once the Holy Spirit comes into our lives, then all things change – no more hostility towards God and His law, but a desire to submit to it, exactly what Ezekiel 36 says. If anyone doesn't have the Spirit of Christ, they are not a Christian.

There is a wonderful picture of the association of preaching with the regenerating work of the Holy Spirit that is set forth in Ezekiel 37:1-14.

Ezekiel 37:1-14

> [1]*The hand of the LORD was upon me, and He brought me out by the Spirit of the LORD and set me down in the middle of the valley; and it was full of bones.* [2]*He caused me to pass among them round about, and behold, there were very many on the surface of the valley; and lo, they were very dry.* [3]*He said to me, 'Son of man, can these bones live?' And I answered, 'O Lord GOD, You know.' Again He said to me, 'Prophesy over these bones and say to them, 'O dry bones, hear the word of the LORD.'* [5]*Thus says the Lord GOD to these bones, 'Behold, I will cause breath to enter you that you may come to life.* [6]*I will put sinews on you, make flesh grow back on you, cover you with skin and put breath in you that you may come alive; and you will know that I am the LORD.'* [7]*So I prophesied as I was commanded; and as I prophesied, there was a noise, and behold, a rattling; and the bones came together, bone to its bone.* [8]*And I looked, and behold, sinews were on them, and flesh grew and skin covered them; but there was no breath in them.* [9]*Then He said to me, 'Prophesy to the breath, prophesy, son of man, and say to the breath, 'Thus says the Lord GOD, 'Come from the four winds, O breath, and breathe on these slain, that they come to life.'* [10]*So I prophesied as He commanded me, and the breath came into them, and they came to life and stood on their feet, an exceedingly great army.* [11]*Then He said to me, 'Son of man, these bones are the whole house of Israel; behold, they say, 'Our bones are dried up and our hope has perished. We are completely cut off.'* [12]*Therefore prophesy and say to them, 'Thus says the Lord GOD, 'Behold, I will open your graves and cause you to come up out of your graves, My people; and I will bring you into the land of Israel.* [13]*Then you will know that I am the LORD, when I have opened your graves and caused you to come up out of your graves, My people.* [14]*I will put My Spirit within you and you will come to life, and I will place you on your own land. Then you will know that I, the LORD, have spoken and done it,' declares the LORD.'"*

This is a magnificent portrayal of God's initiating work of sovereign grace on behalf of those who have no hope in themselves. God, in a vision, takes the prophet (preacher) Ezekiel to a valley of dry bones, asking Ezekiel if these bones can live. Ezekiel says that only God knows this. God then commands Ezekiel to prophesy over the dry bones. In other words, **God told Ezekiel to preach to the dead!** What was the result of the preaching? The bones came together, breath came into them, and then flesh came on the bones. The dry bones came to life! In fact, an exceedingly great army came to life. God explains to Ezekiel the meaning of the vision in that the dry bones was the whole house of Israel, whose hope had perished, but God caused them to come out of their graves. When God supernaturally gives life to the dead, people clearly understand who was responsible for giving them spiritual life. From chapter one of this book, we have come to understand that God is not referring to the Jewish people per se (though not excluding them), for the Christian church is the new Israel of God.

I cannot help but stress the obvious. God commanded a preacher to preach, and in the human man's preaching, God does His marvelous work of regenerating dead souls. **Preaching is the God ordained primary means of the gospel being effective.**

The gospel is the very power of God as Romans 1:16 informs us.

Romans 1:16

> *For I am not ashamed of the gospel, for it is the power of God for salvation to everyone who believes, to the Jew first and also to the Greek.*

The English word, "power," is derived from the Greek word, "*dunamis*." Yes, our English word "dynamite" is derived from the Greek "*dunamis*." What a magnificent illustration of the gospel. It is the very dynamite of God! Nothing is the same once the gospel is proclaimed by the preacher. Either men are condemned in their spiritual rebellion in the preaching of the gospel, or they are transformed by it. This biblical truth should excite every God ordained preacher. As we saw in Romans 10, preachers' feet are beautiful because wherever they go, they carry the dynamite of God – the gospel message. Nothing is the same when the Word of God is preached.

Isaiah 55:10-11

> *[10]For as the rain and the snow come down from heaven, And do not return there without watering the earth and making it bear and sprout, and furnishing seed to the sower and bread to the eater; [11]So will My word be which goes forth from My mouth; It will not return to Me empty, without accomplishing what I desire, and without succeeding in the matter for which I sent it.*

Christ commissions His preachers to proclaim His glorious gospel. The gospel is the good news of God. It is the divine message of how God has graciously and mercifully reconciled sinners to Himself. Those who have been elected to salvation from the foundation of the world will hear the Savior calling them to Himself; others, whom God has chosen to leave in their sin and misery, will not hear Jesus calling unto them. But one thing is certain. One must hear Jesus preaching to his heart in order to be saved, as the Scripture testifies. Whenever Jesus preached, He often ended with the phrase, "He who has ears to hear, let him hear."

John 8:47

> *He who is of God hears the words of God; for this reason you do not hear them, because you are not of God.*

This is a most intriguing passage. What does it mean to "be of God" in order to hear? It means that one must be of God's elect. We see this truth explained in John 6:37-44 and in John 10:25-29.

John 6:37-44

> *[37]All that the Father gives Me will come to Me, and the one who comes to Me I will certainly not cast out. [38]For I have come down from heaven, not to do My own will, but the will of Him who sent Me. [39]This is the will of Him who sent Me, that of all that He has given Me I lose nothing, but raise it up on the last day. [40]For this is the will of My Father, that everyone who beholds the Son and believes in Him will have eternal life, and I Myself will raise him up on the last day. [41]Therefore the Jews were grumbling about Him, because He said, "I am the bread that came down out of heaven." [42]They were saying, "Is not this Jesus, the son of Joseph, whose father and mother we know? How does He now say, 'I have come down out of heaven'?" [43]Jesus answered and said to them, "Do not grumble among yourselves. [44]No one can come to Me unless the Father who sent Me draws him; and I will raise him up on the last day.'*

The passage teaches that God the Father has given some to God the Son. These are God's elect, who were chosen before the foundation of the world (Ephesians 1:3-9) The glorious and comforting truth is that all those whom the Father has given to the Son will most definitely come to the Son, and Jesus will raise them up on the last day, giving them eternal life.

None of God's elect are lost, not one! Every elect person will believe at some point in his life.

Acts 13:48

When the Gentiles heard this, they began rejoicing and glorifying the word of the Lord; and as many as had been appointed to eternal life believed.

All those appointed or ordained to eternal life believe. This is consistent biblical theology. Since dead men are blinded by their sin and enslaved to Satan (II Timothy 2:26), and since they cannot arouse themselves to take hold of God (Isaiah 64:7), and since they are blinded so that they cannot see the gospel (II Corinthians 4:3-4), God must have grace and mercy upon them. God does so by opening their hearts and giving them ears to hear. To be saved one must hear the voice of Jesus.

John 10:25-29

²⁵Jesus answered them, "I told you, and you do not believe; the works that I do in My Father's name, these testify of Me. ²⁶But you do not believe because you are not of My sheep. ²⁷My sheep hear My voice, and I know them, and they follow Me; ²⁸and I give eternal life to them, and they will never perish; and no one will snatch them out of My hand. ²⁹My Father, who has given them to Me, is greater than all; and no one is able to snatch them out of the Father's hand.'

In order to believe in Jesus, one must be one of Jesus' sheep, which is being one of God's elect. In Scripture, believers are referred to as sheep and unbelievers as goats (Matthew 25:31-45). Jesus' sheep will hear the voice of the Good Shepherd and follow Him. So, the sheep do hear Jesus preaching to their hearts; they do have ears to hear because God has enabled them to hear. God has regenerated their dead and stony hearts. I should reiterate a passage mentioned earlier, which is Psalm 110:3, *"Thy people will volunteer freely in the day of thy power."* This is in the context of the Messiah exercising His kingly office by making His enemies His footstool. The primary way that Jesus destroys His enemies is by converting them, that is, by regenerating their hearts and enabling them to voluntarily choose to follow Him. The gospel is indeed the very dynamite of God for His elect. Those chosen to eternal life will hear the gospel in the power of the Holy Spirit and be led to believe.

I Thessalonians 1:4-5

> *⁴Knowing, brethren beloved by God, His choice of you; ⁵for our gospel did not come to you in word only, but also in power and in the Holy Spirit and with full conviction; just as you know what kind of men we proved to be among you for your sake.*

How do men believe in the gospel? First, they must be chosen of God as were many of the Thessalonians who heard Paul's preaching. Preaching is not a mere proclamation of words; it is Spirit anointed words. How did the gospel come? It came in power and in the Holy Spirit, bringing full conviction. All we can say is that there is certain mysteriousness about gospel preaching. Preaching is unlike anything in the world. The Scripture plainly teaches that Jesus preaches to the hearts of His elect through His human preachers. The words of the human preacher are anointed with power by the Holy Spirit. How do men know in their hearts that what they have heard is truth? The Holy Spirit convinces them – they just know. *The Westminster Confession of Faith* affirms this truth in its chapter "Of Holy Scripture" in 1:5:

> We may be moved and induced by the testimony of the Church to an high and reverend esteem of the holy scripture, and the heavenliness of the matter, the efficacy of the doctrine, the majesty of the style, the consent of all the parts, the scope of the whole, (which is to give all glory to God,) the full discovery it makes of the only way of man's salvation, the many other incomparable excellencies, and the entire perfection thereof, are arguments whereby it doth abundantly evidence itself to be the word of God; **yet, not withstanding, our full persuasion and assurance of the infallible truth, and divine authority thereof, is from the inward work of the Holy Spirit, bearing witness by and with the word in our hearts.** (Emphasis mine)

Paul was not the only preacher who came through Thessalonica; therefore, what separated him from all other pretenders?

I Thessalonians 2:13

> *For this reason we also constantly thank God that when you received the word of God which you heard from us, you accepted it not as the word of men, but for what it really is, the word of God, which also performs its work in you who believe.*

The Thessalonians knew that Paul's preaching was the very word of God, and that it was truth to the saving of their souls. They knew because the Holy Spirit convinced them. The Holy Spirit took the apostle's preaching and through it Jesus preached to the hearts of those chosen to salvation. This is true of everyone who has ever heard the gospel and been driven to repent and believe. We know it is truth. The key is the Holy Spirit.

I John 2:20-24, 27

> [20]*But you have an anointing from the Holy One, and you all know.* [21]*I have not written to you because you do not know the truth, but because you do know it, and because no lie is of the truth.* [22]*Who is the liar but the one who denies that Jesus is the Christ? This is the antichrist, the one who denies the Father and the Son.* [23]*Whoever denies the Son does not have the Father; the one who confesses the Son has the Father also.* [24]*As for you, let that abide in you which you heard from the beginning. If what you heard from the beginning abides in you, you also will abide in the Son and in the Father...* [27]*As for you, the anointing which you received from Him abides in you, and you have no need for anyone to teach you; but as His anointing teaches you about all things, and is true and is not a lie, and just as it has taught you, you abide in Him.*

We know the truth of the gospel that Jesus is God in the flesh by the Holy Spirit's anointing. What a blessed reality all of this is to our souls. God was under no obligation to save any of us. We all deserved His eternal destruction in Hell because we all broke His holy law. God is a God of justice, and He cannot act contrary to His own holiness. God doesn't cut breaks to anyone; what He does is send His only begotten Son into this world to assume a nature like ours in order to pay the terrible penalty for our transgressions and credit His perfect righteousness to us, as if it was our own. God the Father has elected some (actually many) to eternal life from the foundation of the world, and through the preaching of the gospel by human preachers, Jesus actually preaches to the hearts of these elect. These elect hear Jesus preaching; they finally see the light of the gospel, not by anything in them, but by the pure grace and mercy of God. God regenerates our darkened hearts; God convicts us of our sins; we mourn over our sins and run to Christ to find forgiveness. We believe everything God says about us and what we must do in order to be saved. This is exactly what happened on the Day of Pentecost. The risen King of kings and Lord of lords, through the preaching of Peter, preached to those Jews who had participated in His crucifixion and brought conviction of sin, so much so that they cried out to Peter, "What must we do?"

The Power of Prayer

Preaching is truly one of the divinely ordained instruments of the church in its spiritual conquest of the world, but there is another weapon, one that is sadly not used as it should be. That weapon is prayer! If only Christians would understand the immense power of prayer in the accomplishment of the Great Commission. In prayer we acknowledge our complete dependence upon our God. After all, God has decreed whatsoever comes to pass in history, and since He has ordained the victory of His gospel, then it is incumbent upon Christ's church to avail herself of the weapon of prayer.

Prayer and God's Eternal Decree

One of the theological questions often debated is the relationship between God's sovereignty and man's responsibility. What value is man's action in a world governed by a sovereign God? If God has decreed whatsoever comes to pass from all eternity, then do our prayers have any impact whatsoever? Critics of Calvinistic theology always want to argue that such an understanding of Scripture negates man's responsibility. In other words, if God has predestined all events, then man strives in vain with regard to God's purposes. If God has predestined men to be saved from all eternity, what value is the preaching of the gospel? The biblical truth is: It is not a matter of either/or, but both. There is no conflict in the mind of God; there is no contradiction in Scripture. Scripture never pits God's absolute sovereignty against man's accountability. We must believe both because both are true. God's sovereignty is clearly seen in Isaiah 46:9-11:

> *[9]Remember the former things long past, for I am God, and there is no other; I am God, and there is no one like Me, [10]Declaring the end from the beginning, And from ancient times things which have not been done, Saying, 'My purpose will be established, and I will accomplish all My good pleasure'; Calling a bird of prey from the east, the man of My purpose from a far country. Truly I have spoken; truly I will bring it to pass. I have planned it, surely I will do it.*

History has already been determined. God has declared the end from the beginning, but this does not mean that man's actions have no impact and consequence. Consider these three passages of the relationship between God's predestinating work and man's accountability. Acts 2:22-23 states:

> [22]*Men of Israel, listen to these words: Jesus the Nazarene, a man attested to you by God with miracles and wonders and signs which God performed through Him in your midst, just as you yourselves know—* [23]*this Man, delivered over by the predetermined plan and foreknowledge of God, you nailed to a cross by the hands of godless men and put Him to death.*

The crucifixion of Jesus was predestined from eternity; nothing could stop it. Jesus understood that He came into this world for this very purpose – to redeem those the Father had given Him from all eternity. The cross was an absolute theological necessity, but whose fault was it that Jesus was crucified? Ungodly men! This truth is also pictured in Acts 4:27-28:

> [27]*For truly in this city there were gathered together against Your holy servant Jesus, whom You anointed, both Herod and Pontius Pilate, along with the Gentiles and the peoples of Israel,* [28]*to do whatever Your hand and Your purpose predestined to occur.*

God is so amazing in that He can predestine to use "evil actions of men" to accomplish His eternal plan without being implicated in their evil actions. God is not the author of sin. An eternal decree that permits men to sin does not theologically impugn the character of God. One of the most dramatic illustrations of the relationship between God's sovereignty and man's accountability is seen in Mark 14:21:

> *For the Son of Man is to go just as it is written of Him; but woe to that man by whom the Son of Man is betrayed! It would have been good for that man if he had not been born.*

Jesus stated that His betrayal leading to His death was proceeding according to what was written, that is, what was prophesied (predestined). And in the same breath, Jesus immediately condemned Judas Iscariot for betraying Him. Judas Iscariot was predestined to be the betrayer of the Lord Jesus, but Judas was totally accountable for his sin; it would have been better never to have been born. Judas could never complain, "Why me, O God, why was I chosen to be the betrayer?" No, Judas understood that his actions were sinful. When he saw what was happening to Jesus, he felt remorse and returned the thirty pieces of silver to the Sanhedrin (the price paid to him for the betrayal), exclaiming, "I have sinned by betraying innocent blood" (Matthew 27:4).

Just because we, as finite men, cannot fathom an infinite God and how both the absolute sovereignty of God functions together with man's accountability, doesn't mean that we deny either of these biblical truths. We need to have humble attitudes and accept what Isaiah 55:8-9 affirms:

> *'For My thoughts are not your thoughts, Nor are your ways My ways,' declares the LORD. 'For as the heavens are higher than the earth, So are My ways higher than your ways and My thoughts than your thoughts.'*

It all makes sense to God, and that is all that matters. It is the height of arrogance for a man to try to outthink God. We must accept this biblical truth: **the same God that has ordained the end has also ordained the means to accomplish that end.** *The Westminster Confession of Faith* affirms this by the following statements:

> God from all eternity did, by the most wise and holy counsel of his own will, freely and unchangeably ordains whatsoever comes to pass: yet so, as thereby neither is God the author of sin, nor is violence offered to the will of the creatures, nor is the liberty or contingency of second causes taken away, but rather established.[19]

> Although, in relation to the foreknowledge and decree of God, the first cause, all things come to pass immutably and infallibly; yet, by the same providence, he ordereth them to fall out according to the nature of second causes, either necessarily, freely, or contingently. God in his ordinary providence maketh use of means, yet is free to work without, above, and against them, at his pleasure.[20]

Nothing catches God by surprise. There is no change in God's ultimate plan; however, God brings about His sovereign decree (plan) often in terms of "second causes." These second causes are the decisions of men freely made according to their own desires, be they good or bad. By contingency, we mean that certain ends are accomplished **if** we do certain things. This is why we can say that God, who ordains the end, often accomplishes it by the use of means (the decisions of men). Positively, men will inherit eternal life **if** they believe in Jesus. God will bring certain things to pass **if** we pray for them.

---

[19]   Westminster Confession of Faith, Chapter 3:1
[20]   Westminster Confession of Faith, Chapter 5:2-3

These theological truths are not some "ivory tower" doctrines that have no bearing on our daily lives, but they are powerfully part of every day life. Predestination does not lend itself to inactivity but to confident activity! If God has ordained the preaching of the gospel to be a means to the salvation of His elect, then it demands that we preach the gospel! Prayer is no useless activity, but a powerful means whereby God brings to pass His eternal decree in human history. Dr. Douglas F. Kelly has made some very astute observations in his great book, *If God Already Knows, Why Pray?* With reference to prayer and the purposes of God, he has said:

> The sovereign God on His throne, who has planned all things from the beginning to the end, has arranged His plan in such a way that the prayers of the saints are one of the major means He uses to accomplish His final goal.[21]

> Whatever it is that prompts us to come to Him, the fact is that God Himself has ordained that these prayers of His people begin to release predestined blessings which would not have flowed down at all had the prayers not occurred.[22]

> One of the ways He carries out His plan is to activate our personality so that we will pray and then take intelligent action, preach, witness, and serve. In all of it, His plan comes more and more to fruition. His goal begins to be reached through both the prayers and the actions of His people. It is because God planned it to be this way that these two truths- God has a sovereign plan, and a believer has genuine power in prayer to effect the supernatural – are not in fact contradictory, but come together in wonderful harmony. People who catch the vision of this glorious sovereign God, who has destined the prayers of His people to be a means of executing His unspeakably wonderful decrees, have a way of transforming the world.[23]

> We can see, therefore, how our prayers can bring about the purposes of God and why we should be faithful to Jesus' teaching to pray, "Thy kingdom come"... we must echo the third petition. Here Jesus teaches us to say, "Your will be done," when we are seeking God's intervention to transform the world. Our prayers are

---

[21] Douglas F. Kelly, *If God Already Knows Why Pray?* (Brentwood, Tennessee: Wolgemuth & Hyatt Publishers, Inc., 1989), p. 62.
[22] Kelly, p. 64.
[23] Kelly, p. 64.

to be governed by His will, in order that His name – and not ours- will be glorified.[24]

When we pray on the basis of the revealed will, we are lining ourselves up with the person of God and thus with the secret purposes of God, His secret purposes are carried out through the praying of His saints on the basis of His revealed will in Scripture… we can know that as we pray, "Thy will be done" on the basis of His written Word, our prayers are being caught up in the eternal purposes of God. There, in the "grinding of the wheels of providence, "they are somehow being used to activate the eternal decrees of God in space-time history."[25]

The Necessity and Power of Intercessory Prayer

James 4:2-3

[2]… You do not have because you do not ask. [3]You ask and do not receive, because you ask with wrong motives, so that you may spend it on your pleasures.

Not only are we to assail the throne of grace with our prayers but we must have our motives aligned with God's purposes. We know from Scripture that the Lord intends to have His gospel spread to the four corners of the earth and for the nations to be discipled. Intercessory prayer for the gospel to be successful is a godly prayer. When we align our prayers with God's glory, then we can be amazed at what God does through our prayers. Let's consider two great biblical examples.

Exodus 32:7-14

[7]Then the LORD spoke to Moses, "Go down at once, for your people, whom you brought up from the land of Egypt, have corrupted themselves. [8]They have quickly turned aside from the way which I commanded them. They have made for themselves a molten calf, and have worshiped it and have sacrificed to it and said, 'This is your god, O Israel, who brought you up from the land of Egypt!'" [9]The LORD said to Moses, "I have seen this people, and behold, they are an obstinate people. [10]Now then let

---

[24]   Kelly, p. 65.
[25]   Kelly, p. 67.

Me alone, that My anger may burn against them and that I may destroy them; and I will make of you a great nation." [11]*Then Moses entreated the LORD his God, and said, "O LORD, why does Your anger burn against Your people whom You have brought out from the land of Egypt with great power and with a mighty hand?* [12]*Why should the Egyptians speak, saying, 'With evil intent He brought them out to kill them in the mountains and to destroy them from the face of the earth?' Turn from Your burning anger and change Your mind about doing harm to Your people.* [13]*Remember Abraham, Isaac, and Israel, Your servants to whom You swore by Yourself, and said to them, 'I will multiply your descendants as the stars of the heavens, and all this land of which I have spoken I will give to your descendants, and they shall inherit it forever.'"* [14]*So the LORD changed His mind about the harm which He said He would do to His people.*

How are we to understand the incident with Israel's idolatry (worshipping the golden calf) and God's determination to destroy them? We learn that Moses' intercessory prayer over a period of forty days did persuade God to change His mind. Was God's immutable decree changed? No. Did Moses' prayer alter what would have been otherwise? Yes. Exodus 32:10 is the key verse – **"Now then let Me alone**, that My anger may burn against them, and that I may destroy them..."** (Emphasis mine). The emphasized phrase of the verse implies that God would respond favorably to Moses' intercessory request if Moses were interceding on Israel's behalf. This passage should excite us about the nature of intercessory prayer. If Moses had chosen not to intercede for Israel, we must believe that God's intention to destroy Israel would have been carried out. However, if Moses had chosen to intercede, which he did, then God would be merciful to Israel. Moses obviously interceded for Israel, having pled for God to remember His covenant promises to Abraham, Isaac, and Jacob. Moses pled for the glory of God's name, and a nation was delivered. One could rightly view this incident as God's encouragement to Moses to pray! This passage should stir us up in interceding for one another in prayer. We might be amazed how much danger we avoided because of the intercessory prayers of a godly person.

Martin Luther wrote: "Prayer is not overcoming God's reluctance, but it is a laying hold of His willingness."[26] Dr. Joseph C. Morecraft, III writes:

> So we see that the sovereignty of God does not make prayer superfluous. On the contrary, it gives prayer an important place as the *divinely decreed means of accomplishing divinely decreed purposes so that all human beings may know that God is the Lord...* The point is this: there are some things God has determined He will not do for His people except through their prayers, and even then, for His own glory, as well as for their benefit.[27]

God has ordained to use intercessory prayer as a means to accomplish His holy will. Israel's sins deserved God's destruction of the nation. We should note that Moses' intercessory prayer was directed towards God's covenant promises. It's as if God was waiting for Moses to remind Him of His faithfulness. Some have said that God loves to be persuaded by His own Word.

Another wonderful example of the power of intercessory prayer is King Hezekiah's prayer for Jerusalem's deliverance from the mighty Assyrian army. The Assyrian empire had destroyed the Northern Kingdom of Israel in 722 B.C. and had invaded Judah, overcoming all the fortified cities of Judah. This seemingly invincible army, an army that had conquered all other nations, had laid siege to Jerusalem. An insulting letter from the Assyrians was sent to King Hezekiah for the purpose of intimidation and persuading them to surrender without a fight. The account is recorded in II Kings 19.

II Kings 19:10-19

> [10]*Thus you shall say to Hezekiah king of Judah, "Do not let your God in whom you trust deceive you saying, 'Jerusalem will not be given into the hand of the king of Assyria.'* [11]*Behold, you have heard what the kings of Assyria have done to all the lands, destroying them completely. So will you be spared?* [12]*Did the gods of those nations which my fathers destroyed deliver them, even Gozan and Haran and Rezeph and the sons of Eden who were in Telassar?* [13]*Where is the king of Hamath, the king of*

---

[26]   Joseph C. Morecraft, III, *Authentic Christianity: An Exposition of the Theology and Ethics of the Westminster Larger Catechism,* Vol. 5, (Powder Springs, GA: Minkoff Family Publishing and American Vision Press, 2010) p. 523.

[27]   Morecraft, p. 524.

Arpad, the king of the city of Sepharvaim, and of Hena and Ivvah?'" [14]Then Hezekiah took the letter from the hand of the messengers and read it, and he went up to the house of the LORD and spread it out before the LORD. [15]Hezekiah prayed before the LORD and said, "O LORD, the God of Israel, who are enthroned above the cherubim, You are the God, You alone, of all the kingdoms of the earth. You have made heaven and earth. [16]Incline Your ear, O LORD, and hear; open Your eyes, O LORD, and see; and listen to the words of Sennacherib, which he has sent to reproach the living God. [17]Truly, O LORD, the kings of Assyria have devastated the nations and their lands [18]and have cast their gods into the fire, for they were not gods but the work of men's hands, wood and stone. So they have destroyed them. [19]Now, O LORD our God, I pray, deliver us from his hand that all the kingdoms of the earth may know that You alone, O LORD, are God."

From a human perspective, Hezekiah knew that militarily Jerusalem stood no chance against the invading Assyrians, but did this lead Hezekiah to despair? No! It drove him to pray one of the greatest prayers of all time. Hezekiah takes this insulting letter and spreads it out before the Lord in God's house, the place where God manifested His presence in the old covenant. Hezekiah wants his God to see what these pagans were saying about his God! While the Assyrian letter was designed to intimidate Hezekiah, the great king aptly reminds God who the insult is really directed towards. Jehovah has been reproached, and God's name has been challenged. Hezekiah does not question what the Assyrians have done to other nations and their gods. However, Hezekiah reminds God that the gods of these other nations are no gods at all; they are the work of men's hands. Hezekiah's prayer is one that seeks God to vindicate His holy name! Hezekiah pled with God to deliver Jerusalem for the sake of His name so that all nations may know that there is only one true God, namely Jehovah. This was the greatness of Hezekiah's intercessory prayer; it was designed to exalt the true God above all others. Consequently, God sends word to Hezekiah via the great prophet Isaiah that God has heard his prayer and determined to deliver Jerusalem. We should not miss this vital point that God says, *"For I will defend this city to save it for My own sake and for My servant David's sake"* (II Kings 19:34). In this case, God determines not to use His people in the fight, but Jehovah will exclusively take on the Assyrians. The glorious deliverance is recorded in II Kings 19:35-37:

[35]Then it happened that night that the angel of the LORD went out and struck 185,000 in the camp of the Assyrians; and when

men rose early in the morning, behold, all of them were dead.
[36]So Sennacherib king of Assyria departed and returned home,
and lived at Nineveh. [37]It came about as he was worshiping in
the house of Nisroch his god, that Adrammelech and Sharezer
killed him with the sword; and they escaped into the land of
Ararat. And Esarhaddon his son became king in his place.

Christians need to understand the power of intercessory prayer and utilize it in the extension of Christ's kingdom. As the Lord's instrument for world dominion, the church must wield the divinely ordained weapons of spiritual warfare.

Ephesians 6:17-20

[17]And take the helmet of salvation, and the sword of the Spirit,
which is the word of God. 18With all prayer and petition pray at
all times in the Spirit, and with this in view, be on the alert with
all perseverance and petition for all the saints, [19]and pray on my
behalf, that utterance may be given to me in the opening of my
mouth, to make known with boldness the mystery of the gospel,
[20]for which I am an ambassador in chains; that in proclaiming it
I may speak boldly, as I ought to speak.

This beautifully shows the correlation of wielding the sword of the Spirit, the Word of God, with the ministry of intercessory prayer. This intercessory prayer is to be persistent and for all the saints. As Christians, we all desperately need each other's prayers in our personal fight against the wiles of the devil, but we also need prayers in the mission of the church. Paul wanted prayer on his behalf for what purpose? It was for him **to boldly preach the gospel**, even if he is an ambassador in chains.

Romans 15:30-33

Now I urge you, brethren, by our Lord Jesus Christ and by the
love of the Spirit, to strive together with me in your prayers to
God for me, that I may be rescued from those who are
disobedient in Judea, and that my service for Jerusalem may
prove acceptable to the saints; so that I may come to you in joy
by the will of God and find refreshing rest in your company. Now
the God of peace be with you all. Amen.

Paul urges the church in Rome to "strive together" with him in their prayers to God for him. The Greek word for strive together is *sunagonizomai*. This is a combination of two words *agonizomai* and *sun*. The preposition *sun* conveys "together with." The word *agonizomai* conveys the idea of contending for victory in the public games. It commonly came to mean to fight, to wrestle with great pains, straining to achieve victory in the contest. Bringing this to our text and understanding the spiritual meaning, we see that Paul urges intercessory prayer on his behalf in his preaching. In doing so, the faithful prayers of the saints are really contending **with** Paul in his struggles to preach the gospel.

So often, Christians do not understand the dynamic of prayer. Paul says that our prayers on his behalf place us **spiritually with him in the struggle.** We can rightly refer to those who engage in these intercessory prayers as prayer warriors. We are fighting with all those for whom we are praying. This should have sweeping ramifications in praying for missions.

I must ask my reader, "How serious are you about prayer?" If God has promised the victory of the gospel in the present age, if Jesus is reigning victoriously at the Father's right hand, if God promises that all His enemies will be subjugated, and if Jesus is empowering His church, then what is stopping us from praying for this victory? It must be laziness, which should shame us. It must be a lack of faith in His promises, which should shame us.

Believing and persistent prayer is the foundation in one sense for the great success of the gospel; it is the energizing agent that Christ uses to extend His dominion over the nations. It is the calling upon our sovereign Lord to do what He has promised! Prayer demonstrates our complete dependence upon our Lord to accomplish His glorious purposes. Since the Scripture pictures the church as an offensive army assailing the gates of hell, we should see prayer as the absolutely essential supply line to keep the army pressing on to its victory. Cut the supply line and one causes the advancing army to grind to a halt. Our enemy will do what he can to discourage Christ's church to pray. With believing and persistent prayer combined with the faithful preaching of the gospel, the domain of darkness, Satan's citadel, will be overcome, and those residing in darkness will be set free and led to Christ's obedience.

Exercising Faith in God's Promises through Prayer

If there was one area of the Christian life that is woefully inadequate, it would be that of exercising true biblical faith. So many Christians sin by having a lack of faith. One of the saddest things is that we often spiritualize away the necessity of having faith. We unbiblically qualify our petitions to such a degree that there is no need for real faith as a necessity in receiving whatever we pray.

Hebrews 11:6 exhorts us, *"And without faith it is impossible to please God, because anyone who comes to him must believe that he exists and that he rewards those who earnestly seek him."* If we are to have a dynamic prayer life we must have faith. What is the real nature of faith? Hebrews 11:1 states, *"Now faith is being sure of what we hope for and certain of what we do not see."* Faith is a channel that links the unseen reality with the seen reality. Faith allows us to rest with confidence that we possess a reality yet unseen. When we pray, we must learn to be assured that our prayers will be answered as we desire. Of course, this assumes that other conditions for powerful praying are being exercised simultaneously.

Faith is a mental conviction arising from a heart that yearns after Christ. However, faith has an objective element in that faith is not so much a conjuring of desired hope independent of anything else. Genuine biblical faith is not in us but in the one who is able to do great and mighty things. What counts is not so much faith itself as it is the object of faith. Of course biblical faith never divorces the proper object of faith from the one exercising it. Who is the proper object of our faith? It is the Lord Jesus Christ!

We can see how reliance upon the source of faith is vital by observing the incident of Peter's walking on water recorded in Matthew 14:22-31. Peter could not have walked on water by his own ability. He was granted power to perform a supernatural act based upon his faith in Jesus. Who is the sole dispenser of that power? Peter demonstrated dependency upon the authority and power of Jesus when he said, *"Tell me to come to you on the water"* (v. 28). Peter's faith was not in his own ability but in the object of his faith. Where did Peter go wrong when he began to sink? It was when he took his eyes off Jesus, the source of his power. The problem is that Peter began to look at the circumstances. Verse 30 says that he began to sink when he saw the wind and became afraid. The circumstances should have made no difference, seeing that Jesus is Lord over all. By looking at the wind Peter forgot whose power was enabling him to walk on water. What did Jesus say to Peter when He saved him? He said, *"You of little faith, why did you doubt?"* (v.31). Unbelief or doubt is essentially the failure to recognize and constantly rely upon the object of our faith - a God who is faithful to His Word.

The above incident raises the question as to the meaning of Jesus' statement, *"You of little faith."* There is another incident whereby Jesus rebuked his disciples. In Matthew 8:23-26 the disciples were in a boat with Jesus when a great storm arose, seemingly threatening their lives. What is disturbing to the disciples is that Jesus was sleeping through the storm. When they woke Jesus, accusing Him of not caring, Jesus replied, *"You of little faith, why are you so afraid?"* (v.26). One lesson we learn is that fear and faith cannot coexist. Where one is, the other is absent. Thus, whenever we are afraid, it demonstrates that we lack faith. The solution is to confess the sin and to trust in the source of our deliverance. Does the phrase, "littleness of faith," mean that we need to have more faith or to have it increased? Littleness of faith should not be interpreted in a quantitative way (of how much) but in a qualitative way (the very nature of it). Unbelief is never because we don't have enough faith, necessitating the increase of it, but it is the failure to exercise the nature of faith. Jesus clarifies this in the episode concerning the forgiving of a brother in Luke 17:3-6. Jesus exhorts us that we are obligated to repeatedly forgive a man who sins against us and who keeps asking for forgiveness. The disciples responded by saying "increase our faith!" (v. 5) Jesus replied, *"If you have faith as small as a mustard seed, you can say to this mulberry tree, 'be uprooted and planted in the sea' and it will obey you"* (v. 6). The point is - the disciples didn't need more faith; they simply needed to exercise faith regardless of its size.

In Matthew 17:18-20, we see Jesus rebuking His disciples for the littleness of faith in their inability to cast out a demon from a boy. Again, Jesus said that if they had faith the size of a mustard seed mountains could move at their command and that nothing would be impossible for them (vs. 20, 21).

It is noteworthy that Jesus uses the mustard seed as His illustration because the mustard seed is one of the smallest seeds, but it grows into one of the largest trees. The point is this: even a little faith in the divine promise, when genuine in quality, will accomplish great things just as a mustard seed grows into a great tree. If we but have a grain of true faith nothing is impossible. It doesn't take much when it is genuine. Thus, the littleness of faith means the failure to exercise what faith we have, not that we need to have it increased.

The faith that was required in Matthew 17:18-20 was a confidence in divine revelation, namely, that in Jesus' name the disciples were to cast out demons. It was a lack of faith in this direct command where they fell short. Jesus had promised them the power to cast out demons earlier (Matthew 10:8). The great tragedy in "littleness of faith" or "doubt" is that it refuses to heed to the clear promises of God. When we act upon Jesus' commands, that is, when we exercise faith in the promises, the apparently impossible becomes a reality.

We must, however, keep in proper focus the relationship between the one who exercises faith and the one who supplies the power and brings to reality what faith clings to. "Nothing will be impossible to you" must be seen in this light. No task assigned, such as casting out demons, is impossible when the person receiving the command is and remains in trustful contact with God. Biblical faith is the recognition that God is the source of all power and blessing. When we have any faith at all, we have all the ingredients intact to do the seemingly impossible.

Who moves the mountain? Is it God or us? In the ultimate sense, it is God because it is His power, but in another sense we do through the exercise of our faith. Perhaps the best way to see it is that God works out His divine purposes in the world through the agency of His people. We can see this in the Gospel of Jesus Christ. Who does the saving? It is God alone. But who preaches that Gospel which saves? It is human beings (Romans 10:13-15). Matthew Henry has stated it well when he said, *"an active faith can remove mountains, not of itself, but in the virtue of a divine power engaged in a divine promise, both which faith fastens upon."*[28]

Do we really believe God's Word? Do we really and truly believe that the gospel will be victorious in history? Has God promised it? Since He has, then it demands **our believing and persistent prayer!**

Persevering in Believing Prayer

Powerful praying begins with a divine promise and faith in that promise, and then the prayer warrior will not let go of that promise and perseveres in that faith through persevering prayer.

James 4:2 states, *"... You do not have, because you do not ask God."* Some Christians have the notion that some of their requests are so mundane that it is a waste of God's precious time even to ask. Of course, this attitude reflects a faulty theological view. The person who doesn't ask doesn't receive; it is as simple as that.

---

[28]   Matthew Henry's Commentary on Matthew 17:20.

In Matthew 7:7-11 and in Luke 11:9-13 we see Jesus giving three **commands**: ask! seek! and knock! Jesus exhorts us to do these three things. It is important to note that in the original Greek these three commands are in the present tense, which infers a **continual** performance. We can see the quality of persistence taught in these passages. The petitioner is **constantly** asking, seeking, and knocking. The Greek grammar indicates that those who continually do these things will be continually receiving, finding, and having the door opened.

Great power in prayer comes from exercising faith. Jesus made this clear in several passages. In Matthew 21:21, 22 Jesus said:

> *[21] I tell you the truth, if you have faith, and do not doubt, not only can you do what was done to the fig tree, but you say to this mountain, 'Go, throw yourself into the sea,' and it will be done. [22] And all things you ask in prayer, believing, you shall receive.*

In Mark 11:22-24 Jesus said:

> *[22] Have faith in God. I tell you the truth, [23] if anyone says to the mountain, 'Go, throw yourself into the sea', and does not doubt in his heart but believes that what he says will happen, it will be done for him. [24] Therefore I tell you,* **whatever you ask for in prayer, believe that you have received it, and it will be yours** (Emphasis mine).

Where there is true faith it is impossible for the answer not to come. We must remember Jesus' words, "believe that you have received." Jesus will fulfill the promise that is given. Faith knows this and thereby it prays great things. It lays hold of God's boundless promises and says they are mine! Faith is the pledge or forerunner of the coming answer.

In Mark 11:24 the Greek grammar is clear in revealing that the asking and praying are to be a **constant** practice. As we are continually engaged in prayer, we are **commanded** to believe. In fact the grammar says we are to keep on believing. The thrust of the passage is that as we keep on praying and believing, we **have received** our requests. The verb "have received" conveys the thought of completed action. Isn't this wonderful - we are to keep on believing that we have received what we are asking while we are praying. We may not actually see it for the time being, but we are assured that our Heavenly Father has already given the request. The actual manifestation of the prayer request is yet to come, which is according to God's timetable, not ours. This answers why certain requests are seemingly delayed. It isn't because God has not heard nor has not already granted the request; it is because He always works to His glory according to His plan. God wants to build godly character in our lives. By delaying the actual realization of the prayer, God often determines the real nature of our faith. Are we patient? Are we willing to persevere in prayer? Also, God often has granted one of our desires, not according to our timetable but according to His, and we realize that it was more glorifying to God through an apparent delay. Genuine faith doesn't despair when God delays the bringing to fruition the request; faith continues to believe and thanks God that the request has already been granted. Faith says, "I know God will bring to pass, in due time, my request according to His glory."

Doubt is the great robber of powerful praying. Doubt blocks the channel to the unlimited blessings of God, while faith allows the free flowing of those blessings. We need to begin to see the seriousness of doubt; it is a grievous sin. James 1:6, 7 says that the man who doubts and who doesn't believe in his prayer is double-minded and unstable in all his ways. The picture that James portrays is a mind so filled with uncertainty and indecision that it cannot properly choose. The grievousness of doubt is that it insults the living God. Doubt assaults the very glory of God's perfections! Doubt refuses to accept God's readiness to make good all His promises to those who ask; therefore, it assaults the **faithfulness** of God. We must remember that the essence of prayer is the laying hold of God's promises made to us. Believing prayer is a means by which these promises are realized. James 1:7 assures us that the one who doubts **will not receive anything** from the Lord. Doubting is the sin of unbelief!

Jesus taught His disciples that they must persevere in prayer. In Luke 18:1-8 we see:

> *[1]Now He was telling them a parable to show that at all times they ought to pray and not to lose heart, [2]saying, "In a certain city there was a judge who did not fear God and did not respect man. [3]There was a widow in that city, and she kept coming to him, saying, 'Give me legal protection from my opponent.' [4]For a while he was unwilling; but afterward he said to himself, 'Even though I do not fear God nor respect man, [5]yet because this widow bothers me, I will give her legal protection, otherwise by continually coming she will wear me out.'" [6]And the Lord said, "Hear what the unrighteous judge said; [7]now, will not God bring about justice for His elect who cry to Him day and night, and will He delay long over them? [8]I tell you that He will bring about justice for them quickly. However, when the Son of Man comes, will He find faith on the earth?"*

When it comes to world missions and the fulfilling of the Great Commission, we must be persistent in our intercessory prayers for God's preachers. We must fight the temptation of looking at the dismal circumstances that we often see and despairing, wondering when the knowledge of the Lord will cover the earth as the waters cover the sea. We must believe in the promises and persevere in praying for greater revivals! This brings us to the nature of our prayer requests. God is under no obligation to grant any arbitrary prayer request simply because we believe it. Power in prayer comes through praying consistently in God's revealed will, consistent with His purposes. We must pray in Jesus' name, which is more than simply praying through Him as our mediator.

We Must Ask according to God's Will

There is a difference in praying in conformity with God's will as opposed to praying that God's will be done, which may override our request. When we pray, we are to pray in light of God's revealed will, which is not only accessible to us but commanded that we know. We are to discern God's will as best as we can **before** we pray, so that when we do pray, we can, in faith, receive exactly what we asked. As we pray there should be no doubt as to the legitimacy of our prayer; otherwise, we should not be praying for that request.

It is discouraging to see Christians say they will pray for God's will about a matter in which God has already revealed His will. I John 5:14, 15 is highly instructive for us:

> *[14]This is the assurance we have in approaching God; that if we ask anything according to His will, he hears us. [15]And if we know what he hears us - whatever we ask - we know that we have what we asked of him.*

One cannot separate this passage from the preceding verses, which deal with the assurance of our salvation. Verse 13 affirms that all who genuinely believe in Christ can absolutely know they have eternal life. This same assurance in absolutely knowing that we have eternal life is also true of approaching God in prayer.

The Greek grammar is very helpful, again. The verbs "ask" and "hear" are in the present tense, inferring a continual asking and hearing. The Greek word for "know" is highly significant. There are in John's epistle two words for "know." *Ginosko* is used to refer to knowledge gained through personal experience, and *oida* is an absolute knowledge of certainty. The word which was used in verse 13 for knowing that we have eternal life is the word *oida.* It is the same word that is used in verse 14 which means that we can know with absolute certainty that God hears our prayers. Moreover, in verse 15, the grammar reveals that we **keep on knowing with certainty** that God **keeps on hearing:** therefore, we keep on having **whatever** we have asked. The verb "asked" in verse 15 is in another Greek tense, which demonstrates an action which has been completed in the past but whose result remains in the present. We can see that God never forgets what we have prayed for and is continually bringing to pass, in the present, whatever we have prayed for in the past, if we persist in the asking.

The prevailing condition for our certainty in receiving whatever we ask is that we continually ask in accordance with God's will. It should be obvious that God's will cannot refer to God's hidden counsel. It has to refer to God's revealed will. We see this taught in the following passages: Psalm 40:8, 143:10; Matthew 12:50; John 7:17; Romans 12:2. If it doesn't mean this, then how can we know with certainty? How can we know that we will receive exactly what we prayed for? To interpret the meaning of "according to His will" to infer an uncertainty and a yielding to some hidden plan of God severely distorts the passage, actually making it self-contradictory. God's continual hearing of our prayers is contingent upon asking in conformity with God's will. Also, the realization of our prayers is directly contingent upon God's hearing. Not knowing God's revealed will breaks the necessary chain of events. John's purpose is to stir in us boldness and confidence. He is saying that we should have the boldness to say to the Father that we know we are asking according to His will, and we know that He hears us. We are confident that He hears us no matter what we request. It is by faith that we know we have the desired answer. John also wants us to persevere in prayer because knowing with certainty gives us the courage to continue despite the apparent circumstances. If we are uncertain as to whether our petitions are in accordance with God's will, we cannot be comforted with the promise, "We know that we have what we asked of him."

One of the greatest hindrances to powerful prayer is the mistaken notion that we can rarely know with certainty what God's will is. This is false. God's will is revealed in the pages of Holy Scripture. This truth is brought out in the *Westminster Confession of Faith* in 1:6:

> The whole counsel of God concerning all things necessary for His own glory, man's salvation, faith and life, is either expressly set

down in Scripture, or by good and necessary consequences may be deduced from Scripture...

The trouble is that so few Christians take the time to be saturated with the Word of God. The result is that their prayer life is thwarted. Again, faulty theology leads to faulty praying. In God's Word, God has revealed His precious promises to us. The Christian must claim by faith these promises through prayer. Thus, whatever he asks within the limits of God's revealed will, he may confidently expect to receive. The prayer of faith does not proclaim its desire to God, leaving the decision to God. This is a submission to God for cases only where we cannot know God's will. The prayer of faith that we are called to exercise is finding God's promises in His Word and pleading for those promises until they come to pass. Faith is the exertion of the will, resting on God's promises and saying, "I must have it." We must realize that such a will is not arrogance; it is not self-centeredness, nor is it failure to submit to God. On the contrary, such a will is true submission, honoring God. It is only when the Christian has surrendered to Christ's Lordship that he receives the freedom to will what he desires. Once the Christian has yielded to God's revealed purpose, as his own purpose and desire, God wants him to exercise his will for His glory. The Christian lives only for his heavenly Father's interests. He seeks his Father's will above his own. Thus, God entrusts His kingdom work to those children by saying, "What do you desire?" It is often only slothfulness in the guise of humility that we profess to have no will. No, true humility is always accompanied by strong faith. In knowing God's will, faith boldly claims the fulfillment of the promise, "You shall ask whatever you will, and it shall be done unto you."

We are normally to expect an answer to our every prayer in the way we pray it. If there is no answer to our request, it is because we haven't prayed correctly. We are then to diligently look for what sin is inhibiting or blocking that channel of blessing. We must confess it and repent of it.

Before we leave this section concerning the nature of praying in accordance with God's will, I said that this qualification is not normally found in exhortations for powerful prayer. We must ask whether it is explicitly wrong to pray as such. The answer is, no, only as long as we are unable to discern beforehand from Scripture what is most glorifying to God. For example, an unemployed man needs to provide for his family. The man wonders if a certain job prospect can be claimed by faith. It would be difficult to pray the prayer of faith, seeing that this particular job may not be the most glorifying to God or the best job to provide for his family's needs. We must be careful in limiting God in the precise way He is to be glorified. Perhaps the best prayer in this situation is to say to God that you do not know if this is the best job, but you do know for sure that God will provide some means to satisfy your family's needs. The whole point is that the godly Christian, who is living in conformity with God's law, will be careful in how and for what he prays. He normally restricts his prayers to the areas where he knows the will of God.

We Must Pray in Jesus' Name

Sad to say, many Christians who pray ending their prayers with the phrase, "in Jesus name," don't understand its meaning and are often guilty of violating it, even though they say it. In John 14:13 and in 16:23, 24 we see Jesus saying He will grant **whatever** we ask in prayer if we ask in His name. It should be apparent that simply mouthing the words "in Jesus name" has no magical significance. To appreciate the meaning of this phrase, we must first appreciate the significance of the concept of "name." Throughout the Bible, names indicate nature, character, mission, and ministry. For example, the names of God in Scripture denote God Himself as He is revealed to us and as He desires to be known by us. God has revealed His nature and character to His people through His names. The names of God are associated with God's honor and glory (Psalm 8:1; 132:2). Sometimes God's name is used as synonym for His various perfections, namely His faithfulness (Isaiah 48:9), His grace (Psalm 23:3), and His honor (Psalm 79:9).

Praying in Jesus' name means that we recognize all that His name implies. First, it implies His deity and His Lordship. Praying in Jesus' name means we are in union with His purpose for this world. Many a Christian has read the unlimited promises in these passages and has attempted to use them for his own selfish desires. The result is disappointment and discouragement. The problem is that they have separated the promise from its context. The promise is the free use of His name in conjunction with **doing His works**. It is the Christian who lives only for Jesus' work and kingdom that has the right to appropriate the promise of receiving whatever he asks. We cannot use Jesus' name to make Jesus the servant of our own pleasures or comfort. Effective and powerful prayer is characteristic of every Christian who prays for that which is needed in the service of the Lord's interests, not his own. Thus, praying in Jesus' name is aligning us with His nature, character, and mission. Yes, the promises are limitless, but are we truly praying in His name?

Second, we are acknowledging His mediatorship, meaning that it is only through Jesus Christ that we can approach a Holy God. Jesus is the only way to fellowship with God (John 14:6). As our great high priest, He enables us to boldly approach the throne of grace (Hebrews 4:14-16). We should carefully note that it is **only** through Jesus Christ that God the Father can hear and answer prayer. Be gone with the unscriptural idea that God hears the prayers of anybody, as long as they are sincere. Vague prayers to some unbiblical notion of God are indeed in vain.

A most thrilling passage that combines the necessity and duty of preaching and prayer is Isaiah 62:6-7.

Isaiah 62:6-7

> *⁶On your walls, O Jerusalem, I have appointed watchmen; all day and all night they will never keep silent. You who remind the Lord, take no rest for yourselves; ⁷and give Him no rest until He establishes and makes Jerusalem a praise in the earth.*

This is a magnificent passage urging God's people, particularly watchmen on Jerusalem's walls, to assail the throne of God with believing and relentless prayer until God's glorious purpose for His church comes to pass in the earth. The passage presumes that Jerusalem will be a praise in the earth; hence, victory for the church is pictured, but this reality comes to pass through the faithful application of the means that God has appointed for His church. Prayer is the energizing agent for the success of the gospel.

Matthew Henry makes these pertinent observations about this Isaiah passage:

> Plenty of the means of grace--abundance of good preaching and good praying (*v. 6, 7*), and this shows the method God takes when he designs mercy for a people; he first brings them to their duty and pours out a spirit of prayer upon them, and then brings salvation to them.

> … that ministers may do their duty as watchmen. It is here spoken of as a token for good, as a step towards further mercy and an earnest of it, that, in order to what he designed for them, he would set *watchmen on their walls who should never hold their peace.*

> They must never hold their peace; they must take all opportunities to give warning to sinners, in season, out of season, and must never betray the cause of Christ by a treacherous or cowardly

silence. They must never hold their peace at the throne of grace; they must *pray, and not faint,* as Moses lifted up his hands and kept them steady, till Israel had obtained the victory over Amalek, Exod. xvii. 10, 12.

... God's professing people must be a praying people, must be public-spirited in prayer, must wrestle with God in prayer, and continue to do so: "*Keep not silence;* never grow remiss in the duty nor weary of it." *Give him no rest*--alluding to an importunate beggar, to the widow that with her continual coming wearied the judge into a compliance. God said to *Moses, Let me alone* (Exod. xxxii. 10), and Jacob to Christ, *I will not let thee go except thou bless me,* Gen. xxxii. 26. (3.) God is so far from being displeased with our pressing importunity, as men commonly are, that he invites and encourages it; he bids us to cry after him; he is not like those disciples who discouraged a petitioner, Matthew xv. 23. He bids us make pressing applications at the throne of grace, and *give him no rest,* Luke xi. 5, 8. He suffers himself not only to be reasoned with, but to be wrestled with. (4.) The public welfare or prosperity of God's Jerusalem is that which we should be most importunate for at the throne of grace; we should pray for the good of the church. [1.] That it may be safe, that he would *establish* it, that the interests of the church may be firm, may be settled for the present and secured to posterity... We must persevere in our prayers for mercy to the church till the mercy come; we must do as the prophet's servant did, go yet seven times, till the promising cloud appear, 1 Kings xviii. 44. It is a good sign that God is coming towards a people in ways of mercy when he pours out a spirit of prayer upon them and stirs them up to be fervent and constant in their intercessions.[29]

John Calvin makes these observations on Isaiah 62:6-7:

And here we see that the external agency of men is joined with the efficacy of the Holy Spirit; for, although the Lord alone is the author and finisher of the work, yet he brings forward instruments which he employs for rearing the building of the Church. This reminds us that we ought not to lose courage, even when we see nothing but ruin and wretchedness and desolation; but it is our

---

[29] Matthew Henry's Commentary on Isaiah 62:6-7.

duty to pray that the Lord will restore her, which he also promises that he will do.[30]

When Christians pray, especially God's anointed ministers of the gospel, powerful things are placed in motion. As Dr. Douglas Kelly said, our prayers, in some mysterious way, activate Gods' eternal decrees in space-time history.

One of the most exciting things for the Christian today is to see how his great God has worked in times past. One of the most thrilling periods of history was the work of God during the 18th Century in England and America. We saw a great outpouring of His Spirit in the conversions of thousands in the English revivals and in America in what came to be known as the First Great Awakening. We see in this period of history a great combination of the two divinely ordained weapons of spiritual warfare – preaching and prayer.

Jonathan Edwards' Response to a Call to Prayer

In my opinion, one of Jonathan Edwards' most profound works was published in Boston, Massachusetts in 1748. The title was: *A Humble Attempt to Promote the Agreement and Union of God's People Throughout the World In Extraordinary Prayer For a Revival Of Religion And The Advancement Of God's Kingdom On Earth According To Scriptural Promises And Prophecies Of The Last Time.* Such long titles were not unusual during that time period. This work simply came to be known as *A Humble Attempt.* The long title says it all. Edwards was clearly a postmillennialist. In this small work, Edwards masterfully sets forth the glorious promises of Scripture, and he passionately calls upon Christians to pray these promises into reality. This work was his response to a plea from several Scottish ministers for the church of the Lord Jesus to engage in earnest prayer for a great outpouring of His Spirit to revive the church and extend Christ's kingdom throughout the world. The plea was referred to as a "Memorial." Edwards explains the motivation of the Scottish ministers in sending out their "Memorial:"

> In October, A. D. 1744, a number of ministers in Scotland, taking into consideration the state of God's church and of the world of mankind, judged that the providence of God, at such a day, did loudly call upon such as were concerned for the welfare of Zion,

---

[30]   Calvin's Commentary on Isaiah 62:6-7.

to united extraordinary applications to the God of all grace, suitably acknowledging him as the fountain of all the spiritual benefits and blessings of his church, and earnestly praying to him, that he would appear in his glory, and favor Zion, and manifest his compassion to the world of mankind, by an abundant effusion of his Holy Spirit on all the churches, and the whole habitable earth, to revive true religion in all parts of Christendom, and to deliver all nations from their great and manifold spiritual calamities and miseries, and bless them with the unspeakable benefits of the kingdom of our glorious Redeemer, and fill the whole earth with his glory. Consulting one another on the subject, they looked upon themselves, for their own part, obliged to engage in this duty; and, as far as in them lay, to persuade others to the same: and to endeavor to find out and fix on some method, that should most effectually tend to promote and uphold such-extraordinary application to heaven among God's people.[31]

The "Memorial" sent by the Scottish ministers was a call for the next two years for churches to have some set times for earnest prayer for the express purpose of seeing Christ's kingdom extended. Congregations, families, and prayer societies were encouraged to participate. Saturday evenings, Sabbath mornings, and the first Tuesday of each month were to be set aside.

I think it is no coincidence that this call to pray coincided with what the Lord was simultaneously doing in the English speaking world through the preaching of George Whitefield and others. With the completion of the first two years, a number of the Scottish ministers decided to print the "Memorial" and distribute it abroad. Edwards says that the "Memorial" was sent to nearly 500 churches in Massachusetts Bay, New Hampshire, Connecticut, Rhode Island, New York, New Jersey, Pennsylvania, Maryland, Virginia, Carolina, and Georgia.

---

[31]   Edwards, *A Humble Attempt*. There is no page notation since I have worked from an online version of this work.

Edwards was encouraging ministers to preach frequently on the importance and necessity of prayer for the coming of our Lord's kingdom. The preface to Edwards' *Humble Attempt,* which was written by the editors of his book, is a magnificent expression of the postmillennial hope. Here are some of the excerpts from this preface:[32]

> The ruin of Satan's miserable kingdom, and the advancement of the universal and happy reign of Christ on the earth, were included, and hinted at, in the sentence denounced on the serpent, that the seed of the woman should bruise his head. What was a terrible threatening to Satan, in the surprised ears of our first guilty parents, implied a joyful prophecy, to keep them from despair, and enliven their hopes, for themselves and their descendants, of obtaining by this seed of hers an eternal triumph over him who had so sadly foiled them. And it is likely, that their hope and faith immediately arose laid hold on the reviving prophecy, earnestly desired its happy accomplishment, and transmitted it to their posterity.

> But though this prophecy was at first only delivered in the form of a threatening to Satan, it was afterwards directly given in the form of a promise to Abraham, though still in general terms, that in his seed should all the nation of the earth he blessed. Yet this general promise was more clearly by degrees explained in the following ages, to mean a DIVINE KING, no other than the SON OF GOD assuming human nature of the seed of Abraham, Isaac, Jacob, and David that should be born of a virgin in Bethlehem of Judah, and at first despised, abused, rejected, and put to death; but should rise to immortal life, ascend to heaven, and thence extend his blessed kingdom over all nations, not by outward force but inward overcoming influence, by his word and Spirit making them his willing people in the day of his power, and reigning in glorious light and holiness, love and peace, for ever: and the advancement of this universal and happy reign has been the earnest desire and prayer of the saints in all ages to the present day.

> But how great the honor, and how lively the encouragement, given in Scripture to those their prayers, by representing them as offered by CHRIST himself with the fragrant incense of his own merits and intercession, on the golden altar before the throne, and ascending together in one grateful perfume to GOD!

---

[32]   Editorial preface to *A Humble Attempt.*

... To promote the increase and constancy of these acceptable prayers, is the great intention both of the pious memorial of our reverend and dear brethren, in Scotland, and of the worthy author of this exciting essay. And this design we cannot but recommend to all who desire the coming of this blissful kingdom in its promised extent and glory, in this wretched world... May GOD pour out on all his people abundantly the Spirit of grace and supplications, and prepare them for the amazing changes hastening on the earth, both for previous trials and for following glories.

What a wonderful preface to this great work. These editors understood clearly the promises of Scripture. The defeat of Satan was promised, and Christ was seen on His throne reigning victoriously in the crushing of Satan's miserable kingdom. The church was to be inspired by the prophetic hope of Christ's triumph in the earth with His gospel. They understood the central role of the church in this victory. The triumph was achieved by the powerful internal working of the Holy Spirit through the ministry of the Word. These men understood that this great work of God would be a fulfillment of Psalm 110:3 whereby God would make men willing in the day of His power. They understood that God achieved His foreordained purposes through means, and one of the foremost means was that of prayer.

To Edwards, the victory of the gospel was a prophetic assurance rooted in Christ's Kingship. Citing Hebrews 1:2 and 2:8, the nations were given to Him as His inheritance. He understood Romans 4:13 as the distinct promise of Christ as heir of the world's nations. This would be expressed through the propagation of the gospel and the power of the Spirit. The prophetic promise that every knee would bow to King Jesus was not restricted to the final Day of Judgment, but the effect of the spread of the gospel. Isaiah 45:22-23 associates gospel victory with every knee bowing. The text states:

> [22]*Turn to Me, and be saved, all the ends of the earth; for I am God, and there is no other.* [23]*I have sworn by Myself, the word has gone forth from My mouth in righteousness and will not turn back, that to Me every knee will bow, every tongue will swear allegiance.*

Indeed, the victory of the gospel is rooted in a Divine oath! The phrase "has gone forth from My **mouth**" should be seen as expressing that truth emphasized earlier in the imagery of Revelation 19:15 where a sharp sword protruding from Christ's mouth smites the nations, of Isaiah 11:4

where a rod from Messiah's mouth strikes the earth, and where the breath of His lips slays the wicked. I wish all Christians understood these prophetic passages as Edwards did and acted in response as he and others. **God has guaranteed the victory by an oath!** It is a dereliction of Christian duty not to believe and act upon this.

Edwards cites Daniel 2 and 7 as prophetic promises of the widespread extension and victory of Christ's kingdom. He cited Isaiah 11:9 as the strongest expression of the universality of the knowledge of true religion throughout the habitable world – *"The earth shall be full of the knowledge of the Lord, as the waters cover the sea."* Edwards writes about this promise:

> "The earth shall be full of the knowledge of the Lord, as the waters cover the sea." Which is as much as to say, as there is no place in the vast ocean where there is not water, so there shall be no part of the world of mankind where there is not the knowledge of the Lord; as there is no part of the wide bed or cavity possessed by the sea, but what is covered with water, so there shall be no part of the habitable world that shall not be covered by the light of the gospel, and possessed by the true religion. Waters are often in prophecy put for nations and multitudes of people. So the waters of the main ocean seem sometimes to be put for the inhabitants of the earth in general, as in Ezekiel's vision of the waters of the sanctuary, (Ezekiel 47) which flowed from the sanctuary, and ran east, till they came to the ocean, and were at first a small stream, but continually increased till they became a great river; and when they came to the sea, the water even of the vast ocean was healed, (verse 8.) representing the converse of the world to the true religion in the latter days.[33]

Edwards cites Jeremiah 10:11 as a promise of heathen idolatry being abolished. The renowned missionary to India, William Carey, carried to India a copy of Edwards' *A Humble Attempt,* and he made a similar comment of what God would do to the idols of India. Jeremiah 10:11 reads:

> *Thus you shall say to them, 'the gods that did not make the heavens and the earth shall perish from the earth and from under the heavens.'*

---

[33]   Edwards.

Like many of his fellow preachers, Edwards believed in the restoration of national Israel per the promise set forth in Romans 11, but it would be a restoration taking place during this age, not as dispensational premillennialists believe.[34]

Edwards expresses beautifully how the promise of gospel victory motivates Christians to prayer and action. He writes:

> That the church of God, under all preceding changes, should have this consideration to encourage her, and maintain her hope, and animate her faith and prayers, from generation to generation, that God has promised, her reuse should finally be maintained and prevail in the world. (Emphasis mine)

Edwards understood that God is most ready to grant prayer requests that are consistent with His purposes:

> The infinite goodness of God's nature is the more gratified, the grand design of our redemption is the better answered, Jesus Christ, the Redeemer, has the greater success in his undertaking and labors; and those desires which are expressed in prayer for the most excellent blessings, are the most excellent desires, and consequently such as God most approves of, and is most ready to gratify.

> The Scriptures do not only direct and encourage us, in general, to pray for the Holy Spirit above all things else but it is the expressly revealed will of God, that his church should be very much in prayer for that glorious outpouring of the Spirit, which is to be in the latter days and for what shall be accomplished by it. God, speaking of that blessed event, Ezekiel 36 under the figure of "cleansing the house of Israel from all their iniquities, planting and building their waste and ruined places, and making them to become like the garden of Eden, and filling them with men like a flock, like the holy flock, the flock of Jerusalem in her solemn feasts," he says, verse 37. "Thus saith the Lord, I will yet for this be inquired of by the house of Israel, to do it for them." Which doubtless implies it is the will of God, that extraordinary prayerfulness in his people for this mercy should precede the bestowment of it.

---

[34]   During the 18th Century, there was no view known as Dispensational Premillennialism. This erroneous belief would not be propagated until nearly a century later. The restoration of the Jews would come to pass due to the faithful preaching and praying of the church.

There is perhaps no one thing that the Bible so much promises, in order to encourage the faith, hope, and prayers of the saints, as this which affords to God's people the clearest evidences that it is their duty to be much in prayer for this mercy. For, undoubtedly, that which God abundantly makes the subject of his promises, God's people should abundantly make the subject of their prayers. It also affords them the strongest assurances that their prayers shall be successful. With what confidence may we go before God, and pray for that, of which we have so many exceeding precious and glorious promises to plead![35]

Edwards views Isaiah 62:6-7 as probably the greatest incentive for preachers to pray for the success of the gospel. He writes:

I know of no place in the Bible, where so strange an expression is made use of to signify importunity in prayer as is used in Isaiah 62:6, 7.

Where the people of God are called upon to be importunate for this mercy: "Ye that make mention of the Lord, keep not silence, and give him no rest, till he establish and till he make Jerusalem a praise in the earth." flow strong is the phrase! And how loud is this call to the church of God, to be fervent and incessant in their cries to him for this great mercy! How wonderful the words used, concerning the manner in which such worms of the dust should address the high and lofty One that inhabits eternity! And what encouragement is here, to approach the mercy-seat with the greatest freedom humble boldness, earnestness, constancy, and full assurance of faith, to seek of God this greatest favor that can be sought in Christian prayer![36]

Edwards rightfully saw the first three petitions of the Lord's Prayer as expressed commands for the church to pray in order to see the glorious success of Christ's kingdom in this world. He wrote:

... So that the three first petitions of the Lord's prayer are, in effect, no other than requests for bringing on this glorious day - And as the Lord's prayer begins with asking for this, in the three first petitions, so it concludes with it in these words, "For thine is the kingdom, and the power, and the glory, for ever. Amen." Which words imply a request, that God would take to himself his

---

35   Edwards.
36   Edwards.

great power, and reign, and manifest his power and glory in the world. Thus Christ teaches us, that it becomes his disciples to seek this above all other things, and make it the first and the last in their prayers, and that every petition should be put up in subordination to the advancement of God's kingdom and glory ill the world.[37]

One of the greatest encouragements to the church is the fact that if God burdens the hearts of His people to pray. This then is evidence that He is about to do marvelous things.

Revelation 11:15-17:

> [15]*Then the seventh angel sounded; and there were loud voices in heaven, saying, "The kingdom of the world has become the kingdom of our Lord and of His Christ; and He will reign forever and ever."* [16]*And the twenty-four elders, who sit on their thrones before God, fell on their faces and worshiped God,* [17]*saying, "We give You thanks, O Lord God, the Almighty, who are and who were, because You have taken Your great power and have begun to reign."*

Edwards believes that a proper application of Revelation 11:15-17 is:

> By the prayers of his saints; this gives us great reason to think, that whenever the time comes that God gives an extraordinary spirit of prayer for the promised advancement of his kingdom on earth - which is God's great aim in all preceding providence's, and the main thing that the spirit of prayer in the saints aims at - then the fulfillment of this event is nigh.[38]

Concluding Remarks on Preaching and Prayer

The church must recover a truly biblical understanding of prophetic promises. God has sworn to see His enemies defeated. Why don't we believe these promises? It's a lack of faith and zeal. It is unthinkable to fathom the only true God having His purposes thwarted in this world; it is equally unfathomable to think that God has ordained the failure of His church. The eternal Son of God came into this world to redeem a fallen race, and He secured the victory. His gospel must be victorious because He has all authority and power in the universe. Jesus reigns with omnipotent

---

[37]   Edwards.
[38]   Edwards.

power from the Fathers' right hand. He sits on David's throne as promised. He stretches forth His royal scepter and His enemies are utterly destroyed. The primary way that He destroys His enemies is by converting them, by bringing captive every thought of those in bondage to sin and Satan to His obedience by making them willing in the day of His power. Jesus has commanded His church to go forth and disciple the nations. He has promised to be with them to the end of the world, thereby guaranteeing their success. Jesus has equipped His church with divinely powerful weapons to accomplish the Great Commission. These are preaching and prayer. We must engage in believing and earnest prayer for His gospel to prevail, understanding that Jesus does preach to the hearts of men through His faithful preachers.

We now turn our attention to historical examples of the victory of the gospel. We will look at some of the great preachers of the past 300 years and how God used them to assault the gates of hell.

Chapter 5

Great Preachers and Past Revivals

This chapter is a survey of the ministerial labors of some of the greatest preachers in church history. I have included this chapter for the express purpose of demonstrating how the biblical principles set forth in earlier chapters are flushed out in actual preaching ministries.

All the preachers mentioned in this chapter were distinctly Calvinistic in their theological commitments. Several of the preachers were postmillennial in their eschatological outlook. These men were some of the greatest evangelistic preachers of all time, thereby, dispelling the myth often propagated by today's Arminian adherents. The myth is that to be Calvinistic means that one is against evangelism. This viewpoint shows a woeful lack of understanding Calvinism and an acute unawareness of church history. A Calvinistic commitment actually is a significant aid and incentive to evangelism because it recognizes the power of the One who guarantees the salvation of His elect. Since God is sovereign and has decreed the end from the beginning and has promised the success of the gospel in this age prior to Christ's Second Coming, it is no surprise that these preachers who believed this exuded a great confidence in what God could do through their faithful preaching.

Much attention is given in this chapter to the ministry of George Whitefield for several reasons. His ministry is clearly an example of how God gives gifts to men for the purpose of achieving His eternal purposes, specifically in the evangelization of the world. Whitefield's ministry revolved around preaching, and it demonstrated that this method was and still is God's primary means of advancing the gospel. Though God saves men through private reading of the Scripture and one- on- one witnessing, the overwhelming testimony in studying church history is that God normally uses a preacher to bring about conversions to Christ. Whitefield was by no means a perfect man; no Christian is. He was a sinner saved by grace. Whitefield knew this and passionately led men to see the depth of their sins and the necessity of trusting only in Jesus for the salvation of their souls.

The Dawn of the English Revivals and the First Great Awakening

Fortunately, there is an ample amount of material from this historical period. Of course, the challenge to all historians is to get it right. The best that any responsible historian can do is to look at documentary evidence, giving much weight to letters, diaries, and other written material of the period by those directly associated with the events. Having said this, George Marsden makes this very important observation about historians:

> As one astute historian has recently reminded us, "objectivity is not neutrality." Even the fairest observers have biases and blind spots. They have (and they ought to have) interests. The best way to deal with these universal phenomena is to acknowledge one's point of view rather than posing as a neutral observer.[1]

Marsden affirms his presuppositions by stating his admiration for aspects of Edwards' theology, though not endorsing all of it. He acknowledges his own commitment to a Christian faith in the tradition of the Augustinian and Reformed tree. One of things I found appreciative about Marsden's massive work on Edwards (600 pages) is his attempt to be objective regarding the historical data. He is not trying to romanticize Edwards or this historical period. It is evident that Marsden has done his research by observing his many footnotes and source material. But again, in attempting to be objective, there is no question that a writer is selective in his research. No two historians, writing on the same subject and dealing with the same sources, will say exactly the same thing. They have their own analyses of the data and can present this to the reader in such a way in order to emphasize their own perspectives. However, it is encouraging when one finds a general agreement among various writers. This lends certain credibility to all these writers demonstrating that they have not severely twisted the data.

Another work from which I have drawn is Arnold Dallimore's massive two volume masterpiece on George Whitefield titled, *George Whitefield: The Life and Times of the Great Evangelist of the 18th Century Revival*. Like Marsden, Dallimore has drawn from a voluminous amount of material. There is no question that Dallimore admired Whitefield, but this enthusiasm did not restrain him from being as objective as possible in his assessment of Whitefield's ministry.

---

[1]   George M. Marsden, *Jonathan Edwards: A Life*, (New Haven & London: Yale University Press, 2003), p.5.

I want to reiterate Marsden's observation that objectivity is not neutrality. As one who has engaged in his fair share of theological debate, I have observed that men will muster quotations from original sources to buttress their perspective. I have then gone to many of these sources only to find that some of these quotations were taken out of context thereby skewing the facts. This is most disconcerting, and what it means is that we must be diligent to do our own research, especially when there are theological differences.

Significant movements in history don't happen in some kind of spiritual vacuum. God does hear the prayers of a righteous man (James 5:16). As I noted earlier, God does hear godly prayers and determines to use them in His timetable, not ours. Great outpourings of God's Spirit, bringing revival, are normally preceded in prayer with the confidence that God will accomplish His purposes in the world.

One of the notable Puritans of the 17th Century was Samuel Rutherford, a Scottish delegate to the great Westminster Assembly. Rutherford's monumental work, *Lex Rex*, which was a biblical refutation to the notion of the divine right of kings, had a tremendous impact a century later in the American colonies, providing a biblical basis for the cause of American independence. As Rutherford lay dying at St. Andrews in 1661, his undaunted faith in God's promises was exhibited despite what was culturally happening around him. Ian Murray, in his book, *The Puritan Hope,* sets forth these words of Rutherford:

> Twenty-six years later, when Rutherford lay dying at St. Andrews, in 1661, he spoke with the same anticipation. Though he had lived to see Christ's covenanted cause in Scotland reduced to near ruin with the restoration of Charles II, and though for himself he could say "there is nothing now betwixt me and the resurrection but paradise," he had not lost sight of promises respecting the Church on earth: "We cannot but say it is a sad time to this land at present, it is a day of darkness and rebuke and blasphemy. The royal prerogative of Christ is pulled from his head. Yet we are to believe, Christ will not so depart from the land, but a remnant shall be saved; and he shall reign a victorious conquering King to the ends of the earth. O that there were nations, kindreds, tongues, and all the people of Christ's habitable world, encompassing his

throne with cries and tears for the spirit of supplication to be poured down upon the inhabitants of Judah for that effect."[2]

Murray observes:

> In connection with the Church's responsibility in this regard, there was no duty higher in Puritan esteem than the duty of prayer. The seasons when the kingdom of Christ is rapidly to spread in the earth are not revealed, but they will come in answer to prayer.[3]

Murray refers to one of the Scottish martyrs, Walter Smith, who died on the scaffold along side of Donald Cargill on July 27, 1681. In 1679, Smith had drawn up rules for praying societies. Smith wrote:

> As it is the undoubted duty of all to pray for the coming of Christ's kingdom, so all that love our Lord Jesus Christ in sincerity, and know what it is to bow a knee in good earnest, will long and pray for the out-making of the gospel promises to his Church in the latter days, that King Christ would go out upon the white horse of the gospel, conquering and to conquer, and make a conquest of the travail of his soul, that it may be sounded that the kingdoms of the world are become his, and his name called upon from the rising of the sun to its going down. (1) that the old offcasten Israel for unbelief would never be forgotten, especially in these meetings, that the promised day of their ingraffing again by faith may be hastened... (2) that the Lord's written and preached world [may be sent] with power, to enlighten the poor pagan world, living in black perishing darkness without Christ and the knowledge of his name.[4]

I trust that the reader recognizes what I noted in an earlier chapter as the proper interpretation of Revelation 6 and 19. It was a common Puritan belief that the imagery in Revelation of Christ riding on a white horse going forth conquering to conquer is properly understood as occurring in the present age.

---

[2]   Ian H. Murray, *The Puritan Hope: A Study in Revival and the Interpretation of Prophecy*, (Edinburgh, Scotland: The Banner of Truth Trust, 1971), p. 98, who quotes from Rutherford's "Testimony to the Covenanted Work of Reformation from 1638 to 1649 in Britain and Ireland, which is found in the early editions of his *Letters*.

[3]   Murray, p. 99.

[4]   Murray, p. 102.

The Puritan Thomas Goodwin (a chaplain to Oliver Cromwell) wrote in his work *The Return of Prayers*:

> There may be some prayers which you must be content never yourselves to see answered in this world, the accomplishment of them not falling in your time: such as those you haply make for the calling of the Jews, the utter downfall of God's enemies, the flourishing of the gospel... all which prayers are not yet lost, but will have answers: for as God is an eternal God, and Christ's righteousness an "everlasting righteousness," and therefore of eternal efficacy, Daniel 9:24, so are prayers also, which are the work of the eternal Spirit of Christ, made to that God in his name, and in him are eternally accepted, and therefore may take place in after ages.[5]

Goodwin also made this great comment regarding the importance of prayer:

> There is a common treasure of the church, not of their merits, but of their prayers. There are bottles of tears a-filling, vials a-filling to be poured out for the destruction of God's enemies. What a collection of prayers hath there been these many ages towards it! And that may be one reason why God will do such great things towards the end of the world, even because there hath been so great a stock of prayers going for so many ages, which is now to be returned.[6]

I must reiterate the significant theological truth regarding godly praying. Just because we may not see the impact of our prayers even in our lifetime does not mean that these prayers are fruitless. We must have faith that our glorious God hears them and will answer them in His timetable. Mark 11:24 states, "*Therefore I tell you, whatever you ask for in prayer, believe that you have received it, and it will be yours.*" We must learn to see with the eyes of faith! This was true of the renowned Calvinist commentator, Matthew Henry. In a sermon entitled "England's Hopes," preached on January 1, 1707 from Isaiah 63:4, "The year of my redeemed is come," Henry speaks of a coming fulfillment of this prediction:

> The year of the revival of primitive Christianity in the power of it, will be the year of the redeemed. This we wish, we hope, we long to see, both at home and abroad... When the bounds of the church

---

[5]   Murray, pp. 102-103.
[6]   Murray, p. 103 who quoted from *Works of Thomas Goodwin*, Vol. 3, pp. 365-66.

will be enlarged by the conversion of Pagan and Mahometan nations to the faith of Christ, and the spreading of the gospel in foreign parts... Pray for the outpouring of the Spirit upon us from on high and then the year of the redeemed would soon come... But if the year of the redeemed should not come in our days; if the carcasses of this generation should fall in this wilderness, as justly they may for our unbelief and murmuring, and we should not go over Jordan to see that goodly mountain, and Lebanon; yet let it suffice us, that those who shall come after us shall enter into that rest. Joseph dies in Egypt, but lay his bones in confidence that God will surely visit Israel."[7]

In these comments, we see his exuding confidence in the promises of God, even when we may not see them coming to pass in our lifetime. Henry had the eyes of faith and still prayed great prayers for God to do a marvelous thing. One of the privileges that we presently have is that we can see with historical retrospect. We can see what God did after Matthew Henry died. It is no coincidence that in the year of Matthew Henry's death, 1714, the Lord brought into this world a man whose preaching would rock the English speaking world. George Whitefield was born in 1714. In his thirty years of preaching, God would use Whitefield and others to bring countless thousands in England and America to saving faith in Christ. Whitefield is recognized by historians as a central figure in the English revivals and the First Great Awakening.

We presently have the privilege to see the impact of a man's labors upon one who would come after him, who many have viewed as the greatest preacher in the history of the church since the apostle Paul. We never know the full impact of our faithful efforts for the cause of Christ. Matthew Henry had no idea of the impact of his commentary. It is still bringing edifying illumination to Christians nearly 300 years after his death. Amazingly, Henry encouraged Christians, in his sermon referred to earlier, to pray for the great blessings promised in Scripture. One who would be immensely impacted by his commentary was one born in the year of his death. George Whitfield acknowledged his indebtedness to Matthew Henry's commentary. In his masterful treatise on the life and ministry of Whitefield, Arnold Dallimore refers to Whitefield's use of Matthew Henry's commentary. Dallimore comments on Whitefield's practice:

---

[7] Murray, pp. 112-13, who quotes from *The Complete Works of Matthew Henry, 1859,* Vol. 1, p.465.

There he is at five in the morning, in the room above Harris' bookstore. He is on his knees with his English Bible, his *Greek New Testament* and Henry's *Commentary* spread out before him. He reads a portion in the English, gains fuller insight into it as he studies words and tenses in the Greek and then considers Henry's explanation of it all. Finally, there comes the unique practice that he has developed: that of "praying over every line and word" of both the English and the Greek till the passage, in its essential message has veritably become part of his own soul.[8]

In fact, Whitefield in the pulpit was but a reflection of Whitefield in the study. The hours on his knees with the Bible, the Greek New Testament and some rich Puritan volume spread out before him, were his preparations for this pressing and powerful ministry. So fully had he drunk of the wells of Biblical exposition in Matthew Henry that much of his public utterance was little more than the thought of the great commentator – thought that had become assimilated in his own mind and soul, and poured forth spontaneously both as he prepared and as he preached his sermons.[9]

Dallimore states that Whitefield paid £7 (equal to the wages received by a laboring man for fifteen or sixteen weeks of work) for a copy of Matthew Henry's commentary.

Isn't God amazing how He unites His servants together in ways we cannot fathom, even after their death? Matthew Henry earnestly prayed for his God to bring to pass a great outpouring of His Spirit even on future generations, and God answered part of that prayer in the life of George Whitefield, who built upon the labors of Matthew Henry. It's as if God in the hour of Matthew Henry's death said, "My servant, I will bring into this world one that will be part of your earnest prayer; I will give the world George Whitefield who will take what you did in faithfulness to Me and through him I will transform the English speaking world."

---

[8]   Arnold Dallimore, *George Whitefield: The Life and Times of the Great Evangelist of the 18th Century Revival,* Vol.1, (Edinburgh, Scotland: The Banner of Truth Trust, 1970), pp. 82-83.

[9]   Dallimore, p. 128.

Spiritual Conditions Leading Up to the English Revivals
and the First Great Awakening

One of the advantages of studying history is that we have the blessing of seeing how God works through multiple generations. It is not uncommon for Christians to bemoan the spiritual state of their time. Sometimes we mistakenly think that we are unique in the history of the world. This is a lesson that many dispensational premillennialists desperately need to learn. Present discouraging events are not signs of the imminent return of Christ, but they are often indications that the church needs to be more faithful and earnest in prayer. But of course, if one's theological perspective teaches them to look upon the church as an utter failure, then this unbiblical perspective will cause the church to stagnate and have no real cultural influence. This doesn't change the overall plan of God; God simply raises up those who really believe in His glorious promises and who will pray them into fruition.

Both Ian Murray and Arnold Dallimore allude to the sad spiritual conditions in England prevalent in the period from 1660-1740. Murray quotes from J.B. Marsden's *The History of the Later Puritans* regarding the spiritual climate in England during this time:

> When the Puritans were expelled, they carried with them the spiritual light of the Church of England... Religion in the Church of England was almost extinguished, and in many of her parishes the lamp of God went out. The places of the ejected clergy were supplied with little regard even to the decencies of the sacred office: the voluptuous, the indolent, the ignorant, and even the profane, received Episcopal orders, and like a swarm of locusts overspread the Church.[10]

Ian Murray comments on the spiritual climate in many English pulpits:

> In less than half a century, according to the opinion of Skeats who describes conditions around 1720, 'the doctrines of the great founders of Presbyterianism could scarcely be heard from any Presbyterian pulpit in England.[11]

---

[10] Murray, p. 109, who quoted J.B. Marsden, *The History of the Puritans, 1852*, p. 473 and p.470.

[11] Murray, p. 108.

The erroneous philosophy of Deism was decimating the churches. Murray alludes to a quote from Thomas Halyburton, professor of Divinity at St. Andrews in 1712. Halyburton says:

> O sirs! I dread mightily that a rational sort of religion is coming in among us; I mean by it, a religion that consists in a bare attendance on outward duties and ordinances, without the power of godliness; and thence people shall fall into a way of serving God which is mere deism, having no relation to Christ Jesus and the Spirit of God.[12]

Dallimore believed that the churches of the 18th Century had failed; they had failed in not believing in Scriptural authority, in their lack of earnestness, and in their lack of power. Whitefield and the Wesleys, among others, complained of the general malaise and spiritual corruption in society. Lord Chesterfield addressed Parliament in 1737 regarding the obscenity of the theater. He said:

> When we complain of the licentiousness of the stage, "I fear we have more reason to complain of the general decay of virtue and morality among the people."[13]

In 1732 London's foremost religious paper, *The Weekly Miscellany*, published an article deploring the decadent prevailing conditions:

> … atheism was scattered broadcast throughout the kingdom… vice was profitable to the state; … the country would be benefited by the establishment of public stews; and that polygamy, concubinage, and even sodomy were not sinful.[14]

Writing in 1738, Archbishop Secker asserted:

> In this we cannot be mistaken, that an open and professed disregard to religion is become, through a variety of unhappy causes, the distinguishing character of the present age. This evil has already brought in such dissoluteness and contempt of principle in the higher part of the world, and such profligate intemperance and fearlessness of committing crimes in the lower, as must, if this torrent of impiety stop not, become absolutely fatal.[15]

---

[12]   Murray, p. 111.
[13]   Dallimore, p. 28.
[14]   Dallimore, p. 31.
[15]   Dallimore, p. 31.

Methodism and the English Revivals

To understand the English revivals, one must understand the rise of Methodism as a movement within the established church – the Church of England, also known as the Anglican Church. Also, we need to understand the significant role that religious societies in England played in the English revivals. In 1673 Dr. Anthony Horneck, a minister in the Anglican Church, preached a series of what was dubbed as "awakening sermons." This led to some young men gathering in small groups in fixed locations for the purpose of mutual encouragement. These fixed local groups were termed as society rooms. The activities in these rooms included prayer, Bible reading, and the study of religious books. They also went out and ministered to the poor at their own expense.

The Church of England did recognize the value in these society rooms but laid out various rules to govern these activities. These societies by 1730 had grown to nearly a hundred in London alone, not to mention another hundred scattered among various English towns. While the spiritual vitality of the Church of England began to wane, these societies became what we would term today as "evangelical" centers. The spiritual revivals that emerged under the ministries of Whitefield, the Wesley brothers, and others, were nurtured in many respects in these societies.

With George Whitefield's conversion to Christ, he was used to lead other young people to Christ, who then formed themselves into a small society for the purpose of mutual edification. It met every evening of the week where Psalms were sung, the Bible read, and various theological books read that focused upon personal growth in holiness. Whitefield would normally "exhort" for about an hour during these meetings. He hesitated to call it "preaching" because it was outside the official parameters of the established church. The founding of this society was an historic event because it was the first "Methodist" society in a permanent sense.

The Meaning of "Methodist"

While the name of John Wesley is viewed as synonymous with Methodism, and while many have viewed John and his brother Charles as the founders of Methodism, this is historically not completely accurate. Certain scholars who have researched the large number of documents of that historical period would concur that George Whitefield (1714-1770) was viewed in his time as the founder of Methodism and the originator of one of its most notable distinctives - open air preaching. Arnold Dallimore, in his massive two volume work on Whitefield, writes:

> Of this movement Whitefield was the central figure... among his contemporaries he was regarded as both the leader and founder of the movement – the leader and founder of Methodism. For instance, the Countess of Hertford writing in 1739 to the Countess of Pomfret who was then on the Continent, said, "I do not know whether you have heard of our new sect who call themselves Methodists. There is one Whitefield at the head of them – a young man under five and twenty."[16]

The term "Methodist" was first applied to the "Holy Club of Oxford." This included George Whitefield, John and Charles Wesley, and other young men when they were students at Oxford. The term "Methodist" was essentially a term that others applied to those in the Holy Club, and it wasn't always a flattering term much like how believers in Jesus were first called "Christians" at the church in Antioch. Succinctly, it simply meant "a strict method of living;" hence, those who adhered to this method were called, "Methodists." It entailed a rigorous search for holiness. This method of living at the Holy Club consisted of fasting until 3PM on Wednesdays and Fridays, receiving communion once each week, studying and discussing the Greek New Testament, reading of the Classics in the members' rooms, and visiting prisoners and the sick. It was an attempt to bring their lives under strict discipline – a strict method of living. Interestingly, Whitefield and the Wesleys later said that their participation originally in the Holy Club was a vain attempt at self righteousness that led all of them to spiritual despair until God genuinely saved them by applying His regenerating influence upon their souls. Later, the term "Methodist" was adopted by George Whitefield, who after his conversion, referred to himself and others as "Methodists." Consequently, those who followed him and those who adhered to the same beliefs that he preached were known as "Methodists." The English revivalists of the 18th Century were known as "Methodists."

Arnold Dallimore remarks that Whitefield, in many regards, was the founder of Methodism. Later, John Wesley would apply the name to his society, and he would become known as the founder of Methodism only because he outlived Whitefield by twenty-one years and because of the Methodist denominations that would eventually spring from his societies that were officially organized after his death in 1791.

---

[16] Dallimore, p.381.

Both George Whitefield and John Wesley officially remained as ordained ministers in the Church of England during their lifetimes. As Arnold Dallimore points out, Whitefield never thought of forming a new denomination.[17] Methodism was essentially a term used to designate what we today would term as "evangelical." Most of those in England who viewed themselves as Methodists during this period of time were still members of the Church of England. In 1739 if one were to ask the common man in Bristol, London, and Gloucester, England what do Whitefield and the Methodists believe, he would say, "They claim everybody must be born again."[18]

As we shall set forth in the following sections, the English revivals of the 18th Century began under Whitefield's ministry of which he would soon incorporate John and Charles Wesley. However, it would not be long until there was a significant split between Whitefield and the Wesleys over the doctrine of predestination; thereby, leading to a split in the Methodist movement.

Whitefield's ministry as an "evangelist" began while the Wesleys were still in the American colony of Georgia. The Wesleys were not yet genuinely converted to Christ by the time Whitefield began to become a national sensation in England. Whitefield popularized the open air preaching method. He then led the Wesleys to participate in this method after their conversion. Whitefield was the first to organize the religious societies into a movement.

The Ministry of George Whitefield

One cannot view the English revivals and the First Great Awakening in the American colonies of the 18th Century without knowing something of the incredible ministry of George Whitefield (1714-1770). He was born in 1714 at the Bell Inn, Southgate Street, in Gloucester, England. His parents were considered upper middle class; however, the economic climate of the Whitefield household was dramatically impacted with Thomas Whitefield's sudden death at age thirty-five. George was only two years old at the time. Having contracted measles at an early age, one of the lasting effects of the disease was a permanent misfocus of his eyes that

---

17   Dallimore, p.383.
18   Dallimore, Vol. 1, p.345.

made him look somewhat cross-eyed. During his ministry, his detractors often ridiculed him by referring to him as "Dr. Squintum."

According to his own autobiography, Whitefield referred to his boyhood as follows:

> Lying, filthy talking, and foolish jesting I was much addicted to, even when very young. Sometimes I used to curse, if not swear. Stealing from my mother I thought no theft at all, and used to make no scruple of taking money out of her pocket before she was up. I have frequently betrayed my trust, and have more than once spent money I took in the house, in buying fruits, tarts, etc., to satisfy my sensual appetite. Numbers of Sabbaths have I broke, and used generally to behave myself very irreverently in God's sanctuary. Much money I have spent in plays and the common entertainments of the age. Cards and reading romances were my heart's delight. Often have I joked with others in playing roguish tricks.[19]

The previous comment is mentioned solely for the purpose of demonstrating how Whitefield depicted his own life prior to his conversion. The biblical doctrine of regeneration, whereby the darkened heart held in captivity to sin is transformed into a heart dominated by the power of the Holy Spirit, would become a major doctrine that marked Whitefield's preaching and the Methodist revivals.

George's mother expected more from him than her other children, seeing special promise in him. George wrote that his mother was very concerned about his education, preparing him for a university education at Oxford.

As a young boy, George was enamored with the theatre. Though but a boy of thirteen and fourteen, he became so enthralled with his roles that he would act them out prior to going to school. He would spend days perfecting his role. He soon manifested a gifted imagination and intense emotion. He also possessed an exceptional elocution and memory that are essential for a good actor and orator. It was quite evident that God was preparing a man uniquely fitted for becoming what many have considered the greatest evangelist and preacher since the apostle Paul.

George's mother remarried when he was eight years old. His step father became proprietor of the Bell Inn and custodian of endowments left to the

---

[19]   Dallimore, pp. 46-47.

children by Thomas. His step father mismanaged most everything to the point that his mother lost all hope of sending George to Oxford. After six years of turmoil, Elizabeth divorced her husband and had to leave the Bell Inn.

Despite all the financial hardships, George learned that he could attend Oxford University and defray his college costs by working as a servant. As a seventeen year old, George fell into a life of slothfulness and began to keep bad company, but then he began to become more conscious of trying to reform his life through religious activity. He became diligent at studying the classics and studying the Greek New Testament. He became much disciplined in this religious way of life, but as he would later testify, he was void of the new birth in Christ. We can learn a very valuable lesson in this. Religious zeal should not necessarily be interpreted as being a genuine Christian. The Pharisees during Jesus' ministry were vivid illustrations of religious zealots who were white washed tombs, per Jesus' assessment of them.

At eighteen years of age, George would enroll in the prestigious colleges of Oxford University in the year 1732. His position as a servant did not grant him all the privileges of other students, but then this was the only way for him to attend Oxford.

During this period in Oxford's history, there was a considerable decline in the religious and moral nature of the university. George applied himself most earnestly to his studies but found himself a very lonely person, desiring some spiritual friends. For a period of a year, George watched a group of students who were referred to by other students as "the despised Methodists." George was impressed with these students who would courageously work their way through a crowd of ridiculing students to take the Holy Eucharist. He wanted to follow their good example and be acquainted with them. Finally, George's serious demeanor caught the attention of one of these students. His name was Charles Wesley, who then introduced George to the other Methodist men. This group was referred to as "The Holy Club of Oxford."

Within a year, Charles' brother, John Wesley, would join the Holy Club. This was the beginning of a lifetime of friendships (though greatly strained at times) between George Whitefield and John and Charles Wesley. The Wesley brothers were noted for their academic prowess and self-assertion. The Wesley brothers were highly opinionated and were often strongly disliked by others. John Wesley had a proclivity towards dominating those around him, and soon, John became the leader of the Holy Club. Those in the club took the Eucharist every Sunday, fasted each Wednesday and Friday and hallowed Saturday as the Sabbath of preparation for the Lord's Day. Those in the Holy Club were intensely loyal to the Church of England. The group frequently sought to persuade others to attend church; they regularly visited prisons and the Poor House, often contributing to a fund to help these inmates. Unfortunately, it was the belief of the Holy Club that somehow these actions themselves aided in the salvation of their souls. In other words, the Holy Club sought salvation by good works. This was Whitefield's perspective about his days in the Holy Club after he was truly converted to Christ.

Arnold Dallimore comments that the Holy Club of Oxford was not famous, not evanglical, and not the beginning of the revival. He says that the Methodism of Oxford would die out with the dispersion of its members in 1735. Dallimore states that the Methodism of the revival was born in 1737 and 1739 under the dynamic ministry of Whitefield assisted by the Wesley brothers. He insists that the Methodism of Oxford and the revivals were completely different. The Holy Club knew nothing of the grace taught in the Scriptures – it was an iron-clad religion of human effort.[20]

The spiritual dissatisfaction of the Holy Club, which later was expressed by most all of its members, was first seen in George Whitefield. Whitefield was greatly impacted by Henry Scougal's book *The Life of God in the Soul of Man*. Whitefield later commented about the book's impact upon him.

> God showed me that I must be born again, or be damned! I learned that a man may go to church, say his prayers, receive the sacrament, and yet not be a Christian. How did my heart rise and shudder, like a poor man that is afraid to look into his account-books, lest he should find himself a bankrupt.

> Shall I burn this book? Shall I throw it down? Or shall I search it? I did search it; and, holding the book in my hand, thus addressed the God of heaven and earth; "Lord, if I am not a Christian, or if I am not a real one, for Jesus Christ's sake, show me what Christianity is that I may not be damned at last!"

> God soon showed me, for in reading a few lines further, that, "true religion is a union of the soul with God, and Christ formed within us," a ray of Divine light was instantaneously darted in upon my

---

[20]   Dallimore, Vol.1, p. 72.

soul, and from that moment, but not till then, did I know that I must become a new creature.[21]

Aroused by this book's admonitions, Whitefield searched for the life which he yearned for. Mistakenly, he still was seeking salvation by human effort by becoming more austere in his external behavior. This only made him more miserable, losing hope. He spent many nights in bed groaning under intense spiritual burden. He soon withdrew himself from his friends. He began to practice extreme fasting during the Lent season and became so sickly that his physician put him to seven weeks of bed rest.

Finally, the saving grace of the Lord Jesus came to Whitefield in its glorious, soul liberating splendor. Whitefield wrote of his true conversion:

> God was please to remove the heavy load, to enable me to lay hold of His dear Son by a living faith, and by giving me the Spirit of adoption, to seal me even to the day of everlasting redemption. O, what joy - unspeakable - even joy that was full of and big with glory, was my soul filled, when the weight of sin went off, and an abiding sense of the pardoning love of God, and a full assurance of faith, broke in upon my disconsolate Soul! Surely it was the day of mine espousals – a day to be had in everlasting remembrance! At first my joys were like a spring tide, and overflowed the banks![22]

Later in life, Whitefield reflected on the momentous occasion by saying:

> I know the place! It may be superstitious, perhaps, but whenever I go to Oxford I cannot help running to that place where Jesus Christ first revealed himself to me and gave me the new birth.[23]

I find it most interesting that some Christians likewise remember the place where the Lord came to them in His sovereign saving power. Whitefield remembered the place at Oxford University. My maternal great, great grandfather (William Audiss who became a Primitive Methodist preacher in England and America) remembered vividly the date of his conversion (March 31, 1839) at Little Hale chapel in Lincolnshire, England. And I remembered the place of my conversion in my dormitory room at the University of Utah in 1969.

---

[21]   Sermon, "All Men's Place," published in *Sermons on Important Subjects by the Reverend G. Whitefield,* quoted in Dallimore, Vol.1, p. 73.

[22]   Dallimore, p. 77. Dallimore derived this information from George Whitefield's Journals, p. 58.

[23]   Dallimore, *Whitefield's Journals,* p. 58.

I have provided this information about Whitefield's life in the Holy Club at Oxford and his conversion experience for the purpose of better understanding the nature of the Methodist revivals of the 18th Century.

The change in Whitefield was dramatic. The gloom and fear were gone; he was enthusiastic about his new found relationship with Christ. His whole understanding of the Scriptures changed, and prayer became a precious thing to him. He meditated upon the Scriptures, praying over them on a daily basis. In reality, Whitefield was simply putting to practice the glorious truths of Psalm 1 where the Psalmist says that he takes delight in the law of the Lord, meditating upon it day and night. The result being that such a person would be like a tree planted by the rivers of water and prospering in all that he does. As Whitefield wrote, "I got more true knowledge from reading the Book of God in one month than I could ever have acquired from all the writings of men."[24]

Whitefield applied himself diligently to his English Bible and the reading of his Greek New Testament. He also diligently studied Matthew Henry's commentary on the Bible.[25] Other books of great value to him were: Joseph Alleine's 1671 work *Alarm to the Unconverted* and Richard Baxter's 1657 work *Call To the Unconverted.*[26]

If one wants to learn something about a man, then discover what he reads. Whitefield's preaching obviously was rooted in what he read. The practice of Whitefield was: he was on his knees with his English Bible, his Greek New Testament, and Matthew Henry's commentary spread out before him. He studied the English text, and then read it in Greek gaining insight into the words and tenses, and then he considered what Matthew Henry said about the text. He prayed over every line of the text until the essential meaning became a part of his soul. This diligent preparation was the stage upon which Whitefield would preach forty or more hours a week with little preparation. During his ministry that spanned thirty years, the average number of sermons per week for these thirty years was about twelve sermons a week! This is a staggering number averaged over thirty years! And, if one reads some of these sermons, they were hardly little homilies.

---

[24] Dallimore, p. 81. *Whitefield's Journals*, p. 60.
[25] Whitefield read through Matthew Henry's commentary four times - the last time on his knees. Charles Spurgeon stated, "Every minister ought to read it entirely and carefully through once at least." Whitefield paid a friend £7 for Henry's commentary. This amounted to a laboring man's wage for sixteen weeks.
[26] Richard Baxter (1615-1691) was one of the most noted Puritan pastors and authors. Baxter was a passionate preacher, who "preached as never sure to preach again, and as a dying man to dying men." His book *The Reformed Pastor*, has remained a classic for over 300 years.

Those who heard him preach were astounded by the power, the vivid illustrations, and the intensity that he would preach his sermons often with tears, and normally without referring to any notes!

Whitefield became increasingly convinced that he should be ordained in the Church of England in order to preach the Word. He had a sobering view of the nature of the ministry. He wrote:

> Oh, it is a dreadful office! ... I am fully persuaded it is His will that I should take Orders, and a strong conviction that God immediately calls me. I began to think that if I held out any longer, I should fight against God.[27]

He studied the Church of England's confessional document known as *The Thirty Nine Articles,* and he went to Scripture to see if they were biblical. He was convinced that they were. His ordination was on June 20, 1736 when he was only twenty-two years old.

His friends kept encouraging him to preach, and his first sermon was in the Church of St. Mary de Crypt. About 300 people gathered to hear him, consisting of his former school mates, members of the religious society, his mother, his siblings, certain town fathers, and other friends. He preached from Ecclesiastes 4:9-12 on the necessity of mutual assistance in the Christian life, emphasizing the necessity of being regenerated and living a holy life. According to those present, Whitefield spoke with great clarity and power. There were many hearts deeply affected by the sermon. Whitefield felt that he was empowered from on high with gospel authority.

What was about to transpire was simply astounding. His preaching in England would simply startle the nation. In his book on George Whitefield, Luke Tyerman wrote:

> In 1737 Whitefield's appearance, voice and pulpit eloquence drew around him thousands…in a succession of public services which literally startled the nation. He was a new phenomenon in the Church of England. All eyes were fixed upon him. His popularity in Bristol, London, and other places was enormous. His name became a household word. Thousands and tens of thousands were making enquiries concerning him. His position was perilous.

---

[27]   Dallimore, p. 91. *Whitefield's Journals,* p. 67.

Popular favour might have ruined him, but the grace of God preserved him.[28]

Whitefield's Startling Ministry in England, Scotland, and America

As we examine the amazing ministry of George Whitefield, we must understand this one great fact- God raises up His heralds of the gospel. While men can somewhat improve their oratorical skills and improve the biblical content of their sermons, in the final analysis, preachers are born not made, meaning that they are called and equipped by the Lord Jesus. They are His gifts to the world. Ephesians 4:7-13 states:

> [7]*But to each one of us grace was given according to the measure of Christ's gift.* [8]*Therefore it says, "When He ascended on high, He led captive a host of captives, and He gave gifts to men."* [9]*(Now this expression, "He ascended," what does it mean except that He also had descended into the lower parts of the earth?* [10]*He who descended is Himself also He who ascended far above all the heavens, so that He might fill all things.)* [11]*And He gave some as apostles, and some as prophets, and some as evangelists, and some as pastors and teachers, for the equipping of the saints for the work of service, to the building up of the body of Christ; until we all attain to the unity of the faith, and of the knowledge of the Son of God, to a mature man, to the measure of the stature which belongs to the fullness of Christ.*

---

[28] Dallimore, p. 102.

Preachers of the gospel are gifts of Christ to His church. Since Jesus is going forth conquering to conquer by defeating all His enemies through the sword coming out of His mouth, it is no surprise that the Lord of glory gives such men as George Whitefield to His church. Since preachers are the tools through which Jesus preaches, the Lord will orchestrate the lives of men to lead them in such a way so as to achieve His sovereign purposes. Proverbs 16:9 beautifully states: *"The mind of man plans his way, but the Lord directs his steps."* This truth is vividly seen in Whitefield's life. He did not set out to have some startling ministry. In fact, upon his ordination, Whitefield determined to obtain his Master's degree from Oxford being fully content in a life of academics, but the Lord had other plans for him. Whitefield was being encouraged to supply the pulpit at the Chapel of the Tower of London. He was reluctant to take the position and wrote:

> I said, Lord, I cannot go! ... I pleaded to be at Oxford two or three
> years more and intended to make an hundred and fifty sermons...
> I said, I am undone, I am unfit to preach in thy great name! Send
> men not, I pray, Lord, send me not yet![29]

His ministry at the Tower lasted two months, but he was gaining popularity. Many young men from the religious societies were drawn to hear Whitefield speak on "the new birth." After his short ministry, he returned to Oxford with great joy to engage himself in academic life again. Whitefield wrote:

> Oh what delightful life did I lead here! What communion did I
> daily enjoy with God! How sweetly did my hours in private glide
> away in reading and praying over Matthew Henry's *Comment on
> the Scriptures.* Nor was I alone happy, for several dear youths
> were quickened greatly and met daily in my room to build each
> other in their most holy faith.[30]

While at Oxford, another Holy Club man, Charles Kinchin, persuaded Whitefield to minister at Dummer in Hampshire. Many of the parishioners were poor and illiterate. At first, the highly educated Whitefield felt very uncomfortable among such people, but he learned a lesson that would prove invaluable in a ministry that God was preparing for him. Whitefield remarked that he learned more from an afternoon's visit with such people as a week of study.

---

[29]   Dallimore, Vol. 1, p. 104 who quotes from Sermon, "The Good Shepherd," *Sermons of the Rev. George Whitefield*, p. 733.
[30]   Dallimore, p. 106 who quotes from *Whitefield's Journals*, p. 78.

It was while at Dummer that Whitefield would make a decision that affected his entire ministerial career. He would decide to be a missionary to the American colony of Georgia at the encouragement of his Holy Club friend, John Wesley. John and his brother Charles with others had made a voyage to Georgia. Wesley had written a letter to the Holy Club from Georgia requesting assistance. Wesley's letter had first been read by Whitefield while he was ministering at the Tower of London. Wesley wrote another letter to Whitefield while he was at Drummer. Whitefield determined that this was his calling- to be a missionary to Georgia. With this decision, he ceased further study at Oxford making preparations to set sail for America. There was one problem which proved to be of monumental significance. He would be detained for nearly a year because a ship was not available.

Here was the hand of providence revealed. While visiting Gloucester he was requested to preach for two Sundays before large congregations. At Bristol he found himself preaching every day of the week and twice on Sundays. Soon, the churches became crowded to the point of overflowing to hear this remarkable twenty-four year old preacher. Those with spiritual concerns were continually seeking his counsel, and lucrative offers were being made to entice him to remain in Bristol. His popularity was steadily growing. People would walk a mile just to hear him. The churches were overflowing. People from all sorts of denominations were flocking to hear him. As his popularity was growing, Whitefield informed people that they might soon not see him ever again because of his commitment to go to Georgia as a missionary. Such news caused multitudes to be overcome with tears with the thought of losing such a preacher.

While still waiting for an opportunity to leave for Georgia, his ministry kept growing. The crowds were huge that sought to hear him and thousands would be turned away because there was no room in the churches for them. Whitefield said that he was now preaching nine times a week. This ministry lasted for four months. As 1737 drew to a close, a ship was now available to sail for Georgia. When one thinks about it, it is absolutely amazing. He gives up a ministry in England during the midst of being a national sensation to honor his commitment to the Wesleys that he would come to Georgia. Despite lucrative financial offers to stay in London to preach, he still left and spent 1738 in Georgia.

The Spiritual Conversions of John and Charles Wesley

We cannot faithfully give a recounting of the English revivals without commenting briefly on the conversions and ministries of John and Charles Wesley. As noted previously, the Wesleys had become friends with Whitefield during their early days at the Holy Club of Oxford, and John Wesley had successfully sought to persuade Whitefield to come to Georgia.

While Whitefield's ship, the *Whitaker,* was in the harbor at the port of Deal waiting to sail to America, amazingly, the ship, the *Samuel,* sailed in carrying John Wesley from America. It was not a happy occasion for John Wesley. He had returned in abject despondency, having been a failure in Georgia. Things had not gone well for John. He learned a painful but vital spiritual and blessed lesson – salvation is not by human effort. In his own Journals, John Wesley is very frank:

> What have I learned? Why, what I the least of all suspected, that I who went to America to convert others, was never myself converted to God.[31]

A major turning point in his life occurred on the voyage over to America. A very violent storm arose that seemed to threaten the ship. The English passengers were screaming in terror for fear of their lives including Wesley. Some of the passengers were of a German sect known as the Moravians. They (men, women, and children) exhibited a profound calmness in the midst of the storm by singing a hymn of trust and praise. This so impressed John that he inquired of them what kind of relationship with God could provide such peace. He realized he had nothing like them. While in Georgia, one of the Moravian leaders, Augustus Spangenberg answered some of John Wesley's questions by directing some questions back to John: Does the Spirit of God bear witness with your spirit that you are a child of God? Do you know Jesus Christ? Do you know He has saved your soul? John had no answers, but it left a lasting impression on him to ponder.

While in Georgia, John Wesley was involved in a budding love affair that never materialized. John's vacillation caused the woman, Sophia Hopkey, to suddenly marry another man, which deeply wounded him. In a very foolish maneuver, John denied communion to her. Sophia's husband was

---

31   Dallimore, p. 145 quoting John Wesley's *Journal*, Vol. 8, p. 288.

incensed and sued him for a £1000 for defamation of character, and a notice was issued for his arrest. Under cover of night, John escaped to Charleston, South Carolina where he quickly sailed for England. Needless to say, John never returned to America.

Trying to preach while being an unconverted person is a mind boggling endeavor for those of us who are preachers. From what well spring will the unconverted preacher draw from? To show the effect of unconverted preaching, Wesley recounted this sad assessment given about his own preaching while in Georgia. A Georgian magistrate by the name of Horton said this to John while in Georgia:

> I like nothing you do. All your sermons are satires upon particular persons, therefore I will never hear you more; and all the people are of my mind, for we won't hear ourselves abused. Besides, they say they are Protestants. But as for you, they cannot tell what religion you are of... And then your private behavior – all the quarrels that have been here since you came have been long of you. Indeed, there is neither man nor woman in the town who minds a word you say.[32]

One can understand why John Wesley viewed himself as a complete failure. These were devastating words to be said to a person, much less a preacher!

Whitefield spent almost all of 1738 in Georgia, and his reception by the Georgians was dramatically different than what Wesley experienced. Back in England, the Anglican clergy that held Whitefield in contempt hoped that his departure would cause his influence to die. They were greatly mistaken. Before departing for America, Whitefield had committed to a publisher, James Hutton, the rights to publish his sermons. Nine of Whitefield's sermons were produced in one volume. Other publishers also published Whitefield's nine sermons. These publications kept the memory of Whitefield ever before the nation. The religious societies were growing with enthusiastic attendees. This revival that characterized the religious societies alarmed the clergy that were opposed to Whitefield. These societies had no desire of Anglican clergy leadership; hence, they were becoming somewhat autonomous. A common question presented to these clergymen by those in the societies was – "Have you been born again?" One prominent Anglican clergyman at Oxford began to publicly criticize

---

[32]   Dallimore, p. 149 who quoted from John Wesley's *Journal*, Vol. 1, p. 234.

the doctrine of the new birth. Other clergymen sought to have the religious societies banned altogether for fear of what influence they would have.

This hostility of the religious leaders towards the Methodist revival was painfully reminiscent of Jesus' encounters with the Pharisees, the religious leaders who Jesus referred to as "white washed tombs."

After returning in defeat and seeing the fruit of Whitefield's ministry, John Wesley was amazed. Whitefield's ministry was bearing fruit even in his absence. All these things began to weigh heavily upon him. Wesley remarks:

> This, then, have I learned in the ends of the earth- that I am fallen short of the glory of God: that my whole heart is altogether corrupt and abominable... that, alienated, as I am from the life of God, I am a child of wrath, and heir of hell;... that, having the sentence of death in my heart, and having nothing in or of myself to plead, I have no hope but that of being justified freely through the redemption that is in Jesus'; I have no hope, but that if I seek I shall find Christ, and be found in Him, not having my own righteousness, but that which through faith of Christ, the righteousness which is of God by faith.[33]

Charles Wesley, John's brother, was essentially in the same spiritual bondage. He was a preacher that really did not know Christ. Both John and Charles sought out the Moravian missionary, Peter Bohler, who was in England at the time. Bohler said to John, "My brother! My brother! That philosophy of yours must be purged away."[34] Bohler was referring to John's attempts at earning salvation by good works.

Charles Wesley had a similar experience with Peter Bohler. Charles wrote:

> He asked me, "Do you hope to be saved?" "Yes!" "For what reason do you hope it?" "Because I have used my best endeavours to serve God." He shook his head and said no more. I thought him very uncharitable, saying in my heart, "What? Are not my endeavors a sufficient ground of hope? Would he rob me of my endeavors? I have nothing else to trust to."

---

[33] Dallimore, pp. 179-180, who quotes from John Wesley's *Journal*, Vol. 1, pp. 423-424.
[34] Dallimore, p. 180, quoting Wesley's *Journal*, p.440.

John Wesley also said:

> I was strongly convinced that the cause of my uneasiness was unbelief, and that the gaining a true, living faith was the one thing needful for me. But still I fixed not this faith on its right object: I meant only faith in God, not faith in or through Christ. Again, I knew not that I was wholly devoid of this faith, but only thought I had not enough of it. So that when Peter Bohler... affirmed of true faith in Christ, that it had those two fruits inseparably attending it, dominion over sin and constant peace or from a sense of forgiveness, I was quite amazed and looked upon it as a new gospel.[35]

While both John and Charles were making headway to a certain degree, they were seeking faith as opposed to seeking Christ. Charles was thinking that this coming of faith might be associated with some kind of visible presence of Christ. John was looking for an experience accompanied by some emotional response. He was having trouble thinking that a person could have a sense of forgiveness without a feeling.

By May of 1738 both the Wesley's were in a miserable spiritual condition. Charles spent several weeks in a bed ridden condition. A friend of Charles Wesley, William Holland, who was a commercial printer, brought him a copy of Martin Luther's *Commentary on the Galatians*. This proved to be of immense value to Charles. The book of Galatians is a masterful treatise on justification by faith and not by works. Reading this commentary by Luther led to William Holland's conversion to Christ. Then, according to Charles Wesley, on Sunday May 21, 1738, the Lord chased away the darkness of his unbelief. Upon his conversion, the future great hymn writer wrote what is still considered over 300 years later as one of the greatest hymns of the Christian faith. He penned these famous lines:

> And can it be that I should gain
> An interest in the Savior's blood?
> Died he for me, who caused his pain?
> For me, who Him to death pursued?
> Amazing love! How can it be
> That Thou, my God, should'st die for me!
> Long my imprisoned spirit lay
> Fast bond in sin and nature's night;
> Thine eye diffused a quick'ning ray;
> I woke; the dungeon flamed with light;

---

[35] Dallimore, p. 181, quoting John Wesley's *Journal. Are*

> My chains fell off, my heart was free,
> I rose, went forth, and follow'd Thee.

That evening, John Wesley wrote, "I received the surprising news that my brother had found rest to his soul. His bodily strength returned also from that hour." But John was still despondent. On Wednesday of the following week, he happened upon the verse, "Thou art not far from the kingdom of God." He attended a service at St. Paul's cathedral, and as the choir sang, "Out of the deep have I called unto Thee, O Lord; Lord, hear my voice. O let Thine ears consider well the voice of my complaint." He found the words and expression of his own deep desires. On Wednesday evening John went to a society meeting at Aldersgate Street, where William Holland was reading Martin Luther's preface to the epistle to the Romans. Holland himself had just been converted seven days earlier. As Holland was reading about faith in Christ, John Wesley felt in that moment that he received the faith that he so longed for.

What's amazing is that within a span of a week three people were brought to a saving knowledge of Christ by reading a commentary by Luther on the books of Galatians and Romans.

John could not wait to tell his brother Charles. At 10PM on that Wednesday evening, Charles writes that "My brother was brought in triumph by a troop of our friends, and declared, 'I believe!' We sang the hymn with great joy and parted with prayer."

Charles began to proclaim "salvation by faith" to everyone he could reach. He even went to the prisons to speak to condemned men. He led one black man to Christ, and then as many of these prisoners were led to the gallows, Charles was preaching to them up to the very moment of their execution. In the days ahead, Charles continued to boldly proclaim his new found faith in Christ, and the poetic gifts that he possessed soon became directed to producing hymns that are still sung today.

John Wesley began to preach on faith wherever he could. His first sermon after his conversion was on I John 5:5 – "And who is the one who overcomes the world, but he who believes that Jesus is the Son of God."

The Onset of Open Air Preaching

Upon returning from his first American trip, Whitefield was very pleased that the effects of his preaching the year before were bearing fruit. He was most pleased with the conversions of the Wesley brothers and appreciated the ministry they were having. While his friends were enthusiastic about Whitefield's return to England, his foes were not rejoicing. He was not permitted to preach in various Anglican churches, a most sad turn of events. This did not deter Whitefield from his determination to preach wherever he could. At least four churches were still open to him. In a period of fifty-six days, he preached fifty-seven times in seventeen different churches, obviously preaching everyday during this period.

The religious societies proved to be the most receptive to his ministry; therefore, these societies were gaining influence. Whitefield commented that within a week he had preached nine times and exhorted eighteen times. Whitefield distinguished "preaching" from "exhortation," meaning that he preached in churches and exhorted in the religious societies. In modern terminology, he would have viewed the religious societies as "para-church" organizations. These groups obviously had value, but they were not the same as the "visible church."

The Holy Club had taken on a different dimension; they had been born again! The self righteous attempts toward earning salvation that had first marked the Holy Club at Oxford had given way to the transforming power of the gospel. Whitefield wrote about the activities of the Holy Club:

> ... Everything else was carried on with great love, meekness and devotion. We continued in fasting and prayer till three o'clock and then parted with the full conviction that God was going to do great things among us. Oh, that he would make us vessels pure and holy, and meet for our master's use![36]

While the ministries of Whitefield and the Wesleys were growing, the opposition from the Anglican clergy was also growing. Whitefield noted that the opposition often was directed toward his emphasis upon the doctrine of the new birth. Whitefield wrote:

> … Set up till near one in the morning with my honored brother and fellow laborer, John Wesley, in conference with two clergymen of the Church of England, and some other strong opposers of the doctrine of the new birth. God enabled me, with great simplicity, to declare what He had done for my soul, which made them look upon me as a madman... They believe only in an

---

[36] Dallimore, p. 222 from Whitefield's *Journals,* p. 96.

outward Christ, we further believe that he must be inwardly formed in our hearts also.[37]

His concern was realized when St. Mary's at Islington Church, where he preached his first sermon, denied him access to the church. Having been denied this pulpit, he wrote:

And since the self-righteous men of this generation count themselves unworthy, I go out into the highways and hedges, and compel harlots, publicans and sinners to come in, that my Master's house may be filled.[38]

With Whitefield's growing popularity, the sanctuaries of church buildings were becoming inadequate. There were times that nearly a thousand people were in the churchyard trying to hear him. Zealous for wanting to reach people with the gospel, Whitefield began to think of an innovative way of reaching the multitudes:

This put me first upon thinking of preaching without doors. I mentioned it to some friends who looked upon it as a mad notion. However, we kneeled down and prayed that nothing may be done rashly.[39]

Despite the feelings of some friends who thought the prospect of open air preaching as a crazy endeavor, Whitefield continued to entertain the thoughts that this method could remedy the problem of Anglican churches being closed to him. He exclaimed, "The churches are closed against me, 'Bless God, the fields are open!'"[40]

Though Whitefield would take open air preaching to heights heretofore not seen, his open air preaching was not the first. A Welshman, Howell Harris, had for three years been exhorting his fellow-countrymen through field preaching. Whitefield had heard of Harris' endeavors and wrote several letters to him beginning in December 1738. Harris was not an ordained minister, and this fact had prompted strong opposition from the clergy.

The exchange of letters between Whitefield and Harris began a very close friendship and corroboration of gospel laboring. Being unordained, Harris refused to practice any kind of formal sermonizing. He often stood before

---

[37]   Dallimore, p. 226 from Whitefield's *Journals*, pp. 203-204.
[38]   Dallimore, p. 287 who quotes Whitefield's *Journals*, p. 259.
[39]   Dallimore, p. 229 from Whitefield's *Journals, p. 200.*
[40]   Dallimore, p. 230.

his congregations with no prepared message. There were instances where his services lasted for six hours with no break.[41]

Howell Harris formed his first society in 1736, and by 1739, there were nearly thirty such societies in Wales.[42] Harris' ministry was considered the beginning of Welsh Calvinistic Methodism. About four years later, he and George Whitefield would officially form the Welsh Calvinistic Methodist body. Harris' ministry was often met with hostility from civil magistrates threatening to imprison him, and mobs were often threatening to harm him. Twice Harris applied for ordination, but he was adamantly opposed. Though opposed by the Anglican clergy, Harris viewed his evangelistic endeavors as part of the institutional church.

In many regards, Howell Harris was the pioneer of Methodist field preaching. He was the first to form a number of societies and link them together in a permanent organization. John Wesley's work was patterned after Harris, and Whitefield was deeply indebted to his example.[43]

Shortly after Whitefield's correspondences with Howell Harris, he determined to make the momentous step to engage in open air preaching. While considered unorthodox, the Church of England actually permitted this method, particularly where missionary activity was being performed.

Again, Whitefield's decision to engage in open air preaching was not a rash decision. It was out of a sense of urgency to proclaim the gospel and as a means to solve logistical problems of people wanting to hear his preaching. The momentous date was February 7, 1739. He began in Bristol, England. From a human perspective, the district known as "Kingswood" that bordered the city of Bristol was a very unlikely place to begin. It was a place where the working class citizen spent long hours, facing danger and disease. It was notorious for being so dangerous that strangers did not wander into it. This fact did not deter Whitefield in the slightest. In several days, crowds from 3,000 to 10,000 had gathered to hear him. Moreover, his preaching was not some common modern day sermon of twenty minutes; it was often one and a half hours! So much for the idea that people cannot sit or stand, much less in the cold, to hear a preacher.

---

[41] Dallimore, p. 241 who quotes R. Bennett, *The Early Life of Howell Harris* (Edinburg, Scotland: Banner of Truth Trust, 1962), p. 41.

[42] Wales is technically its own country that is a part of the United Kingdom, bordered by England in the east and the Atlantic Ocean and the Irish Sea to the west.

[43] Dallimore, p. 246.

When Whitefield preached that Saturday afternoon, it was one of the coldest days in living memory, but he was determined to reach these people. Whitefield wrote:

> Blessed be God! I have now broken the ice! I believe I was never more acceptable to my Master than when I was standing to teach those hearers in the open fields.[44]

Whitefield had determined to only continue open air preaching for eight weeks before he sailed again for America. He was looking for someone to take over his Bristol work. He had held thirty meetings a week in Bristol with crowds totaling between 40,000 to 50,000.

One needs to understand the nature of the spiritual climate of the time and the way that the Church of England conducted its ministry. Parishes are geographical areas that serve as the religious centers for worship. It is the smallest and most fundamental aspect of the Church of England. Dioceses are geographical areas consisting of various parishes; therefore, all of England is divided up into various parishes and dioceses. Each parish is ministered by a local priest referred to as a vicar or rector. All religious activity in a parish then is under the governing authority of the parish rector.

Whenever Whitefield entered a parish he requested the use of the church since he was an ordained Anglican clergyman. If he was allowed, he availed himself of the opportunity. If he was denied, then he would preach wherever he could, be it on a street corner or in an open field.

With his successful preaching in Bristol, Whitefield turned his attention to London. Anglican pulpits in London were being denied him. With this rejection, Whitefield believed that God was compelling him to the open fields as well. In London there was an eighteen acre park called Moorfields. The Moorfields was known for its bear-baiting[45], its lewd shows, wrestling, dog fights, and a blood sport known as cudgel fighting.[46] It was hardly a park where respectable parents would take their children

---

[44] Dallimore, p. 256 who quotes *Whitefield's Journals*, p.216.
[45] It is a cruel form of entertainment. Arenas for this purpose were called bear-gardens, consisting of a circular high fenced area, the "pit," and raised seating for spectators. A post would be set in the ground towards the edge of the pit and the bear chained to it, either by the leg or neck. A number of well-trained hunting dogs would then be released, being replaced as they tired or were wounded or killed. In some cases the bear was let loose, allowing it to chase after animals or people.
[46] Cudgel playing was a type of blood sport competition that entailed a long wooden stick called a "cudgel" that opponents used to hit one another.

for a nice picnic. Large numbers would gather each evening and on Sundays. In one sense, it was an ideal place where there were many people but very dangerous. Some of the brethren from the Fetter Lane Society, hearing about Whitefield's success in Bristol, attempted open air preaching in the Moorfields. They brought a table on which to stand, but the result was not what they desired. The mob soon broke the table into pieces and sent them running for fear of their lives.

This was the setting that awaited Whitefield. He entertained thoughts as to whether he should attempt such a daring venture, knowing the type of people gathered in this place. The decision was made to proceed, and public notice was given of the date he would come and preach. This first day was documented:

> Public notice having been given… upon coming out of the coach he found an incredible number of people assembled. Many had told him that he should never come again out of that place alive. He went in, however, between two of his friends, who, by the pressure of the crowd were soon parted entirely from him and were obliged to leave him to the mercy of the rabble. But these, instead of hurting him, formed a lane for him, and carried him along to the middle of the Fields (where a table had been placed which was broken in pieces by the crowd) and afterwards back again to the wall that then parted the upper and lower Moorfields; from when he preached without molestation to an exceedingly great multitude.[47]

The Anglican clergy continued in their denunciation of Whitefield, and one Anglican clergyman, Dr. Joseph Trapp, made Whitefield the subject of his sermon, denouncing Whitefield's ministry. This public denunciation only spurred Whitefield to continue.

One of the other areas of London where Whitefield preached to thousands was at Kennington Common. It was an area of about twenty acres where many public hangings were carried out and where a permanent scaffold existed. If the Moorfields was a tough place, Kennington Common was known for its brutality. As some described the inhabitants, it was where the lowest of the lowest social strata gathered. But, it was to such people that Whitefield was moved with compassion to reach their souls. On one occasion Whitefield wrote that thirty thousand gathered to hear him

---

[47]   Dallimore, pp. 287-288 quoting John Gilles, *Memoirs of the Life of the Reverend George Whitefield*, p. 42.

preach. On another occasion, Whitefield believed eighty thousand gathered to hear him, stating that it was the largest crowd he had ever seen. On this occasion, a large scaffold was made for him to preach from.

While Whitefield may not have been run out of the area for fear of his life, there were occasions where unruly portions of the crowd would throw rocks, and at times, parts of dead animals at him. On one occasion, Whitefield was hit with a rock leaving a deep cut in his head. There were times when cursing mobs would beat on the doors of Whitefield's Tabernacle[48] and attack the congregation. What was most discouraging was that these vicious attacks, especially where Christians were assaulted indoors, were often with the full knowledge of civil authorities who did nothing to stop it. Things would have been worse, if it had not been for the faithful and courageous efforts of the Countess of Huntingdon[49] who used her influence to exhort the civil authorities to do their civic duty to protect people from ruthless mobs. She cast the shield of protection around her own ministers and obtained relief from the highest authorities. When she journeyed throughout the country, her very name was sufficient to strike terror into the enemies of the cross and to attract thousands to see the illustrious lady.

John Wesley Begins Open Air Preaching

The person that Whitefield turned to was none other than John Wesley. Whitefield wrote Wesley saying, "You must come and water what I have planted." Whitefield introduced John Wesley to his open air congregation at Bristol. Somewhat astounded, Wesley wrote to his friend Hutton saying:

> Brother Whitefield expounded on Sunday morning to six or seven thousand at the Bowling Green; at noon to much the same number

---

[48]   As Whitefield's ministry was growing, some "Protestant Dissenters" built a meeting house in the Moorfield district that would serve as an indoor meeting place, sheltering the people from the wind and rain.

[49]   One would be remiss in any study of the rise of English Methodism to neglect the incredible influence of Selena Hastings, the Countess of HuntingdonError! Bookmark not defined.. She deserves to have her name enshrined with all the notable revivalists of the 18th Century. She did as much as any to advance the cause of evangelical Christianity during her life. She was a product of the MethodistError! Bookmark not defined. revivals, and used her vast wealth to promote the cause of Christ as much as anyone in the entire history of the Christian church. Her estate house was used for the purpose of having Whitefield and others preach to the nobility. She used her personal wealth to build over 200 chapels and pay the salary of the ministers of all of them. Her charitable contributions to Christians causes in England and America were profound.

at Hanham Mount, and at five to, I believe, 30,000 from a little mount on Rose Green.[50]

I could scarce reconcile myself at first to this strange way of preaching in the fields, of which he set me an example on Sunday; having been all my life (till very lately) so tenacious of every point relating in decency and order, that I should have thought the saving of souls almost a sin if it had not been done in the church.[51]

Arnold Dallimore comments on the differences between Whitefield and Wesley in their open air preaching:

While Whitfield was probably as greatly gifted for the open air preaching as any man in Christian history, Wesley, whose talents fitted him admirably for the Oxford classroom, was not particularly suited to addressing the crowds in the fields. His voice, though apparently a rich tenor, lacked the organ tones of Whitefield's, and his manner of preaching, while intense in its earnestness, had not the popular appeal of Whitefield's dramatic oratory.[52]

The crowds that followed Wesley were a tenth of the numbers flocking to hear Whitefield; Wesley was much more fitted for the society rooms.

While George Whitefield and John Wesley were personal friends, and while Whitefield introduced Wesley to open air preaching, theological differences began to emerge between them and within two years a separation had occurred.

John Wesley began to preach sermons openly attacking the doctrine of predestination, a doctrine taught in the Church of England's *Thirty Nine Articles* and in *The Westminster Confession of Faith*.[53] While in Bristol, Wesley began to publicly criticize this doctrine. During this time, Wesley began to notice some rather odd emotional outbursts occurring in the crowd. People were experiencing convulsive seizures of sorts – a phenomenon that Wesley thought was God's approval on his ministry. It had only been four weeks since Whitefield had turned over his Bristol

---

[50]   Dallimore, p. 274 who quotes John Wesley's *Letters*, Vol. 1, p. 289.
[51]   Dallimore, who quotes John Wesley's *Journal*, Vol. 2, p. 167.
[52]   Dallimore, p. 277.
[53]   *The Westminster Confession of Faith* was approved in 1647 and ratified by acts of Parliament in 1649. The *Westminster Confession of Faith* serves as the doctrinal constitution of many Reformed and Presbyterian churches throughout the world. It is the constitution of the RPCUS, the denomination that I, John M. Otis, am a member of.

ministry to Wesley that Wesley began to attack the doctrine of predestination. Wesley's sermon against predestination was the first sermon to drive a wedge in the Methodist movement. Whitefield, Howell Harris, and the Countess of Huntingdon were all staunch believers in this doctrine. What was odd was that Wesley began to assert that any belief in predestination made preaching a vain work and a detractor to manifesting good works. He was scathing in his attack on this doctrine insisting that it was full of blasphemy, making the Lord Jesus Christ a hypocrite and deceiver of people. The clear implication was that Whitefield's preaching was incompetent and inadequate – a rather startling belief seeing that there was none of the era more evangelistic than George Whitefield!

Wesley's sermon against predestination, a view that openly contradicted the church that Wesley was a part of and a view that was held close to Whitefield's heart, was of vast importance in the history of Methodism. His sermon marked the actual beginning of Wesley's own movement with all of the historical implications flowing out of it. Wesley had his sermon on "free grace" immediately published. One of the most interesting but perplexing things is that Wesley tied together his sermon against predestination and the strange emotional phenomena as clear proof that God was sanctioning his ministry and that he was theologically correct. Wesley wrote:

> Dear Jemmy – You seem to forget what I told you: (1) that, being unwilling to speak against Predestination, we appealed to God, and I was commanded by lot to preach and print against it; (2) that the very first time I preached against it explicitly, the power of God so fell on those that heard, as we have never known before, either in Bristol or London, or elsewhere.[54]

While Whitefield was engaged in open air preaching opportunities in London at the Moorfields and Kennington Commons, he still knew nothing of Wesley's open attacks on the doctrine of predestination. Upon learning of Wesley's attacks, Whitefield immediately wrote Wesley:

> I hear, Honoured Sir, that you are about to print a sermon against predestination. It shocks me to think of it! What will be the consequences but controversy? If people ask my opinion, what shall I do? I have a critical part of me to act. God enable me to behave aright! Silence on both sides will be best. It is noised

---

[54]   Dallimore, p. 314 who quotes *Wesley's Letters*, Vol. 1, p. 307.

abroad already that there is a division between you and me, and my heart within me is grieved.[55]

But, Wesley had already printed the sermon, exclaiming, "Here I fix my foot!" The theological division was now in place in the Methodist movement, much to the great sorrow of George Whitefield.

One of the other doctrines that John Wesley began to publicly endorse and put in print was *A Plain Account of Christian Perfectionism*. This adherence to this doctrine provided additional basis for division between Wesley and Whitefield. What was Wesley teaching by this doctrine? He was teaching that the sin nature could become completely eradicated and the soul entirely sanctified. Though he resisted using the term "absolute" holiness, he continually used the words, "all," "whole," and "entire." Count Zinzendorf, the founder of the Moravians and whose influence was profound in Wesley's life, was very blunt in his criticism of Wesley. Upon hearing of Wesley's teaching on perfectionism, Zinszendorf called Wesley a false teacher and deceiver of souls. Zinzendorf had a conversation with John Wesley as follows:

> I acknowledge no inherent perfection in this life. This is the error of errors! I persecute it through all the world with fire and sword! I trample upon it, I destroy it! Christ is our only perfection! All Christian perfection is faith in the blood of Christ. It is imputed, not inherent. We are perfect in Christ: we are never perfect in ourselves.[56]

Not only did Wesley find himself at odds with Whitefield and Zinzendorf, but he was alienating himself from other leaders of the Methodist movement. John Cennick and Howell Harris greatly debated Wesley on this doctrine of perfectionism.

Whitefield began to see that Wesley's views on predestination and now on perfectionism were beginning to drive a wedge in the Methodist movement. Whitefield wrote Wesley:

> Honoured Sir, how could you tell that some who came to you "were in a good measure sanctified?" What fruits could be

---

[55]   Dallimore, p. 315 who quotes *The Methodist Magazine*, 1849, p. 165.
[56]   Dallimore, p. 318 who quotes *Wesley's Journal*, Vol. 2, p. 488.

produced in one night's time? "By their fruits," says our Lord, "shall you know them."[57]

The gap was now widening in the Methodist movement. Those who followed Whitefield were known as Calvinistic Methodists, and those who followed John Wesley and his brother Charles were known as Arminian Methodists. Whitefield and Howell Harris were instrumental in forming the Welsh part of the Methodist Movement, known as the "Calvinistic Methodist Association." They held their first Methodist Conference eighteen months before Wesley held his first Arminian based Methodist Conference.

During this period, we must be aware that both the Calvinistic and Arminian groups bore the name, "Methodist." By now, the term "Methodism" meant a fervent manner of life and a belief in evangelical doctrine. John Wesley increasingly began to use the word "Methodist" and eventually dropped the term, "United Societies."

Calvinistic and Arminian Branches of Methodism

As mentioned, theological drifts separated Whitefield and Wesley. Methodism now had two expressions – Calvinistic and Arminian branches by 1744. But both branches were still viewed to be within the Church of England. Both Whitefield and Wesley were ordained Anglican ministers. Whitefield realized that he could not officially organize with John Wesley, but he believed that the two could still preach to multitudes the great doctrines of the rebirth and justification by faith alone in Christ. Interestingly, both Whitefield's "Tabernacle" church and John Wesley's "The Foundery" were only a few miles from each other in London.

It is important to note this vital point. Today's emphasis upon evangelism, revivals, and the like are touted as fundamentally Arminian in theology, which is true for the most part. A common notion today is that one cannot be avidly evangelistic without being Arminian, that somehow Calvinism and evangelism are diametrically opposed.

Presbyterians and others who firmly believe in the doctrines of grace[58] (also known as the "Five Points of Calvinism") have been viewed as being

---

[57]   Dallimore, p. 319 who quotes *The Methodist Magazine*, p. 165.

anti-evangelistic. What is ironic is that some of the greatest evangelists in history were Calvinists. George Whitefield was staunchly a believer in the "Five Points of Calvinism" and regularly preached them. Who could ever accuse what many think was the greatest evangelist since the apostle Paul as anti-evangelistic? The Presbyterian pastor, Samuel Davies, was a contemporary of Whitefield. His ministry brought much revival to Virginia, being known as "the apostle to Virginia." Davies was also a thorough going Calvinist. One of the greatest Presbyterian American evangelists of the early to mid 19th Century was the renowned Daniel Baker, whose preaching in the northern but primarily southern states was very similar to George Whitefield's preaching. Baker was a powerful, fiery preacher who also was a Calvinist. Hence, the notion that the doctrines of grace are inhibitors to evangelism is a historical falsehood.

The renowned English preacher of the 19th Century, Charles Haddon Spurgeon, was a firm believer in the doctrines of grace and was simultaneously vigorous in evangelistic zeal. Spurgeon wrote:

> There is no soul living who holds more firmly to the doctrines of grace than I do, and if any man asks me whether I am ashamed to be called a Calvinist, I answer—I wish to be called nothing but a Christian; but if you ask me, do I hold the doctrinal views which were held by John Calvin, I reply, I do in the main hold them, and rejoice to avow it.[59]

Regarding his indebtedness to Whitefield, Spurgeon said:

> There is no end to the interest which attaches to such a man as George Whitefield. Often as I have read his life, I am conscious of distinct quickening whenever I turn to it. He lived. Other men seem to be only half alive; but Whitefield was all life, fire, wind, force. My own model, if I may have such a thing in due

---

[58]   "The Doctrines of Grace" is a term that is often associated with the term, "The Five Points of Calvinism." The term did not originate with John Calvin. It actually became associated with the Synod of Dordt in 1618-1619 that met over fifty years after Calvin's death. Historically, what became known as the five points of Calvinism were first known as the five points of the Synod of Dort in refutation to the five points of the Arminians that found expression in the theology of Jacob Arminius, a Dutch theologian who took exception to "Reformed Theology" that came out of the Protestant Reformation. These counter points of the Synod of Dort came to be known as the "Five Points of Calvinism." A common acronym for these points is known as "Tulip." The doctrines of grace were as follows: total depravity, unconditional election, limited atonement, irresistible grace, and the perseverance of the saints.

[59]   Curts and Jennings, *The Autobiography of Charles H. Spurgeon* Vol. 1, (Cincinnati - Chicago - St. Louis, 1898), p. 172.

subordination to my Lord, is George Whitefield; but with unequal footsteps must I follow in his glorious track.[60]

The two theological systems of Calvinism and Arminianism differ over how God applies His saving grace to sinners and the nature of one's ability as a sinner to believe in Jesus. While the differences are significant in this respect, both can preach Christ alone, calling men to repent and believe in Jesus alone for their salvation. This fact is probably why Whitefield often exhorted John Wesley not to make their theological differences a litmus test for reaching sinners for Christ. In other words, just because a man may not fully understand how God applies His saving grace to a sinner doesn't mean that God's saving grace hasn't come to a man.

Whitefield's American Ministry

George Whitefield made a total of seven voyages to America.[61] He was in America during these time frames: 1738, 1739-1741, 1744-1748, 1751-1752, 1754-1755, 1763-1765, 1769-1770. While Whitefield was not the origin of revivalism in the colonies, his 1739 visit to the New England colonies surely fueled the flames of what God had already begun several years earlier. In 1734-1735 a revival broke out in Northampton, Massachusetts under the preaching and ministry of Jonathan Edwards. Edwards would publish a report of this revival titled *A Faithful Narrative of the Surprising Work of God.* By 1738 Boston printers had already published three editions of Edwards' account and copies had reached London, England. George Whitefield had read Edwards' *Faithful Narrative* by the time he came to the New England colonies in 1739.

As I have sought to emphasize, any true revival begins with godly people praying for the Lord to pour out His Spirit. Not only did faithful prayers precede the revivals in England, but they also preceded revivals in the American colonies. In the summer of 1734, several Boston pastors agreed to propose days of prayer and fasting in their congregations. The pastors urged their people to humble themselves and ask forgiveness for not being more faithful in their use of the means of grace. The pastors urged their people to ask God for an effusion of his Spirit to revive the

---

[60]   Curts and Jennings, Vol. 2, p.66.

[61]   It took anywhere from a month to a month and a half to sail from England to America, and there were some instances where the storms were so violent that Whitefield thought he might perish at sea.

power of godliness among them.[62] During that summer, nothing of revival had yet occurred in Boston; however, the Boston pastors were receiving reports of an awakening under Jonathan Edwards at Northampton. This news encouraged the prayer warriors to continue in their prayers for a revival to spread throughout the country.

In 1738 some Boston pastors had received reports from England of Whitefield's phenomenal ministry and wrote him requesting him to come to Boston. A ministry that was always dear to the heart of Whitefield was the creation of an orphanage in the colony of Georgia. It would be a life long effort of raising money for the orphanage. When Whitefield came to America in 1739, he decided to first go to the geographic center of the colonies, Philadelphia. From there he would go to the other largest of the New England cities such as New York and Boston.

Whitefield arrived in Philadelphia on Friday November 2, 1739. He read prayers at the Church of England on Sunday and made acquaintances with some Presbyterian and Baptist ministers on Monday. He preached in the Church of England church on Tuesday and dined with Thomas Penn (son of William Penn) on Wednesday. On Thursday evening, he held his first open air service from the Philadelphia Court House stairs to a crowd of about 6000.[63]

It was in Philadelphia that Whitefield made his acquaintance with Benjamin Franklin, which became a life long cordial friendship. Benjamin Franklin, upon hearing Whitefield, remarked:

> Every accent, every emphasis, every modulation of voice, was so perfectly well turned and well placed, that, without being interested in the subject, one could not help being pleased with the discourse; a pleasure of much the same kind with that received from an excellent piece of musick.[64]

---

[62] Hamilton, Hill, *History of the Old South Church*, Vol. 1, (Boston: Houghton, Mifflin and Company, 1890), p. 503.

[63] Dallimore, Vol. 1, p. 432 who quoted from *Whitefield's Journals*, p. 343.

[64] Dallimore, p. 116, who quotes from *Memoirs of the Life and Writings of Benjamin Franklin*, Vol. 1, p. 87.

The ability of Whitefield to captivate an audience was best expressed by Benjamin Franklin. One of the dear projects to George Whitefield was an orphanage house in Georgia. He was always asking for a donation for this cause during his preaching. Franklin recounted this incident concerning Whitefield's desire to have people donate to the orphanage cause:

> I did not disapprove of the design, but, as Georgia was then destitute of materials and workmen, and it was proposed to send them from Philadelphia at a great expense, I thought it would have been better to have built the house here, and brought the children to it. This I advised; but he was resolute in his first project, rejected my counsel, and I therefore refused to contribute. I happened soon after to attend one of his sermons, in the course of which I perceived he intended to finish with a collection, and I silently resolved he should get nothing from me, I had in my pocket a handful of copper money, three or four silver dollars, and five pistoles in gold. As he proceeded I began to soften, and concluded to give the coppers. Another stroke of his oratory made me ashamed of that, and determined me to give the silver; and he finished so admirably, that I emptied my pocket wholly into the collector's dish, gold and all. At this sermon there was also one of our club, who, being of my sentiments respecting the building in Georgia, and suspecting a collection might be intended, had, by precaution, emptied his pockets before he came from home. Towards the conclusion of the discourse, however, he felt a strong desire to give, and applied to a neighbor, who stood near him, to borrow some money for the purpose.[65]

One of the amazing things about Whitefield's preaching was the apparent power of his voice to carry significant distances. Franklin[66] was skeptical of the newspaper accounts coming out of England that Whitefield was

---

[65] Quoted from www.raleighcharterhs.org/faculty/bnewmark/AP%20History/BenjaminFranklinon GeorgeWhitefield.htm.

[66] One of the saddest realities is that Benjamin Franklin, despite his friendship with Whitefield and hearing him preach, never embraced the Savior that Whitefield so eloquently and powerfully preached. Franklin said, "Mr. Whitefield used, indeed, to pray for my conversion, but he never had the satisfaction of believing that his prayers were heard. Ours was a mere civil friendship, sincere on both sides, and lasted to his death." A month before Franklin's death at age 84 in 1790, he responded to Yale president, Ezra Stiles, who asked him about his views of Jesus Christ. Franklin replied, "I think the system of morals and His religion, as he left them to us, the best the world ever saw or is likely to see... and I have with most of the present Dissenters in England, some doubts as to His divinity; tho' it is a question I do not dogmatize upon, having never studied it, and I think it needless to busy myself with now, when I expect soon an opportunity of knowing the truth with less trouble." Within a little over a month from making that statement, Franklin would pass into eternity without faith in Christ. What a great tragedy indeed! He would soon know the truth but in a way that he would regret for all eternity.

preaching to crowds of twenty-five thousand. Franklin wrote about Whitefield's preaching from the courthouse in Philadelphia:

> He preached one evening from the top of the Court House steps, which are in the middle of Market-street, and on the west side of Second-street, which crosses it at right angles. Both streets were filled with his hearers to a considerable distance. Being among the hindmost in Market-street, I had the curiosity to learn how far he could be heard, by retiring backwards down the street towards the river, and I found his voice distinct till I came near Front-street, when some noise in that street obscured it. Imagining then a semicircle, of which my distance should be the radius, and that it were filled with auditors, to each of whom I allowed two square feet, I computed that he might well be heard by more than thirty thousand. This reconciled me to the newspaper accounts of his having preached to twenty-five thousand people in the fields.[67]

Franklin was so impressed with Whitefield's abilities, and being one who always was looking for a business enterprise, decided to become Whitefield's principal publisher of his sermons in America. A printer once told Franklin that he could have sold a thousand sermons of Whitefield. In May 1740 Benjamin Franklin printed the first volumes of Whitefield's *Journals and Sermons*. He and Whitefield had developed a subscription and distribution network of merchants and booksellers which included James Franklin, John Smith, Benjamin Elliot, and Charles Harrison in Boston. Elliot purchased 250 sets and Harrison received 1,000 volumes.[68] The fifteen booksellers in Boston competed aggressively with each other to sell Whitefield's books before, during and after his tour to New England. Some published their own editions. In the peak revival year, 1740, Whitefield wrote or inspired thirty-nine titles, or 30 percent of all works published in America. From 1739 to 1742, one of the largest publishers in the colonies, Daniel Henchman of Boston, spent more than 30 percent of his printing budget on producing the evangelist's books.[69] News accounts in the *Boston Weekly News-Letter* and other sources all contributed to advance publicity for Whitefield. Rev. Thomas Prince of Boston noted the influence of all this printed publicity: "Accounts of the Rev. Mr. Whitefield as they *successively* arrived before his appearance

---

[67]   Dallimore, Vol. 1, p. 439.

[68]   Frank Lambert, *"Pedlar in Divinity": George Whitefield and the Transatlantic Revivals* (Princeton, N.J.: Princeton University Press, 1994), 123 which is taken from an internet article titled, Emmanuel Research Review Issue No. 24 - January/February 2007 - History of Revivalism in Boston.

[69]   Lambert, p. 128.

here... prepar'd the Way for his Entertainment and successful Labours among us."[70]

While in Philadelphia, William Tennent paid a visit to Whitefield, which prompted Whitefield to later write:

> He and his sons are secretly despised by the generality of the Synod, as Mr. Erskine and his brethren are hated by the judicatories of Edinburgh, and as much as the Methodist preachers are by their brethren in England. Though we are but few and stand alone, as it were like Elijah, yet I doubt not the Lord will appear for us and make us more than conquerors.[71]

After nine days in Philadelphia, Whitefield traveled to New York. At New Brunswick, he made his acquaintance with Gilbert Tennent, suggesting that they travel together to New York. There developed a mutual esteem between these two preachers. Upon hearing Gilbert Tennent preach, Whitefield commented:

> I never before heard such a searching sermon. He convinced me more and more that we can preach the gospel no further than we have experienced the power of it in our own hearts. Being deeply convicted of sin at his first conversion, he has learned experimentally to dissect the heart of a natural man. Hypocrites must either soon be converted or enraged at his preaching... He is a son of thunder and does not fear the faces of men.[72]

Upon reaching New York, Whitefield was denied use of the pulpit of the Church of England by Rev. Vessey who did not appreciate at all Whitefield's ministry. Whitefield's practice, as an ordained Church of England minister, was to first go to his denomination's churches. Only when denied the pulpits, did he go elsewhere, although he began to receive numerous requests to preach in various other churches. With this particular refusal in New York, he preached in a field and received an invitation by Dr. Pemberton at Wall Street Presbyterian Church.

An anonymous writer[73] published a letter to the *New England Journal* of his observations of Whitefield's preaching. Similar to what happened among English crowds that heard Whitefield, those who came to hear him

---

70 Lambert, p. 127.
71 Dallimore, Vol. 1, p. 433 who quotes from *Whitefield's Journals*, p. 344.
72 Dallimore, Vol. 1, p. 434 who quotes from *Whitefield's Journals*, pp. 347-48.
73 Dallimore says that some of the contemporaries of the time thought that the anonymous writer was Rev. Pemberton of the Presbyterian Church.

preach were divided into two groups – one that was very serious and attentive and the other that stood on the outskirts of the audience giggling, scoffing, talking, and laughing.

The anonymous writer gives us a glimpse of Whitefield's preaching in America, which was similar to observers in England. In hearing Whitefield at the Presbyterian Church, he wrote:

> I never in my life saw so attentive an audience. Mr. Whitefield spoke as one having authority: all he said was *demonstration, life, and power*. The people's eyes and ears hung on his lips. They greedily devoured every word. I came home astonished. Every scruple vanished; I never saw or heard the like; and I said within myself, surely God is with this man of truth!

> …He is of sprightly cheerful temper and acts and moves with great agility. The endowments of his mind are very uncommon. His wit is quick and piercing, his imagination lively and florid; and, as far as I can discern, both are under the direction of an exact and solid judgment. He has a most ready memory and, I think, speaks entirely without notes. He has a clear and musical voice, and a wonderful command of it. He uses much gesture, but with great propriety. Every *accent* of his voice, and every *motion* of his body, speaks, and both are natural and unaffected. If his delivery be the product of art, 'tis certainly the perfection of it, for it is entirely concealed. He has great mastery of words, but studies *much plainness of speech.*

> ... He speaks much the language of the New Testament; and has an admirable faculty in explaining the Scriptures… He expresses the highest love and concern for the souls of men; and speaks of Christ with the most affectionate appropriation – *My Master*!

> … He prays most earnestly, that God would destroy all that *bigotry* and party zeal that has divided Christians. He supposes some of Christ's flock are to be found under every denomination… He declares that his whole view in preaching is to bring men to Christ, to deliver them from their false *confidences*, to raise them from their dead formalities, to revive primitive Christianity among them; and if he can he will leave them to their

liberty, and they may go to what church, and worship God in what form they like best.[74]

Upon leaving New York, Whitefield's itinerary would take him up the New England coast, but before leaving New York, he would write a letter to Jonathan Edwards at Northampton, desiring to meet him. Part of Whitefield's letter states:

> I am but a stripling, but the Lord chooses the weak things of this world to confound the strong. I should rejoice to be instructed by you.[75]

On September 19, 1740, Whitefield arrived in Boston where he met with Governor Belcher, who was moved to tears during their personal meetings together. While in Boston, Whitefield met with Anglican clergy who questioned him on his beliefs. They questioned whether he should be meeting with persons of other denominations. Whitefield recounted the nature of the questioning:

> … One of them began with me for calling "that Tennent and his brethren *faithful* ministers of Jesus Christ." I answered, "I believed they were." They then questioned me about the validity of the Presbyterian ordination. I replied, "I believe it was valid."[76]

His alienation among many of his Anglican brethren was augmented when he engaged in further discussion with the Anglican Commissary in Boston, Dr. Cutler. Whitefield commented to Dr. Cutler:

> … I saw regenerate souls among the Baptists, among the Presbyterians, among the Independents, and among the Church folk – all children of God, and yet all born again in a different way of worship.[77]

---

[74]   Dallimore, Vol. 1, pp. 435-36 who quotes from Prince, 1743, pp. 361-63. We can see from Whitefield's practice that this set somewhat a precedent among future evangelists, especially those of the 20th Century in encouraging people to go to the churches of their choice since there were people of all sorts who heard him. While I cannot say that this was a good practice on Whitefield's part, it is understandable in one sense. Whitefield's goal was to reach as many people as possible with the gospel. It is clear from his sermons and correspondences that he was a Calvinist in his theology and preached the doctrines of grace, but he was not out to start a new denomination. He would remain loyal to the Church of England; it was many Anglican pulpits that refused their pulpits to him, not liking what he preached.

[75]   Dallimore, Vol. 1, p. 437 who quotes from *The Works of George Whitefield*, Vol. 1, (Edinburgh: Banner of Truth, 1976), p. 121.

[76]   Dallimore, Vol. 1, p. 529 who quotes from *Whitefield's Journals*, pp. 456-57.

[77]   Dallimore, Vol. 1, p. 530 who quotes *Whitefield's Journals*, pp. 457-59.

He preached at Brattle Street Church where 2,000 people quickly gathered to hear him. Rev. Thomas Prince[78] observed that Whitefield preached in the demonstration of the Spirit and power. When it came to application, Prince said that Whitefield would address himself to the audience in such a tender, earnest, and moving way to come to the Redeemer that the assembly simply melted into tears.[79] On Saturday afternoon September 20, he spoke to 5,000 people on Boston Common.[80] On Sunday afternoon, he spoke to a huge crowd of 12,000-15,000 people at the Boston Common.[81] When Whitefield spoke in Boston churches, they were often crowded with people squeezed into the pews, standing in the aisles, filling the pulpit area and stairways, and stretching to look in the windows. On one occasion at the Old South Church, the crowd was so immense that Whitefield had to enter through a window.[82]

On Wednesday September 24, Whitefield went over to Cambridge and spoke twice at Harvard Yard to a large audience (numbered at 7000) of students, teachers, and a great number of ministers from nearby areas. President Holyoke of Harvard said of the work of Whitefield and Gilbert Tennent:

> Indeed, these two pious and valuable men of God, who have been laboring more abundantly among us, have been greatly instrumental, in the hands of God, to revive this blessed work; and many, no doubt have been savingly converted from the error of their ways, many more have been convicted, and all have been in some measure roused from their lethargy.[83]

Harvard College, founded in 1636, was the oldest institution of higher learning in America, having been created for the purpose of training clergymen. After Whitefield's preaching at Harvard, Benjamin Coleman wrote, "At Cambridge the college is a new creature; the students full of God."[84] In June 1741 the Harvard visiting committee of the overseers commented, "They find of late an extraordinary and happy impressions of

---

[78] Rev. Thomas Prince was an American clergyman, scholar, and historian noted for his historical text, *A Chronological History of New England, in the Form of Annals*. He was an avid supporter of the First Great Awakening, who invited Whitefield to preach at his Old South Church in Boston. In 1743 he wrote *An Account of the Revival of Religion in Boston in the Years 1740-1743.*

[79] Hill, Vol. 1, p. 506.

[80] Edwin Scott Gaustad, *The Great Awakening in New England* (New York: Harper & Brothers, 1957), 26. *Quoting The Boston Weekly News-Letter*, 25 Sept. 1740.

[81] Hill, Vol. 1, p. 506.

[82] Dallimore, Vol.1, p. 533.

[83] Hill, Vol. 1, p.508 footnote.

[84] Hill, Vol. 1, p. 510 footnote.

a religious nature have been made on the minds of a great number of students."[85]

On Sunday, October 12, 1740, his final day in Boston, Whitefield preached to an estimated 23,000 on the Boston Common as his farewell sermon. Whitefield wrote that this was probably the largest gathering of people in America up to that time. Those present exceeded the entire population of Boston (17,000 in 1740). He said that numbers, great numbers, melted into tears when he talked of leaving them.[86]

What was the effect of Whitefield's preaching in Boston? Luke Tyerman summarized it:

> This wondrous movement continued a year and a half after Whitefield's departure from Boston. Thirty Religious Societies were instituted in the city. Ministers, besides attending to their usual work, preached in private houses almost every night. Chapels were always crowded. The very face of the town seemed to be strangely altered... Dr. Coleman in a letter to Dr. Isaac Watts, "our Sabbaths are joyous, our churches increase and our ministers have new life and spirit in their work."[87]

Massachusetts governor, Jonathan Belcher, was highly impressed with Whitefield and escorted him in his coach from one location to another. The governor was already known for his Christian character and determination to apply biblical principles as a civil ruler. This is manifested in Rev. William Cooper's sermon before the governor and the two houses of the Massachusetts government on May 28, 1740 (several months before Whitefield's Boston tour).[88] On one occasion, while Whitefield was in Boston, Gov. Belcher said, "Mr. Whitefield, do not spare rulers, any more than ministers, no, not the chief of them." Another time after one of Whitefield's sermons, Gov. Belcher stated, "I pray God, I may apply what has been said to my own heart. Pray, Mr. Whitefield, that I may hunger and thirst after righteousness."[89] A newspaper stated, "Mr. Whitefield has not a warmer friend anywhere than in the first man among us. Our Governor can call him nothing less than the Apostle Paul. He has shown

---

[85]   Justin Winsor, editor, *The Memorial History of Boston*, 4 vols. (Boston: Ticknor and Company., 1881), 1:234 as quoted from Emmanuel Research Review Issue No. 24 - January/February 2007 - History of Revivalism in Boston.

[86]   Dallimore, Vol. 1, p. 534 who quotes from *Whitefield's Journals*, p. 472.

[87]   Dallimore, Vol. 1, p. 536 who quotes Tyerman's *Whitefield*, Vol. 1, p. 425.

[88]   See this book's Appendix A for William Cooper's great sermon titled *The Honors of Christ Demanded of the Magistrate*.

[89]   Dallimore, Vol. 1, p. 536 who quotes from *Whitefield's Journals*, p. 475.

him the highest respects and carried him in his coach from place to place; and could not help following him fifty miles out of town."[90]

On Monday morning, October 13, Whitefield continued his whirlwind tour of New England, preaching over 175 sermons.[91] By Friday of that week, Whitefield had reached Northampton where both he and Jonathan Edwards were looking forward to meeting with one another. As noted earlier, Whitefield had read Jonathan Edwards' *A Faithful Narrative of the Surprising Work of God,* recounting a revival that occurred in Northampton in 1734-1735. Whitefield recounted his four day stay at Northampton:

> Their pastor's name is Edwards, successor and grandson to the great Stoddard, whose memory will always be precious to my soul, and whose books entitled, "A Guide to Christ," and "Safety of Appearing in Christ's Righteousness," I would recommend to all... Mr. Edwards is a solid, excellent Christian, but at present weak in body... Saturday, Oct. 18 at Mr. Edwards' request, I spoke to his little children, who were much affected... Sunday, Oct. 19. Felt great satisfaction in being at the house of Mr. Edwards. A sweeter couple I have not yet seen. Their children were not dressed in silks and satins, but plain, as becomes the children of those who, in all things, ought to be examples of Christian simplicity. Mrs. Edwards is adorned with a meek and quiet spirit...[92]

Edwards would later state that Whitefield's visit with his girls bore much fruit.[93] And, Whitefield's preaching had a great impact on Jonathan and Sarah Edwards, as well as all those in the town. On Sunday, Jonathan wept during the whole sermon according to Whitefield who wrote:

> Preached this morning, and good Mr. Edwards wept during the whole time of exercise... Oh, that my soul may be refreshed with the joyful news, that Northampton people have recovered their

---

[90] Dallimore, Vol. 1, p. 537 who quotes from a Postscript to the *South Carolina Gazette*, No. 361. This issue contained serial accounts of Whitefield's ministry in Boston, written at the request of Josiah Smith, Whitefield's defender at Charleston. In publishing these accounts Smith doubtless intended they should be news to Whitefield's multitude of friends in the southern Colonies and also that they should serve as an additional rebuttal to Commissary Garden.

[91] Harry S. Stout, "Whitefield, George," *Dictionary of Christianity in America,* ed. Daniel G. Reid (Downers Grove, Ill: Intervarsity Press, 1990), p. 1252.

[92] Dallimore, Vol. 1, pp. 537-38 who quotes from *Whitefield's Journals,* p. 475.

[93] Marsden, p. 207.

first love, that the Lord has revived His work in their souls, and caused them to do their first works.[94]

Jonathan Edwards was weeping as he was reminded of Northampton's former revival. Regarding this 1740 visit, Edwards would later write:

> Mr. Whitefield preached four sermons in the meeting-house (besides a private lecture at my house). The congregation was extraordinarily melted by each sermon, almost the whole assembly being in tears for a great part of the time. Mr. Whitefields' sermons were suitable to the circumstances of the town; containing just reproofs of our backslidings, and in a most moving and affectionate manner, making use of our great profession and great mercies, as arguments with us to return to God, from whom we had departed. Immediately after this, the minds of the people in general appeared more engaged in religion, shewing a great forwardness to make religion the subject of their conversation, and to embrace all opportunities to hear the Word preached... In about a month there was a great alteration in the town, both as to the revival of professors, and awakening of others...[95]

From Whitefield's preaching at Northampton we have an account of the style of Whitefield's preaching from the perspective of Sarah Edwards who wrote a letter to her brother to prepare him for Whitefield's preaching in his area. Sarah wrote:

> Dear Brother James,
>
> I want to prepare you for a visit from the Rev. Mr. Whitefield, the famous preacher of England. He has been sojourning with us a week or more, and, after visiting a few of the neighbouring towns, is going to New Haven, and from thence to New York. He is truly a remarkable man, and during his visit has, I think, verified all that we have heard of him.
>
> He makes less of the doctrines [of grace] than our American preachers generally do, and aims more at affecting the heart. He is a born orator. You have already heard of his deep-toned, yet clear and melodious voice. O it is perfect music to listen to that alone! And he speaks so easily, without any apparent effort. You remember that David Hume thought it worth going twenty miles

---

94   Dallimore, Vol. 1, p. 538 who quotes *Whitefield's Journals*, pp. 476-77.
95   Dallimore, Vol. 1, p. 538 who quotes from Prince's, *Christian History*, Vol. of 1743, p. 368.

to hear him speak; and Garrick said, 'He could move men to tears or make them tremble by his simple intonations in pronouncing the word Mesopotamia.'

Well, this last was a mere speech of the play-actor; but it is truly wonderful to see what a spell this preacher often casts over an audience by proclaiming the simplest truths of the Bible. I have seen upward of a thousand people hang on his words with breathless silence, broken only by an occasional half-suppressed sob. He impresses the ignorant, and not less the educated and refined. It is reported, you know, that as the miners of England listened to him the tears made white furrows down their smutty cheeks, and so here our mechanics shut up their shops, and the day-labourers throw down their tools to go and hear him preach, and few go away unaffected.

A prejudiced person, I know, might say that this is all theatrical artifice and display; but not so will any one think who has seen and known him. He is a very devout and godly man, and his only aim seems to be to reach and influence men the best way. He speaks from a heart all aglow with love, and pours out a torrent of eloquence which is almost irresistible. Many, very many persons in Northampton date the beginning of new thoughts, new desires, new purposes, and a new life, from the day on which they heard him preach of Christ and this salvation.[96]

As an aside, I should clarify something about Sarah's statement, "He makes less of the doctrines of grace than our American preachers generally do, and aims more at affecting the heart." While Whitefield's preaching may not have been expositions on the doctrines of grace like others, he wholeheartedly believed them and preached them. Whitefield's strained relationship with John and Charles Wesley was precisely over the doctrines of grace.

In his book, George Marsden makes this observation of the different preaching styles of Whitefield and Edwards:

In public, Whitefield was a born actor. He preached without notes, had a splendid voice that Benjamin Franklin calculated could readily be heard by 25,000, and was a master of painting vivid pictures that would draw an audience emotionally into the theme

---

[96] Dallimore, Vol. 1, pp. 538-39 who quotes from Tyerman's *Whitefield,* Vol. 1, pp. 428-29.

of the text… Seldom did he preach a sermon in which he did not weep and reduce multitudes to tears. Edwards, despite his efforts to emulate his grandfather, had still not learned to preach with notes only, let alone extempore without them. He could depict some powerful images, but he seldom sustained them. The power of his preaching came from his relentless systematic delineation of al the implications of his theme. Although his personal intensity could hold audiences spellbound, his voice was weak. He almost never referred to himself or his own experiences.[97]

Whitefield had five more visits to America with the last being from 1769-1770, where he died in Massachusetts. His influence upon America was phenomenal.

Whitefield's Scottish Ministry

As with most places that Whitefield traveled, his preaching would have remarkable success in Scotland. During the time period from 1741-1768, he would make a total of fifteen visits to Scotland. The first began on July 24, 1741 when he set sail for Edinburgh.

Scotland had a rich Protestant and Presbyterian heritage reaching back to John Knox's ministry during the 16th Century. Scotland had sent some of the finest delegates to the Westminster Assembly in 1643. Some of these most influential delegates were Samuel Rutherford, Robert Ballie, and George Gillespie. *The Solemn League and Covenant* was a tremendous document that was essentially a treaty between England and Scotland for the preservation of the reformed religion in Scotland according to the word of God, and was a polemic against popery and prelacy. With the onset of the 17th Century and while lip service was made to the *Westminster Confession of Faith*, spiritual life was at low ebb. With the publication the old Puritan book *The Marrow of Modern Divinity,* a split occurred in the Church of Scotland between the moderates (who vigorously opposed the book) and the lesser group, the evangelicals. The book advocated personal preaching, a life of spiritual joy, and evangelistic zeal. The evangelicals were calling for a return to true biblical doctrine and gospel zeal. Two of the leading figures among the evangelicals were Ebenezer and Ralph Erskine. They were the first to invite Whitefield to Scotland. Their

---

[97]   Marsden, p. 206.

churches were crowded, and they were also doing field preaching before large crowds.

During the 1730's, the Erskines and others of similar thinking were suspended from the ministry. They then formed "The Associate Presbytery," which later became "The Secession Church." Upon hearing of the Erskine's activity in Scotland, Whitefield corresponded to the Erskines in 1739. Ralph Erskine wrote Whitefield stating:

> Come, if possible, dear Whitefield, come. There is no face on earth I would desire more earnestly to see than you...Yet I would desire it *only* in a way that, I think, would tend most to the advancing of our Lord's kingdom, and the reformation work, among *our* hands. Such is the situation... among us, that, unless you come with a design to meet and abide with us of "The Associate Presbytery"... I would dread the consequences of your coming, lest it should seem equally countenance our persecutors. Your fame would occasion a flocking to you, to whatever side you turn; and if it should be in their pulpits, as no doubt some of them would urge, we know how it would be improven against us.[98]

We learn additional information about Whitefield's ministry in general by his reply to Ralph Erskine. Whitefield wrote:

> This I cannot altogether agree to. I come only as an occasional preacher, to preach the simple Gospel to all who are willing to hear me, of whatever denomination. It will be wrong of me to join in a reformation as to church government, any further than I have light given me from above... I write this that there may not be the least mis-understanding between us. I love and honour "The Associate Presbytery"... But let them not be offended, if, in all things, I cannot immediately fall in with them.[99]

---

98   Dallimore, Vol. 2, p. 86 who quotes from Tyerman's *Whitefield*, Vol. 1, pp. 504-05.
99   Dallimore, Vol. 2, p. 86 who quotes from Tyerman's *Whitefield*, Vol. 1, p. 505.

Upon Whitefield's arrival in Scotland on July 29, 1741, it was not the Erskines who met him but a group of the Evangelicals. Whitefield did meet with the Associate Presbytery, but it did not go well. The Erskines wanted him to only preach for them and to persuade him to leave the Church of England. This Whitefield would not do; so he parted from them. He would later explain what he meant by having a catholic spirit:

> ... I believe the Church of Scotland to be the best constituted National Church in the world; but, then, I would bear and converse with all others, who do not err in fundamentals, and who give evidence that they are true lovers of the Lord Jesus. This is what I mean by a *catholic spirit.*[100]

Upon his second visit to Scotland, Whitefield preached at Cambusang, which was on the outskirts of Glasgow. An immense crowd gathered to hear him. One Scottish preacher who participated in the revival that occurred here was William McCulloch who did not possess great pulpit skills, but he was a man of great earnestness and prayer. Through him the societies for prayer became greatly strengthened.

During Whitefield's third visit to Scotland in 1748, it was marked by a serious decline in his personal health that would plague him the rest of his life. He had apparently burst a blood vessel in his throat straining to preach against the wind. Henceforth, he would experience pain in breathing the remainder of his life until his death in 1770, but considering when this occurred, he still preached for another twenty-two years.

Whitefield's Departure into Glory

The departure from this life into eternal glory for George Whitefield came on a Sunday morning on September 30, 1770. He was only fifty-five years

---

[100]   Dallimore, Vol. 2, p. 92 who quotes from *Letters of George Whitefield, 1734-42,* p. 515. With regards to his views on church government, and with the greatest respect and admiration that I have for him, this is one area of weakness in that he did not believe that Scripture taught any particular form of church government. I do believe the Scripture mandates a Presbyterian form of church government. Some of the greatest defenses of this can be found in two books. The first is a 1646 work put together by the ministers of Sion College in London titled *Jus Divinum Regiminis Ecclesiastici: The Divine right of Church Government.* The second work is an 1856 work by Thomas Witherow titled *The Apostolic Church: Which is it?* Whitefield always remained in the Church of England. He viewed his ministry as encompassing all who would hear the gospel. In this regard, his catholic spirit is commendable; he simply wanted as many people as possible to hear and believe in the gospel. Whitefield understood that the gospel transcends all denominational affiliations, and in this sense, he was right. With this being true, however, the Scripture does teach a Presbyterian form of church government.

old. His ministry had spanned nearly thirty years. He died in Newburyport, Massachusetts.

The end of this remarkable man's life was only fitting. His last sermon, which some said was one of his best, was two hours in length. His text was II Corinthians 13:5 on "examine yourselves, whether ye be in the faith." This was in the open air. It was almost as if he had a sense of his impending death. One who heard his sermon that day wrote the following of what Whitefield actually preached:

> "I go," he cried, "I go to a rest prepared; my sun has arisen, and by aid from Heaven has given light to many. It is now about to set – no, it is about to rise to the zenith of immortal glory. Many may outlive me on earth, but they cannot outlive me in Heaven. Oh, thought divine I shall soon be in a world where time, age, pain, and sorrow are unknown. My body fails, my spirit expands. How willingly would I live to preach Christ! But I die to be with Him!"[101]

Following this two hour sermon, Whitefield traveled to the home of the Rev. Jonathan Parsons, the pastor of the Old South Presbyterian Chruch at Newburyport, Massachusetts. Parsons is said to have asked Whitefield at the supper hour, "I asked Mr. Whitefield how he felt himself after his journey. He said, "He was tired, therefore he supped early, and would go to bed."[102]

By the time Whitefield was retiring to go to bed, the street in front of Parsons' house was filled with people. As Whitefield was ascending the stairs to his bedroom, several people at the door begged him to preach. Not wanting to turn them away, Whitefield stood on the landing with a candle in hand, preaching Christ. He kept preaching until the candle flickered out and died away.

The last recorded account of someone seeing Whitefield alive was Richard Smith who said he saw Whitefield reading his Bible with Dr. Watt's Psalms lying open before him. Whitefield asked for some water and then knelt down by his bedside to pray. At about 2 AM, he awakened wanting some cider to drink. Smith said he was panting for breath. Smith wished he would not preach so often, but Whitefield replied, "I had rather wear out than rust out." At quarter past four he awakened exclaiming, "My asthma,

---

[101] Dallimore, Vol. 2, pp. 503-504.
[102] Dallimore. who quotes from John Gilles, *Memoirs of the Life of the Reverend George Whitefield*, p. 270.

my asthma is coming on... I am almost suffocated, I can scarce breathe; my asthma quite chokes me." At five o'clock, Whitefield arose to open the window for air. Soon he turned to Richard Smith saying, "I am dying... soon the doctor came in only to witness the great evangelist take his last breath at six o'clock.[103]

One of the world's greatest preachers since the apostle Paul went to his heavenly reward. How true was his statement made earlier during the day- "I will soon rise to the zenith of immortal glory." The news of his death spread quickly throughout New England. Some New Englanders said that if he died in America he should be buried beneath the pulpit of Newburyport Presbyterian Church, and so he was.

As Whitefield's coffin was placed at the foot of the pulpit, Rev. Mr. Daniel Rogers made a moving prayer and openly confessed that he owed his own conversion to the labors of the dear man of God. Then he cried out, "Oh my father, my father!" then stooped and wept though his heart would break, and the people wept all through the place. Then he recovered and finished his prayer, and sat down and wept.

Memorial services were held in various places where he had preached. The official memorial service was preached in London by none other than John Wesley. Before parting on his last voyage from England to America, Whitefield had informed Robert Keen that if he were to die in America, he wished John Wesley to preach his funeral sermon. Wesley's sermon was from the Scripture, "Let me die the death of the righteous, and let my last end be like his" (Numbers 23:10).

Part of Wesley's sermon reads:

> If it be enquired, what was the foundation of this integrity, or of his sincerity, courage, patience, and every other valuable and amiable quality, it is easy to give an answer... It was no other than faith in a bleeding Lord; faith of the operation of God... It was the love of God shed abroad in his heart by the Holy Ghost, which was given unto him, filling his soul with tender, disinterested love to every child of man.
>
> From this source arose that torrent of eloquence, which frequently bore down all before it, from this, that astonishing force of persuasion, which the most hardened sinners could not resist. This

---

[103]   Dallimore. p. 271 of Gilles.

it was which often made his head as waters, and his eyes as a fountain of tears. This it was which enabled him to pour out his soul in prayer, in a manner peculiar to himself, with such fullness and ease united together, with such strength and variety, both of sentiment and expression.

I may close this head with observing what an honour it pleased God to put upon His faithful servant, by allowing him to declare His everlasting Gospel in so many various countries, to such numbers of people, and with so great an effect on so many of their precious souls .

Have we read or heard of any person since the apostles, who testified the Gospel of the grace of God, through so widely extended a space, through so large a part of the habitable world? Have we read or heard of any person, who called so many thousands, so many myriads of sinners to repentance? Above all, have we read or heard of any, who has been a blessed instrument in the hand of God, of bringing so many sinners from darkness to light, and from the power of Satan unto God?[104]

Whitefield's Uniqueness and Legacy

Scores of Londoners, who were being spiritually starved, turned to religious societies. This was the ecclesiastical climate to which George Whitefield was immersed. His preaching style and sermons stood in stark contrast to many of his fellow Anglican clergy. His sermons were marked with clarity that most could understand. The well spring of his sermons came from an intense personal holiness that marked him. He simply poured forth with great boldness biblical truths that he personally cherished. His love for Christ and zeal for His glory could not help but be manifested in his sermons. One of the most outstanding characteristics of his preaching was his conveyance of truth as one having authority from God. Whitefield viewed himself as Christ's herald, but then this is what every true preacher is – a herald of truth originating from the King of the universe. Many of Whitefield's hearers viewed him as a messenger from heaven. Some referred to him as "The Seraph."

The chief characteristics of his preaching were its biblical content, its doctrinal emphasis, and its simplicity. His most distributed sermon was

---

[104] Dallimore, p. 532 who quotes Tyerman's *Whitefield*, Vol. 2, pp. 616-617.

titled *The New Birth*. One of his most theological of his early sermons was titled "*Of Justification By Christ*." This two fold emphasis on the Spirit's transforming power by regeneration and the necessity of us being justified by God's free grace constituted the primary thrust of Whitefield's ministry.

His sermons were marked with great conviction and with such clarity that most could understand. Amazingly, he declared that he was preaching nothing but the basic doctrines of the Church of England, that is, the *Thirty-Nine Articles*. As mentioned earlier, Whitefield's life was marked by great personal holiness that just overflowed into his preaching. His zeal for the truth, and the excitement which he conveyed in his sermons was contagious. Simply put, people were starving for biblical truth and Whitefield fed them. Wherever he preached, crowds followed, wanting to hear more.

Believers and unbelievers both marveled at Whitefield's preaching. Henry St. John, Viscount Bolingbroke (1678-1751), who "professed himself a deist," was forced to exclaim, after hearing Whitefield preach:

> The most extraordinary man of our times, the most commanding eloquence, unquenchable zeal, and unquestionable piety.[105]

David Hume, agnostic philosopher, heard Whitefield preach and made these comments about his preaching and one of his sermons:

> Mr. Whitefield is the most ingenious preacher I ever heard; it is worth going twenty miles to hear him... After a solemn pause Mr. Whitefield thus addressed his numerous auditory: "the attendant angel is just about to leave the threshold of this sanctuary and ascend to heaven. Shall he ascend and not bear with him the news of one sinner among all this multitude reclaimed from the errors of his way? To give the greater effect to this exclamation he stamped with his foot, lifted hand and eyes to heaven, and gushing with tears, cried aloud, "Stop Gabriel! Stop, ere you enter the sacred portals, and yet carry with you the news of one sinner converted to God!" He then, in the most simple but energetic language described what he called the Saviour's dying love to sinful man, so that almost the whole assembly was melted into tears. This

---

[105] Willard Connely, *The True Chesterfield: Manners—Women—Education* (London: Cassell and Co. Ltd., 1939), p. 179.

address was accompanied with such animated yet natural action that it surpassed anything I ever saw or heard in any preacher.[106]

Shortly after the evangelist's death, Augustus Montague Toplady (1740-1778), author of the famous hymn "Rock of Ages, Cleft for Me," and Calvinist apologist, remembered him as "the apostle of the English empire."[107]

J.I. Packer has mentioned three areas that marked Whitefield's success as a preacher. Packer states:

> First, the Anglican evangelist addressed his hearers simply as fellow human beings, so that distinctions of rich and poor, educated and uneducated, ceased to matter. Whitefield spoke in such a way that he was readily understood and appreciated by the poor and uneducated as well as by the wealthy and learned.
>
> Then, he put spiritual issues to his hearers as one who transparently loved them and longed for them to be delivered out of the bondage of sin. "He speaks from a heart all aglow with love," Sarah recalled. And many who came to mock the preacher and laugh at his doctrine went away sobered and ultimately converted as they heard of the love of God in Christ for sinners and felt that love through the medium of Whitefield's impassioned preaching.[108]

Harry S. Stout viewed Whitefield's impact on America as America's first cultural hero. "By 1750 virtually every American loved and admired Whitefield and saw him as their champion."[109] And, William Cooper, who

---

[106]   Dallimore, Vol.2, p. 274 who quoted from J.P. Gledstone, *Life and Travels of George Whitefield*, 1871, pp. 378-379. Hume, Bolingbroke, and Benjamin Franklin, all were astounded at Whitefield's preaching but never embraced the Jesus that Whitefield so passionately preached. This only proves that salvation is truly a gift of God, and unless one has ears to hear, having had his heart regenerated by the Holy Spirit,, one can never believe in Christ. These men heard Whitefield mightily preach, but they never heard Jesus preaching to them through the anointed preacher.

[107]   "A Concise Character of the Late Rev. Mr. Whitefield", *The Works of Augustus Toplady, B.A.* (London: J. Chidley, 1837), p. 494.

[108]   "George Whitefield: Man Alive. A Review Article," *Crux*, 16, No.4 (December 1980), p. 26.

[109]   Harry S. Stout, "Heavenly Comet," *Christian History*, pp. 13-14. Harry Stout is Professor of History, Religious Studies, and American Studies at Yale Divinity School. He is a noted historian for this time period. He has published *The New England Soul: Preaching and Religious Culture in Colonial New England* (1986) and *George Whitefield, Divine Dramatist* (1991), and several edited books, including *New Directions in American Religious History* (1997) with Darryl Hart, *Religion in American History: A Reader* (1997). He is the General Editor of the Works of Jonathan Edwards (Yale Press); the Co-Director with Jon Butler of the Center for Religion and American Society at Yale.

died when Whitefield was twenty-nine years of age, called him "the wonder of the age."[110]

John Newton (the one who wrote the famous hymn *Amazing Grace*) was a contemporary of Whitefield and the Wesleys. Concerning Whitefield, Newton said:

> ... what a change has taken place throughout the land within little more than 30 years... and how much of this change has been owing to Mr. Whitefield's labours, is well known to many who have lived throughout this period... the Lord gave him a manner of preaching, which was peculiarly his own. He copied from none, and I never met anyone who could imitate him with success... his familiar address, the power of his action, his marvelous talent in fixing the attention even on the most careless, I need not describe to those who have heard him, and to those who have not, the attempt would be in vain. Other ministers could, perhaps, preach the gospel as clearly, in general say the same things, but no man living could say them in his way.[111]

Arnold Dallimore captured the essence of Whitefield's success as a preacher. He said:

> Yes it would be very misleading to assume that there was anything of a mere performance in Whitefield's preaching. On the contrary, it was the utter lack of anything artificial, and its burning sincerity which were its most noticeable qualities. His delivery was simply the outflow of that spiritual passion which inflamed his whole life.
>
> These are, however, but the human explanations of Whitefield's success. They reveal the possession of exceptional abilities, but his effectiveness lay not in his eloquence nor his zeal. As we look back from our present standpoint we see that God's chosen time to "arise and have mercy upon Zion... yea, the set time (had) come," and that in raising up Whitefield, He had granted upon him and his ministry "a mighty effusion of the Holy Ghost;" and it was this, the Divine power, which was the first secret of his success.[112]

One of the most striking features about Whitefield was his humility. He was not out for self-glory. At age twenty he shuttered at the thought of

---

[110]　Michael Haykin, "The Revived Puritan: The spirituality of George Whitefield (1714-1770)."

[111]　Dallimore, Vol. 2, pp. 531-532, 533-534.

[112]　Dallimore, Vol. 1, pp. 116-117.

entering the ministry, knowing the awesome responsibility attached to it. With the immensity of the crowds that would gather to hear him, it would be a great temptation to be filled with pride. Whitefield in renouncing any desire to form an organization associated with his name, said, "Let the name of Whitefield perish, but Christ alone be glorified, I wish only to be simply the servant of all."[113] While Whitefield was human and a sinner, he understood the temptations in this respect. He wrote:

> I used to plead with Him to take me by the hand and lead me unhurt through this fiery furnace. He heard my request and gave me to see the vanity of all commendations but His own.[114]

The effect of Whitefield's preaching was profound, to put it mildly. He was the original founder of Methodism. It has its roots in him. Sir James Stephen said this about Whitefield's preaching:

> The fervor with which he habitually spoke, the want of all aids to the voice... and the toil of rendering himself distinctly audible to thousands and tens of thousands, and... The result is among the most curious of well authenticated marvels. If the time spent in traveling from place to place in some brief intervals of repose in preparation be subtracted, his whole life may be said to have been consumed in the delivery of one continuous, scarcely interrupted sermon.[115]

Augustus Toplady said of Whitefield:

> It appears from a little account book, wherein that great man of God, the Rev. Mr. George Whitfield, minuted the times and places of his ministerial labors, that he preached upwards of 18,000 sermons, from the era of his ordination to that of his death.[116]

These 18,000 sermons do not include what Whitefield termed "exhortations" in society rooms.

He possessed an amazing ability to simplify spiritual truths that reached all strata of society; yet he particularly appealed to children from reports regarding his preaching in the Moorfields of London. Whitfield's *Works* that were published shortly after his death contained fifty-seven sermons.

---

[113]   Dallimore, Vol. 2, p. 518.
[114]   Dallimore, Vol. 2, p. 517.
[115]   Dallimore, Vol. 2, p. 522 who quotes Sir James Stephen, *Essays in Ecclesiastical Biography*, pp. 384-385.
[116]   Dallimore, who quotes *The Works of Augustus Toplady*, 1844, p. 495.

All of these but one were preached before he passed the age of thirty-three. Forty-two of the fifty-seven sermons were produced before he was aged twenty-five.[117]

Johnathan Edwards said, "He impresses the ignorant, and not less the educated and refined." Charles Wesley said of him that he was wise beyond his years. And only as poetic Charles Wesley could say:[118]

> From strength to strength our young Apostle goes
> Pours like a torrent, and the land o'erflows,
> Resistless wins his way with rapid zeal
> Turns the world upside down, and shakes the gates of hell!

Arnold Dallimore has this astute observation about the scope and the unparalleled oratorical skills that Whitefield possessed:

> Are there any persons (before the electrical amplification of sound) who regularly made themselves heard by congregations of 10,000 and sometimes of 20,000 and 30,000? Is there nay man, the aggregate of whose hearers throughout his lifetime, equals the total number of those addressed by Whitefield.. The lives of the orators of antiquity and of the greatest preachers of the Christian era leave little doubt that as to the number reached, both in single instances and in the totality of the lifetime, Whitefield stands alone... And a further extraordinary feature of Whitefield's ministry is manifest in the *breadth of its appeal.* Most ministers prove able to preach effectively to but one class of hearers. But Whitefield was equally effective among all... Moreover, the children were attracted. He possessed an almost childlike simplicity which drew children to him.[119]

Edwin C. Dargan who devoted a lifetime to the history of preaching said about Whitefield:

> The history of preaching since the apostles does not contain a greater or worthier name than that of George Whitefield.[120]

---

117 Dallimore, p. 525.
118 Dallimore, Vol. 1, p. 282.
119 Dallimore, Vol. 2, pp. 523-524.
120 Dallimore, Vol. 2, p. 536 who quotes E.C. Dargan, *A History of Preaching*, (Grand Rapids, MI: Baker Books, 1954), Vol. 2, p. 307.

What are the lessons we can learn from Whitefield's life and ministry? Arnold Dallimore makes these insightful observations:

> **Whitefield speaks to us about the power of the gospel.** It was not the so called "Social Gospel" but the gospel of redeeming grace. The gospel is the need of this present hour. Not the partial gospel which characterizes so much of today's evangelicalism, but the whole gospel that declares the majesty and holiness of God, the utter helplessness of man, the necessity of repentance, and a salvation that is manifested, not in a mere profession, but in the miracle of a new life.
>
> **Whitefield speaks to us about the primacy of preaching.** It is widely declared today that preaching is passé, that it must give way to dialogue and discussion and that it is a mark of pride for a man to stand before a congregation as though he had something authoritative to say. But biblical preaching is precisely that- the declaration of an authoritative message – a message founded upon an inerrant Book. True preaching is not as discussion, but a proclamation; not dialogue, but the asserting of "Thus saith the Lord!" True preaching should arise from a broken heart, should be alive with a mighty and compelling urgency, and should overflow with compassion.
>
> **Whitefield speaks to us about true Revival.** Much is said today about Revival and all manner of human attempts are made to bring it about. There is the resort to showmanship, sensationalism and musical entertainment and the effort to evoke confession without any basis in doctrine or conviction, and all of these, after a brief flurry of excitement, markedly fall. Whitefield's life teaches us that Revival is a sovereign work of God, a supernatural work, a mighty outpouring of the Holy Spirit.[121]

Regarding the great lessons for us to learn from the 18th Century revival, Ian Murray states:

> None was more important than the practical demonstration that scriptural preaching, accompanied by the power of the Spirit of God, is **the** divine means for extending the kingdom of Christ. This was to be the significant theme of Roland Hills's sermon when he preached at the foundation of the first interdenominational missionary society of modern times in 1795.

---

[121] Dallimore, Vol. 2, pp. 536-537.

Having spoken of the glorious revivals of the past, he declared: "What has been done, shall be done. God will ever stand by his own truth, and if he be for us, who can be against us? Preaching the Gospel of the kingdom does all the work."[122]

Concluding Remarks Regarding Whitefield

In the annals of Christian preaching, Whitefield truly does remain in a class by himself. As John Newton said, others could preach biblical truth as clear and often with more detailed content as Whitefield, but no one could preach it like him. He was a vivid display of God's gifts to His church. There was a profound simplicity to the man. He manifested an unrelenting commitment to preaching. He, as probably no other man besides the apostle Paul, lived and breathed preaching. It is no exaggeration that he literally wore himself out in preaching. Many times his friends kept insisting that he must lessen his schedule; it was way too demanding. The fact that he averaged twelve sermons a week during a thirty year ministry is simply mind boggling. Though he did not know that His master would bring him home within a few hours of this statement, Whitefield's response to Richard Smith's plea to lessen his preaching schedule was, "I would rather wear out than rust out." For years, it was manifest to many that he was literally killing himself in his rigorous preaching. Whitefield surely exemplified the Puritan Richard Baxter's famous dictum- "I preached as never sure to preach again, and as a dying man to dying men." With the apostle Paul, Whitefield could say, *"For if I preach the gospel, I have nothing to boast of, for I am under compulsion; for woe is me if I do not preach the gospel"* (I Corinthians 9:16).

In typical Whitefield fashion, he preferred for his name to perish so that the name of the Lord Jesus would be magnified. Well, Proverbs 10:7 and Psalm 112:6 surely apply to the life of George Whitefield - the memory of the righteous is blessed and will be remembered forever. Nearly two and a half centuries later, the name, Whitefield, still shines brightly among the saints.

---

[122] Ian Murray, pp. 127-128.

Characteristics of the First Great Awakening

One thing that was most apparent about the First Great Awakening and those revivals in England and Scotland was that preaching was the focal point. It was the public proclamation of the gospel and fundamental doctrines pertaining to growth in holiness that marked these revivals. And, much prayer preceded these revivals – prayers that pled with God to pour out His Spirit. Why study these revivals? We can learn from history how God has worked in the past. We can learn from both the positive and negative aspects of these revivals. The history of these revivals provides a backdrop from which we can evaluate future events. Hopefully, we can learn from certain mistakes in order to avoid duplicating them in the future. We can learn how the greatest enemy of the gospel operates, the devil. We can learn how he counterattacks in the midst of a great work of God.

Today we have the privilege of historical retrospect. We can assess historical events from their overall scope, noting both their positive and negative aspects. We can assess the events from documents of the period, correspondences, and diaries of the revivalists. In 1851 Charles Hodge, noted theologian of Princeton Seminary, published his work *The Constitutional History of the Presbyterian Church in the United States of America: Part II – 1741-1788.* Chapter 4 of his book is titled *The Great Revival of Religion 1740-45.* He has given, in my opinion, one of the better assessments of the positive and negative impacts of the First Great Awakening in America. Hodge seeks to give a fair analysis. His negative observations are actually taken from what some of the revivalists themselves said, particularly Jonathan Edwards. Another good recounting of this revival is one of the several biographies of Jonathan Edwards by George M. Marsden titled *Jonathan Edwards: A Life.* Marsden has some very insightful comments regarding the emotionalism associated with various aspects of the revival and some of the issues that led to a split in the churches.

In Charles Hodge's assessment of the First Great Awakening, he affirmed that the doctrinal content of the revivalists such as George Whitefield, William and Gilbert Tennent, Samuel Blair, Samuel Davies, and others was solid Reformation based doctrine. Hodge quoted Turnbull as saying:

> The doctrines preached by those famous men. who were owned as the principal instruments of this remarkable revival of God's work, were the doctrines of original sin, regeneration by the supernatural influences of the Divine Spirit, and of its absolute

necessity; of effectual calling, of justification by faith, wholly on account of the imputed righteousness of Christ; of repentance towards God, and faith towards our Lord Jesus Christ; of the perseverance of the saints, of the indwelling of the Holy Spirit in them, and of its divine consolation and joy.[123]

Charles Hodge was dealing with issues that arose in the Presbyterian Church in the wake of the First Great Awakening; however, the issues that led to a certain division in this church were similar to other groups such as the Congregationalists. In 1740, Samuel Blair and Gilbert Tennent presented complaints to the Presbyterian synod. Their complaints focused upon their perception that there was a prevalent laxity and lack of zeal in the preaching of the gospel among the synod's ministers even to the point that they questioned the salvation of many of them.

Hodge refers to the decline in Puritan New England with the passing of the first generation. He quoted Increase Mather who in 1678 said:

The body of the rising generation is a poor, perishing, unconverted, and (unless the Lord pour down his Spirit) an undone generation. Many are profane, drunkards, swearers, lascivious, scoffers at the power of godliness, despisers of those that are good, disobedient. Others are only civil and outwardly conformed to good order by reason of their education, but never knew what the new birth means.[124]

Hodge assessed the leading characteristics of the revivals. There was a deep conviction of sin that resulted from clearly apprehending the condemning nature of God's law. People came to understand the depth of their sinful corrupt natures and the guilt of their sins. There was an acknowledgement of God's justice in condemning them for their sins and their utter helplessness in themselves to change this. There was a clear apprehension of God's mercy shown in the Lord Jesus in the preaching of the gospel message. There was a sense of being reconciled to a holy God only on the basis of Christ's merits. Among those affected by the revivals, there was a delight in God's law, a desire to obey God's will, and a desire to love the brethren. **Hodge acknowledged that the essential features of a genuine revival were: a conviction of sin, faith in Christ, joy and peace in believing this, and a holy life.** In the truest sense, the revivals

---

[123] Charles Hodge, *The Constitutional History of the Presbyterian Church in the United States of America: Part II – 1741-1788,* (Philadelphia: Presbyterian Board of Education, No. 266 Chestnut St, 1840). Information from this source was found at: http://www.tracts.ukgo.com/hodge_revivals1.pdf.

[124] Hodge.

that were associated with what has come to be known as the First Great Awakening were a true work of God the Holy Spirit.

Gilbert Tennent stated that the ministry of Rev. Frelinghuysen of the Dutch Reformed Church in the year 1720 was marked by great blessings. The nature of his preaching revolved around the nature of original sin, repentance, and the nature and necessity of conversion.[125]

Hodge noted an incident with George Whitefield in Philadelphia in 1739. One former Episcopalian minister publicly stood up and warned people of Whitefield's preaching, stating that Whitefield's emphasis upon the necessity of the imputed righteousness of Christ would be a deterrent to good works. At this point, Whitefield pointed the audience to several passages that proved the need for Christ's imputed righteousness but refused to openly debate the issue in a church meeting. This demonstrates that the doctrines of the Reformation were faithfully being preached by most of these revivalist preachers.

Hodge pointed out what Samuel Blair said about the revival at his church in Fagg's Manor, Pennsylvania:

> Mr. Blair insisted much in his preaching upon the miserable state of man by nature, on the way of recovery through Jesus Christ, on the nature and necessity of faith, warning his hearers not to depend upon their repentance, prayers, or reformation; nor to seek peace in extraordinary ways, by visions, dreams, or immediate inspirations, but by an understanding view and believing persuasion of the way of life, as revealed in the gospel, through the suretyship, obedience and sufferings of Jesus Christ. His righteousness they were urged to accept as the only means of justification and life.[126]

In the revival that occurred in Boston through the preaching of Whitefield and Davenport, Hodge pointed to what Thomas Prince of the Old South Church said about the revival:

> Mr. Prince says he met with only one or two persons who talked of their impulses; that he knew of no minister who encouraged reliance on such enthusiastic impressions. "The doctrinal principles, he adds, of those who continue in our congregations, and have been the subjects of the late revival, are the same as they

---

[125]   Hodge.
[126]   Hodge.

all along have been instructed in, from the Westminster Shorter Catechism, which has generally been received and taught in the churches of New England, from its first publication, for one hundred years to the present day; and which is therefore the system of doctrine most generally and clearly declarative of the faith of the New England churches."[127]

Hodge then described what others said about Gilbert Tennent:

As a preacher he had few equals. His reasoning powers were strong; his expressions nervous and often sublime; his style diffusive; his manner warm and pathetic, such as must convince his audience that he was in earnest; and his voice clear and commanding. "When I heard Mr. Tennent," says the celebrated Dr. Hopkins, then a student in Yale College, "I thought he was the greatest and best man, and the best preacher that I had ever seen or heard."[128]

In assessing the overall impact of the preaching during the First Great Awakening, Hodge said that it was genuinely godly. He stated:

The deliberate judgment of such men as Edwards, Cooper, Colman, and Bellamy, in New England; and of the Tennents, Blair, Dickinson, and Davies, in the Presbyterian Church, must be received as of authority on such a subject. These men were not errorists or enthusiasts. They were devout and sober-minded men, well versed in the Scriptures and in the history of religion.

They had their faults, and fell into mistakes; some of them very grievous; but if they are not to be regarded as competent witnesses as to the nature of any religious excitement, it will be hard to know where such witnesses are to be found. Besides the testimony of these distinguished individuals, we have that of a convention of about ninety ministers met at Boston, July 7, 1743. Similar attestations were published by several associations in Connecticut and elsewhere. The Presbyteries of New Brunswick and New Castle, and the whole Synod of New York, repeatedly and earnestly bore their testimony to the genuineness and value of this revival.[129]

---

[127]   Hodge.
[128]   Hodge.
[129]   Hodge.

In his analysis of the preaching of the First Great Awakening, Hodge continued to observe the following:

> The contemporary accounts of the doctrines inculcated by the zealous preachers of that day, fully sustain the statement just quoted. Edwards mentions that his sermon on justification by faith, though it gave offence to many, was greatly blessed, and that it was on the doctrine therein taught, the revival was founded in its beginning and during its whole progress. In the account of the revival at Plymouth, we are told that the doctrines principally insisted upon, were the sin and apostasy of mankind in Adam; the blindness of the natural man in things of God; the enmity of the carnal mind; the evil of sin, and the ill desert of it; the utter inability of fallen man to relieve himself; the sovereignty of God, his righteousness, holiness, truth, power, eternity, and also his grace and mercy in Christ Jesus; the way of redemption by Christ; justification through his imputed righteousness received by faith, this faith being a gift of God, and a living principle that worketh by love; legal and evangelical repentance; the nature and necessity of regeneration.[130]

Hodge referred to the comments of a Rev. Mr. M'Gregore, pastor of the Presbyterian Church at Londonderry, New Hampshire:

> As the Assembly's Shorter Catechism has been all along agreeable to the known principles of the New England churches, and has been generally received and taught in them as a system of Christian doctrine agreeable to the Holy Scriptures, wherein they happily unite; it is a great pleasure to us that our Presbyterian brethren who came from Ireland, are generally with us in these important points, as also in the particular doctrines of experimental piety arising from them, and the wondrous work of God agreeable to them, at this day making its triumphant progress through the land.
>
> The doctrines which the promoters of this work teach are the doctrines of the gospel, of the Apostles' Creed, of the Thirty-nine Articles of the Church of England, and of the *Westminster Confession of Faith*.
>
> More particularly these men are careful to teach and inculcate the great doctrine of original sin, in opposition to Pelagius, Arminius,

---

[130]   Hodge.

and their respective followers: that this sin has actually descended from Adam, the natural and federal head, to all his posterity proceeding from him by ordinary generation; that hereby the understanding is darkened, the will depraved, and the affections under the influence of a wrong bias, to that degree that they are utterly indisposed to anything that is spiritually good; that man, as a sad consequence of the fall, has lost all power in things spiritual.

They teach likewise, with due care, the doctrine of the imputation of the righteousness of the second Adam, Jesus Christ; that this righteousness is apprehended and applied by faith alone, without the deeds of the law; that the faith which justifies the soul is living and operative. They teach that this faith is the gift of God; that a man cannot believe by any inherent power of his own. As to regeneration, they hold it to be absolutely necessary, that the tree must be made good before the fruit be so; that unless a man undergo a supernatural change by the operation of the Holy Ghost upon his soul, or be born of water and of spirit, he cannot enter into the kingdom of God.[131]

Hodge went on to discuss another important aspect of the First Great Awakening. What about its effects? He said:

The second criterion of the genuineness of any revival is the nature of the experience professed by its subjects. However varied as to degree or circumstances, the experience of all true Christians is substantially the same. There is and must be a conviction of sin, a sense of ill-desert and unholiness in the sight of God, a desire of deliverance from the dominion as well as penalty of sin; an apprehension of the mercy of God in Jesus Christ; a cordial acquiescence in the plan of redemption; a sincere return of the soul to God through Christ, depending on his merits for acceptance. These acts of faith will ever be attended with more or less of joy and peace, and with a fixed desire and purpose to live in obedience to the will of God.

We must, therefore, look further than mere professions or detail of experiences, for evidence of the real character of this work. We must look to its effects. The only satisfactory proof of the nature of any religious excitement, in an individual or a community, is its permanent results. What then were the fruits of this revival?

---

[131]   Hodge.

Hodge directed us to what William Tennent said:

> Mr. William Tennent says that the subjects of this work, who had
> come under his observation, were brought to approve of the
> doctrines of the gospel, to delight in the law of God, to endeavour
> to do his will, to love those who bore the divine image; that the
> formal had become spiritual; the proud, humble; the wanton and
> vile, sober and temperate; the worldly, heavenly-minded; the
> extortioner, just; and the self-seeker, desirous to promote the glory
> of God.[132]

It is noteworthy what Hodge said about Jonathan Edwards' view of the
effect of the First Great Awakening:

> President Edwards, in his Thoughts on the Revival, written in
> 1743, says, there is a strange alteration almost all over New
> England among the young. Many, both old and young, have
> become serious, mortified and humble in their conversation; their
> thoughts and affections are now about the favour of God, an
> interest in Christ, and spiritual blessedness. The Bible is in much
> greater esteem and use than formerly. The Lord's Day is more
> religiously observed. There has been more acknowledgment of
> faults and restitution within two years, than in thirty years before.
> The leading truths of the gospel are more generally and firmly
> held; and many have exhibited calmness, resignation, and joy, in
> the midst of the severest trials.[133]

Some Problems Emerging During the English Revivals and the First Great Awakening

While Hodge speaks very highly of the solid biblical preaching of most of
the revivalists in America, he observed what he perceived as some of the
errors that attended the revival. He said:

> If the evidence was not perfectly satisfactory, that this remarkable
> and extended revival was indeed the work of the Spirit of God, it
> would lose almost all its interest for the Christian church. It is
> precisely because it was in the main a work of God that it is of so
> much importance to ascertain what were the human or evil
> elements mixed with it, which so greatly marred its beauty and

---

[132]   Hodge.
[133]   Hodge.

curtailed its usefulness. That there were such evils cannot be a matter of doubt.

The single consideration, that immediately after this excitement the state of religion rapidly declined, that errors of all kinds became more prevalent than ever, and that a lethargy gradually settled on the churches, which was not broken for near half a century, is proof enough that there was a dreadful amount of evil connected with the revival.

Was such, however, actually the case? Did religion thus rapidly decline? If this question must be answered in the affirmative, what were the causes of this decline, or what were the errors which rendered this revival, considered as a whole, productive of such evils? These are questions of the greatest interest to the American churches, and ought to be very seriously considered and answered.

That the state of religion did rapidly decline after the revival, we have abundant and melancholy evidence. Even as early as 1744, President Edwards says, "the present state of things in New England is, on many accounts, very melancholy. There is a vast alteration within two years."

God, he adds, was provoked at the spiritual pride and self-confidence of the people, and withdrew from them, and the enemy has come in like a flood in various respects, until the deluge has overwhelmed the whole land. There had been from the beginning a great mixture, especially in some places, of false experiences and false religion with true; but from this time the mixture became much greater, and many were led away into sad delusions.

In another letter, dated May 23, 1749, he says, "as to the state of religion in these parts of the world, it is, in general, very dark and melancholy." In the preceding October, when writing to Mr. Erskine of Edinburgh, he communicates to him an extract from a letter to himself, from Governor Belcher of New Jersey, who says, "The accounts which I receive from time to time, give me too much reason to fear that Arminianism, Arianism, and even Socinianism, in destruction to the doctrines of grace, are daily propagated in the New England colleges."[134]

---

[134] Hodge.

Despite the fact that the revivals associated with the First Great Awakening bore marks of a genuine work of God with solid doctrines of the Reformation being preached, what went wrong? Charles Hodge said that something must have been wrong, even under the watchful eye of Jonathan Edwards. Hodge stated:

> There must have been many spurious conversions, and much false religion which at the time were regarded as genuine. This assumption is nothing more than the facts demand, nor more than Edwards himself frequently acknowledged. There is the most marked difference between those of his writings which were published during the revival, and those which appeared after the excitement had subsided.[135]

Problems with Excessive Emotionalism and Clergy Schism

George Marsden, in his book on the life of Jonathan Edwards, documents what he considers some of the problems that emerged during the First Great Awakening. The problems were two fold: excessive emotionalism and schism among the clergy regarding their perspectives on the revivals. Jonathan Edwards openly acknowledged some of the problems and sought to remedy them by several of his books in addition to various preaching opportunities where he was able to address the issues. Unusual phenomena were occurring in the congregations among the various revivalist preachers. These phenomena were being manifested not only in the revivals associated with the First Great Awakening in America, but they were also being seen in England and Scotland. Depending upon who the revivalist preachers were, the magnitude and frequency of these phenomena varied. They were seen in the preaching of Whitefield, Edwards, the Wesley brothers, the Erskines in Scotland, and others to name a few. These phenomena were more common among those who viewed such things as a sign of God's approval. This was particularly true of John Wesley in England. Arnold Dallimore comments that in England in 1739, these strange phenomena were almost entirely limited to the ministry of John Wesley.[136] According to Luke Tyerman, The difference between Whitefield and Wesley over these manifestations is that early on, they were never seen in Whitefield's preaching but occurring later after they showed up in Wesley's preaching. Whitefield looked upon these manifestations with suspicion and dislike. There was often weeping and

---

[135]   Hodge.
[136]   Dallimore, Vol. 1, p. 325.

sobbing in Whitefield's audiences that sometimes became so loud that it almost drowned his voice, but the effect was not so much as to overtake the person.[137]

What were these strange phenomena? They were ecstatic manifestations among various people in the audience such as outcries of anguish and/or joy, convulsions, rages, seizures, and fainting. How were these experiences to be evaluated? Were they the work of God, of the devil, or solely of human origin? If they were of the Holy Spirit, were these experiences always expected to be present? Was there some kind of social expectation? What is the relationship of the mind to the body? How was one to distinguish between Holy Spirit induced feelings over against Satanic ones? Often times, how one answered these questions determined whether one was sympathetic or unsympathetic to the revivals.

Concerning these outbursts, one of the closest to John Wesley was the preacher, John Cennick, who said about these experiences:

> At first no one knew what to say, but it was soon called the pangs of the new birth, the work of the Holy Ghost, casting out the old man, etc., but some were offended and left the Societies entirely when they saw Mr. Wesley encourage it. I often doubted it was not of the enemy when I saw it, and disputed with Mr. Wesley for calling it the work of God; but he was strengthened in his opinion after he had wrote about it to Mr. Esrskine in Scotland, and had received a favourable answer.[138]

John Wesley wrote Ralph Erskine in Scotland, asking his opinion of the emotionalism being manifested during his preaching. Erskine had also experienced some of this during his preaching as well. Erskine gave Wesley this assessment:

> All the outward appearances of people's being affected among us may be reduced to these two sorts: one is, hearing with a close, silent attention, with gravity and greediness, discovered by fixed looks, weeping eyes, and sorrowful or joyful countenances; another sort is, when they lift up their voice aloud, some more depressedly, and others more highly; and at times the whole multitude in a flood of tears, all as it were crying out at once, till their voice be ready to drown the minister's, that he can scarce be

---

[137]   Luke Tyerman, *The Life of the Rev. George Whitefield.* Vol. 1, (London: Hodder and Stoughton, 1876), p. 264.
[138]   Tyerman, p. 326.

heard for the weeping noise that surrounds him. The influence on some of these, like a landflood, dries up; we hear of no change wrought; but in others it appears in the fruits of righteousness and the tract of a holy conversation.[139]

Joseph Humphreys was one of John Wesley's earliest assistants and also witnessed emotional outbursts in his own ministry. Humphreys said:

I think the case was often this; the word of God would come with a convincing light and power into the consciences of sinners, whereby they were *so far* awakened, as to be seized with dreadful terrors. The rebellion of their natures would be raised; the peace of the strong man armed would be diminished; hell within would begin to roar; the devil, that before, being unmolested, lay quiet in their hearts, would now be stirred up and be most outrageously angry, because of this convincing light and power of the word. Hence, I believe, proceeded some of these agonies of body.[140]

John Cennick witnessed an incident where a man, during his preaching, became violently seized and foamed at the mouth. Six men could not hold him down. The man would tear away from their arms as in hellish agony. Cennick said he saw others sweat profusely, their necks and tongues swelling and twisting out of all shape. Some prophesied, and some uttered the worst of blasphemies against our Saviour.[141]

These weird occurrences so troubled Cennick that he recounted going into the woods weeping before the Lord. Cennick said the Lord's presence seemed to calm him, and he became more convinced to preach nothing but Him and His righteousness. With that, Cennick said that all fits and crying disappeared wherever he preached, but the differences of opinion between him and John Wesley over these matters still continued.

While John Wesley generally looked upon these outbursts favorably, there were times that even he became afraid. Wesley went to a house of a young woman in Kingswood where two or more persons were holding a woman. Wesley described it as a horrific sight. She was pale in the face with multitudes of distortions in her body. The woman kept screaming, "I am damned, damned; lost forever. Six days ago you might have helped me. But it is past. I am the devil's now. I have given myself to him. His I am.

---

[139] Dalllimore, Vol. 1, p. 324 who quoted from Wesley's *Journal*, Vol. 2, pp. 230-231.
[140] Dallimore, Vol. 1, p. 324 who quoted from Tyerman's *Whitefield*, Vol. 1, p. 226.
[141] Dallimore, Vol. 1, p. 327. That which was witnessed by Cennick was probably demonic possession, particularly the blasphemies against Jesus coming from such people.

Him I must serve. With him I will go to hell..." She then began to pray to the devil. John said he was joined by his brother Charles at nine o'clock, and they prayed for two hours for the woman. Eventually, the woman quieted and began to praise God.[142]

On other occasions, John Wesley witnessed bizarre behavior. These people became very violent when the name Jesus was mentioned. Wesley said that this person would scream with horrid laughter, mixed with blasphemy grievous to hear. Eventually after much prayer, this person's pains disappeared.

We learn several things from the above accounts. It appears that one can categorize the phenomena into three categories: 1) those emotionally affected in a more restrained manner, 2) those who openly and profusely expressed their emotions, and 3) those that manifested bizarre behavior, which appears to be demonic possession.

One thing that was consistent with virtually all the revivalists was an emphasis upon bringing conviction of sins due to having transgressed God's commandments. Vivid imagery was often employed to show the sinner's spiritual danger. In short, people were shown to be sinners, having no hope without Christ and that the only remedy for their pitiful plight was to believe in Jesus for the salvation of their souls.

It is interesting that John Wesley's brother Charles began to think that some of these outbursts were feigned. Charles wrote:

> Some stumbling-blocks, with the help of God, I have removed, particularly the fits. Many, no doubt, were, at our first preaching, struck down, both body and soul, into the depth of distress. Their *outward affections* were easy to be imitated. Many counterfeits I have already detected.[143]

As one tries to assess what actually was happening during revivalist preaching, whether it was in England, Scotland, or America, one thing becomes apparent – they all appeared to be independent of each other for the most part. During the 18th Century there was no telegraph, radio, television, and audio recordings. There would only be newspaper accounts, personal journals, and letters. While some of the personal journals were published and distributed such as with Whitefield, how many average

---

[142]   Dallimore, Vol.1, p. 329 who quotes from John Wesley 's *Journal*, October 23, p. 298.
[143]   Dallimore, Vol. 1, p. 329 who quotes Charles Wesley's *Journal*, August 5, 1740.

people would have readily known what was happening in distant cities, especially in different countries? It is understandable that in one locale the word could spread from one town to another. This would explain why these phenomena would more often show up among certain revivalists who readily approved of all kinds of emotional outbursts. In other words, certain behavior is expected and sanctioned. However, the commonality of these experiences would not be easily explained when there was a distance of thousands of miles spanning a vast ocean. On the average, it took a month to travel from England to America. This means that letters and any kind of correspondences took this long. Consequently, when Whitefield and Edwards were preaching, there was no way for those in either country to readily know what was happening elsewhere, especially the average person. Also, the evidence clearly shows that there were revivals occurring simultaneously in America, England, and Scotland. With this being the case, how can we explain common emotional phenomena?

These common human experiences can be explained on a human and supernatural level. On a human level, there are common emotional responses to various stimuli. Upon hearing of tragic stories, is not weeping common, especially among women? Is not hope and joy a common human emotion when certain things are said that are designed to elicit that kind of response? Human beings are emotional creatures. George Whitefield was a master at creating vivid imagery. The common opinion of varied observers of Whitefield's preaching was that the audience was often fixated on him, hanging on every word proceeding from his mouth. Probably the best example of this is what happened to Lord Chesterfield who frequently heard Whitefield. Whitefield was explaining the great imminent danger that lost sinners are in. He was vividly animating an old man being led by a little dog on a cord, who feels his way by tapping the ground with a cane. Directly before him lies a great chasm, but before he reaches the precipice, the old man loses the dog's chain, and as he reaches the precipice, he loses his cane. He lurches forward to retrieve it, but his foot falls on empty air. At this point, Lord Chesterfield, overcome with visualizing the imminent danger of the old man, leaps out of his seat crying, "He's gone! He's gone!" There is nothing necessarily wrong with this kind of preaching; in fact, I think it is great preaching. As we shall see later, the most famous sermon of Jonathan Edwards was his *Sinners in the Hands of an Angry God* preached at Suffield, Massachusetts. Edwards was not an animated preacher like Whitefield, Gilbert Tennent, and others; however, the imagery that Edwards used did have a profound impact on the congregation, so much so that the weeping was so loud and pervasive in the congregation that he could not finish his sermon. In today's society, television and movies do the exact same thing. Do we not cry at certain scenes? Are we not inspired by visual scenes of the underdog triumphing over seemingly insurmountable obstacles? Filmmakers understand human psychology and use it. Well, preachers and "motivational speakers" understand it as well, not to say that they are necessarily trying to manipulate an audience.

What about common human experiences on a supernatural level? We know from Scripture that biblical preaching brings about genuine conviction of sin when God sovereignly goes to save sinners (e.g. Peter's sermon on the Day of Pentecost where 3000 were spiritually pierced in the heart). There is a supernatural work of the Holy Spirit which can elicit an emotional response, and there is another supernatural reality that can attend to the preaching of God's word.

Satan is a genuine supernatural reality, whether men acknowledge him or not. Some of the accounts of what was happening during various revivalist preaching can be attributed to demonic activity, such as contortions of body and certain seizures. Fainting and some seizures do not necessarily imply demonic activity because some people can emotionally work themselves into such a state; however, other bizarre behavior is demonic. We have ample examples in the Scripture. Certain bodily illnesses are demonic related such as muteness (Matthew 9:32; Luke 11:14) and blindness (Matthew 12:22). When Jesus approached certain demon possessed people, the demon would cry out (Luke 4:33); therefore, spontaneous outbursts during preaching could be demonically related. Certain bizarre behavior where one appears to be out of their mind can be demonic (Mark 5:15). Seizures can be demonic (Luke 8:29). Incidents of being slammed to the ground with convulsions can be demonic (Luke 9:42). Obviously, not every incident as listed is demonic related, but it can be. The fact that these types of bizarre emotional behavior attended sound preaching lends one to think there was a good possibility that Satan was seeking to counterfeit the work of God and disrupt the preaching of God's word. We do know that Satan can disguise himself as an angel of light (II Corinthians 11:14).

Regardless of the actual source of the emotional phenomena associated with revivalist preaching, it did cause problems; it did lead to schism among various clergymen; and it did provide fodder for enemies of the revivals to discredit them.

It should be noted that Edwards would later comment that the revival that first occurred in Northampton in 1734-35 did not manifest itself with such emotionalism as did this one in 1741. Also, George Whitefield had already preached at Northampton in the fall of 1740.

In May 1741 Jonathan Edwards recorded what was happening in his town of Northampton:

> A sermon was preached to a company at a private house. Near the conclusion of the exercise one or two persons that were professors were so greatly affected with a sense of the greatness and glory of divine things, and the infinite importance of the things of eternity, but they were not able to conceal it; the affection of their minds overcoming their strength, and having a very visible effect on their bodies.

> The affection... was quickly propagated through the room: many of the young people and children that were professors appeared to be overcome with a sense of the greatness and glory of divine things, and with admiration, love, joy and praise and compassion to others that looked upon themselves as in the state of nature; and many others at the same time were overcome with distress about their simple and miserable state and condition; so that the whole room was full of nothing but outcries, faintings and such like. [144]

By midsummer 1741, Edwards indicated that between sixteen to twenty-six young people met at his house. He said that the meeting was blessed with extraordinary affections so intense that many were overcome. Ecstatic experiences soon spread from such meetings to the Sabbath services themselves. Outcries sometimes filled the assembly. Several times many of the congregation stayed after the services to meet with those who were overcome, praying and singing as the wondrous contagion spread.[145] Smaller gatherings at homes were most intense. "It was a very frequent thing to see a house full of outcries, faintings, convulsions and suchlike, both with distress, and also with admiration and joy."[146]

---

[144] Marsden, p. 217
[145] Marsden, p. 218.
[146] Marsden, p. 217.

Marsden points out that ecstatic manifestation began to mark many towns in New England where the phenomena equaled or surpassed that at Northampton. For instance, the Rev. Jonathan Parsons, one of the pastors turned itinerant during the awakening, reported an incident that occurred on Election Day, May 14, 1741. When the young people of his parish normally would have been rumbling, they instead attended his preaching:

> Under the sermon, many had their countenances changed; the thoughts seem to trouble them, so that the joints of their warnings were loosed, and her knees smote one against another. Great members cried out loud in the anguish of their souls. Several stout men fell as the like can have been discharged; and the ball had made its way through their hearts. Some young women were thrown into hysteric fits.[147]

It seemed as though spiritual hysteria was spreading throughout all of New England. In several towns, full church memberships were rising at phenomenal rates, even in those churches that were strict in rules for church membership.[148]

It is worth noting that during the revivals Jonathan Edwards knew that with the magnitude of the spiritual awakening, Satan would seek to counter it with excesses and self-delusions, but he said that there was nothing to do but seize the hour.[149]

We have noted previously that the preaching styles of Whitefield and Edwards were quite different. Whitefield preached without notes and was very animated, while Edwards needed notes and was not animated in his delivery. But, this did not mean that Edwards could not captivate an audience. One of Edwards' admirers described his delivery as follows:

> Easy, natural and very solemn. Yet not a strong, loud voice; but appeared with such gravity and solemnity, and spake with such distinctness, clearness and precision; his words were so full of ideas, set in such a plane and striking light, that few speakers have been so able to demand the attention of an audience as he." Through sheer intensity regenerated emotion. "His words often discovered a great degree of inward fervor, without much noise or

---

[147] Marsden, p. 218 who quoted Jonathan Parsons account dated April 14, 1744 regarding Lyme, Connecticut.

[148] Marsden, p. 218. He cites quotations from Tracy, *Great Awakening*, pp. 120-212, giving quotations from mostly contemporary sources, especially Prince's *Christian History*, who provided accounts of such phenomena in many places.

[149] Marsden, p. 219.

external emotion, and fell with great weight on the minds of his hearers. He even made a little notion of his head or hands in the desk, but spake so as to discover the motion of his own heart, which tended in the most natural and effectual manner to to move and affect others.[150]

Jonathan Edwards is probably best known for his sermon *Sinners in the Hands of an Angry God.* The sermon was preached at nearby Suffield, Massachusetts on July 8, 1741. Suffield had been experiencing a revival already, having the previous Sunday added ninety-five persons to its communicant roles.

Edwards himself found the doctrine of God's eternal punishment to be difficult, but since it was in God's word, it must be preached. The subject of the sermon was that God was holding sinners in his hands, delaying the horrible destruction that the rebellious justly deserve. Despite His unfathomable mercy, God still remains the just Judge who must condemn sinners for their rebellion against Him. God in His amazing mercy is still pleading with sinners and keeping them from falling. God permits hate and injustice to be their own reward; sinners love being in darkness and revel in their rebellion against God.

The extraordinary nature of this sermon was the sustained imagery that Edwards used to challenge his audience. He employed multiple images designed to force his hearers to come to no other realization but how dangerous it was to remain in an unconverted state and face the fires of hell. Relentlessly, Edwards used image after image of the horrors of God's judgments. "Your wickedness makes you as it were heavy as lead, and to tend downwards with great weight and pressure toward hell." "All your righteousness" can have no more effect "than a spider's web would have to stop a falling rock."[151]

Then came the infamous passage:

> The God that holds you over the pit of hell, much as one holds a spider, were some loathsome insect, over the fire, abhors you, and is dreadfully provoked; his wrath towards you burns like fire; he looks upon you as worthy of nothing else, but to be cast into the fire; he is of purer eyes than to bear to have you in his sight; you

---

[150] Marsden, p. 220 who quotes from Hopkins, *The Life and Character of the Late Reverend Mr. Jonathan Edwards, (Boston 1765)*, pp.47-48.

[151] Marsden, p. 223 who quotes an excerpt from Edwards' sermon, *Sinners in the Hands of an Angry God.*

are 10,000 times so abominable in his eyes as the most hateful venomous serpent is in ours. You have offended him infinitely more than ever a stubborn rebel did his prince: and yet 'tis nothing but his hand that holds you from falling into the fire every moment: 'tis to be ascribed to nothing else, if you did not go to hell the last night... but that God's hand has held you up: there is no other reason to be given why you haven't gone to hell since you have sat here in the house of God, provoking his pure eyes by your sinful wicked manner of attending his solemn worship: yea, there is nothing else that is to be given as a reason why you don't this very moment drop down to hell. Oh sinner! Consider the fearful danger you are in.[152]

An eyewitness account of the sermon was as follows:

Edwards, who had been building the intensity of the sermon, had to stop and ask for silence so that he could be heard. The tumult only increased as the "shrieks and cries were piercing and amazing." As Edwards waited, the wails continued, so there was no way that he might be heard. He never finished the sermon. Wheelock offered a closing prayer, and the clergy went down among the people to minister among them individually. "Several souls were hopefully wrought upon that night," Stephen Williams recorded, "and oh the cheerfulness and pleasantness of their countenances." Finally the congregation was enough under control to sing and affecting hymn, hear a prayer, and be dispersed.[153]

When Isaac Watts received the printed version of the sermon, he wrote on his copy: "A most terrible sermon, which should have had a word of Gospel at the end of it, though I think 'tis all true."[154] Most interestingly, Edwards had preached the identical sermon before to his own congregation in Northampton, but there was no similar impact as there was in Suffield. In the sermon preached before his own congregation, Edwards did end with a gospel plea. We should remember that at Suffield he never got to finish his sermon because of the pervasive emotional state of the congregation.

---

[152] Marsden, p. 223 who quotes an excerpt from Edwards' sermon, *Sinners in the Hands of an Angry God.*

[153] Marsden, pp. 220-21 who quotes from Samuel Hopkins, *The Life and Character of the Late Reverend Mr. Jonathan Edwards* (Boston 1765), pp. 47-48.

[154] Marsden, p. 224 who quoted from Ola Winslow, *Jonathan Edwards, 1703-1758* (New York: Macmillan, 1940), p. 192, from Watts' handwritten comment on title page of volume, owned by Forbes Library, Northampton.

As noted earlier, there appears to be a difference of the revivals of 1734-35 and the ones in the early 1740s. Deacon Lyman of Northampton stated in 1739 that he was troubled with the extravagant outcries and bodily effects that were so common among the various itinerant preachers. Goodman was quite familiar with the 1734-1735 Northampton revival and saw a significant difference between the two revivals.[155]

By spring 1741, controversy was spreading regarding the various emotional manifestations associated with the revivals. In a letter to Deacon Lyman, Edwards concluded that there were "some imprudences... and irregularities, as there always was, and always will be in the imperfect state." Yet the awakening as a whole had "clear and incontestable evidences of a true divine work." Edwards allowed no room for doubt:

> If this ben't the work of God, then I have all my religion to learn over again, and know not what use to make of the Bible. [156]

He would publicly proclaim the same at Yale on September 10, 1741.

Yale College at New Haven, Connecticut was becoming a center for the controversy. Not only was there the issue of how to understand these ecstatic manifestations associated with the revivals, but several of the revivalist itinerant preachers that spoke at Yale were insinuating that many of the clergy were unconverted as well as a good portion of the Yale faculty. It did not help that George Whitefield had preached on the dangers of the unconverted ministry when he preached at Yale, and made the following comments:

> Nay most that preach, I fear do not experimentally know Christ... and as for the colleges of Harvard and Yale, "their light is become darkness, darkness that can be felt, and is complained of by the most godly ministers."[157]

This greatly offended friends of the colleges, and Whitefield would later have to do a considerable amount of "damage control" to get back into the good graces of many people. Years later Whitefield would write:

> In my former Journal, taking things by hearsay too much, I spoke and wrote rashly of the colleges and ministers of New England, for which, as I have done it when at Boston last from the pulpit, I

---

[155] Marsden, p. 228.
[156] Marsden, p. 231.
[157] Marsden, pp. 231-32 who quotes from George Whitefield, *A Continuation of the Reverend Mr. Whitefield's Journal: The Seventh Journal* (London 1741), pp. 54-55.

take this opportunity of asking public pardon from the press. It was rash and uncharitable and though well-meant, I fear did hurt.[158]

Yale president, Thomas Clapp, who at first welcomed the awakening, was fast becoming disillusioned. With itinerant preachers insinuating that ministers and faculty were suspect as to their relationship with Christ, he instituted a ban on allowing itinerant preachers at Yale.[159]

The situation at Yale was exacerbated with a young itinerant revivalist preacher, James Davenport. He was an extremist, to say the least. In 1740 he had traveled with Whitefield and Gilbert Tennent in New York and New Jersey. Davenport shared the same negative perspective on the spiritual state of New England's clergy and New England's overall spiritual state. Davenport, in his own journeys along the Connecticut coast, was relentless in his widespread condemnation of virtually all ministers, even those ministers who had a general reputation for godliness. He would march along to his services singing with his "head thrown back, and his eyes staring up to heaven." His meetings during commencement week in New Haven generally lasted until 10 or 11 at night. The general perspective from many was that these meetings lacked all decorum. At one of these late-night commencement week gatherings, as one critic described it, all order had disappeared, "some praying, some exhorting and testifying, some singing, some screaming, some crying, some laughing and some scolding, made the most amazing confusion that ever was heard."[160]

The Yale College trustees were most grieved over Davenport's outright encouragement to students to defy their teachers. Unfortunately, at that time, one of the brightest students, David Brainerd, was caught up in being very judgmental.[161]

As disillusionment about the impact of the revivals was mounting, Jonathan Edwards came to Yale in an attempt to bring a balanced understanding. Edwards warned against spiritual pride and the dangers of "being led by impulses and strong impressions." In 1740 Edwards had noticed in Whitefield a propensity to depend upon strong impressions from God and had admonished him concerning it. Whitefield later said that the admonishment was deserving. Edwards, in his Yale address, admonished

---

158   Dallimore, Vol. 1, p. 552 who quotes from *Whitefield's Journals,* p. 462, footnote.
159   Marsden, p. 233.
160   Marsden, p. 232 who quotes from an anonymous letter from Stonington, Connecticut, *Boston Weekly Post-Boy,* (July 29, 1741).
161   Marsden, p. 233.

students of their disdain of human learning, and he admonished them strongly of their censorious spirit.

Having addressed the problems associated with certain aspects attending to the revivals, Edwards discussed what constituted sufficient evidences of a genuine work of the Holy Spirit. The distinguishing marks of a genuine work of God are: love for Jesus, renouncing worldly lusts and ambitions, a love of Scripture, as the truth, and true Christian love. But then, Edwards also exhorted the Yale establishment to be very circumspect in their criticism of the revivals lest they be found opposing God. Edwards said that those insisting on "pretended prudence" to see if the awakening bore consistent good fruit are like "fools waiting at the riverside to have the water all run by." Edwards insisted that there were clear evidences of true conversions, but with these, there would be counter attacks by Satan. Those who seriously questioned the revivals should take care lest they be guilty of the unpardonable sin.[162]

Sarah Edwards' Personal Ecstatic Experiences

Ecstatic manifestations were showing up in various revival settings, and they showed up in Jonathan Edwards' own house. His wife Sarah recounted her own ecstatic experiences first occurring on January 20, 1742. For two weeks she was caught up in this state where she repeatedly was physically overwhelmed by her spiritual raptures, sometimes leaping involuntarily to praise God and more often so overcome by joys and transports that she physically collapsed. Jonathan was out of town on a scheduled preaching tour except for the first two days. Upon his return, what was Jonathan Edwards' perspective on Sarah's experiences? He was actually pleased with them, writing down a detailed account from her recollections. Sarah could specify the day and hour that she had them. Interestingly, these experiences occurred while her house was filled with guests, her own seven children, and some servants. Never did she neglect her domestic duties. These ecstatic moments would occur often at night when she retired to meditate on Scripture, but they also occurred in the presence of others and visiting ministers. According to George Marsden, Jonathan was so impressed by Sarah's spiritual example that he incorporated a disguised version of her account into a long treatise that he

---

[162] Marsden, p. 237 who quotes from Jonathan Edwards, *Distinguishing Marks, Works, 4:271-73.*

was writing titled *Some Thoughts Concerning the Present Revival of Religion* as a sequel to *The Distinguishing Marks*.[163]

Edwards used Sarah's experiences as perfectly fitting for the highest of spiritual standards. The importance of taking a close look at Sarah Edwards' narrative is because it is not typical of what today we consider "charismatic" manifestations. There was no speaking in tongues; she was not "slain in the Spirit" by someone laying hands on her. There was no "holy laughter or barking." Moreover, Jonathan Edwards will argue that these experiences of his wife were not uncommon among some others during the First Great Awakening. If we presume that these ecstatic experiences are legitimate expressions of a godly Christian (which some might question), then, if God were to send another great revival in our time, we might see people having similar experiences. One thing should be noted, and it is quite significant. These specific experiences occurred during sound biblical teaching where gospel truths were clearly enunciated, and where Reformation doctrines were powerful preached. They also occurred while people were reading Scripture or hearing it expounded in family settings.

The following excerpts are from Sarah Edwards' own detailed recollections to her husband:[164]

> On Tuesday night, Jan. 19, 1742, "observes Mrs. Edwards," I felt very uneasy and unhappy, at my being so low in grace. I thought I very much needed help from God, and found a spirit of earnestness to seek help of him, that I might have more holiness. When I had for a time been earnestly wrestling with God for it, I felt within myself great quietness of spirit, unusual submission to God, and willingness to wait upon him, with respect to the time and manner in which he should help me, and wished that he should take his own time, and his own way, to do it.

> The next morning, I found a degree of uneasiness in my mind, at Mr. Edwards's suggesting, that he thought I had failed in some measure in point of prudence, in some conversation I had with Mr. Williams of Hadley, the day before. I found, that it seemed to bereave me of the quietness and calm of my mind, in any respect

---

163   Marsden, p. 240.

164   This accounting is taken from Sarah Edwards' Narrative found found in [excerpt from Dwight, Sereno. *The Works of President Edwards: With a Memoir of His Life.* Vol. I. (New York: G. & C. & H. Carvill. 1830. 171-186.], http://xroads.virginia.edu/~ma05/peltier/conversion/pierpont2.html.

not to have the good opinion of my husband. This, I much disliked in myself, as arguing a want of a sufficient rest in God, and felt a disposition to fight against it, and look to God for his help, that I might have a more full and entire rest in him, independent of all other things. I continued in this frame, from early in the morning until about 10 o'clock, at which time the Rev. Mr. Reynolds went to prayer in the family.

I had before this, so entirely given myself up to God, and resigned up every thing into his hands, that I had, for a long time, felt myself quite alone in the world; so that the peace and calm of my mind, and my rest in God, as my only and all sufficient happiness, seemed sensibly above the reach of disturbance from any thing but these two: First, My own good name and fair reputation among men, and especially the esteem, and just treatment of the people of this town; Secondly, And more especially, the esteem, and love and kind treatment of my husband. At times, indeed, I had seemed to be considerably elevated above the influence of even these things; yet I had not found my calm, and peace and rest in God so sensibly, fully and constantly, above the reach of disturbance from them, until now.

While Mr. Reynolds was at prayer in the family this morning, I felt an earnest desire that, in calling on God, he should say, *Father*, or that he should address the Almighty under that appellation: on which the thought turned in my mind--Why can I say, *Father*?--Can I now at this time, with the confidence of a child, and without the least misgiving of heart, call God my Father? This brought to my mind, two lines of Mr. Erskine's Sonnet: "I see him lay his vengeance by, and smile in Jesus' face."

I was thus deeply sensible, that my sins did loudly call for vengeance; but I then by faith saw God "lay his vengeance by, and smile in Jesus' face." It appeared to be real and certain that he did so. I had not the least doubt, that he then sweetly smiled upon me, with the look of forgiveness and love, having laid aside all his displeasure towards me, for Jesus' sake; which made me feel very weak, and somewhat faint.

In consequence of this, I felt a strong desire to be alone with God, to go to him, without having any one to interrupt the silent and soft communion, which I earnestly desired between God and my own soul; and accordingly withdrew to my chamber. It should have been mentioned that, before I retired, while Mr. Reynolds was praying, these words, in Romans viii. 34, came into my mind *"Who is he that condemneth; It is Christ that died, yea rather that is risen again, who is even at the right hand of God, who also maketh intercession for us;"* as well as the following words, *"Who shall separate us from the love of Christ,"* etc., which occasioned great sweetness and delight in my soul.

But when I was alone, the words came to my mind with far greater power and sweetness; upon which I took the Bible, and read the words to the end of the chapter, when they were impressed on my heart with vastly greater power and sweetness still. They appeared to me with undoubted certainty as the words of God, and as words which God did pronounce concerning me. I had no more doubt of it, than I had of my being.

Melted and overcome by the sweetness of this assurance, I fell into a great flow of tears, and could not forbear weeping aloud. It appeared certain to me that God was my Father, and Christ my Lord and Savior, that he was mine and I his. Under a delightful sense of the immediate presence and love of God, these words seemed to come over and over in my mind, "My God, my all; my God, my all." The presence of God was so near, and so real, that I seemed scarcely conscious of any thing else.

The peace and happiness, which I hereupon felt, was altogether inexpressible. It seemed to be that which came from heaven; to be eternal and unchangeable. I seemed to be lifted above earth and hell, out of the reach of every thing here below, so that I could look on all the rage and enmity of men or devils, with a kind of holy indifference, and an undisturbed tranquility. At the same time, I felt compassion and love for all mankind, and a deep abasement of soul, under a sense of my own unworthiness.

At night, my soul seemed to be filled with an inexpressibly sweet and pure love to God, and to the children of God; with a refreshing consolation and solace of soul, which made me willing to lie on the earth, at the feet of the servants of God, to declare his gracious dealings with me, and breathe forth before them my love, and gratitude and praise.

On Tuesday night, especially the latter part of it, I felt a great earnestness of soul and engagedness in seeking God for the town, that religion might now revive, and that God would bless Mr. Buell to that end. God seemed to be very near to me while I was thus striving with him for these things, and I had a strong hope that what I sought of him would be granted. There seemed naturally and unavoidably to arise in my mind an assurance, that now God would do great things for Northampton.

On Wednesday morning, I heard that Mr. Buell arrived the night before at Mr. Phelps's, and that there seemed to be great tokens and effects of the presence of God there, which greatly encouraged, and rejoiced me. About an hour and a half after, Mr. Buell came to our house, I sat still in entire resignedness to God, and willingness that God should bless his labours here as much as he pleased; though it were to the enlivening of every saint, and to the conversion of every sinner, in the town. These feelings continued afterwards, when I saw his great success; as I never felt the least rising of heart to the contrary, but my submission was even and uniform, without interruption or disturbance. I rejoiced when I saw the honour which God put upon him, and the respect paid him by the people, and the greater success attending his preaching, than had followed the preaching of Mr. Edwards immediately before he went to Leicester. I found rest and rejoicing in it, and the sweet language of my soul continually was, "Amen, Lord Jesus! Amen, Lord Jesus!"

At 3 o'clock in the afternoon, a lecture was preached by Mr. Buell. In the latter part of the sermon, one or two appeared much moved, and after the blessing, when the people were going out, several others. To my mind there was the clearest evidence, that God was present in the congregation, on the work of redeeming love; and in the clear view of this, I was all at once filled with such intense admiration of the wonderful condescension and grace of God, in returning again to Northampton, as overwhelmed my soul, and immediately took away my bodily strength… We remained in the meeting-house about three hours, after the public exercises were over. During most of the time, my bodily strength was overcome; and the joy and thankfulness, which were excited in my mind, as I contemplated the great goodness of God, led me to converse with those who were near me, in a very earnest manner.

When I came home, I found Mr. Buell, Mr. Christophers, Mr. Hopkins, Mrs. Eleanor Dwight, the wife or Mr. Joseph Allen, and Mr. Job Strong, at the house. Seeing and conversing with them on the Divine goodness, renewed my former feelings, and filled me with an intense desire that we might all arise, and, with an active, flowing and fervent heart, give glory to God. The intenseness of my feelings again took away my bodily strength.

The words of one Dr. Watts's Hosannas powerfully affected me; and, in the course of the conversation, I uttered them, as the real language of my heart, with great earnestness and emotion: "Hosanna to King David's Son, "Who reigns on a superior throne."

And while I was uttering the words, my mind was so deeply impressed with the love of Christ, and a sense of his immediate presence, that I could with difficulty refrain from rising from my seat, and leaping for joy. I continued to enjoy this intense, and lively and refreshing sense of Divine things, accompanied with strong emotions, for nearly an hour; after which, I experienced a delightful calm, and peace and rest in God, until I retired for the night; and during the night, both waking and sleeping.

I awoke in the morning of Thursday, January 28th, in the same happy frame of mind, and engaged in the duties of my family with a sweet consciousness, that God was present with me, and with earnest longings of soul for the continuance, and increase, of the blessed fruits of the Holy Spirit in the town. About nine o'clock, these desires became so exceedingly intense, when I saw numbers of the people coming into the house, with an appearance of deep interest in religion that my bodily strength was much weakened, and it was with difficulty that I could pursue my ordinary avocations.

Those who were near raised me, and placed me in a chair; and, from the fulness of my heart, I expressed to them, in a very earnest manner, the deep sense I had of the wonderful grace of Christ towards me, of the assurance I had of his having saved me from hell, of my happiness running parallel with eternity, of the duty of giving up all to God, and of the peace and joy inspired by an entire dependence on his mercy and grace. Mr. Buell then read a melting hymn of Dr. Watts, concerning the loveliness of Christ, the enjoyments and employments of heaven, and the Christian's earnest desire of heavenly things; and the truth and reality of the things mentioned in the hymn, made so strong an impression on my mind, and my soul was drawn so powerfully towards Christ and heaven, that I leaped unconsciously from my chair.

I seemed to be drawn upwards, soul and body, from the earth towards heaven; and it appeared to me that I must naturally and necessarily ascend thither. These feelings continued while the hymn was reading, and during the prayer of Mr. Christophers, which followed. After the prayer, Mr. Buell read two other hymns, on the glories of heaven, which moved me so exceedingly, and drew me so strongly heavenward, that it seemed as it were to draw my body upwards, and I felt as if I must necessarily ascend thither. At length my strength failed me, and I sunk down; when they took me up and laid me on the bed, where I lay for a considerable time, faint with joy, while contemplating the glories of the heavenly world. After I had lain a while, I felt more perfectly subdued and weaned from the world, and more fully resigned to God, than I had ever been conscious of before.

I was entirely swallowed up in God, as my only portion, and his honour and glory was the object of my supreme desire and delight. At the same time, I felt a far greater love to the children of God, than ever before. I seemed to love them as my own soul; and when I saw them, my heart went out towards them, with an inexpressible endearedness and sweetness.

That night, which was Thursday night, Jan. 28, was the sweetest night I ever had in my life. I never before, for so long a time together, enjoyed so much of the light, and rest and sweetness of heaven in my soul, but without the least agitation of body during the whole time. The great part of the night I lay awake, sometimes asleep, and sometimes between sleeping and waking. But all night I continued in a constant, clear and lively sense of the heavenly sweetness of Christ's excellent and transcendent love, of his nearness to me, and of my dearness to him; with an inexpressibly sweet calmness of soul in an entire rest in him. I seemed to myself to perceive a glow of divine love come down from the heart of Christ in heaven, into my heart, in a constant stream, like a stream or pencil of sweet light.

My soul remained in a kind of heavenly Elysium. So far as I am capable of making a comparison, I think that what I felt each minute, during the continuance of the whole time, was worth more than all the outward comfort and pleasure, which I had enjoyed in my whole life put together. It was a pure delight, which fed and satisfied the soul. It was pleasure, without the least sting, or any interruption. It was a sweetness, which my soul was lost in.

Mr. Sheldon came into the house about 10 o'clock, and said to me as he came in, "The Sun of righteousness arose on my soul this morning, before day;" upon which I said to him in reply, "That Sun has not set upon my soul all this night; I have dwelt on high in the heavenly mansions; the light of divine love has surrounded me; my soul has been lost in God, and has almost left the body." This conversation only served to give me a still livelier sense of the reality and excellence of divine things, and that to such a degree, as again to take away my strength, and occasion great agitation of my body.

So strong were my feelings, I could not refrain from conversing with those around me, in a very earnest manner, for about a quarter of an hour, on the infinite riches of divine love in the work of salvation: when, my strength entirely failing, my flesh grew very cold, and they carried me. I felt at the same time an exceedingly strong and tender affection for the children of God, and realized, in a manner exceedingly sweet and ravishing, the meaning of Christ's prayer, in John xvii.21, *"That they all may be one, as though Father art in me, and I in thee, that they also may be one in us."* This union appeared to me an inconceivable, excellent and sweet oneness; and at the same time I felt that oneness in my soul, with the children of God who were present with me and set me by the fire.

So conscious was I of the joyful presence of the Holy Spirit, I could scarcely refrain from leaping with transports of joy. This happy frame of mind continued until two o'clock, when Mr. Williams came in, and we soon went to meeting. He preached on the subject of the assurance of faith. The whole sermon was affecting to me, but especially when he came to show the way in which assurance was obtained, and to point out its happy fruits. When I heard him say, that *those, who have assurance, have a foretaste of heavenly glory,* I knew the truth of it from what I then felt: I knew that I then tasted the clusters of the heavenly Canaan: My soul was filled and overwhelmed with light, and love, and joy in the Holy Ghost, and seemed just ready to go away from the body.

In the forenoon, I was thinking of the manner in which the children of God had been treated in the world - particularly of their being shut up in prison--and the folly of such attempts to make them miserable, seemed to surprise me. It appeared astonishing, that men should think, by this means, to injure those who had such a kingdom within them. Towards night, being informed that Mrs. P---- had expressed her fears least I should die before Mr. Edwards' return, and he should think the people had killed his wife; I told those who were present, that I chose to die in the way that was most agreeable to God's will, and that I should be willing to die in darkness and horror, if it was most for the glory of God.

My soul remained, as on Thursday night, in a kind of heavenly Elysium. Whether waking or sleeping, there was no interruption, throughout the night, to the views of my soul, to its heavenly light, and divine, inexpressible sweetness. It was without any agitation or motion of the body. I was led to reflect on God's mercy to me, in giving me, for many years, a willingness to die; and after that, for more than two years past, in making me willing to live, that I might do and suffer whatever he called me to here; whereas, before that, I often used to feel impatient at the thought of living.

When I arose on the morning of the Sabbath, I felt a love to all mankind, wholly peculiar in its strength and sweetness, far beyond all that I had ever felt before. The power of that love seemed to be inexpressible. I never before felt so far from a disposition to judge and censure others, with respect to the state of their hearts, their sincerity, or their attainments in holiness, as I did that morning.

The road between heaven and my soul seemed open and wide, all the day long; and the consciousness I had of the reality and excellence of heavenly things was so clear, and the affections they excited so intense, that it overcame my strength, and kept my body weak and faint, the great part of the day, so that I could not stand or go without help. The night also was comforting and refreshing. I had a strong sense of the infinite worth of Christ's approbation and love, and at the same time of the grossness of the comparison; and it only astonished me, that any one could compare a smile of Christ to any earthly treasure.--Towards night, I had a deep sense of the awful greatness of God, and felt with what humility and reverence we ought to behave ourselves before him. Just then Mr. W---- came in, and spoke with a somewhat light, smiling air, of the flourishing state of religion in the town; which I could scarcely bear to see. It seemed to me, that we ought greatly to revere the presence of God, and to behave ourselves with the utmost solemnity and humility, when so great and holy a God was so remarkably present, and to rejoice before him with trembling.--In the evening, these words, in the Penitential Cries, --"THE COMFORTER IS COME!"--were accompanied to my soul with such conscious certainty, and such intense joy, that immediately it took away my strength, and I was falling to the floor; when some of those who were near me caught me and held me up.

 How should I feel, if our house and all our property in it should be burnt up, and we should that night be turned out naked; whether I could cheerfully resign all to God; and whether I so saw that all was his, that I could fully consent to his will, in being deprived of it? and that I found, so far as I could judge, an entire resignation to his will, and felt that, if he should thus strip me of every thing, I had nothing to say, but should, I thought, have an entire calm and rest in God, for it was his own, and not mine.

My former impressions of heavenly and divine things were renewed with so much power, and life and joy, that my strength all failed me, and I remained for some time faint and exhausted. After the people had retired, I had a still more lively and joyful sense of the goodness and all-sufficiency of God, of the pleasure of loving him, and of being alive and active in his service, so that, I could not sit still, but walked the room for some time, in a kind of transport.

Jonathan Edwards' Account of Sarah Edwards' Experiences[165]

As mentioned previously, Jonathan Edwards thought that the experience of his wife was the emotional response of a godly Christian to the majesty of God, but while there were similarities of his wife's experiences with others, they should not necessarily be seen as normative for all people.

---

[165] Sereno, Some of these comments are also found in Edwards' work titled, *Some thoughts Concerning the Present Revival of Religion 1742.*

Edwards' accounting of these kinds of experiences was as follows:

> I have been particularly acquainted with many persons that have
> been the subjects of the high and extraordinary transports of the
> present day; and in the highest transports of any of the instances
> that I have been acquainted with, and where the affections of
> admiration, love and joy, so far as another could judge, have been
> raised to a higher pitch than in any other instances.

> I have observed or been informed of, the following things have
> been united, viz. a very frequent dwelling for some considerable
> time together, in such views of the glory of the divine perfections,
> and Christ's excellencies, that the soul in the mean time has been
> as it were perfectly overwhelmed, and swallowed up with light
> and love, and a sweet solace, rest and joy of soul, that was
> altogether unspeakable; and more than once continuing for five or
> six hours together, without any interruption, in that clear and
> lively view or sense of the infinite beauty and amiableness of
> Christ's person, and the heavenly sweetness of his excellent and
> transcendent love; so that (to use the person's own expressions)
> the soul remained in a kind of heavenly Elysium, and did as it
> were swim in the rays of Christ's love, like a little mote swimming
> in the beams of the sun, or streams of his light that come in at a
> window; and the heart was swallowed up in a kind of glow of
> Christ's love, coming down from Christ's heart in heaven, as a
> constant stream of sweet light, at the same time the soul all
> flowing out in love to him; so that there seemed to be a constant
> flowing and reflowing from heart to heart.

> The soul dwelt on high, and was lost in God, and seemed almost
> to leave the body; dwelling in a pure delight that fed and satisfied
> the soul; enjoying pleasure without the least sting, or any
> interruption; a sweetness that the soul was lost in; so that (so far as
> the judgment, and word of a person of discretion may be taken,
> speaking upon the most deliberate consideration) what was
> enjoyed in each single minute of the whole space, which was
> many hours, was undoubtedly worth more than all the outward
> comfort and pleasure of the whole life put together; and this
> without being in any trance, or being at all deprived of the exercise
> of the bodily senses.

> And the like heavenly delight and unspeakable joy of soul,
> enjoyed from time to time, for years together; though not
> frequently so long together, to such an height. Extraordinary views

of divine things, and religious affections, being frequently attended with very great effects on the body, nature often sinking under the weight of divine discoveries, the strength of the body taken away, so as to deprive of all ability to stand or speak; sometimes the hands clinched, and the flesh cold, but senses still remaining; animal nature often in a great emotion and agitation, and the soul very often, of late, so overcome with great admiration, and a kind of omnipotent joy, as to cause the person (wholly unavoidably) to leap with all the might, with joy and mighty exultation of the soul; the soul at the same time being so strongly drawn towards God and Christ in heaven, that it seemed to the person as though soul and body would, as it were of themselves, of necessity mount up, leave the earth and ascend thither.

These effects on the body did not begin now in this wonderful season, that they should be owing to the influence of the example of the times, but about seven years ago; and began in a much higher degree, and greater frequency, near three years ago, when there was no such enthusiastical season, as many account this, but it was a very dead time through the land. They arose from no distemper catched from Mr. Whitefield, or Mr. Tennent, because they began before either of them came into the country; they began as I said near three years ago, in a great increase, upon an extraordinary self dedication, and renunciation of the world, and resignation of all to God, made in a great view of God's excellency, and high exercise of love to him, and rest and joy in him; since which time they have been very frequent; and began in a yet higher degree, and great frequency, about a year and an half ago, upon another new resignation of all to God, with a yet greater fervency and delight of soul; since which time the body has been very often fainting, with the love of Christ; and began in a much higher degree still, the last winter, upon another resignation and acceptance of God, as the only portion and happiness of the soul, wherein the whole world, with the dearest enjoyments in it, were renounced as dirt and dung, and all that is pleasant and glorious, and all that is terrible in this world, seemed perfectly to vanish into nothing, and nothing to be left but God, in whom the soul was perfectly swallowed up, as in an infinite ocean of blessedness.

Since which time there have often been great agitations of body, and an unavoidable leaping for joy; and the soul as it were dwelling almost without interruption, in a kind of paradise; and very often, in high transports, disposed to speak of those great and glorious things of God and Christ; and the eternal world, that are in view, to others that are present, in a most earnest manner, and with a loud voice, so that it is next to impossible to avoid it. These effects on the body not arising from any bodily distemper or weakness, because the greatest of all have been in a good state of health.

This great rejoicing has been a rejoicing with trembling, i. e. attended with a deep and lively use of the greatness and majesty of God, and the persons' own exceeding littleness and vileness. Spiritual joys in this person never were attended, either formerly or lately, with the least appearance of any laughter or lightness of countenance, or manner of speaking; but with a peculiar abhorrence of such appearances in spiritual rejoicings, especially since joys have been greatest of all. These high transports when they have been past, have had abiding effects in the increase of the sweetness, rest and humility that they have left upon the soul; and a new engagedness of heart to live to God's honor, and watch and fight against sin.

Which growth has been attended, not only with a great increase of religious affections, but with a wonderful alteration of outward behaviour, in many things, visible to those who are most intimately acquainted, so as lately to have become as it were a new person; and particularly in living so much more above the world. and in a greater degree of steadfastness and strength in the way of duty and self denial, maintaining the Christian conflict against temptation, and conquering from time to time under great trials; persisting in an unmoved, untouched calm and rest, under the changes and accidents of time.

What has been felt in late great transports is known to he nothing new in kind, but to be of the same nature with what was felt formerly, when a little child of about five or six years of age; but only in a vastly higher degree. These transporting views and rapturous affections are not attended with any enthusiastic disposition, to follow impulses, or any supposed prophetical revelations; nor have they been observed to be attended with any appearance of spiritual pride, but very much of a contrary disposition, an increase of a spirit of humility and meekness, and a disposition in honor to prefer others.

I say, it is worthy to be observed, that there were these two things in a remarkable manner felt at that time, viz. a peculiar sensible aversion to judging of others that were professing Christians of good standing in the visible church, that they were not converted, or with respect to their degrees of grace; or at all intermeddling with that matter, so much as to determine against and condemn others in the thought of the heart; it appearing hateful, as not agreeing with that lamblike humility, meekness, gentleness and charity, which the soul then, above other times, saw the beauty of, and felt a disposition to. The disposition that was then felt was, on the contrary to prefer others to self, and to hope that they saw more of God and loved him better; though before, under smaller discoveries, and feebler exercises of divine affection, there had been felt a disposition to censure and condemn others. And another thing that was felt at that time, was a very great sense of the importance of moral social duties, and how great a part of religion lay in them.

The things already mentioned have been attended also with the following things, viz. an extraordinary sense of the awful majesty and greatness of God, so as oftentimes to take away the bodily strength; a sense of the holiness of God, as of a flame infinitely pure and bright, so as sometimes to overwhelm soul and body; a sense of the piercing all seeing eye of God, so as sometimes to take away the bodily strength; and an extraordinary view of the infinite terribleness of the wrath of God, which has very frequently been strongly impressed on the mind, together with a sense of the ineffable misery of sinners that are exposed to this wrath, that has been overbearing.

the strength of the body very often taken away with a deep mourning for sin, as committed against so holy and good a God, sometimes with an affecting sense of actual sin, sometimes especially indwelling sin, sometimes the consideration of the sin of the heart as appearing in a particular thing, as for instance, in that there was no greater forwardness and readiness to self denial for God and Christ, that had so denied himself for us; yea, sometimes the consideration of sin that was in only speaking one word concerning the infinitely great and holy God, has been so affecting as to overcome the strength of nature. A very great sense of the certain truth of the great things revealed in the gospel; an overwhelming sense of the glory of the work of redemption, and the way of salvation by Jesus Christ; the glorious harmony of the divine attributes appearing therein, as that wherein mercy and truth are met together, and righteousness and peace have kissed each other; a sight of the fullness and glorious sufficiency of Christ, that has been so affecting as to overcome the body.

Sometimes the sufficiency and faithfulness of God as the covenant God of his people, appearing in these words, I AM THAT I AM, in so affecting a manner as to overcome the body. A sense of the glorious, unsearchable, unerring wisdom of God in his works, both of creation and providence, so as to swallow up the soul, and overcome the strength of the body. A sweet rejoicing of soul at the thoughts of God's being infinitely and unchangeably happy, and an exulting gladness of heart that God is self sufficient, and infinitely above all dependence, and reigns over all, and does his will with absolute and uncontrollable power and sovereignty; a sense of the glory of the Holy Spirit, as the great comforter, so as to overwhelm both soul and body.

The thoughts of the perfect humility with which the saints in heaven worship God, and fall down before his throne, have often overcome the body, and set it into a great agitation.

Now if such things are enthusiasm, and the fruits of a distempered brain, let my brain be evermore possessed of that happy distemper! If this be distraction, I pray God that the world of mankind may be all seized with this benign, meek, beneficent, beatifical, glorious distraction! If agitations of body were found in the French prophets, and ten thousand prophets more, it is little to their purpose who bring it as an objection against such a work as this, unless their purpose be to disprove the whole of the Christian religion.

The great affections and high transports that others have lately been under, are in general of the same kind with those in the instance that has been given, though not to so high a degree, and many of them, not so pure and unmixed, and so well regulated.

Those that do not think such things as these to be the fruits of the true spirit, would do well to consider what kind of spirit they are waiting and praying for, and what sort of fruits they expect he should produce when he comes. I suppose it will generally be allowed that there is such a thing as a glorious outpouring of the Spirit of God to be expected, to introduce very joyful and glorious

times upon religious accounts; times wherein holy love and joy
will be raised to a great height in true Christians.

But if those things that have been mentioned be rejected, what is
left that we can find wherewith to patch up a notion, or form an
idea, of the high blessed, joyful religion of these times? What is
that any have a notion of, that is very sweet, excellent and joyful,
of a religious nature, that is entirely of a different nature from
these things?

From Jonathan Edwards' analysis, it is quite apparent that he did not frown
on such emotional experiences if what he witnessed reflected the following
things. The following is a summary of his analysis:

1) There was a sense of being overwhelmed with God's glorious
   perfections, with a sense of God's majesty and greatness
   accompanied with the individual's perception of his/her
   unworthiness before God.
2) There was a sense of being overwhelmed with the glory of
   Christ's redeeming work.
3) There was a spirit of humility and of self-denial whereby the
   person sincerely sought to put the interests of others ahead of his
   own.
4) There was a genuine desire to renounce worldliness.
5) There was a sincere desire to see the salvation of the unconverted.
6) There was a genuine desire to love others by not sinfully judging
   them, and a desire to be diligent in good works toward one's
   neighbor.
7) There was no imitating the experiences of others due to the
   preaching of such men like Whitefield and Gilbert Tennent.
8) These ecstatic manifestations were **not** associated with an
   unbiblical notion of following impulses (so called leadings of the
   Spirit) or supposed prophetic revelations.

Edwards assessed these experiences primarily in light of those things that
predicated them and the fruit that flowed from them. In other words, if
such godly thinking and behavior is the basis and fruit of a deranged mind,
then he wants such a deranged mind.

When Edwards wrote his *Some Thoughts Concerning the Present Revival
of Religion 1742*, he was ultimately seeking to give biblical reasons

justifying the revivals as a true work of the Holy Spirit, although he admitted that there were various problems and sinful tendencies that emerged. Edwards was also seeking to provide a biblical refutation to one of Boston's leading clergyman, Charles Chauncy. Chauncy was fast becoming Edwards' chief antagonist of the revivals and was having a significant amount of success in persuading others that the revivals were fraught with all kinds of problems.

What were some of the problems that Edwards acknowledged? They can be generally classified as follows:

1) A spiritual pride arising among some.
2) The errors of some friends of the revival in not setting limits or regulations in the expressions of emotions, thereby leading to a lack of order and a disruption of public worship.
3) The ungodly manifestations of a censorious spirit towards others, especially towards those that were actually God fearing.
4) The adoption of wrong principles such as those thinking they can have inspired revelations from God and other misuse of Scripture to justify the following of various impulses by pleading that they were simply following the leading of the Spirit.
5) The losing of the importance of family worship.
6) The dangers of having "lay preachers."

Edwards had great biblical insight into these problematic areas. Today, we can glean much from his analysis. All of these observations and exhortations are found in his book *Some Thoughts Concerning the Present Revival of Religion: And The Way In Which It Ought To Be Acknowledged And Promoted, Humbly Offered To The Public In A Treatise On That Subject* [166]

The Error of Undiscerned Spiritual Pride

Probably the greatest error that Edwards saw in connection with the Great Awakening was what he called - undiscerned spiritual pride. He saw this sin in some preachers who were zealous in promoting the revivals. And do

---

[166]   All of the direct quotes in the following sections are taken from an online copy of Edwards' *Some Thoughts Concerning the Present Revival of Religion: And The Way In Which It Ought To Be Acknowledged And Promoted, Humbly Offered To The Public In A Treatise On That Subject.* It can be found at http://www.prayermeetings.org/files/Jonathan_Edwards/JE Some Thoughts Concerning The Present Revival.pdf.

we not have similar problems in our time with certain men, who are theologically correct in certain respects but who then promote their views with extreme harshness? Edwards stated the problem:

> The first and the worst cause of errors that prevail in such a state of things is spiritual pride. This is the main door by which the devil comes into the hearts of those who are zealous for the advancement of religion.
>
> The spiritually proud man is full of light already. He does not need instruction and is ready to despise the offer of it. But, if this disease be healed, other things are easily rectified. The humble person is like a little child, he easily receives instruction. He is jealous over himself, sensible how liable he is to go astray, and therefore, if it be suggested to him that he does so, he is ready most narrowly and impartially to inquire. Nothing sets a person so much out of the devil's reach as humility, and so prepares the mind for true divine light without darkness, and so clears the eye to look on things as they truly are; Psalm 25:9, "The meek will he guide in judgment."
>
> The spiritually proud person is apt to find fault with other saints, that they are low in grace and to be much in observing how cold and dead they are and being quick to discern and take notice of their deficiencies. But the eminently humble Christian has so much to do at home and sees so much evil in his own heart and is so concerned about it, that he is not apt to be very busy with other hearts.
>
> Some who have spiritual pride mixed with high discoveries and great transports of joy, disposing them in an earnest manner to talk to others, are apt in such frames to be calling upon other Christians about them and sharply reproving them for their being so cold and lifeless. In a contrariety to this, it has been the manner in some places, or at least the manner of some persons, to speak of almost everything that they see amiss in others in the most harsh, severe, and terrible language. It is frequent with them to say of others' opinions or conduct or advice — or of their coldness, their silence, their caution, their moderation, their prudence, etc. — that they are from the devil or from hell. That such a thing is devilish or hellish or cursed and that such persons are serving the devil or the devil is in them, that they are soul-murderers and the like; so that the words devil and hell are almost continually in their mouths. And such kind of language they will commonly use, not only towards

wicked men but towards them whom they themselves allow to be the true children of God and also towards ministers of the gospel and others who are very much their superiors. And they look upon it as a virtue and high attainment thus to behave themselves. "Oh," say they, "we must be plain-hearted and bold for Christ, we must declare war against sin wherever we see it, we must not mince the matter in the cause of God and when speaking for Christ."

And shall the meanest of the people be justified in commonly using such language concerning the most excellent magistrates or the most eminent ministers? I hope nobody has gone to this height. But the same pretense of boldness, plain-heartedness, and declared war against sin will as well justify these things as the others.

Spiritual pride takes great notice of opposition and injuries that are received and is apt to be often speaking of them and to be much in taking notice of their aggravations either with an air of bitterness or contempt... There has been a great deal too much talk of late among many of the true and zealous friends of religion about opposition and persecution.

Ministers who have been the principal instruments of carrying on this glorious revival of religion, and whom God has made use of to bring up his people as it were out of Egypt, should take heed that they do not provoke God as Moses did by assuming too much to themselves and by their intemperate zeal to shut them out from seeing the good things that God is going to do for his church in this world.

The Error of the Lack of Order and Disruption of Public Worship by Excessive Enthusiasts

While Edwards gave a certain defense of ecstatic manifestations due to a person's comprehension of the great doctrinal truths of Scripture, he did not sanction the disruption of public worship that promoted disorder in the assembly of God. Edwards stated:

Speaking in the time of the solemn worship of God; as public prayer, singing, or preaching, or administration of the Sacrament of the Holy Supper, or any duty of social worship should not be allowed. I know it will be said, that in some cases, when persons are exceedingly affected they cannot help it; and I believe so too; but then I also believe and know by experience that there are several things which contribute to that inability besides merely and absolutely the sense of divine things upon their hearts. Custom and example or the thing being allowed have such an influence that they actually help to make it impossible for persons under strong affections to avoid speaking. If it was disallowed and persons, at the time that they were thus disposed to break out, had this apprehension that it would be very unbecoming for them so to do, it would contribute to their ability to avoid it. Their inability arises from their strong and vehement disposition; and, so far as that disposition is from a good principle, it would be weakened by this thought, viz. "What I am going to do will be for the dishonor of Christ and religion." And so the inward vehemence that pushed them forward to speak would fall, and they would be enabled to avoid it. This experience confirms.

There ought to be a moderate restraint on the loudness of persons' talking under high affections; for if there be not, it will grow natural and unavoidable for persons to be louder and louder without any increase of their inward sense; till it becomes natural to them, at last, to scream and halloo to almost every one they see in the streets when they are much affected. But this is certainly very improper and what has no tendency to promote religion.

There should also be some restraint on the abundance of talk under strong affections; for, if persons give themselves an unbounded liberty to talk just so much as they feel an inclination to, they will increase and abound more and more in talk beyond the proportion of their sense or affection; till at length it will become ineffectual on those that hear them and, by the commonness of their abundant talk, they will defeat their own end.

Edwards differentiates between the various ecstatic experiences of those in the Great Awakening. Some are tied with being overwhelmed with the glorious perfections of God, while others are absorbed in a self centered approach to the Faith. Edwards stated:

Another thing that is often mixed with the experiences of true Christians, which is the worst mixture of all, is a degree of self-righteousness or spiritual pride. This is often mixed with the joys of Christians. Their joy is not purely the joy of faith or a rejoicing in Christ Jesus but is partly a rejoicing in themselves. There is oftentimes in their elevations a looking upon themselves and a viewing their own high attainments; they rejoice partly because they are taken with their own experiences and great discoveries which makes them in their own apprehensions so to excel...

Sometimes, for want of persons distinguishing the ore from the pure metal, those experiences are most admired by the persons themselves and by others that are not the most excellent. The great external effects and vehemence of the passions and violent agitations of the animal spirits is sometimes much owing to the corrupt mixture (as is very apparent in some instances) though it be not always so. I have observed a great difference among those of high affections who seem disposed to be earnestly talking to those about them. Some insist much more in their talk on what they behold in God and Christ, the glory of the divine perfections, Christ's beauty and excellency and wonderful condescension and grace and their own unworthiness and the great and infinite obligations that they themselves and others are under to love and serve God. Others insist almost wholly on their own high privileges, their assurance of God's love and favor, and the weakness and wickedness of opposers and how much they are above their reach. The latter may have much of the presence of God, but their experiences do not appear to be so solid and unmixed as the former. And there is a great deal of difference in persons' earnestness in their talk and behavior. In some it seems to come from the fullness of their hearts and from the great sense they have of truth. They have a deep sense of the certainty and infinite greatness, excellency, and importance of divine and eternal things attended with all appearances of great humility.

Edwards even assigned some of the ecstatic experiences to the work of the devil. He stated:

I have seen it thus in an instance or two in which this vehemence at length issued in distraction. And there have been some few instances of a more extraordinary nature still, even of persons finding themselves disposed earnestly to talk and cry out, from an unaccountable kind of bodily pressure without any extraordinary view of anything in their minds or sense of anything upon their hearts; wherein probably there was the immediate hand of the devil.

Christians therefore should diligently observe their own hearts as to this matter and should pray to God that he would give them experiences in which one thing may bear a proportion to another that God may be honored and their souls edified thereby; and ministers should have an eye to this in their private dealings with the souls of their people.

It is chiefly from such a defect of experiences that some things have arisen which have been pretty common among true Christians of late, though supposed by many to have risen from a good cause; as particularly, talking of divine and heavenly things and expressing divine joys with laughter or light behavior. I believe in many instances such things have arisen from a good cause, as their *causa sine qua non*. High discoveries and gracious joyful affections have been the *occasion* of them; but the proper *cause* has been sin, even that odious defect in their experience whereby there has been wanting a sense of the awful and holy majesty of God as present with them, and their nothingness and vileness before him, proportionable to the sense they have had of God's grace and the love of Christ.

And the same is true in many cases of unsuitable boldness; a disposition to speak with authority, intemperate zeal, and many other things that sometimes appear under great religious affections. And sometimes the vehemence of the motion of the animal spirits, under great affections, is owing in considerable measure to experiences being thus partial. I have known it in several instances that persons have been greatly affected with the dying love of Christ and the consideration of the happiness of the enjoyment of him in heaven and other things of that nature, and their animal spirits at the same time have been in great emotion; but in the midst of it they have had such a deep sense of the awful, holy majesty of God as at once composed them and quieted animal nature without diminishing their comfort, but only has made it of a better and more solid nature. When they have had a sense both of the majesty and grace of God one thing has as it were balanced another and caused a more happy sedateness and composure of body and mind.

Experiences, thus qualified, will be attended with the most amiable behavior, will bring forth the most solid and sweet fruits, will be the most durable, and will have the greatest effect on the abiding temper of the soul.

Edwards was sensitive to the excessive emotional experiences that did not truly glorify God and contributed to a degeneration of overall experiences:

> What I mean is something diverse from the mere decay of experiences or their gradually vanishing by persons losing their sense of things; viz. experiences growing by degrees worse and worse in their kind, more and more partial and deficient; in which things are more out of due proportion and also have more and more of a corrupt mixture; the spiritual part decreases, and the other useless and hurtful parts greatly increase. This I have seen in very many instances, and great are the mischiefs that have risen through want of being more aware of it.

> It appears to me very probable that many of the heresies that have arisen and sects that have appeared in the Christian world in one age and another with wild enthusiastic notions and practices began at first by this means, that it was such a degenerating of experiences which first gave rise to them or at least led the way to them. — Nothing in the world so much exposes to this as an unheeded spiritual pride and self-confidence and persons being conceited of their own stock without an humble, daily, and continual dependence on God.

The Error of Unjustly Censuring Others

Edwards found the manifestation of a censorious spirit among some of the preachers, particularly the lay preachers, most disconcerting. The attitude of some college students, particularly those at Yale and Harvard, was also grievous. Edwards stated:

> And here the first thing I would take notice of is censuring professing Christians of good standing in the visible church as unconverted. I need not repeat what I have elsewhere said to show this to be against the plain, frequent, and strict prohibitions of the Word of God. It is the worse disease that has attended this work, most contrary to the spirit and rules of Christianity, and of the worst consequences.

> … So, when they have heard any minister pray or preach, their first work has been to observe him on a design of discerning him, whether he be a converted man or no; whether he prays like one that feels the saving power of God's Spirit in his heart, and whether he preaches like one that knows what he says.

... There has been an unhappy disposition in some ministers toward their brethren in the ministry in this respect which has encouraged and greatly promoted such a spirit among some of their people... Indeed it appears to me probable that the time is coming when awful judgments will be executed on unfaithful ministers and that no sort of men in the world will be so much exposed to divine judgments. But then we should leave that work to Christ who is the searcher of hearts and to whom vengeance belongs; and not, without warrant, take the scourge out of his hand into our own. There has been too much of a disposition in some, as it were, to give ministers over as reprobates, being looked upon as wolves in sheep's clothing: which has tended to promote and encourage a spirit of bitterness towards them and to make it natural to treat them too much as if they knew God hated them. If God's children knew that others were reprobates it would not be required of them to love them: we may hate those that we know God hates: as it is lawful to hate the devil and as the saints at the day of judgment will hate the wicked.

... The worst enemies of this work have been inwardly caused by this practice. They have made a shield of it to defend their consciences and have been glad that it has been carried to so great a length; at the same time that they have looked upon it and improved it as a door opened for them to be more bold in opposing the work in general.

The Error of Depending on Impulses and Believing One Has Inspired Revelation

In pointing out these kinds of errors, Edwards' analysis is applicable to today's practices in many "charismatic" churches. While various charismatic denominations were not officially in existence during Edwards' time, the erroneous views were becoming apparent in certain Congregational, Presbyterian, and Baptist churches. Edwards' comments upon the "leading of the Spirit" are timeless. Edwards stated:

One erroneous principle, than which scarce any has proved more mischievous to the present glorious work of God, is a notion that it is God's manner in these days to guide his saints, at least some that are more eminent, by inspiration or immediate revelation. They suppose he makes known to them what shall come to pass hereafter, or what it is his will that they should do, by impressions made upon their minds either with or without texts of Scripture, whereby something is made known to them that is not taught in the Scripture. By such a notion the devil has a great door opened for him; and if once this opinion should come to be fully yielded to and established in the church of God, Satan would have opportunity thereby to set up himself as the guide and oracle of God's people and to have his Word regarded as their infallible rule and so to lead them where he would and to introduce what he pleased and soon to bring the Bible into neglect and contempt. Late experience, in some instances, has shown that the tendency of this notion is to cause persons to esteem the Bible as in a great measure useless.

This error will defend and support errors. As long as a person has a notion that he is guided by immediate direction from heaven, it makes him incorrigible and impregnable in all his misconduct... This great work of God has been exceedingly hindered by this error...

It is strange what a disposition there is in many well-disposed and religious persons to fall in with and hold fast this notion. It is enough to astonish one that such multiplied, plain instances of the failing of such supposed revelations in the event do not open every one's eyes. I have seen so many instances of the failing of such impressions that would almost furnish a history.

They have been made upon the minds of apparently eminent saints and with an excellent heavenly frame of spirit yet continued and made with texts of Scripture that seemed exceeding apposite, yea, many texts following one another, extraordinarily and wonderfully brought to the mind, and the impressions repeated over and over. And yet all has most manifestly come to nothing to the full conviction of the persons themselves. God has in so many instances of late, in his providence, covered such things with darkness that one would think it should be enough quite to blank the expectations of those who have been ready to think highly of such things. It seems to be a testimony of God that he has no design of reviving revelations in his church and a rebuke from him to the groundless expectations of it.

And why cannot we be contented with the divine oracles, that holy, pure Word of God which we have in such abundance and clearness now since the canon of Scripture is completed? Why should we desire to have anything added to them by impulses from above? Why should we not rest in that standing rule that God has given to his church which, the apostle teaches us, is surer than a voice from heaven? And why should we desire to make the Scripture speak more to us than it does? Or why should any desire a higher kind of intercourse with heaven than by having the Holy Spirit given in his sanctifying influences, infusing and exciting grace and holiness, love and joy, which is the highest kind of intercourse that the saints and angels in heaven have with God and the chief excellency of the glorified man Christ Jesus?

Some that follow impulses and impressions indulge a notion that they do no other than follow the guidance of God's Word because the impression is made with a text of Scripture that comes to their mind. But they take that text as it is impressed on their minds and improve it as a new revelation to all intents and purposes; while the text, as it is in the Bible, implies no such thing...

Here are the propositions or truths entirely new that those words do not contain. These propositions, That it is God's mind and will that such a person by name should arise at such a time and go to such a place and that there he should meet with discoveries, are entirely new propositions, wholly different from those contained in that text of Scripture.

Edwards' comments on the leading of the Spirit are extremely helpful. He correctly demonstrates what the Spirit's leading truly consists of. It must lead to actual godliness in keeping the Lord's precepts. He stated:

Those texts of Scripture that speak of the children of God as led by the Spirit have been by some brought to defend such impulses; particularly Romans 8:14, "For as many as are led by the Spirit of God, they are the sons of God:" and Gal. 5:18, "But if ye are led by the Spirit, ye are not under the law." But these texts themselves confute them that bring them...A man may have ten thousand such revelations and directions from the Spirit of God and yet not have a jot of grace in his heart...If a person has anything revealed to him from God or is directed to anything by a voice from heaven or a whisper or words immediately suggested to his mind, there is nothing of the nature of grace merely in this...

There is a more excellent way in which the Spirit leads the sons of God that natural men cannot have; and that is by inclining them to do the will of God and go in the shining path of truth and Christian holiness from a holy, heavenly disposition which the Spirit of God gives them and which inclines and leads them to those things that are excellent and agreeable to God's mind, whereby they "are transformed by the renewing of their minds and prove what is that good, and acceptable and perfect will of God," (Romans12:2).

The Spirit of God enlightens them with respect to their duty by making their eye single and pure, whereby the whole body is full of light. The sanctifying influence of the Spirit of God rectifies the taste of the soul, whereby it savors those things that are holy and agreeable to God's mind; and, like one of a distinguishing taste, it chooses those things that are good and wholesome and rejects those that are evil.

And thus the Spirit of God leads and guides the meek in his way, agreeable to his promises. He enables them to understand the commands and counsels of his Word and rightly to apply them...

The leading of the Spirit which God gives his children, and which is peculiar to them, is that teaching them his statutes and causing them to understand the way of his precepts which the psalmist so very often prays for, especially in the 119th Psalm: and not in giving them new statutes and new precepts.

The Error of Lay-Preachers

Edwards saw much error in an untrained preacher, which he called, a "lay preacher or exhorter." Edwards stated:

Another thing in the management of which there has been much error and misconduct is lay-exhorting; about which there has been an abundance of disputing, jangling and contention. In the midst of these disputes, I suppose that all are agreed as to these two things, viz. 1. That all exhorting one another by laymen is not unlawful or improper; but, on the contrary, that such exhorting is a Christian duty. And, 2. I suppose also, all will allow that there is some kind or way of exhorting and teaching which belongs only to the office of teachers.

... If there be any way of teaching that is peculiar to that office, then for others to take that upon them is to invade the office of a minister; which doubtless is very sinful and is often so represented in Scripture.

... The two ways of teaching and exhorting, the one of which ought ordinarily to be left to ministers and the other of which may and ought to be practiced by the people, may be expressed by those two names of *preaching* and *exhorting* in a way of Christian conversation.

There is a certain authority that ministers have and should exercise in teaching as well as in governing the flock. Teaching is spoken of in Scripture as an act of authority, 1 Timothy 2:12. In order to a man's preaching, special authority must be committed to him, Romans 10:15, "How shall they preach, except they be sent?" Ministers in this work of teaching and exhorting are clothed with authority as Christ's messengers, Malachi 2:7, as representing him, and so speaking in his name and in his stead, 2 Corinthians 5:18-20. And it seems to be the most honorable thing that belongs to the office of a minister of the gospel that to him is committed the work of reconciliation, and that he has power to preach the gospel as Christ's messenger and speaking in his name. The apostle seems to speak of it as such, 1 Corinthians 1:16, 17. Ministers, therefore, in the exercise of this power, may clothe themselves with authority in speaking or may teach others in an authoritative manner, Titus 2:15, "These things speak and exhort, and rebuke with all authority: Let no man despise thee." But the common people, in exhorting one another, ought not thus to exhort in an authoritative manner.

When private Christians take it upon them in private meetings to act as the masters or presidents of the assembly, and accordingly from time to time to teach and exhort the rest, this has the appearance of authoritative teaching.

Despite Jonathan Edwards' attempts at distinguishing the good and bad parts of the First Great Awakening, the damage had already been done. As Edwards had noted, the friends of the revivals had also proved to be a target for opposition. Charles Chauncy was the junior pastor to Thomas Foxcroft at the First Church in Boston. He was fast becoming the spokesman for the minority who were resistant to the revivals. The problems identified by Chauncy were the same things that Edwards sought to address: the error of imposing a standardized test for determining a heartfelt experience, the excessive emotionalism, and the existence of lay people exhorting and claiming authority. By 1742 Chauncy was openly critical of the revivals. Chauncy wrote:

> Scores or even hundreds of people would shriek, swoon, or fall into fits. In the same house of worship and at the same time, some would be praying, some exhorting, some singing, some clapping their hands, some laughing some crying, some shrieking and roaring out. Often the worst effects, and Chauncey observed, would be at night. "It is at evening, or more late in the night with only a few candles in a meeting house, that there is a screaming and shrieking to the greatest degree, and the persons thus unaffected are generally children, young people, and women. Anyone who dared criticize any of these improprieties would be dismissed as "an opposing the spirit, the child of the devil."[167]

---

[167]   Chauncy, Charles. *A Letter from a Gentleman in Boston, to Mr. George Wishart, One of the Ministers of Edinburgh, Concerning the State of Religion in New England* (Edinburg, 1742). The letter was dated Aug. 4, 1742.

It did not help the cause of the revival with James Davenport's continued schismatic behavior. By the end of May 1742, citizens of Stratford, Connecticut issued a complaint against Davenport and Benjamin Rory for behavior that was contributing to church schism. The association of local pastors interviewed Davenport and came to the conclusion that he was out of control. The association issued a strong rebuke for his excesses and obstinate attitude. Virtually all the pastors of Boston signed the document, including a great champion of the revival, Benjamin Coleman, who was the first to sign this document.[168] Another champion of the revival, Thomas Prince, wrote:

> A "disputatious spirit most grievously prevailed amongst us" and that "every party" as "sadly guilty" of lamentable acrimony.[169]

This public rebuke of Davenport did not deter him from his schismatic behavior. By March 6, 1742, Davenport led a separatist group comprised of about 100 young people in a ceremonial religious book burning to signal their purity from the corrupt New England establishment. The books included leading Puritan and congregational works in divinity, such as those by John Weibel, Increase Mather, and Benjamin Coleman. The next day, turning to the problem of idolatry, Davenport ordered his people to burn jewelry, wigs, cloaks, nightgowns, and any item of clothes that Davenport said they loved too much. A more moderate New Light advocate intervened and raised the possibility that Davenport might be possessed by the devil.[170]

After two months of forbearance, the Boston authorities had heard enough. They gathered sufficient evidence of Davenport's schismatic behavior and issued a warrant for his arrest.[171] With this action, Davenport began to take notice of the rebuke of his fellow friends of the revival. Jonathan Edwards played a major role in aiding Davenport to see the error of his ways. Edwards encouraged Davenport to make a public, humble, and suitable recantation of his errors. Davenport issued such a recantation in a letter that he gave to Solomon Williams for publication. In this letter, Davenport retracted his judging people unconverted, separatism, lay preaching, and to listening to impulses supposedly as messages from God. Now he believed that in his zeal for these errors and other nonessentials he had been led by

---

[168]   Marsden, p. 272 who cites "Declaration with Regard to the Rev. James Davenport and His Conduct", by the associated pastors of Boston and Charlestown, July 1, 1742.

[169]   This follows Tracy's well documented account, *Great Awakening*, pp. 243-48. Tracy's quotation from Prince on p.240 is from *Christian History*, Vol. 2, p. 248.

[170]   Marsden, p. 275.

[171]   The quotations attributed to Davenport are from a Grand Jury testimony of August 19-20, 1742.

a false spirit, especially in the matter of the book and clothes in New London.[172]

By 1743, the First Great Awakening was waning. More and more lay preachers were condemning those who they perceived as unconverted clergy. Separatist groups were forming where ecstatic experiences were seen as normative. Some of these radical separatist groups became Baptist and Congregational churches. By May 1742, Connecticut began to pass anti-itinerant laws in an attempt to curb the proliferation of enthusiastic evangelists.

The divisions were now in place between what came to be termed as "New Lights" vs "Old Lights."[173] In the "New Light" camp was Jonathan Edwards and others who looked upon the revival as a positive thing despite certain problematic elements. In the "Old Light" camp was Charles Chauncy and others who saw the revival as primarily a negative influence.

George Marsden summarizes the differences as follows:

> At a 1743 meeting, the Old Lights, finding themselves with a slight majority through the meeting into a turmoil by drafting a testimony of the pastors of the churches in the province of Massachusetts Bay condemning a member of the practices associated with the awakening, including reliance on impulses which they compared to Antinomianism, unguided itinerancy, lay preaching, separatism, censorious judgment of who is "unconverted," and enthusiastic disorders. Almost everyone agreed in renouncing these errors, but the friends of the Awakening insisted that these condemnations be balanced by one's condemning Arminianism as well as Antinomianism and especially by praise for the legitimate blessings of the Awakening. After heated debate and complicated attempts at redrafting, the Old Lights prevailed.[174]

In response to the "Old Lights" prevailing in 1743, the "New Lights" organized a counter convention consisting of around forty pastors, of whom the most prominent were Jonathan Edwards, Benjamin Coleman, Thomas Prince, Joseph Sewell, William Cooper, Thomas Foxcroft, and

---

[172] Marsden quotes from "The Rev. Mr. Davenport's Retraction, "July 28, 1744. This information came from a letter Edwards had sent to Eleazar Wheelock dated July 13, 1744.

[173] This is to be distinguished from the differences in "New School" and "Old School" Presbyterianism in the 19th Century.

[174] Marsden, p. 279.

Joshua Gee. In this convention, they greatly praised the fundamental value of the awakening while condemning the excesses.

It is interesting how the differences between these two sides focused around the differences between Jonathan Edwards and Charles Chauncy. Chauncy had no use whatsoever with emotional displays of any kind. Edwards did not disdain certain expressions if carefully regulated. Underlying the differences between Edwards and Chauncy on the awakening was a crucial philosophical issue. "The plain truth is," wrote Chauncey, "an *enlightened* mind, and not *raised affections*, ought always to be the guide of those who call themselves men; and this, in the affairs of religion, as well as other things."[175] Chauncy saw religious affections as principally related to one's animal nature that needed to be restrained by the highest faculty in man – reason. Edwards, while viewing reason as the noblest and highest faculty, also saw true religious affections as stemming from a regenerated heart. It is most interesting to note George Marsden's distinction between Edwards and Chauncy. Marsden states:

> Chauncy was aware of the underlying debate, who was coming from the Aristotelian (and Thomistic) tradition, which argued that we should follow the dictates of reason. Edwards was of the more Augustinian "voluntarist" camp which viewed a person guiding by affections of the will. The voluntarist emphasized that the intellect, without true affections, was insufficient for true religion. The proper affections of the will must reign in tandem with intellectual truth. The intellectual lust, by contrast, saw the affections at first of all unruly emotions, which could serve the good only when brought into submission to properly informed reason. [176]

By May 1743, Edwards wrote a letter to Rev. James Robe of Kilsyth, Scotland indicating that New England had now become fractured into two parties. Edwards stated in this letter:

> We have not such joyful news to send you; the clouds have lately thickened. New England was now sadly divided into two parties...very much owing to imprudent management in the friends of the work, and a corrupt mixture which Satan has found means to introduce, and are manifold simple errors, by which we have grieved and quenched the Spirit of God.[177]

---

[175]   Marsden, p. 281.
[176]   Marsden, pp. 282-283.
[177]   Marsden p. 284 quoted from Edwards to James Robe, May 12, 1743, *Works*, 16:109.

Edwards laid the blame for the subsiding of the revival at the feet of the friends of the revival. It was the radical "New Lights" with their misguided emphases that led many into arrogant self-delusion. In his letter to Rev. Robe, Edwards gave this summary of the two revivals that he had seen come and go:

> Gentleness and genuine self renouncing humility were far better evidences of true saintliness then were merely intense experiences. Edwards explained, "But experience plainly shows, that it is not the degree of rapture and ecstasy, but the nature and kind that must determine us in their favor." Genuine raptures would be accompanied not by a "noisy showy humility," but rather by "deep humiliation, brokenness of heart, poverty of spirit, mourning for sin, solemnity of spirit, a trembling reverence towards God, tenderness of spirit, self jealousy and fear, and great engagedness of heart, after holiness of life, and readiness to esteem others better than themselves."[178]

Edwards had preached a series of sermons to his congregation at Northampton, instructing them on the place of religious affections in the Christian life. Over the next several years he revised and extensively expanded these into his *Treatise on Religious Affections*, which finally appeared in 1746. This careful exposition was immediately reprinted in England and remains the most widely read and admired of his theological works.[179]

In his work *Treatise on Religious Affections*, Edwards stated that church history was replete with examples of how friends of true religion often do more damage to their cause than their open enemies. Edwards believed that Satan capitalized on certain aspects of the revival. While believers were resisting open opposition in front of them, the devil came in behind them and gave a fatal stab unseen. Satan's strategy was to counterfeit true religious experience with religious experience in the unregenerate with the most pernicious forms of self aggrandizement. Edwards wrote:

> By this means Satan brings then, even the friends of religion, insensibly to themselves, to do the work of enemies, by destroying religion, in a far more effectual manner, then open enemies can do.[180]

---

[178] Edwards letter to Rev. James Robe, May 12, 1743.
[179] Marsden, pp. 284-285.
[180] Marsden, p. 285 who quotes from Edwards, *Treatise on Religious Affections*, *Works*, 2:86-89.

In a roundabout way, Edwards was refuting Charles Chauncy's views on religious affections. Edwards insisted that true religion consisted in holy affections and that Scripture consistently stresses the proper manifestation of affections such as fear, hope, love, hatred, desire, joy, sorrow, gratitude, compassion, and zeal.[181] Edwards insisted that the new birth (regeneration) changed the entire man by changing his heart thereby changing what he loves. Edwards stated:

> Affections that are truly spiritual and gracious, do arise from those influences and operations on the heart, which are *spiritual, supernatural, and divine.*[182]

In his *Treatise on Religious Affections*, Edwards lamented over some of his supposed converts. He wrote:

> It has been a common thing in the church of God, for such bright professors that are received as eminent saints, among the saints, to fall away and come to nothing... How great therefore may the resemblance be, as to all outward expressions and appearances, between an hypocrite and a true saint.[183]

Edwards insisted that the way to judge the genuineness of one's faith was not by looking at one's feelings but by one's practice, that is, by one's fruit. Marsden makes this important observation:

> Edwards concluded *Religious Affections* by answering the objection that the emphasis on practice might seem like a new legalism. To the contrary, he said, it was all carefully premised on standard Calvinistic doctrine that a general work of grace would lead to keeping God's commandments. Edwards was dedicated to the old New England way that celebrated grace and lived by law. He was not going to let revival enthusiasm displace that balance which was disciplined into the very marrow of his bones.
>
> Edwards especially feared Satan's ability to subvert the awakening by appealing to human self-centeredness. The inflated go was the devil's playground, and in revival times his favorite boy was to simulate evangelical experience. Edwards refused a blanket condemnation of the reliance on personal testimony that would become normative for evangelicalism, but he had already seen

---

[181] Marsden, p. 285 who quotes from Edwards, *Treatise* on *Religious Affections*, pp. 95, 96, 97, and 102.

[182] Marsden, p. 287 who quotes from Edwards, *Treatise* on *Religious Affections*, p. 197.

[183] Marsden, p. 287 who quotes from Edwards, *Treatise* on *Religious Affections*, pp. 87, 185.

how Satan could use the contagiousness of revival enthusiasm as a means of exporting a human egotism.

The concluding sentences of Edwards's religious affections stated it would become fashionable for men to show their Christianity, more by an amiable distinguished behavior, then by an abundant and excessive declaring their experiences.[184]

Concluding Thoughts on the 18th Century Revivals

There is much to learn from church history, both from its successes and failures. We see how our sovereign Christ exercises dominion over the earth, and how He has used His church to advance His purposes in the world by giving gifts to His church. He raises up and anoints His heralds, His preachers.

We still live in a fallen world. Though men are redeemed out of their bondage to sin and Satan, errors can still manifest themselves in the Lord's church. Those who have closely studied the English revivals and the First Great Awakening in America have acknowledged that there was great good done with thousands of people genuinely saved. And yes, we must learn from mistakes that were made, but as Jonathan Edwards insisted, we must not judge the whole in light of the errors of various parts.

It may be true that the revivals in America were short lived, with the First Great Awakening lasting from 1740-1744, but this is no overriding criterion by which we should assess its impact. The millennial age is one of spiritual warfare. Satan's domain is being plundered. Should we not expect the great adversary to put up some fight even though he is a defeated foe in principle?

The Scripture pictures Jesus as King of kings and Lord of lords, going forth conquering to conquer. The gospel is truly God's *dunamis*, His dynamite. The English and American cultures were languishing in spiritual darkness. The sovereign Lord was pleased to anoint His heralds to proclaim good news to the afflicted and liberty to the captives. Just as the apostle Paul was sent forth to turn men from darkness to light and from the dominion of Satan to God, so did the great preachers of the 18th Century

---

[184]   Marsden, p. 289 who quotes from Edwards, *Treatise* on *Religious Affections*, p. 451.

go forth storming the gates of hell with the gospel, bringing every thought captive to Christ's obedience. Their message was simple. One must be born again, and one must run to Christ alone for salvation.

As Charles Hodge noted, the content of many of the revivalist preachers was solid Reformation based doctrine, emphasizing the doctrines of original sin, the necessity of regeneration, of effectual calling, of justification by faith, of a justification based solely on the imputed righteousness of Christ, of the need for repentance, and of the need of manifesting fruit indicative of one's justified state.

We cannot predict how men respond to the power of the gospel. Is God's saving grace and its apprehension lifeless? If there is joy in heaven with the conversion of one lost soul, should we not expect joy in the lives of those freed from their spiritual bondage? When the gospel came with great convicting power to thousands of Jews in Jerusalem through the anointed preaching of Peter, the hearers were pierced to the heart. We are not told how or if these people responded similarly to those convicted by the preaching of Christ's heralds of the 18th Century. In Jesus' parable of the Pharisee and the Publican, Jesus said that the Publican could not even lift his eyes to heaven but beat his breast saying, "God, be merciful to me, the sinner!"

The problems manifested among some during these revivals are the same errors that we must be vigilant to avoid. We must never make the experiences of some as normative for all. Assuming that the experiences of some are genuine expressions of a heart rendering gratitude to God, we must never minimize the power of example. If godliness is supposed to be seen in crying and fainting, then there is the tendency for others to think that this behavior is how one should behave. Such ecstatic expressions become the sign of the Holy Spirit's power. We see this today in certain charismatic churches where speaking in tongues is seen as normative for those truly filled with the Spirit. Being "slain in the Spirit" is viewed as normative in such churches. To think that social pressure is not being applied to people in such churches is naivety.

Jonathan Edwards' analyses of the errors that began to be duplicated during the revival are exactly the same errors we must avoid today. We must avoid the great sin of spiritual pride; we must resist entertaining the false use of Scripture to justify some subjective impulse; we must not think that just anyone can be authorized to publicly preach the Word; and we must avoid a judgmental spirit, thinking that unless people measure up to our expectations of godliness, they cannot be godly men.

Having the privilege of historical retrospect, we can see what came of Charles Chauncy's opposition to the First Great Awakening. While some of his observations of the excesses of the revival had some merit, his theological framework was fatally flawed, and the accusations made against him by some "New Light" preachers that he was unconverted might not have been exaggerated. Chauncy was no fan of George Whitefield. Whitefield was a Calvinist while Chauncy was an Arminian. But not all Arminians went to the extent that Chauncy later did. In 1784, Chauncy published his book titled *The Mystery Hid from Ages and Generations, or, the Salvation of All Men; The Grand Thing Aimed at in the Scheme of God*. In this 402 page book, Chauncy gave a supposed exegetical defense for the belief that all men will eventually be saved.[185] He detested the idea of an eternal place of torment. It is no wonder that Chauncy opposed the preaching of Edwards and Whitefield.

It is noteworthy that the Unitarian/Universalist Church claims Charles Chauncy as a precursor to Unitarianism. Unitarian minister, Jack D. Bryant writes:

> Although Chauncy and Mayhew were not Unitarians, they had laid the theological ground work by proclaiming: [a] commitment to logic and reason in theology, a biblicism that was strict but that demanded critical and historical analysis, and an overriding concern for moral aspiration as the focal point of the Christian religion.[186]

On the Unitarian and Universalist Association of Churches webpage, one can find this tribute to Charles Chauncy:

> Thanks in no small part to Chauncy's life and work, by 1804 a liberal Christian view was the dominant one in Boston. This complex conservative man had inadvertently sparked a new American liberal theological tradition: American Unitarianism.[187]

---

[185] I have skimmed this book by Charles Chauncy and found it most disconcerting. I have never read a book that sought to use Scripture to advance views so antithetical to biblical doctrines. Chauncy's exegesis is seriously flawed in numerous places. The great damage that Chauncy did was to provide a supposed biblical defense for what later became standard Unitarian/Universalist beliefs. Eventually, Unitarian/Universalists jettisoned the Bible, but it was Chauncy that provided a basis for doing so.

[186] Rev. Jack D. Bryant, "Unitarian and Universalist Theological History" found at: http://hopeuu.org/rootsessays/UU%20Theological%20History. Jack Bryant is presently minister of the Hope Unitarian Church in Tulsa, OK.

[187] This quote found at: www.uua.org/re/tapestry/adults/moves/workshop5/workshopplan/stories/153053.shtml

A lecture given on August 25, 2002 at the Unitarian Society of Hartford, Connecticut by W. Robert Chapman is most illuminating on Chauncy's contributions to the eventual rise of Unitarianism. Portions of his lecture are as follows:[188]

> At their inception, both Unitarians and Universalists shared a common theological enemy known as Calvinism. As the religion of the New England Puritans, Calvinism had deeply affected the fabric of American living and thinking. It was a vital theology, prone to different emphases and interpretations, one that was adapted in remarkable ways to the necessities of American spiritual life.
>
> Meanwhile, another more gradual change was taking place among many of the clergy of Boston and eastern Massachusetts. Still part of the churches of the "Standing Order" of New England, established by the Puritans on a Calvinist basis, these ministers began to doubt the doctrines of Calvinism, especially that of Election. They began to emphasize God's benevolence, humankind's free will, and the dignity rather than the depravity of human nature. This trend was accelerated by the religious upheavals that had begun with the Great Awakening in New England in the 1740s. The emotional excesses of the revival, and the threats that the many itinerant preachers posed to the established clergy, caused a reaction that forced many of the Boston-area ministers into a deeper commitment to liberal and rational theology. The vast majority of these Harvard-educated clergy adopted Arminianism, the belief that mankind was free to accept or reject God's grace.
>
> A few of the established Congregational churches evolved into Universalist societies, but the greater number of Universalist churches were comprised of the lower classes of New England society…Although they shared certain beliefs in common, the Unitarians increasingly looked to nonbiblical sources for inspiration. The Universalists, on the other hand, maintained a more pious biblical orientation.
>
> Few opposed the intense revival that swept New England in the 1740s with the tenacity and vehemence of the Rev. Charles Chauncy, pastor of Boston's First Church. A serious and scholarly

---

[188]   This lecture can be found in its entirety at: http://www.ushartford.com/ fatherhoodofman.html.

man educated at Harvard, given to neither great emotion nor large ambition, Chauncy found in the Great Awakening not only a source of personal passion in his dissent to it but a role of leadership in a movement that neither he nor anyone else in New England had contemplated. Chauncy was able to transmute his vigorous dissent into a positive set of ideas, falling loosely into three major categories: (1) a commitment to logic and reason in theology, (2) a biblicism that was strict but that demanded critical and historical analysis, and (3) an overriding concern for moral aspiration as the focal point of Christianity.

The emotional excess of the revivals was the target of liberal criticism, because it differed from the rational concept of religion that crystallized in the late eighteenth century. In an important sense, the seedbed for this rational religion was in the larger intellectual revolution of Sir Isaac Newton, whose reputation among a good many eighteenth-century Christian thinkers is best expressed by Alexander Pope:

NATURE, and Nature's laws lay hid in Night: God said, *Let NEWTON be!* and all was Light.

The new science held out the promise of a growing discovery of an ordered, benevolent universe, the product of a rational and benevolent God, intent on demonstrating his qualities through the perfection of nature. A system based on learning, reason, and order certainly had a great attraction for those skeptical of the intuition, passion, and disorder found in revivals.

Liberals consistently attacked Calvinism on the related issues of Original Sin and Election to salvation, doctrines that in their view undermined human moral exertion. The idea of the taint of Adam, communicated to all people regardless of their action or character, seemed to deny the possibility of the moral life; the idea of God's preordained selection of a few to salvation, regardless of their character or action, seemed to undercut the motivation for it. The liberals countered with a moral system that affirmed human capability, as evidenced in the moral sense, and even those writings that did not attack Calvinism by name contributed to the liberal revolt by contributing to a positive counter-theory.

Jonathan Mayhew's *Seven Sermons*, preached in 1748, offers a very good sense of the developing liberal moral philosophy.

Mayhew based his series on a firm rejection of all creeds and a corresponding insistence on private judgment as the necessary arbiter of religious opinion. The cornerstone of the whole series of sermons was an argument for human ability to make moral distinctions and act on that knowledge. As Mayhew saw him, God was "perfect in all those moral qualities and excellencies which we esteem amiable in mankind."

In rehabilitating human nature, Mayhew and the other liberals were not asserting the actual goodness of humankind but the *potential* for goodness in human nature.

Charles Chauncy and Jonathan Edwards were destined to "lock horns." At the feet of Charles Chauncy and Jonathan Meyhew, we can lay the beginnings of the New England slide into the darkness of Unitarian Universalism. Ellis Sandoz describes Charles Chauncy as "The most influential clergyman in Boston of his time and—apart from Jonathan Edwards the elder—in all New England."[189]

Chauncy would co-pastor and then pastor the First Church of Boston for sixty years! It was evident at the outset that there were problems with Chauncy's theology. His theological "Achilles Heel" was his belief that "reason" and "revelation" was the guide for religious life. The plain truth was, wrote Chauncy:

> An *enlightened mind* , and not *raised affections*, ought always be the guide of those who call themselves men; and this, in the affairs of religion, as well as other things.[190]

Jonathan Edwards' view of Chauncy's low view of human affections was expressed as:

> Some make philosophy instead of the Holy Scriptures their rule of judging of this work… particularly the philosophical notions they entertain of the nature of the soul, its faculties and affections.[191]

I would concur again with Jonathan Edwards' argument – don't judge the whole by some errors of the part. Chauncy would prove himself, in my

---

[189]   Ellis Sandoz. *Political Sermons of the American Founding Era, 1730-1805*. Indianapolis: Liberty Press, 1991: Foreword.

[190]   Charles Chauncy, *Seasonable Thoughts on the State of Religion in New England: A Treatise in Five Parts*, 1743, p. 327.

[191]   Jonathan Edwards, *Some Thoughts Concerning the Present Revival of Religion in New England, Works*, 4:296-297.

opinion, to be a wolf in sheep's clothing, but Jonathan Edwards and other various revivalists of the First Great Awakening were seeking to reach men with the glorious gospel, despite some of the attending mistakes that redeemed fallen men can sometimes make.

This leads us to consider another great preacher of the 18th Century.

Samuel Davies – "The Apostle to Virginia"

One of the contemporaries of both George Whitefield and Jonathan Edwards was Samuel Davies of Virginia (1723 –1761). He personally viewed his ministry as insignificant in many ways; however, during his short life of thirty-seven years, he did have a profound affect in Virginia, earning the later designation as "the apostle of Virginia." The renowned English preacher of the 20th Century, Dr. Martyn Lloyd-Jones, once told an American audience, "You Americans do not know the greatest preacher your country has ever produced." He then pronounced the name- Samuel Davies.[192]

Samuel Davies was born in Newcastle County, Delaware in 1723. What a blessing for him to have been born in a Christian home where his mother was particularly godly. His mother named him Samuel, after the biblical prophet Samuel. Davies would later say, "I am a son of prayer, like my namesake." His relationship with his mother throughout his life was a very strong one. His mother would outlive him, and at his death, it is recorded that when his body was in the coffin, she gazed on it attentively and then exclaimed, "There is the son of my prayers and my hopes, my only son, my only earthly supporter, but there is the will of God, and I am satisfied."[193]

By the age of fifteen, he was convinced that he was justified by faith. He made a profession of faith and joined the Presbyterian Church. With his parents being unable to financially provide for Samuel's education, a learned Welsh minister, Mr. Morgan, paid for his tuition when Samuel

---

[192]   This was a comment made by Dr. Lloyd-Jones in 1967 while addressing an audience at Westminster Theological Seminary. It is referenced in Ian Murray's book, *Revival and Revivalism*, pp. 24-25.

[193]   This was in a footnote listed as [Editor of the Board] of the sermon preached by Samuel Finley, D.D. who was Davies' successor as President of the College of New Jersey. The sermon was titled, "Disinterested and Devoted Christians" preached by him at Nassau Hall, Princeton, May 28, 1761.

Blair opened his famous school at Fagg's Manor, Pennsylvania. This is where he completed his education.[194] It is of value to know something of the man who Samuel Davies viewed as one of the best preachers he ever knew. Learning something of the mentor gives insight into the pupil. Samuel Davies was trained in the congregation of Samuel Blair, and Blair gave accounts of revival in Pennsylvania and New Jersey during the First Great Awakening. In his *A Short and Faithful Narrative of the Late Remarkable Revival of Religion*, Blair gave some insight of how the revival impacted his own congregation. He said:

> Those awakened were much given to reading the Holy Scriptures and other good books... It was a peculiar satisfaction to people to find out how exactly the doctrines they heard preached, harmonize with the doctrines maintained and taught by great and godly men in other parts and former times. There was an earnest desire in people often opportunities for public worship and hearing of the word.[195]

Blair did document some strange occurrences among those affected in his congregation. It would be those same strange occurrences that happened elsewhere during the First Great Awakening that caused a split among the clergy of the time in how they viewed the awakening. Blair explained some of these strange experiences in his congregation during the summer of 1740:

> There was manifest evidence of impressions on the hearers, and many times the impressions were very great and general; several would be overcome and fainting; others deeply sobbing hardly able to contain, others crying in a most dolorous manner, many others more silently weeping, and a solemn concern appearing in the countenances of many others. And sometimes the soul exercises of some, comparatively but few, would so far affect their bodies as to occasion some strange, unusual bodily motions.[196]

The type of preaching that Blair did that summer when the revival was underway was solid gospel preaching with an emphasis on a person grasping the gravity of his sins and the necessity of repentance and faith in Christ's imputed righteousness. Samuel Davies had nothing but the greatest praise for his mentor, Samuel Blair. Davies said that in terms of

---

[194] Rev. William Henry Foote, *Sketches of Virginia: Historical and Biographical*, (Philadelphia: William S. Martien, 142 Chestnut Street, 1850). Viewed online at
http://quod.lib.umich.edu/m/moa/aja2527.0001.001/169?page=root;size=100;view=image.
[195] Foote, p. 110.
[196] Foote, p. 111.

the preachers that he heard in England none of them came close to his old master as to the matter of their discourses and the impression produced by their delivery.[197] Blair was also viewed as an admirable preacher, a superior teacher, and a good writer.[198]

The impact of Blair's ministry would find great fruit in the ministry of his pupil, Samuel Davies. Davies was licensed to preach by Newcastle Presbytery in 1746. In 1747 tragedy struck his home with the death of his wife and son. He spent considerable time filling pulpits wherever he could, and in the spring of 1748, he received an earnest call from the heads of 150 families in Hanover County,[199] Virginia. He accepted the call, and it was not long before there was considerable fruit in his ministry. The distances between the meeting houses in Hanover County were significant, some being more than thirty miles from one another. In many regards, Davies was a circuit rider preacher in Hanover County. One of the original frame buildings in which Davies preached is still standing in Louisa County. Robert L. Dabney's ancestors were connected to this, the Providence Church, and Dabney himself served this congregation in his first pastoral charge almost 100 years after Davies. In his writings, Dr. Dabney often mentions Davies with the highest praise and in connection with the greatest men such as Augustine and Whitefield.[200]

In 1748 over 300 people joined the church and were admitted to the Lord's Table, and one of the most notable things about Davies' ministry in Hanover County was his ministry to the Negroes where over 300 were regular attendees of his services. In the next century, Archibald Alexander said that he had seen Negroes born in Africa who were baptized by Davies, taught to read, and given books to them by the imminent preacher. Some of the books given to the Negroes were Watson's *Body of Divinity,* Boston's *Human Nature in its Fourfold State,* Luther's commentary on Galatians, Flavel's works, Alleine's *Alarm to the Unconverted,* Baxter's *Call to the Unconverted,* and Issac Watts' *Psalms.*[201] These were substantial theological works given to these Negroes who were being taught to read.

---

[197]   Foote, p. 145.
[198]   Foote, p. 144.
[199]   Hanover County was twelve miles north of Richmond.
[200]   Thomas Talbot Ellis, *Samuel Davies: Apostle of Virginia*, Part 1. This was an internet article found at: http://www.graceonlinelibrary.org/biographies/samuel-davies-apostle-of-virginia-part-i-of-ii-by-thomas-talbot-ellis/
[201]   Ellis article.

Those that visited Hanover County remarked that many people under Samuel Davies' ministry were spiritually flourishing. News of what was happening in Virginia reached Jonathan Edwards in Massachusetts who wrote:

> I have heard lately a credible account of a remarkable work of conviction and conversion among whites and negroes at Hanover, Virginia, under the ministry of Mr Davies, who is lately settled there, and has the character of a very ingenious and pious young man.[202]

The work in Virginia was growing so rapidly that the first presbytery (Hanover) in Virginia was organized in 1755 with Davies as the first moderator. The stability of the work was of such a nature that the absence of Davies' one year trip to England obviously did not jeopardize his ministry.

In 1751 the trustees of the College of New Jersey (today called Princeton) petitioned the Synod of New York that was meeting in Newark, New Jersey to raise funds for the college. When it became evident that colonial money was insufficient to sustain the college, the trustees again petitioned the synod of New York for it to appoint two of its members, Samuel Davies and Gilbert Tennent to travel to England and Scotland for the expressed mission of soliciting funds for the college.

Davies and Tennent departed in November 1753 and returned in February 1755. Their trip was immensely successful, passing all expectations in the amount of money that was raised.[203] It was George Whitefield who had initially encouraged a delegation to come to England for this purpose. The great Christian philanthropist and revivalist, the Countess of Huntingdon, was a significant contributor to the College of New Jersey.

We do not know how many times Samuel Davies may have heard George Whitefield preach when Whitefield made his first visit to America in 1740. It was probably multiple times because Davies was Samuel Blair's pupil, and Whitefield preached at Fagg's Manor. It is quite clear that Davies greatly admired the ministry of Whitefield. In Davies' plea to the Bishop of London for the cause of Dissenters[204] in Virginia, we first get a glimpse

---

[202] Foote, p. 172.
[203] They would raise £3000, which was equal to the wages of a laborer for more than a hundred years of work in terms of 18th Century buying power.
[204] Dissenters were any Christians who broke away from the established church, the Church of England. The Puritans were among the first English dissenters. Listed among the dissenting churches would be the Congregationalists, Presbyterians, Baptists, and Quakers to name but a

of Davies' respect for Whitefield. In his plea, Davies makes these comments about Whitefield:

> Your Lordship huddles me promiscuously with the methodists, as though I were of their party. I am not ashamed to own that I look upon Mr. Whitefield as a zealous and successful minister of Christ; and as such countenance him. I love him, and I love your lordship.[205]

Davies and Tennent arrived in London on Christmas Day, 1753. Upon learning of their arrival, Whitefield invited them that night to use his home during their stay in London. Davies' journal date for December 26, 1753 reads:

> Mr. Whitefield having sent us an invitation last night to make his house our home during our stay here; we were perplexed what to do lest we should blast the success of our mission among the dissenters, who are generally disaffected to him. He spoke in the most encouraging manner as to the success of our mission, and in all his conversation discovered so much zeal and candour, that I could not but admire the man as the wonder of the age! When we returned, Mr Tennent's heart was all on fire; and after we had gone to bed, he suggested that we should watch and pray, and we rose and prayed together till about 3 o'clock in the morning.[206]

There is an interesting entry in Davies' diary regarding his attendance at Whitefield's London meeting house called "The Tabernacle." Davies' January 1, 1754 entry reads:

> Went in the Evening to hear Mr. Whitefield in the Tabernacle, a large, spacious building. The assembly was very numerous, tho' not equal to what is common. He preached on the parable of the barren fig tree, and tho' the discourse was incoherent, yet it seemed to me better calculated to do good to mankind than all the accurate, languid discourses I have heard. After sermon enjoyed his pleasing conversation at his house.[207]

---

few. The Act of Toleration of 1689 permitted the existence of these churches with certain stipulations.

[205] Foote, p. 199.
[206] Foote, p. 244.
[207] Foote, p. 245.

There were differences of opinion between Whitefield and Davies/Tennent on the best methods of soliciting funds for the College of New Jersey. Davies in his January 14, 1754 entry wrote:

> Spent an hour with Mr. Whitefield, he thinks we have not taken the best method in endeavouring to keep in with all parties, but should "come out boldly," as he expressed it, which would secure the affections of the pious people whom we might expect the most generous contributions.[208]

I must mention the following story only because it is commonly associated with Samuel Davies. Writers and preachers commonly refer to this story as one of the greatest examples of the boldness of Davies' preaching. The story goes as follows:

> Davies' fame as a preacher was so great in London that news reached King George II that a dissenting minister from the colony of Virginia was attracting notice and drawing very crowded audiences. When the king expressed a strong desire to hear him, his chaplain invited Davies to preach in the royal chapel. He is said to have complied and preached before the royal family and many of the nobility. As Davies was preaching, the king was seen speaking at different times to those around him. While the king was speaking, Mr. Davies paused and became silent. He then looked in the direction of the king and is said to have exclaimed, "When the lion roars, the beasts of the forest all tremble; and when King Jesus speaks, the princes of the earth should keep silence." The remark was well taken, and afterwards the king explained that he was so impressed with the solemn manner and true eloquence of the preacher that he was constrained to express his astonishment and approval to those around him. He professed to feel anything but irreverence. Davies ever afterwards had a high regard for the king as may be learned from the sermon he preached on the occasion of the death of George II.

The reason preachers love this story is because of the courageous stand of Davies and the primacy of preaching over the kings of the earth. Earthly kings must all bow to the word of the King of kings and Lord of lords and show respect before Him. These are surely great and precious biblical

---

[208]   Foote, p. 247.

truths; however, here is the problem: the best evidence is that the story is dubious.[209] The highest probability is that it never happened!

Sadly, when Davies and Tennent, being Presbyterians, traveled throughout England, it was not the Presbyterians that he often found fellowship with. Davies found many of the English Presbyterians in a dismal spiritual condition. Many times he found greater Christian fellowship in the coffee houses frequented by Independents and Baptists. He wrote:

> The Independents and Baptists are more generally Calvinists, than the Presbyterians, though I fear some of them are tainted with Antinomianism.[210]

---

[209] Whenever one finds the citing of this story, even in seminary journals, there is no historical documentation cited. In one seminary journal article, the author in a footnote simply says, "During his year in England he actually did preach for King George II." Unfortunately, this is not historical documentation but an unfounded opinion. The monumental problem with this story is that Samuel Davies' daily detailed journal of his year trip never mentions his preaching in the royal chapel before King George II. This was his only trip to England. Davies recounted numerous preaching occasions and social events, but no mention of this significant of an event. While there are a few gaps in his journal, nothing is said of preaching before the king.

Another problem with the story is that it specifically mentions that Davies was a dissenting minister from Virginia. If Davies was concerned about his image of being publicly associated with George Whitefield, that it could damage his chances of raising money for the College of New Jersey, imagine the social "fall out" of a dissenting minister admonishing the head of the Church of England to pay attention to the sermon. It surely would have been headlines in London newspapers. The evidence throughout Davies' journal is that he is ever mindful of not unduly offending anyone. In a January 20, 1754 journal entry, Davies comments on hearing Gilbert Tennent preach for a Presbyterian minister. Davies was pleased with the simplicity of Tennent's sermon, but commented, "Heard Mr. Tennent P.M., preach an honest and plain sermon; and while I was pleased with its simplicity, I was uneasy lest its bluntness might be offensive." Now, if Davies is uneasy about the bluntness of Tennent's sermon in a Presbyterian London pulpit, what are the chances of him openly rebuking the King of England by supposedly stopping his sermon when he noticed the king talking during it? The evidence is virtually undeniable that the oft told event never happened.

Moreover, the story indicates that Davies had these crowded audiences when he preached which prompted King George II to invite him to his chapel. This is not Davies' perspective when he first arrived in England. In a Dec. 30, 1753 entry, Davies mentions that he filled the pulpit of a Baptist minister in London. Davies writes: "It is grievous to see how small the congregations are in this vast city." In other words, people were not flocking to hear him preach.

I have discussed this matter with a Christian historian who stated that he has no idea of the origin of the story and that it is undocumented. If not factual, who fabricated it? No one knows. My guess is that it would be good fodder for dissenting bodies to perpetuate – one of their dissenting ministers telling the head of the established church to be silent, but then, that is only speculation on my part. In conclusion, my opinion is that it is best for preachers not to use this story, as good as it appears to be. We need to strive for accuracy as much as possible and not mislead people.

[210] December 30, 1753 journal entry as found in Foote, p. 244.

It is worth noting Davies' perspective of the English Methodists:

> The despised Methodists with all their foibles do have more of the spirit of religion than any sect of people in this island.[211]

Though Davies boarded his ship for its return trip to America in November of 1754, it took nearly six weeks before he got out of England. The account of his return voyage is most illuminating. Davies recounted the perils of sea voyages in those days. They encountered a massive forty-eight hour storm where Davies honestly showed his struggle with maintaining faith in a sovereign God and moments of sheer terror where there was a self resignation that he would perish at sea. Davies expressed an attitude that the godliest of men have often expressed in the face of imminent mortal danger:

> I was in a careless, guilty frame when the storm came on: and I never felt so deeply the terrors of being seized by danger or death in such a frame. The sight of death frowning upon me on every side, threw my mind into a ferment like that of the ocean around me. Sometimes indeed I have some intervals of serenity in resignation: but generally my views were gloomy, my fears outrageous, and my heart faint. I endeavored to commit myself to God, and resigned my dear family to His care: but alas! I could not do it with cheerfulness. I never appeared to myself so helpless in all my life: confined to a little vessel, in the midst of mountainous seas, and a dreadful distance from land, and no possible prospect of escaping death, if any accident should befall the ship. I could do nothing but lie in bed, hearing the howl of winds and roar of waves without, and tossed from side to side by the motion of the vessel, which sometimes ruled so violently that she lay almost on her beam ends, and I was afraid she would not recover. The waves broke over her so as to wash the men from one side of the deck to the other, and dashed in through the dead-lights into the cabin. I often fell upon my face praying in a kind of agony, sometimes for myself, sometimes for the unhappy ship's company, and sometimes for my dear destitute family, whom the nearest prospect of death could not cross from my heart.[212]

During his absence from Virginia, hostilities had already commenced on the frontier during May 1754 in what became the French and Indian War that aligned the French and Indians against the English. Davies

---

[211] October 27, 1754 journal entry as found in Foote, p. 275.
[212] February 7, 1755 journal entry as found in Foote, p. 280.

demonstrated his English patriotism by preaching a sermon on the day that the Virginia Legislature designated as a day of fasting and prayer (March 5, 1755). He preached on the text, Daniel 4:25. The sermon title was, "The Most High Ruleth the Kingdom of Men and Giveth it to whom He Will." It was a decidedly Christian and patriotic sermon designed to excite his audience towards true piety and love of country. With General Braddock's monumental defeat on July 10, 1755 and the brutality that the Indians showed, fear spread especially to frontier regions. On July 20, 1755, Davies preached from Hanover County on the text, Isaiah 22:12-14 where God was calling for His people to weep and wail for their sins. Davies called upon people to courageously defend their colony. In August 1755, Davies preached a sermon (based on II Samuel 10:12) to the volunteer company of Virginia, raised to defend people on the frontier. In this sermon, Davies made this comment about the famous incident of Colonel George Washington's amazing protection during Braddock's defeat:

> I may point out to the public that heroic youth, Col. Washington, whom I cannot but hope Providence has hitherto preserved in so signal a manner, for some important service.[213]

In this and other sermons during this time period, Davies along with others demonstrated the vital public role that preachers had in society. The heralds of the King of kings were to carry out a prophetic role to the civil magistrate and to the public in general. The church often was the rallying instrument in the cause of righteousness and in their calls for public repentance for national sins.

As a true minister of the gospel, Davies yearned for bringing the gospel to poor whites and particularly to poor Negroes. In March 1755 Davies wrote to his friends in England who were part of "The Society in London for Promoting Religious Knowledge among the Poor." His desire was to encourage them to raise funds to purchase Bibles and theological works for him to distribute throughout Virginia. In his letter, Davies stated:

> Though there are very few of the white people in this colony in abject poverty, yet there are many in such low circumstances, that they cannot spare money to purchase good books, and many more so stupidly ignorant and insensible of their want of instruction, and deem it an unnecessary charge, and so excuse themselves from it as a needless expense... but the poor neglected Negroes, who are so far from having money to purchase books, that they themselves are the property of others; who were originally African savages,

---

[213]   Foote, p. 284.

and never heard of Jesus or his gospel, till they arrived at the land of their slavery in America, and their masters generally neglect, and whose souls none care for, as though immortality were not a privilege, and to them with their masters,-these poor unhappy Africans are objects of my compassion and I think the most proper objects of the society's charity.[214]

Davies' letter was received with great enthusiasm in England. Society members raised considerable sums to purchase the books alluded to earlier. When the books arrived in Virginia, Davies was overwhelmed with the magnitude of the generous supply of books. Some 400-500 books were distributed to the Negroes alone. Davies affectionately wrote to his benefactors:

On this occasion I also enlarged upon a new topic of conviction, both of the slaves themselves and their masters. Since persons at so great a distance, who had no connection with them, were so generously concerned to Christianize the poor Negroes, and had been etc. much pains and expense for that end, then how much more concerned, how much more zealous, and industrious should their masters be and how much more to the poor Negroes to be concerned for themselves? And how much more aggravated would be the guilt and ruin, if they persisted in obstinate infidelity and wickedness, after so much pains had been taken with them for their conversion? This I found afterwards proved a very popular topic of conviction, and made some impressions upon the minds of not a few.

For some time after this, the poor slaves, whenever they could get an hour's leisure from their masters, would hurry away to my house, and received the charity with all the genuine indications of passionate gratitude which unpolished nature could give, in which affectation and grimace would mimic in vain. The books were all very acceptable, but none more so than the Psalms and Hymns, which enabled them to gratify their peculiar taste for psalmody. Sundry of them have lodged all night in my kitchen, and sometimes when I waked to about two or three o'clock in the morning, a part of sacred harmony ported to my chamber, and carried my mind away to heaven. In this seraphic exercise, some

---

[214]   Foote, p. 285.

of them spend almost the whole night. I, sir, you and their other benefactors could hear any of these sacred concerts.[215]

This thrilling story about what was happening in the backwoods of Virginia under the ministry of Samuel Davies shows how God works through means to achieve His sovereign purposes. God raises up men of vision who yearn for the souls of the lost and disadvantaged. These Christian visionaries are the mediators between those of worldly means and those in need. One of the great passages on the godly use of wealth is seen in I Timothy 6:17-19 which says:

> [17]*Instruct those who are rich in this present world not to be conceited or to fix their hope on the uncertainty of riches, but on God, who richly supplies us with all things to enjoy.* [18]*Instruct them to do good, to be rich in good works, to be generous and ready to share,* [19]*storing up for themselves the treasure of a good foundation for the future.*

While it is true that one cannot take his earthly wealth to heaven; nonetheless, it is a biblical truth that a wealthy Christian can have his good works, based on the godly use of that wealth, laid up in heaven for him. One of the greatest examples of this in Christian history is Selena Hastings, the Countess of Huntingdon. She was a contemporary of Whitefield and Davies and used her great wealth to promote Christian causes both in England and America. She was a great supporter of the College of New Jersey in America and for the evangelization of Negroes. She stands with the greatest of the revivalists of the 18th Century in every respect.

In terms of efforts and successes to evangelize colonial Negroes, there is no greater name than that of Samuel Davies, and his name was cherished by numerous Negroes generations later.

The last phase of Samuel Davies' ministry was one that removed him from being a pastor in Virginia to the presidency of the College of New Jersey. With the death of Jonathan Edwards as the president of the college, the trustees turned to one who had so ably pled the college's cause in England and who had labored so faithfully in promoting the gospel in Virginia. When the trustees first presented their desire to have Davies as their new president, Davies turned them down, preferring his ministry in Virginia. The trustees asked a second time but received the same refusal, and finally

---

[215]   Foote, p. 289.

with a third request, he began to wonder if it was not his duty to consider God's leading of him to a new ministry. He cherished his ministry with the saints of Hanover, but then he also saw the great potential and pivotal role that the college had in advancing religion in the colonies. Davies decided to commit the matter to the Synod of New York that met in May 1759. The Synod dealt with the arguments from the College of New York and the pleas from Davies' Virginia congregation for him to remain as their pastor. After careful consideration and prayer, the Synod decided to dissolve Davies' pastoral relationship in order for him to become the president of the College of New Jersey. In July 1759, he began his duties as the new president and was officially inaugurated into the position in September 1759. For two years, he would give himself totally to the cause of the college. He rose early and studied late. He was very popular among the students, who often preferred to hear Davies in chapel instead of invited guests.

At the age of thirty-seven, the Lord God, the giver of life, determined to bring His faithful servant to glory. On February 4, 1761, he died of a brief bout with pneumonia, leaving behind a second wife, three sons, two daughters, and his mother. His January 1, 1761 sermon was seemingly prophetic. His sermon text was – "This year thou shalt die," based on Jeremiah 28:16. In his sermon Davies stated that "It is not only possible-but highly probable, that death may meet *some* of us within the compass of this year."

His life was relatively short, and his ministry only spanned a total of fifteen years. Yet, his impact was unforgettable. William Henry Foote assesses Davies' impact:

> McKamie stands as the father of the Presbyterian Church in America; Davies as the apostle of Virginia. To no one man, in a religious point of view, does the state owe as much; no one can claim a more affectionate remembrance by Christian people. His residence in the state is an era in its history. To Virginia we look for the record and fruits of his labors. The Virginia Synod claims him as her spiritual father. The Virginia creed in politics acknowledges his principles of religious freedom and civil liberty. His influence on politics was indirect, but not the less sure. The sole supremacy of Christ in the church,-the authority of the word of God,-the equality of the ministers of religion,-and individual rights of conscience,-principles for which he pled before the general court, and in the defense of which he encountered such men as Pendleton, Wythe, Randolph, and a whole host of the aristocracy, are now a part and parcel of the religious and political

creed of an overwhelming majority of the citizens of the "ancient dominion." He demonstrated the capability of the Church of Christ to sustain itself, not only without the fostering aid of the state, but under its oppressive laws. He showed the patriotism of true religion;-and in defending the principles of Presbytery, he maintained what Virginia now believes to be the inalienable rights of man.[216]

Like so many godly heralds, though dead, yet he speaks. Davies' sermons went through several editions in the United States and England, and for fifty years after his death they were among the most widely read in the English language.[217] The first five volumes of sermons were printed in London from 1767-71, and the best known American edition is a three volume set, which appeared in New York in 1851.

The Calvinistic, Theonomic, and Postmillennial Nature of Samuel Davies' Sermons

The sermons of Samuel Davies were wonderful expositions of the gospel of the Lord Jesus Christ. They were powerfully evangelistic, as the historical record demonstrates. His commitment to the doctrines of *The Westminster Confession of Faith* are clearly expressed in his sermons. In modern vernacular, we can say that his sermons were Calvinistic, theonomic,[218] and postmillennial. The best way to demonstrate this is simply to give various excerpts from some of his sermons.

Thoroughly Calvinistic

Just as Calvinism or the doctrines of grace found ample expression in the preaching of George Whitfield, they also found in Samuel Davies. We see these biblical truths in two of his sermons *The Success of the Ministry of the Gospel, Owing to a Leading of Divine Influence* (November 19, 1757), and *The Method of Salvation Through Jesus Christ* (October 2, 1757).

---

[216]   Foote, pp. 304-305.
[217]   Davies biography from *A Princeton Companion*.
[218]   When I use the word theonomic, I am expressing the views of the Westminster divines that the general principles of the law of God as found in the Old and New Testaments are not only normative but commanded for modern society.

In his sermon on the success of the ministry of the gospel, Davies clearly demonstrated the sovereignty of God in the salvation of sinners. One of the misnomers that people have about Calvinism is that they think God's sovereignty militates against human responsibility, but Davies showed that God's sovereignty incorporates human means, particularly the preaching of the gospel. Davies says:

> The design of God in all his works of creation, Providence, and grace, is to advance in securing the glory of his own name; and, therefore, though he makes use of secondary causes as the instruments of his operations, yet their advocacy depends upon his superintending influence.

> So, in the world of grace, God uses a variety of suitable means to form degenerate sinners into his image, and fit them for a happy eternity... ministers are sowers sent out into the wild field of the world, with the precious seed of the word... it is by the use of painful industry, that they can expect to improve this wilderness into a fruitful field; the Lord is pleased to pour out his Spirit from on high, at times, to render their labors successful...

> But alas, they meet with disappointments enough to convince them that all their labors will be in vain—if a sovereign God denies the influence of his grace. The agency of his Holy Spirit is as necessary to fructify the Word, and make it the seed of conversion, as the influences of heaven are to fructify the earth and promote vegetation! A zealous Paul may plant the Word, and an eloquent Apollos may water it; one may attempt to convert sinners to Christianity, and the other to build them up in faith—but they are both nothing, as to the success of their labors—unless God gives the increase! That is, unless he affords the influence of his grace to render their attempts successful in begetting and nourishing living religion in the hearts of men.

> The metaphors used in sacred Scripture to illustrate this case, sufficiently prove the degeneracy of mankind, and their entire opposition to the gospel. They are represented as spiritually DEAD, Ephesians 2:1; John 5:25; that is, though they are still capable of the exercises of reason and animal actions, yet they are really destitute of a supernatural principle of spiritual life, and incapable of suitable exercises towards God. And can a Paul or an Apollos quicken the dead with convictive arguments, with strong persuasions, or tender and passionate expostulations? No! None

but He can do it—whose Almighty voice bade Lazarus come forth.

Sinners are also represented as BLIND. 2. Corinthians 4:4. Now what can feeble mortals do to give sight to the blind? We can exhibit divine things before them; we can expose the horrid deformity of sin, and its tremendous consequences; we can display the glories of God, the beauty of holiness, and the allurements of redeeming love. But, alas! all this is but like showing pictures to the blind. We cannot open their blind eyes; we cannot communicate such views of things to their minds as are in any measure adequate to the things themselves.

What can tender arguments avail—to break hearts of stone? What can the best reasoning do—to overcome headstrong obstinacy to the Gospel? What can hearty persuasions do—to extirpate inveterate, implacable enmity towards God? Romans 8:7. What can the greatest eloquence do—to charm deaf adders that stop their ears? Psalm 58:4. The Israelites might as well pretend to overthrow the walls of Jericho with the sound of rams' horns, as we with our feeble breath to overthrow the strongholds of Satan in the hearts of sinners! It is the divine agency alone—which gives the success in both cases. Clay cannot open the eyes of the blind, except in his Almighty hands, who could form a world out of nothing—and who can work without or against means as easily as with them.

What was the success of Peter's sermon (Acts 2) in the conversion of 3,000 but the accomplishment of those promises in Joel and Zechariah? "I will pour out my Spirit upon all flesh." (Joel 2:28, 29.) "I will pour out upon the house of David, and upon the inhabitants of Jerusalem, the Spirit of grace and of supplication, and they shall look," etc. Zechariah 12:10. These promises were substantially renewed by Christ, to encourage the drooping apostles, John 16:8-10. "I will send the Spirit; and when he has come—he will convince the world," etc. All their miraculous powers were not sufficient for the conviction of mankind, without the agency of the divine Spirit; but by this, that promise of the Father to his Son was accomplished: "Your people shall be willing in the day of your power." Psalm 110:3.

The remark is this: That the promises of God to bestow blessings upon us, do not render needless our most vigorous endeavors to obtain them. And, on the other hand, that our most vigorous endeavors do not supersede the influences of the Spirit to work in us the dispositions we are laboring after! Or, that that may be consistently enjoined upon us as a duty, which is promised by God's free favor; and vice versa. This may be illustrated by various instances.God commands us as strictly to circumcise our hearts, to make ourselves new hearts and new spirits, (Jeremiah 4:4,) and to cleanse ourselves from moral pollution, (Isaiah 1:16,) as if this were wholly our work, and he had no efficiency in it. In the meantime, he promises as absolutely to circumcise our hearts to love him, to give us new hearts, and to purge us from all our filthiness, and from all our abominations; as though he performed all the work without our using means!

Now we are sure these things are consistent; for the sacred oracles are not a heap of contradictions. And how does their consistency appear?

Why, thus: it is our duty to use the most vigorous endeavors to obtain those graces promised, because it is only in the use of vigorous endeavors, that we have reason to expect divine influences. And yet these endeavors of ours do not in the least work those graces in us, and therefore there is certainly as much need of the promised agency of divine grace to effect the work— as if we should do nothing at all. Our utmost endeavors fall entirely short of it, and do not entitle us to divine assistance; and this we must have a humble sense of, before we can receive the accomplishments of such promises as the effect of free grace alone. But we should continue in these endeavors, because we have no reason to hope for the accomplishment of the promises, in a course of sloth and negligence.

This point may be illustrated by the consistency of the use of the means and the agency of providence in the natural world. God has peremptorily promised, that "while earth remains, seed-time and harvest shall not cease," Genesis 8:22. But this promise does not render it needless for us to cultivate the earth. Nor does all our cultivation render this promise needless; for all our labor would be in vain without the influence of divine providence; and this influence is to be expected only in the use of labor.

Accordingly we find: The unsuccessfulness of the gospel is often resolved into the withholding or withdrawing of the influences of divine grace, as one cause of it. Thus Moses resolves the obstinacy of the Israelites under all the profusion of wonders that had attended them, into this, as one cause of it: "The Lord has not given you a heart to perceive, and eyes to see, and ears to hear, unto this day." Deuteronomy 29:2-4. If none believe the report of the gospel, it is because the arm of the Lord is not revealed, Isaiah 53:1. If the mysteries of the kingdom of heaven are hidden from the wise and prudent, while they are revealed to babes—it is because God in his righteous judgment and sovereign pleasure, hides them from the one, and reveals them to the other! Matthew 11:25, 26.

We must indeed be cautious that we do not infer from the Scriptures any such horrid doctrine as this: that men are compelled to sin, and pushed on to ruin, by a necessitating decree, or the resistless impulse of Providence; or that, though they were disposed to turn to God, they are judicially kept back and hindered by the divine hand. This would be contrary to the whole current of Scripture, which charges the sin and ruin of sinners upon themselves... But yet that God, in denying them his grace, does not act merely as an arbitrary sovereign—but as a just judge, punishing them for their sin in abusing the blessings he has bestowed upon them, by judicially withdrawing the aids of his grace, and withholding farther influences.

His hardening the heart, blinding the eyes, etc., of sinners, signify his withdrawing the influences of grace which they have abused, his withholding those additional influences which might irresistibly subdue their obstinacy, and his allowing them to fall into circumstances of temptation. These passages do but strongly and emphatically express thus much: thus much they may mean, without casting any injurious reflections upon God; and less than this they cannot mean—or they would have no meaning at all.

From the whole, then, we find that the doctrine of the reality and necessity of divine influences to render the administrations of the gospel effectual for saving purposes, is a doctrine clearly taught in the sacred oracles.

This point might be illustrated farther, by a history of the various periods of the church, from the apostolic age to the present time; but it would be too tedious; and what has been offered is sufficient to convince us that it is not by power, nor by might—but by the

Spirit of the Lord Almighty, that the interests of true religion are carried on. Zechariah 4:6.

How essential and important, the doctrine of divine influence is to the church of God. The very life, and the whole success of the gospel depends upon it! And since this necessarily supposes the utter depravity and spiritual impotence of human nature in its fallen state, that doctrine also must be frequently and plainly inculcated.

That when we enjoy the ministrations of the gospel in the greatest purity and plenty, we should not place our trust upon them—but wholly depend on the influence of divine grace for the success. We are apt to think, if we had but such a minister among us—how much good would be done! It is true, that faithful and accomplished ministers are singular blessings to the places where they labor, because it is by their instrumentality that the Lord is accustomed to work: but still let us remember, that even a Paul or an Apollos are nothing, unless the Lord gives the increase.

In his sermon titled *The Method of Salvation through Jesus Christ* (October 2, 1757), Davies masterfully and biblically dealt with common objections raised against Calvinistic doctrines. He anticipated what his audience may be thinking:

But before I proceed any farther, I would remove one stumbling-block out of your way. You are apt to object, "You teach us that faith is the gift of God, and that we cannot believe of ourselves; why then do you exhort us to believe? Or how can we be concerned to endeavor that which it is impossible for us to do?"

In answer to this, I grant the premises are true; and God forbid that I should so much as intimate that faith is the spontaneous growth of corrupt nature, or that you can come to Christ without the Father's drawing you: but the conclusions you draw from these premises are very erroneous. I exhort and persuade you to believe in Jesus Christ, because it is while such means are used with sinners, and by the use of them, that it pleases God to enable them to comply, or to work faith in them. I would therefore use those means which God is pleased to bless for this end. I exhort you to believe in order to set you upon the trial; for it is putting it to trial, and that only, which can fully convince you of your own inability to believe; and until you are convinced of this, you can never expect strength from God.

I exhort you to believe, because, sinful and enfeebled as you are, you are capable of using various preparatives to faith. You may attend upon prayer, hearing the gospel, and all the outward means of grace with natural seriousness; you may endeavor to get acquainted with your own helpless condition, and, as it were, put yourselves in the way of divine mercy; and though all these means cannot of themselves produce faith in you—yet it is only in the use of these means, that you are to expect divine grace to work it in you: never was faith yet produced in one soul, while lying supine, lazy, and inactive!

I hope you now see good reasons why I should exhort you to believe, and also perceive my design in it; I therefore renew the proposal to you, that you should this day, as guilty, unworthy, self-despairing sinners—receive of the only begotten Son of God as your Savior, and fall in with the gospel-method of salvation; and I once more demand your answer. I would by no means, if possible, leave the pulpit this day until I have effectually recommended the blessed Jesus, my Lord and Master, to your acceptance. I am strongly bound by the vows and resolutions of my recent sick bed—to recommend him to you; and now I would endeavor to perform my vows. I would have us all this day, before we part, consent to God's covenant, that we may go away to our houses—justified with God!

To this I persuade and exhort you, in the name and by the authority of the great God, by the death of Jesus Christ for sinners, by your own most urgent and absolute necessity, by the immense blessings proposed in the gospel, and by the heavy curse denounced against unbelievers!

But I expect, as usual, some of you will refuse to comply with this proposal. This, alas! has been the usual fate of the blessed gospel in all ages and in all countries; as some have received it, so some have rejected it. That old complaint of Isaiah has been justly repeated thousands of times; "Who has believed our report? and to whom is the arm of the LORD revealed?" Isaiah 53:1. And is there no reason to pour out the gospel from a broken heart over some of you, my dear people? Are you all this day determined to believe? If so, I pronounce you blessed in the name of the Lord; but if not, I must denounce your doom!

Be it known to you then from the living God, that if you thus continue in unbelief—then you shut the door of mercy against yourselves, and exclude yourselves from eternal life. Whatever splendid appearances of virtue, whatever amiable qualities, whatever seeming good works you have—the express sentence of the gospel lies in full force against you, "Whoever does not believe stands condemned already, because he has not believed in the name of God's one and only Son!" John 3:18. "Whoever rejects the Son will not see life, for God's wrath remains on him!" John 3:36. This is your doom repeatedly pronounced by him whom you must own to be the best friend of sinners; and if he condemns you—then who can justify you?

And now does not all this move you? Are you not alarmed at the thought of perishing; of perishing by the hand of a Savior rejected and despised; perishing under the stain of his profaned blood; perishing not only under the curse of the law—but under that of the gospel, which is vastly heavier? Oh! are you hardy enough to venture upon such a doom? This doom is unavoidable if you refuse to comply with the proposal now made to you.

I must now conclude the treaty; but for my own acquittance, I must take witness that I have endeavored to discharge my commission; whatever reception you give it. I call heaven and earth, and your own consciences to witness, that life and salvation, through Jesus Christ, have been offered to you on this day! And if you reject it, remember it; remember it whenever you see this place; remember it whenever you see my face, or one another; remember it, that you may witness for me at the supreme tribunal, that I am clear of your blood! Alas! you will remember it among a thousand painful reflections millions of ages hence, when the remembrance of it will rend your hearts like a vulture! Many sermons forgotten upon earth—are remembered in hell, and haunt the guilty mind forever. Oh that you would believe, and so prevent this dreadful effect from the present sermon!

Is Calvinistic preaching antithetical to evangelism? Is it some horrible doctrine from the pits of hell, as some Arminian preachers today want to convince us? Let the resounding answer of history silence the gainsayers. Let the thousands upon thousands of men, women, and children led to Jesus Christ by Whitefield and Davies answer the critics! Let the hundreds of Negro slaves, though in human bondage but spiritually set free, answer the critics!

Thoroughly Postmillennial

Throughout this book, I have endeavored to set forth the biblical/exegetical basis for the victory of the gospel during this present age prior to Christ's physical Second Coming at the end of the world, commonly known as postmillennialism. Though the term, "postmillennial" may not have been commonly used in the 18th Century, can we confidently say that Samuel Davies was a postmillennialist? I will simply let the extended excerpts from two of his sermons answer the question. First, let's consider his October 16, 1757 sermon titled *The Happy Effects of the Pouring Out of the Spirit:*

> I need not tell you how gloomy and discouraging the prospect is before us, from the growing power of the French—from their great influence with the Indian savages—from the naked and defenseless state of our country—from the dastardly, secure spirit that prevails among the generality, and from many causes that I need not name. These things are too public and notorious for me to enlarge upon them. Alas! who is ignorant of them? though but few lay them properly to heart.
>
> The great inquiry I would now employ your time and thoughts about, is, What is the best remedy in this melancholy case? This, I think, we may clearly discover in the verses I have read to you.
>
> The Holy Spirit of God is represented in the Scriptures as the original fountain of all the real goodness and virtue which is to be found in our degenerate world; the only author of reformation, conversion, sanctification, and every grace included in the character of a saint, or a godly man. The pouring out of the Spirit is a Scripture phrase, which signifies a plentiful communication of his influence to effect a thorough reformation. It is not a distilling, or falling in gentle drops, like the dew; but a copious effusion, or pouring out, like a mighty shower, or torrent that carries all before it.
>
> Now, as the communication of the Spirit is necessary to produce a reformation, so a large communication, or outpouring of the Spirit, is necessary to produce a public, general reformation; such as may save a country on the brink of ruin, or recover one already laid desolate.
>
> Without this remedy, all other applications will be ineffectual; and the distempered nation will languish more and more, until it is at

length dissolved. Until this outpouring of the Spirit, says the prophet, "briers and thorns shall come upon the land; and the houses of joy, the palaces, and towers—shall be heaps of ruins, dens for wild beasts, and pastures for flocks!" Until that blessed time comes—no means can effectually repair a broken state, or re-people a desolate country.

But when that blessed time does come—then what a glorious revolution—what a happy alteration follows! Then says the prophet, "The wilderness shall be a fruitful field, and the fruitful field be counted for a forest. Then judgment shall dwell in the wilderness, and righteousness remain in the fruitful field: and the work of righteousness shall be peace, and the effect of righteousness, quietness and assurance forever; and my people shall dwell in a peaceable habitation, and in sure dwellings, and in quiet resting-places." These are the blessed peaceful effects of the outpouring of the Spirit; and these effectually cure all the ravages of war, and ensure a lasting peace, with all its blessings.

The word here rendered poured generally signifies to be made naked, that is— to be revealed in full power. This may be illustrated by that expression in Isaiah "The Lord has made bare his holy arm in the eyes of all the nations;" that is, has given an illustrious display of his Power. The sense is the same, however we render it; namely, a full exertion of the power of the Spirit to produce a reformation.)

Thus, you see, the outpouring of the Holy Spirit is the great and only remedy for a ruined country! This is the only effectual preventive of national calamities and desolations, and the only sure cause of a lasting and well-established peace. This is the truth I now intend chiefly to illustrate.

There are some also who complain, that our country cannot be safe or prosperous without a general reformation; that it cannot be expected that the undertakings of a guilty, impenitent people, ripe for the judgments of God, can succeed, until their repentance is in some measure as signal and public as their sin. Thus far we look; but, unless we look farther, we do not go to the bottom of things. As all our measures are not likely to be successful without a reformation; so we may despair of ever seeing a thorough, general reformation, unless The Spirit is poured upon us from on high.

And yet they sinned on still, impenitent and unreformed: no general reformation was carried on by all these means; and even under the hardships of captivity, they still continued to be the same incorrigible sinners. Hence God complains of them, "But whenever they were scattered among the nations, they brought dishonor to my holy name," as they had done before in their own land. Ezekiel 36:20. And what was lacking all this time for their effectual reformation? Why, the Spirit was not yet poured upon them from on high; and while he was absent, they continued unreformed, and their country desolate.

But when the time for their restoration came—then the Spirit was poured out. Thus their restoration and the effusion of the Spirit are connected in the divine promise: "I will take you from among the heathen, and gather you out of all countries, and will bring you into your own land. Then will I sprinkle clean water upon you," (the usual emblem of Divine influences, John 7:38, 39,) and you shall be, clean; and I will put my Spirit within you." Ezekiel 36:24-27. And when this promise was fulfilled, what was the consequence? Why a glorious public reformation followed, of which you see an account in the books of Ezra and Nehemiah. They returned to their own land as weeping penitents, according to Jeremiah's prediction, which seems to have had its primary accomplishment in this event. "The children of Israel shall come, they and the children of Judah together, going and weeping" (this is a description of the march of the captives in their return to their own country,) they shall go and seek the Lord their God: they shall ask the way to Zion, (Zion, the place where the house of God once stood, which they are eager to rebuild) with their faces thitherward, saying, Come, let us join ourselves to the Lord in a perpetual covenant that shall not be forgotten." Jeremiah 50:4, 5. And when they were thus brought to repentance, what a happy revolution followed! The scattered captives were collected; they restored their ruined church and state, and again became a free and flourishing people. And what happened to them will also happen to us, and all nations of the earth in all ages, in like circumstances.

In illustrating the subject I have principally in view, I intend only to offer a few arguments to prove the absolute necessity of a general outpouring of the Spirit, to effect a general reformation.

The arguments for this truth, with which the holy Scriptures furnish us, are so many, that I can only select a few; and they shall be chiefly such as refer to nations—and not to individuals, or private people; asserting the Holy Spirit to be the only author of public national reformation, as well as of the conversion of particular people.

And, therefore, "until The Spirit is poured out from on high," they will never grow and flourish. Faith, repentance, and every grace are the free gift of God, wrought by the Holy Spirit. Ephesians 2:8; Philippians 1:29; Acts 5:31, and 11:18; 2 Timothy 2:25; 2 Corinthians 5:17, 18. In short, not one soul, much less a whole nation—can be effectually reformed without the power of God. If even a well-disposed Lydia gave a believing attention to the things spoken by Paul, it was because the Lord opened her heart. Acts 16:14. "No man can come unto Christ—unless the Father draws him." John 6:44.

Then the most solemn preaching, and the most alarming providences have no effect; but men continue blind and stupid under the clearest instructions, and the loudest warnings! They grow harder and harder, instead of being refined in the furnace of affliction!

But on the other hand, when the Spirit is poured out from on high—then the cause of true religion and virtue is promoted, almost without means; then sinners are awakened by a word; then true religion catches and circulates from heart to heart, and bears down all opposition before it. Peter had preached many a sermon before that which we find recorded in Acts 2; and his Lord and master had preached many a one—but with very little success. But now by one short discourse, no fewer than three thousand are converted in a few minutes among a hostile, prejudiced multitude, some of whom had been accessory to the death of Jesus Christ but a few days before!

And whence this happy turn? Peter himself will tell you, it was because then was fulfilled the ancient prophecy of Joel, "I will pour out my Spirit upon all flesh." Acts 2:16, 17; Joel 2:8. Then, too, was fulfilled the promise of the blessed Jesus to his disciples; "I will send the Spirit unto you; and when he has come—he will reprove the world of sin, of righteousness, and of judgment." John 16:7, 8. It was this which rendered the progress of the gospel so rapid and irresistible through the world, in spite of the most powerful opposition from all quarters in that age; which, in times seemingly more favorable, has languished and lost ground!

It is my happiness to be able to furnish you with an instance of the like nature, in the review of my own short life. About sixteen years ago, in the northern colonies, when all religious concern was much out of fashion, and the generality lay in a dead sleep in sin, having at best but the form of godliness—but nothing of the power; when the country was in peace and prosperity, free from the calamities of war, and epidemic sickness; when, in short, there were no extraordinary calls to repentance; then suddenly, a deep, general concern about eternal things spread through the country; sinners, startled out of their slumbers—broke off from their vices, began to cry out, What shall I do to be saved? and made it the great business of their life to prepare for the world to come. Then the gospel seemed almighty, and carried all before it. It pierced the very hearts of men with an irresistible power. I have seen thousands at once melted down under it; all eager to hear as for life, and hardly a dry eye to be seen among them!

Many have since backslidden, and all their religion has come to nothing, or dwindled away into mere formality. But, blessed be God, thousands still remain as shining monuments of the power of divine grace in that glorious day. That harvest did not continue very long: and now, in the very same places, and under the same ministry, or a better—there are hardly any appearances of it; though Providence has given them so many alarms of late, and such loud calls to repentance.

But, on the other hand, it is lamentably evident, there has not been of late any such general outpouring of the Spirit, as is necessary to produce a public national reformation: which is the only cure for a nation so far gone as ours. We have lost ground indeed before our enemies, and been almost everywhere worsted: but I am afraid that vice has stood its ground against the artillery of the gospel; or if it has lost in one place, it has gained in another.

We need a general public reformation: and we shall always need it, "until The Spirit is poured upon us from on high." Alas! this need is little thought of; but it is by so much the more dangerous and lamentable. Never will our country and nation be safe, never will Britain or Virginia be out of the reach of some executioner of divine vengeance, until there be a public general reformation: and never will there be such a reformation, "until The Spirit is poured upon us from on high."

At the outset of the French and Indian War, Samuel Davies preached the following sermon in Hanover County on May 9, 1756 – *The Mediatorial Kingdom and Glories Of Jesus Christ.* As I read this sermon, I was simply overwhelmed by the depth of content and the unwavering commitment to all the salient features of what we commonly refer to as postmillennialism. As one reads his sermon, are not most of the basic points of this book in this sermon? It was his confidence in the gospel, empowered by the risen Christ that spurred Davies on in his missionary activity.

The following are extended excerpts from this incredible sermon based on the text, Psalm 2:12-14:

> *"Do homage to the Son, lest He become angry, and you perish in the way, for His wrath may soon be kindled. How blessed are all who take refuge in Him."*

In my text you hear one entering a claim to a kingdom, whom you would conclude, if you regarded only his outward appearance, to be the meanest and vilest of mankind. To hear a powerful prince, at the head of a victorious army, attended with all the royalties of his character, to hear such an one claim the kingdom he had acquired by force of arms, would not be strange. But here the despised Nazarene, rejected by his nation, forsaken by his followers, accused as the worst of criminals, standing defenceless at Pilate's bar, just about to be condemned and hung on a cross, like a malefactor and a slave, here he speaks in a royal stile, even to his judge, *I am a King: for this purpose was I born; and for this cause came I into the world.* Strange language indeed to proceed from his lips in these circumstances! But the truth is, a great, a divine personage is concealed under this disguise; and his kingdom is of such a nature, that his abasement and crucifixion were so far from being a hindrance to it, that they were the only way to acquire it. These sufferings were meritorious; and by these he purchased his subjects, and a right to rule them.

The greatest kings of the Jewish nation, particularly David and Solomon, were types of him; and many things are primarily applied to them, which have their complete and final accomplishment in him alone. It is to him ultimately we are to apply the second psalm: *I have set my king,* says Jehovah, *upon my holy hill of Zion. Ask of me, and I will give thee the heathen for thy inheritance, and the utmost parts of the earth for thy possession.* Psalm ii. 6, 8.

If we read the seventy-second psalm we shall easily perceive that one greater than Solomon is there. In his days shall the righteous flourish; and abundance of peace so long as the moon endureth. All kings shall fall down before him; all nations shall serve him. His name shall continue for ever; his name shall endure as long as the sun: and men shall be blessed in him; and all nations shall call him blessed. Psalm lxxii. 7, 11, 17.

The hundred and tenth psalm is throughout a celebration of the kingly and priestly office of Christ united. *The Lord,* says David, *said unto my Lord,* unto that divine person who is my Lord, and will also be my Son, *sit thou at my right hand,* in the highest honour and authority, *until I make thine enemies thy footstool.* Rule thou in the midst of thine enemies. *Thy people shall be willing in the day of thy power,* and submit to thee in crowds as numerous as the drops of morning dew. Psalm cx. 1–3.

The evangelical prophet Isaiah is often transported with the foresight of this illustrious king, and the glorious kingdom of his grace: *Unto us a child is born, unto us a son is given; and the government shall be upon his shoulder; and he shall be called— the Prince of Peace. Of the increase of his government and peace there shall be no end, upon the throne of David and upon his kingdom, to order and to establish it with judgment and with justice, from henceforth even for ever.* Isaiah ix. 6, 7.

This is he who is described as another David in Ezekiel's prophecy, Thus saith the Lord, I will take the children of Israel from among the heathen. And I will make them one nation—and one king shall be king to them all—even David my servant shall be king over them. Ezekiel xxxvii. 21, 22, 24. This is the kingdom represented to Nebuchadnezzar in his dream, as a stone cut out without hands, which became a great mountain, and filled the whole earth.

And Daniel, in expounding the dream, having described the Babylonian, the Persian, the Grecian, and Roman empires, subjoins, *In the days of these kings,* that is, of the Roman emperors, *shall the God of heaven set up a kingdom, which shall never be destroyed: and the kingdom shall not,* like the former, *be left to other people; but it shall break in pieces and consume all these kingdoms, and it shall stand for ever.* Daniel ii. 34, 35, 44. There is no character which our Lord so often assumed in the days of his flesh as that of the Son of Man; and he no doubt alludes to a majestic vision in Daniel, the only place where this character is given him in the Old Testament: *I saw in the night visions,* says Daniel, *and behold, one like the Son of Man came to the Ancient of Days, and there was given to him dominion, and glory, and a kingdom, that all people, nations, and languages, should serve him: his dominion is an everlasting dominion, which shall not pass away, and his kingdom that which shall not be destroyed,* Daniel vii. 13, 14, like the tottering kingdoms of the earth, which are perpetually rising and falling.

This is the king that Zechariah refers to when, in prospect of his triumphant entrance into Jerusalem, he calls the inhabitants to give a proper reception to so great a prince. *Rejoice greatly, O daughter of Zion; shout, O daughter of Jerusalem: behold thy King coming unto thee,* &c. Zechariah ix. 9. Thus the prophets conspire to ascribe royal titles and a glorious kingdom to the Messiah. And these early and plain notices of him raised a general expectation of him under this royal character. It was from these prophecies concerning him as a king, that the Jews took occasion, as I observed, to look for the Messiah as a temporal prince; and it was a long time before the apostles themselves were delivered from these carnal prejudices.

This royal character Christ himself assumed, even when he conversed among mortals in the humble form of a servant. *The Father,* says he, *has given me power over all flesh.* John xvii.2. Yea, *all power in heaven and earth is given to me.* Matthew xxviii. 16. The gospel-church which he erected is most commonly called the kingdom of heaven or of God, in the evangelists: and when he was about to introduce it, this was the proclamation: *The kingdom of heaven is at hand.* Under this character also his servants and disciples celebrated and preached him. Gabriel led the song in foretelling his birth to his mother. *He shall be great, and the Lord shall give unto him the throne of his father David; and he shall reign over the house of Jacob for ever: and of his kingdom there shall be no end.* Luke i. 32, 33. St. Peter boldly tells the murderers of Christ, *God hath made that same Jesus whom you crucified, both Lord and Christ,* Acts ii. 36. *and exalted him, with his own right hand, to be a Prince and a Saviour.* Acts v. 31.

And St. Paul repeatedly represents him as advanced *far above principality, and power, and might, and dominion, and every name that is named, not only in this world, but also in that which is to come: and that God hath put all things under his feet, and given him to be head over all things to his church.* Ephesians i. 21, 22. Philippians ii. 9–11. Yea, to him all the hosts of heaven, and even the whole creation in concert, ascribe *power and strength, and honour and glory.* Revelation v. 12. Pilate the heathen was over-ruled to give a kind of accidental testimony to this truth, and to publish it to different nations, by the inscription upon the cross in the three languages then most in use, the Latin, Greek, and Hebrew: *This is Jesus of Nazareth, the King of the Jews*; and all the remonstrances of the Jews could not prevail upon him to alter it. Finally, it is he that wears *upon his vesture, and upon his thigh, this name written, King of kings, and Lord of lords,* Revelation xix. 16. and as his name is, so is he.

Thus you see, my brethren, by these instances, selected out of many, that the kingly character and dominion of our Lord Jesus runs through the whole Bible. That of a king is his favourite character in which he glories, and which is the most expressive of his office. And this consideration alone may convince you that this character is of the greatest importance, and worthy of your most attentive regard.

It is the mediatorial kingdom of Christ that is here intended, not that which as God he exercises over all the works of his hands: it is that kingdom which is an empire of grace, an administration of mercy over our guilty world. It is the dispensation intended for the salvation of fallen sinners of our race by the gospel; and on this account the gospel is often called the kingdom of heaven; because its happy consequences are not confined to this earth, but appear in heaven in the highest perfection, and last through all eternity. Hence, not only the church of Christ on earth, and the dispensation of the gospel, but all the saints in heaven, and that more finished œconomy under which they are placed, are all included in the kingdom of Christ.

The whole universe is put under a mediatorial head; but then, as the apostle observes, *he is made head over all things to his church,* Ephesians i. 22. that is, for the benefit and salvation of his church. As Mediator he is carrying on a glorious scheme for the recovery of man, and all parts of the universe are interested or concern themselves in this grand event; and therefore they are all subjected to him, that he may so manage them as to promote this end, and baffle and overwhelm all opposition.

And therefore Christ, as a Mediator, is made the head of all the heavenly armies, and he employs them as *his ministering spirits, to minister to them that are heirs of salvation.* Heb. i. 14. These glorious creatures are always on the wing ready to discharge his orders in any part of his vast empire, and delight to be employed in the services of his mediatorial kingdom. This is also an event in which the fallen angels deeply interest themselves; they have united all their force and art for near six thousand years to disturb and subvert his kingdom, and blast the designs of redeeming love; they therefore are all subjected to the controul of Christ, and he shortens and lengthens their chains as he pleases, and they cannot go an hair's breadth beyond his permission.

The scriptures represent our world in its state of guilt and misery as the kingdom of Satan; sinners, while slaves to sin, are his subjects; and every act of disobedience against God is an act of homage to this infernal prince. Hence Satan is called *the God of this world,* 2 Corinthians iv. 4. *the prince of this world,* John xii. 31. *the power of darkness,* Luke xxii. 53. *the prince of the power of the air, the Spirit that now worketh in the children of disobedience.* Ephesians ii. 3. And sinners are said to be *taken captive by him at his will.* 2 Timothy ii. 26.

Hence also the ministers of Christ, who are employed to recover sinners to a state of holiness and happiness, are represented as soldiers armed for war; not indeed with carnal weapons, but with those which are spiritual, plain truth arguments, and miracles; and *these are made mighty through God to the pulling down of strong holds, casting down imaginations, and every high thing that exalteth itself against the knowledge of God, and bringing into captivity every thought to the obedience of Christ.* 2 Corinthians x. 3, 4, 5. And christians in general are represented as *wrestling, not with flesh and blood, but against principalities, against powers, against the rulers of the darkness of this world, against spiritual wickednesses in high places.* Ephesians vi. 12.

Hence also in particular it is that the death of Christ is represented not as a defeat, but as an illustrious conquest gained over the powers of hell; because, by this means a way was opened for the deliverance of sinners from under their power, and restoring them into liberty and the favour of God. By that strange contemptible weapon, the cross, and by the glorious resurrection of Jesus, he *spoiled principalities and powers, and made a shew of them openly, triumphing over them.* Col. ii. 15. *Through death,* says the apostle, *he destroyed him that had the power of death; that is, the devil.* Heb. ii. 14. Had not Christ by his death offered a propitiatory sacrifice for the sins of men, they would have continued for ever under the tyranny of Satan; but he has purchased liberty, life, and salvation for them; and thus he hath destroyed the kingdom of darkness, and translated multitudes from it into his own gracious and glorious kingdom.

As for the sons of men, who are more immediately concerned in this kingdom, and for whose sake it was erected, they are all its subjects; but then they are of different sorts, according to their characters. Multitudes are rebels against his government; that is, they do not voluntarily submit to his authority, nor choose they to do his service: they will not obey his laws. But they are his subjects notwithstanding; that is, he rules and manages them as he pleases, whether they will or not. This power is necessary to carry on successfully his gracious design towards his people; for unless he had the management of his enemies, they might baffle his undertaking, and successfully counteract the purposes of his love. The kings of the earth, as well as vulgar rebels of a private character, have often set themselves against his kingdom, and sometimes they have flattered themselves they had entirely demolished it. But Jesus reigns absolute and supreme over the kings of the earth, and over-rules and controls them as he thinks proper; and he disposes all the revolutions, the rises and falls of kingdoms and empires, so as to be subservient to the great designs of his mediation; and their united policies and powers cannot frustrate the work which he has undertaken.

But besides these rebellious involuntary subjects, he has (blessed be his name!) gained the consent of thousands, and they have become his willing subjects by their own choice. They regard his authority, they love his government, they make it their study to please him, and to do his will. Over these he exercises a government of special grace here, and he will make them the happy subjects of the kingdom of his glory hereafter. And it is his government over these that I intend more particularly to consider. Once more, the kingdom of Jesus is not confined to this world, but all the millions of mankind in the invisible world are under his dominion, and will continue so to everlasting ages.

I cannot forbear reading to you one of the most majestic descriptions of this all-conquering hero and his army, which the language of mortality is capable of. Revelation xix. 11, 16. *I saw heaven open,* says St. John, *and behold a white horse,* an emblem of victory and triumph, *and he that sat upon him was called Faithful and True.* How different a character from that of mortal conquerors! "And in righteousness he doth judge and make war." War is generally a scene of injustice and lawless violence; and those plagues of mankind we call heroes and warriors, use their arms to gratify their own avarice or ambition, and make encroachments upon others. Jesus, the Prince of Peace, makes war too, but it is in righteousness; it is in the cause of righteousness he takes up arms. The divine description proceeds: *His eyes were as a flame of fire; and on his head were many crowns,* emblems of his manifold authority over the various kingdoms of the world, and the various regions of the universe. *And he was clothed with a vesture dipt in blood,* in the blood of his enemies; *and his name was called, The Word of God: and the armies which were in heaven, followed him upon white horses, clothed in fine linen, white and clean:* the whitest innocence and purity, and the beauties of holiness are, as it were, the uniform, the regimentals of these celestial armies. *And out of his mouth goeth a sharp sword, that with it he should smite the nations: and he shall rule them with a rod of iron; and he treadeth the wine press of the fierceness and wrath of Almighty God; and he hath on his vesture and on his thigh a name written, King of kings, and Lord of lords.* In what manner the war is carried on between the armies of heaven and the powers of hell, we know not; but that there is really something of this kind, we may infer from Revelation xii. 7, 9. *There was war in heaven: Michael and his angels fought against the dragon; and the dragon fought and his angels, and prevailed not, neither was there place found any more in heaven. And the great dragon was cast out, that old serpent called the Devil and Satan.*

Engaged in hard conflict with temptations from without, and the insurrections of sin from within. Sometimes, alas! they fall; but their General lifts them up again, and inspires them with strength to renew the fight. They fight most successfully upon their knees. This is the most advantageous posture for the soldiers of Jesus Christ; for prayer brings down recruits from heaven in the hour of difficulty. They are indeed but poor weaklings and invalids; and yet they overcome, through the blood of the Lamb; and he makes them conquerors, yea more than conquerors. It is the military character of christians that gives the apostle occasion to address them in the military stile, like a general at the head of his army. Ephesians vi. 10–18. *Be strong in the Lord, and in the power of his might. Put on the whole armour of God, that ye may be able to stand against the wiles of the devil. Stand therefore, having your loins girt about with truth, and having on the breastplate of righteousness, and your feet shod with the preparation of the gospel of peace; above all, taking the shield of faith, wherewith ye shall be able to quench all the fiery darts of the wicked. And take the helmet of salvation, and the sword of the spirit, which is the word of God, praying always with all prayer and supplication.* The ministers of the gospel in particular, and especially the apostles, are soldiers, or officers, in the spiritual army.

Hence St. Paul speaks of his office, in the military stile; *I have,* says he, *fought the good fight.* 2 Timothy iv. 7. *We war,* says he, *though it be not after the flesh.* The humble doctrines of the cross are our weapons, and these are mighty through God, *to demolish the strong holds of the prince of darkness, and to bring every thought into a joyful captivity to the obedience of faith.* 2 Corinthians x. 3–5. *Fight the good fight,* says he to Timothy. 1 Timothy vi. 12. And again, *thou therefore endure hardness, as a good soldier of Jesus Christ.* 2 Timothy ii. 3. The great design of the gospel-ministry is to rescue enslaved souls from the tyranny of sin and Satan, and to recover them into a state of liberty and loyalty to Jesus Christ; or, in the words of the apostle, *to turn them from darkness to light, and from the power of Satan unto God.* Acts xxvi. 18. Mortals indeed are very unequal for the conflict; but their success more conspicuously shews that the *excellency of the power is of God:* and many have they subdued, through his strength, to the obedience of faith, and made the willing captives of the cross of our divine Immanuel.

The kingdoms of the world have their rise, their progress, perfection, declension, and ruin. And in these things, the kingdom of Christ bears some resemblance to them, excepting that it shall never have an end.

Its rise was small at first, and it has passed through many revolutions in various ages. It was first founded in the family of

Adam, but in about 1600 years, the space between the creation and the flood, it was almost demolished by the wickedness of the world; and at length confined to the little family of Noah. After the flood, the world soon fell into idolatry, but, that this kingdom of Christ might not be destroyed quite, it was erected in the family of Abraham; and among the Jews it continued until the coming of Christ in the flesh. This was indeed but the infancy of his kingdom, and indeed is seldom called by that name. It is the gospel constitution that is represented as the kingdom of Christ, in a special sense. This was but very small and unpromising at first. When its founder was dying upon Calvary, and all his followers had forsaken him and fled, who would have thought it would ever have come to any thing, ever have recovered? But it revived with him; and, when he furnished his apostles with gifts and graces for their mission, and sent them forth to increase his kingdom, it made its progress through the world with amazing rapidity, notwithstanding it met with very early and powerful opposition. The Jews set themselves against it, and raised persecutions against its ministers, wherever they went. And presently the tyrant Nero employed all the power of the Roman empire to crush them. Peter, Paul, and thousands of the christians fell a prey to his rage, like sheep for the slaughter. This persecution was continued under his successors, with but little interruption, for about two hundred years.

This gracious kingdom makes but little way in Virginia. The calamities of war and famine cannot, alas! draw subjects to it; but we seem generally determined to perish in our rebellion rather than submit. Thus it has been in this country from its first settlement; and how long it will continue in this situation is unknown to mortals: however, this we may know, it will not be so always. We have the strongest assurances that Jesus will yet take to him his great power, and reign in a more extensive and illustrious manner than he has ever yet done; and that the kingdoms of the earth shall yet become the kingdoms of our Lord and of his Christ. There are various parts of the heathen world where the gospel has never yet been; and the Jews have never yet been converted as a nation; but both the calling of the Jews and the fulness of the gentiles, you will find plainly foretold in the 11th chapter to the Romans; and it is, no doubt, to render the accomplishment of this event the more conspicuous, that the Jews, who are dispersed all over the world, have, by a strange, unprecedented, and singular providence, been kept a distinct people to this day, for 1700 years; though all other nations have been so mixt and blended together, who were not half so much dispersed into different countries, that their distinct original cannot be traced. Posterity shall see this glorious event in some happy future period.

How far it is from us, I will not determine: though, upon some grounds, I apprehend it is not very remote. I shall live and die in the unshaken belief that our guilty world shall yet see glorious days. Yes, my brethren, this despised gospel, that has so little effect in our age and country, shall yet shine like lightning, or like the sun, through all the dark regions of the earth. It shall triumph over heathenism, Mahometism, Judaism, popery, and all those dangerous errors that have infected the christian church. This gospel, poor negroes, shall yet reach your countrymen, whom you left behind you in Africa, in darkness and the shadow of death, and bless your eyes with the light of salvation: and the Indian savages, that are now ravaging our country, shall yet be transformed into lambs and doves by the gospel of peace. The scheme of Providence is not yet completed, and much remains to be accomplished of what God has spoken by his prophets, to ripen the world for the universal judgment; but when all these things are finished, then proclamation shall be made through all nature, "That Time shall be no more:" then the Supreme Judge, the same Jesus that ascended the cross, will ascend the throne, and review the affairs of time: then will he put an end to the present course of nature, and the present form of administration. Then shall heaven and hell be filled with their respective inhabitants: then will time close, and eternity run on in one uniform tenor, without end. But the kingdom of Christ, though altered in its situation and form of government, will not then come to a conclusion.

Thoroughly Theonomic

How do we define justice? Whose laws should govern our land? Davies advocated the fundamental tenets of what today would be termed, "theonomy." His sermon was titled *Divine Government—The Joy of Our World.*

Here are some excerpts of this great sermon:

My present design is: To illustrate this glorious truth, that Jehovah's supreme government is a just cause of universal joy.

For that end I shall consider the divine government in various views, as legislative, providential, mediatorial, and judicial; and show that in each of these views—the divine government is matter of universal joy.

The Lord reigns upon a throne of LEGISLATION. "Let the earth rejoice; let the multitude of islands be glad!" He is the one supreme LAWGIVER, James 4:12, and is perfectly qualified for that important trust. Nothing tends more to the advantage of civil society—than to have good and just laws established, according to which mankind are to conduct themselves, and according to which their rulers will deal with them. Now the supreme and universal king has enacted and published the best laws for the government of the moral world, and of the human race in particular. Let the earth then rejoice that God has clearly revealed his will to us, and not left us in inextricable perplexities about our duty to him and mankind.

Again, "let the earth rejoice; let the multitude of islands be glad," that these laws are suitably enforced with proper sanctions. The sanctions are such as befit a God of infinite wisdom, almighty power, inexorable justice, untainted holiness, and unbounded goodness and grace! And they are such as are agreeable to the nature of reasonable creatures formed for an immortal duration.

"Let the earth rejoice; let the multitude of islands be glad," on account not only for the rewards of obedience to the law—but also for this tremendous penalty; for it flows not only from justice—but from goodness, as well as its promise of rewards for obedience. The penalty annexed to the law, will not be executed from a malignant pleasure in the misery of the creature—but it is annexed from a regard to the happiness of mankind, and will be executed upon individuals for the extensive good of the whole—as well as for the honorable display of the divine purity and justice.

But to proceed: "Let the earth rejoice; let the multitude of islands be glad," that the divine laws reach the inner man, and have power upon the hearts and consciences of men. Human laws can only regulate our external conduct at best—but the heart in the meantime may be disloyal and wicked! Now this defect is supplied by the laws of the King of heaven, which are spiritual. They require a complete uniformity and self-consistency in us—so that heart and life may agree: and therefore they are wisely framed to make us entirely good.

2. The Lord reigns by his PROVIDENCE. "Let the earth therefore rejoice; and the multitude of islands be glad." The Providence of God is well described in our shorter Catechism: "It is his most holy, wise, and powerful preserving and governing all his creatures, and all their actions." To particularize all the instances of providential government which may be matter of joy to the earth, would be endless; therefore I shall only mention the following: Let the earth rejoice; and the multitude of islands be glad, that the Lord reigns over the kingdoms of the earth, and manages all their affairs according to his sovereign and wise pleasure!

We sometimes hear of wars, and rumors of wars, of thrones tottering, and kingdoms falling, of the nations tumultuously raging and dashing in angry conflict, like the waves of the boisterous ocean. In such a juncture we may say, "The LORD reigns, he is robed in majesty; the LORD is robed in majesty and is armed with strength. The world is firmly established; it cannot be moved. Your throne was established long ago; you are from all eternity. The seas have lifted up, O LORD, the seas have lifted up their voice; the seas have lifted up their pounding waves. Mightier than the thunder of the great waters, mightier than the breakers of the sea—the LORD on high is mighty. Your statutes stand firm, O LORD!"   Psalm 93:1-5

Sometimes the ambition of foreign power, or the encroachments of domestic tyranny, may threaten our liberties, and persecution may seem ready to discharge its artillery against the church of God; while every pious heart trembles for the ark, lest it should be carried into the land of its enemies. But the Lord reigns! let the earth, let the church rejoice! "The eternal God is her refuge, and underneath her are the everlasting arms!" Deuteronomy 33.27. He will overrule the various revolutions of the world for her good; and the united powers of earth and hell shall not prevail against her! Though the frame of nature should be unhinged, we may find refuge in our God. But the LORD reigns! Let the earth be glad! contingent events are at his disposal, and necessity at his control. The smallest things are not beneath the notice of his providence, and the greatest are not above it. Those diseases and misfortunes which seem to happen by chance—are commissioned by the Lord of all! And those which result evidently from natural causes—are sent by his almighty will. He says to one, "Go!" and it goes; and to another, "Come!" and it comes! He orders the devastations that are made by the most raging elements. If flames lay our houses in ashes—they are kindled by his breath. If hurricanes sweep through our land, and carry desolation along with them—they but perform his will, and can do nothing beyond it! His hand hurls the thunder, and directs it where to strike! An arrow or a bullet shot at a venture in the heat of battle—is carried to its mark by divine direction!

The Lord reigns upon a throne of GRACE! "Let the earth rejoice; let the multitude of islands be glad!" It is the mediatorial government of the Messiah, which the Psalmist had more immediately in view; and this is the principal cause of joy to the earth and its guilty inhabitants. This is a kind of government peculiar to the human race; the holy angels do not need it, and the fallen angels are not favored with it. This is invested in the person of Immanuel, "who is made head over all things to his church," Ephesians 1:22; "to whom all power in heaven and earth is given," Matthew 11:27, and 28:18. This is the kingdom described in such magnificent language in Daniel 2:44, 45, and 7:14; Luke 1:32-33. Hence that Jesus who was mocked with a crown of thorns, and condemned as a criminal at Pilate's bar, wears on his vesture and on his thigh this majestic inscription, "KING OF KINGS, AND LORD OF LORDS!" Revelation 19:16.

And behold, I bring you glad tidings; this kingdom of God has come unto you, and you are called to become its subjects, and share in its blessings. Wherever the gospel is preached, there Jehovah sits upon a mercy-seat in majesty tempered with condescending grace. From thence he invites rebels who had rejected his government, to return to their allegiance; and passes an act of grace upon all who comply with the invitation. To his throne of grace he invites all to come, and offers them the richest blessings. From thence he publishes peace on earth, and good will towards men. From thence he offers pardon to all who will submit to his government, and renounce their sins—those weapons of rebellion. From thence he distributes the influences of his Spirit to subdue obstinate hearts into cheerful submission, to support his subjects under every burden, and furnish them with strength for the spiritual warfare. He subdues their rebellious corruptions, animates their languishing graces, and protects them from their spiritual enemies!

He enacts laws for the regulation of his church, appoints ordinances for her edification, and qualifies ministers to dispense them. He has ascended up on high; he has received gifts for men; and these he has distributed, and given: "some apostles; and some prophets; and some evangelists; and some pastors and teachers— for the perfecting of the saints, for the work of the ministry, for the edifying of the body of Christ," Ephesians 4:8, 11, 12.

How happy are we, who we live under the mediatorial administration! under the empire of grace! "Let the earth rejoice; let the multitude of islands be glad upon this account!" And let us pray that all nations may become the willing subjects of our gracious Sovereign.

If this administration of grace had not yet been erected, in what a miserable situation should we have been! guilty, miserable, and hopeless! Let us rejoice that the King of heaven, from whom we had revolted, has not allowed us to perish without remedy in our sinful rebellion—but holds out his scepter of grace to us—that we may touch it and live.

Samuel Davies was a great Presbyterian preacher of the 18th Century. We now turn our attention to another great Presbyterian preacher of the 19th Century – Daniel Baker.

Daniel Baker- The Great American Presbyterian Preacher of the 19th Century

One of the greatest evangelists of the 19th Century is little known by many people. His name is Daniel Baker (1791-1857). His longest ministry in one place was only nine years. His preaching ministry spanned some forty years. He preached the gospel throughout the North and South and finally in Texas where he died. Professor Douglas Kelly wrote the following about Baker's ministry in light of Isaiah 52:7:

> There could not be a better way of characterizing the effects of the life and preaching of this great Southern evangelist... than this

verse about beautiful feet hastening with glad tidings across waste places.[219]

The primary source for this section on Daniel Baker's life is the book *Making Many Glad: The Life and Labours of Daniel Baker* by his son William M. Baker. William Baker states in the preface to this book that he persuaded his father to write the narrative or autobiography of his life. This is incorporated in William's book. William accessed the various letters and journal of his father.

Daniel was born in 1791 at Midway, Georgia. He lost his mother while he was only an infant, grieving that he never knew a mother's smile, and he was orphaned at age eight with the death of his father. Daniel viewed his childhood as one where he had deep religious impressions but not evangelical ones. He viewed himself as self-righteous and was greatly disturbed by a dream where he found himself in hell. After many months of fearing the worst, he picked up a hymn book where he was moved by several stanzas. With resolve, he goes into a grove to pray where he finds God's saving grace.

He worked in Savannah, Georgia for three years at a dry goods and grocery store. At age nineteen, he was at a prayer meeting where he determined that he wanted to give his life to the gospel ministry, but he had no means of earning an education, nor did he know how to obtain it. While conversing with his brother one day, his brother mentioned that a Rev. C. Gildersleeve had visited Dr. Moses Hoge, President of Hampton Sidney College near Richmond, Virginia. Dr. Hoge inquired if Rev. Gildersleeve knew of any pious young man who wished to become a Presbyterian minister but who had no financial means of pursuing it.

Daniel viewed this as a providential act of God to have him pursue the gospel ministry. In 1811 he arrived at Hampton Sidney College. The sermons of President Hoge had a great impact upon him as well as the reading of *Witherspoon on Regeneration*. Daniel came to cherish the thought that God's saving grace was free, sovereign, and discriminating.

In a Sunday, December 14, 1812 journal entry, Daniel stated:

A goodly number of the pious students of this Seminary have united, (prompted, I hope, by a pure and fervent zeal,) and have

---

[219] This quote is on the back cover of a biography on Baker's life, titled *Making Many Glad: The Life and Labours of Daniel Baker* by his son William M. Baker. The quote is from *Preachers with Power*, p. 3.

formed a praying society, to be held every Sunday afternoon, in this neighborhood, for the benefit of the poor, ignorant, and too much neglected negroes.[220]

Daniel recounted how a sermon by Dr. Hoge challenged him that he did not possess certain necessary qualities needed for a preacher of God's word. This journal entry dated July 31, 1813 gives us a glimpse into Daniel Baker's view of preaching:

Dry, logical sermons, with rounded periods, delivered in a cold, formal, and heartless manner, I can never relish, however beautified by the superficial elegances of composition; and I question if the good effects which flow from such preaching will be sufficient to compensate the minister for all his care, labour, and refinement. I love warm, animating, lively, *evangggelominos* preaching, full of fire, breathing love and compassion. O may I never become cold, lifeless, sentimental preacher, but may I imitate the zeal of a Whitefield, the tenderness of a Hervey, the affection of a Baxter and blend all with the pure, sound, evangelical principles of Doddridge.

O shall I ever be honoured as the ambassador of the living God- shall I ever be called to preach the unsearchable riches of this, my crucified, my risen, my dear, my glorious Redeemer? I humbly hope so. O if I should, may I go forth in the fullness of the blessings of the gospel of Christ, with burning love, flaming zeal, tender compassion, and a melting heart.[221]

During the winter of 1813, Daniel enrolled in the College of New Jersey at Princeton.[222] The spiritual climate of this college was quite dismal according to Baker. He wrote:

At this time religion was at a very low ebb in the College. There were about one hundred and forty-five students, and of these, only six, so far as I knew, made any profession of religion, and even two of these six seemed to care very little about the matter; for, although four of us, Price, Allen, Biggs, and myself, agree to meet

---

[220]   William M. Baker, *Making Many Glad: The Life and Labours of Daniel Baker*, (Edinburgh: Banner of Truth Trust, 2000), p. 57.
[221]   Baker, pp. 61-62.
[222]   New Light Presbyterians established the College of New Jersey in 1746. In 1756, the college moved to Princeton, NJ. It was later renamed Princeton University in 1896.

every evening for what was called family prayer, they kept aloof.[223]

The Beginning of the Revival

A study of revivals throughout church history reveals one definite axiom – **it starts with earnest prayer followed by faithful action.** This is exactly what happened during the college days of Daniel Baker. Baker and his other three students were dubbed the "Religiosi" by the rest of the student body.[224] Because of the widespread decadence of the spiritual state of the college student body, Baker and his friends decided to engage in weekly prayer for the express purpose of seeing a revival at the college. One thing we can learn from this is that one never knows when God will answer the prayers in the affirmative. Baker wrote:

> At the commencement of the third session, as our prayers seemed not to have been heard, I was somewhat doubtful about continuing our weekly prayer- meeting, but, very happily, my associates were clear for continuing it, and it was well; for although we knew it not, the blessing was nigh, even at the doors.

> At this time the war was still raging with Great Britain; and by the President of the United States, James Madison, all day was set apart for fasting, humiliation, and prayer. I recollect that day well. My feelings were much excited; and, after engaging in private devotions, I proposed to my room-mate that we should spend the whole day, as far as practicable, in visiting from room to room, and converse with our fellow students on religious matters; and I recollect distinctly saying to my room-mate, "Brother B., what does the Bible say? – "Is not this the fast that I have chosen, to loose the bands of wickedness? Come," added I, "and let us do what we can to break the bands of wickedness this day." The proposition was also made to P. and A., who occupied the room just under ours; they cordially concurred, and we had four warm-hearted missionaries in College that day. We went from room to room, conversing on the subject of religion only.[225]

---

[223]   Baker, p. 64.
[224]   Baker, p. 65.
[225]   Baker, pp. 65-66.

Baker stated that the college president, Dr. Green, made a report to the Trustees of the college documenting the causes of the revival that soon broke out:

> The few pious youth who were members of College before the revival, were happily instrumental in promoting it. They had, for more than a year, been earnestly engaged in prayer for this event. When they perceived the general and increasing seriousness, several of them made an agreement to speak privately and tenderly to their particular friends and acquaintances, on the subject of religion. And what they said was, in almost every instance, not only well received, but those with whom they conversed became immediately and earnestly engaged in those exercises which it is hoped have issued in genuine piety.[226]

The impact was gradual at first, but it then quickly gained momentum. The evening of their missionary activity saw eight new faces at the "family prayer." Just like in other revivals, sometimes it gains momentum through the conversion of one notable sinner. Such was this case. Baker wrote:

> The next day an event occurred which produced a considerable excitement amongst the students, and served to increase the religious interest greatly. One of the students, W. J., a very profane young man, but of a warm heart, with great oratorical powers, had been out at a tavern the night before, with some others, gambling. Returning to college at a late hour, he was arrested on the campus by an officer of College, who, laying his hand upon him, said, "Ah, my young man! Have I got you?" The moment this was said, W. J. (as he told me afterwards) was struck under conviction of sin. He felt that he had violated the laws of his Maker, as well as the laws of College. He was suspended by the faculty; but it being known that he was under conviction, he was permitted to remain on the college grounds for some two or three days. Much of this time was spent by the "young orator" in telling his fellow students what a great sinner he had been, and urging them all to attend to the salvation of their souls, as the one thing needful. That night the room in which we held our family worship was crowded. A little after we changed our place of meeting to the largest room in College, and that was nearly full; some seventy or eighty students being present.

---

[226] Quoted in Baker, p. 66.

> The interest in the college continued to increase, and in about a week from the day of the national fast, I made this record in my diary, "thank God! we can now say, there is a revival of religion in Nassau Hall College." Yes, our prayers had been answered at last, and the Lord had done for us far more than we ever dared hope for.[227]

Baker said that the revival continued until the end of the session with about forty-five students profoundly affected. They were regularly testifying with each other what God had done for them. While others at the college were impacted in some way, Baker stated that he believed forty-five were genuinely converted, and twenty or thirty would later become ministers of the gospel. One of them became known by the British press as the greatest divine alive.[228]

After leaving college at Princeton, Baker went to study theology under Rev. Hill at Winchester, Virginia. Some of his tasks were exhorting during Wednesday evening meetings and Sabbath days. Believing in the value and power of prayer, Baker established prayer meetings every Friday evening at his house. He said these prayer meetings were the birthplace of many souls. During this period of time, he with others started a Sabbath school which was held at 3:00 P.M. every Sabbath Day. It was attended eventually by nearly 200 people. In the female academy, he met his future wife, Elizabeth. They were married on March 28, 1816.

A momentous day occurred in the fall of 1816. Daniel Baker was licensed to preach by the Presbytery of Winchester. Concerning his licensure, Baker wrote:

> I am now about to go forth to preach the everlasting gospel to poor, perishing sinners; to proclaim liberty to the captive, and the opening of the prison to those that are bound; to proclaim the acceptable year of the Lord... I ask not to be rich in silver and gold, and to be admired and caressed; I ask to be rich in faith and good works, and to be blessed and owned in my labours of love. I ask not to be exempted from grievous trials and persecutions, but I ask grace to glorify thee in the hour of trial; grace to be useful, grace to be triumphant in death, and grace to reach, at length, the

---

[227] Baker, pp. 67-68.
[228] Baker never identifies who this person was.

Mount Zion above, where I may forever sing the triumphs of my dearest Lord.[229]

It seems that his trials immediately began at his licensure at presbytery. Baker stated that Rev. Hill had neglected to guide him in his theological studies, giving him no books except *Butler's Analogy*. Baker said he made great use of the Shorter Catechism (Westminster). There were some at the presbytery meeting who greatly opposed his licensure. However, a Mr.W. was pleased to say, "The Lord had licensed me."[230]

Almost immediately his sermons began to have a genuine impact upon people. Baker said, "Awakening influences went abroad in a most remarkable manner." People would gather at Rev. Muir's house where six to eight people came weeping, inquiring what they must do in order to be saved. Baker spoke at a monthly concert meeting held at a Methodist church. He said about 100 people came up to him, and he exhorted them for about thirty minutes to serve the Lord.

In a visit to his brother in Savannah, Georgia he was asked to preach for a Dr. Kollock who had been impressed with Baker's preaching. Baker remained in the area for about two weeks preaching at differing locations where great crowds gathered to hear him.

In March 1818, Baker was ordained and installed as pastor of the united congregations of Harrisonburg and New Erection, Virginia. While at Harrisonburg, he taught school for about three years. One of his students, Gessner Harrison, who later became a distinguished professor at the University of Virginia, would later write this about Daniel Baker's influence upon him and others:

> For some years of my boyhood I was a pupil of the late Rev. Daniel Baker, D.D. and have always regarded him as having displayed in a very eminent degree, some of the best qualities of a teacher of youth... his heart was in the work of training them in useful knowledge and virtue, would hardly convey an adequate idea of the enthusiastic zeal with which he labored in his school... he simply mingled firmness with kindness, that his pupils so universally and so greatly loved and respected him.[231]

---

[229] Baker, pp. 91-92.
[230] Baker, p. 93.
[231] Cited in Baker, p. 98.

A major turning point in Baker's life occurred in 1820 when he became burdened to become a missionary. He resigned his pastorate in Harrisonburg and began preaching in various churches in Washington D.C. During this period of time, he was offered two calls to be pastor of the Second Presbyterian Church in Washington D.C., and a call to be pastor of the Independent Presbyterian Church in Savannah, Georgia. The salary for the Savannah church was quite large while the one in Washington was small. Baker chose the small salary and accepted the call in Washington. Concerning Baker's ministry in Washington, D.C. a Baptist brother would later write after Baker's death the following tribute of Baker's ministry:

> I remember him well. During a residence of five years in and near Washington, District of Columbia, I frequently attended at his place of worship. I preferred his ministry, not because it was the most intellectual, but because it was spiritual, fervent, and enforced by a consistent life. He was a man of prayer; he preached to save souls; he walked with God. [232]

An interesting event occurred one Sabbath while preaching in his church in Washington D.C. Baker wrote:

> One Sabbath afternoon, just as I had announced my text, which was this- "Ephraim is a cake not turned" – John Quincy Adams, the Secretary of State, stepped in, and walking up the aisle, took his seat near the pulpit. The reverence[233] which I had for this great man, the singularity of the text, and my want of due preparation, all united to disconcert me; I was thrown off my balance, and preached, as I then thought, and still think, a very indifferent discourse. It had, however, one excellence, not found in most of my sermons – it was very short; not more than twenty or twenty-five minutes long. When I finished, I was excessively mortified, and thought I would never see the Secretary of State in that church again; but, to my astonishment, the next week I was told he had rented one of the best pews in the church... I soon had the

---

232   Cited in Baker, p. 107.

233   The reason for Baker's reverence or respect for John Quincy Adams was probably based on these facts about him when he was Secretary of State under the presidency of James Monroe. As a diplomat, Adams played an important role in negotiating many international treaties, most notably the Treaty of Ghent, which ended the War of 1812. As Secretary of State, he negotiated with the United Kingdom over America's northern border with Canada, negotiated with Spain the annexation of Florida, and authored the Monroe Doctrine. According to some historians he was one of the greatest diplomats and secretaries of state in American history. John Quincy Adams, the son of the second President of the United States, John Adams, would later become the sixth president of the United States serving one term from 1825-1829.

pleasure of hearing - that Mr. Adams had taken a pew; and that was not all – soon after, the Secretary of State became one of the most efficient trustees of my church, and one of the best friends I ever had... Mr. Adams never failed to be in his pew on Sabbath afternoon, whatever might be the weather, and was a most attentive hearer... After he took a pew in my church, and became a trustee, it seemed to come more into notice... and so did General Jackson, then a Senator.[234]

While in his pastorate in Washington, D.C., an elder of his church once wrote this about Baker's preaching:

> Whenever he appeared in the pulpit, the audience saw that he was not preaching himself, but Jesus Christ.. His delivery was very earnest, and generally his discourses were practical in their character. His power of endurance was very remarkable, and he was always ready to preach whenever and wherever opportunity offered. **He was deeply impressed with a conviction of the importance of meetings for prayer to the spiritual prosperity of a church**; and on such occasions eh was most earnest in his addresses, and devout in his supplications... It was impossible to fail in discovering that the Holy Spirit was dwelling in and communing with him.
>
> Dr. Baker possessed, in an eminent degree, the spirit of a missionary. Gentle as he was in spirit, he was stranger to the emotion of fear, and no 'lions in the way' would have turned him aside from unblenching progress in the path to which duty led. (Emphasis mine).[235]

During his tenure in Washington, Baker published *A Scriptural View of Baptism,* which was extensively circulated and soon followed by his *Baptism in a Nutshell.* This last small book was a definitive treatment on the proper mode and objects of baptism (in support of infant baptism).

The salary from the Washington congregation became insufficient for him to provide for his family. This necessitated him in having to accept a position as clerk in the office of the General Land Office. He hated to do this because it took so much time from his love of ministering. When a new commissioner took charge, there was a significant reduction in clerks.

---

[234] Baker, pp. 107-108. The reference to General Jackson was Andrew Jackson who would become the seventh President of the United States after John Quincy Adams.

[235] Cited in Baker, pp. 113-114.

A lottery was used to determine which clerks would be dismissed. In this lottery, Baker's name was drawn, meaning he had to go. Suddenly, his financial base was cut in half. Just when his situation looked very bleak, a second call was issued to him from the Independent Presbyterian Church in Savannah, Georgia, which he accepted.

While in Savannah, Baker received two letters from John Quincy Adams and Andrew Jackson indicating that they would like to see him back in Washington; however, he would never go back but to the end of his life, he regarded the members of the church with great affection, referring to them as his "first love."

While using Savannah as a base, Baker had preaching opportunities in South Carolina where significant crowds gathered to hear him. He indicated that some eighty people professed Christ, one of whom was an eighty-six year old man who had heard many sermons from the renowned George Whitefield but never professed Christ. But, at this late age, God used another herald, Daniel Baker, to reap the harvest of the seed sown many years earlier.

Interestingly, people from all sorts of denominations came to hear Baker preach, and often, it was others besides the Presbyterians that were most influenced by his preaching.

It was during this period that Baker desired to resign his pastorate and become a preacher for a missionary society in Georgia. He asked his presbytery if it would consider making him its missionary and use him as it saw fit. He indicated that he would entrust himself to God's providence for his financial support. His presbytery approved his idea, and Daniel Baker now became evangelist at large with quite an extensive field. For two years he preached protracted meetings in Georgia at Midway, St. Marys, Augusta, Athens, and Macon. In Florida, he preached at St. Augustine, Tallahassee, Monticello, Quincy, and Mariana.

A man in Tallahassee made these observations about Baker's evangelistic preaching:

> There were few men hardened enough to resist these appeals... His appeals were so kind, so earnest, so evidently sincere, that, whatever other effects they produced, his impenitent hearers could not resist the impression that the speaker was their friend. And this was one secret, so far as human agency was concerned, of this great power over his audience. But there was something more in his discourses than sincerity and earnestness. They were prepared

with great labour and care, and the manner of uttering every sentence thoroughly studied. They were not exactly committed to memory, but every thought was so well fixed and arranged in his mind, that it was never omitted nor introduced out of its proper place. His sermons had consequently all the order and compactness of written discourses, with the ease and freedom of extemporary appeals.

Another secret of Mr. Baker's power, was his uniform habit of earnest communion with God, in his closet, before he delivered his message to the people from the desk. [236]

Baker preached in Montgomery, Alabama and also in Columbia, South Carolina. A student at Columbia Theological Seminary wrote the following about Baker's preaching during one of his meetings in May, 1832. These meetings were well attended by Presbyterians, Methodists, and Baptists. The student's observations were:

He often looked over his manuscript before preaching, but he frequently dispensed with notes in the pulpit. His voice was clear and strong, his utterance easy and fluent, his manner very earnest and animated; and when in the full flow of his subject, amid revival scenes, he was strikingly eloquent and impressive... As far as I had opportunity to observe, and now recall his method in revivals, his first aim was to arouse Christians, and elicit much fervent and persevering prayer. I personally knew a circle that, during the revival at Columbia, on more than one occasion, spent the whole night in prayer. His application of truth was very plain and pungent, without being harsh and repulsive.[237]

The sermons he preached in Columbia, South Carolina were published as his *Revival Sermons.* The same observer of these sermons said:

These sermons were delivered with simplicity and power, but with an unction that seemed to impress his hearers with the conviction that really he was an ambassador from heaven, and spoke "the words of truth and soberness."... I have heard many of the most eloquent men of our country in the pulpit, but I have never heard one who, to the same extent, could rivet the attention of the sinner, draw him insensibly to the conclusion that he was "a fool-consummate fool;" harrow up his soul, force him to think, and

---

[236]   Cited in Baker, pp. 161-162.
[237]   Cited in Baker, pp.169-170.

> lead him to pray... for he was not what the world terms an
> eloquent man, but it was , as I believe, that unction from on high,
> which, reflected from his heart on his countenance and manner,
> fastened on the hearer the conviction that he was in truth God's
> ambassador.[238]

For two years, Baker estimated that he had preached on the average two
sermons per day for this period of time with an estimated 2500 people
professing Christ. Baker's son stated the following about his preaching
style and presence:

> He always spoke on a perfectly natural key and easy pitch of
> voice; he knew nothing of throat problems despite the voluminous
> amount of preaching, and often in the open air. His manner in the
> pulpit was as natural and easy as in the parlour; he stood in the
> pulpit as one who had something important to say. His effort was
> to present divine truth with transparent clearness, and let that truth
> work its own results. In a discourse, his voice and manner ran
> through a wide range –statement of subject, reasoning, solemn
> denunciation, tearful entreaty- but in all he was natural, perfect so;
> it was only a man conversing with his friends most earnestly in
> regard to their soul's salvation.[239]

These observations of Daniel Baker's preaching are very similar to how
George Whitefield preached. After all, Baker did once say that he wanted
to have the zeal of a Whitefield, which apparently he did possess.

It is most interesting that he regarded the preaching of the word of God of
such great importance that he did not permit disturbances during the
preaching:

> He never hesitated, in the midst of a sermon, to rebuke any
> disorder. If any outcry, the result of religious emotion, was made,
> he would pause, and say in a solemn manner, "The Lord is in his
> holy temple, let all the earth keep silence before him:" a course
> which never failed to still even the most excited. He could bear a
> babe crying in the congregation, but misconduct on the part of one
> old enough to know better, he would never permit. On one
> occasion, after once or twice rebuking a rude boy, he said at last,
> "Little boy, go home, and tell your mother you deserve a good
> whipping;"and, as the boy went out with his singular message, the

---

[238]   Cited in Baker, p. 176.
[239]   Baker, p. 181.

speaker continued his discourse. Pausing, and addressing himself to them, he said, with the utmost solemnity, "Young men, at the bar of God, in judgment, you will answer for your conduct this day."[240]

With regard to his livelihood, Baker had told his presbytery that, as an evangelist, he was willing to trust in God's providence. During the two years of this protracted preaching, the free will offerings amounted to nearly what he would have earned in his pastorate.

Concerning money matters, Baker was determined not to incur a debt that he did not quickly satisfy. He was a very generous man as per this story told of him by his son:

> It need scarce be added, that he contributed to all deserving objects, up to, and even beyond his means. A widow applied to him in her distress for ten dollars; he hesitated for a moment, and then enclosed twenty in a note to her, knowing her great necessity. It was ten dollars more than he could afford; and he considered it a marked providence when, on going to the office to mail the note, he took from his box an anonymous letter to himself, containing just ten dollars, as a donation. The prayer of Agur was his prayer, and it was answered – to the day of his death he knew "neither poverty nor riches."[241]

Over the next several years he served pastorates in Nashville, Tennessee, Frankfort, Kentucky, and Tuscaloosa, Alabama. In 1838, Dr. John Breckinridge approached Baker with the belief that Baker was the right man to plant Presbyterian churches in the newly established republic of Texas. Baker concluded that if his presbytery in Alabama approved the notion and committed financial support for him to go to Texas, then he would consider it his duty to do so. The presbytery unanimously voted to make Baker its missionary to Texas. Interestingly, in going to Texas, Baker took a letter of introduction to General Sam Houston from Andrew Jackson, with whom he had had a cordial relationship while in Washington D.C.

Baker's first taste of Texas was at Galveston Island, arriving there on February 26, 1840. Baker noted that Christians were very few. He resided in the home of Dr. Roberts. His first effort was the distribution of many

---

[240] Baker, pp. 185-186.
[241] Baker, p. 189.

tracts that he had brought, and he began to preach daily during the week, and three times on the Sabbath. He also addressed the Sabbath school which he was pleased to see had already been established. There is an interesting story Baker tells of encountering some young boys playing marbles on the Sabbath. We get a glimpse of Baker's view of the Sabbath which was common among many in those days. He stated:

> Walking along the streets of Galveston on a Sabbath day, I came up to a large group of boys who were playing marbles. "Hey boys," said I, "playing marbles on Sunday!" "O, we are in Texas," one of them replied. "Well, but boys," replied I, "don't you know that God can see you in Texas, as well as in the States?" Putting my hand in my pocket, I pulled out a good many little books, and, whilst giving, I talked very kindly to the boys; and winding up, I pleasantly remarked, "Boys, it is not right to play marbles on Sunday; you had better go to Sunday school"- pointing to the place. I then left them, bidding them good–by; but I had gone only a few steps when several of them called to me aloud, and said, "We won't play marbles any more on Sunday; we will go to Sunday school, sir."[242]

One of the great biblical truths about the relationship of prayer to evangelism is that God often uses the prayers of godly parents to bring about the salvation of wayward children. A beautiful example of this was related by Baker:

> One day I took a stroll out of town, and whilst walking on the beach on the south side of the island, I unexpectedly came up to a military station, where some thirty soldiers were on the look-out for Mexicans, who were expected to invade Texas about this time. On conversing with them I found that no one had ever preached to them, or given them a Bible, or tract, or anything of the kind. Each could with but too much truth, say, No man cared for my soul.
>
> Having obtained permission from the commander, who was very polite, I distributed tracts amongst them, and preached to them near the strand, in the open air. As there were no seats for their accommodation, they stood before me in military order. In the midst of my discourse, a new thought occurred, and leaving my theme, I addressed them to this effect: "Soldiers, here you are, in this new and wild country, far away from the means of grace. I think likely that you are all quite careless and unconcerned about

---

[242] Baker, pp. 229-230.

your soul's salvation. And yet, after all, I wonder if some of you have not pious mothers in the old States, who love you, and pray for you, and weep over you." Passing my eyes rapidly over the faces of the soldiers, I noticed one particularly who was prodigiously wrought upon. His lips quivered; every muscle was in motion; tears ran down his cheeks. Much excited myself, said I, "Soldier, come here, I want to talk to you." Leaving the ranks, he came to me, and we two retiring a short distance, I said to him, "Soldier, have you not a pious mother in the States?" Bursting into tears, he replied, "Yes, sir, a very pious mother, a member of the Methodist Church in Pennsylvania." As I spoke to him about the blessed Savior, and the way of salvation through him, he wept aloud – so loud that his voice might have been heard for several hundred yards. After giving such instruction and encouragement as I thought the case called for, and after finishing the discourse which I had commenced, I returned to my lodgings in Galveston.

Two days after, I visited the same military station again, and had the happiness to find that soldier rejoicing in Christ. His mother's prayers, it would seem, have been answered, and I, as a missionary, was sent into this frontier land to call home a wandering son. To God be all the praise! This, it seems, was the first person who ever professed conversion on Galveston Island.[243]

Baker's story brings out a great biblical truth. God does answer prayer. God does attend to the prayers of godly parents, and no parent should ever give up praying for an unbelieving child as long as that child is alive. As long as there is life, there is hope! Baker was so correct when he said that he was a missionary sent by God into a wild land in answer to a godly mother's prayers. Romans 10:14-15 states:

> [14]*How then shall they call upon Him in whom they have not believed? And how shall they believe in Him whom they have not heard? And how shall they hear without a preacher?* [15]*And how shall they preach unless they are sent? Just as it is written, "How beautiful are the feet of those who bring glad tidings of good things!"*

Baker was eager to visit the interior of Texas, but he was apparently not desirous to make Texas a permanent residence. His mission he says was to

---

[243] Baker, pp. 230-231.

preach, organize churches, form temperance societies, and Sabbath schools. He believed there were only six Presbyterian ministers in all of Texas; however, there were a much larger number of Methodists, and an unknown number of Baptists. Before leaving Galveston Island, Baker commented that he thought there were two or three people soundly converted, one being a lady of high respectability who had never heard a single sermon before until she heard him. And Baker wrote:

> And there is the case of a Texan soldier, a poor wanderer brought back by my instrumentality, that has touched my heart, insomuch that I thought it well I had come all the way to Texas, if it were only for the sake of that poor wandering sheep. Bless the Lord![244]

Jesus did say in Luke 15:4:

> *What man of you, having an hundred sheep, if he lose one of them, doth not leave the ninety and nine in the wilderness, and go after that which is lost, until he find it?*

While in Texas, he had opportunities for personal evangelism. Baker recounted an episode with a Major B in Columbia, Texas. This man was an avowed infidel who was in the custom of cursing preachers and lawyers. Baker described a breakfast with the man:

> Reaching the chair assigned to me, just at the right time, I remarked, "Major, with your permission I will ask a blessing" – and not allowing him time to say, no, it was all over before he was aware that a thing had been done at his table which probably had never been done before… The Major has been out-generaled this time! He took it, however, all in good part; and as we rose from the table, and were going into another room by ourselves, he remarked, "I don't believe in the Bible, sir; it will do for women and children. But maybe I am wrong." "Ah! Major B.," said I, "Maybe you are wrong." I then went on for some fifteen or twenty minutes with all the force and power of language which I could command, showing him the fearful consequences of a mistake being made in a matter of such immense importance; especially as no mistake could be rectified after death. He listened to me in silence, and was as a child subdued; and when I closed, he shook me by the hand most cordially, and, inviting me to call upon him whenever I passed that way, he bade me farewell. For my fare he

---

charged nothing. This case convinced me that any man, however wicked, may be approached, if it be done in the right way.[245]

The Texas frontier presented all kinds of unique events for Daniel Baker. From his perspective it was indeed – the wild, wild west.

The town of Washington, Texas was noted for its lack of concern for religion despite the faithful labors of a Methodist preacher in town. Baker recounted the story of mock prayer meetings that were held on Friday nights by the town's rabble. He indicated an event that should have put fear into the hearts of such rabble, but it didn't. During one such mock prayer meeting, a half drunk man began mimicking a certain preacher with the entire crowd laughing hysterically. During this time, a pistol was drawn and accidentally went off. The bullet pierced a man's heart killing him instantly. As Baker related, this death did not deter the continual mocking on other days.[246]

Baker did refer to a remarkable conversion of a Captain C. who had no respect at all for religion. He described the man's conversion:

> On a certain day, a gentleman riding over the settlement, noticed a beautiful spot, and remarked, "Captain C., that is a beautiful place for a church." "Don't talk about churches," said Captain C.; "if you do, you will drive me out of this country." I said he was profane, very; and yet he was made a trophy of grace, and became one of the humblest and most devoted Christians I ever knew. How? The case was this. I was preaching a sermon from these words, "Tekel, thou art weighed in the balances, and art found wanting." When I came to weigh profane swearers, amongst other things, I remarked: "An old writer has said, 'The devil sometimes turns fisherman; when he fishes for ordinary sinners, he is willing to go to some expense; he baits his hook with the riches of the world, the honours of the world, and the pleasures of the world; but when he fishes for profane swearers, he throws them the naked hook; - cheap in the devil's account.'" This was carried like an arrow to his heart. He was deeply convicted, and a few days after, was a happy convert. "Captain C.," said I, "what first set you to thinking?" "O, Mr. Baker," replied he, "the idea of the devil's catching me with a naked hook. I could not stand that, sir."[247]

---

[245]   Baker, pp. 242-243.
[246]   Baker, p. 246.
[247]   Baker, pp. 247-248.

What this story demonstrates is that the gospel is indeed the "dunamis" (power) of God as the Scripture states. It also demonstrates that the usual method of God convicting men is under the **preaching of the Word by one officially sent to preach.**[248]

In the early 1840's, Baker's labors in Texas were very time consuming, meaning that he was frequently away from his family. For the benefit of his family, he decided to take a pastorate in Holly Springs, Mississippi where he stayed nine years. To supplement his income he engaged in preaching tours throughout the state and into Tennessee, going as far as East Tennessee. His preaching itinerary was enormous at this time – some seventy sermons a month![249]

In June 1848, Baker made the decision to resign his pastorate in Holly Springs, Mississippi and return to Texas. Baker's Calvinistic understanding of Scripture is clearly shown from this journal entry while in Victoria, Texas:

> Had prayer meeting at half-past eight; some tenderness. Preached to an overflow in house; some twenty or thirty without. In the afternoon preached a Calvinistic sermon. Well received. At night, an overflowing house and great solemnity.[250]

While in Austin, Texas, Baker gives a most humorous plea for the best preachers to come to Texas. He stated:

> Permit me here to repeat a remark made in my former report, "Let inferior preachers be retained in the East; let talented ones be sent to the West... In Texas, the people will not come out on week-days, and not very well on Sabbath-days, unless they think the preacher is 'worth hearing.'"[251]

In 1849 his presbytery began considering the establishment of a Presbyterian college in Texas. And, it was at this time that Baker began to plead with men to come to Texas for the fields were white to harvest. His presbytery approved the idea of a Presbyterian college and named it Austin College in honor of Stephen F. Austin, the great Texas pioneer. The

---

[248]   This is not to say that God doesn't convert people in other ways such as in personal reading, one on one evangelism, etc. It simply states that official preaching is the normative method that God uses.

[249]   Baker, p. 306.

[250]   Baker, p. 339.

[251]   Baker, pp. 350-351.

purpose for the college was that Texas might have a native ministry that would endure for generations.

During this period, Baker had opportunities to preach as far as Brownsville, Texas, which is virtually on the Mexican border. He indicated that large crowds came to hear him, and he said that he was probably the first regular Protestant preacher of any denomination to preach in Brownsville. He even thought that he might be the first gospel voice up the Rio Grande. He stated:

> ...That it was the first time in his life that he had known a Presbyterian minister to be ahead of the Methodists![252]

In the formation of Austin College, Daniel Baker became an official representative (fundraiser) for the college. This opened up preaching tours in 1850 to Houston, Galveston, New Orleans, Memphis, Cincinnati, Philadelphia, Princeton, New York, Easton, Brunswick, Newark, Brooklyn, Wilmington, Washington City, Baltimore, Georgetown, Savannah, Augusta, Freehold, and Mobile. As one can see, it was a monumental preaching tour on behalf of Austin College.

In 1851 and 1852, he engaged in a second and third tour respectively to solicit funds for Austin College. During his third tour, he visited again Columbia, South Carolina where he had had great success in his evangelistic preaching years earlier. One of the most generous contributors to Austin College was the president of the college in Columbia. This was none other than the renowned Southern Presbyterian preacher and theologian, Dr. James Henley Thornwell. Baker wrote:

> ... Almost wherever I go, I meet with those who were brought in under my ministry many years ago, several of whom are even ministers of the gospel, of whom I had never heard before. Even in the pulpit I am spoken of in a manner which almost overwhelms

---

[252]   Baker, p. 408. This is an interesting comment because as I stated earlier in this chapter, Methodism originally was aggressively evangelistic under the ministries of Whitefield and others, who referred to themselves as Calvinistic Methodists. During the 1790's, the Methodist denomination was formed under the leadership of John Wesley. From the organization of the Methodist Church, two groups of Methodists eventually arose during that period of time: Wesleyan and Primitive Methodists. The Primitive Methodists were aggressively evangelistic. It is interesting that my maternal great, great grandfather, William Audiss, was converted in England under the ministry of Primitive Methodists and became a minister in that denomination for sixty years (1840-1900). He eventually moved his family of ten to America and settled in Wisconsin. His journal of his evangelistic preaching has been a treasured possession of mine, and it formed the basis of my last book titled *Retracing the Beautiful Steps*. In 2008, I had the privilege to go to England and retrace his preaching circuit in Lincolnshire, England. This book can be obtained by going to www.triumphantpublications.com.

me. Only think, Dr. Thornwell made an announcement to the students of South Carolina College after this manner: "In consequence of the tender relations which exist between many of your parents and the Rev. Dr. Baker, who has just addressed you, you are no doubt desirous to know his appointments; I will therefore state, &c.&c." ... Wherever I go I am received with open arms. My spiritual children, especially, seem so glad to see me. Sometimes I feel almost overwhelmed![253]

A pastor of the Darlington Church in South Carolina wrote in October 1852 the following observations of Daniel Baker's doctrinal commitment and preaching style. The significance of this quote shows the indisputable Calvinistic commitment of Baker, and it brings out that this was indicative of all his preaching wherever he went. Daniel Baker was a living testimony that Calvinistic preaching was and is thoroughly biblical and powerful to the saving of souls. Those of the 21st Century who think Calvinism is antagonistic to vigorous evangelism are simply misinformed of history. The Darlington pastor wrote:

> Our spacious church was crowed day and night to its utmost capacity, to the close. People of all denominations flocked to hear the stranger from Texas; even some of the Jews came to hear him explain the Old Testament prophecies....The professed converts are chiefly, if not entirely, the children of pious parents, children of the covenant. A majority of them are young men, and promise much usefulness in the Church. The good Spirit seems to have paved the way for the earnest preaching of the stranger from Texas; they were a people prepared of the Lord. **Dr. Baker's preaching is eminently Calvinistic.** The doctrines of our church- the divine sovereignty, election, total depravity, vicarious atonement, and efficacious grace, were prominently exhibited... Great stillness and solemnity characterized the large assemblies. It was truly an interesting spectacle to behold a sea of uplifted faces, with many streaming eyes, directed towards the speaker, as the words of eternal life fell from his lips....
>
> It may be mentioned here as a singular fact, **that such Arminians as heard his doctrinal discourses concurred in them as the gospel truth**... The truth is, Dr. Baker presented these doctrines so clearly, both as to their foundation and inferences; proved them so from reason, revelation, and Christian experience, as to make it

---

[253]   Baker, pp. 439-440.

evident that they are indeed the gospel itself, in all its freeness and fullness, in all its sweetness and power. His whole aim was to do as Scripture does – exalt God, and humble man – place the almighty Sovereign and the offending subject in their actual relations to each other; and this, in order to show how infinite the love of God in stooping to save, and absolutely essential the need, and certain the salvation of such a Savior. (Emphasis mine)[254]

The Darlington pastor continued to make his observations of Daniel Baker's preaching:

It is especially gratifying to state that the distinctive points of our Old-school theology were clearly, fully, and faithfully preached.... But so far as my observation has extended, I am free to say that I think the religious movement among us is due mainly to the plain, frank, undisguised presentation of these great doctrines in their own solemn Scripture attire. The sovereign purpose of God in election, the vicarious atonement of Christ, the total inability of the sinner, the instantaneous work of regeneration, the perseverance of the saints; these, in all their glorious beauty and sweetness to the believer, in all their startling terror to the sinner, were set forth, without reserve, as the counsel of God. The singularly happy arguments and illustrations of the venerable Texan who was with us, and his peculiar skill in detecting where these great doctrines underlie the Christian's peace and joy, disarmed all gain sayings, and untied the hearts of different denominations in perfect harmony. A beautiful and cordial union prevails: Presbyterians, Methodists, and Baptists, commingled their tears under the droppings of a sublime Calvinistic theology. The scene was novel and intensely engaging. Truly our great doctrines are all involved in the plan of redemption, and all true Christians feed upon them. May all our brethren be encouraged to lay aside a trembling delicacy, and, grasping the sharp tools of the word of God with a firm faith, as wise builders, build up the walls of our spiritual temple.[255]

During his third preaching tour, Baker preached throughout North Carolina. Baker wrote:

Immense congregations attend upon my preaching – every Sabbath perhaps three thousand people come from a great

---

[254]   Baker, pp. 459-461.
[255]   Baker, pp. 463-464.

distance, and I am told there has not been such a glorious revival in North Carolina for the last fifty years. To God be the glory... In the eleven protracted meetings which I have attended in North Carolina recently, something more than six hundred persons have been hopefully converted, of whom nearly three-fourths are males, from fourteen to seventy years of age.[256]

In a letter to his son, Baker speaks of the success of his ministry throughout his years:

During this whole tour I have preached Him incessantly, and with positive love kindling and glowing in my heart; frequently with tears streaming down my cheeks! I think this has been one secret of the success: 'Him that honoureth me will I honour; but he that despiteth me shall be lightly esteemed.' Remember my son, this saying of your father, that the sermon that does not distinctly present Christ in the beauty and glory of his mediatorial character, is no better than a cloud without water, a casket without a jewel, a shadow without the substance, or the body without the soul. Thin of what Paul says, 'God forbid that I should glory, save in the cross of our Lord Jesus Christ' – and again, 'Christ is all and in all.' Think of it in your pulpit and in your study; when you lie down and when you rise up; when you go out and when you come in.[257]

Baker also wrote this extremely helpful observation about effective preaching. He said:

But if my preaching was crowned with a remarkable blessing, I believe one reason was this: Bearing in mind that the 'Word of God' and not the word of man, is quick and powerful, I was as a man of one book, and that book the Bible; and taking the hint from an inspired Apostle, I made Jesus Christ, and him crucified, my constant theme. This was certainly Paul's great doctrine; this was his battle-axe; and influenced by his example, I seized upon this heavenly-tempered weapon, and wielded it as well as I could. And here, my brother, permit me, as an old soldier of the cross, to say, that after long experience and close observation, I have come to

---

[256]   Baker, pp. 483-484, 486. It is interesting that Baker viewed 3000 people attending his preaching as huge. In one sense it is huge, but it was still vastly smaller than the 25,000- 40,000 that at times gathered to hear Whitefield preach a century earlier.

[257]   Baker, pp. 487-488.

the settled conclusion, that no doctrine has more power to soften the heart and subdue the soul than this.[258]

In speaking about the revivals in North Carolina under his preaching, it was of such magnitude that the North Carolina presbytery wanted to declare a special day of thanksgiving. One who witnessed the revivals in North Carolina wrote:

> Never has it been our privilege before to witness such a scene in the house of God- never, at least, one that gave so many unequivocal evidences of a genuine work. The congregations were most orderly and solemn; no shouting, not an outcry was heard that could possibly beget an artificial or mere sympathetic excitement; and no effort chiefly for such a purpose was once made. Nay, in proportion to the depth of feeling pervading the assembly, was the solemnity of its silence. It sometimes appeared as if the Spirit of God was actually brooding visibly upon the people, chastening and subduing their emotions, till almost a breath was audible. The visit and labours of Dr. Baker in our midst have also been greatly blessed in confirming and reanimating the people of God; for surely there is much that is eminently contagious in his warmth of love to the Saviour, gentleness of spirit, and comprehensive charity.[259]

We learn much about powerful preaching from this other observation of Daniel Baker's preaching:

> We had head much of the Doctor even in boyhood, but not till recently were we favored with the rare pleasure of witnessing ourselves his peculiar powers as a minister of the gospel... He is eloquent in a faith and an unction that seem to know no ebb; eloquent in a zeal and earnestness that beams in a face whose benignity once looked upon can never be forgotten; eloquent in a long life of energy and ripe experience that stands without a parallel in the present age, that is only comparable to that of Wesley or Whitefield, or the Apostles. What a relief it is – or to use one of his own favorite expressions, 'how delightful' it is to listen to such a man after sitting for years under the less animated and genial, the less practical and more purely argumentative sermonizing generally prevalent, and in many places sadly

---

[258]   Baker, pp. 505-506.
[259]   Baker, p. 509.

distorted from the simplicity of the Savior, to the stiff, lofty intellectuality of the modern heroic school.

Do men love simplicity, especially in matters of great and lasting moment, such as the salvation of the soul? – he orders his style, his manner, and practical overwhelming logic, with a plainness and simplicity that is truthfully eloquent, whole all is dressed in language whose purity and taste make it classic.

In the mysterious providence of God, it is only in long and rare intervals that such men are given to the world, and they always seem to come just in time to re-illustrate the forgotten simplicity of truth, and its dignity as well.[260]

Another wrote:

No minister of our Church was more beloved by the brethren than this venerable servant of God. No one was more deserving of veneration.[261]

And still another related an incident that demonstrated the power of God that often was associated with Baker's preaching:

There is one instance in which he was the means of the instantaneous conviction, and we trust, the true conversion of one who habitually and openly ridiculed the religion of Jesus and his people. Dr. Baker had been preaching at the place referred to for several days, and a revival of religion followed. This mocker of all that is holy went to the meeting on purpose to seek for something for which he might deride him, and those who were then led to see their danger, and to fly to the 'Rock of ages' for safety, under his powerful preaching.

The services of the day had commenced when he entered the church. He took his seat in front of the pulpit. All was silence, save the voice of the preacher proclaiming the conditions of eternal life to that dying assembly, and the groans that would now and then escape from some agonizing penitent. It seemed that that was indeed the house of God, and that the Holy Spirit was there working in the hearts of the people. The engaging manner of Dr. Baker soon attracted and riveted his attention. The awful truths

---

[260]   Baker, pp. 509-510, 511.
[261]   Baker, p. 511.

preached that day soon aroused his sleeping conscience, and convinced him of sin. His hard heart was softened, and the stern, the notorious scoffer, was subdued to tears. The man of God descended from the sacred desk, bringing the word of life with him, entered into conversation with the weeping man, and showed him that if he only would repent and come to Christ, he would forgive all his sins, and save him. He who had always before left the house of worship with a sneer of derision on his proud lips, on that day left an humble penitent, weeping aloud as he rode away. He found peace in the wounds of a sacrificed Savior – became a minister of the gospel in the Baptist denomination- led a consistent and useful Christian life; and from that day forward found his greatest delight in the fellowship of those whom before he had despised.[262]

Another person made this observation of Baker's preaching:

I have heard more finished orators- remarks one, concerning his preaching at this time- men whom it was more pleasant to hear; but I have seldom heard an orator who made his hearers understand him better or who gave them less room, or less occasion, in fact, to dodge the conclusions which he came. He is composed, and thoroughly in earnest... It is the distinctive feature of his preaching, that he speaks not to a conception of his hearers, but to his hearers... Each is made to feel that the himself is the object, and that then and there, in view of the hopes of heaven and powers of hell alone, and upon his own responsibility, he must accept them or reject them.[263]

William Baker makes this notation about his father's preaching:

He was not such a novice as to forget for an instant, that in whatever degree he excelled, it was solely and only the Spirit of God working in and by him; and this effectually cures any tendency on the part of those who loved and esteemed him most, to exalt him above measure. Place beside him the least successful minister in the Church – in whatever degree he excelled that minister, who can be so blind as not to know, that it was simply because a sovereign God had given to the one a larger measure of the Holy Spirit than to the other? Our wonder is not at the man,

---

[262] Baker, pp. 512-514.
[263] Baker, p. 514.

but at the wonderful working of the Holy Ghost in him and by him.[264]

We must never forget what William Baker wrote. The great outpourings of the Holy Spirit do not rest in the persuasive words of men, but in the sovereign bestowal of God. In one sense, this is a great comfort. The ultimate victory of the gospel isn't dependent upon us. It doesn't negate our responsibility, but it demonstrates the true source of the gospel's power.

Daniel Baker's ministry spanned some forty years, which took him North, South, East, and West. The normally resilient Baker was wearing out. On January 7, 1857 he resigned the office of President at Austin College. During his tenure for Austin College, he had brought in an incredible $100,000, which was a huge amount for that time. Most of this was money donated as a result of his preaching tours.

On November 22, 1857, Daniel filled the pulpit of his son's church in Austin.[265] As it turned out, he would preach his last sermon on November 29, 1857. On that day, he preached in the morning, afternoon, and evening. He was very hoarse that day and could barely speak at night. Incredibly, in rising to refer to his text that evening, which was Philippians 2:6-11, he commented that he was about to preach a sermon which, if he knew when he was to die, he would choose this text because it had much to do with Christ. At the request of an elder of the Austin church, Baker preached on Christ the mediator, which was sermon three in his published work, *Revival Sermons.* Those present during this sermon observed that he struggled through the sermon due to his hoarseness. It was the last time in a forty year preaching ministry that he would herald the beauties of Christ his Savior.

On the following Sabbath, December 6, 1857, Daniel was too ill to attend services. When his son William returned from church, Daniel commented that he had great delight as he sat at his window looking at the church and thinking that he had a son preaching there the glorious gospel and felt that he was more than willing to let go of this world. During the following

---

[264] Baker, p. 517.
[265] His son was William, the author of the book about his father had graduated from Princeton College in 1846 and from Princeton Seminary in 1848. In 1850 he became the organizing pastor of the First Presbyterian Church of Austin, Texas. He served in that capacity until 1865. In 1866, he asked his presbytery to dissolve his pastoral relationship with the Austin church. William was a unionist, and after the War Between the States, he moved his family to the North where he served churches in Ohio and Massachusetts. His one biography was that of his father. He also wrote twelve novels, mostly about his Texas experiences. He died in 1883.

week, Daniel's health continued to deteriorate. On Thursday December 1, Daniel was struggling to breathe. William had left to get the physican. Earlier, Daniel had said to his son:

> William, my son, if I should die, I want this epitaph carved on my tomb – "Here lies Daniel Baker, Preacher of the Gospel. A Sinner Saved by Grace." "Remember," he added, "A Sinner Saved by Grace." [266]

Even then his son did not realize that his father's death was imminent. William had returned with the physician. As Daniel was laboring for breath, it was evident that the ashen hue of death was upon his face. He said to William:

> "My son," he exclaimed, reaching out his arms to his son as he entered the door, "My son, my dear son, you are back in time to see your father die!"[267]

William cradled his father in his arms, pleading with the Lord to spare such a mighty servant, but it was not to be. His son wrote:

> Seated there, in the full vigor of his remarkable general health, in the unclouded use of his intellect, more composedly even than in his usual addresses to the throne of grace, he lifted his eyes to heaven, and exclaimed, in the serene exercise of a perfect faith, "Lord Jesus, into thy hands I commend my spirit!" As the last word passed his lips, he closed his eyes on earth, to open them for ever on the face of that Savior, whom, not having seen, he so loved.[268]

Upon the word of Daniel Baker's death, a leading statesman upon the floor of the Texas Legislature on that occasion stated:

> It becomes my painful duty to announce to this house the sudden and unexpected intelligence of the death of one of Texas ' public benefactors; the Rev. Daniel Baker is no more!... I consider the death of Dr. Baker a public calamity. He is justly entitled to the claim and rank of one of Texas' benefactors... Possessed of a catholic spirit, of universal love and benevolence towards his fellow-men, he was prompted thereby to extend his sphere of usefulness as wide as possible. There has been scarcely a State in

---

[266] Baker, p. 558.
[267] Baker, p. 559.
[268] Baker, p. 559.

the Union but has heard his eloquent pleadings in behalf of religion and all the great moral interests of society.[269]

When the news of his death reached Huntsville, Alabama, the editor of the paper who was a long acquaintance of Baker stated:

> The news of the sudden death of Dr. Baker came like an earthquake on our citizens last Monday night... Who is left to fill thy place here? - not one. Men like our venerable friend are only made once in an age... He died at his post. Truly a great man has fallen in Israel.[270]

As the word spread of Daniel Baker's death across cities, towns, villages, and scattered cabins on frontier territory, grief was manifested with the loss of the beloved preacher. The Lord gives and the Lord takes away. King Jesus reigns from on high and has given gifts to men, foremost of which are His heralds of the gospel whose footsteps are indeed beautiful, for wherever they trod, glad tidings are proclaimed- Jesus is ever ready to loosen the bonds of tyranny and set men free.

Charles Haddon Spurgeon (1834-1892)
The Prince of Preachers

Any discussion of great preachers of the past would be deficient without the name, Charles Haddon Spurgeon. He was the renowned English preacher of the 19th Century. He has been dubbed "the prince of preachers" and "the last of the Puritans."

His own conversion to Christ at age fifteen was in a little Primitive Methodist[271] chapel in Colchester on January 6, 1850. He is best known as the pastor of London's Metropolitan Tabernacle, and upon its completion in 1861, it was the largest church edifice of its day, seating 5000 people and standing room for another 1000 people. He often preached ten times a

---

[269]   Baker, pp. 540-541.

[270]   Baker, p. 541-542.

[271]   I have a great interest in Primitive Methodism because my maternal great, great grandfather, William Audiss, was a Primitive Methodist preacher. Upon his conversion to Christ in 1839, he would faithfully preach the gospel for sixty years (30 years in England and then 30 years in Wisconsin). In 2008, I had the privilege to retrace his English preaching circuit. My story of this journey and William Audiss' personal preaching diary can be found in my book entitled, *Retracing the Beautiful Steps*. This book can be purchased from my publishing website at www.triumphantpublications.com.

week, and during his ministry spanning some thirty years, it is estimated that he preached to over 10 million people! His weekly sermons, which sold for a penny each, were widely circulated and still remain one of the all-time best selling series of writings published in history. He is best known as a "Reformed Baptist."[272] Spurgeon stands shoulder to shoulder with all the great preachers of history in that his main focus in his preaching was the person of Jesus Christ, the only mediator between Christ and man.

Spurgeon's childhood was not lacking in godly influence, but despite this great heritage, Spurgeon was fifteen years old before he was brought to saving faith. Both his father and grandfather were English independent congregational ministers. Young Charles was no stranger to many Puritan works. At age six, he first read *Pilgrim's Progress* and would read it 100 times. Spurgeon testified that one of the most significant books he read as a child was *Foxes Book of Martyrs.*

Due to family financial hardships, Charles would be raised by his grandparents up until age seven when he returned to his parent's home. Charles' godly mother faithfully instructed her children in the Scriptures. His mother would diligently pray individually for her children,[273] and her prayer for Charles was "O that my son might live for Thee." We must never discount the prayers of a godly mother for her children. Though yet unconverted to Christ, a noteworthy event took place when Charles was ten years old. A visiting missionary, Pastor Richard Knill, was impressed at young Charles' ability to read the Scriptures with great emphasis. After breakfast, Pastor Knill took Charles for a walk in the garden where he discussed the Lord and His service with young Charles. They knelt together and Pastor Knill earnestly prayed for Charles, and before the preacher's departure, he called the Spurgeon family together. He sat young Charles on his knee and said, "I do not know how, but I feel a solemn presentiment that this child will preach the gospel to thousands and God will bless him to many souls. So sure am I of this that when my little man preaches in Surrey Music Hall, and he will do one day, I should like him to promise me that he will give out the Hymn commencing 'God moves in a mysterious way, His wonders to perform.'"[274]

---

[272] A Reformed Baptist is one who is Baptist in his understanding of church polity and the sacraments but adhering to the Calvinistic doctrines of grace in his doctrine of salvation.

[273] Charles was one of seventeen children, nine of whom died in infancy.

[274] Quoted from "Charles Spurgeon: The Puritan Prince of Preachers" found at http://www. tecmalta.org/tft350.htm. The fulfillment of Pastor's Knill's request would take place when Charles was twenty-one years old. This story is most interesting to me because a similar thing

Spurgeon's Conversion

The story of Charles Spurgeon's conversion to Christ is not unusual in terms of how our sovereign God moves in amazing and mysterious ways to bring His elect to saving faith. Despite his godly upbringing, it was not until a snowy day in 1850 that he would be transferred from the kingdom of darkness to the kingdom of our blessed Redeemer. Like so many others, young Spurgeon believed that he must do something special to make himself worthy of salvation. Spurgeon recounted:

"Before I came to Christ, I said to myself, 'It surely cannot be that, if I believe in Jesus, just as I am, I shall be saved? I must feel something; I must do something.' I could pour scorn upon myself to think of some of the good resolutions I made!...Oh, the many times that I have wished the preacher would tell me something to do that I might be saved! Gladly would I have done it, if it had been possible... Yet that simplest of all matters - believing in Christ crucified, accepting His finished salvation, being nothing, and letting Him be everything, doing nothing but trusting to what He has done - I could not get a hold of it. Once I thought there was salvation in good works, and I laboured hard, and strove diligently to preserve a character for integrity and uprightness; but when the Spirit of God came into may heart, 'sin revived, and I died.' That which I though had been good, proved to be evil; wherein I fancied I had been holy, I found myself to be unholy. I discovered that my very best actions were sinful, that my tears needed to be wept over, and that my prayers needed God's forgiveness. I discovered that I was seeking after salvation by the works of the law, that I was doing all my good works from a selfish motive, namely, to save myself, and therefore they could not be acceptable to God... "What a struggle that was which my young heart waged

---

happened to my great, great grandfather, William Audiss, when he was ten years old. Though his parents were not Christian, William Audiss, had pious grandparents who on one occasion prayed over him, "God bless this little boy and make him a blessing to the world." And William Audiss recounted as a ten year old of being at a small Primitive Methodist prayer meeting where the adults prayed over him saying, "God bless this little boy." William Audiss' conversion to Christ would occur at age eighteen in a small Primitive Methodist chapel in Little Hale, Lincolnshire, England. While William Audiss was still in England, he was a contemporary of Charles Spurgeon. William ministered in Lincolnshire, England which is about 125 miles north of London. William Audiss' ministry was nothing of the magnitude of Spurgeon's but then what matters is one's faithfulness to what has been given him. Both Spurgeon and my great, great grandfather were faithful stewards of that which was bestowed to them.

In 2008, I had the blessed privilege of preaching from the same pulpit as my great, great grandfather 167 years later to the day. Up until two weeks before my English trip, I had no idea that this chapel even existed.

against sin! When God the Holy Ghost first quickened me, little did I know of the precious blood which has put my sins away, and drowned them in the depths for ever. But I did know this, that I could not remain as I was... When I was in the hand of the Holy Spirit, under conviction of sin, I had a clear and sharp sense of the justice of God. Sin, whatever it might be to other people, became to me an intolerable burden. It was not so much that I feared hell, as that I feared sin; and all the while, I had upon my mind a deep concern for the honour of God's name, and the integrity of His moral government. I felt that it would not satisfy my conscience if I could be forgiven unjustly. But then there came the question - 'How could God be just, and yet justify me who had been so guilty?' I was worried and wearied with this question; neither could I see any answer to it.[275]

Young Spurgeon's thinking was not unusual. The story has been told over and over of a person raised in a Christian family, having sat under sound preaching, but whose heart has not yet been subdued to Christ. The testimonies of George Whitefield and of John and Charles Wesley are similar. All of these future preachers were at one time deluded with a view of self righteousness, thinking that diligent religious effort was the essence of Christianity, only to find that such thinking was vanity. Salvation is an act of God's free sovereign grace and mercy whereby He convinces us of our sin and misery and the futility of our works righteousness, thereby driving us to Christ's unmerited righteousness imputed to us and received by faith alone.

The decisive event in God's wonderful plan for His elect occurred on a snowy day, January 6, 1850. An outbreak of fever in the school of Newmarket brought Charles' first term to an early termination before its appointed time. This precipitated an early return home for the winter holidays. Because of the snowy weather, Charles was prevented from accompanying his father to Tollesbury. On this day, Charles was led to a small Primitive Methodist chapel in Artillery Street not far from their home. In his autobiography, Spurgeon recounted that momentous day:

I sometimes think I might have been in darkness and despair until now had it not been for the goodness of God in sending a snowstorm, one Sunday morning, while I was going to a certain place of worship. When I could go no further, I turned down a side

---

[275]   *The Early Years,* Banner of Truth Trust, pp. 69, 70, as quoted in http://www.tecmalta.org/tft350.htm.

street, and came to a little Primitive Methodist Chapel. In that chapel there may have been a dozen or fifteen people. I had heard of the Primitive Methodists, how they sang so loudly that they made people's heads ache; but that did not matter to me. I wanted to know how I might be saved, and if they could tell me that, I did not care how much they made my head ache. The minister did not come that morning; he was snowed up, I suppose. At last, a very thin-looking man, a shoemaker, or tailor, or something of that sort, went up into the pulpit to preach. Now, it is well that preachers should be instructed; but this man was really stupid. He was obliged to stick to his text, for the simple reason that he had little else to say. The text was,— "LOOK UNTO ME, AND BE YE SAVED, ALL THE ENDS OF THE EARTH."

He did not even pronounce the words rightly, but that did not matter. There was, I thought, a glimpse of hope for me in that text. The preacher began thus — "My dear friends, this is a very simple text indeed. It says, 'Look.' Now lookin' don't take a deal of pains. It ain't liftin' your foot or your finger; it is just, 'Look.' Well, a man needn't go to College to learn to look. You may be the biggest fool, and yet you can look. A man needn't be worth a thousand a year to be able to look. Anyone can look; even a child can look. But then the text says, 'Look unto *Me.* "Ay!" said he, in broad Essex, "many on ye are lookin' to yourselves, but it's no use lookin' there. You'll never find any comfort in yourselves. Some look to God the Father. No, look to Him by-and-by. Jesus Christ says, 'Look unto *Me.*' Some on ye say, 'We must wait for the Spirit's workin'. 'You have no business with that just now. Look to *Christ.* The text says, 'Look unto *Me.* '"

Then the good man followed up his text in this way: "Look unto Me; I am sweatin' great drops of blood. Look unto Me; I am hangin' on the cross. Look unto Me; I am dead and buried. Look unto Me; I rise again. Look unto Me; I ascend to Heaven. Look unto Me; I am sittin' at the Father's right hand. O poor sinner, look unto Me! look unto Me!"

When he had gone to about that length, and managed to spin out ten minutes or so, he was at the end of his tether. Then he looked at me under the gallery, and I daresay, with so few present, he knew me to be a stranger. Just fixing his eyes on me, as if he knew all my heart, he said, "Young man, you look very miserable." Well, I did; but I had not been accustomed to have remarks made from the pulpit on my personal appearance before. However, it was a good blow, struck right home. He continued, "and you always will be miserable—miserable in life, and miserable in death,—if you don't obey my text; but if you obey now, this moment, you will be saved." Then, lifting up his hands, he shouted, as only a Primitive Methodist could do, "Young man, look to Jesus Christ. Look! Look! Look! You have nothin' to do but to look and live." I saw at once the way of salvation. I know not what else he said,—I did not take much notice of it,—I was so possessed with that one thought. Like as when the brazen serpent was lifted up, the people only looked and were healed, so it was with me. I had been waiting to do fifty things, but when I heard that word, "Look!" what a charming word it seemed to me! Oh! I looked until I could almost have looked my eyes away. There and then the cloud was gone, the darkness had rolled away, and that moment I saw the sun; and I could have risen that instant, and sung with the most enthusiastic of them, of the precious blood of Christ, and the simple faith which looks alone to Him. Oh, that somebody had told me this before, "Trust Christ, and you shall be saved." Yet it was, no doubt, all wisely ordered, and now I can say,— "Ever since by faith I saw the stream Thy flowing wounds supply, Redeeming love has been my theme, And shall be till I die."[276]

Spurgeon's conversion to Christ was a supreme example of God's sovereign work of grace through the foolishness of preaching. As Spurgeon mentioned, the man that preached that day was hardly an articulate man who didn't even pronounce the words correctly. Moreover, it was not the first time that he had heard this text, but it was the first time that he heard Jesus preaching to his heart. His conversion was a glowing testimony to the biblical truth – the gospel is the power of God unto salvation. Spurgeon wrote:

I have no doubt that I heard, scores of times, such texts as these - 'He that believeth and is baptized shall be saved;' 'Look unto Me, and be ye saved, all the ends of the earth;' 'As Moses lifted up the serpent in the wilderness, even so must the Son of man be lifted up: that whosoever believeth in Him should not perish, but have everlasting life;' yet I had not intelligent idea of what faith meant. When I first discovered what faith really was, and exercised it - for with me these two things came together, I believed as soon as ever

---

[276]   Charles Spurgeon, *Autobiography*, Vol. 1.

> I knew what believing meant - then I though I had never before heard the truth preached. But, now, I am persuaded that the light often shone on my eyes, but I was blind, and therefore thought that the light had never come there.[277]

To demonstrate the value of a preacher in comparison to that of good books, Spurgeon wrote:

> The books were good, but the man was better. The revealed Word awakened me, but it was the preached Word that saved me; and I must ever attach peculiar value to the hearing of the truth, for by it I received the joy and peace in which my soul delights.[278]

In recognizing the gospel as the very power of God unto salvation, the sinner who hears Jesus preaching to his heart through the earthly preacher understands the preaching as not the preaching of human wisdom but the words of God. Spurgeon states:

> Before my conversion, I was accustomed to read the Scriptures to admire their grandeur, to feel the charm of their history, and wonder at the majesty of their language; but I altogether missed the Lord's intent therein. But when the Spirit came with His Divine life, and quickened all the Book to my newly-enlightened soul, the inner meaning shone forth with wondrous glory... I was not in frame of mind to judge God's Word, but I accepted it all without demur; I did not venture to sit in judgment upon my Judge, and become the reviser of the unerring God. Whatever I found to be in His Word, I received with intense joy.[279]

Spurgeon's Call to Preach

It is simply astounding to see how God marvelously works in men's lives to make them His heralds of the gospel. Even before they have professed Christ, the Lord is orchestrating events in the lives of His elect to have them where He wants them. Every genuine Christian knows in his heart of hearts that God is sovereign in his salvation. Even before Spurgeon would finally hear Jesus preaching to his heart in that small Primitive Methodist chapel on a snowy day in 1850, the Lord God had prepared the young man for His service. All those Puritan books that Spurgeon had read in his

---

[277]   *The Early Years*, Banner of Truth Trust, pp. 84-85, as quoted in www. tecmalta.org/tft350.htm.
[278]   *The Early Years*, p. 87, as quoted in http://www. tecmalta.org/tft350.htm.
[279]   *The Early Years*, p. 107.

grandfather's house came to memory. The visiting preacher recognized exceptional ability in the ten year old Spurgeon and believed that one day God would raise up this child to be the herald to thousands.

We must not forget what the Lord says in Psalm 139:14-16:

> *[14]I will give thanks to Thee, for I am fearfully and wonderfully made; wonderful are Thy works, and my soul knows it very well. [15]My frame was not hidden from Thee, when I was made in secret, and skillfully wrought in the depths of the earth. [16]Thine eyes have seen my unformed substance; and in Thy book they were all written, the days that were ordained for me, when as yet there was not one of them.*

The Lord ordains His preachers, and even in there unbelieving state, He is orchestrating events to His utmost glory. The apostle Paul understood that he was ordained to one day be the apostle to the Gentiles. Galatians 1:15-16 states:

> *[15]But when He who had set me apart, even from my mother's womb, and called me through His grace was pleased [16]to reveal His Son in me, that I might preach Him among the Gentiles, I did not immediately consult with flesh and blood.*

Paul's stint in Judaism was all in the permissive will of God, and one day the Lord would use it for Paul to be more effective in his preaching.

The same was true with George Whitefield as noted earlier. Before his conversion, Whitefield had an amazing talent for conveying stories with vivid imagery that God one day would channel into making him a preacher unlike any other.

With respect to Charles Spurgeon, God would use him to preach his first sermon at the age of sixteen to a small congregation of farm laborers in a thatched chapel in Teversham. He joined St. Andrews Baptist Church and became a village preacher. It was not long before it was evident to many that Charles was no ordinary preacher. He possessed exceptional oratorical skills, and within eighteen months. His reputation had spread to London. People came for miles to listen to the boy preacher. In 1857, Spurgeon was invited to preach to the largest audience of his life (24,000) on the occasion of a national day of fasting.

As noted previously, in 1861 the 5000 seat Metropolitan Tabernacle was built and was usually filled each Lord's Day.

Like Whitefield, whom he admired greatly, Spurgeon was a compelling and charismatic preacher. Like Whitefield, he was very animated in his story telling. It was not unusual for him to run from one side of the platform to the other to graphically tell a story. His stories were very pertinent to where people were, and they appreciated it. Like Whitefield, Spurgeon had his critics who thought his mannerisms were inappropriate; they viewed his preaching style as not dignified.

Spurgeon's preaching schedule was often very heavy (10 times a week), and in the midst of this, he was known to have read six books a week, remembering much of what he had read. His personal library contained 12,000 volumes.[280]

Spurgeon's Sunday sermons were normally delivered extemporaneously often with only a page outline before him. His sermons were taken down by shorthand by a secretary appointed by the congregation. His sermons were revised on Monday morning and published every Thursday, being translated into several languages. By 1865 Spurgeon's sermons were selling 25,000 copies per week. These sermons were distributed weekly up until 1917, which is remarkable because he died in 1892. By 1917 the total copies sold totaled over 100 million! He edited a monthly magazine called *The Sword and Trowel*.[281] He wrote several books and commentaries and produced sermon notes and lecture notes for his students.

In many regards, Spurgeon can be viewed as the most widely read preacher in history. His *New Park Street Pulpit* and *The Metropolitan Tabernacle Pulpit: The Collected Sermons of Spurgeon* fill sixty-three volumes. His sermon series stands as the largest set of books by a single author in the history of the Christian church. He spent twenty years studying the Psalms and wrote *The Treasury of David*, often considered by many as his greatest work.

The center stage of Spurgeon's sermons was always directed to glorifying the atoning work of Jesus Christ. Spurgeon wrote:

> I have always considered, with Luther and Calvin, that the sum and substance of the gospel lies in that word substitution - Christ standing in the stead of man. If I understand the gospel, it is this: I

---

[280]   Taken from "Charles Spurgeon: The Puritan Prince of Preachers" found at www.reformationsa.org/articles/CH%20Spurgeon.htm.

[281]   When I was a seminary student at Reformed Theological Seminary from 1975-1979, I came across copies of the *Sword and Trowel* which was still being produced. The magazine now featured modern writers but with many articles originally written by Spurgeon. After nearly forty years, I still have many copies of this magazine in my library.

deserve to be lost for ever; the only reason why I should not be damned is, that Christ was punished in my stead, and there is no need to execute a sentence twice for sin. On the other hand, I know I cannot enter heaven unless I have a perfect righteousness; I am absolutely certain I shall never have one of my own, for I find I sin every day, but then Christ had a perfect righteousness, and He said, " There, poor sinner, take My garment, and put it on; you shall stand before God as if you were Christ, and I will stand before God as if I had been the sinner; I will suffer in the sinner's stead, and you shall be rewarded for works which you did not do, but which I did for you." I find it very convenient every day to come to Christ as a sinner, as I came at the first. "You are no saint," says the devil. Well, if I am not, I am a sinner, and Jesus Christ came into the world to save sinners. Sink or swim, I go to Him; other hope I have none. By looking to Him, I received all the faith which inspired me with confidence in His grace; and the word that first drew my soul - "Look unto Me" - still rings its clarion note in my ears. There I once found conversion, and there I shall ever find refreshing and renewal.[282]

How could Spurgeon accomplish so much? It was not unusual for his daily routine to consist of eighteen hours per day!

Notable Attendees to Spurgeon's Preaching

English Prime Minister, William Gladstone, frequented Spurgeon's preaching along with members of the Royal Family and members of Parliament. Gladstone was criticized for receiving the dissenting preacher at 10 Downing Street for breakfast or lunch on various occasions. Gladstone was known as a man of principle and prayer.

Some of the other visitors to Spurgeon's church were the famous missionary David Livingstone and the American evangelist, D.L. Moody. When Moody first arrived in London in 1867, he immediately went to Metropolitan Tabernacle. When back home, he was asked as to whether he visited the great cathedrals and other tourist sites in London. Moody said, "No, but I've heard Spurgeon!"[283]

---

[282] *The Early Years*, p. 94.
[283] "Charles Spurgeon: The Puritan Prince of Preachers." It is interesting that Moody was a staunch Arminian while Spurgeon was a staunch Calvinist.

Spurgeon was a contemporary with Hudson Taylor, founder of the China Inland Mission and George Muller, the famous founder of orphanages. Spurgeon spent time with each man. Spurgeon paid several visits to George Muller and his orphanage. Spurgeon was astonished at Muller's stories of living by faith. They often spent whole days together encouraging each other to have faith in God's wonderful promises.

Being a man of principle, he would stand for biblical truth in his Baptist denomination even to the point of great controversy. He stood against the growing tide towards Liberalism. This controversy became known as the "Downgrade Controversy." This was at great cost to his physical health.

Spurgeon as the Calvinist Preacher

When the Metropolitan Tabernacle was first opened in 1861, Spurgeon's first series was on the Five Points of Calvinism. Spurgeon dispelled the myth as much as did George Whitefield that Calvinists are not evangelistic. But then, we must always be careful what we mean by our designations. What I mean by the term, "Calvinist" is not what some have falsely termed as "Calvinist." Today, some erroneously think that Calvinism utterly denies human responsibility, that it is some type of hopeless fatalism that it denies the free offer of the gospel, and therefore it is antithetical to evangelistic endeavors. Spurgeon helps clarify where he stands on these questions by the following quotes:

> The old truth that Calvin preached, that Augustine preached, that Paul preached, is the truth that I must preach to-day, or else be false to my conscience and my God. I cannot shape the truth; I know of no such thing as paring off the rough edges of a doctrine. John Knox's gospel is my gospel. That which thundered through Scotland must thunder through England again.[284]

> There is no soul living who holds more firmly to the doctrines of grace than I do, and if any man asks me whether I am ashamed to be called a Calvinist, I answer—I wish to be called nothing but a Christian; but if you ask me, do I hold the doctrinal views which were held by John Calvin, I reply, I do in the main hold them, and rejoice to avow it.[285]

---

[284]   Charles Spurgeon, *A Defense of Calvinism* , found at http://www.spurgeon.org/ calvinis.htm.
[285]   Spurgeon.

Concerning the relationship of God's absolute sovereignty in salvation and man's responsibility, Spurgeon said:

> The system of truth revealed in the Scriptures is not simply one straight line, but two; and no man will ever get a right view of the gospel until he knows how to look at the two lines at once. For instance, I read in one Book of the Bible, "The Spirit and the bride say, Come. And let him that heareth say, Come. And let him that is athirst come. And whosoever will, let him take the water of life freely." Yet I am taught, in another part of the same inspired Word that "It is not of him that willeth, nor of him that runneth, but of God that sheweth mercy." I see, in one place, God in providence presiding over all, and yet I see, and I cannot help seeing, that man acts as he pleases, and that God has left his actions, in a great measure, to his own free-will. Now, if I were to declare that man was so free to act that there was no control of God over his actions, I should be driven very near to atheism; and if, on the other hand, I should declare that God so over-rules all things that man is not free enough to be responsible, I should be driven at once into Antinomianism or fatalism. That God predestines, and yet that man is responsible, are two facts that few can see clearly. They are believed to be inconsistent and contradictory to each other. If, then, I find taught in one part of the Bible that everything is fore-ordained, *that is true*; and if I find, in another Scripture, that man is responsible for all his actions, *that is true*; and it is only my folly that leads me to imagine that these two truths can ever contradict each other. I do not believe they can ever be welded into one upon any earthly anvil, but they certainly shall be one in eternity. They are two lines that are so nearly parallel, that the human mind which pursues them farthest will never discover that they converge, but they do converge, and they will meet somewhere in eternity, close to the throne of God, whence all truth doth spring.[286]

Spurgeon also dealt with the charge that Calvinism leads to unholy living. Spurgeon wrote:

> It is often said that the doctrines we believe have a tendency to lead us to sin. I have heard it asserted most positively, that those high doctrines which we love, and which we find in the Scriptures, are licentious ones. I do not know who will have the hardihood to make that assertion, when they consider that the holiest of men

---

[286]   Spurgeon.

have been believers in them. I ask the man who dares to say that Calvinism is a licentious religion, what he thinks of the character of Augustine, or Calvin, or Whitefield, who in successive ages were the great exponents of the system of grace; or what will he say of the Puritans, whose works are full of them? Had a man been an Arminian in those days, he would have been accounted the vilest heretic breathing, but now *we* are looked upon as the heretics, and they as the orthodox. *We* have gone back to the old school; *we* can trace our descent from the apostles. It is that vein of free-grace, running through the sermonizing of Baptists, which has saved us as a denomination. Were it not for that, we should not stand where we are today. We can run a golden line up to Jesus Christ Himself, through a holy succession of mighty fathers, who all held these glorious truths; and we can ask concerning them, "Where will you find holier and better men in the world?" No doctrine is so calculated to preserve a man from sin as the doctrine of the grace of God. Those who have called it "a licentious doctrine" did not know anything at all about it.[287]

I especially like what Spurgeon has to say about Arminians. Sometimes in their great zeal, my fellow Calvinists will erroneously relegate any Arminian to a state of unbelief. Spurgeon's words are very timely:

But far be it from me even to imagine that Zion contains none but Calvinistic Christians within her walls, or that there are none saved who do not hold our views. Most atrocious things have been spoken about the character and spiritual condition of John Wesley, the modern prince of Arminians. I can only say concerning him that, while I detest many of the doctrines which he preached, yet for the man himself I have a reverence second to no Wesleyan; and if there were wanted two apostles to be added to the number of the twelve, I do not believe that there could be found two men more fit to be so added than George Whitefield and John Wesley. The character of John Wesley stands beyond all imputation for self-sacrifice, zeal, holiness, and communion with God; he lived far above the ordinary level of common Christians, and was one "of whom the world was not worthy." I believe there are multitudes of men who cannot see these truths, or, at least, cannot see them in the way in which we put them, who nevertheless have

---

[287] Spurgeon.

received Christ as their Saviour, and are as dear to the heart of the God of grace as the soundest Calvinist in or out of Heaven.[288]

Spurgeon on the Relationship of Preaching to Evangelism

One of Spurgeon's most significant works, in my opinion, was his book entitled *The Soul Winner*. This book is a wonderful presentation of the necessity of preaching in the reaching of the lost with the gospel. The prefatory note to his book states that the first six chapters contained his college lectures to ministerial students. This is followed by four addresses delivered to Sunday school teachers, open-air preachers, and friends gathered for prayer meetings at Metropolitan Tabernacle. The remaining part of the book consists of sermons for the purpose of encouraging Christians to be engaged in winning lost souls for Christ. Spurgeon viewed soul winning as the chief business of the Christian minister, and his book is a masterpiece in this respect. Every preacher of the gospel should look carefully at the practice of one of the Lord's great heralds of the gospel and learn. I have included extensive quotes from Spurgeon's book on soul winning because it demonstrates that which was not only true of Spurgeon's preaching but that which marked all those that I have included in this chapter on great preachers. There is much similarity in these men, and Spurgeon has captured the essence of great preaching.

Preaching and the Doctrines of Grace

Some have mistakenly thought that preaching the Calvinistic doctrines of grace are a deterrent to evangelism. Spurgeon understood that the doctrine of man's total depravity is central in driving men to the gospel. Spurgeon wrote:

> Men need to be told that, except divine grace shall bring them out of their enmity to God, they must eternally perish; and they must be reminded of the sovereignty of God, that He is not obliged to bring them out of this state, that He would be right and just if He left them in such a condition, that they have no merit to plead before Him, and no claims upon Him, but that if they are to be saved, it must be by grace, and by grace alone. The preacher's work is to throw sinners down in utter helplessness, that they may be compelled to look up to Him who alone can help them.

---

[288] Spurgeon.

The best attraction is the gospel in its purity. The weapon with which the Lord conquers men is the truth as it is in Jesus. The gospel will be found equal to every emergency; an arrow which can pierce the hardest heart, a balm which will heal the deadliest wound. Preach it, and preach nothing else. Rely implicitly upon the old, old gospel. You need no other nets when you fish for men; those your Master has given you are strong enough for the great fishes, and have meshes fine enough to hold the little ones. Spread these nets and no others, and you need not fear the fulfilment of His Word, "I will make you fishers of men." [289]

While Spurgeon would have disdained the modern emphasis upon theatrics, like Whitefield and others, he saw the biblical relationship between intellectual apprehension of truth and one's emotions. He said:

A sinner has a heart as well as a head; a sinner has emotions as well as thoughts; and we must appeal to both. A sinner will never be converted until his emotions are stirred. Unless he feels sorrow for sin, and unless he has some measure of joy in the reception of the Word, you cannot have much hope of him. The Truth must soak into the soul, and dye it with its own colour. The Word must be like a strong wind sweeping through the whole heart, and swaying the whole man, even as a field of ripening corn waves in the summer breeze. Religion without emotion is religion without life... But, still, we must mind how these emotions are caused. Do not play upon the mind by exciting feelings which are not spiritual. [290]

You and I must continue to drive at men's hearts till they are broken; and then we must keep on preaching Christ crucified till their hearts are bound up; and when this is accomplished, we must continue to proclaim the gospel till their whole nature is brought into subjection to the gospel of Christ. [291]

One the doctrines that permeated in the messages of the great preachers of the past, as was found in Whitefield and Baker, was that of the necessity of regeneration by a sovereign God. The doctrine of God's sovereign

---

[289]   Charles Spurgeon, *The Soul Winner*, pp. 9, 10, found at http://www.thesoulwinner.org/ebooks/The%20Soul%20Winner%20-%20Spurgeon.pdf. The page numeration is that which is in the electronic version, not the printed copy.

[290]   Spurgeon, *The Soul Winner*, p. 10.

[291]   Spurgeon, *The Soul Winner*, p. 11.

regeneration was one of the central messages in George Whitefield's evangelistic preaching. Spurgeon wrote:

> A new and heavenly mind must be created by omnipotence, or the man must abide in death. You see, then, that we have before us a mighty work, for which we are of ourselves totally incapable. No minister living can save a soul; nor can all of us together, nor all the saints on earth or in heaven, work regeneration in a single person... the marvels of regeneration which attend our ministry are the best seals and witnesses of our commission.[292]

While no preacher can bring about regeneration, the preacher should recognize the fruit of God's regenerating grace among those to whom he is heralding the gospel. Spurgeon stated:

> As this God-begotten spiritual life in men is a mystery, we shall speak to more practical effect if we dwell upon the signs following and accompanying it, for these are the things we must aim at. First, regeneration will be shown in *conviction of sin.* This we believe to be an indispensable mark of the Spirit's work; the new life as it enters the heart causes intense inward pain as one of its first effects. Though nowadays we hear of persons being healed before they have been wounded, and brought into a certainty of justification without ever having lamented their condemnation, we are very dubious as to the value of such healings and justifying.

> God never clothes men until He has first stripped them, nor does He quicken them by the gospel till first they are slain by the law. When you meet with persons in whom there is no trace of conviction of sin, you may be quite sure that they have not been wrought upon by the Holy Spirit; for "when He is come, He will reprove the world of sin, and of righteousness, and of judgment." When the Spirit of the Lord breathes on us, He withers all the glory of man, which is but as the flower of grass, and then He reveals a higher and abiding glory. Do not be astonished if you find this conviction of sin to be very acute and alarming; but, on the other hand, do not condemn those in whom it is less intense, for so long as sin is mourned over, confessed, forsaken, and abhorred, you have an evident fruit of the Spirit.[293]

---

[292] Spurgeon, *The Soul Winner,* p. 13.
[293] Spurgeon, *The Soul Winner,* p. 13.

The previous comment is noteworthy in our understanding of the emotionalism often associated with the revivals of the 18th Century. While Jonathan Edwards warned of being deceived by various emotions, he sanctioned them if they were responses of hearts broken by a sense of their sins in response to seeing how one has been slain by the law of God.

Not only was the doctrine of regeneration foremost in Whitefield's preaching, but the doctrine of justification by faith alone in Christ's imputed righteousness was equally emphasized. Such an emphasis finds great acceptance in Spurgeon's preaching:

> The production of faith is the very centre of the target at which you aim. The proof to you that you have won the man's soul for Jesus is never before you till he has done with himself and his own merits, and has closed in with Christ. Great care must be taken that this faith is exercised upon Christ for a complete salvation, and not for a part of i Salvation by grace is eternal salvation. Sinners must commit their souls to the keeping of Christ to all eternity; how else are they saved men? Alas! according to the teaching of some, believers are only saved in part, and for the rest must depend upon their future endeavours. Is this the gospel? I trow not. Genuine faith trusts a whole Christ for the whole of salvation. Is it any wonder that many converts fall away, when, in fact, they were never taught to exercise faith in Jesus for eternal salvation, but only for temporary conversion? [294]

Preaching and Repentance

Spurgeon's emphasis on gospel preaching is a far cry from what is spoken from many a pulpit today. Today's "wishy washy" moralisms are anything but the gospel that is the power of God unto salvation. Where is the call to repentance these days? Spurgeon understood it very well when he said:

> Together with undivided faith in Jesus Christ there must also be *unfeigned repentance of sin.* Repentance is an old-fashioned word, not much used by modern revivalists… True conversion is in all men attended by a sense of sin, which we have spoken of under the head of conviction; by a sorrow for sin, or holy grief at having committed it; by a hatred of sin, which proves that its dominion is ended; and by a practical turning from sin, which shows that the life within the soul is operating upon the life without. True belief

---

[294] Spurgeon, *The Soul Winner,* p. 14.

and true repentance are twins: it would be idle to attempt to say which is born first... No sinner looks to the Saviour with a dry eye or a hard heart. Aim, therefore, at heart-breaking, at bringing home condemnation to the conscience, and weaning the mind from sin, and be not content till the whole mind is deeply and vitally changed in reference to sin.[295]

Preaching and Godly Fruit

One of the great tragedies of modern evangelistic methods is the shallowness of what is expected in those professing Christ. The notion is: if I pray this prayer, or walk the aisle, then I am automatically saved. Spurgeon cautioned very strongly:

> Another proof of the conquest of a soul for Christ will be found in a *real change of life*. If the man does not live differently from what he did before, both at home and abroad, his repentance needs to be repented of; and his conversion is a fiction... The Scripture says, "He that committeth sin is of the devil." Abiding under the power of any known sin is a mark of our being the servants of sin, for "his servants ye are to whom ye obey." Idle are the boasts of a man who harbours within himself the love of any transgression.[296]

Spurgeon is hardly speaking about a work's salvation paradigm. No, he is simply stating that where there is no fruit of sanctification, then there is no tree of justification. We are not saved by our works, but then we are not saved without them. A justified life always leads to a sanctified life, though not perfectly. Spurgeon wrote:

> There must also be a *willingness to obey the Lord in all His commandments*. It is a shameful thing for a man to profess discipleship and yet refuse to learn his Lord's will upon certain points, or even dare to decline obedience when that will is known. How can a man be a disciple of Christ when he openly lives in disobedience to Him?

> If the professed convert distinctly and deliberately declares that he knows his Lord's will but does not mean to attend to it, you are not to pamper his presumption, but it is your duty to assure him that he is not saved... Jesus must be received as King as well as

---

[295] Spurgeon, *The Soul Winner*, p. 15.
[296] Spurgeon, *The Soul Winner*, pp. 15- 16.

Priest; and where there is any hesitancy about this, the foundation of godliness is not yet laid. [297]

Preaching and the Godly Preacher

While it is true that God the Holy Spirit is the saving agent in preaching, Spurgeon identifies several qualities that should be present among Christ's heralds. Spurgeon mentions that the preacher should **be a man of holy character**. Spurgeon stated:

> I am sure you would say, first of all, that *a man who is to be a Soul-winner must have holiness of character...* No wise man would pour his wine into foul bottles... An unholy ministry would be the derision of the world, and a dishonor to God.[298]

> He delights especially in humility amongst His ministers. It is an awful sight to see a proud minister... True humility will lead you to think rightly about yourselves, to think the truth about yourselves. In the matter of soul-winning, humility makes you feel that you are nothing and nobody, and that, if God gives you success in the work, you will be driven to ascribe to Him all the glory, for none of the credit of it could properly belong to you... Why should God give blessing, and then let you run away with the glory of it? The glory of the salvation of souls belongs to Him, and to Him alone.[299]

Preaching with Confidence and Authority

One of the things that has marked great preachers of the past is that they really and truly believe that they are heralds of the living God. While there should be humility among preachers, there is a sense among great preachers that they are indeed the "heralds" of the great king, that they have a special word from the King of kings. This marked Whitefield and Baker's preaching, and it was true of Spurgeon. In this regard, Spurgeon wrote:

> You must have faith, brethren, about your call to the ministry; you must believe without question that you are really chosen of God to

---

[297] Spurgeon, *The Soul Winner*, pp.16-17.
[298] Spurgeon, *The Soul Winner*, pp.20-21.
[299] Spurgeon, *The Soul Winner*, pp.23-24.

be ministers of the gospel of Christ. If you firmly believe that God has called you to preach the gospel, you will preach it with courage and confidence; and you will feel that you are going to your work because you have a right to do it.

If you have genuine faith in your call to the ministry, you will be ready, with Luther, to preach the gospel even while standing within the jaws of the leviathan, between his great teeth.

You must also believe that the message you have to deliver is God's Word... If you adopt this style, "I think this is a truth, and as a young man I beg to ask your kind attention to what I am about to say; I am merely suggesting," and so on, if that is your mode of preaching, you will go to work the easiest way to breed doubters.

You must also believe in the power of that message to save people... I like to go to the pulpit feeling, "This is God's Word that I am going to deliver in His name; it cannot return to Him void; I have asked His blessing upon it, and He is bound to give it, and His purposes will be answered, whether my message is a savour of life unto life, or of death unto death to those who hear it."

That is the essential point, you must believe in God and in His gospel if you are to be a winner of souls; it does seem that the most likely instrument to do the Lord's work is the man who expects that God will use him, and who goes forth to labour in the strength of that conviction. When success comes, he is not surprised, for he was looking for it.[300]

It must be quite clear to your hearers that you have a firm belief in the truths that you are preaching; otherwise, you will never make them believe them. Unless they are convinced, beyond all question, that you do believe these truths yourselves, there will be no efficacy and no force in your preaching. No one must suspect you of proclaiming to others what you do not fully believe in yourself; if it should ever be so, your work will be of no effect.[301]

If the Lord has sent you to preach the gospel, why should you make any apologies? Ambassadors do not apologise when they go

---

[300] Spurgeon, *The Soul Winner*, pp.26-28.
[301] Spurgeon, *The Soul Winner*, p. 34.

to a foreign court; they know that their monarch has sent them, and they deliver their message with all the authority of king and country at their back.[302]

One of the things that have marked great preachers is fearlessness. No preacher is worth a grain of salt if he isn't ready to die at any moment for uncompromisingly preaching the truth. The heralds of the gospel are the spokesmen of the living Christ, and are willing to preach the truth no matter the consequences, like John the Baptist. In this regard, Spurgeon said:

> Now, brother, feel ready to say just anything that God gives you to say, irrespective of all the consequences, and utterly regardless of what the "hypers" or the lowpers or anybody else will think or do.[303]

Preaching with Earnestness

One of the things that has marked every great preacher is their earnestness. They believed their preaching was so important that it would be tragic not to plead with men with great force to heed God's words. Spurgeon stated:

> The command to the man who would be a true servant of the Lord Jesus Christ is, "Thou shalt love the Lord thy God with all thy heart, and with all thy soul, and with all thy strength, and with all thy mind." If a man is to be a soul-winner, there must be in him intensity of emotion as well as sincerity of heart. You may preach the most solemn warnings, and the most dreadful threatenings, in such an indifferent or careless way that no one will be in the least affected by them; and you may repeat the most affectionate exhortations in such a half-hearted manner that no one will be moved either to love or fear. I believe, brethren, that for soul-winning there is more in this matter of earnestness than in almost anything else.

> I believe, brethren, that for soul-winning there is more in this matter of earnestness than in almost anything else. I have seen and heard some who were very poor preachers, who yet brought many souls to the Saviour through the earnestness with which they delivered their message… It was not what the preachers said, so

---

[302]   Spurgeon, *The Soul Winner*, p. 41.
[303]   Spurgeon, *The Soul Winner*, p. 32.

much as how they said it, that carried conviction to the hearts of their hearers. The simplest truth was so driven home by the intensity of the utterance and emotion of the man from whom it came that it told with surprising effect.

That is what you must do with your sermons, make them red-hot; never mind if men do say you are too enthusiastic, or even too fanatical, give them red-hot shot, there is nothing else half as good for the purpose you have in view. We do not go out snow-balling on Sundays, we go fire-balling; we ought to hurl grenades into the enemy's ranks.[304]

Something needs to be said of Spurgeon's previous comments. Someone might think that it is all about being a good actor. This isn't true; Spurgeon deplored the idea of coming into the pulpit and becoming a theatrical actor. One of the worst things a preacher could ever do is to present God's precious word in a boring manner. Now of course, one doesn't have to scream or shout to be effective, but delivery of sermons is an important aspect of preaching. We are naïve if we think that delivery in public speaking is irrelevant. I could ask the reader a question, "Do you like monotone messages, or energetic ones?"

Preaching That is Relevant

The purpose of preaching, and particularly evangelistic preaching, is to make God's word clear and relevant to the congregation. The preacher should not be in the pulpit to impress people with his education, his scholarship per se. Great preachers have always sought to reach the common man, that is, to make the sermon relevant and understandable. It was true of Whitefield and Spurgeon. Spurgeon made these observations:

...We must preach in what Whitefield used to call "market language" if we would have all classes of the community listening to our message. Then, when they do come in, we must preach interestingly.[305]

When I was a seminary student, I saw this truth vividly exemplified in the preaching of one my seminary professors who I admired the most. The professor was regarded as a brilliant man and one of the greatest apologists of our time. He was very demanding of his students in class, but on several

---

[304] Spurgeon, *The Soul Winner*, pp. 35-36.
[305] Spurgeon, *The Soul Winner*, pp. 46-47.

occasions, my wife and I heard him preach at a local church where we worshipped on the Lord's Day. We were amazed how simple but profound his message was to this Presbyterian congregation. He had a gift to take great theological truths and make them very understandable to the average Christian in the pew. This professor/preacher understood the true nature of preaching. He was not in the pulpit to impress people with his brilliance but to communicate biblical truth in a clear and relevant way to God's people.

Preaching That is Instructive

There are two things that every preacher must keep before him. One, as noted previously, he must preach in an interesting and relevant manner. This could be dubbed as preaching with "heat." Second, the preacher must preach truth. This could be dubbed as preaching with "light." Spurgeon had some very timely remarks in this respect:

> There must be light as well as fire. Some preachers are all light, and no fire, and others are all fire and no light; what we want is both fire and light. I do not judge those brethren who are all fire and fury; but I wish they had a little more knowledge of what they talk about, and I think it would be well if they did not begin quite so soon to preach what they hardly understand themselves. It is a fine thing to stand up in the street, and cry, "Believe! Believe! Believe! Believe! Believe! Believe!" Yes, my dear soul, but what have we to believe?
>
> The sermons that are most likely to convert people seem to me to be those that are full of truth, truth about the fall, truth about the law, truth about human nature, and its alienation from God, truth about Jesus Christ, truth about the Holy Spirit, truth about the Everlasting Father, truth about the new birth, truth about obedience to God, and how we learn it, and all such great verities. Tell your hearers something, dear brethren, whenever you preach, tell them something, tell them something![306]

---

[306]   Spurgeon, *The Soul Winner*, p. 48.

Preaching Must be Christ Centered

Spurgeon understood with all great preachers the most important thing in preaching. Preachers are heralds of the living and reigning Jesus Christ, King of kings and Lord of lords. The Scripture clearly teaches that Christ preaches through earthly preachers (Romans 10:14-15). Jesus is the central theme of the Bible; He is the golden thread, as it were, that runs throughout all Scripture. On the day of His resurrection, Jesus told two of His disciples on the road to Emmaus this vital biblical truth:

> *O, foolish men and slow of heart to believe in all that the prophets have spoken! Was it not necessary for the Christ to suffer these things and to enter into His glory? And beginning with all the prophets, He explained to them the things concerning Himself in all the Scriptures.* (Luke 24:25-27)

In exhorting his students, Spurgeon said:

> Let your sermons be full of Christ, from beginning to end crammed full of the gospel... People have often asked me, "What is the secret of your success?" I always answer that I have no other secret but this, that I have preached the gospel, — not about the gospel, but the gospel,—the full, free, glorious gospel of the living Christ who is the incarnation of the good news. Preach Jesus Christ, brethren, always and everywhere; and every time you preach be sure to have much of Jesus Christ in the sermon. You remember the story of the old minister who heard a sermon by a young man, and when he was asked by the preacher what he thought of it he was rather slow to answer, but at last he said, "If I must tell you, I did not like it at all; there was no Christ in your sermon." "No," answered the young man, "because I did not see that Christ was in the text." "Oh!" said the old minister, "but do you not know that from every little town and village and tiny hamlet in England there is a road leading to London?" Whenever I get hold of a text, I say to myself, 'There is a road from here to Jesus Christ, and I mean to keep on His track till I get to Him.'" "Well," said the young man, "but suppose you are preaching from a text that says nothing about Christ?" "Then I will go over hedge and ditch but what I will get at Him." So must we do, brethren; we must have Christ in all our discourses, whatever else is in or not in

them. There ought to be enough of the gospel in every sermon to save a soul.[307]

Preaching and Prayer

In a previous chapter, I have endeavored to drive home this blessed truth – the victory of the gospel in this world is advanced through the faithful use of the divinely powerful weapons of spiritual warfare, namely preaching and prayer. Every mighty preacher of the Lord Jesus has understood this biblical truth. Spurgeon understood that without earnest prayer, we cannot expect to see the great power of God unleashed upon sinners, not that God is limited by human means. The reality is: God has ordained prayer as the very means for His purposes to be realized. Spurgeon wrote:

> Every true pulpit is set up in heaven by which is meant that the true preacher is much with God. If we do not pray to God for a blessing, if the foundation of the pulpit be not laid in private prayer, our open ministry will not be a success...
>
> ... at any rate there must be prayer, much prayer, constant prayer, vehement prayer, the kind of prayer which will not take a denial, like Luther's prayer, which he called the bombarding of heaven; that is to say, the planting a cannon at heaven's gates to blow them open, for after this fashion fervent men prevail in prayer; they will not come from the mercy-seat until they can cry with Luther, *"Vici,"* "I have conquered, I have gained the blessing for which I strove." "The kingdom of heaven suffereth violence, and the violent take it by force." May we offer such violent, God-constraining, heaven compelling prayers, and the Lord will not permit us to seek His face in vain!... *After praying, Elisha adopted the means.* Prayer and means must go together. Means without prayer—presumption! Prayer without means—hypocrisy![308]

The other Sabbath morning, before I entered the pulpit, when my dear brethren, the deacons and elders of this church, gathered about me for prayer, as they are wont to do, one of them said, "Lord, take him as a man takes a tool in his hand when he gets a firm hold of it, and then uses it to work his own will with it." That is what all workers need; that God may be the Worker by them.

---

[307]   Spurgeon, *The Soul Winner*, pp. 53-54.
[308]   Spurgeon, *The Soul Winner*, p. 80.

You are to be instruments in the hands of God; yourselves, of course, actively putting forth all your faculties and forces which the Lord has lent to you; but still never depending upon your personal power, but resting alone upon that sacred, mysterious, divine energy which worketh in us, and by us, and with us, upon the hearts and minds of men.[309]

Concluding Remarks on Preachers

One of the most amazing things is that the Lord of glory preaches through the frailty of mere men. It is a sacred calling, and the preacher's reward does follow after him, but faithful preachers don't labor for the reward they will obtain. They preach for they have a compulsion to do so. Every faithful preacher can say with the prophet Jeremiah, "B*ut if I say, 'I will not remember Him or speak anymore in His name,' Then in my heart it becomes like a burning fire shut up in my bones; and I am weary of holding it in, and I cannot endure it'"* (Jeremiah 20:9). They can say with the apostle Paul, "*For if I preach the gospel, I have nothing to boast of, for I am under compulsion; for woe is me if I do not preach the gospel*" (I Corinthians 9:16).

Preachers are mighty ones in the hands of the living Christ and yet Jesus referred to them as His "little ones" (Matthew 10:42). For any preacher, it is a great privilege to be an instrument of the Lord Jesus in subduing the world to Christ, and yet, it is very humbling. We must remind ourselves that we are but Jesus' "little ones." Our task as preachers is to simply be faithful in proclaiming God's word without compromise. All the glory goes to Christ. Paul understood this when he said, "*I planted, Apollos watered, but God was causing the growth. So then neither the one who plants nor the one who waters is anything, but God who causes the growth*" (I Corinthians 3: 6-7).

Nothing is the same when a preacher shows up. The preacher brings either a blessing or a curse to men. Jesus said, "*The one who listens to you listens to Me, and the one who rejects you rejects Me; and the one who rejects Me rejects the One who sent Me*" (Luke 10:16).

---

[309] Spurgeon, *The Soul Winner*, p. 87.

The feet of the preacher are indeed beautiful, for wherever he goes, he brings glad tidings of good things (Romans 10:14-17). This magnificent passage from Romans 10 is but a paraphrase of Isaiah 52:7. In Isaiah the preacher of salvation is proclaiming – Your God reigns!

Conclusion

The Christian must always strive to look at life with the eyes of faith – faith in the blessed promises of God, a God who cannot lie. From Genesis to Revelation, the abundant testimony of Scripture is the victorious plan of God worked out in precise detail in human history. With the first promise of the Savior in Genesis 3:15 to the culminating event in history with Christ's Second Coming, the great story is: victory in Jesus! It is victory over sin and misery and victory over the devil and his demons. In history, Jesus is going forth conquering and to conquer (Revelation 6:2). There is no such thing as defeat for a sovereign Christ. How can a sovereign God lose? It is an absurd notion. As Revelation 11:15 informs us, *"The kingdom of the world has become the kingdom of our Lord, and of his Christ; and He will reign forever and ever."*

In this book, I have diligently labored to prove exegetically one glorious truth – Jesus is reigning now and is conquering! His Second Coming does not usher in the glorious millennial kingdom. We are in His glorious millennial kingdom right now! His Second Coming is His glorious return to a world subdued at last. As I Corinthians 15:24-25 tells us, *"Then comes the end, when He delivers up the kingdom to the God and Father, when He has abolished all rule and all authority and power. For He must reign until He has put all His enemies under His feet."*

The Day of Pentecost is one of the momentous days in human history. As inspired Peter preached to a crowd who were implicated in Jesus' crucifixion, he boldly preached that King David's prophecy had indeed come to pass. David had prophesied that a seed of his would sit on his throne forever. Peter boldly proclaimed that David actually spoke of that seed as Jesus Christ, risen from the dead and ascended to heaven and sitting at the Father's right hand in power and glory. The glorious promise of Psalm 110:1-3 was coming to pass – *"The Lord says to my Lord: 'Sit at My right hand, until I make Thine enemies a footstool for Thy feet.' The Lord will stretch forth Thy strong scepter from Zion, saying, 'Rule in the midst of Thine enemies.' Thy people will volunteer freely in the day of Thy power; ..."* The Lord Jesus has been coronated as King of kings and Lord of lords; King Jesus has and is stretching forth his strong scepter. He has and is stretching it out mightily through His ordained instrument – His precious bride, the church. The church is the fullness of Christ who fills all in all (Ephesians 1:23). Jesus does have all authority in heaven and earth (Matthew 28:18). And Jesus is with His church to the end of the world empowering her to fulfill His great commission. How can the church be defeated? How can it not but accomplish the task of discipling all the nations? The warrior of Israel is with her! Jesus does preach through His preachers. His preachers, His little ones, are mighty in His power. As they herald the gospel of good news, His people, His elect that is, do volunteer freely in the day of Thy power. The gospel is indeed the *dunamis* (power) of God (Romans 1:16) His gospel goes out with irresistible power. His grace and mercy comes with liberating power to deliver Adam's lost race from its sin and misery. The church does storm the gates of Hell; Hell's gates are impotent before the onslaught of the preached gospel (Matthew 16:18). The church's weapons are divinely powerful to the bringing down of Satan's citadel. With its glorious gospel, the church is bringing all thoughts to the obedience of Christ (II Corinthians 10:3-5) The Lord, through His church, is bringing multitudes out of darkness and transferring them into His glorious light and kingdom (Colossians 1:13-14; Acts 26:15-18).

We must learn to see with the eyes of faith; we must learn to believe in God's blessed promises despite what our present circumstances may look like. We must resist imitating the sin of the children of Israel, who because of their unbelief refused to enter the Promised Land. They chose to believe a bad report of ten spies. They chose to walk by sight and not by faith, and they paid a dear price for this rebellion.

God has promised that one day the knowledge of the Lord will cover the earth as the waters cover the sea (Isaiah 11:9). Do we believe it despite what we presently see? One day "*The mountain of the house of the Lord will be established as the chief of the mountains and will be raised above the hills, and all nations will stream to it, and many peoples will come and say, 'Come, let us go up to the mountain of the Lord, to the house of the God of Jacob; that He may teach us concerning His ways, and that we may walk in His paths'. For the law will go forth from Zion, and the word of the Lord from Jerusalem. And He will judge between the nations, and will render decisions for many peoples, and they will hammer their swords into plowshares, and their spears into pruning hooks. Nation will not lift up sword against nation, and never again will they learn war*" (Isaiah 2:2-4).

Christian, believe God's word! Preacher, preach it with all your might, soul, and strength! Christian, pray for this glorious victory! Through preaching and prayer Jesus goes forth conquering to conquer! Hallelujah!

Appendix

Historical Connections between the First Great Awakening and American Independence

Kenneth Scott Latourette makes these observations about the relationship of the First Great Awakening to the cause for American independence. He writes:

> The Great Awakening was an early stage in a mass conversion of the partially de-Christianized population which characterized the religious history of the Thirteen colonies on the eve of independence and then of the United States. The mass conversion, in part by "revivals" and "evangelistic" preaching for reaching the "unconverted" or "unsaved," was one of the distinguishing features of the Christianity of the United States, and especially of those elements of the population of Protestant, particularly Anglo-Saxon heredity.
>
> Yet it was mainly in the circles of British ancestry which were most committed to what was usually called Calvinism and its doctrine of election that the Great Awakening began and made its chief appeal.
>
> Part of the appeal was due to an alteration in traditional Calvinism which prevailed in New England as an early importation from England. Calvin had held at the evidence is that an individual was among the elect were adherence to correct doctrine, a worthy life, in faithful attendant on the sacraments. In New England it was maintained that the evidences were adherence to correct doctrine worthy life in an experience of salvation this last was akin to pietism. Since experience was essential, and that experience had been that much of the motion, seasons were to be expected when a community was aroused and tides swept through it changing many

individuals. These were those, especially among the clergy, who prayed for such seasons and sought to encourage them.[1]

Brattle Street Church in Boston played a significant role in the history of the United States, especially through the preaching and writing of its pastors. In 1699, Benjamin Coleman became the pastor of the Brattle Street Church (Congregationalist), serving in this capacity until his death in 1747. In 1715, William Cooper became his associate pastor. Both were avid supporters of the First Great Awakening. William Cooper was a close friend and supporter of Jonathan Edwards and wrote the preface to Edwards' famous work in defense of the Great Awakening, *The Distinguishing Marks of a Work of the Spirit of God.*

William Cooper served in his ministerial capacity until his death in 1743. One of the distinctives of his preaching was his biblical view of the relationship of Christianity to the civil government. William Cooper's sermon, *The Honors of Christ Demanded of the Magistrate* was a sermon preached in front of Governor Jonathan Belcher and the two branches of the Massachusetts legislature (the Council and House of Representatives) on May 28, 1740. This sermon clearly set forth a biblical view of civil government. In today's vernacular, this would be viewed as an avid "theonomic" and "postmillennial" sermon.

Massachusetts governor, Belcher, was a conspicuous advocate of advancing Christianity into the civil sphere, and as noted previously, wept during his personal meetings with George Whitefield. William Cooper's sermon was printed by the government printer at the request of the Massachusetts legislature. The central thoughts of the sermon with their foci on the liberties of the people and resistance to tyrants set the stage for much of the rhetoric of the cause for independence.

William Cooper advanced the phrase, "the free exercise of His holy religion." There is a close similarity with what showed up later in the "Free Exercise" clause of the First Amendment to the Constitution. Cooper believed that Christian magistrates are duty bound to use their power for the advancement of Christ's kingdom.

William Cooper's sermon was a masterful exhortation to civil rulers and stands in stark contrast to what people today think should be the relationship of the church to the civil realm. Today, we often hear that

---

[1]   Kenneth Scott Latourette, *A History of Christianity*, Vol. 2 *Reformation to the Present, A.D.1500-A.D.1975*, (New York: Harper & Row Publishers, 1975), p. 958.

pulpits should never be political in any sense. While it may be true that preachers today should exercise great wisdom as to how to direct their congregations in their thinking about political matters, it is wholly incorrect to say that they should never be political. The fact that Jesus is the King of kings and Lord of lords who is reigning at the Father's right hand and subduing all His enemies by the faithful preaching of His heralds of the gospel, should be sufficient in itself that biblical preaching cannot avoid being political.

Cooper's sermon is so magnificent that I am simply going to quote verbatim various excerpts from his printed sermon.[2] This sermon is unabashedly Christian in its content and exhortations to all facets of civil government. Today in the 21st Century, a sermon like this would be viewed by many Christians, by many Christian ministers, and by all non-Christians as outright "radical." Sadly, this is how far we have fallen as the visible church and as a nation. We surely deserve God's judgment upon us. As a nation, we have failed to understand the mindset of many preachers of colonial America.

As previously mentioned, Cooper's sermon is clearly "theonomic" and "postmillennial." It stands as a good application of several portions of *The Westminster Confession of Faith*. It should encourage those of us in our small Presbyterian denomination, the Reformed Presbyterian Church in the United States (RPCUS), that we really are not radical at all. We stand in good company with our forebears. Our distinctives of being theonomic and postmillennial were commonplace among many preachers of colonial America. Chapter 23 of *The Westminster Confession of Faith* finds faithful expression and application in William Cooper's sermon. *Westminster Confession of Faith* chapter 23:1, 3 states:

> God, the supreme Lord and King of all the world, hath ordained civil magistrates, to be, under Him, over the people, for His own glory, and the public good: and, to this end, hath armed them with the power of the sword, for the defence and encouragement of them that are good, and for the punishment of evil doers.

> The civil magistrate may not assume to himself the administration of the Word and sacraments, or the power of the keys of the kingdom of heaven: yet he hath authority, and it is his duty, to take order, that unity and peace be preserved in the Church, that the truth of God be kept pure and entire; that all blasphemies and

---

[2]   This sermon can be found in its entirety at http://www.belcherfoundation.org/honors.htm.

heresies be suppressed; all corruptions and abuses in worship and discipline prevented or reformed; and all the ordinances of God duly settled, administrated, and observed. For the better effecting whereof, he hath power to call synods, to be present at them, and to provide that whatsoever is transacted in them be according to the mind of God.

The following are excerpts of William Cooper's 1740 sermon titled, *The Honors of Christ Demanded of the Magistrate.* Coopers Bible text was Psalm 2:10-12:

Be wise now therefore, O ye kings: be instructed, ye judges of the earth. Serve the Lord with fear, and rejoice with trembling. Kiss the SON, lest He be angry, and ye perish from the way, when His wrath is kindled but a little: blessed are all they that put their trust in Him. (KJV)

Cooper opens with the following comments to his audience, which are the governor and both branches of Massachusetts government:

... We again see the princes, the legislators of the people, even the people of the God of Abraham, gathered together, not only in the State House to dispatch the public business, but [also] in the Lord's house to pay Him their public homage and to learn their duty to Him "by inquiring in his temple" (Psalm 27:4). And since "the shields of the earth do belong unto God", it is fit He should in this way be exalted by them.

... I know Your Excellency [Governor Belcher] and the honorable Councilors, who have ordered me into the sacred desk [the pulpit] on this great occasion, don't expect...from me either an address of compliment [empty flattering] or a lecture in politics, both of which are as distant from my genius [talents] as they would be disagreeable to my character. That which you have called me to, as a Gospel minister, is to direct you from the Word of God and remember [remind] you of your duty as Christian magistrates [rulers], which I shall accordingly endeavor, by Divine help, with all fidelity and a proper deference. And I don't know how I can better do this than from the solemn passage I have just read [which means this]: if then you [have] come together to "hear what God the Lord has to say unto you", the message brought you in His Name, by the unworthiest of His ministers, is this: "Serve the LORD with fear, and rejoice with trembling. Kiss the SON lest He be angry, etc."

The Psalm of which this text is the close, is a prophetic discourse [about] the Kingdom of the Messiah. It foretells the opposition which would be given to that kingdom when it [would] be set up in the world. Though the laws of this kingdom and the administration of it are [in] every way suited to make the subjects [of it] easy and happy, and the nature of it is such that if it did universally obtain [prevail], it would make the kingdoms of this world resemble the Kingdom of Heaven--for it consists in righteousness, and peace, and joy in the Holy Spirit... And this opposition is general, made by all sorts of persons--not only the common [sort], from whom little better is to be expected, but [also] the kings and rulers are engaged in it, as if they thought the reign of Christ would eclipse their glory and diminish their authority. These back their strength and power with policy and counsel: "The kings of the earth set themselves, and the rulers take counsel together, against the Lord, and against his Anointed, saying, Let us break their bands asunder, and cast away their cords from us" (Psalm 2:2, 3).

But for the comfort of all those who have heartily espoused the interests of Christ and are the faithful subjects of His kingdom, the vanity and unsuccessfulness of this [worldly] opposition follow [the world's attempts at thwarting Christ's kingdom]. Their attempts will certainly be defeated, and their counsels baffled, however confident they may be of carrying their point. The Most High controls their rage and derides their folly. "Why do the heathen rage, and the people imagine a vain thing? He that sitteth in the heavens shall laugh: the Lord shall have them in derision" (Psalm 2:1, 4). For the thing they attempt is not only unlikely, but impossible. The Kingdom of Christ is better established than any of the monarchies of the world. It is founded upon an irrevocable decree of God the Father, from which He cannot recede in point of honor.

... No, the opposition will issue [result] not only in a vexatious and shameful disappointment, but in the dreadful, utter and irrevocable ruin of all who are in the cursed confederacy. The honors of this Divine King will be sufficiently vindicated, and they who would not submit to His gracious scepter shall be broken with His iron rod. "Thou shalt break them with a rod of iron, thou shalt dash them in pieces like a potters vessel" (Psalm 2:9)--so suddenly, easily, and irreparably.

Now our text is the application of all this by way of counsel and admonition to persons of the highest rank and order in the world, as [those] more especially concerned in it. And here we may observe, 1. The persons to whom the counsel is addressed; 2. The counsel that is given them; and 3. The arguments and motives with which it is enforced.

... 1. The first thing then that falls under our observation is, The persons to whom the counsel in our text is addressed. And these are the kings and judges of the earth. That is, sovereign princes and their under-officers; all magistrates [rulers], both the supreme and the subordinate; those who have the legislative [i.e., legislators], and those who have the executive power [i.e., governors], in the government of any people.

... Nothing in the world is plainer than this: That it is the mind and will of God that there should be magistracy [government] in the world, that men should be governed by laws and polity, and [that men] should be kept in order by this means.

Surely no one can doubt whether the foundation of civil government is laid in Divine institution who but reads, without a comment, such texts as these: "by me kings reign, and princes decree justice: By me princes rule, and nobles, even all the judges of the earth" (Proverbs 8:15, 16); "Let every soul be subject unto the higher powers. For there is no power but of God: The powers that be are ordained of God" (Romans 13:1-2); "Submit yourselves to every ordinance of man for the Lord's sake: whether it be to the king, as supreme; Or unto governors, as sent by him for the punishment of evildoers, and for the praise of them that do well. For so is the will of God...." (1 Peter 2:13-15).

And this is the dictate of reason, as well as the voice of Scripture. The very light of nature gives a sufficient indication of the mind of God in this matter--for all nations, [no matter] how barbarous [what]soever, have united in some kind of government or other for their common peace and safety, nor can any number of men continue [for] any time without [having] something of law and rule [law and order], which shows that government is from God as the Author of nature.

But how necessary is government, even in the severer restraints of it, for man in his present fallen and corrupt state! To how much greater a height would wickedness rise if there were none to be a "terror to evildoers"! If all men were left to their unrestrained liberty, what an uncomfortable and dangerous place would this world be!

... Therefore, God's good will to men and concern for their happiness appears next to the Gospel and the ministry of it in the institution of magistracy [civil government]--His appointing [determining] that men in their present state should be governed by men... The people of Israel found this [out] by experience in the day when God promulgated His law to them in a way suited to His own majesty and greatness. They could not bear it... And God granted their request and in condescension to their weakness and infirmity when the government over Israel was a theocracy, he used the ministry of men in the management of it.

... What we have spoken of the Divine institutions of government, you all understand to be meant of government itself and not of any particular form or model of it--for one is no more appointed by God than another, but every people are left to judge for themselves, to frame such a Constitution as may best answer the ends of government for them and to alter and change that, too, at discretion and by common consent.

... We have been saying, GOD has in kindness to men appointed that they should be governed by men, yet He has been too good and kind to leave them to be governed by men according to their arbitrary will and pleasure. The end of government is the public peace and safety; when therefore this is neglected and the ordinance of government only made an engine of tyranny and oppression; when the Constitution is subverted, the liberties and properties of the people invaded, their religion and laws made a sacrifice to the superstition, ambition, or coveteousness of the prince that is over them; when this is really the case, as it has been in our own nation, doubtless the remedy is left in their own hands, and every man is under higher and earlier engagements to the community in general than he is to the supreme magistrate [ruler].

He who has freed His people from their spiritual taskmasters has not left them under the power of earthly tyrants. The rules of obedience laid down in the Gospel oblige none to submit to unlawful impositions. It is mentioned to the reproach of Issachar that the men of that tribe wanted the true spirit of liberty...(Genesis 49:14,15).

And though GOD has not prescribed any one form of government in Scripture, yet he has therein given general rules to be observed by all that are in government. The civil magistrate's commission is thus limited by the great Monarch of the world: "He that ruleth over men must be just, ruling in the fear of God" (2 Samuel 23:3).

And that they may not be unmindful of the duties of their station, He has appointed another order of men to be their faithful and humble monitors: I mean, the ministers of religion. For ministers are as truly the magistrates' teachers as magistrates are their governors. And as we must put our people "in mind to be subject to principalities and powers, to obey magistrates" (Titus 3:1), so we must put magistrates in mind to subject to the Lord Jesus Christ and use their power in a subserviency to the interests of His kingdom.

This leads us to the second thing to be considered in the words, which is:

2. The solemn counsel here given to earthly rulers of all degrees: "Serve the LORD"; "Kiss the SON".

The same Person is here meant by the Lord and the Son, namely, the Lord Jesus Christ, God-Man, Mediator.

The duty required is expressed [in] two ways. They must serve Him, as [do] those who are in subjection to Him, in all the instances of devotion and obedience.

I take the words to be comprehensive of the duty of rulers in their double capacity--the private and the public--as Christians and as magistrates [rulers].

1. RULERS are, as men and as Christians, obliged to the general service of Christ, in common with others. And the service of Christ includes in its real inward religion and practical Godliness in all the parts of it.

A Servant of Christ is one who has parted with his old masters, fallen off from his allegiance to and renounced the service of those other lords which "have had dominion over him" --Satan and the world (Isaiah 26:13). He [the Christian ruler] has actually submitted to the government of the Lord Jesus Christ, "taken His yoke upon him", and sworn allegiance to Him (Psalm 119:106). . ...He obeys all His laws and makes His will the rule of all his actions, how contrary [opposite] [what]soever to his own will or humor [inclination], ease, or interest.

MOREOVER, he follows his Divine Master's example and desires to copy the life of the holy Jesus into his own and will follow no man, of what name or figure [status] [what]soever, any farther than he sees him to follow Christ (1 Corinthians 11.1).

The servant of Christ does also resign [give up all] to His conduct [in favor of Christ's lifestyle] and is determined to "follow the Lamb whither soever he goes", and not to "turn away from following after him", whatever opposition and danger may be in the way.

Once more, a true servant of Christ makes the glory of Christ his chief and governing aim, and, both habitually and actually, directs his actions in the best manner he can towards this great end.

… Now, kings and judges are as strictly bound to serve the Lord in all the instances of personal religion and practical Godliness as any of their people. For there is the same Lord over all, who stands in the same relations to them that He does to others, as Creator, Lawgiver, and Judge (Romans 10:12). There is the same infinite distance between Him and them, that there is between Him and the lowest of their subjects. They are under the common obligations of Christians by their birth in and baptism into the Christian Church and their profession of the Christian religion. They must be saved, if ever they are so, upon the same terms and in the same way that others are. In matters of religion, in the concerns of salvation, they are without privilege or dispensation. The Gospel makes no distinction between them and others in these things, but the commands of it are addressed to them in common with persons of lower degrees in life. "Hear this all ye people; give ear, all ye inhabitants of the world: Both low and high, rich and poor together" (Psalm 49:1, 2). "Kings of the earth and all people, princes and all judges of the earth. Both young men and maidens, old men and children; let them praise the name of the Lord" (Psalm 148:11, 12, 13).

If there is any difference, these are more strictly bound to observe the laws of Christ than others because the eminence of their station will make their conversation to be the more observed, and their example will be like to have the greater influence upon [their people]. "A city set upon a hill cannot be hid", was our Savior's observation, and He made it for the sake of that exhortation and charge which follows: "Let your light so shine before men, that they may see your good works, and glorify your Father which is in heaven" (Matthew 5:14, 16).

2. RULERS are to serve the Lord Jesus Christ in their public capacity and in the exercise of their office as magistrates [government officials]. And it is in this capacity more especially that our text addresses them. And so they are to consider themselves as Christ's ministers and stewards, placed in their stations to serve Him and His interests.

THEREFORE, they must not seek themselves and their own things to the neglect of the things of Jesus Christ (Philippians 2:12-21).

… Much less must they carry on any cross designs [malevolent plans] or do anything in opposition to His [Christ's] kingdom or that may damage His interests. They must not therefore persecute His saints, silence His ministers, hinder the free exercise of His holy religion, or do anything that may obstruct the work of the Gospel, as the rulers of the Jews did when they imprisoned the professors [practitioners] of Christianity and forbade the Apostles to preach in the Name of Jesus.

They [rulers] must make no laws that are repugnant to, or inconsistent with, the settled laws of Christ's kingdom. For although GOD has given this power to all kingdoms and nations to make laws for the better support and government of themselves, yet He has not given them leave to repeal any of His own laws, nor to enact anything contrary to them.

… And so are those laws made in any particular kingdom of the world, if they be in the least contrary to any of the common laws of the world, those which the King of kings has made for all mankind--both kings and people to observe. In such a case, the general law is that "we must obey GOD rather than man" (Acts 5:29).

THE BIBLE therefore, which is the great statute book of Heaven, must be consulted by the rulers of a people, and they must frame their administration by the general laws there laid down.

...those in government over GOD's people should acquaint themselves well with His holy Word and should have an inviolable regard [for] the laws of Christ in the whole of their administration.

MOREOVER, CHRISTIAN magistrates [rulers] must employ their power for the advancement of Christ's kingdom. They are in a lieutenancy to Christ, and so they are to concur with Him in carrying on the same design for which all power is given to Him, both in Heaven and Earth (Matthew 28:18).

TRUE, indeed, the care of souls is not committed to the civil magistrate [civil ruler], nor may he extend his power to force article of faith, or modes of worship, on the consciences of men-- for conscience is exempt from every jurisdiction but Christ's, and He alone must reign there. Yet we must not run into the other extreme and say that the magistrate [civil ruler] has nothing to do in matters of religion.

As they rule by Christ, so they are obliged to rule for Him, and therefore to protect and encourage the practice of His holy religion, to guard and defend GOD's sacred Name, day [Sunday], and institutions from the insults of those who would openly profane and trample upon them, and to restrain and punish those vices and immoralities which are as contrary to the laws of Christ as they are to the welfare of societies--for the very end [purpose] of their office is the "punishment of evildoers, and the praise of them that do well" (1 Peter 2:14). And this is the design of their institution [government], that under them we may lead quiet and peaceable lives in all godliness and honesty (1 Timothy 2:2).

In a word: THEY [the rulers] should openly profess the religion of Christ, publicly espouse His cause, and zealously promote it as far as ever their authority and influence will reach, and should strenuously set themselves against everything that is opposite to His interest, against the works and kingdom of the devil which our blessed Savior came into the world to destroy (1 John 3:8).

THERE is a war carried on in this world, between the rightful king and the usurping god of it--between Christ and Satan--and whoever stands neuter [neutral], magistrates, who are Christ's officers, must not. If they do, they are traitors to His crown and government and must expect from Him the highest resentment and the severest punishment. Which leads us to the third and last thing observed in the Words:

3. The arguments and motives with which the Divine counsel here given to the kings and judges of the earth is enforced.

WISDOM is a very requisite qualification in rulers. Without this they will make but a poor figure, and both their persons and authority fall into contempt. Now, to serve the Lord, "Behold! This is wisdom". When rulers do this, they engross all the rules of policy into one. For, this is the way to have the presence of Christ with them in their administration, to direct their counsels, and succeed their endeavors for the public good, without which their own policy and power will be in vain, the wisest schemes will be baffled, and the most promising enterprises defeated... "He that ruleth over men must be just, ruling in the fear of God: And he shall be as the light of the morning, when the sun riseth, even a morning without clouds; as the tender grass springing out of the earth by clear shining after rain" (2 Samuel 23:3-4)--i.e., the religious ruler will be a great common and extensive blessing, like the light and rain of Heaven.

THIS is also the best way to secure and exalt their own character. For, if a serious and strict regard to religion runs through their conduct, both in private and public life--if they appear to act in the fear of God, and with a governing view to the honor of Christ--this will certainly make them look more great and venerable in the eyes of the people than any shining titles or glittering badges of honor which they wear. This will procure them not only outward but inward reverence. When piety is found in conjunction with greatness, the person shines with a diviner luster, and the authority wherewith he is vested strikes into a greater awe and more powerfully constrains submission and obedience. So "Joshua was magnified in the sight of all" Israel (Joshua 4:14).

... MOREOVER, this is the most likely way for them [rulers] to be established and continued in their authority and to have their public opportunities and advantages lengthened out by that GOD in whose bond their times are. For it stands in the Book of GOD as an argument why the king should above all things mind religion: "To the end that he may prolong his days in his kingdom" (Deuteronomy 17:20).

The title and character of "Lord" given to Christ in the text suggests to us these following reasons why the kings and judges of the earth--rulers of all degrees--should serve Him:

1. He is the Lord, and so their authority is derived from Him. It is so with respect to the Constitution of government itself--for dominion and rule are His appointment in the world--the original of power is from Heaven... . In whatever way, by whatever means and methods, men are advanced to their several stations, the Providence of the Lord Jesus Christ is to be acknowledged and adored therein.

... This is a great truth respecting GOD's providential government of the world, which the Psalmist has instructed us in: "Promotion cometh neither from the east, nor from the west, nor from the south: But God is the judge: he putteth down one, and setteth up another" (Psalm 75:6, 7). When there are candidates for an election in the post of government, and a struggle among the electors, the King of the world sits umpire and in a powerful, though invisible, way determines the matter so as to bring about His own counsels and serve His own purpose. "The lot is cast into the lap, but the whole disposing thereof is of the LORD" (Proverbs 16:33). This is a good reason why they who are in public stations should serve Christ in them--because He has placed them where they are.

2. He is the Lord, and so their authority is dependent on Him. They are dependent on Him as to the exercise of their rule. He has not given them an absolute power, but restrained and limited them by certain general rules and instructions to which they must conform. The glory of His supremacy He will not give to another. And they are also dependent on Him as to their continuance in their authority. They hold their places only during [His] pleasure. He that gave them their commission, can revoke or supercede it whenever He pleases.

3. He is the LORD, and so their power is in subservience and subordination unto His (Romans 13:6). They are called "His

ministers." Whatever power they have it is but ministerial, and in order to serve. The honor and power of rulers do not terminate in themselves, as if the design of GOD in the institution of magistracy [government] was only to gratify a few particular men by raising them above the common rank and putting them into authority for their persons' sake and only to make them look great. No! His end is the service that is expected from them to GOD and man, the church and the world. And the dignity is affixed to the person as an encouragement to, and a necessary means of, doing that service. Their places and offices are given them with reference to the duty expected from them. And he is an unworthy servant who, when his Master has put him into an honorable office and given him large encouragement to be faithful in the business of it, only grows proud and insolent and becomes regardless [heedless] of the Master's honor and negligent of His service.

4. RULERS, as well as others, must appear before the Judgment of Christ to give an account, as well of their public as of their private life. *** And here surely is a powerful reason why they should endeavor to acquit themselves as good stewards....

The kings and judges of the earth must not think themselves above the resentment of Christ, or too big for Him to deal with. He will be angry with them as soon as with others, and they will be as little able to stand before His indignation. Whatever prerogatives [power] they may lay claim to here, they will be of no service to them in the day of death and the Day of Judgment.[He will execute His righteous displeasure against them if they refuse to honor Him now--for in proportion to the talents which men have neglected or misimproved in this world will be the degrees of wrath inflicted on them in the next.

On the other hand, the happiness of this submission to Christ is: BLESSED "are all they who trust in Him". In a word, all they who have ruled for Christ in their several orders of government shall at the consummation of all things "reign with Him for ever and ever", set down with Him on His throne, even as He is set down with His Father on His throne. An honor and blessedness this, ineffable, inconceivable! What an incentive is this to the men of ambition who seek and court honor! But, oh! Where is the faith of it? The thing is future and invisible; therefore few believe it and seek after it, though it be not the less real and certain.

Having set forth the biblical duties for civil rulers and their obligation to advance the gospel of Christ, Cooper now personally addresses Governor Jonathan Belcher. This personal address is very touching, and should cause us today to weep that we don't have such men to run for high offices of the land. Concerning Governor Belcher, Cooper states:

WHEREFORE,

1. In the first place, let the counsel of Heaven which has been given be acceptable to your EXCELLENCY [Governor Belcher], to whom with a most respect it is now addressed.

AND it is our great pleasure and happiness this day that we can address our Governor in Chief [Jonathan Belcher] as one who has openly chosen the LORD to serve Him, and that in the way of these churches. Suffer me then, SIR, to remind you that you publicly devoted yourself to the service of the exalted Son of GOD when you had just entered into the world in superior outward circumstances and advantages, and it was with great pleasure to your own and your father's friends and the friends of religion then to observe it--from the hopes it gave them that Christ and His people here would afterwards have much service from you, by the will of GOD: And doubtless you look upon your covenant obligations to be strengthened by the honors to which Christ in His Providence has since advanced you.

A servant of Jesus Christ is a character which kings and governors have no reason to be ashamed of--a title which they should be ambitious of [attaining]--for it will be found [to be] their truest honor when all the glory of this world shall vanish like a blaze in straw, and will turn to their greatest advantage when all the prerogatives [powers] they were possessed of here will be forgotten and useless.

The honor of Christ and His interest are very much concerned in Your Excellency's conduct and administration. Religion is not in such a state at this day, but it needs the example of the greatest among us to render it more reputable and honorable. But while Your Excellency [Governor Belcher] is seen to pay a solemn regard to the day of GOD [Sunday], to attend with reverence and devotion upon His public worship, and to live in the practice of those private and public virtues which adorn the Christian character, this will go far to prevent its falling into further contempt and neglect.

ESPECIALLY if together with this, the honors of the government, which are so much at Your Excellency's disposal, are conferred on true piety and not given in course or out of compliment. I humbly conceive Your Excellency cannot give a better sanction and security to the religion that remains among us than by the wise distinction in your commissions. And here, I think we should be ungrateful to GOD and Your Excellency if we did not acknowledge the countenance and encouragement which the religion of the country has received under Your Excellency's administration, from your example and authority here.

PROVIDENCE has placed Your Excellency [Governor Belcher] over a people who stand in a special relation to Christ and are a distinguished part of the lot of His inheritance. And all your faithful services to them, He will accept as done to Him. For I trust we are still beloved for our fathers' sake and for the sake of a precious number through the land who are yet faithful with the saints.

… And suffer me to say, Sir, the distressed state of this people at this day loudly calls for your paternal compassion, your wise councils, and best endeavors for their relief.

… IF now I have gone too far in what I have said, I must rely on your...goodness to forgive me. The Searcher of hearts knows it proceeds, as from an ardent affection [for] my dear country, so from a sincere personal regard [for] Your Excellency, and an unfeigned desire that Your Excellency may long sit easy in the chair of government, and this people sit with delight under your shadow.

YOUR power, honor, and influence, employed for Christ and for His people, this, SIR, will be a crown which no man can take from you. This will give you undisturbed serenity in a recess from the cares and burdens of government, and cause the blessings of an obliged people to follow you into retirement--or it will brighten the shades of death to you and carry you from the chair of government to the sepulcher of your fathers with the public praises and lamentations and will finally give you a blessed part in the noble triumphs of the saints of the Most High...

At this point in Cooper's sermon, he now begins to address the legislative and judicial branches of the Massachusetts Commonwealth:

> 2. LET this Word of God be in the next place addressed with all decency to the honorable His MAJESTY'S COUNCIL and the honorable House of REPRESENTATIVES, this day in General Court assembled. AND here I would first of all apply myself to you as having the power of election to be exercised this day. It is an affair of no small importance you are to transact this afternoon: To elect His Majesty's Council for the Province [Massachusetts]. These, in the frame of our government, do, as it were, stand between the king and the people, both of which do in a sort meet in them, and while they are to guard the prerogative [rights] of the one, they are to preserve the privilege [liberty] of the other. They are one branch of the legislature, and bear a distinct part in the framing and enacting of our laws.
>
> Let me tell you, Gentlemen, your votes are not your own; you vote for Christ and for His people, and therefore must look to the qualifications of those you vote for. "Thou shalt provide out of all the people, able men, such as fear God, men of truth, hating covetousness, and place such over them, to be rulers" (Exodus 18:21). Men of a general character for capacity, integrity, public spiritedness, and piety. Men of a genius [talent] for government, and who understand the civil and religious interests of their people. True men who will act upon principle and not be daunted by frowns nor clamors. Men not governed by narrow and selfish views, but who can generously sacrifice their private interest to that of the public when they stand in competition. And men who appear to act in the fear of GOD in their private life--for only such will act for His glory in a public station, and they are the most likely to be favored with the divine presence and blessing.
>
> AMIDST these cares which will now press upon you, you will not forget that you are the guardians of religion, but will do what you can to maintain the kingdom of Christ among us in its light, purity, and glory. It is for the sake of the church that the world stands, and Christ is head over all things for the church. Therefore they that rule by Him should employ their care and power for that in the first and chief place. You will therefore think it your duty to strengthen the hands and encourage the hearts of the faithful minister of Christ, and do your part that there may be a succession of such in times to come by supporting the means of education and cherishing the college [Harvard College] from whence the

churches look for their supply. Your generous smiles on that society we thankfully acknowledge as an instance of your just care that religion and learning may still flourish among us.

WHETHER any new laws need to be brought forward for the suppression of our growing immoralities, you, Gentlemen,...can best judge. But what will the best laws signify without a vigorous execution?

Permit me to say to Your Honors [the Executive branch of government, the Judges of the courts, and justices in the counties]: You are Christ's officers and ministers and must act for Him in that part of government which His Providence has assigned you.

LET your courts therefore be always opened in His Name: I mean that you pay Him your public homage, and adore Him as the supreme King, Lawgiver, and Judge by solemn and open prayer. This is done, I suppose, in our several Courts of Justice through the land. And I think that all the officers of the court and those who have business at it should be ordered reverently to attend.

In civil causes, let there be shown the most steady impartiality and irreproachable integrity. The charge which King Jehosaphat gave to his judges is the charge of the King of Heaven to you: "Take heed what ye do; for ye judge not for man, but for the LORD, who is with you in the judgment: Wherefore now let the fear of the LORD be upon you, take heed and do it: for there is no iniquity with the LORD our God, nor respect of persons, nor taking of gifts" (2 Chronicles 19:6, 7). And in criminal cases, let the edge of the law be sharpened in proportion to the nature of the crime and the boldness of the transgressor. While you sit on the seat of judgment, sinners should behold your face as the face of God which is set against them that do wickedly. And the day of Assize [court day] should be a little image of that day when the Lord will come "to judge the world in righteousness and the people with His truth,"and shall "render indignation and wrath, tribulation and anguish, to every soul of man that doth evil." The judge on the bench should be worthy of that commendation which Christ gave to the angel of the church of Ephesus: "I know thy works:...how thou canst not bear them which are evil" (Revelation 2:2).

Justices of the Peace, you have the law on your side. Our Governor [Jonathan Belcher] has lately called upon and charged you in a seasonable proclamation. Good people do bless you. And GOD will accept and reward you! So Jehoshaphat encouraged the ministers of justice under his government to a resolute discharge of their duty. "Deal courageously, and the LORD shall be with the good" (2 Chronicles 19:11).

To everyone in Massachusetts: LET me exhort you then to thankfulness that you live under Christian magistrates [rulers], who are a "terror not to good works, but to the evil", and who countenance religion by their example as well as authority.

This sermon reflected the Christian political thought of one of the great champions of the First Great Awakening. From the available evidence, William Cooper's Christian political thought found a safe depository in the life of his son, Samuel Cooper, who eventually followed in his father's ministerial footsteps and, upon the death of Benjamin Coleman in 1747, became the pastor of Brattle Street Church, serving in this capacity from 1747-1783. Samuel would have learned much from his father regarding the relationship of Scripture to civil government. Samuel Cooper would exert a monumental influence on colonial thinking over a thirty-six year period. According to Fredrick Mills, Samuel Cooper was minister to no less than one-fourth of Boston's merchants and more than half of Boston's selectmen, among whom were John Adams, Samuel Adams, John Hancock, James Bowdoin, and James Otis, Jr. Cooper's views helped fuel ideas that dominated the cause for American independence. He spoke on common themes such as "constitution," "civil and religious liberty," "no man has a natural claim of dominion over his neighbors," and "that these states are innocent of the blood that hath been shed... we have stood upon the ground of justice, honor, and liberty, and acted merely a defensive part."

Samuel Cooper is also well known for his 1780 election sermon titled, *A Sermon on the Day of Commencement of the Constitution*. It was preached before his excellency John Hancock (governor), and the Senate and House of Representatives of the Commonwealth of Massachusetts on October 25, 1780, being the day of the commencement of the Constitution and inauguration of the new government of the commonwealth of Massachusetts. According to Ellis Sandoz,[3] this sermon was seen as a

---

3   Quoted in "The Pulpit and the Patriots; The Influence of Calvin, the Puritans, and the Pulpit in the American Revolution," found at http://leonardooh.wordpress.com/2010/07/05/the-pulpit-and-

model for a patriotic sermon. Cooper corresponded several times with Benjamin Franklin who said about Cooper: "Your candid, clear, and well written letters, be assured, are of great use."[4]

Of particular interest to me is that one of Samuel Cooper's patriotic associates was James Otis, Jr. James Otis is my sixth generation removed great uncle. Until doing research for this book, I was unaware of James Otis' ties with the First Great Awakening. I was well aquainted with his contributions to the cause of American independence but unaware of any of his religious views, which are quite scarce. I found this most interesting information about James Otis' early college days at Harvard College. In speaking about the impact of the First Great Awakening and particularly George Whitefield's 1740 preaching at Harvard, Allen states:

> And yet if Henry Flynt is to be believed, the Great Awakening preachers put the students "in great concern as to their Souls and Eternal State." A group of students that included Russell and Otis "prayed together, sung Psalms and discoursed together two or three at a time and read good books... Samuel Fayerweather, later to be a missionary of the Society for the propagation of the gospel in Rhode Island said that... Otis may have been absorbed in Whitefield's revivalist fervor – after all, he was only 15 years old – but as with so many sudden conversions, the effects were fleeting.[5]

In my research on James Otis, I cannot find much further information on his religious views per se. I have been unable to uncover why Samuel Fayerweather thought James Otis' conversion to be fleeting. I do know that James Otis and his wife joined the Old South Church[6] in Boston in 1756 where years earlier George Whitefield had preached. This is the church where Whitefield had to enter through a window due to the large crowd.

James Otis shared the same political views as William and Samuel Cooper. He had graduated in the same class at Harvard in 1743 with Samuel Cooper. He has been an obscure figure in the history of the United States.

---

the-patriots-%e2%80%93-the-influence-calvin-the-puritans-and-the-pulpit-had-on-the-american-revolution/.

[4]   Franklin Paul Cole, *They Preached Liberty*, p. 38.

[5]   Nathan A. Allen, *Arsonist: The Most Dangerous Man in America*, (Westport, Connecticut: Griffins Wharf Productions LLC, 2011), p. 36.

[6]   As with many churches of New England, the Old South Church of Boston eventually gave way to Unitarianism. It is a very sad story to see where once great gospel light had shone brightly, grievous theological error had now displaced it.

Today, he is recognized by political and legal scholars as being the inspiration behind the Fourth Amendment to the Constitution, which is part of the Bill of Rights that guards against unreasonable searches and seizures. Historians view him as igniting one of the sparks of the American War for Independence. These scholars all focus on a four hour speech delivered by the Massachusetts politician, and former customs official, to the Superior Court in Boston in 1761.

Concerning James Otis, Jr., Brandon Hopkins states:

> In the introduction to a series of biographical sketches written for the National Gallery on the leaders of the pre-Revolutionary era, Lillian Miller describes the philosophical impact that Otis had on the Patriot movement: In denouncing the writs [of assistance], James Otis, Jr., not only condemned what he believed to be their illegality as 'the worst instrument of arbitrary power, the most destructive to English Liberty, and the fundamental principles of the constitution,' but in doing so he argued that every man had a 'right to his life, his liberty...his property.' Furthermore, he defined these rights as 'written on [man's] heart, and revealed to him by his maker.' They were, Otis maintained, 'inherent, inalienable, and indefensible by any laws, pacts, contracts, covenants, or stipulations, which man could devise...' Spoken in 1761, the idea that these words express was to become so deeply ingrained in the minds and hearts of Americans in all parts of the colonies that it would animate the explosive chain of events recounted in this narrative, and [fifteen] years later find fuller and finer utterance in the Declaration of Independence.[2]

James Otis, Jr. would become renowned in his time for his inspiring speech against Writs of Assistance. Writs of Assistance were *general* search warrants which allowed colonial customs officials to "break open shops, cellars, and houses to search for prohibited goods, and merchandise on which duties had not been paid" without having to consult a judge, describe the goods being searched for or their suspected location, or provide any evidence that such goods even existed. Appointees of customs officials serving such Writs could legally search the premises of any

---

[2]   Brandon Hopkins, *James Otis, Jr's Attack on Writs of Assistance: A Turning Point in the Life of John Adams and the Birth of Indepedence in America*, The Concord Review, 2004, p.22. as quoted in Lillian Miller, In the Minds and Hearts of the People, Prologue to the American Revolution 1760-1774 (Greenwich, Connecticut: New York Graphic Society, 1974) p. 10.

individual they chose on the basis of suspicion alone without having to provide any evidence supporting the necessity of their actions.[3]

John Adams, later to become our second American President, as an eyewitness of Otis' speech in 1761 stated the following:

> Otis was a flame of fire; with a promptitude of classical allusions, a depth of research, a rapid summary of historical events and dates, a profusion of legal authorities, a prophetic glance of his eye into futurity, and a rapid torrent of impetuous eloquence, he hurried all away before him. American Independence was then and there born. The seeds of patriot and heroes to defend the vigorous youth were then and there sown. Every man of an immense crowded audience appeared to me to go away, as I did, ready to take arms against Writs of Assistance. Then and there was the first scene of the first act of opposition to the arbitrary claims of Great Britain. Then and there the child Independence was born. In fifteen years he grew to manhood and declared himself free...I do say in the most solemn manner, that Mr. Otis' oration against Writs of Assistance breathed into this nation the breath of life.[4]

This was John Adams' eyewitness account of Otis' speech:

> Otis opened his four hour attack with these memorable words: "May it please your Honors...I will to my dying day oppose with all the power and faculties God has given me, all such instruments of slavery on the one hand, and villainy on the other, as this writ of assistance is. It appears to me the worst instrument of arbitrary power, the most destructive of English liberty and the fundamental principles of the constitution, that ever was found in an English law book."[5]

Otis would continue his attack of Writs of Assistance:

> Everyone with this writ may be a tyrant in a legal manner, also may control, imprison, or murder anyone within the realm... Every man may reign secure in his petty tyranny, and spread terror and desolation around him, until the trump of the archangel shall

3   Hopkins, p.30.
4   William Tudor, *The Life of James Otis of Massachusetts* [First published 1823] (New York, Da Capo Press, 1970), p. 61.
5   John Adams, "Letter to William Tudor, 29 March 1817." John Adams, *The Founding Fathers*, pp. 54-55. John Adams, "Notes taken during the Writs of Assistance Trial, February 1761," and *The Founding Fathers*, pp. 55-56.

excite different emotions in his soul... Now one of the most essential branches of English liberty is the freedom of one's house. A man's house is his castle; and whilst he is quiet, he is as well guarded as a prince in his castle. This writ, if it should be declared legal, would totally annihilate this privilege. Custom house officers may enter our houses when they please; we are commanded to permit their entry. Their menial servants may enter, may break locks, bars, and everything in their way: and whether they break through malice or revenge, no man, no court, can inquire. Bare suspicion without oath is sufficient....[6]

General writs, Otis argued, were a direct violation of the natural rights of man, which were incorporated into the English constitution as fundamental laws in the old Saxon laws, the Magna Carta, and in 50 confirmations of it in Parliament. Charles I lost his head, and James II lost his throne due to their violations of these basic rights. Otis asserted that the security of these rights to life, liberty, and property, had been the object of all the struggles against arbitrary power in every age. Otis declared: All precedents are under control of the principles of the law.... No Acts of Parliament can establish such a writ. Though it should be made in the very words of the petition, it would be void. An act against the Constitution is void.. It is the business of this court to demolish this monster of oppression and to tear into rags this remnant of Star Chamber tyranny.[7]

William Tudor gives us this insight into Otis' thinking:

Otis argued that natural rights could never be denied to British subjects in either England or America because they were thoroughly incorporated into British constitutional law and the provincial or colonial charters. Otis also soundly condemned the idea of "virtual representation." Our ancestors as British subjects, and we, their descendants, as British subjects, were entitled to all those rights by the British constitution, as well as by the law of nature, and our provincial charter, as much as any inhabitant of London . . . or any part of England; and were not to be cheated out of them by any phantom of 'virtual representation' or any other fiction of law or politics.... These rights were inherent and inalienable. That they could never be surrendered or alienated, but

---

[6]   John Adams, pp.65-67.
[7]   John Adam's "Notes," pp. 56-57.

by idiots or madmen, and all acts of idiots and lunatics were void, and not obligatory by all the laws of God and man.[8]

According to William Tudor, Otis spoke vehemently against the *tyranny of taxation without representation*:

> From the energy with which [Otis] urged this position, that 'Taxation without representation was tyranny,' it came to be a common maxim in the mouth of everyone. And with him it formed the basis of all his speeches and political writings."[9] Otis also believed that "expenditures of public money without appropriations by the representatives of the people, were arbitrary, unconstitutional and therefore tyrannical."[10]

According to Brandon Hopkins, Otis was an instant hero after the speech. John Adams' sons would describe the impact of Otis' speech in the colonies against Writs of Assistance:

> The effect of the argument was electrical, although the interest upon which it could immediately operate was necessarily limited to the colony where the question arose. It was not like the Stamp Act, which bore at once upon the property and passions of the people of all the colonies. The introduction of the writs of assistance would in the first instance have affected only the rights of a few merchants of Boston and Salem. But the principle of tyranny was in it, and it was the natural precursor of the Stamp Act.[11]

Brandon Hopkins would write:

> Otis's efforts in the legislature, in the press, in the caucuses of Boston, and in towns all over Massachusetts and the rest of New England over the next 10 years led directly to the downfall of Hutchinson and his court party and to the Revolutionary War. By eloquently and forcefully establishing the principle that "taxation without representation was tyranny" and that public expenditures not approved by representatives of the people were tyrannical, Otis created a broad sense of watchfulness and a widely held disposition to resist vehemently every encroachment of the civil

---

[8] Tudor, p. 71.
[9] Tudor, pp. 76-77.
[10] Tudor, p. 118.
[11] John Quincy Adams and Charles Francis Adams, *The Life of John Adams* [First Published 1871] (New York: Haskell House Publishers, Ltd., 1968), p. 82.

liberties guaranteed to British subjects. Tudor says, "The public was taught to look at principles, and to resist every insidious precedent inflexibly." Tudor believed that it was Otis's influence which led Edmund Burke, an influential English Whig politician who supported the American Revolution but was critical of the French Revolution and wrote the widely-read book *Reflections on the Revolution in France*, to make these comments regarding the unusual watchfulness of the people of the British North American colonies that became the United States.[12]

Chief Justice Dana once spoke of James Otis contributions when he said:

He was one of those who first opposed the demands of a tyrannical government, and opened the path through which his successors followed with so much applause, while he was prevented by disease and the infirmities of nature from taking a part in the events succeeding his early exertions. For ten years Mr. Otis was looked upon as the safeguard and ornament of our cause, and the splendor of his intellect threw into the shade all the great contemporary lights. The cause of American Independence was for a long time identified abroad with the name of Otis, and it was thought, foolishly enough, that if he were taken away, that would perish.[13]

The reason that James Otis is not better known is due to the following. Because of his stand against British tyranny, loyalists hated him in the colonies. In 1770, he went into a British Coffee house and a loyalist aided by a number of Army, Navy, and revenue officials beat him to near death with a cane. Otis suffered serious head wounds from which he never fully recovered. During the years to follow, he would have fits of insanity and during some of those he would burn his papers. The patriot, Samuel Adams, would recount that it was quite sad to see America's great intellect reduced to insane fits. The great light was reduced to virtual anonymity.[14]

The manner of James Otis' death is quite extraordinary. He once confided in his sister – "My dear sister, I hope when God Almighty, in His righteous providence, shall take me out of time into eternity, that it will be by a flash of lightning." The irony is that it is the exact way that God chose to remove him from this world. On May 23, 1783, while telling a story to his

---

[12] Hopkins, p.45.
[13] William Otis, "A Genealogical and Historical Memoir of the Otis Family in America, (Chicago, 1924), p. 100.
[14] Otis, p.101.

family at his home in Andover, Massachusetts, Otis was standing at a doorway when a storm arose. It is said that he looked up at the gathering clouds and at that moment a bolt of lightning struck him, killing him instantly. No one else in the room was hurt, and there were no marks on his body. It was bizarre to say the least. Upon hearing of Otis' death, John Adams, who was then Minister to France, wrote:

> It was with very afflicting sentiments I learned of the death of Mr. Otis, my worthy master. Extraordinary in death, as in life, he left a character that will never die while the memory of the American Revolution remains, whose foundation he laid with an energy, and with those masterly abilities, which no other man possessed."[15]

President John Adams would later write:

> I have been young and now am old, and I solemnly swear, I have never known a man whose love of his country was more ardent or more sincere; never one who suffered so much; never one whose services for ten years of his life were so important and essential to the cause of his country as those of Mr. Otis from 1760-70.[16]

In a letter to Hezekiah Niles on the meaning of the War of American Independence dated February, 13, 1818, John Adams listed in importance those who contributed the most to the cause of American independence from 1760-1766:

> It was not until after the annihilation of the French dominion in America that any British ministry had dared to gratify their own wishes, and the desire of the nation, by projecting a formal plan for raising a national revenue from America, by parliamentary taxation. The first great manifestation of this design was by the order to carry into strict executions those acts of parliament, which were well known by the appellation of the *acts of trade*, which had lain a dead letter, unexecuted for half a century, and some of them, I believe, for nearly a whole one.
>
> This produced, in 1760 and 1761, an awakening and a revival of American principles and feelings, with an enthusiasm which went on increasing till, in 1775, it burst out in open violence, hostility, and fury.

---

[15]   Otis, p. 102.
[16]   Otis, p. 99.

> The characters the most conspicuous, the most ardent and influential in this revival, from 1760 to 1766, were, first and foremost, before all and above all, James Otis; next to him was Oxenbridge Thacher; next to him, Samuel Adams; next to him, John Hancock; then Dr. Mayhew; then Dr. Cooper and his brother.[7]

As an orator, it was said of Otis that he was bold, argumentative, impetuous, and commanding, with an eloquence that made his own excitement irresistibly contagious. As a lawyer, his knowledge and ability placed him at the head of his profession. As a scholar, he was rich in acquisition and governed by a classic taste. As a statesman and civilian, he was sound and just in his views. As a patriot, he resisted all the allurements that might weaken the cause of that country to which he devoted his life and for which he sacrificed to it. The future historian of the United States, in considering the foundation of American Independence, will find that the corner stone must be inscribed with the name of James Otis.[17]

It is one thing to be a great patriot, advocating principles consistent with Scripture, and it is another to be one who is in a right relationship with Christ, who is King of kings and Lord of lords. I can only hope that my great uncle's experience at Harvard College in 1740 under the preaching of George Whitefield was indicative of a true conversion. I can only hope that James Otis' close relationship with Rev. Samuel Cooper was that shared by brothers in Christ, seeking to apply biblical principles to all of life.

As Christian political thinking was being developed and growing in colonial America prior to the War for American Independence, George Whitefield's influence in America was substantial. He would make five more visits to America before his death in 1770, which occurred in Massachusetts. According to Jerome Mahaffey, who authored the book, *Preaching Politics: The Religious Rhetoric of George Whitefield and the Founding of a New Nation*, Whitefield directed the growth of an American collective religious identity that lay underneath the emerging political ideology that fueled the War for American Independence.

---

[7]   Adam's letter as quoted on http://tmh.floonet.net/articles/adams.shtml.
[17]   William Otis, p. 103.

Bible Verses Index

Index

Bibliography

(n.d.). Retrieved 2012, from uua.org:
www.uua.org/re/tapestry/adults/moves/workshop5/workshopplan/s
tories/

Adams, J. Q. (n.d.). Retrieved 2012, from
http://tmh.floonet.net/articles/adams.shtml

Adams, J. Q., & Adams, C. F. (1968). *The Life of John Adams*. New York:
Haskel House Publications, Ltd.

Allen, N. A. (2011). *Arsonist: The Most Dangerous Man in America*.
Westport: Griffins Wharf Productions LLC.

Allis, O. T. (1977). *Prophecy and the Church*. Philadelphia: Presbyterian
and Reformed Publishing.

Bahnsen, G. (1999). *Victory in Jesus: The Bright Hope of
Postmillennialism*. Texarkana: Covenant Media Press.

Bruce, F. F. (1964). *The Epistle to the Hebrews*. Grand Rapids: William B.
Eerdmans Publishing Co.

Bryant, J. D. (n.d.). *Unitarian and Universalist Theological History*.
Retrieved 2012, from hopeuu.org:
http://hopeuu.org/rootessays/UU%20Theological%20History

Calvin, J. (1981). *Calivin's Commentaries*. Grand Rapids: Baker Book
House.

Calvin, J. *New Testament Commentaries on I Corinthians*.

Calvin, J. *New Testament Commentaries on Matthew, Mark and Luke*.

Calvin, J. *Old Testament Commentary*.

Calvin, J. (1973). *The Epistles of Paul the Apostle to the Romans*. Grand
Rapids: Eerdmans Publishing Company.

Calvin, J. (1973). *The Epistles of Paul the Apostle to the Romans and to the Thessalonians.* Grand Rapids: William B. Eerdmans Publishing Co.

Chafer, L. S. (1985). Dispensationalism. In C. I. Crenshaw, & I. G. Gunn, *Dispensationalism Today, Yesterday and Tomorrow.* Memphis: Footstool Publications.

Chauncy, C. (1742). A Letter from a Gentleman in Boston, to Mr George Wishart, One of the Ministers of Edinburgh, Concerning the State of Religion in New England. Edinburg.

Connely, W. (1939). *The True Chesterfield: Manners - Women - Education.* London: Cassell and Co. Ltd.

Crenshaw, C. I., & Gunn, I. G. (1985). *Dispensationalism Today, Yesterday, and Tomorrow.* Memphis: Footstool Publications.

Dallas Theological Seminary Doctrinal Statement. (n.d.).

Dallimore, A. (1970). *George Whitefield: The Life nd Times of the Great Evangelist of the 18th Century Revival.* Edinburgh: The Banner of Truth Trust.

DeHann, M. R. (1996). *The Second Coming of Jesus.* Grand Rapids: Kregel Publications.

Delitzsch, K. &. (1977). *Commentary on the Old Testament.* Grand Rapids: William B. Erdmans Publishing Co.

DeMar, G. (1999). *Last Day's Madness.* Atlanta: American Vision.

Dunn, J. (1988, April 30). San Antonio Fundamentalist Battles Anti-Semitism. *Houston Chronicle .* Houston, TX.

Dwight, S. (1830). *The Works of President Edwards: With a Memoir of His Life.* New York: G. & C. & H. Carvill.

Edwards, J. (n.d.). A Humble Attempt.

Edwards, J. (n.d.). *Some Thoughts Concerning the Present Revival of Religion: And the Way In Which It Ought To Be Acknowledged and Promoted.* Retrieved August 2012, from Prayermeetings.org: http://www.prayermeetings.org/files/Jonathan_Edwards/JE Some Thoughts Concerning The Present Revival.pdf

Ellis, T. T. (n.d.). Samuel Davies: Apostle of Virginia. Retrieved 2012, from http://www.graceonlinelibrary.org/biographies/samuel-davies-apostle-of-virginia-part-i-of-ii-by-thomas-talbot-ellis/

Evans, W. *Outline Study of the Bible.*

Falwell, J. (1981). *Fundamentalist Phenomenon.* Garden City: Doubleday.

Fatherhood of Man. (n.d.). Retrieved 2012, from ashartford.com: http://www.ushartford.com/ fatherhoodofman.html

Feinberg, C. L. Millenialism: The Two Major Views. In Crenshaw, & Gunn.

Fisher, G. R. (n.d.). *The Other Gospel of John Hagee: Zionism and Ethnic Salvation.* Retrieved from http://www.pfo.org/jonhagee.htm

Foote, W. H. (1850). Sketches of Virginia: Historical and Biographical. Philadelphia, PA. Retrieved 2012, from http://quod.lib.umich.edu/m/moa/aja2527.0001.001/169?page=root;size=100;view=image

Gaustad, E. S. (1957). *The Great Awakening in New England.* New York: Harper & Brothers.

Gentry, K. L. (1989). *The Beast of Revelation.* Tyler: Institute for Christian Economics.

Gordon, S. D. (n.d.). Quiet Talks with World Winners, Chapter 6: World-Winning - The Past Failure. Retrieved 2012, from Rapture Ready: http://raptureready.com/resource/gordon/gordon39.html

Hamilton, H. (1890). *History of the Old South Church.* Boston: Houghton, Mifflin and Company.

Henry, M. (1972). *Commentary of the Whole Bible.* Wilmington: Sovereign Grace Publications.

Henry, M. (1972). *Matthew Henry's Commentary of the Whole Bible.* Wilmington: Sovereign Grace Publishers.

Hodge, C. (1840). The Constitutional History of the Presbyterian Church in the United States of America: Part II - 1741-1788. Philadephia, PA: Presbyterian Board of Education. Retrieved from http://www.tracts.ukgo.com/hodge_revivals1.pdf

House, W., & Ice, T. (1988). *Dominion Theology: Blessing or Curse: An Analysis of Christian Reconstruction.* Portland: Multnomah Press.

Ice, T. (n.d.). The Holy Spirit and the Pretribulational Rapture. Retrieved from www.according2prophecy.org/hsrap.html

Jennings, C. a. (1898). *The Autobiography of Charles H. Spurgeion.* Cincinnati - Chicago.

Joseph C. Morecraft, I. (2010). *Authentic Christianity: An Exposition of the Theology and Ethics of the Westminster Larger Catechism.* Powder Springs: Minkoff Family Publishing and American Vision Press.

Kelly, D. F. (1989). *If god Already Knows Why Pray?* Brentwood: Wolgemuth & Hyatt Publishers, Inc.

Lambert, F. (1994). *Pedlar in Divinisy: George Whitefield and the Transatlantic Revivals.* Princeton: Princeton University Press.

Larkin, C. (1918). *The Second Coming of Christ.* Philadelphia: Rev. Clarence Larkin Estate.

Latourette, K. S. (1975). *A History of Christianity.* New York: Harper & Row Publishers.

Lindsey, H. (1997). *The Apocalypse Code.* Palos Verdes: Western Front.

Lindsey, H. (1973). *There's a New World Coming.* Santa Ana: Vision House Publishers.

Mantey, D. a. (1927). *A Manual Grammar of the Greek New Testament.* Toronto: The Macmillian Company.

Marsden, G. M. (2003). *Jonathan Edwards: A Life.* New Haven & London: Yale University Press.

Miller, L. (1974). *In the Minds and Hearts of the People, Prologue to the American Revolution 176-1774.* Greenwich: New York Graphic Society.

Murray, I. H. (1971). *The Puritan Hope: A Study in Revival and the Interpretation of Prophecy.* Edinburgh: The Banner of Truth Trust.

Murray, J. (1959). *Epistle to the Romans.* Grand Rapids: Eerdmans Publishing Company.

Otis, W. (1924). *A Genealogical and Historical Memoir of the Otis Family in America.* Chicago.

Pentecost, J. D. (1958). *Things to Come: A Case Study in Bilbical Eschatology.* Grand Rapids: Zondervan.

Riddlebarger, K. (2003). *A Case for Amillenialism: Understanding the End Times.* Grand Rapids: Baker Books.

Sandoz, E. (1991). *Sermons of the American Founding Era, 1730-1805.* Indianapolis: Liberty Press.

Scofield Reference Bible. (1945). New York: Oxford University Press.

Scofield, C. I. (1967). *The New Scofield Reference Bible.* New York: Oxford Press.

Smith, C. (1978). *Future Survival.* Santa Ana: Word for Today.

Spurgeon, C. (n.d.). A Defense of Calvinism. Retrieved 2012, from http://www.spurgeon.org/ calvinis.htm

Spurgeon, C. (n.d.). The Soul winner. Retrieved 2012, from http://www.thesoulwinner.org/ebooks/The%20Soul%20Winner%20-%20Spurgeon.pdf

Stout, H. S. (1990). George Whitefield. In D. G. Reid, *Dictionary of Christianity in America.* Downers Grove: Intervarsity Press.

Symington, W. *Messiah the Prince, or the Mediatorial Dominon of Jesus Christ.* Still Waters Revival Books.

Terry, M. S. (1974). *Biblical Hermeneutics: A Treatise on the Interpretation of the Old and New Testaments.* Grand Rapids: Zondervan Publishing.

The Pulpit and the Patriots; The Influence of Calvin, the Puritans, and the Pulpit in the American Revolution. (n.d.). Retrieved 2012, from Leonardooh.wordpress.com: at http://leonardooh.wordpress.com/2010/07/05/the-pulpit-and-the-patriots-%e2%80%93-the-influence-calvin-the-puritans-and-the-pulpit-had-on-the-american-revolution/.

Tudor, W. (1970). *The Life of James Otis of Massachusetts.* New York: Da Capo Press.

Tyerman, L. (1876). *The Life of the Rev. George Whitefield.* London: Hodder and Stoughton.

Walvoord, J. F. *The Holy Spirit.*

Walvoord, J. F. The Millennial Kingdom. In Crenshaw, & Gunn.

Winsor, J. (1881). *The Memorial History of Boston.* Boston: Ticknor and Company.

Triumphant Publications

This publishing ministry was started in 1995 for the purpose of disseminating distinctly Reformed literature. We are committed to sound biblical doctrine in keeping with *The Westminster Confession of Faith.*

All these other books and booklets written by John M. Otis are available at www.triumphantpublications.com

Unveiling Freemasonry's Idolatry

Danger In the Camp: "An Analysis and Refutation of the Heresies of the Federal Vision Movement"

Retracing the Beautiful Steps

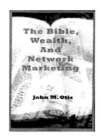

The Bible, Wealth and Network Marketing

Glorifying God With Your Wealth

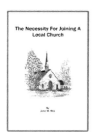

The Necessity For Joining A Local Church

Do You Really
Know the Gospel?

The Praying Christian:
God's Warrior

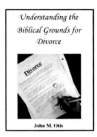

A Biblical
Understanding of
Divorce

Distinctives of
Biblical
Presbyterianism

Where Do You Stand?

The companion tract to
"Do You Really Know
the Gospel?"

Who is the Genuine
Christian?

Sold in bundles of 25